Before Photography

Interdisciplinary German Cultural Studies

Edited by
Irene Kacandes

Volume 29

Before Photography

German Visual Culture in the Nineteenth Century

Edited by
Kirsten Belgum, Vance Byrd and John D. Benjamin

DE GRUYTER

ISBN 978-3-11-110458-4
e-ISBN (PDF) 978-3-11-069644-8
e-ISBN (EPUB) 978-3-11-069662-2
ISSN 1861-8030

Library of Congress Control Number: 2020949068

Bibliographic information published by the Deutsche Nationalbibliothek
The Deutsche Nationalbibliothek lists this publication in the Deutsche Nationalbibliografie; detailed bibliographic data are available on the Internet at http://dnb.dnb.de.

© 2022 Walter de Gruyter GmbH, Berlin/Boston
This volume is text- and page-identical with the hardback published in 2021.
Cover image: AKG Images/"Berlins neue Anschlag-Säulen". Lithographie, um 1855, von P.G. Nordmann nach dem Entwurf von Gehtmann.
Typesetting: Integra Software Services Pvt. Ltd.
Printing and binding: CPI books GmbH, Leck

www.degruyter.com

Acknowledgments

There were many discussions and organizations that contributed to the creation of this volume about German visual culture in the nineteenth century. The first conversation that plumbed the importance of considering the visual culture of nineteenth-century German-speaking Europe took place in the context of a course on "Book Illustration Processes to 1900" offered by Terry Belanger of the Rare Book School at the University of Virginia in the fall of 2016. That conversation continued in a larger setting and with more participants in a seminar on "Critical Nineteenth-Century Visual Cultural Studies" at the German Studies Association conference in 2017. The following year those ideas were expanded further and with the contributions of additional scholars at a symposium held in the Department of Germanic Studies at the University of Texas at Austin. That symposium was supported by generous funding from the German Academic Exchange Service (DAAD), the Texas Chair for German Studies, and several other units of the University of Texas at Austin including the Department of History, the Department of Art and Art History, the Texas Language Center, the Center for Design and Creative Technologies, and the Center for European Studies. Their contributions were vital to the intellectual exchange that led to this volume. The editors also thank Irene Kacandes, editor of the Interdisciplinary German Cultural Studies series at De Gruyter, for her support of this endeavor and her assistants at De Gruyter, Anja-Simone Michalski, Lydia White, and Myrto Aspioti. Finally, the editors want to thank all of the individuals involved in those preliminary events, including those whose work did not make its way directly into this volume, but whose ideas and comments inspired us and encouraged us to continue this project. Particular thanks are, of course, due to our contributors for their persistence, their patience with our process, and their inspiring work.

Contents

Acknowledgments —— V

Kirsten Belgum
Introduction: Before Photography —— 1

Part 1: Ways of Seeing

John D. Benjamin
Ways of Seeing —— 15

Kathrin Maurer
Ballooning as a Technology of Seeing in Jean Paul's "Des Luftschiffers Giannozzo Seebuch" (1801) —— 17

Christian A. Bachmann
Through the Eyepiece and What Visual Satire Found There —— 39

Vance Byrd
Enacting the Past: Nineteenth-Century Illustrated Periodicals and Painted Panoramas —— 65

Peter M. McIsaac
Visual Cultures of Popular Anatomy Exhibition: The Role of Visitor Environment in Shaping the Impact of Public Health Education —— 95

Part 2: Materials and Media

John D. Benjamin
Materials and Media —— 127

Catriona MacLeod
Cut-Ups on the Edges of the Photographic Century —— 129

Trevor Brandt
Printed Pilgrimage: *Spiritual Labyrinths* in the German-American Home —— 157

J. P. Short
Arc of the Anemone: Modeling Nature from the *Wunderkammer* to the *Warenwelt* —— 181

David Ciarlo
The Traveling Cliché: Circulation and Fixity in Engraved Representations of Ethnographic "Others" —— 205

Part 3: Image and Text

John D. Benjamin
Image and Text —— 241

Antje Pfannkuchen
Image, Language, Science: Hieroglyphs and the Romantic Quest for Primordial Truth —— 243

Agnes Hoffmann
A Poetics of Scaling: Adalbert Stifter and the Measures of Nature Around 1850 —— 267

Matthew O. Anderson
Adventure from Concentrate: Visual Interventions in German Youth Adaptations of James Fenimore Cooper's *Leatherstocking Tales* —— 293

Epilogue

Kirsten Belgum
Scans, Databases, and Apps: Using Twenty-First-Century Technology to Study Nineteenth-Century Visual Culture —— 323

Contributors —— 347

Bibliography —— 351

Index —— 379

Kirsten Belgum
Introduction: Before Photography

The last three decades have seen a wealth of scholarship on the subject of visual culture, including collections of foundational essays, field-defining journals, and original monographs on specific themes.[1] The study of visual culture, as a broad and interdisciplinary academic field, has yielded important insights into a diverse and wide-ranging set of phenomena. In the early decades of the field, scholarly investigations focused predominantly on photography, cinema, and electronic media.[2] Since 2000 they have increasingly focused also on digitally produced and mediated material, such as video games and images exchanged via social media.[3]

---

[1] Building on early important social analyses by art historians such as Michael Baxandall and Svetlana Alpers and on work by scholars trained in the field of literary studies such as W. J. T. Mitchell, the field of visual culture studies emerged in the 1980s. Some introductory works appeared in the mid 1990s. See Chris Jenks, ed., *Visual Culture* (New York: Routledge, 1995) and *The BLOCK Reader in Visual Culture* (New York: Routledge, 1996). By 1996 the field was the subject of a public debate that appeared in the "Visual Culture Questionnaire" published in the journal *October*. In the Anglo-American context, introductions to the field, useful anthologies, and journals began to appear shortly thereafter. These included Nicholas Mirzoeff, ed., *The Visual Culture Reader* (New York: Routledge, 1998); Nicholas Mirzoeff, *An Introduction to Visual Culture* (New York: Routledge, 1999); and the *Journal of Visual Culture* (founded in 2002). In German-speaking Europe, the field emerged a bit later with the rise of media studies and *Bildwissenschaft* (as distinct from *Kunstgeschichte*). In the past decade an increasing number of works have appeared there that seek to articulate the place of visual fields of study or the interdisciplinary uses of such investigations. These include: the introductory volume with the striking use of the plural noun form, Marius Rimmele and Bernd Stiegler, *Visuelle Kulturen / Visual Culture* (Hamburg: Junius, 2012); *Handbuch Literatur & Visuelle Kultur*, ed. Claudia Benthien and Brigitte Weingart (Berlin: De Gruyter, 2014); and Gerhard Paul, *Das visuelle Zeitlater: Punkt und Pixel* (Göttingen: Wallstein Verlag, 2016).
[2] Nicholas Mirzoeff famously began his *Introduction to Visual Culture* with the proclamation: "Modern life takes place onscreen," by which he meant film, television, video, and the Web 1.0 at that point. Mirzoeff, *An Introduction to Visual Culture*, 1.
[3] The number of works is far too large to list here, but regarding just the last two items, a glance at the volumes in the University of Minnesota Press series on "Electronic Mediations" reveals (as of February 2020) at least two works dedicated to visual culture and the internet and six to video games: https://www.upress.umn.edu/book-division/series/electronic-mediations. The *Journal of Visual Culture* has devoted an entire issue (with eleven contributions) to internet memes alone and the journal's "virtual issues" function displays four articles in response to the search for "video games." https://journals.sagepub.com/page/vcu/collections/virtual-issues/video-games.

https://doi.org/10.1515/9783110696448-001

Less attention, however, has been devoted to earlier periods within the field of visual culture studies.[4]

The present volume emerged from a series of conversations among scholars who work on visual cultural practices in the German-speaking world of the nineteenth century.[5] It is intended to fill a gap in existing scholarship by focusing on the complex, diverse, and important processes related to visual cultural production and dissemination in that century. As will become clear in the essays that follow, new processes of bringing images to viewers included the growth of the periodical press with printed images using lithography and steel engravings. They also involved novel institutions for displaying images to large audiences in public, such as panoramas or hygiene exhibitions. They included the use of devices that enabled the portrayal of previously unseen perspectives, such as aerial views from hot air balloons or magnification using advanced scientific instruments. In drawing attention to such innovation, this volume attends to the centrality of visual culture both as it relates to social, historical, aesthetic, and technological developments and as it has been analyzed and interpreted from a range of academic disciplines. In particular, it is predicated on the fact that the nineteenth century was both a fertile period of development and growth in visual culture and a time during which visual objects and images were for the first time readily available and accessible to broad and diverse audiences.

---

[4] To be sure, the work of Baxandall and Alpers on the social history of art in the early modern period contributed to the emergence of visual culture studies as a field. Despite her early hopes for the broad historical scope of visual culture studies, Michael Holly has recently bemoaned the trend of focusing predominantly on the present: "I thought: there will be lots of new questions about the past; the past will live again. But it did not happen, perhaps because of the centrality of photography and film." "Histories: Anglo-American Visual Studies, 1989–1999," in *Farewell to Visual Studies*, ed. James Elkins, Sunil Manghani, and Gustav Frank (University Park, PA: Pennsylvania State University Press, 2015), 46. A notable exception to this focus on photography and more recent visual media was the journal launched in 2003 under the title *Living Pictures: The Journal of the Popular and Projected Image before 1914*, https://www.tandfonline.com/toc/repv20/current. Yet, despite its professed focus on early popular visual culture within two years it extended the end of its "period" to 1930 when its title changed to *Early Popular Visual Culture*. Its self-described focus includes photography and cinema: see https://www.tandfonline.com/action/journalInformation?show=aimsScope&journalCode=repv20. Another useful resource is the anthology *The Nineteenth-Century Visual Culture Reader*, ed. Vanessa R. Schwartz and Jeannene M. Przyblyski (New York: Routledge, 2004).

[5] As we mention in the acknowledgments, some of these conversations took place in a seminar at the 2017 annual meeting of the German Studies Association and at a symposium organized at the University of Texas at Austin in 2018.

Thus, while we recognize the importance of questions engendered by the rise of photographic, filmic, electronic, and, most recently, digital visual media, this volume is an invitation to examine the rich terrain of visual culture that arose prior to these innovations. We have entitled this volume "Before Photography" because its chapters engage with processes and products that emerged in a period prior to the widespread use of photomechanical reproduction of images, including those that continued to play a dominant role in cultural forums even as access to photography became more affordable and thus widespread. The idea behind this volume is to recover that context in a field that tends to privilege more recent media and to explore the place and contributions of those earlier forms of visual culture for German studies dealing with the nineteenth century.

The focus on "German" visual culture as articulated in our volume's sub-title also requires some explanation. To be sure, recent scholarship about cultural and social phenomena has questioned the usefulness of the nation-state as the main geographical and political context of investigation. For example, generative work in the field of history, such as that by Sebastian Conrad and Jürgen Osterhammel, has taken a turn toward global as well as transnational developments.[6] This focus has yielded important insights about the deeply interconnected aspects of economic, political, and social interactions across broad geographical regions.[7] And yet, even in the face of such interlinked economic and social forces, we suggest that taking the nation as a point of departure can be a useful enterprise. As many of the essays in this volume demonstrate, it is often precisely within the framework of a national culture that the events, connections, and interactions that challenge and cross over political boundaries become most apparent.

That said, it is important to clarify that our volume takes not the political, but the cultural focus of a German nation as its starting point in order to provide some coherence to a phenomenon, since "visual culture" is broad and potentially unwieldy. The term "German" in our title is a convenient shorthand to designate the German cultural nation rather than a nation-state or any one state. It refers generally to the German lands of Central Europe, including Austria and the German-speaking parts of Switzerland. But, as will become apparent in the contributions, it also identifies ties from Central Europe to communities and interests

---

6 Sebastian Conrad, *Globalisierung und Nation im Deutschen Kaiserreich* (Munich: Beck, 2006). Jürgen Osterhammel, *Die Verwandlung der Welt: Eine Geschichte des 19. Jahrhunderts* (Munich: Beck, 2010). See also their collaboration on Germany in *Das Kaiserreich transnational: Deutschland in der Welt, 1871–1914*, ed. Sebastian Conrad and Jürgen Osterhammel (Göttingen: Vandenhoeck & Ruprecht, 2004).
7 The global perspective has also explicitly made its way into visual culture studies. See Zoya Kocur, *Global Visual Culture: An Anthology* (Oxford: Wiley-Blackwell, 2011).

abroad, be they artists working in other European countries, German-speaking immigrant groups in North America, commercial ventures connected to numerous disparate geographical locations around the world, or colonial enterprises and political interests in Africa. Some chapters in this volume also point out that transnational connection in nineteenth-century visual culture was not unidirectional. Some discuss works and images whose main audience resided outside of Central Europe, and others focus on materials that might have eventually been brought to the German lands but originated elsewhere. Taken together these essays make clear that focusing on "German" visual cultural objects and practices can reveal the complex and extensively transnational character of the century that has often been called the age of nationalism.

The chapters in this volume transcend not only geographical boundaries, but also disciplinary borders as well. Their authors hail from a range of academic disciplines and this attests to the importance of visual culture in two ways. First, it suggests that elements, examples, artefacts, and aspects of visual culture can be productively illuminated from a wide range of interpretive and analytical perspectives. We will say more about this below with regard to our organization of the chapters. Second, the existing scholarly work of our contributors reveals the perceived significance of visual cultural materials for answering research questions in diverse disciplines. Several of our contributors have already published cutting-edge monographs in the last decade that address important questions related to visual artefacts from the German states of Central Europe in the nineteenth century. As historians, both David Ciarlo and J. P. Short have examined works of visual culture in the context of German colonialism.[8] Peter McIsaac, who works in the field of museum studies, has published on the role of collecting and assembling collections in modernity.[9] Two contributors trained in literary studies have written monographs that focus on visual representations of German history: Kathrin Maurer has examined school atlases, illustrated books, and photography to uncover spatial representations of the German past, while Vance

---

8 David Ciarlo, *Advertising Empire: Race and Visual Culture in Imperial Germany* (Cambridge, MA: Harvard University Press, 2011), John Phillip Short, *Magic Lantern Empire: Colonialism and Society in Germany* (Ithaca, NY: Cornell University Press, 2012). Indeed, the number of new works on nineteenth-century German colonial history in particular that have focused on visual culture is so large that *German History* dedicated a review essay in 2017 to the topic. Minu Haschemi Yekani and Ulrike Schaper, "Pictures, Postcards, Points of Contact: New Approaches to Cultural Histories of German Colonialism." *German History* 35, no. 4 (December 2017): 603–623, https://doi.org/10.1093/gerhis/ghx106
9 Peter McIsaac, *Museums of the Mind: German Modernity and the Dynamics of Collecting* (University Park, PA: Pennsylvania State University Press, 2007).

Byrd has explored the function of panoramas in public and private life and the ancillary texts that circulated around them as ways to engage with history in the nineteenth century.[10] As a scholar who works both in art history and literary studies, Catriona MacLeod has written about the relationship between sculpture and literature.[11] Christian Bachmann's work includes scholarship on periodicals and music as well as the metamediality and materiality of comics in the nineteenth and twentieth centuries, while Antje Pfannkuchen has written about acoustic as well as visual and textual media in the Romantic era.[12]

Engagement with visual aspects of the nineteenth century has also been central to the recent work of our other contributors. Agnes Hoffmann completed her dissertation on landscape aesthetics in literature, visual arts, and anthropology around 1900 and has revised it for publication.[13] Matthew O. Anderson's dissertation investigated issues of education and entertainment in early nineteenth-century illustrated children's literature in Germany, and Trevor Brandt's master's thesis in museum studies and material culture addressed both the visual and the haptic aspects of religious broadsides that came to America with early German-speaking immigrants.[14] In other words, this volume introduces new projects from established scholars and work from younger scholars who are beginning to leave their mark on this area of research.

A note about terminology is useful here: in this volume, we have chosen to refer to visual objects and related practices as visual culture. We hold that the

---

10 Kathrin Maurer, *Visualizing the Past: The Power of the Image in Nineteenth-Century Historicism* (Berlin: De Gruyter, 2013) and Vance Byrd, *A Pedagogy of Observation: Nineteenth-Century Panoramas, German Literature, and Reading Culture* (Lewisburg, PA: Bucknell University Press, 2017).
11 Catriona MacLeod, *Fugitive Objects: Sculpture and Literature in the German Nineteenth Century* (Evanston, IL: Northwestern University Press, 2011).
12 Christian A. Bachmann, *Macht der Musik: Musik in Karikatur, Bildergeschichte und Comic, 1830–1930* (Berlin: Ch. A. Bachmann Verlag, 2017); Antje Pfannkuchen, "When Nature Begins to Write Herself – German Romantics Read the Electrophore" (PhD dissertation, New York University, 2010) which is currently being revised for publication, and from which a version of chapter two has appeared as Antje Pfannkuchen, "A Matter of Visibility – Georg Christoph Lichtenberg's Art and Science of Observation." *Configurations* 24, no. 4 (2016): 375–400.
13 Agnes Hoffmann, *Landschaft im Nachbild: Imaginationen von Natur in der Literatur um 1900 bei Henry James und Hugo von Hofmannsthal*, Rombach Litterae 245 (Baden-Baden: Rombach, 2020).
14 Matthew O. Anderson, "Bildung and Bilder? Text, Illustration, and Adventure in Popular German Children's Books of the Early Nineteenth Century" (PhD dissertation, University of Texas at Austin, 2019); Trevor Brandt, "Perplexion and Pleasure: the *Geistlicher Irrgarten* Broadsides in the German-American Printshop, Home, and Mind" (MA thesis, University of Delaware, 2017). Available at: http://udspace.udel.edu/handle/19716/21797.

term 'culture' is necessary for accounting for this diverse and disparate set of practices. We, in turn, refer to the investigations and analyses of this material as visual culture studies, resulting in a terminological distinction between the objects/practices of visual culture and their study that not all scholars make consistently.[15] For example, while in some of the chapters included here the focus of attention might be on an image, in others the materiality, including the three-dimensionality, of visual objects constitutes a significant element of the analysis. Thus, the discussion of these objects is not limited to their visuality, but includes their role as visual cultural objects. This is true even for pages or printed sheets containing images that might seem to be merely two-dimensional representations of other objects. As the following chapters point out, the books, magazines, and even broadsides and re-used paper in a papercut have a third dimension that includes tactile operations. Such engagement with these items goes beyond the sense of vision. To be sure, no one term can adequately capture all the ways in which such materials might be used: picked up, turned, rotated, folded, or handled. By adding the term "culture" to the "visual" of these materials we insist on their rich and complex embeddedness in a multi-sensory world.

Numerous scholars and theorists have approached the concepts of visuality, visibility, image, and other central terms in myriad essays and books in the past three decades.[16] In soliciting contributions to this volume (and to the seminar and symposium that preceded it), we did not set any expectations about specific

---

[15] Some scholars prefer the term "visual studies." See James Elkins, *Visual Studies: A Skeptical Introduction* (New York: Routledge, 2003) or, more recently, *Farewell to Visual Studies*, ed. James Elkins, Sunil Manghani, and Gustav Frank (University Park, PA: The Pennsylvania State University Press, 2015). There is other disparity in the use of terminology. Nicholas Mirzoeff, for example, has used the term "visual culture" for both the object and the area of study. Nicholas Mirzoeff, "The Subject of Visual Culture," in *The Visual Culture Reader*, 2nd ed. (New York: Routledge, 2002), 6. Margaret Dikovitskaya uses the terms "visual culture" and "visual studies" interchangeably to designate the field of research. Margaret Dikovitskaya, "Major Theoretical Frameworks in Visual Culture," *The Handbook of Visual Culture*, ed. Ian Heywood and Barry Sandywell (New York: Berg, 2012), 68.

[16] Useful brief introductions include Jessica Evans and Stuart Hall, "What is Visual Culture?" in *Visual Culture: The Reader* (Thousand Oaks: Sage Publications, 1999), 1–7; Nicholas Mirzoeff, "The Subject of Visual Culture," in *The Visual Culture Reader* (New York: Routledge, 2002), 3–23; or Barry Sandywell and Ian Heywood, "Critical Approaches to the Study of Visual Culture: An Introduction to the Handbook," in *The Handbook of Visual Culture* (New York: Berg, 2012), 1–56. The "Visual Culture Questionnaire" published in the journal *October* in 1996 first revealed how diverse the answers are to the questions: what is visual culture and what is visual culture studies. Dikovitskaya's set of interviews with scholars a decade later makes clear that diversity still reigned. Margaret Dikovitskaya, *Visual Culture: The Study of the Visual after the Cultural Turn* (Cambridge, MA: The MIT Press, 2006).

aspects or modes of visual mediation that we wanted contributors to include or address. As a result, the volume also does not attempt to define visual culture studies as a certain set of analytical or interpretive practices. Indeed, our only guiding principle was that the visual materials and images discussed should help to reveal the range and diversity of modes that predated the rise of photography. Of course, given the advent of photography in the 1820s and the mass reproducibility of photographs by the 1880s, we anticipated that photography would in some of the chapters also serve as a foil against which other visual culture in the later part of the century was produced, disseminated, and received.

At the same time, we also did not intend to exclude traditional forms of art that have been the mainstay of art historical analysis over the decades. Yet, the ways in which hand-made art emerges in this volume does not relate to works that made their way into museum or gallery collections, but rather as painting that intersected with literary production, as glass works that circulated in commercial, scientific, and educational domains, or as papercuts that provided an intimate and personal alternative to, as well as commentary on, the aesthetic practice of sculpture.[17] Indeed, we were most interested in exploring precisely the connections between visual cultural objects and their environments, be they productive and reproductive forces, aspects of accessibility and dissemination, the engagement with viewers and audiences, large or small. Some of these are issues that would have been readily available to contemporary viewers of visual culture and thus might contribute to a richer historical understanding of the place and function of such objects in the nineteenth century. But, as some of the chapters will show, another approach to this material is to uncover the ways in which systems of production and distribution and reception were not at all obvious to contemporaries. Some investigations tell us more about the way visual culture worked and was socially networked than might have been apparent at the time.

As such, this volume makes no claims to providing either a comprehensive or a representative introduction to visual culture before the dominance of photographic reproduction. The contributions do not follow any particular theoretical directions or methodologies. And yet, even in the face of the broad range of work included here some common issues emerge. The chapters often point to productive overlap or intersections regarding research questions, aspects of production, new technologies, markets, and networks of dissemination, reception, or use. As a

---

[17] An early essay that focuses specifically on the set of processes that enables the creation, dissemination, and reception of visual culture, serves as one model for these kinds of questions. See John A. Walker and Sarah Chaplin, "Production, Distribution, and Consumption Model," in *Visual Culture: An Introduction* (Manchester: Manchester University Press, 1997), 65–80.

whole, the volume promises to provide readers with a sense of the enormous diversity of visual culture that was produced and consumed in the course of the nineteenth century and that for decades existed alongside, but was often more readily available and prominent than, photography. In the process the volume introduces readers to a range of interpretive questions and practices that we hope will be illuminating and inspiring.

As mentioned above, the volume includes work by scholars from fields as disparate as history, art history, museum studies, cultural studies, literary studies, and book and media studies. The subjects and the related modes or affordances of visual presentation investigated in their chapters are equally wide-ranging. They include philosophical ruminations on symbols and forms of graphic representation (Pfannkuchen on hieroglyphs); questions of the limits and manner of aesthetic expression in writing and painting (Hoffmann on the work of Adalbert Stifter); the literary preoccupation with both real and imagined human flight and the concomitant aerial vantage point it yields (Maurer on Jean Paul); the use and marketing or display of three-dimensional models for scientific investigation and health education (Short on Blaschke glass works of marine animals and McIsaac on wax figures from hygiene exhibitions); history and public representations of war (Byrd on panoramas and the press); the impact of scientific and technological apparatuses on formal innovation in printed caricatures (Bachmann on satirical magazines) or on the concept of scale (Hoffmann on Stifter); innovations in the printing of broadsides as they pertain to gendered religious practice (Brandt on the *Geistliche Irrgarten*); the depiction of adventure and moral lessons in illustrated books for youngsters (Anderson on illustrated Cooper editions); the intricate commentary of hand-made visual works about literature, prominent personas, or artistic networks (Macleod on papercuts); and the recycling and retooling of colonial images across time (Ciarlo on a range of publications). Some of the visual works under consideration here were meant to be touched, turned, folded, and manipulated; others were large in format or scale and meant to be viewed in public, often in the presence of others. Some were delicate or highly personal, meant only for special observers, while others were printed in large quantities and distributed by publishers and booksellers. Some objects were expensive, unique, and fragile; others involved thought constructs that were open to change and shifting conceptions. In the foreground of each chapter, however, is the issue of interaction between forms of visual culture and other issues, be they texts, scientific questions, commercial concerns, technology, or recent history.

To highlight some of the elements that we consider central to the visual culture of the nineteenth century we have clustered the contributions to this volume into three general categories. The first, "Ways of Seeing," establishes a broad conceptual overview of the era, focusing on novel approaches to visual culture. The chapters in that first cluster present specific examples of how the affordances of media and form changed over the course of the nineteenth century due to technological and social developments and consequently altered the way visual culture was seen. The second cluster, "Materials and Media," includes work that interacts with other modes of meaning in materials in the nineteenth century. The chapters in this section explore how materials are repurposed and how their forms and functions change as a result. Related to this is the way in which materials reflect social and technological shifts. The third cluster, "Image and Text," narrows the focus on the interaction of visual cultural materials to two prominent modes and considers the relationship of the visual to the verbal, of image to text.

Each section begins with an introductory orientation that both explains the category itself and why each paper was included in that section. These introductions were written by John D. Benjamin, a scholar who approaches visual culture studies via theories of reading multimodal texts,[18] especially twentieth- and twenty-first-century comics.[19] As a result, his perspective on these works that investigate nineteenth-century cultural objects illuminates the field and the issues raised here from a temporal distance, but one that also reveals the continuity of these pre-photographic forms into the subsequent centuries.

While this set of clusters reveals some of the issues central to each chapter, they are not meant to imply that there are not others that could have been selected or that other essays would not have generated different categories. We encourage readers to move among the various sections rather than limit themselves to following the structure of the book. We mention here only a few of the other issues that cross over the clustering we have presented here. One is the attention to gender, including the gender of the artists, authors, and producers of visual culture (MacLeod), the users and recreators (Brandt), or the visitors and spectators (McIsaac). Another is public forms of display or exhibition of visual works (Byrd, McIsaac). The technologies of print culture, including their innovations, limits, and affordances, and the phenomenon of seriality, also appear in numerous chapters (Bachmann, Byrd, Ciarlo, Anderson, Belgum). And the transnational spread and dissemination of visual material is relevant for many as well (Bachmann, Byrd, MacLeod, Brandt, Short, Ciarlo, Pfannkuchen, Anderson, Belgum). The commercial nature of many visual projects arises frequently, be it regarding the sale of works or the use of visual images to

---

18 John D. Benjamin, "Reading the German Graphic Novel: Understanding Learners' Readings of Multimodal Literary Comics" (PhD dissertation, University of Texas at Austin, 2019).
19 See, for example, John D. Benjamin, "Relocating the Text: *Mosaik* and the Invention of a German East German Comics Tradition," *The German Quarterly* 92, no. 2 (Spring 2019): 148–165.

promote other products (Byrd, Short, Anderson, Belgum). This theme could be contrasted with the focus on philosophical and aesthetic experimentation (Maurer, MacLeod, Pfannkuchen, Hoffmann) or with the creation of visual material in the interest of scientific knowledge and understanding (McIsaac, Short, Pfannkuchen, Hoffmann) or socio-political commentary (Bachmann, Byrd). This brief list of alternative themes could be considerably expanded. A host of other forms of visual cultural production and consumption that were important elements of nineteenth-century experience could have been included in the volume as well if space were unlimited. We think here, for example, of objects related to travel and tourism (postcards, maps, or scenic books) or performance (theater posters or stage and costume design). In other words, this volume does not purport to be the final word, but rather a reminder that rich veins of material and related research questions from the period before 1900 remain to be mined. It is a call for more work on the fascinating and innovative period of visual culture prior to the advent of photography, film, and electronic and digital modes of production and dissemination.

Finally, as an epilogue to the three sections, we include a short contribution on new digital tools for looking at the culture of the nineteenth century. A volume about visual culture published in the year 2020 would be remiss if it did not address the perspective that the present moment provides scholars and consumers of objects from previous eras. Not only do the amount and kinds of visual culture that have been produced since the pre-photographic period impact our ways of viewing earlier material, but recent means for viewing, archiving, and searching for such works can also leave their mark on how, why, and in what ways we study pre-photographic visual culture.

Bibliography

Alpers, Svetlana, Emily Apter, Carol Armstrong, Susan Buck-Morss, Tom Conley, Jonathan Crary, Thomas Crow et al. "Visual Culture Questionnaire." *October* 77 (Summer 1996): 25–70.

Anderson, Matthew O. "Bildung and Bilder? Text, Illustration, and Adventure in Popular German Children's Books of the Early Nineteenth Century." PhD diss., University of Texas at Austin, 2019.

Bachmann, Christian A. *Macht der Musik: Musik in Karikatur, Bildergeschichte und Comic, 1830–1930*. Berlin: Ch. A. Bachmann, 2017.

Benjamin, John D. "Reading the German Graphic Novel: Understanding Learners' Readings of Multimodal Literary Comics." PhD diss., University of Texas at Austin, 2019.

Benjamin, John D. "Relocating the Text: *Mosaik* and the Invention of a German East German Comics Tradition." *The German Quarterly* 92, no. 2 (Spring 2019): 148–165.

The BLOCK Reader in Visual Culture. New York: Routledge, 1996.

Brandt, Trevor. "Perplexion and Pleasure: The *Geistlicher Irrgarten* Broadsides in the German-American Printshop, Home, and Mind." MA thesis, The University of Delaware, 2017. The University of Delaware Library (1015314042). http://udspace.udel.edu/handle/19716/21797.

Byrd, Vance. *A Pedagogy of Observation: Nineteenth-Century Panoramas, German Literature, and Reading Culture*. Lewisburg, PA: Bucknell University Press, 2017.

Ciarlo, David. *Advertising Empire: Race and Visual Culture in Imperial Germany*. Cambridge, MA: Harvard University Press, 2011.

Conrad, Sebastian, and Jürgen Osterhammel, eds. *Das Kaiserreich transnational: Deutschland in der Welt, 1871–1914*. Göttingen: Vandenhoeck & Ruprecht, 2004.

Conrad, Sebastian. *Globalisierung und Nation im Deutschen Kaiserreich*. Munich: Beck, 2006.

Dikovitskaya, Margaret. "Major Theoretical Frameworks in Visual Culture." In *The Handbook of Visual Culture*, edited by Ian Heywood and Barry Sandywell, 68–89. New York: Berg, 2012.

Dikovitskaya, Margaret. *Visual Culture: The Study of the Visual after the Cultural Turn*. Cambridge, MA: MIT Press, 2006.

Early Popular Visual Culture. 2003–present.

Elkins, James. *Visual Studies: A Skeptical Introduction*. New York: Routledge, 2003.

Elkins, James, Sunil Manghani, and Gustav Frank, eds. *Farewell to Visual Studies*. University Park: Pennsylvania State University Press, 2015.

Evans, Jessica, and Stuart Hall. "What is Visual Culture?" In *Visual Culture: The Reader*, edited by Jessica Evans and Stuart Hall, 1–7. Thousand Oaks: Sage, 1999.

Handbuch Literatur & Visuelle Kultur. Edited by Claudia Benthien and Brigitte Weingart. Berlin: De Gruyter, 2014.

Haschemi Yekani, Minu, and Ulrike Schaper. "Pictures, Postcards, Points of Contact: New Approaches to Cultural Histories of German Colonialism." *German History* 35, no. 4 (December 2017): 603–623, https://doi.org/10.1093/gerhis/ghx106.

"Histories: Anglo-American Visual Studies, 1989–1999." In *Farewell to Visual Studies*, edited by James Elkins, Sunil Manghani, and Gustav Frank, 43–55. University Park: Pennsylvania State University Press, 2015.

Hoffmann, Agnes. *Landschaft im Nachbild: Imaginationen von Natur in der Literatur um 1900 bei Henry James und Hugo von Hofmannsthal*. Rombach Litterae 245. Baden-Baden: Rombach, 2020.

Jenks, Chris, ed. *Visual Culture*. New York: Routledge, 1995.

Journal of Visual Culture. 2002–present.

Kocur, Zoya. *Global Visual Culture: An Anthology*. Oxford: Wiley-Blackwell, 2011.

MacLeod, Catriona. *Fugitive Objects: Sculpture and Literature in the German Nineteenth Century*. Evanston, IL: Northwestern University Press, 2011.

Maurer, Kathrin. *Visualizing the Past: The Power of the Image in Nineteenth-Century Historicism*. Berlin: De Gruyter, 2013.

McIsaac, Peter M. *Museums of the Mind: German Modernity and the Dynamics of Collecting*. University Park: Pennsylvania State University Press, 2007.

Mirzoeff, Nicholas. *An Introduction to Visual Culture*. New York: Routledge, 1999.

Mirzoeff, Nicholas. "The Subject of Visual Culture." In *The Visual Culture Reader*, edited by Nicholas Mirzoeff, 2nd ed., 3–23. New York: Routledge, 2002.

Mirzoeff, Nicholas, ed. *The Visual Culture Reader*. New York: Routledge, 1998.

Osterhammel, Jürgen. *Die Verwandlung der Welt: Eine Geschichte des 19. Jahrhunderts*. Munich: Beck, 2010.

Paul, Gerhard. *Das visuelle Zeitlater: Punkt und Pixel*. Göttingen: Wallstein, 2016.

Pfannkuchen, Antje. "A Matter of Visibility – Georg Christoph Lichtenberg's Art and Science of Observation." *Configurations* 24, no. 4 (2016): 375–400.

Pfannkuchen, Antje. "When Nature Begins to Write Herself – German Romantics Read the Electrophore." PhD diss., New York University, 2010.

Rimmele, Marius, and Bernd Stiegler. *Visuelle Kulturen/Visual Culture*. Hamburg: Junius, 2012.

Sandywell, Barry, and Ian Heywood. "Critical Approaches to the Study of Visual Culture: An Introduction to the Handbook." In *The Handbook of Visual Culture*, edited by Barry Sandywell and Ian Heywood, 1–56. New York: Berg, 2012.

Schwartz, Vanessa R., and Jeannene M. Przyblyski, eds. *The Nineteenth-Century Visual Culture Reader*. New York: Routledge, 2004.

Short, John Phillip. *Magic Lantern Empire: Colonialism and Society in Germany*. Ithaca, NY: Cornell University Press, 2012.

Walker, John A., and Sarah Chaplin. "Production, Distribution, and Consumption Model." In *Visual Culture: An Introduction*, 65–80. Manchester: Manchester University Press, 1997.

Part 1: **Ways of Seeing**

John D. Benjamin
Ways of Seeing

Before we look closely at the production and reception of visual artefacts in order to characterize German visual culture in the period prior to and during the early moments of photography, we would do well to take a step back and consider the visual understanding of the world as it was coming into being in the nineteenth century. From what new vantage points, through which apparatuses, and according to what novel and mediated assumptions did people see? Artist and critic John Berger focused on this same starting point in his famed 1972 television series and accompanying volume introducing the ideologies of visual culture to the British public when he noted that it is "seeing which establishes our place in the surrounding world" and also that "the way we see things is affected by what we know or what we believe."[1] To understand German visual culture before photography, we can thus begin by asking what those living in the nineteenth century believed, what they knew, and how this conditioned what they saw.

In this first section, four chapters focus on how technological and social developments changed the way the public interacted with artefacts of visual culture in the nineteenth century. By considering the importance and role(s) of visual culture for life at the time and for our current interest in it, this section is an especially appropriate way to begin the volume.

Kathrin Maurer approaches these questions explicitly in the first chapter, "Ballooning as a Technology of Seeing in Jean Paul's 'Des Luftschiffers Giannozzo Seebuch' (1801)." Here she considers the literary and cultural reactions to the development of hot air balloon rides beginning in the eighteenth century. She argues that the balloon enabled people – no longer moored to the earth – to encounter and create new ways of understanding the world below both in a literal sense and through new modes of perception which echoed throughout a wide range of cultural production. She begins by introducing documents of the new ballooning craze, notably examples from the work of Goethe, Kleist, Günderrode, and Stifter, whose own painterly work is the subject of a chapter later in this volume. Maurer's piece then shifts to its primary focus, i.e., Jean Paul's "Des Luftschiffers Giannozzo Seebuch," a fictional travelogue about a balloon trip, to examine these changed perspectives in greater detail.

---

[1] John Berger, *Ways of Seeing* (London: Penguin, 1972), cover–1.

https://doi.org/10.1515/9783110696448-002

The following chapter, Christian A. Bachmann's "Through the Eyepiece and What Visual Satire Found There," considers the uses, origins, and meaning of round frames in early comics and satire magazines from the 1820s to the 1900s and connects these to technologies increasingly widely available in the period before photography. Like Maurer's changed vantage points, Bachmann observes how the ways we "see" through round frames are socio-historically and technologically determined. Just as the commercialization of the hot air balloon enabled perceptual shifts in diverse fields, including visual art and literature, in Bachmann's chapter, the microscope, the telescope, and the laterna magica alter the ways early comics and satirical magazine authors and artists saw and made use of the available forms for their readers.

The third and fourth chapters in this section look at how people interacted with visual material in public spaces and how their historically determined viewing conditions effect meaning. Vance Byrd's contribution, "Enacting the Past: Nineteenth-Century Illustrated Periodicals and Painted Panoramas," considers how the media biographies of panoramas – huge traveling paintings that encircled their viewers providing them the sense that they were in the time and place of important historical moments depicted – and periodicals related to issues of memory and commemoration. This transnational media production presented spectators and readers alike with a new way to visualize history at a pivotal moment coexistent with the rise of nationalism.

Finally, Peter M. McIsaac's chapter, "Visual Cultures of Popular Anatomy Exhibition: The Role of Visitor Environment in Shaping the Impact of Public Health Education," examines how *fin de siècle* anatomy exhibitions, or *Panoptiken* (panoptica) – extensive public displays using anatomical models and human specimens – were created to provide education on health. McIsaac considers how gendered societal norms determined public interaction with the material in various contexts. Like the other chapters in this opening section, McIsaac's sheds light on how the public's views shaped and were shaped by the technologies with which they interacted in a dialectic. And like in Byrd's chapter, McIsaac's investigation of the international circulation of these media, that is, how they were transported around Central Europe to reach large audiences, links well to some of the questions taken up in this volume's following section, "Materials and Media."

Bibliography

Berger, John. *Ways of Seeing*. London: Penguin, 1972.

Kathrin Maurer
Ballooning as a Technology of Seeing in Jean Paul's "Des Luftschiffers Giannozzo Seebuch" (1801)

Ever since the first hot air and hydrogen balloons rose into the sky in late eighteenth-century Europe, writers have been fascinated with these aerial spectacles. In France, Britain, and Germany literary artists wrote about how they witnessed such events or how they poetically imagined these journeys over the clouds. Previous research has focused on balloons in literature from a thematic, discursive, and poetic perspective.[1] This chapter, however, investigates ballooning as a technology of seeing. This topic raises a number of questions: How does the technology of ballooning stimulate new forms of visual perception?[2] What is the relation between the balloon and the viewing subject? How does ballooning shape the human (visual) sensorium? To address these questions, this chapter focuses on Jean Paul's (1763–1825) work "Des Luftschiffers Giannozzo Seebuch" ("Aeronaut Giannozzo's Voyage Diary") (1801).[3] Jean Paul's fictive travelogue about an imagined balloon journey is an excellent source for understanding how modes of seeing are intertwined with balloon technology. In fact, its title, "Seebuch," is a pun with visual implications: The work could be understood to be a journal about nautical

---

[1] Heinz Brüggemann, "Luftbilder eines kleinstädtischen Jahrhunderts: Ekstase und imaginäre Topographie in Jean Paul: *Des Luftschiffers Giannozzo Seebuch*," in *Die Stadt in der europäischen Romantik*, ed. Gerhard von Graevenitz (Würzburg: Königshausen & Neumann, 2000), 127–182; Jürgen Link, "Literaturanalyse als Interdiskursanalyse: Am Beispiel des Ursprungs literarischer Symbolik in der Kollektivsymbolik," in *Diskurstheorien und Literaturwissenschaft*, ed. Harro Müller and Gerhard von Graevenitz (Frankfurt a.M.: Suhrkamp, 1988), 284–307; Florian Welle, *Der irdische Blick durch das Fernrohr: Literarische Wahrnehmungsexperimente vom 17. bis zum 20. Jahrhundert* (Würzburg: Königshausen und Neumann, 2009), 123–144.
[2] My research emphasizes the connection between vision and the balloon as a technology of seeing in Jean Paul's writing. For research on seeing and perception, see Victoria Niehle, "Die ästhetische Funktion des Raumes: Jean Paul Des Luftschiffer Giannozzo Seebuch," in *Raumlektüren: Der Spatial Turn und die Literatur der Moderne*, ed. Tim Mehigan and Alan Corkhill (Bielefeld: transcript, 2013), 69–85, and Monika Schmitz-Emans "Über Bilder und die bildene Kunst bei Jean Paul," in *Jean Paul und die Bilder: Bildkünstlerische Auseinandersetzungen mit seinem Werk: 1783–2013*, ed. Monika Schmitz-Emans and Wolfram Benda (Würzburg: Königshausen & Neumann, 2013), 19–64.
[3] Jean Paul, "Des Luftschiffers Giannozzo Seebuch," in *Jean Paul: Sämtliche Werke*, vol. 3, ed. Norbert Miller (Darmstadt: Wissenschaftliche Buchgesellschaft, 2000), 925–1010. All translations from the German into English are mine.

(die "See" = the "sea") experience (transposed into the sky), and also as a 'Seh-Buch,' (seeing or sight-book) a book about new modes of seeing, perceiving, and understanding the world from above.

A close reading of Jean Paul's "Seebuch" reveals that the technology of ballooning serves as an affective medium that brings about a psychological state of ecstasy in the fictive balloonist. This affective mode introduces new forms of visual perception in Jean Paul's text, and, further, it steers processes not only of seeing, but also of writing. By utilizing theories of technology and vision (Jonathan Crary) and theories of affect (Brian Massumi), as well as recent discussions of the aerial view, this chapter shows that ballooning was not just a discrete technological invention that impacted travel and the vantage points of individual passengers; rather, it played a powerful role in shaping the human sensorium, creating imaginaries, and generating new modes of aesthetic representation. To demonstrate how ballooning can be understood as a technology of seeing, I begin with a brief overview of late eighteenth- and nineteenth-century balloon technology and its appearance in literature.

1 Ballooning, visual culture, and literature

Only a few years before the French Revolution, France served as the stage for realizing the ancient human dream of flying. The Montgolfier brothers, sons of a paper manufacturer, launched their first hot air balloon on 5 June 1783. Lifted by buoyant gases, the balloon demonstrated the viability of 'lighter-than-air' flight and was certainly one of the most important inventions of the time. This first hot air balloon marked a new phase in history: the human exploration and conquest of the aerial sphere by manned flying ships. Since then, engineers, enthusiasts, and entrepreneurs experimented with, improved, developed, and wrote about balloon flying technology. To test the possibility of human survival at such atmospheric heights (approximately 5,200 and 6,600 feet), the first passengers sent up on balloons were animals (sheep and chickens), but, soon, fearless humans took to the air as passengers and captains.[4] The French were hot air balloon aficionados, and in the late eighteenth century such flights became a spectacle for the rich aristocrats at Versailles, who could afford to watch ornamented and Rococo-styled balloons lift into the air. Soon, however,

---

[4] For an historical overview of the early ballooning, see Wolfgang Behringer und Constance Ott-Koptschalijski, *Der Traum vom Fliegen: Zwischen Mythos und Technik* (Frankfurt a. M.: Fischer, 1991), 320.

a mechanic who was not of noble birth, the aeronaut Jean-Pierre Blanchard (1753–1809), changed ballooning from an elitist spectacle into one suited for the general public. Blanchard's sensational crossing of the English Channel in 1785 made him world famous, and ballooning became an entertainment for a mass bourgeois audience.[5] Later in the 1860s, Félix Nadar (1820–1910) became ballooning's popstar; his spectacular journeys and failures still fascinate us today.[6] In Germany, balloon expeditions, while not as highly developed as in France, and often associated with private and commercial enterprises, also became popular. In the mid-nineteenth century, Wilhelmine Reichard (1788–1848), one of the few female aeronauts, ran a lucrative ballooning business, and anyone with money to spare could book a tour with her.[7]

This ballooning craze, which started in the late eighteenth century and lasted well into the nineteenth century, was documented in pamphlets, caricatures, paintings, newspaper articles, treatises, and theories about ballooning. Some early essays about ballooning, such as Thomas Baldwin's *Airopaidia* (1786) addressed the technical, physical, and aesthetic aspects of this technology. Recounting his balloon flight over the British countryside, Baldwin provides scholarly observations about heights, geography, clouds, and vegetation while also describing flying as something utterly sublime and beautiful.[8] Balloons even inspired fashion trends, influencing the design of clothing as well as fine china and porcelain figurines.[9] But most interestingly for my exploration of the balloon as an aesthetic medium, ballooning inspired works of imaginative literature.[10] Whilst in the air, balloonists recited poems and sang hymns about the greatness of ballooning as well as about the generosity of the noblemen above whose properties they sailed. Literature of all kinds about balloons proliferated. Even writers who had never sailed in a balloon, nor seen one with their own eyes, wrote about balloons. An early German author whose reflections on ballooning were particularly influential was Christoph Martin Wieland (1733–1813). Wieland praised the new flying

---

5 See discussion about Blanchard in Eckert, "Zur Geschichte der Ballonfahrt," 80–83.
6 For a history of Nadar's ballooning adventures, see Adam Begley, *The Great Nadar: The Man behind the Camera* (New York: Tim Duggan Books, 2017).
7 See reference to Wilhemine Reichard in Eckert, "Zur Geschichte der Ballonfahrt," 106–110.
8 See discussion about Baldwin in Caren Kaplan, "The Balloon Prospect: Aerostatic Observation and the Emergence of Militarized Aeromobility," in *From Above: War, Violence, and Verticality*, ed. Caren Kaplan and Lisa Parks (New York: Oxford University Press, 2014), 19–40.
9 See reference about balloon fashion in Eckert, "Zur Geschichte der Ballonfahrt," 47–62.
10 Eckhard Schinkel, "Der Ballon in der Literatur," in *Leichter als Luft: Zur Geschichte der Ballonfahrt*, ed. Bernard Korzus and Gisela Noehles (Münster: Westfälisches Landesmuseum für Kunst und Kulturgeschichte, 1978), 200–236.

technology as a product of rational progress in the *Teutsche Merkur*, but also adopted a skeptical attitude towards its popularization. He coined the satirical term 'Aeropetomanie' to describe the public's obsession with balloons during his time.[11] Heinrich von Kleist (1777–1811), Arthur Schopenhauer (1788–1860), and Johann Wolfgang von Goethe (1749–1832) also wrote diary entries, letters, and essays about ballooning. In fact, the last once wrote that he regretted not having invented ballooning himself.[12]

In addition to authors of classical German literature, other intellectuals of the eighteenth century, such as the theologian Daniel Jenisch (1762–1804), the priest and poet Michael Denis (1729–1800), and the writer and etiquette expert Adolph Freiherr von Knigge (1752–1796), also participated in popularizing ballooning as a theme.[13] These authors, however, frequently expressed skepticism about ballooning, denouncing it as a modern technology that enabled humans to compete with God. Others, such as Karoline von Günderrode (1780–1806) praised the cosmic power of the eternal sky and lamented human bondedness to the earth in her poem "Der Luftschiffer" (1804). Ballooning also played a central role, in conjunction with gender roles and emotions, such as in Adalbert Stifter's (1805–1868) famous novella *Der Condor* (1840). Most interesting in the context of this article is the work of Jean Paul, since in comparison to other authors, his writing on ballooning strongly highlights the affective and visual experience of flying. In doing so, Jean Paul shows how balloon technology can shape the human sensorium and even facilitate specific forms of poetic 'balloon-writing.' His writing on ballooning has to be seen in the context of a whole discourse of balloon literature that emerged after the first balloon ascents as well as an extension of his deep interest in vision, image, and seeing.[14]

2 Ballooning and ecstasy

Jean Paul's work "Des Luftschiffers Giannozzo Seebuch" (1801) is an appendix to his novel *Titan* (1800–1803), a 900-page work about the life of the Spanish aristocrat Albano de Cesara. Whereas *Titan* contains some classical elements of

---

[11] Schinkel, "Der Ballon in der Literatur," 201–202.
[12] Schinkel, "Der Ballon in der Literatur," 203.
[13] A discussion about ballooning as a fashion see Schinkel, "Der Ballon in der Literatur," 204–210.
[14] For discourse on ballooning, see Schinkel, "Der Ballon in der Literatur," 200–236, and for Jean Paul's interest in the visual, see Sabine Eickenrodt, *Augen-spiel: Jean Pauls optische Metaphorik der Unsterblichkeit* (Göttingen: Wallstein Verlag, 2013), 254–268.

the traditional *Bildungsroman*, its appendix, the "Seebuch," adheres fully to Jean Paul's romantic, highly self-reflexive style of writing, which uses irony to create ambivalences and double meanings.[15] Titan tells the story of the sentimental education of Cesara, and the appendix's retelling of Giannozzo's catastrophic life provides a mirror for the main novel's ironic reflection on the genre of the *Bildungsroman*, although Giannozzo does not appear as a character elsewhere in *Titan* or in other works by Jean Paul. The "Seebuch" has been compared to Laurence Sterne's (1713–1768) ironic novel *Tristram Shandy* (1759–1767), because of Jean Paul's use of puns, digressions, and exaggerations, and his work's embeddedness in the satirical and picaresque tradition.[16] The "Seebuch" takes on the form of a travelogue, with references to actual places (such as small German duchies and city-states), historical figures (Frederick II), and historical events. The protagonist Giannozzo is the fictive author of this travelogue, while Jean Paul inserts himself into the narrative as an editor figure, named Jean Paul Fr. Richter, who comments on Giannozzo's story from time to time and inserts footnotes in the main text. At the same time, the "Seebuch" interweaves fantastical elements describing the dreamlike and paradisical environment the balloon is traveling through. When the protagonist Giannozzo hovers in his balloon over the small duchies of Germany, he issues a scathing critique of bourgeois society and its narrowminded view of life, its religious rituals, and its lack of intellectualism. Research often highlights this rather misanthropic perspective from which Jean Paul's text articulates a social and political critique of contemporary Germany.[17]

While criticizing society from above, the balloonist enters into a state of ecstasy, which Jürgen Link considers in his work on ballooning a collective symbol.[18] When Giannozzo flies above the clouds, he, not unlike Icarus, is thrilled

---

15 For more information on Jean Paul's self-reflexive style of writing by using humor, irony, and satire, see for example Paul Fleming, *The Pleasures of Abandonment: Jean Paul and the Life of Humor* (Würzburg: Königshausen & Neumann, 2006). For the concept of romantic irony, see Ernst Behler, *Ironie und Literarische Moderne* (Paderborn: Ferdinand Schöningh, 1997).
16 James Vigus, *Shandean Humour in English and German Literature and Philosophy* (London: Taylor and Francis, 2017).
17 Florian Welle, *Der irdische Blick durch das Fernrohr: Literarische Wahrnehmungsexperimente vom 17. bis zum 20. Jahrhundert* (Würzburg: Königshausen und Neumann, 2009), 123–144; Gerald Bär, "Poetische Perspektiven aus dem (Fessel) Ballon: das Jahrhundertereignis als Eventcharakter und seine Fiktionalisierung," in *Transit oder Transformation? Sprachliche und Literarische Grenzerfahrungen: Yearbook of the German Studies Association in Ireland*, ed. Sabine Egger (Konstanz: Hartung-Gorre Verlag, 2016), 29–48.
18 Jürgen Link, "Literaturanalyse als Interdiskursanalyse: Am Beispiel des Ursprungs literarischer Symbolik in der Kollektivsymbolik," in *Diskurstheorien und Literaturwissenschaft*, ed. Harro Müller and Gerhard von Graevenitz (Frankfurt a.M.: Suhrkamp, 1988), 284–307.

with this new aerial experience of heights, and, for him, the view from above is intertwined with intense affects. Brian Massumi defines affect as a "non-conscious experience of intensity," which refers to a pre-discursive and unstructured form of experiences as well as visceral responses and reactions in the subject or viewer.[19] For Giannozzo the sky becomes a wide ocean embodying a type of primordial soup, which puts him into a state of pre-rational trance.[20] The following passage aptly describes this state of ecstasy:

> I glided on, warmly, on an immense silver sea, gathering from the soft foam of fallen stars within a sea, a sea soft and white, like snow-mist, like the scent of light–all the windows of my hut were shimmering – I was completely illuminated. I sailed over the night-earth covered by the cloudy sky, in whose flood the risen moon stood like a swan with its shiny plumage radiating all the waves, before it flew out into the blue.[21]

In this passage, the protagonist elevates himself into the blue sky and has a kind of out-of-body experience, as boundaries and restrictions dissolve. How can one interpret this affective state of ecstasy? In many ways, this moment of elevation is reminiscent of the experience of the sublime, an important aesthetic category we know from philosophers such as Edmund Burke (1729–1797) and Immanuel Kant (1724–1804).[22] Ballooning, for Giannozzo, is literally an "elevating" experience of incomparable and overwhelming beauty. In his writing about ballooning, Wieland had already discussed the sublime aspects of such aerial travel, linking the aesthetic beauty of the view to human progress and the triumph of reason.[23] Jean Paul's aesthetics of ballooning, however, transcends the Enlightenment concept of the sublime. Although ballooning represents an elevating experience for Giannozzo, this aesthetic moment contains no

---

19 Brian Massumi, *Parables for the Virtual: Movement, Affect, Sensation* (Durham, NC: Duke University Press, 2007), 30.
20 See the references in German in Jean Paul's "Seebuch" that were rephrased in the sentence in the main text: "weite lebendige Nachtmeer" (966), "Rausch des Äthers" (961), and "sonnentrunkene Perspektive" (967).
21 "Ich glitt warm angeweht auf einem unabsehlichen silbernen, aus dem zu zarten Schaum geschlagenen Sternen zusammenwallenden Meere weiter – ein Meer, weich und weiß wie Schneenebel, wie Lichtduft – alle Fenster meiner Hütte schimmerten – ich war ganz erleuchtet. Ich schiffte über die Nachterde hingedeckten Wolkenhimmel, in dessen Flut der aufgegangene Mond wie ein Schwan mit seinem Glanzgefieder alle Wogen durchstrahlend stand, eh' er herausflog ins Blaue," Jean Paul, "Seebuch," 967.
22 Edmund Burke, *A Philosophical Enquiry into the Origin of our Ideas of the Sublime and the Beautiful* (Cambridge: Cambridge University Press, 2014); Immanuel Kant, *Kritik der Urteilskraft*, ed. Karl Vorländer (Hamburg: Felix Meiner Verlag, 1990).
23 For a discussion on the sublime, ballooning, and Wieland, see Schinkel, "Der Ballon in der Literatur," 201.

traces of reason or rationality. Rather, being aerial in Jean Paul's texts generates in the protagonist a pre-reflective state of affective intensity. Giannozzo does not equate the thrill of heights with a form of rational sublimity. Instead, Giannozzo views this experience of ecstasy as a prime source of imagination, poesy, and creativity. Referencing Wolfgang Iser, Heinz Brüggemann interprets this moment of ecstasy in Jean Paul's "Seebuch" as a key that unlocks the power of imagination. Through Giannozzo's out-of-body-experience, he gains the freedom and autonomy to generate aesthetic products. Brüggemann comments on this state of ecstasy in the following way:

> The overcoming of gravity, the ascent from the earth in the airship, appears to him [Giannozzo, KM] as a mirror, as a medium, as a condition of the possibility of another form of overcoming confinement, of stepping out of oneself, of outward feeling, and it is realized for him in an ecstatic state, as Iser has called it, to be both in the person and outside of this person, a condition that requires form, in the mask, in the play, in the self-presentation.[24]

Whereas Brüggemann describes the moment of ecstasy as entirely rooted in Giannozzo and his power of imagination, I would like to shift the attention to the role of technology. It is not Giannozzo as the viewing subject who controls the aesthetic process, but rather the technology of ballooning that stimulates the aesthetic and visual sensorium and triggers the process of writing. Thus, the moment of ecstasy and the technology of ballooning are not two different entities, but rather are deeply intertwined. As we shall see, they constitute an entanglement, in which the technology generates modes of experiencing, perceiving, and representing the world.

3 Seeing the world via ballooning

In Jean Paul's "Seebuch," the balloon itself, the so-called envelope, already reminds us of an artificial replica of a human eye because of its rounded shape. But beyond this, the text provides many more connections between the balloon and the human eye. For example, the protagonist notes that the balloon eyeball

---

[24] "Die Überwindung der Schwerkraft, die Auffahrt von der Erde im Luftschiff, erscheint ihm [Giannozzo, KM] als Spiegel, als Medium, als Bedingung der Möglichkeit für eine andere Form, Eingeschlossenheit zu überwinden, aus sich selbst heraus zu treten, der Außerhalb-Befindlichkeit, und sie verwirklicht sich für ihn im ekstatischen Zustand, wie Iser das genannt hat, zugleich in der Person und außerhalb ihrer selbst zu sein, ein Zustand der der Form bedarf, in der Maske, im Spiel, in der Selbstinszenierung." Brüggemann, "Luftbilder," 141.

is covered with a leathery tissue.[25] This tissue is reminiscent of the sclera, the dense skin around the human eye-ball to which the muscles that move the eye are attached. Projected onto the balloon as an artificial eye, these muscles are represented by the ropes fastened to the balloon's basket. Giannozzo describes the basket as a "leathery cube, which has windows on all six sides, including on its floor."[26] Within the balloon's basket the windows constitute the multi-facetted lens through which the world can be observed. This lens opens up a panoramic view (through the side windows) as well as bird's-eye view (through the vertical window on the floor).

In other words, with its windows as a lens, basket as the posterior chamber, and ropes as the optic nerve, the balloon reflects the physiological mechanisms in the human eye. Furthermore, depending on the position of the balloon and the surrounding atmospheric conditions, the lens can adjust its visual acuity. Sometimes the view can be crystal clear against the blue sky; at other times, when it is cloudy and foggy, visibility is low.[27] Giannozzo, as the balloon's captain, seems to be an integral part of this balloon eye. The text references him as the "black head in a green coat."[28] Translating this image into the aesthetics of the artificial balloon eye, this black dot, often described as jumpy and jittery, embodies a twitching black pupil surrounded by a green iris.

This merging of physiological metaphors of seeing and balloon construction highlights the idea that the balloon embodies a technology of seeing, which is able to perceive the world in ways similar to the human eye. This conceptualization of Giannozzo's balloon, thus already anticipates Odilon Redon's painting *The Eye like a strange Balloon mounts towards Infinity* (1882), a visual representation of this idea that would not appear until more than eighty years after Jean Paul's novel.

This function of the balloon is amplified by the fact that Giannozzo's own eyes do not play the main role during his aerial journey, rather his eyesight is overtaken by the giant artificial balloon eye as an instrument or a kind of prosthetic enabling a type of hyper-visibility. As in Odilon's picture, the balloon in Jean Paul's work is portrayed as one gigantic eye dissociated from its physiological situation of seeing and placed into a superhuman context by means of optical technology. To be sure, Redon's eye-balloon is looking upward towards the sky, whereas Jean Paul's balloon-eye is directed downwards (through the view of the floor bottom of the basket) and panoramic (through the view over the

---

25 "mit feinem, aber unbekannten Leder mit Seide überzogen" Jean Paul, "Seebuch," 928.
26 "Lederwürfel, der auf allen sechs Seiten Fenster hat, auch auf dem Fußboden," Jean Paul, "Seebuch," 928.
27 "Ich trat jetzt trübe und wild auf den Brocken hinaus," Jean Paul, "Seebuch," 965.
28 "Schwarzkopf in grünem Mantel," Jean Paul, "Seebuch," 928.

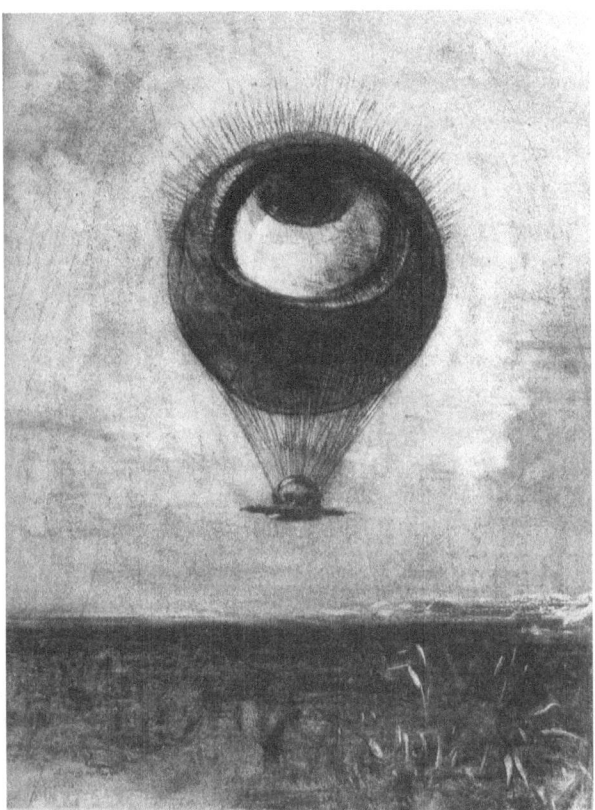

Figure 1: Odilon Redon's painting *The Eye like a strange Balloon mounts towards Infinity* (1882). Permission granted by the Los Angeles County Museum of Art.

railing of the basket sides), but in both cases the technological construction of the balloon itself becomes the instrument of seeing.

How does Jean Paul's balloon perceive the world then? In theories about the aerial, the view from above is often associated with an imperial master gaze, such as in the context of modern warfare. Peter Sloterdijk's theories on verticality and war as well as the most recent discussions about the politics of verticality by Eyal Weizman are examples of this interpretation.[29] However,

---

29 Peter Sloterdijk, *Terror from Air* (Cambridge, MA: The MIT Press, 2009); Eyal Weizman, *Forensic Architecture: Violence at the Threshold of Detectability* (Cambridge, MA: The MIT Press, 2017).

Jean Paul's balloon-eye does not follow a stable vertical perspective, which in turn could be read as a symbol for social and political superiority. Instead, the balloon's mode of seeing perceives the world through three, rather unstable, visual registers: 1) flexible perspective of the observer, 2) flattening, and 3) micro- and macro-vision. In this context, the work by Gerhard Neumann on perceptual techniques is crucial.[30] Neumann focuses on several media (binoculars, microscope, balloon) and their respective effects of distorting a central perspective. My analysis builds on Neumann's work, expanding it by concentrating on the balloon as a technology of seeing that not only distorts the central perspective. It disorients the observer, flattens the represented space, and confuses the focus of seeing.

Let us explore the first visual register of the balloon's mode of seeing: the flexibility of the observer. In Giannozzo's fourteen chapters about his aerial journeys it soon becomes evident that the aeronaut's ability to control the flight path is severely limited. In fact, the balloon itself and its position in the air have a much greater influence on the route than the navigator. And what is seen from the balloon is often highly contingent on how the wind blows; whether the balloon sails south or north is not up to the pilot. Therefore, when describing his experience, Giannozzo often describes his experience as passive: "by unstable blows I let myself sway back and forth over Saxony."[31] The swaying of the balloon produces an unstable, shifting vision. In the eighteenth and nineteenth centuries, hot air balloons' unsteerability was seen as their greatest problem. Pioneers of ballooning struggled to control their balloons' routes, and their trips often ended in disaster, as did the final trip of Jean-François Pilâtre de Rozier (1754–1785), who died when his balloon crashed near Wimereaux in the Pas-de-Calais during an attempt to fly across the English Channel.[32]

In addition, the visual prospect from the balloon is not only unstable and uncontrollable, it also has a kind of flattening effect. Giannozzo describes the view from the balloon as a "surface that extended into infinity."[33] As seen from the balloon the earth appears as flat, suggesting a map-like and topographical representation of the world. The text notes that Giannozzo "maps," i.e., he measures and

---

[30] Gerhard Neumann, "Fernrohr, Mikroskop, Luftballon: Wahrnehmungstechnik und Literatur in der Goethezeit," in *Spektakuläre Experimente: Praktiken der Evidenzproduktion im 17. Jahrhundert*, ed. Helmar Schramm (Boston: Walter De Gruyter, 2006), 345–377.
[31] "vom unsteten Wehen ließ ich mich über Sachsen hin- und herwürfeln," Jean Paul, "Seebuch," 931.
[32] See Eckert, "Zur Geschichte der Ballonfahrt" 13–128.
[33] "Fläche, die ins Unendliche hinausfloß," Jean Paul, "Seebuch," 959.

makes cartographic observations.³⁴ In fact, the topographical flatness of the view from the balloon had already been beautifully shown in the writings of Thomas Baldwin, in *Aeropaidia*. The illustrations as well as Baldwin's descriptions of the ground and the clouds were devoid of spatial depth and horizon. Jean Paul's text likewise eliminates depth, and the earth becomes an endless two-dimensional surface.

> Four and a half thousand feet deep the wide earth – I thought I floated – ran under me, and its broad plate came towards me, whereupon mountains and woodworks and monasteries [. . .] were so wildly confused that a reasonable man above must think that this may only be loose building materials, which you first have to pull apart into a beautiful park.³⁵

This passage highlights the flatness of the view from the balloon, the earth looks like a broad plate. And yet, there is no order on this map; the topographical phenomena are chaotically placed and seemingly provisional. From the perspective of the balloon, the known horizon that ordered the world when percieved at ground level according to a vanishing point is dissolved.

Lastly, the balloon view also has a distorting effect since it can minimize and enlarge the phenomena of the world. That is the third aspect of the visual register of the balloon: the micro- and macro-vision. Giannozzo mentions the miniature cities that can be seen from the balloon.³⁶ This miniaturization of the world was certainly a revolution in perception. Although one could have had similar visual experiences from towers and mountains or through inverted telescopes, the view from a balloon provided a shrinking effect that was unprecedented and not otherwise available in the early nineteenth century. The minimizing impression in Jean Paul's text also has another side: the miniature landscape takes on new shapes and forms that make some objects appear out of proportion. Mountain formations, for example, can look like a giant snake.³⁷ This shift between micro- and macro perspectives is further enhanced by the fact that Giannozzo uses binoculars, yet another prosthetic that can alter human vision. The binoculars make it possible for him to see things that otherwise would remain invisible from the balloon's gondola. For example, Giannozzo uses the binoculars to spy on a couple, whose courtship he disturbs when he accidently lands his balloon on the rotunda where

---

34 "mappiert," Jean Paul, "Seebuch," 959.
35 "Vierhalbtausend Fuß tief rannte die weite Erde – ich glaubte festzuschweben – unter mir dahin, und ihr breiter Teller lief mir entgegen, worauf sich Berge und Holzungen und Klöster [. . .] so wild und eng durcheinanderwarfen, dass ein vernünftiger Mann oben denken musste, das seien nur umhergerollte Baumaterialien, die man erst zu einem schönen Park auseinanderziehe." Jean Paul, "Seebuch," 959.
36 "Zwergenstädte," Jean Paul, "Seebuch," 927.
37 Jean Paul, "Seebuch," 927.

they are meeting.[38] Besides using them to snoop on lovers, Giannozzo labels his binoculars an instrument of war.[39] In fact, he observes a battle, during which the Castle of Blasenstein is about to be attacked by French troops, which works as a reality effect in this rather imaginary and unbelievable story. Giannozzo tries to exchange messages with the French infantry, throwing down letters affixed to stones.[40] On the one hand, this scene points to military discourse about ballooning. Already during ballooning's early phase, there was speculation that balloons could be useful in waging war.[41] In fact, in 1806 Napoleon used balloons for aerial reconnaissance during the Napoleonic Wars – the painting by Francisco Goya (1746–1728) *The Balloon* (1813–1816) aptly captures this militarization of ballooning.[42] On the other hand, the absurd scene of stones falling from above in an attempt at communication in Jean Paul's text exemplifies and ironizes the notion of ballooning as a military technology. Giannozzo himself does not engage in militaristic or nationalistic ambitions, rather he is relieved when his balloon pivots away from the firing battalions. The troops become seemingly invisible and insignificant as the balloon moves off into the endless sky.

These three aspects of the balloon view – the flexible observer position, the flattening, and macro- and micro perspectives – suggest that, in Jean Paul's work, ballooning's primary feature is its irritating dislocation of the human eye by means of technology. The balloon view no longer represents the world within the tradition of a central perspective, which, in broad strokes, organizes and guides the view according to one vanishing point and gives the impression of three-dimensional space. Rather, through the balloon itself, the world is expanded and flattened into an indefinite and diffused space with no clear boundaries.

How can we interpret this change of vision that I observed in my close reading of Jean Paul's work within a theoretical framework of visual studies? According to Jonathan Crary, the early nineteenth century was a decisive time for the construction of new forms of seeing and observers. Technological inventions such as the stereoscope (invented in 1820s and 1830s) and the panorama (the first already constructed in 1787), destabilized the concept of a linear and stable vision. Following Crary implies that the dissolution and critique of the central

---

[38] Jean Paul, "Seebuch," 948.
[39] "Kriegsperspectiv," Jean Paul, "Seebuch," 945.
[40] Giannozzo calls this message form: "letter-stone or letter-quail" ("Brief-Stein oder Brief-Wachtel"), Jean Paul, "Seebuch," 982.
[41] On the military use of balloons, see Walter Locher, "Zur militärischen Nutzung des Ballons," in *Leichter als Luft: Zur Geschichte der Ballonfahrt*, ed. Bernd Korzus (Münster: Landesverband Westfalen-Lippe, 1985), 238–250.
[42] Walter Locher, "Zur militärischen Nutzung des Ballons," 238–250.

perspective did not begin first with the avant-garde movements of the twentieth century; the break in classical representation had already begun much earlier.[43] Crary explains that the camera obscura, despite its closeness to the human eye, does not guarantee a transparent, realistic representation of reality. Although, the camera obscura is often regarded as an instrument of visual truth, Crary makes the point that it is an example of subjectivized vision since it executes a fusion between the photographic apparatus and the observing subject.[44] In fact, he calls the camera obscura an "*assemblage,*" "an object about which something is said and at the time an object that is used."[45] The impact of this human-machine assemblage suggests that there are no fixed boundaries between the perceiving subject and the machine (for example the apparatus of a camera).[46] In other words, for Crary the physiological observer comes into the camera obscura as an autonomous producer of visual experiences.

In similar ways, the optical configuration of Jean Paul's balloon eye, although differing from those of a stereoscope and the panorama (Crary's examples), suggests a technology of seeing that also embodies this element of subjective vision as well as an entanglement between the material object and sensing human. In fact, the balloon and its de-centering modes of vision can be read as another example of Crary's idea of subjective vision. Jean Paul's balloon is reminiscent of an eyeball and prescient of a camera, but it does not provide an "objective" representation of the world. Instead, the balloon is a seeing-machine in Jean Paul's story that illustrates the configuration and subjectivization of human vision by technology. In this regard Crary is in line with Walter Benjamin, who maintained that technology has subjected the human sensorium to a complex kind of training, and that technology can shape our modes of reception, sensing, and experiencing reality.

> During long periods of history, the mode of human sense perception changes with humanity's entire mode of existence. The manner in which human sense perception is organized, the medium in which it is accomplished, is determined not only by nature but by historical circumstances as well.[47]

---

43 Jonathan Crary, *Techniques of the Observer: On Vision and Modernity* (Cambridge, MA: The MIT Press, 1992), 30.
44 Crary, *Techniques of the Observer*, 30.
45 Crary, *Techniques of the Observer*, 31.
46 The term assemblage has its theoretical background in the writings of Gilles Deleuze and Félix Guattari, *A Thousand Plateaus*, trans. Brian Massumi (Minneapolis: University of Minnesota Press, 1993).
47 Walter Benjamin, "The Work of Art in the Age of Mechanical Reproduction," in *Illuminations: Essays and Reflections*, ed. Hannah Arendt and trans. Harry Zohn (New York: Schocken Books, 1968), 222.

The balloon in Jean Paul's text precedes Benjamin's thoughts about the technological shaping of perception as well as the historical construction of vision, since the balloon determines the modes and even contents of perception. The balloon in Jean Paul's text becomes an optical instrument that fuses the subject with the machine. Within this machine-human assemblage, the viewing subject is no longer "alone" in control of sight but is, rather, marginalized and decentralized. Not only can the aeronaut not control how he moves and what he sees, his vision is actually replaced by that of the machine.

In fact, this de-centering of the subject is amplified in the plot of Jean Paul's travelogue by the main character's and narrator's death. The story ends in a catastrophe. Giannozzo's balloon is caught in two thunderstorms above the Swiss Alps and ultimately crashes into the mountains, causing a terrible inferno. Giannozzo dies not only because his balloon falls from the sky, but also because he is gazed upon by two kinds of super-human eyes. On the one hand, he is subject to the deadly and petrifying gaze of a super-human creature, the basilisk.[48] This deadly gaze is also a part of the monstrous balloon: "I opened the airshafts and buried myself in the steam, in which only the basilisk eye of death blinked."[49] On the other hand, he is eliminated by the eye of the sun and its cold and ruthless gaze ["so calm and cold."][50] These two eyes – the mechanical and the godly – annihilate Giannozzo, whose charred corpse (as the editor J. Richter reports in the last paragraph) is discovered in the mountains.

Scholars have interpreted this ending as Jean Paul's anti-idealistic critique of Enlightenment ideas about progress, autonomy, and freedom.[51] The crash of the balloon, and, by extension, the failure of ballooning, can be seen as symbolic of the collapse of the free will of the human subject. These interpretations draw on the text's explicit and scathing critique of Enlightenment philosophy. Giannozzo frequently makes fun of Enlightenment thinkers, such as Schiller and Kant: "enlightened eighteenth-centurists – they embodied Frederick the Great."[52] However, in addition to highlighting the dethroning of the subject, my reading suggests that the subject's sensorium and modes of visual perception cannot be understood as controlled and steered by the individual. This portrayal of the balloon as

---

[48] "Basiliskenauge des Todes," Jean Paul, "Seebuch," 1007.
[49] "Ich riss die Lufthähne auf und vergrub mich in den Dampf, worin nur das Basiliskenauge des Todes seine heissen Silberblicke auf und zutat," Jean Paul, "Seebuch," 1007.
[50] "so ruhig und kalt," Jean Paul, "Seebuch," 1007.
[51] Welle, "Der irdische Blick," 123–144; Link, "Literaturanalyse," 284–307; Brüggemann, "Luftbilder," 127–182.
[52] "aufgeklärte Achtzehnjahrhunderter – sie standen ganz für Friedrich II," Jean Paul, "Seebuch," 950.

a technology of seeing in the "Seebuch" contends that the subject is part of a human-machine assemblage that registers a much more significant and far-reaching crisis of perception and representation.

4 Ballooning as Poiesis

From the very beginning, Giannozzo's ballooning enterprise is also a literary endeavor. Not only does he call his writings "air-ship-diary" ("Luft-Schiffs-Journal"),[53] but each of the fourteen chapters in the diary is devoted to a distinct balloon trip. As a result, the sequence of flights structures the literary text. Giannozzo frequently says that he has to record his experience of being in the air ("I begin again")[54] or that he has to stop recording when his travels have ended for the day.[55] In a meta-reflexive gesture, even the balloon journal's editor is mentioned. The editor appears directly in the main text, which is quite typical for Jean Paul's style of writing: "Now it is enough. As far as the editor is concerned."[56] Thus, the "Seebuch" is not only a private endeavor; it is a literary text intended for an audience. This becomes particularly evident when the literary censor is spotted down below. His name is "Mister von Fahland (indeed a fatal name)."[57] Ironically, the censor carries a book by Jean Paul in his pocket. In this way, the balloon journal is deeply entrenched in the politics of publishing, the literary market, and literary audiences. This literary self-reflexivity is in many ways a common trope in Jean Paul's writing. However, it is interesting that in the "Seebuch," this self-reflexivity is not only connected to textual production, but also to a discourse about seeing, visual perspective, and images. In this context, the image of the balloon simultaneously registers and illustrates a discourse about the possibilities of vision.

Aside from these references to the context of literary production, the balloon journey as a literary endeavor also steers the writing process itself. As shown in the previous section, the balloon, as a type of artificial eye, can perceive the world, which in turn decenters the perspective as well as the visual authority of the subject. This de-centering mode of perception also evokes a specific mode of writing and literary representation, as the following quote demonstrates: "My

---

[53] Jean Paul, "Seebuch," 927.
[54] Jean Paul, "Seebuch," 943.
[55] Jean Paul, "Seebuch," 943.
[56] "Aber nun ists genug. Soweit der Herausgeber," Jean Paul, "Seebuch," 928.
[57] "Herr von Fahland (schon ein fataler Name)," Jean Paul, "Seebuch," 944.

first thought during the flight up was triggered by the word: révénant. One of them happened to say it to me: I thought of the heavenly happiness of being a ghost – then a pandora's box, an Aeolian wind harp [Äolsschlauch] of fantasies opened."[58] A révénant is someone who comes again; a mythological figure of a ghost or an undead person, that haunts the living. Besides this rather demonic connotation, the idea of the révénant also evokes the artificial construction of reality through the process of writing. In Jean Paul's work the balloon as a révénant is present and absent at the same time.

The reconstructed world is present in a literary text through signs, words, letters, and the reader's imaginative power. At the same time, the world in poetic discourse is also absent; it is only there in the form of representation through language. In other words, the balloon as the reappearing révénant instantiates a process of poiesis and constructs a writing scene ("Schreibszene"), to use Rüdiger Campe's term.[59] It is important to understand that the source of this poiesis is not the human subject, the individual author, or Giannozzo as the literary protagonist. Rather, the poetic process is offset by the balloon's sensory capacities. Giannozzo notes that the balloon enables him to shift into different roles and play different characters. The protagonist and narrator Giannozzo can change masks and play charades[60]; the balloon inspires his poetic dreams,[61] such as his absurd fantasy of being a tender and tired beast of prey: "soon I would yawn like a tender shark."[62] Giannozzo's slipping in and out of fictional identities and realities is less steered by the individual, but rather controlled by the balloon, which he frequently refers to as a superhuman aesthetic observer that sees the world from a godly point of view: "Brightly descends the genius from heaven, and the clouds gleam far, when he permeates it and the etheric spirit touches the earth."[63]

In other words, the creative subject determining the literary process is not Giannozzo, but the balloon itself. Giannozzo frequently notes that he does not have the power to steer the balloon in his desired direction. Rather the balloon

---

[58] "Auf den ersten Gedanken der Auffahrt brachte mich das Wort: révénant. Einer sprach es zufällig vor mir aus: ich dachte an das Himmelsglück, ein Gespenst zu sein – da tat sich eine Pandorabüchse, ein Äolsschlauch von Phantasien auf," Jean Paul, "Seebuch," 929.

[59] Rüdiger Campe, "Die Schreibszene: Schreiben," in *Paradoxien, Dissonanzen, Zusammenbrüche: Situationen offener Epistemologie*, ed. Hans Ulrich Gumbrecht and Ludwig Pfeiffer (Frankfurt a. M.: Suhrkamp, 1991), 759–772.

[60] "Geister-Maskenfreiheit," Jean Paul, "Seebuch," 929.

[61] "Idyllen-träume," Jean Paul, "Seebuch," 929.

[62] "bald würd ich als ein sanfter Haifisch gähnen," Jean Paul, "Seebuch," 929.

[63] "Hell steigt der Genius vom Himmel nieder, und das Gewölk erglänzet weit, wenn er es durchdringt und der ätherische Geist berührt die Erde," Jean Paul, "Seebuch," 949.

"rolls back and forth,"[64] and, as in a throw of the dice, can land either here or there. This aerial journey's contingent nature is also reflected in the poetic configuration of Jean Paul's text. The descriptions and observations of life on earth (the observed scenes of the lovers, the parade, life in the small towns) are only possible because the wind has blown the balloon to places from where one can observe them. Thus, the balloon is a sensorial technology of writing that triggers forms of automated subject-less writing, since it controls topics, perspectives, time, the setting, and even the mood.

Just as the aerial maneuvers are bumpy and uncoordinated, so too is the text rhapsodic and disorderly. The events narrated in the aeronautic journal are marked by multiple digressions, which seem to be randomly placed; no linear narrative or chronological structure orders the individual journeys' events. The poetic language often zig-zags, winds, and features numerous abbreviations, a staccato rhythm, and fragmented sentences and thoughts. As if the too-thin air makes the traveler gasp, the text also seems breathless at times: "Brother Graul – this name is much better than your last [. . .]: you certainly opened wide the lax doors of my air cabin and held out the arms in the cold ether bath and the eye in the gloomy blue – heaven!"[65]

Giannozzo frequently laments the disorder of his notes, observations, and records, and the difficulty of keeping up with the task. His description of the aerial view is fragmented, fractured into small incoherent images: "In air-ship diaries there has to be order; I begin again."[66] Giannozzo depicts the earth as seen from above as a type of "theater of the world,"[67] However, this theater does not encapsulate the world as a whole, rather, it opens up many individual perspectives. The mode of seeing changes all the time, from telescopic zooming, micro- and macro perspectives, to a panoramic standpoint, or bird's-eye view. Giannozzo notes: "I was enroute within a turbulent change of scenes."[68] The topics and phenomena he records are not ordered or connected in any logical, causal, or linear fashion, a dissociation that is reflected in the open and disjointed type of writing.

---

64 "würfelt hin und her," Jean Paul, "Seebuch," 931.
65 In German: "Bruder Graul – dieser Name ist viel besser als dein letzter, Leibgeber – du machtest gewiss die Sänftetüren meiner Lufthütte weit auf und hieltest die Arme ins kalte Ätherbad hinaus und das Auge ins düstre Blau – Himmel!" Jean Paul, "Seebuch," 927.
66 In German: "In Luftschiffs-Journalen muss Ordnung sein; ich fange wieder an," Jean Paul, "Seebuch," 931.
67 In German: "Welttheater," Jean Paul, "Seebuch," 959.
68 In German: "allein da ich im wilden Szenenwechsel so hingefahren war," Jean Paul, "Seebuch," 961.

With its break from a classical visual perspective, Jean Paul's balloon-text no longer represents the world as something that can be conveyed in transparent language according to universal, realist parameters. Although the balloon-eye is prescient of a camera, Jean Paul highlights the distortion and instability of such a concept of vision. This destabilization must also be understood as a reflection of broader social-historical processes. In many ways, it becomes clear that the balloon-eye's registering of the world signals a crisis of the subject. De-centered by the flying machine, the subject is no longer in control. Giannozzo occupies the position of an outsider who, looking down with contempt on life in small towns, does not belong there. As Welle has pointed out, the name of Giannozzo's balloon, "lazar house" ("Siechkobel"),[69] referring to a place where sick people are isolated and quarantined, symbolizes his outsider position, which recalls what Foucault termed the "bannopticon."[70] From there the balloonist can no longer make sense of the world, there is no "collective singular,"[71] a common denominator that gives the world meaning. Religion is portrayed in Jean Paul's text as pointless and the sky as empty: "No, no, do not believe that there are paternoster ropes from worlds above me."[72] Idealist moral philosophy does not replace the loss of belief in God, and even the empathic aesthetic moments of the sublime are also ironized as merely hollow echoes of something that has been lost long ago. In other words, all concepts of meaning become empty free-circulating tropes during the balloon's capricious journey. The balloon travels in a diffuse in-between space, which in many ways approximates the transitional period of modernity and the critique of the Enlightenment subject. This reading of the balloon agrees with Link's research about the balloon as a collective symbol of crisis, but it expands this critique by focusing on how the balloon as a technology of seeing highlights a/the crisis of perception and seeing. The Apollonian gaze from above, as Daniel Cosgrove has called this god-like view founded in power, is destabilized and irritated in Jean Paul's "Seebuch."[73]

These observations about Jean Paul's aesthetic representation of the balloon-eye should not be read as a turn towards media theories influenced by

---

[69] Jean Paul, "Seebuch," 931.

[70] Welle, "Der irdische Blick," 30.

[71] Reinhart Koselleck. "Geschichte: Historie," *Geschichtliche Grundbegriffe: Historisches Lexikon zur politisch-sozialen Sprache in Deutschland*, Vol. 2, ed. Otto Brunner, Werner Conze, and Reinhart Koselleck (Stuttgart: Klett, 1972), 647–652.

[72] "Nein, nein, glaubt nicht, Paternosterschnuren von Welten über mir," Jean Paul, "Seebuch," 961.

[73] Daniel Cosgrove, *Apollo's Eye: A Cartographic Genealogy of the Earth in the Western Imagination* (Baltimore: The John Hopkins UP, 2001).

Friedrich Kittler or recent post-humanist accounts about media, affects, and literature, such as in works by Katherine Hayles.[74] Kittler's and Hayles's radical expulsion of the subject in light of technology does not quite match my reflections about ballooning and vision as a sensorial assemblage. As noted above, in the stereoscope (and other optical media), Crary locates the break with classical modes of visual representation long before the avant-garde movement. My investigation aims to point to another "optical" technology, namely, ballooning, and its significant role in distorting and eroding the conditions of possibility for a central perspective. In reckoning with this loss, balloon literature (here, specifically Jean Paul's work) goes even further. It experiments with aesthetic and poetic categories, such as authorship, narrative, and realist representation.

Ballooning and its literary representation also open up a new dimension in the discourse of the aerial that has been understudied in recent research on the view from above: that is the dimension of the aesthetic-sensorial. In his book *Aerial Life* (2010), Peter Adey explores the aerial as an ontological mode of existence similar to Heidegger's "being in the world."[75] Using a materialist and phenomenological approach, Adey shows how the meaning of being aerial is constructed by modern technology, urban space, airports, and aviation. A central concern for Adey is the militarization of the aerial. The discovery of the vertical embodies the imperial and aggressive gaze; a connection that has been discussed in works by Cosgrove and in Sloterdijk's writings on verticality. Ballooning is often seen as a predominantly military technology, which was utilized for warfare in the nineteenth century. Kaplan, in noting that early aerostatic experiences triggered affects of enthusiasm and delight, also mainly approaches ballooning from the prospect of warfare.[76] Although Mark Dorrian, in his writings about the aerial, warns against an oversimplified equation of the aerial with the imperial, he nevertheless embeds the aerial view within a military discourse.[77] Adey, Kaplan, and Dorrian taken together pay little attention to the balloon's modes of vision that go beyond the scopic regime, a term used by scholars of visual studies and that is based on a military and hierarchical gaze from above.[78]

---

[74] Friedrich Kittler, *Aufschreibesysteme 1800/1900* (Wilhelm Fink: Munich, 1985); Kathrine Hayles, *Writing Machines* (Cambridge, MA: The MIT Press, 2002).
[75] Peter Adey, *Aerial Life: Spaces, Mobilities, Affects* (Chichester: John Wiley & Sons), 2010.
[76] Kaplan, "The Balloon Prospect," 1–28.
[77] Mark Dorrian, "The Aerial View: Notes for a Cultural History," *Strates* 13 (2007): 1–17.
[78] Christian Metz, *The Imaginary Signifier: Psychoanalysis and the Cinema*, trans. Celia Britton (Bloomington: Indiana University Press, 1983); Martin Jay, *Downcast Eyes: The Denigration of Vision in Twentieth-Century French Thought* (Berkeley: University of California Press, 1993).

It is this aspect of a disorienting and non-scopic flattened vision I have highlighted in the context of ballooning. This chapter has shown that literature about ballooning can register changes in the human sensorium and that the aesthetic discourse about ballooning opens up an epistemological prism. Literature of ballooning shows that the affective experience of being aerial is not exclusively about power fantasies and military strategies, but rather can demonstrate how technology extends the human sensorium and creates new affective modes of perceiving the world. Thus, balloons should not be seen just as another nineteenth-century technological innovation, but also as generators of perceptive modes, imaginaries, and aesthetic discourses about vision and visuality.

Bibliography

Adey, Peter. *Aerial Life: Spaces, Mobilities, Affects*. Chichester: John Wiley & Sons, 2010.

Baldwin, Thomas. *Airopaidia*. London: J. Flechter, 1786.

Bär, Gerald. "Poetische Perspektiven aus dem (Fessel) Ballon: Das Jahrhundertereignis als Eventcharakter und seine Fiktionalisierung." In *Transit oder Transformation? Sprachliche und Literarische Grenzerfahrungen: Yearbook of the German Studies Association in Ireland*, edited by Sabine Egger, 29–48. Konstanz: Hartung-Gorre, 2016.

Begley, Adam. *The Great Nadar: The Man behind the Camera*. New York: Tim Duggan Books, 2017.

Behler, Ernst. *Ironie und Literarische Moderne*. Paderborn: Ferdinand Schöningh, 1997.

Behringer, Wolfgang, and Constance Ott-Koptschalijski. *Der Traum vom Fliegen: Zwischen Mythos und Technik*. Frankfurt am Main: Fischer, 1991.

Benjamin, Walter. "The Work of Art in the Age of Mechanical Reproduction." In *Illuminations: Essays and Reflections*, edited by Hannah Arendt and translated by Harry Zohn, 217–251. New York: Schocken Books, 1968.

Brüggemann, Heinz. "Luftbilder eines kleinstädtischen Jahrhunderts: Ekstase und imaginäre Topographie in Jean Paul: 'Des Luftschiffers Giannozzo Seebuch.'" In *Die Stadt in der europäischen Romantik*, edited by Gerhard von Graevenitz, 127–182. Würzburg: Königshausen & Neumann, 2000.

Burke, Edmund. *A Philosophical Enquiry into the Origin of our Ideas of the Sublime and the Beautiful*. Cambridge: Cambridge University Press, 2014.

Campe, Rüdiger. "Die Schreibszene: Schreiben." In *Paradoxien, Dissonanzen, Zusammenbrüche: Situationen offener Epistemologie*, edited by Hans Ulrich Gumbrecht and Ludwig Pfeiffer, 759–772. Frankfurt am Main: Suhrkamp, 1991.

Cosgrove, Daniel. *Apollo's Eye: A Cartographic Genealogy of the Earth in the Western Imagination*. Baltimore: John Hopkins University Press, 2001.

Crary, Jonathan. *Techniques of the Observer: On Vision and Modernity in the Nineteenth Century*. Cambridge, MA: MIT Press, 2012.

Deleuze, Gilles, and Félix Guattari. *A Thousand Plateaus*. Translated by Brian Massumi. Minneapolis: University of Minnesota Press, 1993.

Dorrian, Mark. "The Aerial View: Notes for a Cultural History." *Strates* 13 (2007): 1–17.
Eckert, Alfred. "Zur Geschichte der Ballonfahrt." In *Leichter als Luft: Zur Geschichte der Ballonfahrt*, edited by Bernard Korzus and Gisela Noehles, 13–128. Münster: Westfälisches Landesmuseum für Kunst und Kulturgeschichte, 1978.
Eickenrodt, Sabine. *Augen-spiel: Jean Pauls optische Metaphorik der Unsterblichkeit.* Göttingen: Wallstein, 2013.
Fleming, Paul. *The Pleasures of Abandonment: Jean Paul and the Life of Humor.* Würzburg: Königshausen & Neumann, 2006.
Hayles, Katherine. *Writing Machines.* Cambridge, MA: MIT Press, 2002.
Jay, Martin. *Downcast Eyes: The Denigration of Vision in Twentieth-Century French Thought.* Berkeley: University of California Press, 1993.
Kant, Immanuel. *Kritik der Urteilskraft.* Edited by Karl Vorländer. Hamburg: Felix Meiner, 1990.
Kaplan, Caren. "The Balloon Prospect: Aerostatic Observation and the Emergence of Militarized Aeromobility." In *From Above: War, Violence, and Verticality*, edited by Caren Kaplan and Lisa Parks, 19–40. New York: Oxford University Press, 2014.
Kittler, Friedrich. *Aufschreibesysteme 1800–1900.* Munich: Wilhelm Fink, 2003.
Koselleck, Reinhart. "Geschichte: Historie." In vol. 2 of *Geschichtliche Grundbegriffe: Historisches Lexikon zur politisch-sozialen Sprache in Deutschland*, edited by Otto Brunner, Werner Conze, and Reinhart Koselleck, 647–652. Stuttgart: Klett, 1972.
Link, Jürgen. "Literaturanalyse als Interdiskursanalyse: Am Beispiel des Ursprungs literarischer Symbolik in der Kollektivsymbolik." In *Diskurstheorien und Literaturwissenschaft*, edited by Harro Müller and Gerhard von Graevenitz, 284–307. Frankfurt am Main: Suhrkamp, 1988.
Locher, Walter. "Zur militärischen Nutzung des Ballons." In *Leichter als Luft: Zur Geschichte der Ballonfahrt*, edited by Bernd Korzus, 238–250. Münster: Landesverband Westfalen-Lippe, 1985.
Massumi, Brian. *Parables for the Virtual: Movement, Affect, Sensation.* Durham, NC: Duke University Press, 2007.
Metz, Christian. *The Imaginary Signifier: Psychoanalysis and the Cinema.* Translated by Celia Britton. Bloomington: Indiana University Press, 1983.
Neumann, Gerhard. "Fernrohr, Mikroskop, Luftballon: Wahrnehmungstechnik und Literatur in der Goethezeit." In *Spektakuläre Experimente: Praktiken der Evidenzproduktion im 17. Jahrhundert*, edited by Helmar Schramm, Ludger Schwarte, and Jan Lazardzig, 345–377. Berlin: De Gruyter, 2006.
Niehle, Victoria. "Die ästhetische Funktion des Raumes: Jean Pauls 'Des Luftschiffer Giannozzo Seebuch.'" In *Raumlektüren: Der Spatial Turn und die Literatur der Moderne*, edited by Tim Mehigan and Alan Corkhill, 69–85. Bielefeld: transcript, 2013.
Paul, Jean. "Des Luftschiffers Giannozzo Seebuch." In vol. 3 of *Jean Paul: Sämtliche Werke*, edited by Norbert Miller, 925–1010. Darmstadt: Wissenschaftliche Buchgesellschaft, 2000.
Schinkel, Eckhard. "Der Ballon in der Literatur." In *Leichter als Luft: Zur Geschichte der Ballonfahrt*, edited by Bernard Korzus and Gisela Noehles, 200–236. Münster: Westfälisches Landesmuseum für Kunst und Kulturgeschichte, 1978.
Schmitz-Emans, Monika. "Über Bilder und die bildene Kunst bei Jean Paul." In *Jean Paul und die Bilder: Bildkünstlerische Auseinandersetzungen mit seinem Werk; 1783–2013*, edited by Monika Schmitz-Emans and Wolfram Benda, 19–64. Würzburg: Königshausen & Neumann, 2013.

Sloterdijk, Peter, Amy Patton, and Steve Corcoran. *Terror from the Air*. Los Angeles: Semiotext(e), 2009.
Vigus, James. *Shandean Humour in English and German Literature and Philosophy*. London: Taylor and Francis, 2017.
Weizman, Eyal. *Forensic Architecture: Violence at the Threshold of Detectability*. New York: Zone Books, 2017.
Welle, Florian. *Der irdische Blick durch das Fernrohr: Literarische Wahrnehmungsexperimente vom 17. bis zum 20. Jahrhundert*. Würzburg: Königshausen und Neumann, 2009.

Christian A. Bachmann
Through the Eyepiece and What Visual Satire Found There

This chapter discusses circular pictures and frames in nineteenth-century visual satire and graphic narratives from a historical perspective. A cursory examination of round frames shows that they are often used in context with optical devices like the microscope and the telescope and oftentimes specific frames are used to denote discrete types of visual satire.

While the eighteenth century saw the rise of visual satire through the hands of artists such as Thomas Rowlandson (1756–1827), James Gillray (1757–1815), Isaac Cruikshank (1764–1811), and, most notably, William Hogarth (1697–1764), the nineteenth century was the period when visual satire reached an unprecedented bloom. Beginning in 1830, Charles Philipon (1800–1861), famous for his representation of Louis Philippe I (1773–1850) as a pear, included caricatures and visual satire by some of the most acclaimed visual artists of his time in his pathbreaking journals *La Caricature* and *Le Charivari*: Honoré Daumier (1808–1879), Gustave Doré (1832–1883), Grandville (i.e. Jean Ignace Isidore Gérard, 1803–1847), Cham (i.e. Amédée de Noé, 1819–1879), and Draner (i.e. Jules Jean Georges Renard, 1833–1926), to name but a few. Across the Channel, in London, Ebenezer Landells (1809–1860) and Henry Mayhew (1812–1887) founded *Punch, the London Charivari* in 1841, which, after early struggles, became a popular and influential outlet of humor and satire and thrived in a market with numerous competitors that included predecessors of modern American comic strips, such as *Ally Sloper's Half Holiday* or *Comic Cuts* in the last quarter of the nineteenth century. In the 1840s, illustrated satirical magazines started to pop up in the German Confederation. In 1842, one such magazine called *Charivari* was published in Leipzig. The *Fliegende Blätter* by Kaspar Braun and Friedrich Schneider first came out in 1845. After the March Revolution of 1848, when the Carlsbad Decrees of 1819 lessened restrictive censorship laws, a significant number of satirical periodicals were in circulation: *Eulenspiegel* from Stuttgart, *Kladderadatsch* and *Ulk* from Berlin, *Leuchtkugeln* and *Münchener Punsch* from Munich, and *Katzen-Musik, Figaro, Kikeriki, Bombe,* and *Floh* from Vienna. They employed multitudes of artists among whom we find pioneers of visual satire and

Note: Parts of the argument presented here were previously presented in Christian A. Bachmann, *Bilder/Rahmen: Rahmungen in visueller Satire, Bildergeschichte und Comic um 1900* (Hanover: Wehrhahn, 2018), 51–87. All translations are my own unless otherwise noted. I would like to thank the editors for their help finalizing the present chapter.

graphic narrative such as Lothar Meggendorfer (1847–1925), Adolf Oberländer (1845–1923), Hans Schließmann (1852–1920), and Wilhelm Busch (1832–1908).

The origins of many of the themes, gags, and techniques of representation that are staples in visual satire and graphic narrative today lie in the cartoons and stories of these early artists from France, England, and the German Confederation. By way of American satire and humor periodicals like *Puck*, *Truth*, and *Judge*, such themes, gags, and techniques of representation found their way into the American comic strip which sprang to life in the mid-1890s in weekly newspaper supplements published on Sundays. For instance, *Puck*, the first and arguably most famous of these periodicals, was edited by Joseph Ferdinand Keppler (1838–1894), an immigrant from Austria who had worked for Viennese journals before launching the magazine in St. Louis in March of 1871. Thomas Nast (1840–1902), frequently dubbed "The Father of the American Cartoon," was a native of Landau. And Rudolph Dirks (1877–1968), famous for his comic strip *The Katzenjammer Kids*, which debuted in 1897, was born in Heide, a small town in the Prussian province of Schleswig-Holstein.

This history of satire and humor magazines is well known and has been written about at length by David Kunzle, Patricia Mainardi, and Thierry Smolderen, among others.[1] The present chapter investigates a specific, underappreciated feature of nineteenth-century graphic narratives: round frames or *tondos*. It shows how they served as a means of representation and as an instrument of narrative structuring in European visual satire of the nineteenth century and American comics around 1900. I contend that the use of tondos connects those works to contemporary graphic storytelling, which essentially developed around 1900 out of these predecessors. The present example is particularly significant in that microscopic and telescopic images are among the tondos we encounter in nineteenth-century satirical and humor periodicals, which helped introduce the alternation of perspectives into graphic narratives.

European pioneers of cartooning, visual satire, and graphic narrative were not only deeply involved in finding ways to depict political adversaries. An illustrator,

---

[1] Kunzle's important two-volume *History of the Comic Strip* addresses the history of graphic narratives from 1450 to 1900. However, Kunzle does not provide any in-depth discussion of these works due to his study's much broader scope. David Kunzle, *The History of the Comic Strip*. Vol. 2: *The Ninetheenth Century* (Berkeley/Los Angeles/Oxford: University of California Press, 1990). Similarly, Smolderen's *Naissance de la bande dessinée* presents many ideas and concerns that drove the evolution of comic strips. Yet his book does not examine the development of nineteenth-century graphic narrative in comics in any real detail. Thierry Smolderen, *The Origins of Comics: From William Hogarth to Winsor McCay*. Trans. Bart Beaty and Nick Nguyen (Jackson, MS: University Press of Mississippi, 2014).

for example, could turn Louis Philippe I into a pear. The people drawing these visual narratives were also confronted with new technologies and new media. Smolderen notes:

> In the illustrated press of the nineteenth century, comic illustrators camped on the semiotic borders of the rapidly expanding industrial and colonial world. They were on every battlefront, taking note of the emerging technologies brought about by the Industrial Revolution (photographic and microscopic images, X rays, chronophotography, the Kinetoscope) and addressing every significant emerging style [. . .]. Their work was central to visual culture of the period because in their stylized shorthand, comic illustrators always found some way to make humorous sense of the new by hybridizing it with some familiar idiom.[2]

While Europeans' fascination with optical devices used throughout the nineteenth century dates back to around 1600 with the spread of the telescope after Galileo Galilei's (1564–1642) revolutionary *Sidereus Nuncius* of 1610, it is the nineteenth century that takes this inclination to a whole new level. Nineteenth-century Europe is enthralled by pictures, optical devices, and gadgets like the zoetrope, and including panoramas, photography, stereoscopes, and cinema. Consequently, strategies of remediating the imagery generated by these new visual media is of key interest to cartoonists both during and after the nineteenth century. This becomes especially important when dealing with the tondo form based on telescopic and microscopic images.

1 Tondos

Round images and figures have been the exception to the rule for as long as pictures have been hand-painted or printed in codices and books. Working with precious materials such as vellum, scribes and early printers valued space on the page highly and were loath to waste it. Using miniatures, drolleries, and extensive framing, they wanted to make the most of every sheet of parchment. Accordingly, rectangular images were preferable from an economic standpoint because they fit parchment made from hide which, due to the shape of the animal body, is most efficiently cut into rectangular sheets.[3] The same holds true for papyrus because of the triangular shape of the stem of the papyrus plant and the way it is cut into strips and woven to form sheets.

---

2 Smolderen, *The Origins of Comics*, 98.
3 See Jost Amman's depiction of the parchment maker ("der Permennter") in Hans Sachs's book of trades *Eygentliche Beschreibung aller Stände auff Erden, hoher und nidriger, geistlicher und weltlicher, aller Künsten, Handwercken und Händeln* (Frankfurt am Main, 1568).

Once rectangular pages had been established as the standard, somewhat consistent models of how to fill them with images followed. Consider Ulrich Boner's (fl. early fourteenth century) *Der Edelstein*, a collection of fables printed by Albrecht Pfister (ca. 1420–1466) in 1462.[4] This work is considered to be the first printed book illustrated with woodcuts (and the first book printed in German). To achieve a harmonic mise-en-page, Pfister, like manuscript illuminators before him, devised illustrations that spanned the whole column. While the vertical position of the images varies, this width is maintained throughout the *Edelstein*, with the exception of minor deviations due to early printing technology's deficiencies in congruity. Centuries later, satirical periodicals show that publishers preferred using rectangular illustrations to wasting any space on the spreads. Thus, illustrated periodicals keep the white space limited to such an extent that editors often preferred to include nondescript miscellanea to pad out a column rather than leave it unfilled. In the context of print history and the history of illustration, round images that wasted space on the printing form as well as on the printed page are thus significant. It is worthwhile to ask why they were used and what effects they produced.

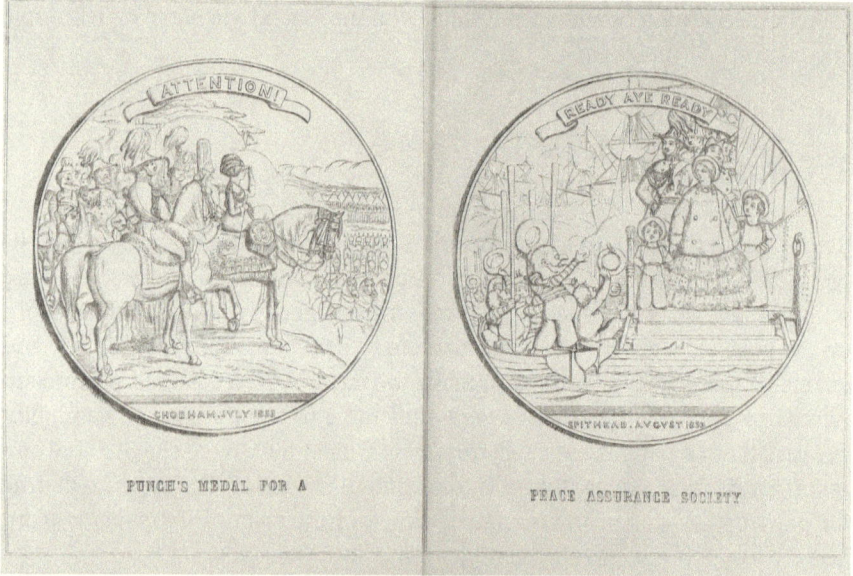

Figure 1: "Punch's Medal for a Peace Assurance Society." *Punch* (1853).

---

4 A copy of *Der Edelstein* is kept at the Herzog August Bibliothek in Wolfenbüttel, Germany, under the identifier 16.1 Eth. 2° [1].

Round images, so-called *tondos* (from Italian *rotondo*, 'round'), have been in use since Antiquity. They were an especially common feature or motif on Greek pottery (e.g. the kylix) in which the round shape of the object lent itself well to circular images and vice versa. In the Italian renaissance, round paintings became a favorite because the tondo incorporated the circle as the ideal of the perfect form, of which Sandro Botticelli's *Madonna of the Magnificat* (1481, Uffizi, Florence) is but one example.[5] The tondo is also used in architectural decoration and can be found on cameos, embroideries, coins, stamps, and medals. Even though there is an abundance of tondos in nineteenth-century everyday life, they were far less common in printing, for the reasons mentioned above. And when they were used, tondos often represented an object of round shape, such as a medal or coin. Take, for instance, *Punch's* "Medal for a Peace Assurance Society," printed in 1853. The satirical medal refers to the military camp at Chobham, Surrey, in 1853 and shows Queen Victoria (1819–1901) and Prince Albert of Saxe-Coburg and Gotha (1819–1861) surveying the troops gathered for parades and maneuvers. The verso depicts Victoria, the Prince Consort, and their children at the Naval Review at Spithead, on 11 August 1853, being greeted by sailors (one of whom appears to be Punch, the periodical's mascot, himself). Two full pages are allocated to the prints and a considerable amount of space around them is left vacant, which distinctly stands out when compared with the regular *Punch* two-column-layout of the same time period that had barely any white space at all (see Figure 1). Similarly, the two identical impressions of a potato dumpling, one seen from a Catholic perspective and one from a Protestant perspective, printed in *Fliegende Blätter* in 1855, are round to resemble an actual dumpling (see Figure 2). Omitting the frame, background, and any kind of decoration foregrounds the object itself and accentuates the minute details that allow the readers, after some comparing, to assert that both images are, indeed, identical (thereby poking fun at the reach of the Reformation). Thus, in printed images, round objects themselves often become tondos.

A different example is a visual satire titled *Locus Sigilli* published in *Kladderadatsch* in 1875: The strongly framed image shows Johann Baptist Sigl (1839–1902), the editor of the anti-Prussian journal *Das Bayerische Vaterland*, standing behind bars. In 1875, Sigl was sentenced to ten months in jail for lèse-majesté.[6] *Kladderadatsch* – based in the then-Prussian capital of

---

[5] See Roberta J. M. Olson, *The Florentine Tondo* (Oxford/New York: Oxford University Press, 2000).
[6] See Paul Hoser, *Das Bayerische Vaterland*, in *Historisches Lexikon Bayerns*, http://www.historisches-lexikon-bayerns.de/Lexikon/Das Bayerische Vaterland, 3 July 2006, accessed 22 Januar 2019.

Zwei Köchinnen werden gesucht.

Eine protestantische Herrschaft in Augsburg sucht eine Köchin protestantischer Religion.

Eine katholische Herrschaft in Augsburg sucht eine Köchin katholischer Religion.

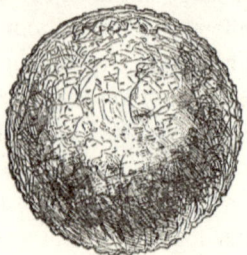
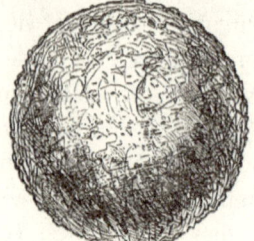

Ein Knödel vom protestantischen Standpunkte.

Ein Knödel vom katholischen Standpunkte.

Figure 2: "Now hiring two cooks." *Fliegende Blätter* no. 513 (1855).

Berlin – sneers: "Mister Sigl has finally found a silent place where he will be of some use to the *German fatherland*."[7] As is often the case, the punchline of *Locus Sigilli* is based on a play on words[8]: In contracts, the *locus sigilli* is the spot reserved for the wax seal and is often marked with a circle, to which the picture here refers. On another level, *Locus Sigilli*, refers to the place (*locus*) where Sigl, the journalist, is incarcerated, i.e., the prison.

    The previous examples illustrate how satirical tondos hearken back to established types of round images. Likewise, round frames can be seen in soap bubbles, which Jacob and Wilhelm Grimm believed portrayed an "image of vicissitude used often and in a variety of ways, a playful inanity."[9] In my view, these forms have an additional layer of meaning worth noting. In 1864, the Viennese *Kikeriki* printed a set of six soap bubble images titled *Vorläufig noch lauter Seifenblasen* (see Figure 3). Inside the bubbles, stacked in the first column of the journal's pages, there are depictions of objects, scenes, and, in one case, a short text, all of which are hard to understand for today's reader as no context is given. Circles and concentric lines as

---

7 "Herr Sigl hat endlich [. . .] eine verschwiegene Stelle gefunden, wo er dem deutschen Vaterland von einigem Nutzen sein dürfte." Anonymous, "Locus Sigilli," *Kladderadatsch* XXVIII no. 18 (18 April 1875): title page.
8 See E. H. Gombrich, "The cartoonist's armory," in *Meditations on a hobby horse and other essays on the theory of art*, 2nd ed. (London: Phaidon, 1971), 127–142.
9 "oft und vielseitig gebrauchtes bild einer unbeständigkeit, einer spielerischen nichtigkeit" (*Deutsches Wörterbuch von Jacob und Wilhelm Grimm* [Leipzig, 1854–1961] vol. 16, col. 191) http://www.woerterbuchnetz.de/DWB?lemma=seifenblase 22 January 2019.

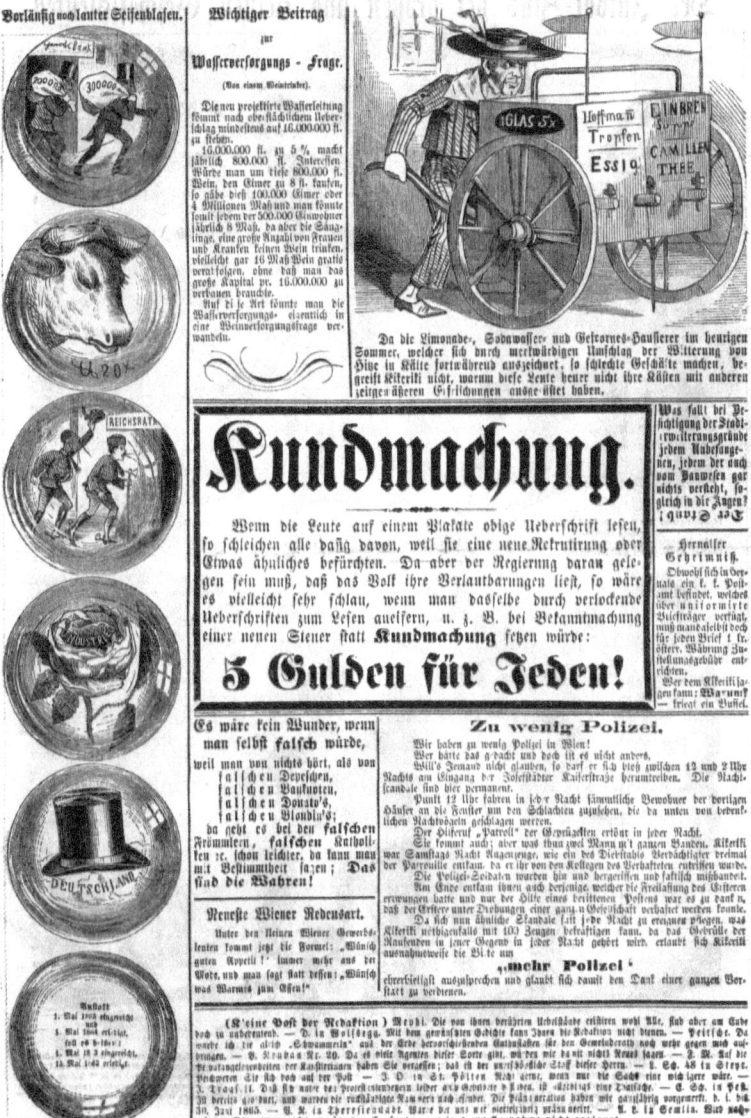

Figure 3: "Soap bubbles for the time being." *Kikeriki* (21 July 1864).

well as representations of a light source reflecting on the bubbles' surfaces convey a sense of plasticity and reflectivity. However, it is the title, operating as a relay, that identifies the images as depictions of soap bubbles. Without it, the bubbles can almost be taken for medals, coins, balls, or bowls. In any case, this example shows that the soap bubble can be turned into a frame that changes the semantics of whatever object it frames. What is shown within a soap bubble, thus, is characterized as a figment or fantasy that is easily spoiled. Apart from being an iconic sign, the etched bubble becomes a symbolic sign when attached to something as a circular frame, which likewise changes the meaning of that which it frames.

That same year, Wilhelm Scholz (1824–1893) published the graphic narrative *Soldat und Diplomat* in *Kladderadatsch* (see Figure 4), which is especially interesting with regard to the semantic function of round frames. Subtitled "Dissolving-views from the Schleswig-Holstein campaign," it deals with the Second Schleswig War between Prussia and Denmark of 1864.[10] Scholz's graphic narrative comprises six circular images each with a black rectangular frame and a caption linking them to events of the war, such as "The Allies occupy Holstein" and "Capture of the fortifications at Dybbøl," etc.[11] As its subtitle points out, Scholz tries to remediate dissolving views, sets of two magic lantern slides that gradually transition into each other. The magic lantern achieves this effect by utilizing two lenses focused on the same spot that can be screened off separately, thus alternating between two finite states, i.e., a landscape during day and night. Scholz draws on the notion of ceaselessly swinging between maxima like a pendulum to convey the idea that the Schleswig-Holstein Question ultimately leads in circles, for which the circular frames of the images can be seen as a metaphor. In the first picture, Scholz presents a diplomat with pen and ink at the ready. In the second image, two soldiers blend together with the diplomat before he gradually 'dissolves' in images two and three and materializes again in pictures five and six. The first picture and the last are nearly identical and the final caption reads accordingly: "Da capo al fine at will."[12] In essence, Scholz emulates some of the visual qualities of dissolving views to liken the graphic narrative to an actual magic lantern screening as well as some of the technical specifications to make a political statement about the state of affairs in the Second Schleswig War.

As late as 1892, the Viennese satirical journal *Die Glühlichter* printed the three-part *Magic lantern slides infused with quotes* [*Laterna magica-Bilder mit*

---

[10] Wilhelm Scholz, "Soldat und Diplomat: Dissolving-views aus dem schleswig-holsteinischen Feldzuge," *Kladderadatsch* XVII, no. 44/45 (25 September 1864): n.p.
[11] "Die Verbündeten besetzten Holstein," "Eroberung der Düppeler Schanzen." Scholz, "Soldat und Diplomat."
[12] "Nach Belieben Da capo al fine." Scholz, "Soldat und Diplomat."

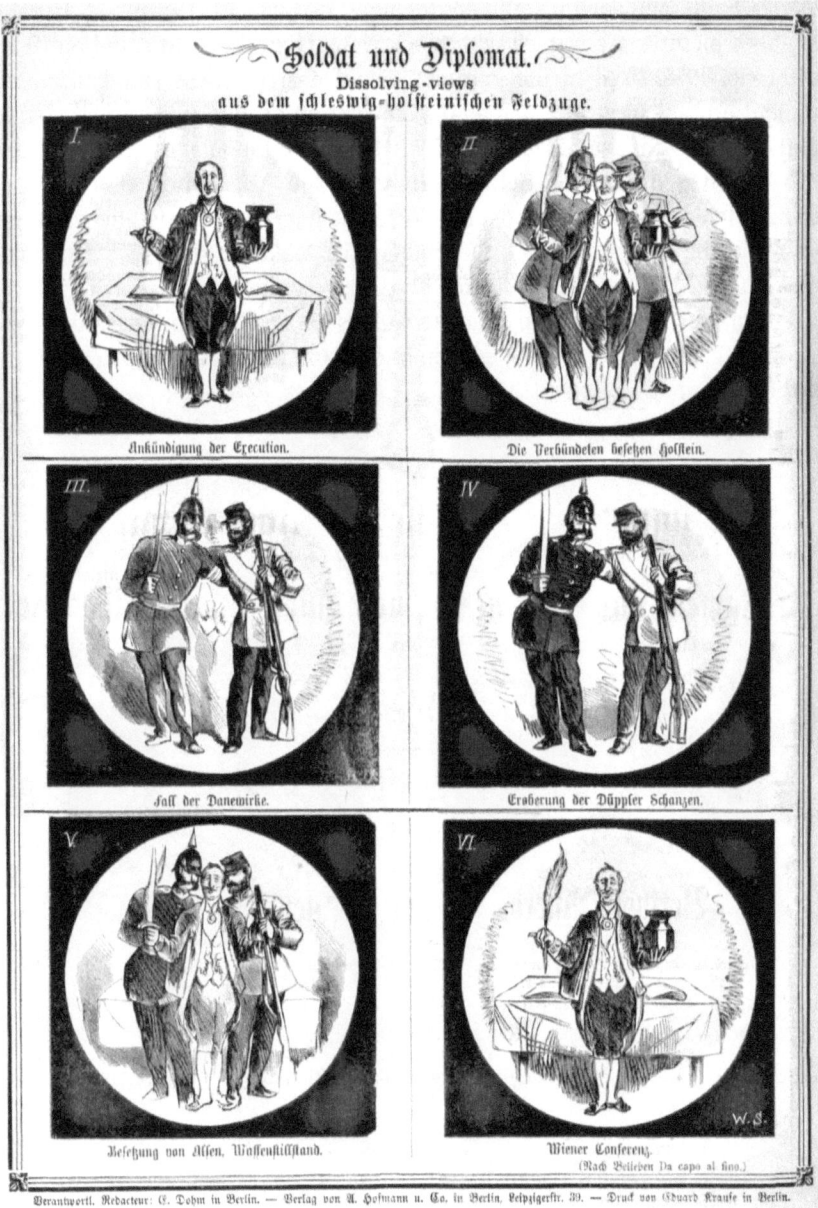

Figure 4: Wilhelm Scholz. "Soldier and diplomat: dissolving-views from the Second Schleswig War." *Kladderadatsch* (25 September 1864).

Citatenaufguß], and each installment included two images (Figure 5).[13] In each case, both pictures are framed with black weighty strokes that stand out from the thinner lines used in the journal's visual design. These satirical images comment on topical news, such as the convention of the Austrian Association of Bakers in Vienna (see Figure 5, left). Attached to the images are quotations by Friedrich Schiller and Heinrich Heine ("The Association of Bakers in Vienna / decided to fight against the Social Democratic Party. / The warhorse rises / and the trumpets ring . . . / Schiller: The Maid of Orleans.")[14] Examples such as these illustrate how nineteenth-century visual satire remediates new types of images, while referring back to well-established authorities and tropes, in order to comment on current events, integrating the old and the new to satirize the present now.

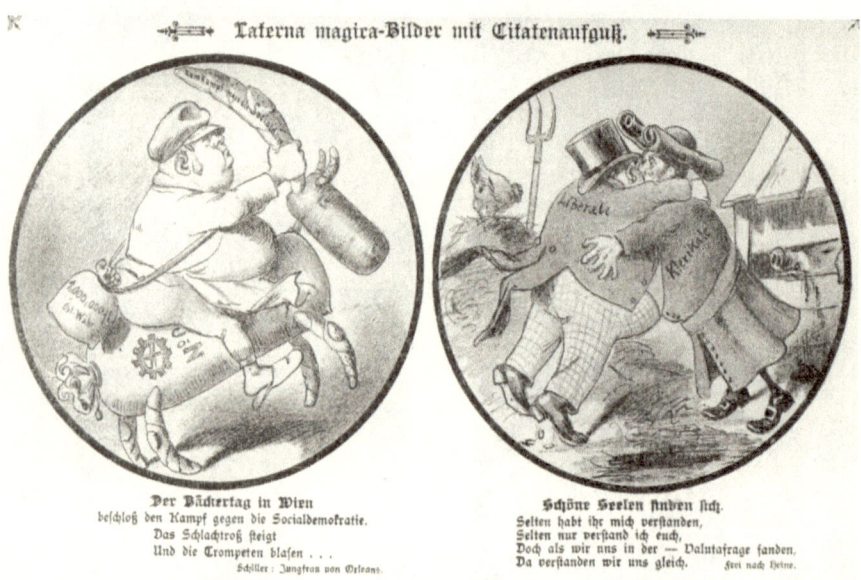

Figure 5: Wilhelm Scholz. "Magic lantern slides infused with quotes." *Kladderadatsch* (25 September 1864).

---

13 Anonymous, "Laterna magica-Bilder mit Citatenaufguß," *Die Glühlichter* III, no. 67 (11 June 1892): 4.
14 "Der Bäckertag in Wien / beschloß den Kampf gegen die Socialdemokratie. / Das Schlachtroß steigt / Und die Trompeten blasen . . . / Schiller: Jungfrau von Orleans".

2 The eyepiece: Microscopic and telescopic satirical imagery

Around 1600, two optical instruments were introduced: the telescope and the microscope. With the first, Galileo Galilei (1564–1642), one of its first makers and users, proved heliocentrism to be true, discovered heretofore unknown stars and unseen moons of Jupiter, and gave a description of the moon's surface (in his literally pathbreaking *Sidereus Nuncius* of 1610). Roughly half a century later, in 1665, Robert Hooke (1635–1702), a prominent member of the Royal Society, published his *Micrographia*, the first substantial discussion of microscopic studies and the Royal Society's first book publication.[15] The book is furnished with excellent engravings, the first images in history to represent the exhilarating intricacies of the bodies of minute life-forms and other miniscule objects invisible to the human eye. Thus, within half a century, man's place in the world had to be thoroughly redefined. As a consequence, man is relegated to a mesocosm, a dissatisfying spot in between large and small details that, due to shortcomings of the human senses, allows neither unhampered access to the exceedingly large objects of the macrocosm, nor to the tiny objects of the microcosm.

2.1 Microscopic imagery

The telescope was quickly adopted for military purposes as well as for marine navigation and became a valued commodity. The microscope, on the other hand, took longer to be accepted. However, as early as 1800, microscopic studies, the activity of marveling at images of magnified fleas and monstrous protozoa in drops of water, became a favorite pastime of the upper class. And because the quality of publicly available water as well as processed foods in cities like London, New York, and Berlin was dubious, wives and housekeepers were advised to examine it under the microscope to make sure that their families were safe. Before the public became acquainted with the idea that invisible life-forms flourish in (drinking) water, spectacular demonstrations with solar microscopes caused quite a stir which, perhaps, is best described by E. T. A. Hoffmann in *Master Flea*. In the 1822 novel, Leuwenhoek, a revenant of the historical Antonie

---

[15] Robert Hooke, *Micrographia: OR SOME Physiological Descriptions OF MINUTE BODIES MADE BY MAGNIFYING GLASSES WITH OBSERVATIONS and INQUIRIES thereupon* (London: Martin & Allesty/Royal Society, 1665).

van Leeuwenhoek (1632–1723) – the best grinder of optical lenses of his time and the discoverer of, among other things, bacteria and red blood cells – gives demonstrations with a solar microscope, a "night-microscope, that, as the sun-microscope by day, like a magic lantern, flung the object, brightly lit up, upon a white ground, with a sharpness and distinctness which left nothing more to be wished."[16] Hoffmann describes the effects of one such presentation in some detail:

> A glance into the hall at once betrayed to the young Pepusch the cause of this horror, which had driven away the people. All within was alive, and a loathsome medley of the most hideous creatures filled the whole room. The race of beetles, spiders, leeches, gnats, magnified to excess, stretched out their probosces, crawled upon their long hairy legs, or fluttered their long wings. A more hideous spectacle Pepusch had never seen.[17]

Upon entering the flea circus, Pepusch beholds fearsome creatures enlarged by Leuwenhoek's sun microscope: bugs, spiders, midges, and mud-dwellers with thin hairy legs and jagged pincers. We find similar depictions in satirical images published in the same period as Hoffmann's story. In 1828, British artist William Heath (1794–1840) published a satirical print titled *MICROCOSM dedicated to the London Water Companies* (see Figure 6). It shows a "MONSTER SOUP commonly called THAMES WATER, being a correct representation [sic] of that precious stuff doled out to us. [. . .] 'Brought Forth All Monstrous, all Prodigious Things, Hydras, and Gorgons, and Chimeras dire.'"[18] These Hydras and Gorgons and Chimeras are a deliberate reference to John Milton's *Paradise Lost* (1668). In the image, we can

---

[16] E. T. A. Hoffmann, *Master Flea*, in *Specimens of German romance: selected and translated from various authors*, vol. II, trans. George Sloane (London: Printed for Geo. B. Whittaker, 1826), 48. "Nachtmikroskop, das wie das Sonnenmikroskop am Tage, einer magischen Laterne ähnlich, den Gegenstand hell erleuchtet mit einer Schärfe und Deutlichkeit auf die weiße Wand warf, die nichts zu wünschen übrig ließ." E. T. A. Hoffmann, *Meister Floh: Ein Märchen in sieben Abenteuern zweier Freunde*, in *Sämtliche Werke in sechs Bänden*, ed. Hartmut Steinecke and Wulf Segebrecht, vol. 6: *Späte Prosa. Briefe: Tagebücher und Aufzeichnungen. Juristische Schriften: Werke 1814–1822*, ed. Gerhard Allroggen et al. (Frankfurt a. M.: Deutscher Klassiker Verlag, 2004), 303–467, here 329.

[17] Hoffmann, *Master Flea*, 49–50. "Ein Blick in den Saal verriet dem jungen Pepusch sogleich die Ursache des fürchterlichen Entsetzens, das die Leute fortgetrieben. Alles lebte darin, ein ekelhaftes Gewirr der scheußlichsten Kreaturen erfüllte den ganzen Raum. Das Geschlecht der Pucerons, der Käfer, der Spinnen, der Schlammtiere, bis zum Übermaß vergrößert, streckte seine Rüssel aus, schritt daher auf hohen, haarigten Beinen, und die greulichen Ameisenräuber faßten, zerquetschten mit ihren zackigten Zangen die Schnacken, die sich wehrten und um sich schlugen mit den langen Flügeln, und dazwischen wanden sich Essigschlangen, Kleisteraale, hundertarmigte Polypen durch einander und aus allen Zwischenräumen kuckten Infusions-Tiere mit verzerrten menschlichen Gesichtern. Abscheulicheres hatte Pepusch nie geschaut." Hoffmann, *Meister Floh*, 330.

[18] William Heath: *MONSTER SOUP commonly called THAMES WATER . . .* (London, 1828).

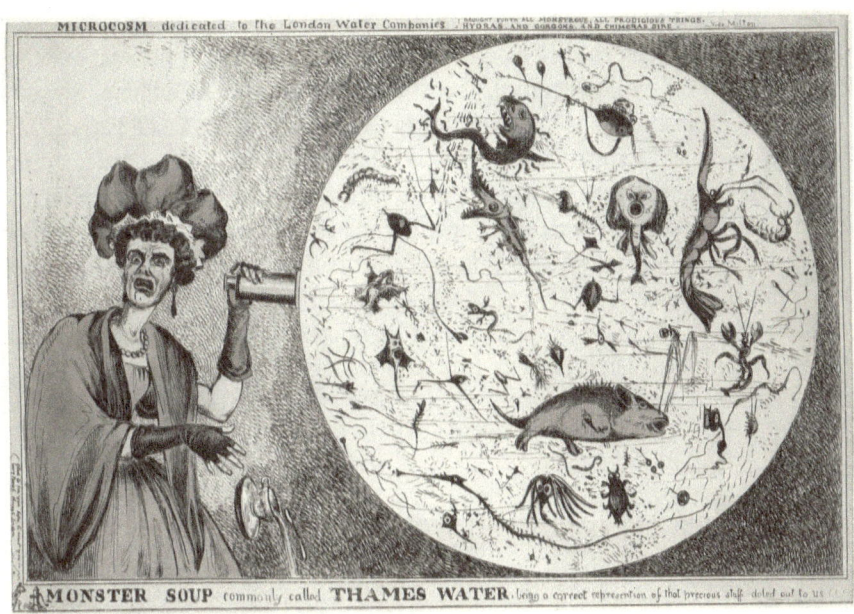

Figure 6: William Heath. "MONSTER SOUP commonly called THAMES WATER . . ." (London, 1828).

identify a well-to-do woman dropping a cup of tea from one hand while holding a microscope in the other. To her right we see a large tondo exhibiting – according to the caption – "Hydras, and Gorgons, and Chimeras dire," aquatic monsters, stingrays, lobsters, crabs, and other creatures. They exist in the water with which the lady's tea was made, as we are meant to gather from the image. To help us understand that the circular shape of the picture on the right shows what the lady is looking at through the microscope, Heath placed the instrument's lens squarely onto the tondo's frame. Looking for a point of reference to which he could moor his visual joke, Heath deliberately chose *Paradise Lost*, arguably one of the most influential descriptions of hell and its minions in literary history. The creatures described by Milton hail from "A Universe of death, which God by curse / Created evil, for evil only good, / Where all life dies, death lives, and nature breeds, / Perverse, all monstrous, all prodigious things, / Abominable, unutterable, and worse."[19] Quoting Milton verbatim, Heath starkly exaggerates the present dangers

---

19 John Milton: *Paradise Lost: A Poem in Ten Books* (London: Simmons, 1668), book 2: 622–626.

and, at the same time, downplays and ridicules the sight of polluted water, suggesting that the worst to be expected is that a lady might spill her tea. Another example from nineteenth-century visual satire can be seen in Wilhelm Scholz's "waterdrop from the Spree" printed in *Kladderadatsch* in 1853 (see Figure 7). It contains aquatic "Gorgons and Chimeras," but also other objects, referencing, among other things, well-known criminal cases, political incidents, and iconic items of the time, including a telescope.[20] Similarly, the editors of *Figaro* printed a page in 1872 showing two sets of six microscopic images each; all twelve show a vast range of items but no water or actual microorganisms.[21]

The first to use such circular frames for microscopic images was Hooke in the aforementioned *Micrographia*. Its first plate (see Figure 8) exhibits three microscopically enlarged objects: the point of a needle, a printed dot, and the edge of a razor blade. It is the last that is framed in a circle. That it does not necessarily have to be framed in this way becomes clear when looking at the needle and the dot which are not framed at all. More to the point, these images are prints based on hand drawings by Hooke which in turn were based on what he saw through the eyepiece; the engravings are by no means first-hand microscopic images. Photography through microscopic objective lenses should not be confused with microphotography, which was pioneered by Richard Hill Norris in the 1850s. Microphotography produces round images because of the circular shape of the objective lenses. If the photographic film or digital sensor is significantly smaller than the lens, this image is cropped to the size and shape of the plate, film, or sensor. Otherwise, a round image can be, and often is, cropped to a rectangular shape. While this results in information lost on the border of the image, it usually affects only those parts of the image that are less sharp and well defined, because optical lenses provide the greatest focus in the center. Of course, none of this applied when Hooke devised a round illustration for the razor blade.

In the *Micrographia*'s illustrations, which were published *before* photography was even invented, there are no technical reasons to explain why a drawing must be round. Hooke's decision, therefore, was based on aesthetics and the intended effects rather than necessity. The art historian Hartmut Böhme has convincingly argued that Hooke's *Micrographia* should be seen as a work of art in and of itself, since it builds upon a deliberate aesthetic program.[22] The picture of

---

[20] Wilhelm Scholz, "Ein Wassertropfen aus der Spree," *Kladderadatsch* VI, no. 12 (13 March 1853), n.p.
[21] Anonymous, "Mikroskopische Studien," *Figaro* XVI, nos. 52–53 (16 November 1872): 209.
[22] Hartmut Böhme, *Natur und Figur: Goethe im Kontext* (Paderborn: Wilhelm Fink, 2016), 347.

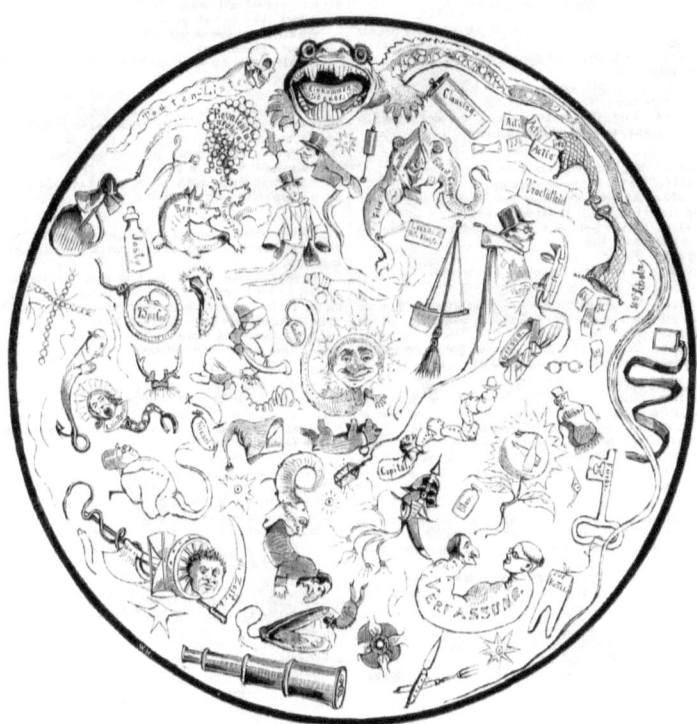

Figure 7: Wilhelm Scholz. "A Drop of Water from the Spree." *Kladderadatsch* (13 March 1853).

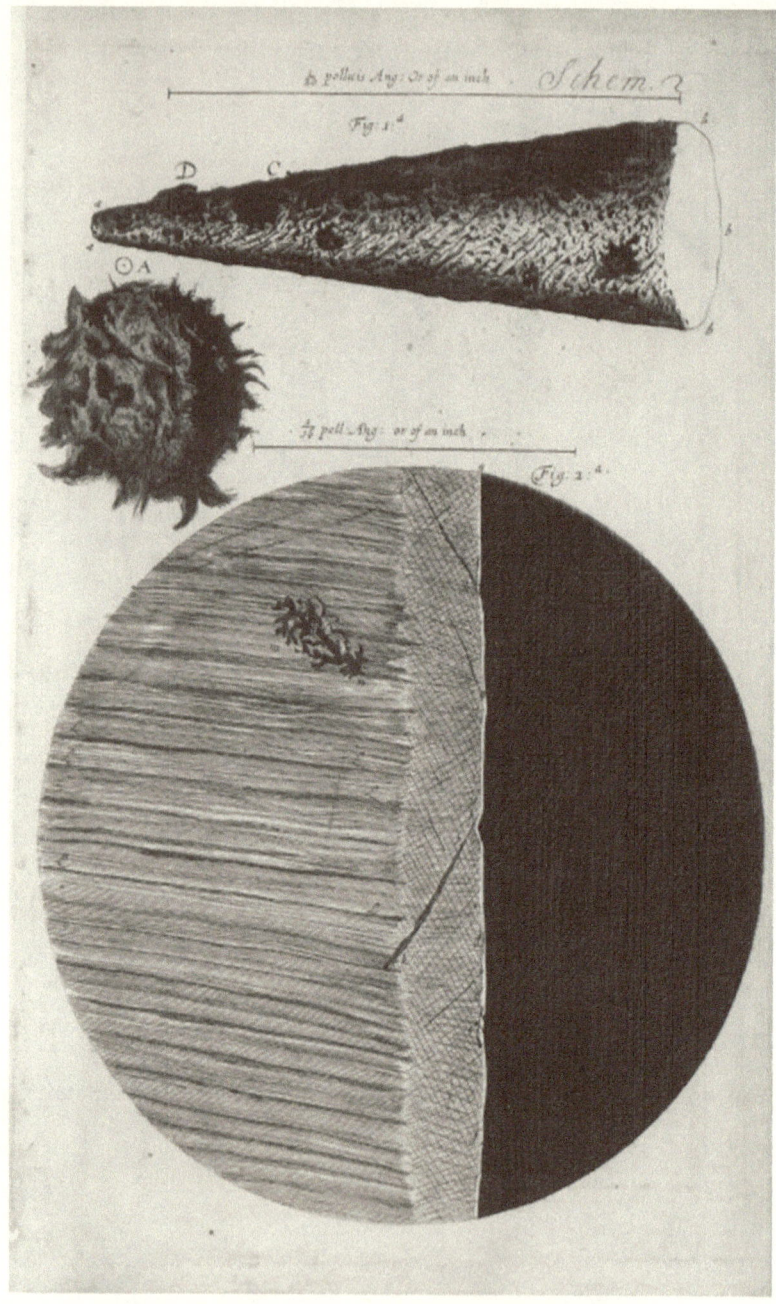

Figure 8: Robert Hooke. *Micrographia*, 1665, plate 1, Figures 1 and 2.

the razor blade is telling because it is clearly and, we can safely assume, knowingly constructed in accordance with the golden ratio. What, then, is the function of the round frame? The art historian Janice Neri explains that it offers the viewers of Hooke's images "an evocation of the experience of looking through the lens of a microscope" itself.[23] This framing style has since become the standard for representing microscopic imagery in print and is used to this day as countless examples from microscopy textbooks to the packaging of children's microscopes strikingly confirm.

In 1892, Franz Albert Jüttner (1865–1926) published a whole page in *Kladderadatsch* titled "Bacteriological research" (see Figure 9).[24] Comprised of three images, the largest one is the backdrop for the other two, and it depicts a microscope stage and an eye peering into the ocular. In the upper left corner, one notes the second image, of which the first appears to be the magnification. In the middle, a rectangular image is situated between them and can be identified as a microscopic picture that depicts what the man in the other two pictures sees through the instrument's ocular lens. This tableau is remarkable because the viewer must shift between three images, which results in alternate views of the magnified object. Looking at the two pictures described first, we see a character from the outside, from a third-person point-of-view. The middle image, however, commands a first-person perspective. As viewers, we have to imagine looking through the microscope and through the eye of the man illustrated in the picture. Jüttner's page thus foregrounds the switching of perspectives much more strongly than Heath's visual satire about pollution in the Thames. Whereas Heath's picture implies two views that are intended to be seen simultaneously, in Jüttner's illustration we see a sequence in which the viewer's perspective is switched twice.

2.2 Telescopic imagery

In 1900, British movie pioneer George Albert Smith (1870–1951) filmed two movies using this same technique for telescopic imagery that cartoonists and comics artists had used before him. In *Grandmother's Reading Glass*, a number

---

[23] Janice Neri, "Between Observation and Image: Representations of Insects in Robert Hooke's 'Micrographia,'" *Studies in the History of Art* 69 (2008), *Symposium Papers XLVI: The Art of Natural History: Illustrated Treatises and Botanical Paintings, 1400–1850*: 82–107, 97.

[24] Franz Jüttner, "Bakteriologische Untersuchungen," *Kladderadatsch* XLV, no. 36 (4 September 1892), n.p.

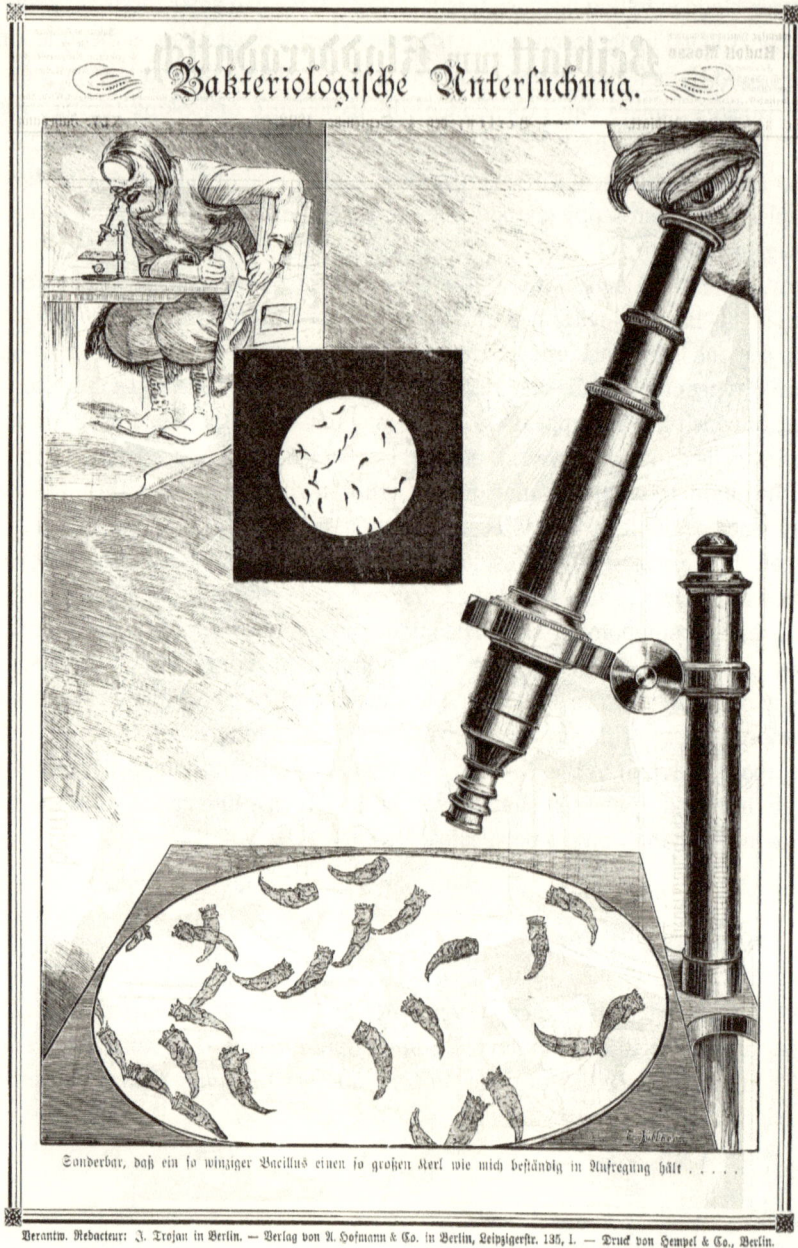

Figure 9: Franz Jüttner. "Bakteriologische Untersuchungen." *Kladderadatsch* (4 September 1892).

of things are looked at through a magnifying glass,[25] and in *As Seen Through A Telescope*, an elderly voyeur peeps at a woman's ankles from afar.[26] By cutting to circular images framed in black and then back again, Smith evokes the idea of the viewer taking the place of the man, looking through his eyes, or making his eyes, and thereby his crime, our own.

Smith was not the first to use this technique for telescopic images. In fact, representations of telescopic images in visual satire date back at least to Hogarth who drew upon *Some of the Principal Inhabitants of ye Moon* for a print that came out in 1788. Similarly, Gustave Doré includes a sequence of seventeen telescopic images in his *Désagréments d'un voyage d'agrément* of 1851.[27] Again, strong black lines are used to frame the tondos and set them apart from the rest of the narrative – none of which is round or framed – and emphasize them as a specific type of remediated image (see Figure 10). In 1858, *Punch* printed a fictitious report about an amateur astronomer trying to photograph the lunar eclipse that year. The illustration shows what appears to be the silhouette of a giant spider against the backdrop of the full moon that turns out to be an ordinary spider dangling in front of the telescope lens (see Figure 11). Much later, in the Tintin-story *The Shooting Star* (1941–1942), Hergé (Georges P. Remi, 1907–1983) used the same gag – and drew it in very much the same manner. Before Hergé, American comics artists had already made use of the technique of switching perspectives exhibited by Jüttner in a number of early comic strips. One example is the almost completely forgotten comic strip titled *Signs of Life Discovered on the Moon!!* (1907) by C. Deball, in which the silhouette of a parrot replaces the spider. Placed squarely in the middle of the nine-panel layout the telescopic tondo attracts the bulk of the reader's attention (see Figure 12).

Already in 1872, the Viennese *Figaro* printed a visual satire titled *Microscopic Studies [Mikroskopische Studien]* (see Figure 13).[28] Similar to Wilhelm Scholz's picture of the water drop from the river Spree, the anonymous artist presents an assortment of different things, figures, and scenes in two series of six individual microscopic pictures each framed in black. The images have short explanatory descriptions attached to them. However, apart from the title it is only the visual appearance of the images that instructs readers to look at them as microscopic images. This is significant because it suggests that readers of the time were already familiar enough with microscopic imagery to understand such an image

---

[25] *Grandmother's Reading Glass*, Dir. George Albert Smith (George Albert Smith Films, 1900).
[26] *As Seen Through A Telescope*, Dir. George Albert Smith (George Albert Smith Films, 1900).
[27] Gustave Doré, *Dés-agréments d'un voyage d'agrément* (Paris: Féchoz & Letouzey, n.y.), 15–17.
[28] Anonymous, "Mikroskopische Studien," 209.

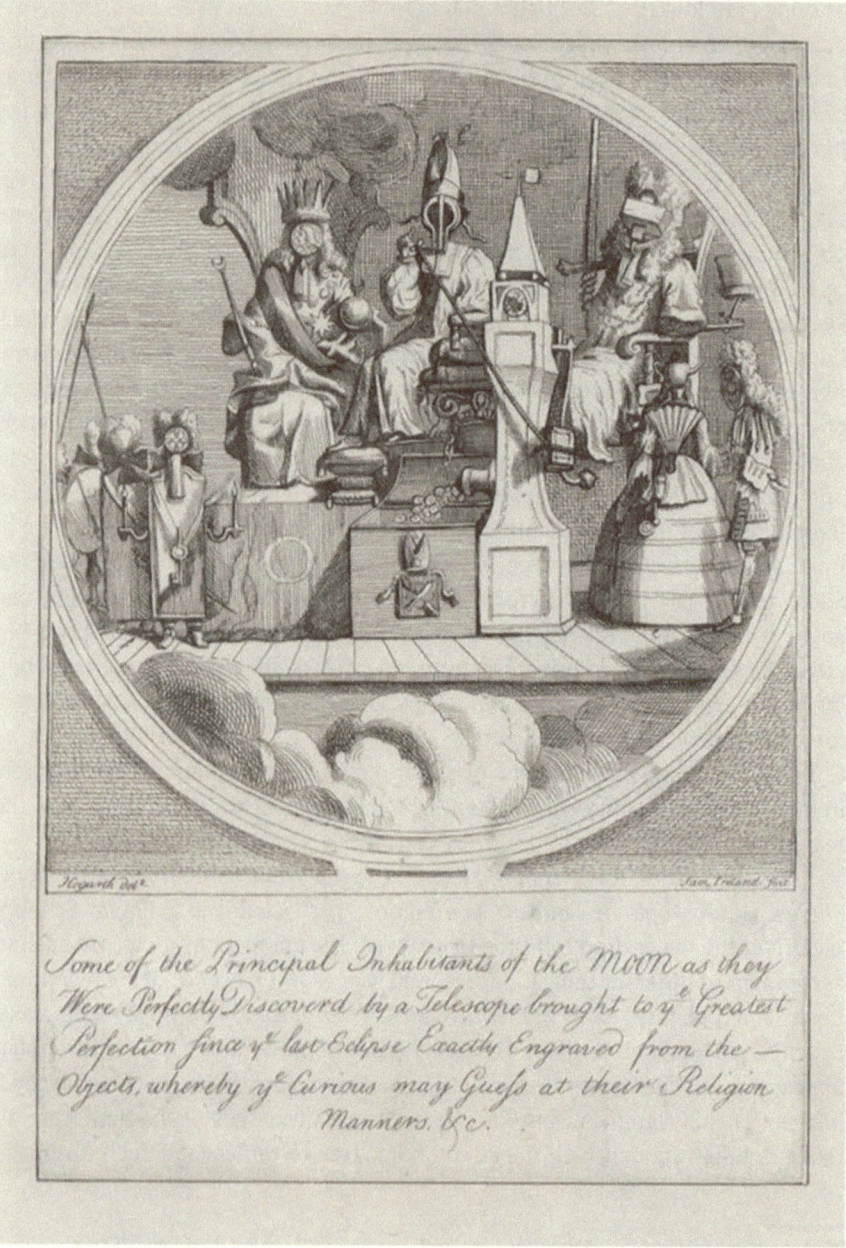

Figure 10: William Hogarth, "Some of the Principal Inhabitants of ye MOON" (London, 1788).

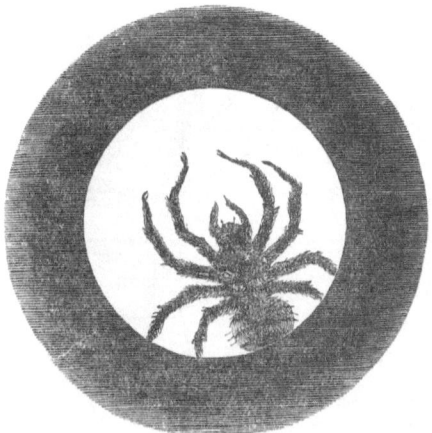

Figure 11: "Alarming Solar Phenomenon," *Punch*, (10 April 1858).

even when it was detached from its typical contents of aquatic monstrosities. Thus, after 1900, this image type could be used in movies and comic strips without further explanation or introduction. That it made readers or viewers switch perspectives may well be a contingent side effect of its integration into narrative, but it surely resonated with audiences more focused on first-person narratives and streams of consciousness.

3 Microscopic views and telescopic prospects

This brief survey of tondos in visual satire can by no means cover the aesthetic range and functions that circular images have in illustrated humor journals – let alone in nineteenth-century visual culture as a whole. To this day, circular imagery is exceptional and commands more of the reader's attention than a rectangular (i.e., regular) illustration would. The modern-day use of tondos to represent Superman's telescopic and microscopic vision is a case in point.[29] The examples I have discussed in this chapter show the immense interest in imaging technology among cartoonists of the nineteenth century. In their mission to comment on social and political events, these artists turned to optical devices like the magic lantern, microscope, and telescope, and so on. Hence, it

---

[29] See Bachmann, *Bilder/Rahmen*, 87.

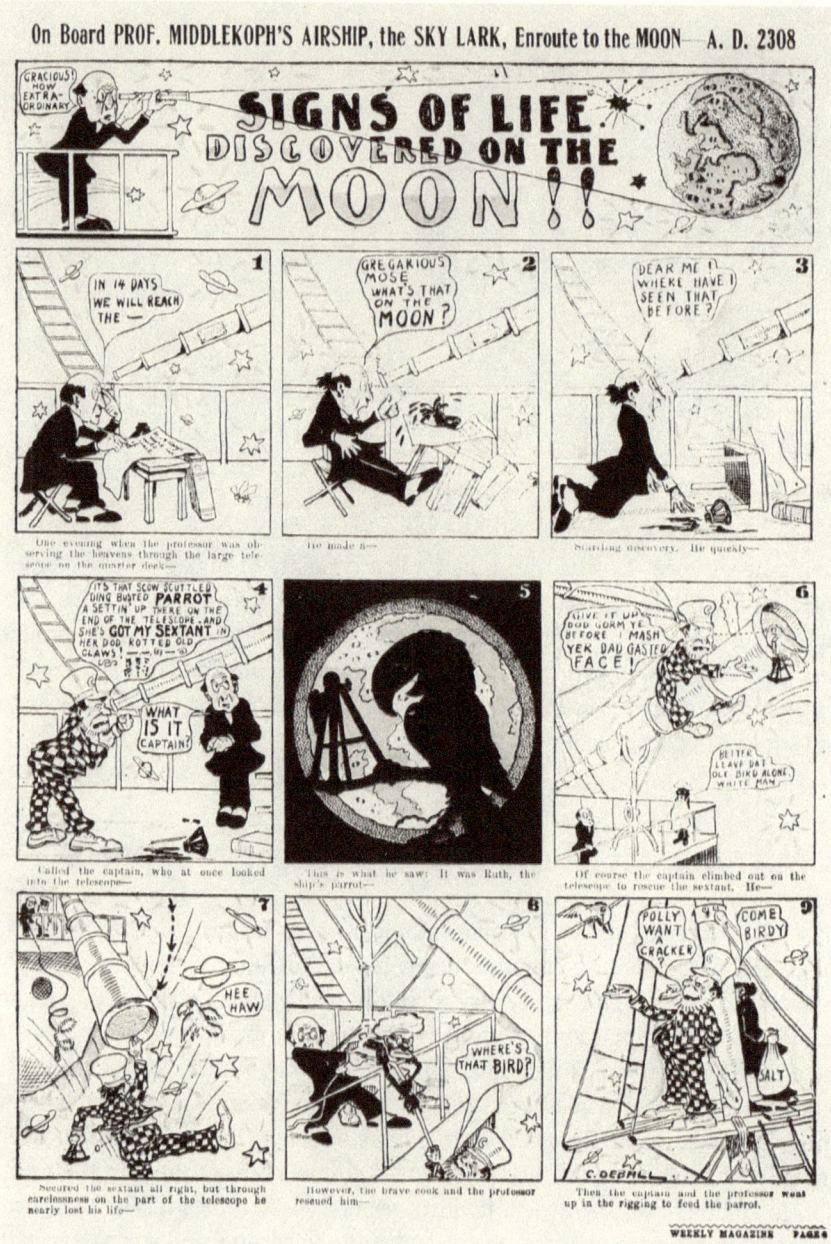

Figure 12: C. Deball. "Signs of Life Discovered on the Moon!!" *Denison Review* (2 October 1907).

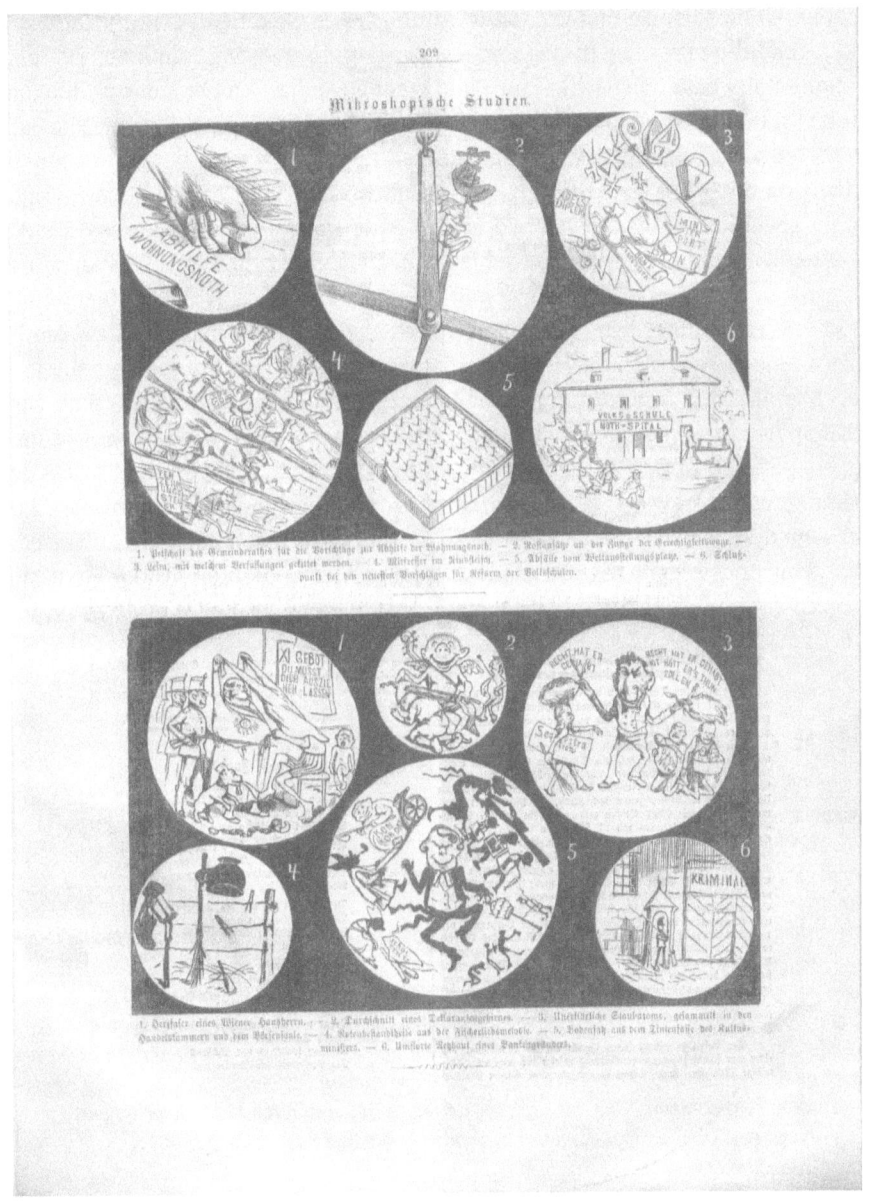

Figure 13: "Mikroskopische Studien" *Figaro* (16 November 1872).

comes as no surprise that the tondo resurfaced in nineteenth-century cartooning, emulating the view through an eyepiece or representing round objects that traditionally bear images like coins and medals, and also other subjects like the (man in the) moon, a favorite topic of cartoonists. At the same time, cartoonists adopted verbal metaphors and transformed them into visual metaphors, much like Gombrich has explained.[30] Consequently, the types of visual satire and their specific framings developed in this period make discrete types of visual satire discernible. Such frames helped viewers identify the type of visual satire the cartoonist wanted to achieve and also conveyed part of their intended effect, e.g., the impression of looking through a telescopic or microscopic ocular.

From these satirical and humorous cartoons, such ways of remediating images found their way into American comics, where they thrive to this day. The examples discussed in this chapter present remediations of new types of images, adapted to fit print technology and aesthetics and established tropes to satirize current events while also being fresh and interesting for readers increasingly exposed to images. And since the same techniques are still used, knowing and recognizing techniques developed (or brought to fruition) in nineteenth-century visual satire before photography helps us better understand today's and possibly future visual satire after photography.

Bibliography

Anonymous. "Laterna magica-Bilder mit Citatenaufguß." *Die Glühlichter* 3, no. 68 (25 June 1892): 4.
Anonymous. "Locus Sigilli." *Kladderadatsch* 28, no. 18 (18 April 1875): title page.
Anonymous. "Mikroskopische Studien." *Figaro* 16, nos. 52–53 (16 November 1872): 209.
Bachmann, Christian A. *Bilder/Rahmen: Rahmungen in visueller Satire, Bildergeschichte und Comic um 1900*. Hanover: Wehrhahn, 2018.
Böhme, Hartmut. *Natur und Figur: Goethe im Kontext*. Paderborn: Wilhelm Fink, 2016.
Doré, Gustave. *Dés-agréments d'un voyage d'agrément*. Paris: Féchoz & Letouzey, n.d.
Gombrich, E. H. "The Cartoonist's Armory." In *Meditations on a Hobby Horse and Other Essays on the Theory of Art*, 2nd ed., 127–142. London: Phaidon, 1971.
Hoffmann, E. T. A. *Master Flea*. In vol. 2 of *Specimens of German romance: Selected and Translated from Various Authors*. Translated by George Soane. London: Geo. B. Whittaker, 1826.
Hoffmann, E. T. A. *Meister Floh: Ein Märchen in sieben Abenteuern zweier Freunde*. In *Sämtliche Werke in sechs Bänden*, edited by Hartmut Steinecke and Wulf Segebrecht. Vol. 6, *Späte Prosa, Briefe, Tagebücher und Aufzeichnungen: Juristische*

---

[30] See E. H. Gombrich, "The Cartoonist's Armory," in *Meditations on a Hobby Horse and Other Essays on the Theory of Art*, 2nd ed. (London: Phaidon, 1971), 127–142.

Schriften: Werke 1814–1822, edited by Gerhard Allroggen et al., 303–467. Frankfurt am Main: Deutscher Klassiker, 2004.

Hooke, Robert. *Micrographia; or, Some Physiological Descriptions of Minute Bodies Made by Magnifying Glasses with Observations and Inquiries Thereupon*. London: Martin & Allesty, 1665.

Hoser, Paul. *Das Bayerische Vaterland*. In *Historisches Lexikon Bayerns*. http://www.historisches-lexikon-bayerns.de/Lexikon/Das Bayerische Vaterland. 3 July 2006. Accessed 22 Januar 2019.

Jüttner, Franz. "Bakteriologische Untersuchungen." *Kladderadatsch* 55, no. 36 (4 September 1892): n.p.

Kunzle, David. *The History of the Comic Strip*. Vol. 2, *The Nineteenth Century*. Berkeley: University of California Press, 1990.

Milton, John. *Paradise Lost: A Poem in Ten Books*. London: Simmons, 1668.

Neri, Janice. "Between Observation and Image: Representations of Insects in Robert Hooke's 'Micrographia.'" *Studies in the History of Art* 69 (2008), *Symposium Papers XLVI: The Art of Natural History: Illustrated Treatises and Botanical Paintings, 1400–1850*: 82–107.

Olson, Roberta J. M. *The Florentine Tondo*. Oxford: Oxford University Press, 2000.

Scholz, Wilhelm. "Soldat und Diplomat: Dissolving-views aus dem schleswig-holsteinischen Feldzuge." *Kladderadatsch* 17, nos. 44–45 (25 September 1864): n.p.

Scholz, Wilhelm. "Ein Wassertropfen aus der Spree." *Kladderadatsch* 6, no. 2 (13 March 1853): n.p.

Smolderen, Thierry. *The Origins of Comics: From William Hogarth to Winsor McCay*. Translated by Bart Beaty and Nick Nguyen. Jackson: University Press of Mississippi, 2014.

Vance Byrd
Enacting the Past: Nineteenth-Century Illustrated Periodicals and Painted Panoramas

The story of Friedrich Wilhelm Heine (1845–1921) and Theodore R. Davis (1840–1894) can help us trace how nineteenth-century visual commemorative culture was established on both sides of the Atlantic. Both men had illustrious careers independent of one another as war reporters and sketch artists before collaborating on commemorative battle panoramas, enormous circular oil paintings that fulfilled a public desire to be surrounded by scenes from the past. Engaged as a special sketch artist for illustrated periodicals during the Franco-Prussian War (1870–1871), Heine helped create a commemorative panorama of the Battle of Sedan in Germany twelve years after the conflict's conclusion. Due to the fame he garnered for this display, he was recruited to the United States in 1885 to run the American Panorama Company. In Milwaukee, he and a team of other German artists created panoramas commemorating battles from the American Civil War (1861–1865), whose execution was supervised and documented in the English-language press by the former Civil War newspaper correspondent and one-time sketch artist Theodore R. Davis.

The collaboration of these former war journalists is important because it invites us to question the "methodological nationalism" of media history and commemorative culture.[1] This means that remembering the American Civil War was not exclusively an American affair or regional concern. The tattered photograph found in a municipal archive in Leipzig showing painters from Vienna and Berlin dressed in Civil War uniforms and standing under an American flag in the company of the Theodore R. Davis in the Milwaukee panorama studio twenty-one years after the conflict's conclusion suggests as much (see Figure 1). It attests to the fact that illustrated journalism and other forms of commemoration the Franco-Prussian War engendered were deeply connected to the emergent business of Civil War celebration in the United States.

Nineteenth-century illustrated periodicals staged media production by establishing the foundation for how contemporaries remembered battles during the Franco-Prussian War and the American Civil War. In these publications, the sketch artist mobilized the readerly imagination to share both how these

---
[1] Sebastian Conrad, *What is Global History?* (Princeton: Princeton University Press, 2016), 3.

https://doi.org/10.1515/9783110696448-005

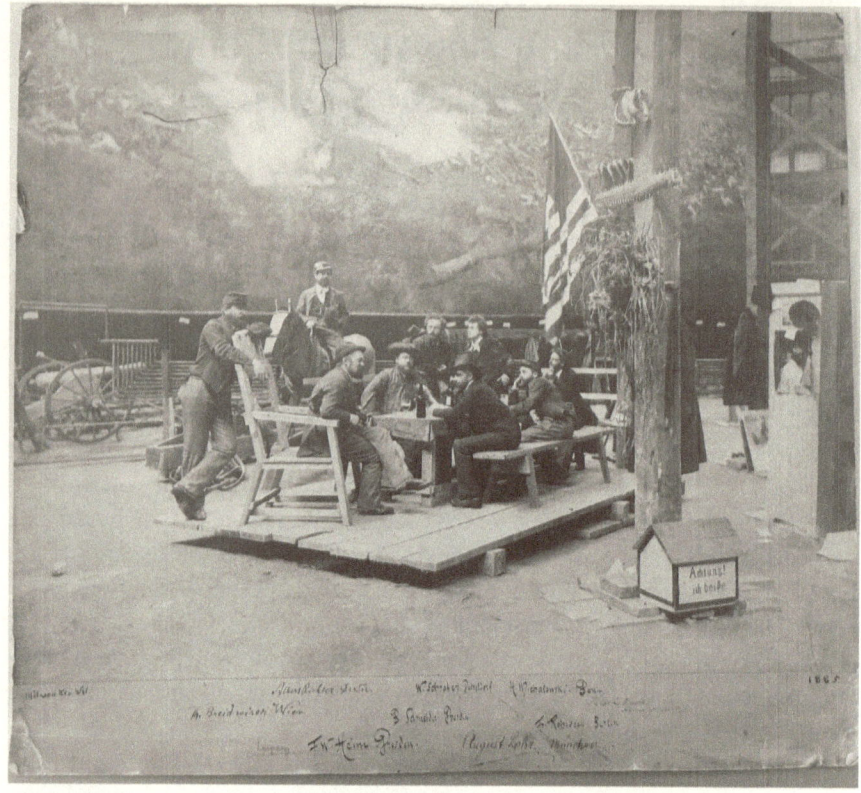

Figure 1: Members of the American Panorama Company in Milwaukee working on the *Missionary Ridge* cyclorama in 1885. The hand-written caption identifies their German or Austrian city of origin. Theodor Breidwiser and Friedrich Rohrbeck are dressed in Civil War uniforms. Theodore R. Davis is seated on the bench at the far right. Darstellung der Anfertigung eines Schlachtenpanoramas. Photographic paper on canvas. 38 x 43 cm (15 x 17 in.). Stadtgeschichtliches Museum Leipzig. Inventar-Nr. f/7/2003.

battles were won and lost, and what was true about what he had witnessed. Descriptions of the roving illustrator behind the lines and on the front captured in cultural periodicals helped elaborate for German readers around the world how to watch war. By first exploring the acts of visualization described in Heine's war coverage I aim to show how the illustrated press cultivated ways of seeing the aftermath of military conflict that paved the way for actual engagement with the recent past in panorama rotundas and on former battlefields. Reading illustrated periodicals, I suggest, became an act of pre- as well as re-enactment. A scholarly engagement with nineteenth-century periodicals and panoramas sets into relief both how the visual history of the Franco-Prussian War and the American Civil War was made, and how these histories were connected.

1 Nineteenth-century journalism and the representation of warfare

The overwhelming violence of warfare became an inescapable reality in the nineteenth century not only for combatants and civilians near battlefields, but also for rapidly expanding reading publics located in the safety of their homes far away.² Since the Franco-Prussian War was mainly fought near the Rhine and in France, and thus far from most German territories, illustrated journalism was an important way for readers across the German lands to follow the conflict. While some newspapers and cultural journals had to rely on remediated images, editors of periodicals with greater resources could provide readers with eyewitness accounts. It was through the focal point of the special artist that these editors attempted to make the historical magnitude of warfare comprehensible for readers through words and original images. As a special artist, Friedrich Wilhelm Heine published war reports for the *Leipziger Illustrirte Zeitung*, *Über Land und Meer*, and *Die Gartenlaube*.³ These cultural periodicals not only reported on the news; their depictions of how editorial and production staff on the home front worked with sketch artists like Heine on the front lines reveal the processes of periodicals and national history in the making.

Ernst Keil's (1816–1878) *Die Gartenlaube: Illustrirtes Familienblatt* [*The Garden Arbor: Illustrated Family Paper*, 1853–1944] was typical in this regard.⁴

---

2 The history of artists representing and reporting on wars is long. A few foundational works include: Jacques Callot's (1592–1635) *Les Grandes Misères et les Malheurs de la Guerre* (1633), Francisco José de Goya y Lucientes (1746–1828) *Los Desastres de la Guerra* (1810–1820, first published 1863), and Constantin Guys's *Our Artist on the Battle-Field of Inkerman* (1855). Hillary Chute, *Disaster Drawn: Visual Witness, Comics, and Documentary Form* (Cambridge, MA: The Belknap Press of Harvard University Press, 2016), 39–40. For her discussion of Constantin Guys, see 63. See also Susan Sontag's discussion of Goya in *Regarding the Pain of Others* (London: Penguin Books, 2003), 36–42.

3 Holger Starke, "Der Empfang der sächsischen Truppen in Dresden am 11. Juli 1871," in *Sachsen in Deutschland: Politik, Kultur und Gesellschaft 1830–1918*, ed. James N. Retallack (Bielefeld: Verlag für Regionalgeschichte, 2000), 143–159, here 145.

4 I cite *Die Gartenlaube* parenthetically with the abbreviation GL, issue number, year, and page number. The original German uses expanded letter spacing for emphasis. I use italics in the English translations. *Die Gartenlaube* changed editorial leadership and publishers several

Die Gartenlaube's editors argued that disseminating the historical truths of military conflict was urgent. To explain the magazine's mission in times of war, its editor juxtaposed the chaos of violent military conflict with the frenetic activity of media production. Keil maintained that providing German readers with "an inexhaustible cornucopia of military-political-feuilletonistic wisdom" (GL 6 [1871]: 98) meant that they need not rely on inaccurate foreign reports and poor translations about the events on the front lines. Keil informed subscribers that the original illustrated and non-illustrated stories they could read in safety with their morning coffee were the product of a tremendous coordinated effort: "*our reporters and sketch artists really sat in the army camp* and not in the editorial office or in an atelier back home" (GL 41 [1870]: 648).[5] The illustrated reports in *Die Gartenlaube* were meant to give rise to a sense of both visual and narrative immediacy to those who had not experienced the war. They could do so because the magazine's correspondents had actually been at the scene.

While transmitting the sense that a correspondent or sketch artist was present during the conflict was a main priority, the magazine also pointed out that coordinated labor *at home* was necessary to contain a flood of words and images during this period of perceived information overload and print saturation.[6] The editorial and production staff established order of "the enormous mass of manuscripts, newspapers, and other printed matter" (GL 6 [1871]: 97). The staff put installment fiction, as well as military-themed reports and letters from the front into dialogue with one-quarter, two-third, full, and double-page engravings in each issue. The magnitude of the war remained hard to grasp, but each issue conveyed how the news was made and stressed that the purpose of illustrated cultural periodicals could be linked to something greater than covering recent battles or other military events. Heine's article describes evocatively how *Die Gartenlaube* reached a broad international readership, which

---

times between 1853 and when it ceased publication in 1937. It was published again as *Die neue Gartenlaube* from 1938 until 1944. Ernst Keil edited *Die Gartenlaube* during the war months of 1870, the focus of this chapter. See *Die Gartenlaube: Illustrirtes Familienblatt* (Leipzig: Keil Verlag, 1853–1884). For a detailed account on war reporting and the national idea in *Die Gartenlaube*, see Kirsten Belgum, *Popularizing the Nation: Audience, Representation, and the Production of Identity in* Die Gartenlaube, *1853–1900* (Lincoln, NE: University of Nebraska Press, 1998), 55–83.

5 "unsere Berichterstattung und Zeichner wirklich im Heerlager und nicht im Redactionsbureau oder im heimischen Atelier saßen, und daß die Redaction keine Opfer gescheut hat, um den Lesern ein möglichst anschauliches Bild des Krieges zu liefern."

6 See essays in *Before Photography* written by Matthew Anderson, Christian Bachmann, and David Ciarlo for more perspectives on nineteenth-century print history.

included German readers living abroad in countries such as in the United States in a timely manner and with remarkable speed. As a result, sketch artists working for *Die Gartenlaube* played no small role in fostering a sense of German national unity and historical awareness wherever the cultural periodical was read.⁷

If we zero in on Heine's illustrated reports in *Die Gartenlaube* during the Franco-Prussian War, we see that the truth he wanted to convey to German readers was comprised of the contradictions witnessed in the wake of military victory. Stories highlighting his own activity of producing hand-drawn sketches are common. By including himself in the reportage, Heine sought to foreground the authenticity of his reporting from the front. For example, in letters addressed to the publisher, which frequently included an engraving of him, Heine took readers on a slow march to the front starting with the departure of troops from a train station in Darmstadt; his reports culminated with Wilhelm I's installation as German Emperor at the Palace of Versailles on 18 January 1871. Heine wrote that no amount of description could convey the level of destruction he witnessed as he approached Paris with the regiment (GL 46 [1870]: 765), yet his war reports did not burden the reader with unpleasant details of injury, death, and destruction. Heine told Keil and, by extension, the periodical's readers how much he enjoyed his métier: "I always like to travel, as you know, and I like to tell stories and sketch what I see" (GL 52 [1870]: 880). With first-person immediacy and pride, Heine, the self-proclaimed "battlefield tourist" (*Schlachtenbummler*) (GL 44 [1870]: 818), reported in installments on the advance of Saxon regiments and the French attacks they faced as they made progress toward Sedan. "Bummeln" in German means to take a leisurely stroll. The entry from Jacob and Wilhelm Grimms' dictionary explains that the neologism was "[a]ttested in the most recent wars, especially used since 1870 for those who used nursing as a pretext to go theatres of war to satisfy their curiosity or to devote themselves to the more enjoyable aspect of life in military quarters and camps."⁸

---

7 Belgum, *Popularizing the Nation*, 53. The articles Heine illustrated about the Franco-Prussian War were read in a vibrant American market for German-language periodicals that had grown since the period of mass German immigration in the 1850s. For more on Germans and the German-language press in the United States during the Civil War, see Walter D. Kamphoefner, Wolfgang Helbich, and Ulrike Sommer, "Introduction," in *News from the Land of Freedom: German Immigrants Write Home*, ed. Walter D. Kamphoefner, Wolfgang Helbich, and Ulrike Sommer (Ithaca: Cornell University Press, 1988), 1–50, here 22. Walter D. Kamphoefner and Wolfgang Helbich, "Introduction," in *Germans in the Civil War: The Letters They Wrote Home*, ed. Walter D. Kamphoefner and Wolfgang Helbich (Chapel Hill: The University of North Carolina Press, 2006), 1–34, here 23.

8 "In den neueren kriegen aufgekommen, besonders seit 1870 für diejenigen gebracht, die unter dem vorwande der krankenpflege sich nach dem kriegsschauplatze begaben, ihre

Duty rather than voyeuristic pleasure determined Heine's work from this perspective. He emphasized that his images told the readership something true about the nature of war: "that's how it is in the war! [. . .] It is the entire truth that I have depicted here for you" (GL 46 [1870]: 765). His assertion was echoed by his editor:

> Our artist, Mr. F. W. Heine from Leipzig has to inform us pictorially about almost all battles and skirmishes on location seen with his own eyes. The present image shows the layman, too, that he does not have before him a product made at home but the truth of experience. (GL 41 [1870]: 688)

Such statements minimize the crucial editorial labor done in Leipzig and elevate how sketch artists like Heine distilled the historical truth out of what they had witnessed on the front. The hand-made scenes published in his articles manifested this "battlefield tourist's" enthusiasm, which at times played down war's violence and asserted German moral character and military dominance. While the time it took to deliver news from the front meant that up-to-date description of the war was unobtainable, the publication delivered truths about how Germans and the French should be remembered instead.

By furnishing readers with scenes they should remember about the conflict, it was the charge of sketch artists like Heine to mobilize the reader's imagination rather than just furnish a neutral account. Some of Heine's illustrated letters from the field focused on what he and his men discovered after a particular battle had been won. Let us take a closer look at how words, images, and page format direct readers to imagine the truth of war.

In an article entitled "In MacMahon's Villa," Heine presented the readership with alternate ways to view what the war had wrought (GL 46 [1870]: 765). There is a French and a German truth, an illustrated one, and alternate ways of watching war that were reserved for the readerly imagination. The first page of Heine's illustrated report was divided into three parts, which interrupt the two-columned text's narrative: Seven lines appear above and nine lines below a three-quarter-page illustration (see Figure 2). With this layout, his verbal account establishes a counterpoint to the image that dominates the page. His words focus on past events in the first sentences: He describes the destruction of mirrors, paintings, and sculptures in MacMahon's villa: Soldiers cut open mattresses and tore apart and burned books. Heine admits that exhausted and

---

neugierde zu büszen oder sich der lustigeren seite des quartier- und lagerlebens zu widmen." In Jacob Grimm and Wilhelm Grimm, eds., *Das deutsche Wörterbuch* (Leipzig: S. Hirzel, 1854–1961), http://dwb.uni-trier.de/de/, here http://www.woerterbuchnetz.de/DWB?lemma=schlachtenbummler

— 765 —

In der Villa Mac Mahon's.

„C'est la guerre!" — „So geht's im Kriege zu! Das wird Ihr Ausspruch sein, Verehrtester" — schreibt uns Herr Fr. Wilh. Heine, unser Feldmaler vor Paris — „wenn Sie das beigegebene Bildchen ansehen. Es ist volle Wahrheit, was ich Ihnen hier dargestellt habe, Landschaft und Staffage, und das, was Sie hier herumliegen und von unseren Soldaten in Nutznießung genommen sehen, ist so ziemlich Alles, was von der

Hof und Hausflur gar nicht zu reden, fanden wir das Innere der Häuser durchweg in dem schauderhaftesten Zustande. Da waren alle Schränke, Commoden, Koffer aufgerissen, der Inhalt lag zerstampft umher, alles nicht Niet- und Nagelfeste von Wand, Fenster und Decke losgebrochen, die kostbarsten Spiegel, Bilder, Sculpturen und oft sogar alle Fensterscheiben entzwei geschlagen, — ja, an einigen Orten traf ich sogar die Polster und Betten aufgeschnitten.

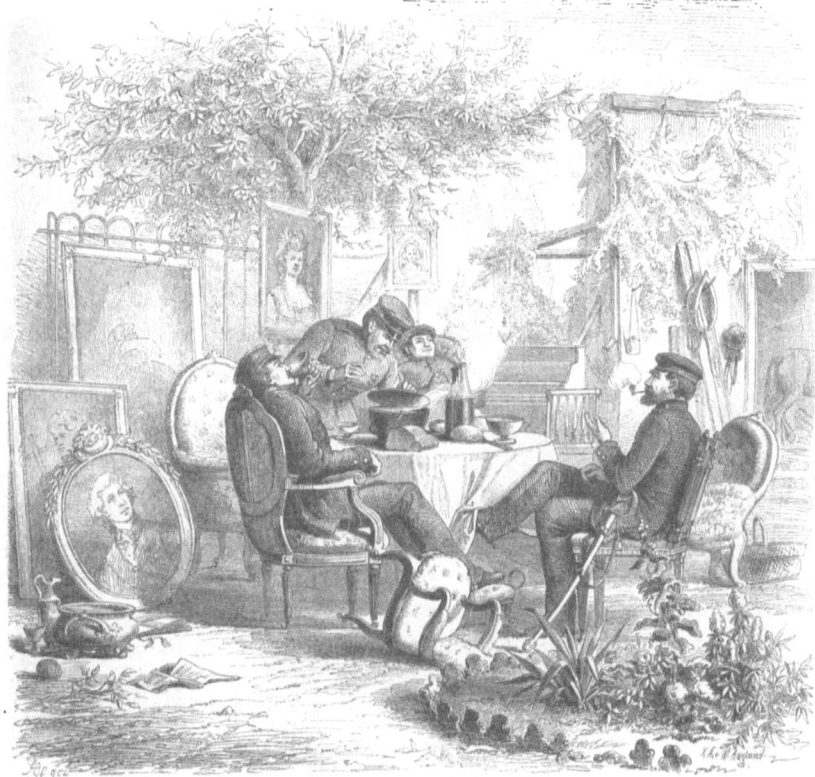

Artilleristen-Frühstück vor Paris.
Nach der Natur aufgenommen von unserem Feldmaler F. W. Heine.

Villa, die man von verschiedenen Seiten als Eigenthum Mac Mahon's bezeichnet, im Parke von Montfermeil bei Paris noch übrig geblieben ist.

Alle Beschreibung und Zeichnung ist nicht im Stande, Ihnen einen Begriff von der Zerstörung zu geben, auf die wir fast mit jedem Schritte rings um Paris stoßen. In Courtry zum Beispiel, von wo mein letzter Brief an Sie abging und wo wir — d. h. unser sächsisches Jägerbataillon — gerade eine Woche lagen, hat das Bataillon sich an die schöne Arbeit gemacht, das ganze Dorf zu säubern und in etwas wohnlichen Stand zu setzen. Von

prachtvolle Uhren zertrümmert, die werthvollsten Bücher zerrissen, zertreten oder halb verbrannt — und dies Alles, weil die ergrimmten Soldaten die Eßwaaren, den Wein, die Cigarren nicht finden konnten, die sie in solchen stattlichen Räumen erwartet hatten. Denn leider ist es Thatsache, daß hier und da auch deutsche Truppen sich zu solchem wilden Treiben verleiten ließen, wenn ihrem Hunger, Durst und Ruhebedürfniß durch die Flucht der Bewohner dieser Ortschaften jede Befriedigung entzogen war. Mit Gewehrkolben, Handbeil und Spaten begann dann ihre Eröffnung und Durchforschung aller Räume der Häuser, Sommerpaläste,

Figure 2: Victorious German artillery soldiers dine al fresco at MacMahon's villa. GL 46 (1870): 765.

hungry Germans occasionally ransacked French residences and villages: "[. . .] it is unfortunately the case that here and there German troops allow themselves to follow such wild drives" (GL 46 [1870]: 765). When this occurs, the French regard these actions as an affront to their culture that strengthens their will: "A great cry of the oppressed civilization will rise up against the disgraceful deeds of the barbarians" (GL 46 [1870]: 766). In previous issues, *Die Gartenlaube* used colonial and racist tropes to call into question France's professed civilization and represent the nation as a physical threat to Prussian political hegemony.[9] By contrast, Heine presents the French fear of German savagery as a material rather than bodily threat. At the conclusion to "In MacMahon's Villa," Heine suggests by making reference to portraits collected in the garden that the Germans maintained their moral respectability: "But chivalry is certainly found in these brave men, for several pictures of women were allocated to an honorable position" (GL 46 [1870]: 766). In Heine's depiction, German soldiers directed their pent-up rage at furniture and not women, at least not those on canvas.

Indeed, his illustration in the middle of the page does not immortalize German barbarians, and there is no destruction on the order Heine said he had witnessed. We have to imagine that such violence would be a French version of what war with the Prussians meant. In an illustration evocative of the open-air domesticity projected by *Die Gartenlaube*'s masthead, Heine instead shows artillery soldiers taking breakfast outdoors on fine porcelain surrounded by portraits from Marshal MacMahon's luxurious villa. This illustration, in which soldiers converse, smoke a pipe, look calmly into the distance, or lift the lid of a cooking pot, seems to contradict Heine's verbal account of the potential for German misdeeds; nothing is burnt or torn asunder. On the next page, the reader learns that Heine found a note cut into the fabric of a billiard table. An act of destruction in and of itself, which is not illustrated, these inscribed words stem from a German fighter who attributed scenes of ruination to the French. Heine responds uncritically and with relief: "I admit to you that these words were a great reassurance to me because the honor of our men must stand above everything else" (GL 46 [1870]: 766). His readers could rest assured, war remained a dignified matter for German troops.

Whereas this image of soldiers at peace dominates the first section, Heine delays further engagement with the picture in the majority of the report. Instead, his retrospective narration takes the reader on a stroll that describes German efforts to build entrenchments that preceded the garden scene depicted in the illustration. During this *Schlachtenbummel*, he did not document the labor of

---

9 See GL 33 (1870): 516–519; GL 37 Beiblatt (1870): 597; GL 40 (1870): 665.

building fortifications in detail or recall conversations these troops might have held about the war or their longing for home. Instead, the plot lines of Heine's report assume a meandering form like his own movements toward Paris. Arriving at an elevated lookout behind a lime quarry north of Gagny, Heine took out a field glass to observe Parisian fortifications, the French pendant to the Germans' labors, and suburbs through the fog. Offering no further comment on the French defensive walls and unsure whether he actually saw St. Denis, Heine addressed the limitations of his own vision:

> While I made every effort to use my sight to catch as much as possible of the long-awaited Babel of the West, an air-balloon of considerable circumference rose from the fog of the cosmopolitan city, floated for a while in one position and then lowered again. It had likely undertaken a reconnaissance flight. That happened at ten o'clock.
>
> (GL 46 [1870]: 766)

While the first section of the report addressed respectable behavior during times of war, his letter from the field related to German readers the dominance of French military and communications technology rather than suggesting superior German military strategy or mastery of the landscape. Nor did his account take on the French perspective and narrate German troop movements, the construction of entrenchments, or skirmishes they might have seen from a position in the hot-air balloon, that is, higher than his own. Instead, the reader is aligned with Heine's imprecise and limited vision and adopts a contemplative mode reminiscent of a travel account. Heine expresses how aesthetically pleasing it was for him and, by extension, for the reader to enjoy his Prussian panoramic view of a combat zone: "My position was so lovely that I did not want to leave it" (GL 46 [1870]: 766).[10] He then impressionistically describes the destruction of the natural environment caused by war and the distant sounds of battle from this panoramic point of view before dedicating a few lines to his German comrades. His words call on the reader's imagination to hear and see the landscape. He singles out valiant German military leaders by name and shares an episode which humorously highlights the cunning of soldiers who had pilfered wine and liqueur. Detailed verbal and pictorial description of the violent fight itself is absent. The battle had concluded before Heine had made it there. It is left for the reader's imagination to fill in these details. Heine slept peacefully that night, and it was on the next morning that he visited MacMahon's Villa: "It was on this stroll that I came upon our image," which he illustrated for his article (GL 46 [1870]: 766).

---

10 "Mein Standort war so schön, daß ich ihn nicht verlassen mochte." Heine's phrase is fascinating because there is more than one coexistent meaning for "Standort," which could refer to a military position or garrison, a political stance, or a point of view.

In Heine's article, images of war's destruction and the panoramic perspective take place in the mind of the reader rather than on the illustrated page. Heine gives his German readers verbal and pictorial imagery they could bear to see. A casual walk onto an active field of war could hardly be possible, but it serves as a rhetorical signal and a narrative strategy to make the violent events of war comprehensible. The truth of the German experience of war gleaned from Heine's stroll communicated a complicated account consisting of reassurances of propriety, a picture of the men in good spirits, and an invitation to imagine the battlefield as a beautiful space in which Germans could advance toward Paris in safety due to a system of entrenchments even while being observed by potentially barbarous French from overhead.

War is violent and gruesome. Some artists chose to represent it that way. Goya, for example, relentlessly directs our attention to drawn scenes of the violent truths of war we cannot bear to see. The caption for the etched copperplate "No se puede mirar" from *Los Desatres de la Guerra* (1810–1820, published 1863) shows how Goya prevents us from disregarding our role as "viewers, looking and looking at others looking upon horror" (see Figure 3).[11] In this plate, drawn bayonet rifles point at two men pleading for mercy while kneeling in front of women cowering in terror. One of these male figures looks directly into the muzzles and pleads for all their lives in the final moments before the shots are to be fired. The man sees the executioners not captured in the plate's frame – we do not.

Heine writes much more about violence than he draws it. Rather than Goya's rhetorical strategy of showing scenes of agony, gruesome violence, and death, such as mutilated bodies impaled by tree trunks, Heine's sober images call for synthesis and attest to the sensibilities and political leanings of his bourgeois German readers. In a letter, "Refuge under the Earth," Heine remarks that more French civilians would have survived the war had they not shot upon Prussian soldiers (GL 44 [1870]: 730), a bloody image he does not present in the illustrated article. Heine shows the release of innocent French women and children and implies via the praying peasant in the foreground and retreating male figures in the illustration's background that the French men were executed (see Figure 4). If these peasant men were killed in response to their attack on the German soldiers, their execution at the hands of Germans is withheld from our view. Here, the illustration should be a comfort to the subscriber reading far away from "the innumerable horrors of this war" (GL 44 [1870]: 730). Heine delivers reassurance and

---

[11] Chute, *Disaster Drawn*, 60. Susan Sontag notes: "Goya's images are a synthesis. They claim: things *like* this happened. [. . .] A photograph is supposed not to evoke but to show. This is why photographs, unlike handmade images, can count as evidence." Sontag, *Regarding the Pain of Others*, 42.

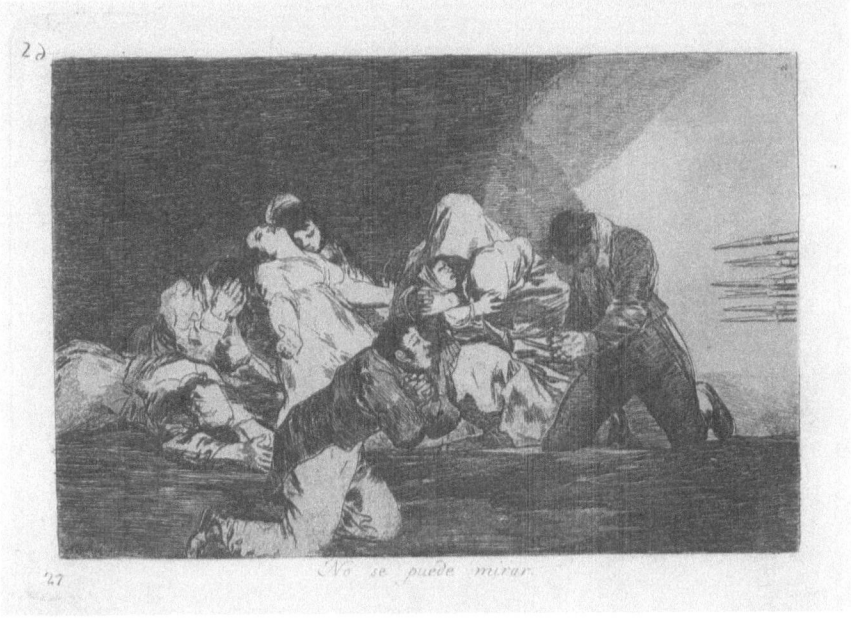

Figure 3: Francisco de Goya y Lucientes, "No se puede mirar," from *Los Desastres de la Guerra* (1810–1820, published 1863). Etching, burnished lavis, drypoint and burin. Plate: 14.5 x 21 cm, sheet: 25.2 x 34.3 cm. The Metropolitan Museum of Art, Rogers Fund and Jacob H. Schiff Bequest, 1922, Accession Number: 22.60.25(26).

atonement for the nation rather than a spectacle of vengeful violence; it is left to the reader to imagine the fate of the male French peasants.

Elsewhere, Heine's illustrations foreground valiant struggles as the German troops press on to the distant village where they all hope to arrive after the offensive. The report "From the Battle near Sedan" (GL 41 [1870]: 687–688) explains the subject matter of Heine's illustration "The 105th Regiment in the Defile at Daigny near Sedan" (see Figure 5) (GL 41 [1870]: 686). In the verbal account, Heine identifies regiments, companies, and battalions with words and sketched numerals; he identifies the French North African (*Zuaven*) troops they faced that day, and marks when military notables fell in battle. The immediate circumstances that led to their tragic deaths are left largely to the imagination through multiple instances of temporal and spatial displacement.

The reader needs the verbal description found at the end of the issue, including spatial and temporal adverbs, to decipher how the sketch artist synthesizes time and space in the illustration's composition. We should not quickly run our

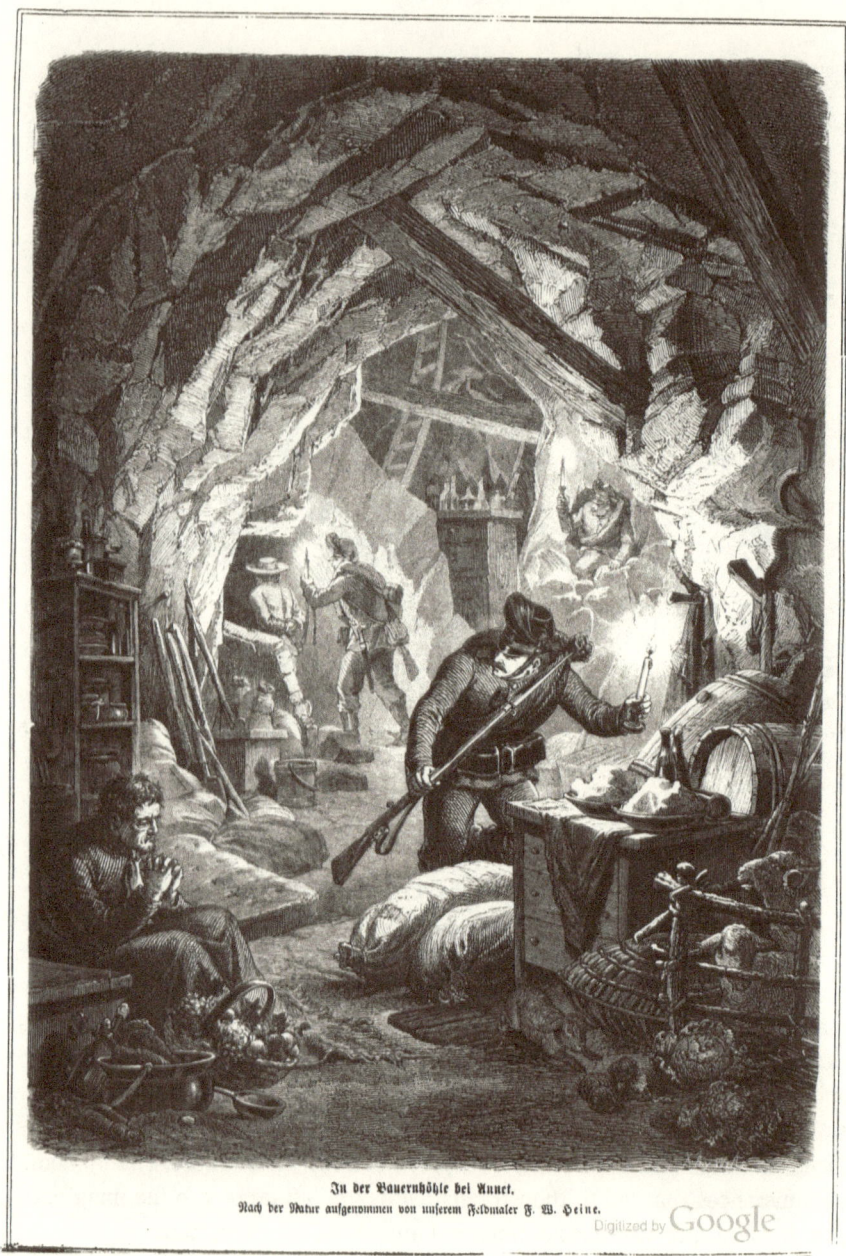

Figure 4: German soldiers moments before executing two French male peasants. GL 44 (1870): 729.

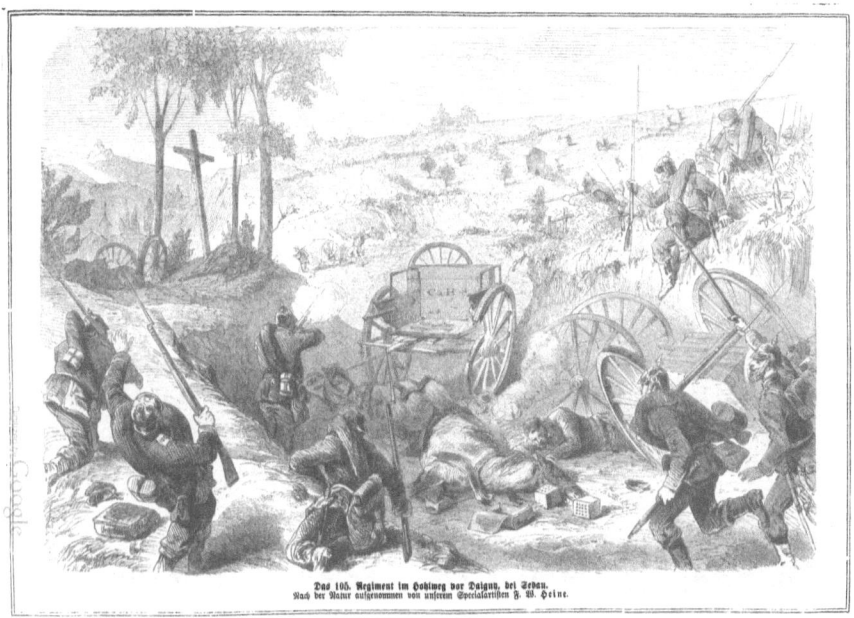

Figure 5: F. W. Heine's illustration of the 105th Saxon Regiment fighting near Daigny. GL 41 (1870): 686.

eyes over his illustrated report. Instead, Heine's description demands that we slow down and use our imagination to let ourselves be absorbed into the action depicted in his verbal description and the full-page engraving. Sequentially recalling where the troops came under fire, Heine invites the reader to imagine spatial depth ("in the closest proximity" and "in the background of our picture to the right") and the passage of time at a given position ("over two hours") before the soldiers continued their advance on Daigny (GL 41 [1870]: 687). For these recollections, Heine refers to locations in the illustration's middle ground where some of these men now lie buried. His words point us to a different section of his battle sketch where the "graves of Saxon heroes in foreign soil" are found in a cemetery in Daigny (GL 41 [1870]: 687). In the periodical's engraving, the reader might be unable to decipher the inscriptions on each fallen officer's grave, but Heine writes that he saved a sketch of each gravestone for future readers ("zum Andenken im Bilde"), a type of private souvenir for the German public, which is not reproduced for examination in this war report (GL 41 [1870]: 687). Heine and the regiment arrive in the French village around five o'clock, and he reflects on the battle he had witnessed: "The victory was great, but the loss of German lives is not lesser and tempers the joy whenever one thinks about it. More next time"

(GL 41 [1870]: 688). Heine's ambivalent remarks about war's violence reveal that there is a drive to show more of it due to reader interest and the periodical's serial form.

Heine's war articles stage nineteenth-century media production, the deliberate process of setting the coordinates for remembering how battles were won and lost during the Franco-Prussian War from the perspective of a war correspondent. Claudia Stockinger observes that already in the weeks immediately *following* the armistice on 31 January and at Versailles on 26 February 1871, *Die Gartenlaube*'s editors turned from current events to the past.[12] However, the articles appearing in a cultural periodical *before* the Prussians had secured victory indicate that a duty to secure memory of these historic events and praise German character was central to the function of illustrated journalism. In this regard, Heine foregrounds his complicated mediating role as a sketch artist *and* witness to violence whose words and images – memoranda – will endure longer than the conflict.

2 Theodore R. Davis's reports on F. W. Heine and the American Panorama Company

German special sketch artists drew upon their experiences and observational techniques developed during the Franco-Prussian War for illustrated periodicals to create different media focused on the memory of the war. Friedrich Wilhelm Heine took his knowledge to the United States, where he worked with the American sketch artist Theodore R. Davis. By focusing on their collaboration, we will observe how the illustrated press influenced in what manner nineteenth-century military conflicts were remembered in painted panoramas. An investigation of Heine and Davis's collaboration is important for understanding how Heine, a German, became a central figure in the production of visual memory of the American Civil War.

The panorama became the prime medium of illusionism in the nineteenth century.[13] Invented in 1787 by Robert Barker (1739–1806), the panorama was a

---

12 "Zugleich beginnt jetzt eine Reihe, die das soeben Erlebte historisierte und aus unterschiedlichen Perspektiven zum Gegenstand kollektiven Erinnerungsinteresses machte: *Erinnerungen aus dem heiligen Kriege.*" Claudia Stockinger, *An den Ursprüngen der populärer Serialität. Das Familienblatt* Die Gartenlaube (Göttingen: Wallstein Verlag, 2018), 323.
13 For a detailed history of panoramas, see Heinz Buddemeier, *Panorama, Diorama, Photographie* (Munich: Wilhelm Fink, 1970); Scott Barnes Wilcox, "The Panorama and Related Exhibitions in London," (M. Litt. thesis, University of Edinburgh, 1976); Stephan Oettermann, *The Panorama:*

bourgeois entertainment form that invited audiences in cities and towns around the world to admire illuminated circular paintings of natural and urban landscapes as well as battle scenes. Often the panorama gave audiences an opportunity to escape everyday life by witnessing scenes from the past. In many cases a panorama exhibition was inflected by patriotic aims of recently formed national states.[14] In the United States, some nineteenth-century panoramas affirmed issues such as slavery, manifest destiny, and westward expansion.[15] Arguments about nation building ring true for most panoramas in the German context, as well. Eight panoramas displayed in Berlin between 1880 and 1914 commemorated Germany's military, colonial, and archaeological conquests. Alexander Kips (1858–1910) and Max Koch's (1859–1930) *Pergamon Panorama* of 1886, stood near Lehrter Stadtbahnhof and could be read against the backdrop of archaeological excavations in Greece and Asia Minor. With its visualization of Attalus I's (269–197 B.C.) victory over the Galatians in 241 B.C., this *Pergamon Panorama* functioned implicitly as a celebration of German victory over the "Gauls" at Sedan and the establishment of the Second German Empire under Prussian authority.[16]

Indeed, the commemoration of the Franco-Prussian War, spurred on by economic rebound in the 1880s, had prompted several German panorama shows to glorify German victory on Sedan Day, a turning point in the Franco-Prussian War leading to the abdication of Emperor Napoleon III. Louis Braun's (1836–1916) panorama, displayed in Frankfurt am Main, celebrated the tenth anniversary of the Battle of Sedan in 1880. Braun, who had worked as a special sketch artist embedded with troops during both the German-Danish War of 1864 and the Franco-Prussian War, created a panorama that foregrounded the heroics of Bavarian – not Prussian – troops in 1870. Anton von Werner (1843–1915), one of the most important representatives of history painting at the time, considered

---

History of a Mass Medium, trans. Deborah Lucas Schneider (New York: Zone Books, 1997); and Bernard Comment, *The Panorama*, trans. Anne-Marie Glasheen (London: Reaktion Books Ltd., 1999). For another perspective on nineteenth-century cultures of exhibition, see Peter McIsaac's chapter in *Before Photography*.

14 Gabrielle Koller, "Panoramen als Orte bürgerlicher Schaulust und Bildung im deutschen Kaiserreich," *Kunst, Nation und Repräsentation*, ed. Brigitte Buberl (Bönen: Kettler, 2007), 87–100, here 87.

15 Peter West, "Introduction to American Panoramas," in *American Panoramas*, edited by Peter West, vol. 5 of *Panoramas, 1787–1900: Texts and Contexts*, edited by Laurie Garrison, Anne Anderson, Sibylle Erle, Verity Hunt, Peter West, and Phoebe Putnam (London: Routledge, 2012), vii–xxiv, here viii–x.

16 Vance Byrd, "Covering the Wound: Panorama Exhibitions and Handmade History," *Seminar* 51, no. 1 (February 2015), 10–27, here 17.

Braun's panorama a provocation because it failed to highlight Prussian military valor. Werner's *Sedan Panorama* (1883–1904), shown in Berlin in the year 1883, opened in response near the rail station at Alexanderplatz in the presence of Wilhelm I.[17] Furthermore, Louis Braun and Hans Peterson's *Panorama of German Colonies*, which, according to the *German Colonial Newspaper*, had attracted 83,000 visitors within a year of its opening in 1885, was praised for its "true to life manner of representation" of the German battlefields in Cameroon and was part of a German colonial-ethnographic museum.[18] As such, looking back to past military victory and looking forward with colonial ambitions were tied to the panorama's function in late nineteenth-century visual culture.

While these panoramas depicted foundational events of the German nation-state, their production followed financial capital and thus extended beyond national borders. The transatlantic production of national memory began a few years after the unification of Germany. The establishment of panorama companies was not based on patriotic interest alone, but also on financial profit. International stock-holding corporations and investors financed the distribution of these late nineteenth-century panoramas. The bankers and businessmen who owned such companies hired painters on a competitive basis to create new ones.[19] The Austrian emigrant William Wehner (1847–1928), a Chicago businessman who wanted to carve out a successful market position for panoramas in the United States, purchased Braun's Sedan panorama in 1884 and transported it from Frankfurt am Main to New Orleans for the Centennial Cotton Exhibition.[20] It went on tour to Cincinnati, Toronto, and Osaka, Japan, afterwards.

Wehner went on to found the American Panorama Company and recruit German panorama painters, most of whom had worked on the Frankfurt Sedan panorama, to come to the United States. Friedrich Wilhelm Heine arrived in Milwaukee in 1885, and other artists arrived from Düsseldorf, Berlin, and Munich in 1886.[21] Panoramas were by no means new to Wisconsin. Godwin and Wilder's *Panorama of the War* and *The Battle Between the Merrimac and Monitor* were the first panoramas of the American Civil War displayed in Milwaukee in 1863. The production of Civil War panoramas continued nearly two decades later in 1884, when Louis Kindt (1832–1923) and Thomas Gardner (1857–1933) executed the

---

[17] For background without an emphasis on global media production, see Koller, "Panoramen als Orte bürgerlicher Schaulust und Bildung," 89.
[18] "Berichtigung," *Deutsche Kolonialzeitung* 3, no. 8 (1886): 254–255, here 254.
[19] Koller, "Panoramen als Orte bürgerlicher Schaulust und Bildung," 88.
[20] Gabrielle Koller, "The European Origins of Milwaukee Panorama Painting." *Milwaukee County History* 1.1–2 (2010): 3–12, here 4–5.
[21] Starke, "Der Empfang der Sächsischen Truppen," 146.

panorama of the *Battle of Lookout Mountain* and founded the Northwestern Panorama Company, which produced battle panoramas of Vicksburg, Shiloh, and Gettysburg.[22] However, Wehner's decision was part of a larger business of commemoration that transformed Milwaukee into a production center for panoramas of the American Civil War in the 1880s.

It should not be surprising that Germans participated in the commemorative cultures of the American Civil War given their relevant role in nineteenth-century American life. By the 1850s, Germans replaced the Irish as the largest immigrant group in the United States.[23] Nearly 1,300,000 people living in the United States at the outbreak of the Civil War came from German-speaking Europe.[24] Most German immigrants in the years leading up to the American Civil War resided in the Northern states, while 70,000 lived in the Confederate states.[25] They were mostly concentrated in the so-called German triangle that extended from Cincinnati to St. Louis to Milwaukee. It is well known that Germans participated in the American Civil War. In fact, one-tenth of Union soldiers had been born in Germany.[26]

Against this backdrop of immigration history and commerce, we recall that illustrated cultural periodicals reflected both on their own status as media archives[27] as well as on their capacity to transmit debates about other media forms.[28] Friedrich Wilhelm Heine's path crossed with that of Theodore R. Davis in this context. Wehner engaged Davis, who had witnessed the Battle of Atlanta on 22 July 1864, as a sketch artist, to advise the members of the American Panorama Company as they produced panoramas of the American Civil War. Davis, a trained wood engraver and acclaimed war correspondent and staff artist for Fletcher Harper's (1806–1877) *Harper's Weekly*, accompanied Heine and August Lohr to Chattanooga, Tennessee, in May 1855, where the German artists prepared location studies for *The Storming of Missionary Ridge*. There, Heine and Davis stayed as

---

[22] See Tom Lidtke, "Panorama Painting in Milwaukee," *Milwaukee County History* 1.1–2 (2010): 13–23.
[23] Kamphoefner, Helbich, and Sommer, "Introduction," 17.
[24] The 1860 census registered 1,276,075 German-born individuals residing in the United States. Kamphoefner and Helbich, "Introduction," 20.
[25] Kamphoefner and Helbich, "Introduction," 2.
[26] More than 200,000 Germans served in the Union army. See Kamphoefner and Helbich, "Introduction," 20.
[27] Gustav Frank, Madleen Podewski, and Stefan Scherer, "Kultur – Zeit – Schrift," *Internationales Archiv für Sozialgeschichte der deutschen Literatur* 34, no. 2 (2009): 1–45, here 1.
[28] Daniela Gretz, "Archen in der Papierflut der Gegenwart: Zur medialen Selbstinszenierung von Zeitschriften als Archiven in der 'Bildungspresse' des 19. Jahrhunderts," in *Sprache und Literatur* 45, no. 2 (2014): 89–107.

guests of the American newspaper publisher Adolph Simon Ochs (1858–1935), the son of Jewish immigrants from Bavaria, who was the owner of the *Chattanooga Times* and later bought the financially troubled *New York Times*.[29]

Like Heine, Theodore R. Davis's writing for nineteenth-century periodicals includes reflection on media production. In 1889, Davis published the essay "How a Battle Is Sketched" in *St. Nicholas: An Illustrated Magazine for Young Folks*.[30] We recall that Davis used pencil and paper as a special sketch artist during the American Civil War. Unlike war photographers who stayed in close proximity to their photography studio and to suppliers, the sketch artist during the American Civil War traveled considerable distances with troop regiments. Carrying pencils and notebooks instead of heavy and messy photography equipment, sketch artists for periodicals provided much more comprehensive and timely coverage of the American Civil War than photography could achieve alone for the illustrated press in this period.[31] These visual reports from the battlefield took two to four weeks to appear as engravings for readers.[32] In the field, battle illustrators made preliminary sketches in an attempt to capture every detail they witnessed. After a battle had ended, they returned to the quiet of the camp or of an occupied house to complete the sketch's depiction, which served as the draft for wood engravers. The special war correspondent's illustration and written notes were then delivered by horse and train to the newspaper office where the illustration process began. There, engravers took individual wood blocks and engraved sections based on the materials the periodical's special artist had prepared in the field and added detail to this picture through the imagination and technical knowledge of uniforms, weapons, horses, and the like. This engraved composite image was bolted back together, reproduced on stereotype or electrotype plates, and printed with adjoining text as part of a magazine issue for distribution to readers.

---

[29] Gustav A. Berger, "Conservation of the Atlanta Cyclorama," in *Conservation within Historic Buildings* (London: International Institute for Conservation, 1980), 155–161, here 155. Niki Lefebvre, "'The Rebels' Last Device': Theodore R. Davis and Faithful Representations of Black Soldiers During the Civil War," in *So Conceived and So Dedicated: Intellectual Life in the Civil War-Era North*, ed. Lorien Foote and Kanisorn Wongsrichanalai (New York: Fordham University Press, 2015), 153–73, here 155.

[30] Susan R. Gannon underscores that *St. Nicholas* was actually regarded as a respectable publication for the entire family. See, "'The Best Magazine for Children of All Ages': Cross-Editing *St. Nicholas Magazine* (1873–1905)." *Children's Literature* 25 (1997): 153–80, here 153 and 155.

[31] Anthony W. Lee, "The Image of War," in *On Alexander Gardner's Photographic Sketch Book of the Civil War* (Berkeley: University of California Press, 2007), 8–51, here 19–24.

[32] Lee suggests that these engravings could appear in print publications in as few as two to three weeks. Lee, "The Image of War," 16–18.

In "How a Battle Is Sketched," Davis intervenes in ongoing nineteenth-century debates about the terms of history and visualization. The visual culture theorist Nicholas Mirzoeff observes that "visuality" has its origins in questions about the "authority to look and visualize a potentially boundless manifold of history."[33] Mirzoeff points out that

> Carlyle coined the terms *visualize* and *visuality* [in 1840] to describe [a] dominant view of Hero over History. Whereas Clausewitz had defined a military strategy of rendering the battlefield as a mental picture [in *On War*, 1832], Carlyle generalized the visualizing of History itself as being the means to order and control it.[34]

In "How a Battle is Sketched," Davis seems interested in correcting the assumption that generals occupy an elevated vantage point during battle and that it is from this perspective that generals provide special artists for newspapers and illustrated magazines the best location from which to sketch the events. Davis argues that, ideally, the general extends the power of his panoramic view to the war illustrator and reporter, who, in turn, can help readers align their vision of battlefield events with the military leader when they read war reports and examine its accompanying engraved images. However, this ideal situation seldom occurs, Davis declares. He explains that it is the scale of battle that makes such panoramic observation or surveillance impossible: "a large army usually covers a wide extent of a country, – wider in fact than could possibly be seen, even with the best field-glass, from any situation less elevated than a balloon high in [the] air."[35] Likewise, Davis argues that a battle is beyond the comprehension of the general present during the event: he is dependent on a network of staff-officers' reports on the ground so that he can see the battle through their collective eyes.[36] Like the general unable to gain a comprehensive view, in turn, Davis argues that the sketch artist on the battlefield "is obliged to visit every accessible point which seems likely to be an important one, and there make a sufficient memorandum" in his pocket-sized notebook.[37] These sketches might reveal the special artist's emotional state during the battle: "jerky marks here and there make it pretty plain that the locality was an unsafe one."[38] Yet these

---

33 Nicholas Mirzoeff, *The Right to Look: A Counterhistory of Visuality* (Durham, NC: Duke University Press, 2011), 2.
34 Mirzoeff, *The Right to Look*, 125.
35 Davis, "How a Battle Is Sketched," *St. Nicholas: An Illustrated Magazine for Young Folks* 16, no. 9 (1889): 661–668, here 661.
36 Davis, "How a Battle Is Sketched," 661.
37 Davis, "How a Battle Is Sketched," 661.
38 Davis, "How a Battle Is Sketched," 667.

"memoranda" help the special artist capture with speed in a heated battle what mattered most and remember it (see Figure 6). After the battle has concluded, he adds annotations and abbreviations that individual readers might identify, such as the names of generals Logan and McPherson.[39]

The memorandum sketchbook allowed war artists to create a preliminary image archive during a battle; details could be filled afterwards at camp. It was a portable aid for the creation of images and allowed the sketch artist more mobility and thus flexibility than a photographer: "whereas special artists could sling portfolios over their shoulders and shimmy up trees or climb rooftops to draw one expansive view after another, photographers' heavy equipment anchored them to the ground, composing (at best) one image every half hour."[40] Photography would be insufficient for the production of such synthetic and highly affective images. Personal yet collective, the visualization of history for Davis seems inseparable from affixing memory on paper for a reading nation.

This article by Theodore R. Davis on sketching battlefields is relevant for understanding his work with Friedrich Wilhelm Heine. In an earlier article in *St. Nicholas*, "How a Great Battle Panorama Is Made," Davis links his experience of Civil War reporting to making field studies for commemorative panoramas. Davis documents his work with Heine and the American Panorama Company in Chattanooga. To prepare a panorama, written accounts of the battles that had been witnessed firsthand had to be studied. Once this written and print archive was created, Davis went to the battlefield and spent at least a month there studying the actual locations where the battle had been fought. Because there were few traces of these conflicts left behind, Davis also had to rely on his "note-books and memory" to "locate all the old roads, houses, earthworks, camps, fields, forests, and troops, as they were on the day of the battle" when he returned to the panorama studio.[41]

Elements from this material and experiential archive were used for a technical and highly theatrical reenactment of the battle scene. Back in Milwaukee, Heine first made a one-tenth scale model of the final rotunda-based panorama. As chief painter, Heine sketched with charcoal on paper, then he and the technical illustrators made more detailed ink drawings on top of the charcoal lines while making constant reference to the sketchbooks and Davis's memory. The charcoal was then dusted off. Davis writes that the completed pen-and-ink drawing would then be enlarged onto a canvas divided into a grid format. In so

---

39 Davis, "How a Battle Is Sketched," 664.
40 Lefebvre, "The Rebels' Last Device," 153–73, here 156.
41 Davis, "How a Great Battle Panorama Is Made," *St. Nicholas: An Illustrated Magazine for Young Folks* 14, no. 2 (1886): 99–112, here 99–100.

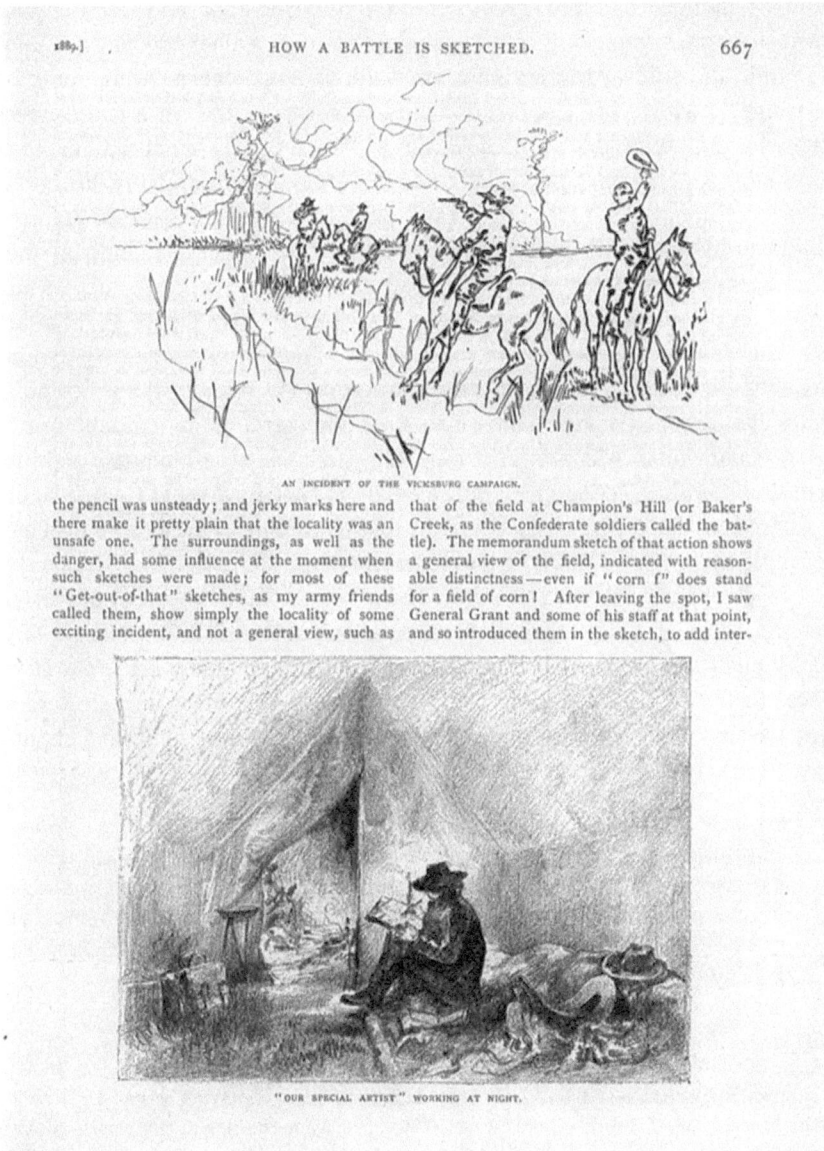

Figure 6: The special correspondent takes his quickly drawn sketches and carefully elaborates details after the day's battle had been fought. Davis, "How a Battle Is Sketched," 667.

doing, panorama painters drew upon tools of observation and representation used since the seventeenth century, such the grid-based techniques common to scientific and military cartographic representation, open-air painting traditions, as well as practices from garden and landscape aesthetics.[42] As a cultural technique for ordering space in the field, these sketched grids permitted the projection, storage, and imagination of three-dimensional worlds onto the canvas' two-dimensional plane for audiences at panorama shows to see (see Figure 7). Outdoors in the garden studio, the members of the panorama company modeled by wearing military uniforms and striking poses with props, such as guns and other military equipment, "relics of the war-days" (see Figure 8).[43] The article then describes how the painting's Belgian linen canvas was prepared and installed for painting and how the studio crew moved about the space on six dolly-like cars on an iron track to do so. A photographic reproduction of the hand-made sketch was projected onto the canvas for the preferred nighttime painting sessions. The problem of the enlarged sketch was that too few figures appeared on the image; Davis's memory and research and the additions of technical illustrators were not sufficient to tell the story of the Battle of Atlanta.

Davis explains in the article how Heine solved this problem. Heine invited veterans of the American Civil War to the panorama studio. In the midst of large-scale media production, they stood on the viewing platform and told stories about their memories of the war (see Figure 9). The war veterans walked around this elevated platform and pointed to sections of the canvas that needed improvement. Davis writes:

> The floor of the platform is chalked and rechalked with diagrams, some referring to which are memoranda of incidents and a variety of data, as well as names and addresses, are pinned to the convenient timber with thumb-tacks. Upon tables will be found sections of the composition, spread out opposite to their location upon the great canvas; field-glasses keep the drawings in place; and the inevitable piece of chalk is there also, ready for instant use.[44]

---

[42] Renzo Dubbini, *Geography of the Gaze in Early Modern Europe* (Chicago: University of Chicago Press, 2002), 3–5; Bernhard Siegert, *Cultural Techniques: Grids, Filters, Doors, and Other Articulations of the Real*, trans. Geoffrey Winthrop-Young (New York: Fordham University Press, 2015), 98. See also, Rosalind Krauss, "Grids," *October 9* (1979): 50–64; Evelyn Onnes-Fruitema and Ron Rombout, "The Origin of the Panorama Phenomenon," in *Panorama Phenomenon* (The Hague: Uitgeverij P/F Kunstbeeld, Panorama Mesdag, and the International Panorama Council, 2006), 11–28, here 16; Peter Galassi, *Corot in Italy: Open-Air Painting and the Classical-Landscape Tradition* (New Haven: Yale University Press, 1991).

[43] Davis, "How a Great Battle Panorama Is Made," 101.

[44] Davis, "How a Great Battle Panorama Is Made," 107.

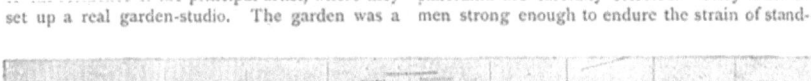

set up a real garden-studio. The garden was a corner-lot separated from the street by a picket-

men strong enough to endure the strain of standing or lying in the same position for some time,

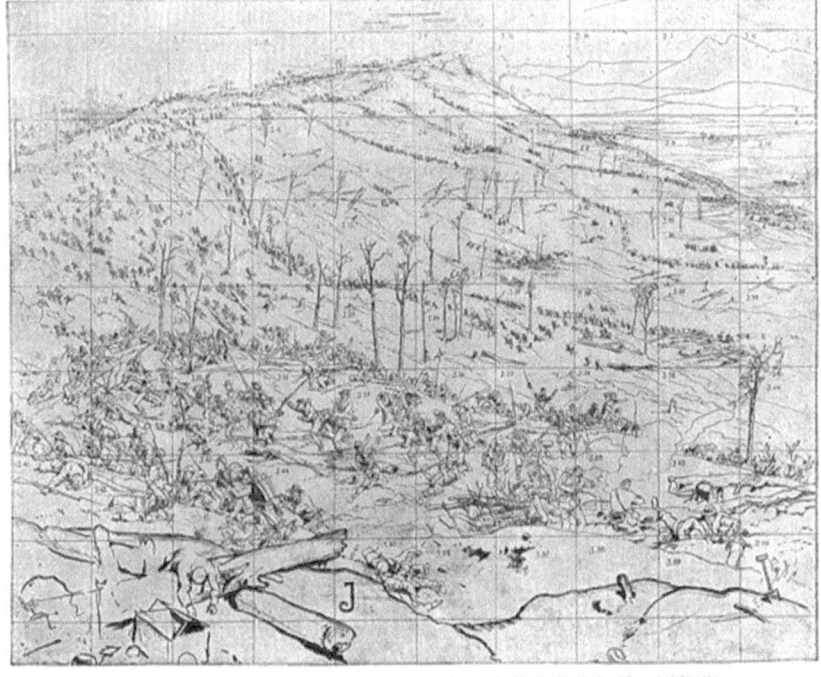

A SECTION (GREATLY REDUCED) OF THE PEN-AND-INK DRAWING, OR FIRST PLAN, OF A PANORAMA.

Figure 7: A location study of a landscape for a painted panorama. Detail from Davis, "How a Great Battle Panorama Is Made," 101.

Rather than the visual perspective of generals and the synthetic reconstructions of sketch artists, the veterans moving about the grid lines combined and condensed multiple moments of remembering and experience within the panorama platform's constricted confines in Milwaukee. The lines of sight of these men corresponded to points of interest in the composition and seemed to imbue the painting with "authenticity." Their recollections of the Battle of Atlanta made the carefully studied and imagined panoramic landscape "truer, more real" as an immersive medium. Davis closes the article complaining that panoramas cannot be, by their very nature, completely historically accurate: "They are fictitious productions, and have in them nothing that a veteran can recognize and explain to those whom he has accompanied to the exhibition for the purpose of showing the

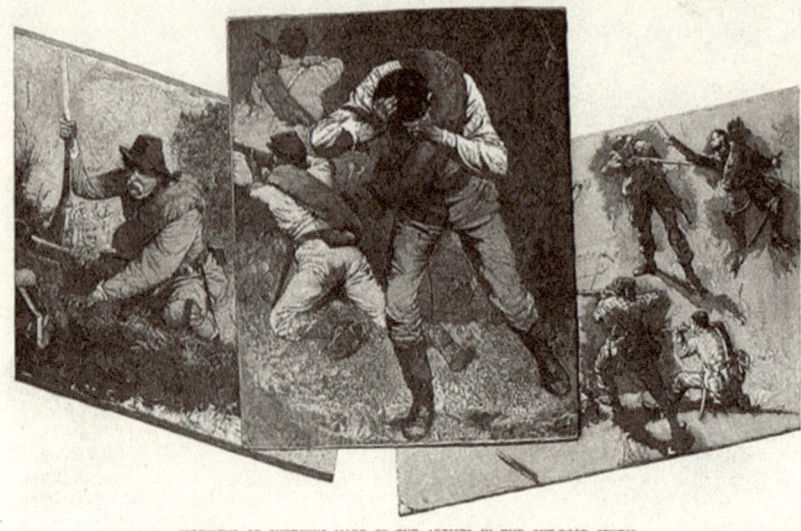

SPECIMENS OF SKETCHES MADE BY THE ARTISTS IN THE OUT-DOOR STUDIO.

Figure 8: The article reproduces artist sketches of costumed German members of the American Panorama Company performing roles for a battle panorama. Detail from Davis, "How a Great Battle Panorama Is Made," 102.

facts that came under his observation as a soldier in the actual battle."[45] In such cases, the veteran becomes the panorama lecturer and the painted medium's "truth of history" much more limited. The promise of panoramic representation of the war can only be reenacted with the aid of experience rather than positivistic documentary accuracy, which Davis rejects as "almost wholly imaginary scenes."[46]

3 Print culture, panoramas, and commemoration

Davis's reporting reveals that truth about war is grounded in the collective endeavors of illustrators, periodical editors, panorama companies, and veterans

---

45 Davis, "How a Great Battle Panorama Is Made," 112.
46 Davis, "How a Great Battle Panorama Is Made," 112. See also Koller, "Panoramen als Orte bürgerlicher Schaulust und Bildung," 90.

high, though they seem to be full life size.

A certain inquisitive old lady, visiting one of the earliest of these panoramas,— "The Battle spectator.

Some very interesting "optical facts" are found in these panoramas. In the "Battle of Mission-

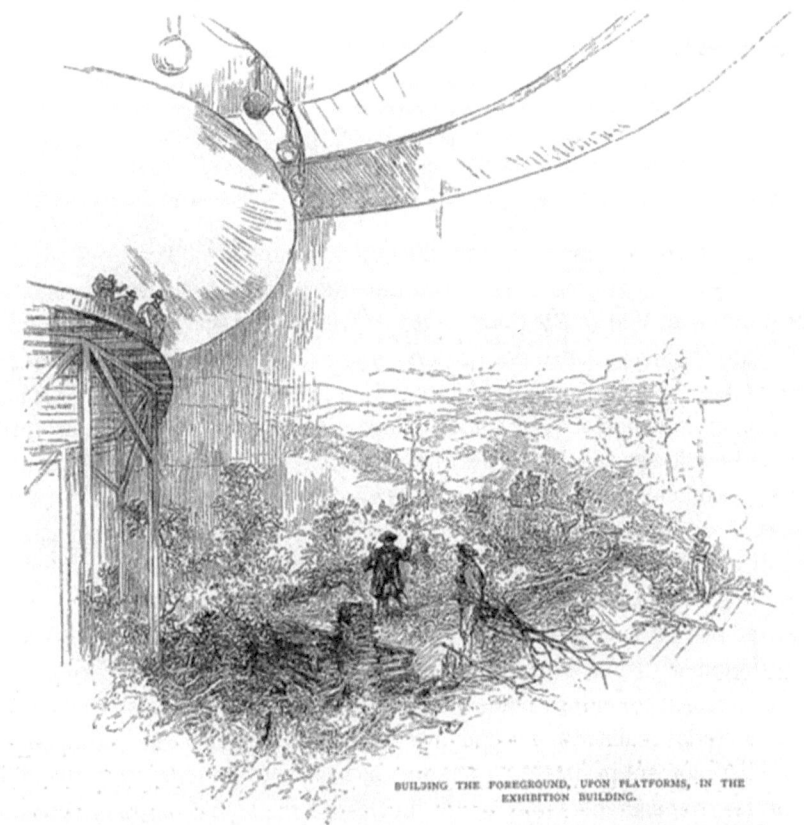

BUILDING THE FOREGROUND, UPON PLATFORMS, IN THE EXHIBITION BUILDING.

of Sedan,"—helped herself over the platform-rail by means of convenient chairs, and trotted down an earth road leading from the platform to the

ary Ridge" there is, near the Craven House, on the side of Lookout Mountain, what appears to the eye to be a steep, open field. Looked at with

Figure 9: The illustration shows how veterans of the American Civil War were invited by members of the American Panorama Company to correct details in the composition. The article adjacent to this image describes how a German visitor to the *Battle of Sedan* panorama reacted to the display's illusionism. Detail from Davis, "How a Great Battle Panorama Is Made," 111.

active during the last third of the nineteenth century to remember the past. In sharing his experience as a reporter tracing the movements of panorama painters on former battlefields, Davis proposes that the presence of Civil War veterans might enhance the truth of Heine's painting. Kirk Savage has written that the public sculptures erected in this period "honor[ed] not only the dead but the living veteran,"⁴⁷ but Davis's article suggests that print culture played no small role in forging these identities, as well. In her reflections on Benedict Anderson's theses on print capitalism and identification, Sara Ahmed writes that

> the circulation of print is what creates common lines or even ties that bind. When citizens read a given paper, they are not necessarily reading the same thing (there are different copies of the paper, and while some might read certain pages, those pages might be overlooked by others), let alone reading the same thing in the same way. Yet the very act of reading means that citizens are directing their attention toward a shared object, even if they have a different view upon that object, or even if that object brings different worlds into view.⁴⁸

Applying Ahmed's phrasing to the illustrated cultural periodicals discussed in this chapter, I suggest that Heine's illustrated reports from the front lines of the Franco-Prussian War in *Die Gartenlaube* as well as this scene in *St. Nicholas* of Civil War veterans gathered on the panorama platform in Milwaukee were "performing the work of alignment."⁴⁹ Rather than presenting an "objective" truth or the illusion that such a "truth" does indeed exist, illustrated periodicals taught readers how to see the recent past in a way that fit a larger national agenda. These periodicals invited nineteenth-century readers to carefully construct scenes of reenactment. With such acts, these sketch artists, panorama makers, periodical editors, and war veterans were entangled in moments in which tradition was being invented, "a process of formalization and ritualization, characterized by reference to the past, if only by imposing repetition."⁵⁰

Panoramas displayed history with grandeur. Individuals and corporations in the nineteenth century made panoramas to create illusionistic realms, in which pictorial realism might convince audiences they have been transported to another moment in time. War panoramas sought to communicate something about the unimaginable violence of war. Despite the ambitious aims of companies like the American Panorama Company, the popularity of panoramas did not last. The *Battle of Atlanta* cyclorama,⁵¹ which Heine painted and whose

---

47 Savage, *Standing Soldiers, Kneeling Slaves: Race, War, and Monument in Nineteenth-Century America* (Princeton: Princeton University Press, 2018), 162.
48 Sara Ahmed, *Queer Phenomenology: Orientations, Objects, Others* (Durham, NC: Duke University Press, 2006), 119–120.
49 Ahmed, *Queer Phenomenology*, 118.
50 Eric Hobsbawm, "Introduction: Inventing Traditions," in *The Invention of Tradition*, ed. E. J. Hobsbawm and T. O. Ranger (Cambridge: Cambridge University Press, 2012), 1–14, here 4.
51 Neologisms with the suffix – orama were given to a wide variety of visual media since the late eighteenth century. A "cyclorama" is a panorama which often includes a three-dimensional diorama space between the canvas and viewing platform. In terms of marketing, the term "cyclorama" was used in the nineteenth century to distinguish this static painted medium from so-called

media production and reception Davis theorized, is the only panorama produced by the Milwaukee painters that stands today. Most of the German panorama painters returned to Germany or left the United States after the work was done, the exhibitions closed, and the panorama companies shut their doors.[52] In Milwaukee, after the American Panorama Company's production facility was sold in 1889, the old building was repurposed as a roller skating rink, ice rink, vaudeville theater, and carriage house before it was razed.

I have argued that nineteenth-century cultural periodicals were influential for cultures of commemoration due to their self-referentiality and archival function. The contrasting temporalities of print media production – the remediated photograph of panorama production integrated into the issue of *St. Nicholas*, for example – reveal how these publications staged these reflections. I made the case that the social, political, and ideological content of nineteenth-century periodicals intersected with the collaborative work of contributors, sketch artists, engravers, editors, and printers. Periodicals and panoramas commented on each other's origins and production, which highlighted the place of both those media in constructing understandings of commemorative culture. In particular, the images of sketch artists fabricating by hand illustrations for war reportage and commemorative panoramas underline how knowledge was stored and transmitted and then further disseminated across media forms. The intersection of periodicals and panoramas reveals how a panorama's virtual environment never really represented any actual place in time.[53] The experience of seeing a panorama composition should remind the viewer of something familiar,[54] a complex performance ultimately contingent on actors willing to see what is not there while permitting others to imagine what history could have been. Engagement with periodicals shows how media *and* history were made.

"moving panoramas," which were mounted on scrolls for a seated viewing audience and were very popular entertainments at the time in the United States of America.
52 Koller, "The European Origins of Milwaukee Panorama Painting," 11.
53 Erik Champion and Bharat Dave, "Dialing up the Past," in *Theorizing Digital Cultural Heritage*, ed. Fiona Cameron and Sarah Kenderine (Cambridge, MA: The MIT Press, 2007), 333–347, here 336.
54 Tom Gunning, "What's the Point of an Index? Or, Faking Photographs," *Nordicom Review* 41, no. 2 (2004): 39–49, here 45.

Bibliography

Ahmed, Sara. *Queer Phenomenology: Orientations, Objects, Others*. Durham, NC: Duke University Press, 2006.
Belgum, Kirsten. *Popularizing the Nation: Audience, Representation, and the Production of Identity in "Die Gartenlaube," 1853–1900*. Lincoln: University of Nebraska Press, 1998.
Berger, Gustav A. "Conservation of the Atlanta Cyclorama." In *Conservation within Historic Buildings*, 155–161. London: International Institute for Conservation, 1980.
"Berichtigung." *Deutsche Kolonialzeitung* 3, no. 8 (1886): 254–255.
Buddemeier, Heinz. *Panorama, Diorama, Photographie*. Munich: Wilhelm Fink, 1970.
Byrd, Vance. "Covering the Wound: Panorama Exhibitions and Handmade History." *Seminar* 51, no. 1 (2015): 10–27.
Champion, Erik, and Bharat Dave. "Dialing up the Past." In *Theorizing Digital Cultural Heritage*, edited by Fiona Cameron and Sarah Kenderine, 333–347. Cambridge, MA: MIT Press, 2007.
Chute, Hillary. *Disaster Drawn: Visual Witness, Comics, and Documentary Form*. Cambridge, MA: Belknap, 2016.
Comment, Bernard. *The Panorama*. Translated by Anne-Marie Glasheen. London: Reaktion Books, 1999.
Conrad, Sebastian. *What Is Global History?* Princeton: Princeton University Press, 2016.
Darstellung der Anfertigung eines Schlachtenpanoramas. Photographic paper on canvas. 38 x 43 cm (15 x 17 in.). Stadtgeschichtliches Museum Leipzig. Inventar-Nr. f/7/2003.
Davis, Theodore R. "How a Battle Is Sketched." *St. Nicholas: An Illustrated Magazine for Young Folks* 16, no. 9 (1889): 661–668.
Davis, Theodore R. "How a Great Battle Panorama Is Made." *St. Nicholas: An Illustrated Magazine for Young Folks* 14, no. 2 (1886): 99–112.
Dubbini, Renzo. *Geography of the Gaze in Early Modern Europe*. Chicago: University of Chicago Press, 2002.
Frank, Gustav, Madleen Podewski, and Stefan Scherer. "Kultur – Zeit – Schrift." *Internationales Archiv für Sozialgeschichte der deutschen Literatur* 34, no. 2 (2009): 1–45.
Galassi, Peter. *Corot in Italy: Open-Air Painting and the Classical-Landscape Tradition*. New Haven: Yale University Press, 1991.
Gannon, Susan R. "'The Best Magazine for Children of All Ages': Cross-Editing *St. Nicholas Magazine* (1873–1905)." *Children's Literature* 25 (1997): 153–180.
Die Gartenlaube: Illustrirtes Familienblatt. Leipzig: Ernst Keil, 1853–1884.
Gretz, Daniela. "Archen in der Papierflut der Gegenwart: Zur medialen Selbstinszenierung von Zeitschriften als Archiven in der 'Bildungspresse' des 19. Jahrhunderts." *Sprache und Literatur* 45, no. 2 (2014): 89–107.
Gunning, Tom. "What's the Point of an Index? or, Faking Photographs." *Nordicom Review* 41, no. 2 (2004): 39–49.
Hobsbawm, Eric. "Introduction: Inventing Traditions." In *The Invention of Tradition*, edited by E. J. Hobsbawm and T. O. Ranger, 1–14. Cambridge: Cambridge University Press, 2012.
Kamphoefner, Walter D., and Wolfgang Helbich. "Introduction." In *Germans in the Civil War: The Letters They Wrote Home*, edited by Walter D. Kamphoefner and Wolfgang Helbich, 1–34. Chapel Hill: University of North Carolina Press, 2006.

Kamphoefner, Walter D., Wolfgang Helbich, and Ulrike Sommer. "Introduction." In *News from the Land of Freedom: German Immigrants Write Home*, edited by Walter D. Kamphoefner, Wolfgang Helbich, and Ulrike Sommer, 1–50. Ithaca, NY: Cornell University Press, 1988.

Koller, Gabriele. "The European Origins of Milwaukee Panorama Painting." *Milwaukee County History* 1, nos. 1–2 (2010): 3–12.

Koller, Gabrielle. "Panoramen als Orte bürgerlicher Schaulust und Bildung im deutschen Kaiserreich." In *Kunst, Nation und Repräsentation*, edited by Brigitte Buberl, 87–100. Bönen: Kettler, 2007.

Krauss, Rosalind. "Grids." *October* 9 (1979): 50–64.

Lee, Anthony W. "The Image of War." In *On Alexander Gardner's Photographic Sketch Book of the Civil War*, 8–51. Berkeley: University of California Press, 2007.

Lefebvre, Niki. "'The Rebels' Last Device': Theodore R. Davis and Faithful Representations of Black Soldiers During the Civil War." In *So Conceived and So Dedicated: Intellectual Life in the Civil War-Era North*, edited by Lorien Foote and Kanisorn Wongsrichanalai, 153–173. New York: Fordham University Press, 2015.

Lidtke, Tom. "Panorama Painting in Milwaukee." *Milwaukee County History* 1, nos. 1–2 (2010): 13–23.

Mirzoeff, Nicholas. *The Right to Look: A Counterhistory of Visuality*. Durham, NC: Duke University Press, 2011.

Oettermann, Stephan. *The Panorama: History of a Mass Medium*. Translated by Deborah Lucas Schneider. New York: Zone Books, 1997.

Onnes-Fruitema, Evelyn, and Ron Rombout. "The Origin of the Panorama Phenomenon." In *Panorama Phenomenon*, 11–28. The Hague: Uitgeverij P/F Kunstbeeld, 2006.

Savage, Kirk. *Standing Soldiers, Kneeling Slaves: Race, War, and Monument in Nineteenth-Century America*. Princeton: Princeton University Press, 2018.

"Schlachtenbummler." In *Das deutsche Wörterbuch*, edited by Jacob Grimm and Wilhelm Grimm. Leipzig: S. Hirzel, 1854–1961. http://dwb.uni-trier.de/de/, here http://www.woer terbuchnetz.de/DWB?lemma=schlachtenbummler.

Siegert, Bernhard. *Cultural Techniques: Grids, Filters, Doors, and Other Articulations of the Real*. Translated by Geoffrey Winthrop-Young. New York: Fordham University Press, 2015.

Sontag, Susan. *Regarding the Pain of Others*. London: Penguin Books, 2003.

Starke, Holger. "Der Empfang der sächsischen Truppen in Dresden am 11. Juli 1871." In *Sachsen in Deutschland: Politik, Kultur und Gesellschaft 1830–1918*, edited by James N. Retallack, 143–159. Bielefeld: Verlag für Regionalgeschichte, 2000.

Stockinger, Claudia. *An den Ursprüngen populärer Serialität: Das Familienblatt "Die Gartenlaube."* Göttingen: Wallstein, 2018.

West, Peter. "Introduction to American Panoramas." In *Panoramas, 1787–1900: Texts and Contexts*, edited by Laurie Garrison, Anne Anderson, Sibylle Erle, Verity Hunt, Peter West, and Phoebe Putnam. Vol. 5, *American Panoramas*, edited by Peter West, vii–xxiv. London: Routledge, 2012.

Wilcox, Scott Barnes. "The Panorama and Related Exhibitions in London." M. Litt. thesis, University of Edinburgh, 1976.

Peter M. McIsaac
Visual Cultures of Popular Anatomy Exhibition: The Role of Visitor Environment in Shaping the Impact of Public Health Education

In the decades before and after 1900, Central Europe was awash in exhibitions featuring hundreds of hyper-realistic, life-sized anatomical models and human specimens. At their most elaborate, these models could take forms known as "anatomical Venuses." These were full-body wax models outfitted with real eyebrows, pubic hair, and jewelry, recumbent on velvet pillows, and with anywhere between forty and two-hundred internal organs that could be removed – as in an operation or autopsy of a seemingly real body – before live audiences. With a pedigree reaching back to the eighteenth-century Italian anatomical modeler Felice Fontana, anatomical Venuses were medical masterpieces that once contributed to professional medical education and continued to form the spectacular core of many popular anatomy collections (see Figure 1.).[1]

Surrounding the Venuses were large numbers of other, visually arresting displays. Packing the room were lifelike torsos modelled to portray the organs of the digestive, circulatory, respiratory, and other key systems of the body, along with waxes vividly depicting male and female reproductive organs. Also *de rigueur* were exhibits containing models and human specimens representing the stages of embryonic and fetal development, culminating in scenes depicting childbirth and complications requiring Cesarean sections, obstetrical forceps, and other medical interventions. Flanking these were dramatic presentations of industrial and other accidents and the first-aid measures available to treat them, a range of surgical interventions, series of busts classified according to prevailing notions of human racial types, medical "abnormalities" (often presented in the

---

[1] Peter M. McIsaac, "Die medizinische Venus: Die performative Basis von anatomischen Zurschaustellungen vor und um 1900," in *Geschlechter Spiel Räume: Dramatik, Theater, Performance und Gender*, ed. Gaby Pailer und Franziska Schößler (Amsterdam: Rodopi, 2011), 313–328. Joanna Ebenstein, *The Anatomical Venus: Wax, God, Death and the Ecstatic* (London: Thames & Hudson, 2016). Kathryn A. Hoffmann, "Sleeping Beauties in the Fairground: The Spitzner, Pedley and Chemisé Exhibits," *Early Popular Visual Culture* 4.2 (2006): 148. Johanna Lang, "Um 1940: Zerlegt und vorgeführt: das Wachsmodell *Eine Figur auf dem Seziertisch liegend*," in *Blicke! Körper! Sensationen! Ein anatomisches Wachskabinett und die Kunst*, ed. Eva Meyer-Hermann (Göttingen: Wallstein, 2014), 107–108.

https://doi.org/10.1515/9783110696448-006

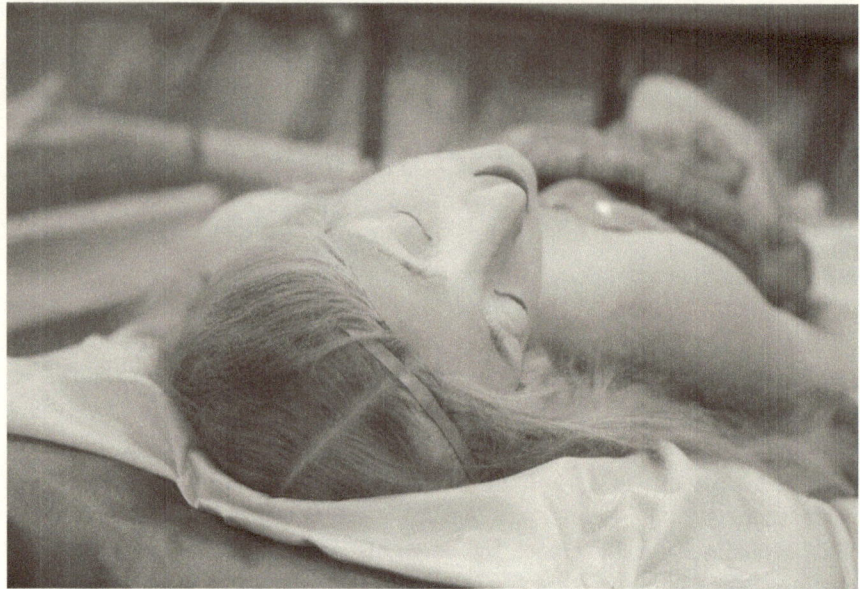

Figure 1: Anatomical Venus, Workshop of Clemente Susini of Florence circa 1780s, The Josephinum, Vienna, Austria. Photo credit: Joanna Ebenstein.

manner of side-shows), and gruesome portrayals of organs affected by cancer, excessive alcohol use, sexually transmitted diseases, and dermatological conditions, typically lacking cures and gorily devastating (see Figure 2).

This latter group was particularly challenging for many visitors, with many anecdotes relating the onset of nausea and even fainting at the sight of arrays of afflicted organs. At once visually compelling and anatomically accurate, these and similar items comprised "anatomical cabinets," the star attraction at the heart of what the public around 1900 knew as the Panoptikum.

The Panoptikum's focus on human anatomy and the medicalized body had a rationale with serious pretensions. The word Panopticum – derived from ancient Greek by the brothers Louis und Gustav Castan, originators of the perhaps best known Panoptikum – was intended to mean "Allesschau," a "show of everything" important about humanity using wax figures.[2] To the *Allesschau* belonged scenes

---

[2] Cornelia Wagner, "Panoptikum: das Wachskabinett als urbane Attraktion," in *Blicke! Körper! Sensationen! Ein anatomisches Wachskabinett und die Kunst*, ed. Eva Meyer-Hermann (Göttingen: Wallstein, 2014), 89–90. "Panopticum" was the term as originally coined by the Castans and was used by their enterprise alone as a kind of trademark. Most other impresarios, commentators and the public used the spelling Panoptikum for other shows and the phenomenon in general.

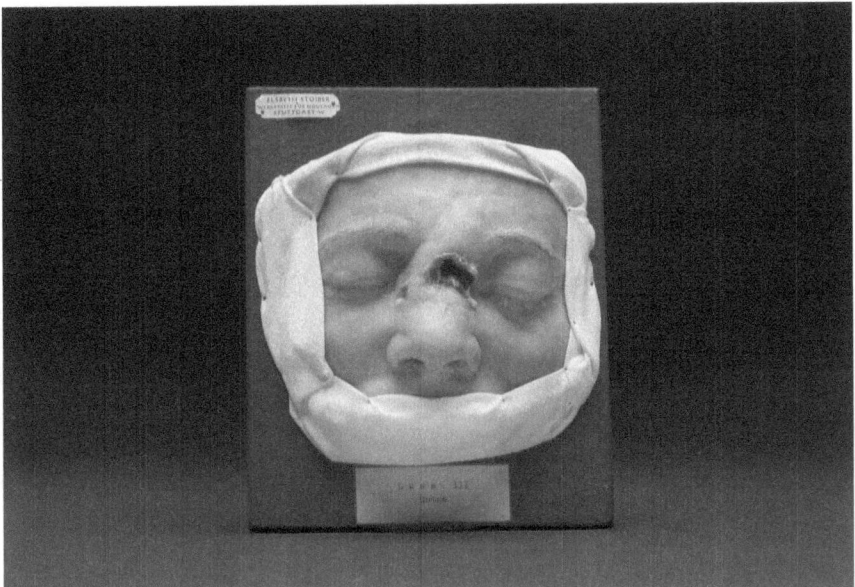

Figure 2: Moulage of syphilitic gumma by Elsbeth Stoiber, around 1926, moulage collection of the Museum of the University of Tübingen (MUT). Photo credit: Museopedia – Valentin Marquardt, CC BY-SA 4.0, https://commons.wikimedia.org/w/index.php?curid=49421687.

of cultural significance (great writers and politicians), orientalist and colonialist imaginings (racist and sexist portrayals of harems located in orientalizing labyrinths, and non-Europeans), and depictions of current events from serial killers to the Captain of Köpenick – a low-level criminal who took the Mayor of Köpenick prisoner and plundered the town's petty cash in 1906 by donning a captain's uniform and getting those who encountered him, including lower ranked soldiers and civilians, to blindly follow his orders. But the main draw for many visitors was the anatomical cabinet (sometimes "extra cabinet," because additional admission was charged), a kind of "museum of human beings" with the trappings of nineteenth-century physical anthropology.[3] Waxes of medical "abnormalities" and non-Europeans were often reminders of "side-show freaks" and *Völkerschau* (a form of ethnological exhibition) performances that were staged in many venues, as attractions both for lay visitors and for experts from local medical and anthropological

---

[3] The German terms often used were "Menschenmuseum" or variants of "ethnologisches/ anthropologisches Museum."

societies who photographed, recorded, and measured performers.[4] Professional legitimation derived as well from using specimens and models whose colorful, three-dimensional hyper-realism made them far more productive than photography for medical researchers. These forms of professional legitimation proved crucial to Panoptiken, allowing impresarios to lay claim to educational purpose in ways that freed them from taxes levied on pure amusements and that lent them the appearance of middle-class propriety that, as I will examine shortly, helped the exhibitions enjoy massive public resonance.[5]

The Panoptikum was only one form of anatomical exhibition targeting a broad public as a particular visual medium around 1900. Beginning in 1902, the German Society to Combat Venereal Disease (which I will refer to using its German acronym, DGBG [Deutsche Gesellschaft für die Bekämpfung der Geschlechtskrankheiten]) launched regular campaigns using exhibitions of wax models to impart knowledge of human reproduction; the biological and social factors that promoted the spread of sexually transmitted diseases; and the ways diseases such as herpes, gonorrhea, and syphilis manifested all over the body. While thematically narrower in scope than Panoptikum cabinets, exhibitions designed to combat sexually transmitted diseases (STDs) had significant overlaps with those cabinets. Both aimed to impart many of the same moralizing messages regarding the relationship of sex to disease, and to support those messages, both predominantly employed moulages, a class of medical wax model usually cast directly from an afflicted patient and then painstakingly painted and outfitted with real eyebrows, pubic hair, and other paraphernalia so as to achieve lifelike verisimilitude (Figure 2). As I will discuss later, the ability of moulages to capture afflictions and conditions with three-dimensional fidelity to their real-life manifestations made them a form of documentation and study superior to photography in medical fields such as dermatology.

Until the outbreak of the First World War and with renewed vigor from 1919 into the late 1920s, STD exhibitions appeared across German-speaking Europe, sometimes as stand-alone installations, sometimes as part of thematically broader exhibitions on public health and anatomy that I will refer to as modern hygiene exhibitions.[6] As organized by a team assembled by Karl August Lingner,

---

[4] See Andrew Zimmerman, *Anthropology and Antihumanism in Imperial Germany* (Chicago: University of Chicago Press, 2001), 15–18.
[5] Medical researchers and anthropologists often testified to the scientific merit of these shows, sometimes voluntarily and sometimes at the request of authorities regulating public morality. On the taxation issue, see Anna Dreesbach, *Gezähmte Wilde: Die Zurschaustellung "exotischer" Menschen in Deutschland 1870–1940* (Frankfurt am Main: Campus, 2005).
[6] I employ the shorthand "modern hygiene exhibitions" because the practice of mounting exhibitions to address topics related to hygiene and public health was at least two decades old

a Dresden-based entrepreneur who had made his fortune using punchy advertising to educate consumers on the health benefits of Odol toothpaste and persuade them to purchase it, modern hygiene exhibitions began to take shape in the years after Lingner's first foray into public health exhibition with a pavilion focused on endemic diseases at the German City Exhibition of 1903.[7] Their breakthrough came with the critical and public success of the 1911 International Hygiene Exhibition in Dresden. Lauded by experts in the press and attracting some 5.5 million visitors from May to October of 1911, this exhibition worked to set the conceptual and exhibitory parameters of what, after many more years of temporary exhibitions throughout the 1910s and 1920s, would become the German Hygiene Museum that opened in Dresden in 1930.[8] Their core approach involved visually compelling models, objects, and graphics designed to facilitate the non-expert comprehension of medical and especially anatomical knowledge. This approach was conceptually and materially very close to that of the DGBG, but overlaps in fact existed not only between modern hygiene and STD exhibitions, but also between these two and the anatomical cabinets of the Panoptikum.

This chapter analyzes these three forms of visually arresting popular anatomy exhibition – anatomical cabinets of Panoptiken; STD exhibitions; and modern hygiene exhibitions – that pervaded Central European culture in the decades before and after 1900. With its focus on these three closely related exhibit types, the chapter seeks not only to delineate the noteworthy reach of these exhibitions as popular visual media, but also to develop a nuanced framework for assessing their approaches and impacts. That these impacts can only be fully grasped by studying all three types together and over time represents part of this chapter's intervention with respect to previous scholarship, which has tended to regard the three exhibitory forms in isolation from each other. Particularly for recent scholars, the striking visuality of Panoptiken objects has fed the notion that they served mostly to satisfy gawking and desires for titillation, whereas for STD and modern hygiene exhibitions, that same visuality, anchored in the same kinds of objects displayed in strikingly similar ways, is

---

before Karl August Lingner's project began. I will treat those aspects of Lingner's approach that qualify as "modern," particularly those related to a type of museum called the *Gegenwartsmuseum* ("museum of the present-day"), later in the essay.

7 As Thomas Schnalke notes, Galewsky had contributed to Lingner's 1903 exhibition and continued work with modern hygiene exhibitors afterward. Thomas Schnalke, *Diseases in Wax: The History of the Medical Moulage* (Chicago: Quintessence, 1995), 121–122.

8 By comparison, the most visited museum of our time, the Louvre, had just over ten million visitors in the year of 2018, itself a record. "Number of visitors to the Louvre in Paris from 2007 to 2018 (in millions)" (Hamburg: Statista Gmbh, 2019). https://www.statista.com/statistics/247419/yearly-visitors-to-the-louvre-in-paris/

instead believed capable of having conveyed important knowledge to visitors. Turning to museum studies approaches and using a performative notion of embodied visitorship, I present new ways of understanding what distinguishes Panoptiken from other forms of anatomical display. Most striking are the changing ways exhibitors regulated the presence of other visitors in exhibition space by gender, changes whose effects became increasingly prominent in and after the 1910s.

My explorations of this terrain are divided into three parts. The first of these begins by delineating the reach of the respective exhibitory forms, showing how they deserve to be regarded as a visually oriented mass medium reaching large audiences across Central Europe. Moving on to their specific commonalities, the second turns to the exhibitions' shared techniques and display objects. Recalling that professional medicine relied heavily on collections of specimens and models in these years, this second part demonstrates that medical models were regarded as authoritative medical specimens the status of which derived from their powerful, three-dimensional visuality and the expert skill in observation and modeling that went into capturing that visuality. At the same time, that visuality was especially valued when it enabled non-experts to comprehend medical issues and their causes. Objects of this kind found their way not just into Panoptiken, but also into STD and modern hygiene exhibitions, into newly emerging museums such as the Deutsches Museum in Munich, and even into professional medical collections as well, ultimately prompting the question of what differentiates these shows from each other.

In analyzing what distinguishes Panoptiken from other forms of anatomical display, I conclude that audience responses depended heavily on changing measures aimed at regulating the morality of exhibition environments. A central tenet in this regard, enshrined in the law well into the 1910s, was the idea that men and women must not be allowed to see sensitive anatomical objects together with members of the opposite sex. When approached in terms of embodied spectatorship, measures that stipulated whether men encountered anatomical displays solely in the company of other men and women in the company of other women ended up becoming a focus of exhibitor experiments designed to enhance particular visitor responses. Changes to these measures from the 1910s on go a long way in elucidating what ends up being different in the traditions in the 1920s. These were the same years when perceptions of the respective exhibition types – i.e., that Panoptiken are predominantly base, and STD and hygiene shows largely educational – take the forms that get handed down to subsequent observers and scholars. Yet especially before the end of the First World War, no one tradition could claim a monopoly on the ability to impart knowledge to non-expert audiences. If visitors to any of the exhibition types I am considering here were in a position to gain knowledge, then Panoptiken also cannot be ruled out as venues capable of imparting insights. By the same token, visitors to STD and modern hygiene exhibitions might have been motivated not to gain enlightenment, but instead to encounter taboo objects and topics. With motivations and methods for the widespread dissemination of anatomical knowledge by exhibitory means tending to overlap with one another as well, many of the delicate issues relating to disease, reproduction and sexuality, and race that gave Panoptiken their allure also informed STD and hygiene shows.

1 The reach of popular anatomical exhibitions as mass medium

A key reason to take stock of popular anatomy exhibitions is their ability to reach larger swaths of the general public than is often recognized, as is particularly the case for Panoptiken. The Panoptikum as exhibition-type in Germany was established by the artistically trained sculptors Louis and Gustav Castan, whose 1869 installation in Berlin's "Red Castle" attained must-see cultural status when it moved to the newly inaugurated Lindenpassage on Friedrichstraße in 1873. As journalist Arthur Eloesser (1870–1938) wrote recalling what visitors to Berlin expected to see when he was a child, "Castan's Panopticum was an utter requirement. It had practically the value of an educational institution and the dignity of going to church. Anyone who came to visit us in Berlin was sent to the aquarium on one day, to Castan's on the other."[9] As scholars commonly note, a show such as Castan's in Berlin could attract 5,000 visitors in a single day.[10] While by no means a small number even by today's standards, Castan's neighbor was the Passage-Panoptikum, a comparably sized rival in the next block of the Friedrichstrasse that competed for visitors from 1888 until 1923, meaning that visitor numbers were significantly higher in the city than just those associated with Castan's.[11] And this was just Berlin. Castan's success – its heyday lasted from the 1870s until its closure during the inflation of the 1920s – led it to found franchises in Cologne, Frankfurt am Main, Dresden, Breslau, Brussels, and Amsterdam. All the while, the cities of Hamburg,

---

9 Arthur Eloesser, "Castan's Ende," *Frankfurter Zeitung und Handelsblatt*, 26 February 1922. 1.
10 Zimmerman, *Anthropology and Antihumanism*, 18.
11 Zimmerman, *Anthropology and Antihumanism*, 15–18. Klaus Gille, *Panoptikum: 125 Jahre zwischen Wachs und Wirklichkeit. Hamburgs Panoptikum und seine Geschichte* (Hamburg: Panoptikum Gebr. Faerber, 2004), 79. Angelika Friederici, *Castan's Panopticum: Ein Medium wird besichtigt* (Berlin: Karl-Robert Schütze, 2009).

Munich, and Vienna had similarly sized, permanent institutions as well as variants containing smaller numbers of similar types of objects. At the same time, popular anatomy was not just a big-city phenomenon. Beyond the permanent offerings were itinerant shows whose scale when, taken together, arguably exceeded that of the permanent shows. According to the sales books of Rudolf Pohl in Dresden, for instance, more than fifty different impresarios plying their shows in large and small cities across Central Europe purchased models and related material from him alone.[12] Each of these, as Johanna Lang's research has shown, would typically visit roughly ten cities a year.[13] While absolute visitor numbers are hard to come by, the ability of many shows to persist for decades indicates lasting resonance with large audiences across the German-speaking world.

A key aspect of this resonance was that it entailed encounters with lifelike objects in space, a feature that exhibitors exploited by creating particular display environments that could only be experienced completely in person. As part of this strategy, Panoptikum exhibitors prevented the circulation of photographs of exhibition space and all but a few select objects, especially in the public realm. Some of the images portrayed figures were regularly found in Panoptikum displays, not just in guidebooks to different Panoptiken, but also in sales materials made available exclusively to exhibitors. A surviving copy of the sales catalog from Dresden anatomical modeler Rudolf Pohl provides at least one photograph of every one of the hundreds of objects available for purchase, with certain prize objects such as anatomical Venuses appearing in multiple variants.[14] For the general public, however, exhibitors worked to limit the ways photographs could circulate in order that their three-dimensional, full color objects would prevail in relation to photography.

Visitor resonance has been more readily recognizable for the STD and modern hygiene exhibitions than has been the case for the forms related to Panoptiken. Particularly impressive were international hygiene exhibitions, which at their largest were capable of drawing millions of visitors in the span of a few months. As I mention above, the International Hygiene Exhibition in Dresden saw 5.5 million

---

[12] Rudolf Pohl, Geschäftsbuch 1901–1919. Archiv des Deutschen Hygiene-Museums Dresden 2009/657. With modelers such as Gustav Zeiller, Emil Eduard Hammer, and also Castan's studios also operating as purveyors, only to name a few, this number is very likely higher, as the number of surviving exhibition guides of otherwise obscure impresarios also suggests.

[13] Johanna Lang, "Die Einführung des Wandergewerbescheins: von reisenden Schaustellern und Beanspruchten Wachsmodellen," in *Blicke! Körper! Sensationen! Ein anatomisches Wachskabinett und die Kunst*, ed. Eva Meyer-Hermann (Göttingen: Wallstein, 2014), 89.

[14] Fotoalbum mit Fotographien aus der Werkstatt Rudolf Pohl. Archiv des Deutschen Hygiene-Museum Dresden 2012/616.

visitors between May and October of 1911, while Düsseldorf's Great Exhibition of 1926 for Healthcare, Social Welfare, and Sports and Exercise recorded more than 7.5 million visitors from May to October of 1926.[15] Numbers of this magnitude rank these exhibitions among the most successful of any in German history to this day.

For the relationship of these exhibitions to the public to be grasped, more than just overall visitor numbers needs to be considered, as can be seen in the example of the 1911 International Hygiene Exhibition (IHE). As press reports from all over Germany document, visitors in 1911 were especially drawn to the pavilions devoted to anatomy ("Der Mensch"), the history of human hygiene, and sexually transmitted disease (a pavilion organized by the DGBG).[16] This particular development, with just a few of the forty-five pavilions receiving overwhelming attention from visitors, was not very well anticipated, though organizers were quick to seize on the emerging situation and to consider calls in the press to transform the temporary show into something lasting. This turn of events was ironic, because IHE organizers originally intended to create an exhibition with no permanent afterlife. Indeed, they explicitly sought to move away from traditional museum forms, particularly as they existed to show art around 1900, because these were perceived to be elitist and inaccessible to any but the most educated of visitors.[17] The exhibition's resonance, however, prompted organizers to explore approaches that, focused particularly on human anatomy and health, would eventually end up contributing to a new form of museum that contemporaries such as publicist Heinrich Pudor called the "museum of the present-day."[18] Unlike traditional museums, the museum of the present-day would present material relevant to everyday life and non-experts, providing whenever possible lay access to knowledge and information in ways also useful

---

15 Große Ausstellung Düsseldorf 1926 Gesundheitspflege, soziale Fürsorge und Leibesübungen, most often known by the German acronym GeSoLei.

16 On the experimental, indeed improvised nature of key aspects of the organizational efforts behind the 1911 IHE, see Claudia Stein's study on the history section. Claudia Stein, "Organizing the History of Hygiene at the International Hygiene-Ausstellung in Dresden in 1911," *NTM. Zeitschrift für Geschichte der Wissenschaften, Technik und Medizin* 22, no. 1 (2014): 355–387. Also Sybilla Nikolow and Thomas Steller, "Das lange Echo der 1. Internationalen Hygiene-Ausstellung in der Dresdner Gesundheitsaufklärung," *Dresdner Hefte* 29, no. 4 (2011): 18.

17 A watershed event catalyzing the move toward new, non-elitist museum types was a conference convened by worker welfare groups in Mannheim in 1903 on the topic "Museums as Sites of Popular Education." Conference attendees leveled critiques as traditional museum forms and attempted to articulate conceptions and approaches that would make informal learning more accessible to those without extensive education.

18 The German term is "Gegenwartsmuseum," first coined in Heinrich Pudor, "Museumschulen," *Museumskunde* 6 (1910): 248–253.

to experts.[19] Rather than "dumb down" expert knowledge, in other words, the aim was to find ways of giving access to undiluted but carefully presented authoritative information.

Such undertakings proved difficult, and for the emerging museum-type, objects and approaches to presenting material capable of operating in the way museum visionaries called for had to be discovered among collections originally made for professional purposes or made for this specific exhibitory purpose. All this took time and testing, lending these exhibitions a provisional quality that could be revised and improved. Indeed, nearly two decades would elapse between the 1911 IHE and the opening of the permanent structure of the German Hygiene Museum in 1930 in Dresden. In that time, hygiene exhibitors pursued a large number of varied temporary exhibitions that refined and updated the formulas that had proved resonant in 1911. Though smaller "solo" shows centered on "Der Mensch" took place in Stuttgart, Darmstadt, and Genoa, hygiene exhibitors also collaborated with organizers of temporary exhibitions such as the 1913 "Adria" exhibition in Vienna. Variants also appeared in the 1926 exhibition on Health, Social Welfare and Exercise (known in German by the acronym GeSoLei) in Düsseldorf and shows dedicated to the military medicine and wounded staged in Berlin, Leipzig, Dresden, Breslau, and Budapest and other cities during WWI. At times, hygiene exhibitors co-organized a variety of exhibitions with the DGBG, whose innovative approaches to exhibition environments and journalistic promotion require attention in their own right.

Although the exposure of the 1911 IHE amplified the status of STD exhibitions, by this point, they had already been mounted for nearly a decade. Consistently capable of getting public attention, STD exhibitions even enjoyed a particular notoriety thanks to the strategies employed by the chief organizer, Eugen Galewsky, in consultation with DGBG founders Albert Neisser, Erwin Lesser, and Alfred Blaschko.[20] Familiar with medical moulages from his professional specialization of dermatology, Galewsky made use of moulages' graphic, at times even gory visuality to incite shock, fear, and disgust in audiences. These emotional responses were designed to promote the position that, in light of diseases that were easily spread and without cures, sex outside of wedlock was to be made frightening and thus deterred. Motivated in large part by a

---

[19] Pudor, "Museumschulen," 248–253. For contemporary perspectives, see Anke te Heesen, *Theorien des Museums. Zur Einführung* (Hamburg: Junius, 2012). Sybilla Nikolow, "'Wissenschaftliche Stillleben' des Körpers im 20. Jahrhundert," in *Erkenne Dich selbst! Strategien der Sichtbarmachung des Körpers im 20. Jahrhundert*, ed. Sybilla Nikolow (Cologne: Böhlau, 2015), 11–46.

[20] Albrecht Scholz, "Bekämpfung der Geschlechtskrankheiten in verschiedenen politischen Systemen," *Hautarzt* 7 (2003): 665.

medical understanding of contagion, the displays aimed to be progressive to the extent that they broached issues related to sex in public settings previously taboo in Wilhemine society. As a 1912 guide put it, "How many people are made miserable due to ignorance of these diseases and their dangers – and yet most avoid getting information – on account of foolish shame."[21] By 1922, the DGBG proclaimed looking back on its record that one of the organization's "greatest contributions consists of doing away with the politics of ignorance and not wanting to know that has previously been associated with venereal diseases."[22]

Complicating these aims were overarching framings that took on a moralizing tone in line with traditional, turn-of-the-century conservative thinking about sexuality and gender roles.[23] As Albrecht Scholz has written, early exhibitions followed mottos, echoed in catalogues and information sheets, such as "vice has such a terrible face / just seeing it is enough to hate it" and "the smart man sees evil and avoids it / the idiot loses sight of it and gets punished."[24] While a basic aspect of DGBG exhibition strategy relied on shocking visitors with painful depictions of disease, the heavy-handedness of these points indicates something less than confidence that visitors would draw the right conclusions from what they are seeing.

While the open moralizing of the early shows seems not to have clashed with their visitor appeal, it is also not clear that visitors sought this sort of lesson. A 1909 STD exhibition in Düsseldorf praised by Roman Catholic observers for being unsurpassed in generating "revulsion at moral lapses" and inspiring abstention as a result of merely seeing "the aftermath of sin" nonetheless attracted over 40,000 people in 16 days.[25] Even for those "who came with lusty

---

21 Karl August Lingner and Arthur Luerssen, Georg Seiring, *Der Mensch: Ausstellung. Ausgewählte Gruppen aus der Internationalen Hygiene-Ausstellung 1911* (Darmstadt, 1912), 43.
22 Eugen Galewsky and Friedrich Woithe, *Die Geschlechtskrankheiten und ihre Bekämpfung* (Dresden: Deutscher Verlag für Volkswohlfahrt, 1922), 143.
23 See Lutz Sauerteig, *Krankheit, Sexualität, Gesellschaft: Geschlechtskrankheiten und Gesundheitspolitik in Deutschland im 19. und frühen 20. Jahrhundert* (Stuttgart: Franz Steiner, 1999) 232–38.
24 Scholz, "Bekämpfung der Geschlechtskrankheiten," 665. Also quoted, without attribution, by Lutz Sauerteig, "'Sex in Wachs,' Gesundheitswissen, Volksaufklärung und Sinneserregung," in *Blicke! Körper! Sensationen! Ein anatomisches Wachskabinett und die Kunst*, ed. Eva Meyer-Hermann (Göttingen: Wallstein, 2014), 169.
25 Sauerteig, "Sex in Wachs," 169. As with Panoptiken, reliable statistics for the total number of visitors are hard to come by, but one DGBG official reported in the 1920s that 700,000 copies of a single information pamphlet had been sold at the exhibitions since their advent, meaning that significant numbers of visitors had been willing to pay for more than just the cost of the exhibition. Scholz, "Bekämpfung der Geschlechtskrankheiten," 665.

feelings," church observers wrote, the only possible effect of seeing open sores and lesioned genitals was "to go home with salubrious shock."[26] Were so many actually completely changing their behavior, however, effects at this scale – 20,000 people a week no longer at risk – should have rapidly eliminated the scourge of sexually transmitted disease. And yet a need for exhibitions clearly remained, indicating that exhibitions needed to be more effective. To achieve this, display techniques and visitor control measures in STD exhibitions tended to move toward ever greater focus on the models on display, doubling down on measures that tried to ensure that visitors were guided to the right conclusions in response to what they were seeing. Textual labeling, for instance, increasingly disappeared from many objects, leaving interpretation to be directed by guidebooks.[27] Looking alone was thus not believed sufficient for changing visitor behavior.

Whatever the stated aims of STD exhibitors, indications abound that moral enlightenment might not have been the sole reason driving visitor interest in STD exhibitions. In the aftermath of the 1911 IHA, the press repeatedly pointed out visitors to the STD pavilion at the IHA and subsequent exhibitions feeling faint, passing out, or having to leave due to nausea.[28] Visitors who made it all the way through the STD pavilion often intoned the refrain that "they had survived 'Galewsky's chamber of horrors (*Schreckenskammer*).'"[29] This label suggests that visitors might have regarded the experience of STD shows less as a place to learn than a place for thrill seeking and extreme experience, perhaps not so far from what more recent viewers of horror films experience, or at the time of these popular anatomy exhibitions, what could be had at Panoptiken, which were reputed to offer gruesome and prurient sights of exactly this nature.[30] As Hamburg physician Hans Harald Schumacher recalled in his memoirs, the pulling back of the curtain covering the moulages at the Hanseatic Panoptikum in Hamburg caused him such visible queasiness that the attendant

---

26 Sauerteig, *Krankheit*, 211. Sauerteig, "Sex in Wachs," 169.
27 Galewsky and Woithe, "Die Geschlechtskrankheiten und ihre Bekämpfung," 144–145.
28 Sauerteig, *Krankheit*, 211–12. Also Sauerteig, "Sex in Wachs," 169. See also "Bericht der Ortsgruppe Hirschberg," *Mitteilungen der DGBG* 10 (1912): 80.
29 On visitors' recollections of Galewsky's chamber of horrors, see Scholz, "Bekämpfung der Geschlechtskrankheiten," 665. Sauerteig, "Sex in Wachs," 168. Schnalke, *Diseases in Wax*, 121–122.
30 On the labeling of the STD pavilion as a "chamber of horrors," see *Offizieller Führer durch die Internationale Hygiene-Ausstellung Dresden 1911 und durch Dresden und Umgebung* (Berlin: Rudolf Mosse, 1911), 38–39.

sent him home.³¹ In fiction, too, STD displays in Panoptiken were associated with just this kind of response. In Ernst von Salomon's novel *Kadetten*, the young protagonist falls unconscious, green-in-the-face while standing before a Panoptikum-vitrine full of models depicting syphilis. In Bertolt Brecht's 1919 "Lux in tenebris," a one-act play centering on a Panoptikum staged to counter STDs and brothel visits, visitors also report feeling "quite sick to their stomachs," falling unconscious, and even having to vomit at seeing the STD displays. Crucially, many visitors sought exactly these experiences, saying that "not being to sleep for a whole night" was part of what they were looking for in coming to these exhibitions.³²

Insofar as STD exhibitions and Panoptikum cabinets produced similar kinds of visitor responses that include the possibility of thrill seeking, the question arises as to what, exactly, distinguishes the two forms of display. For scholars such as Albrecht Scholz and Lutz Sauerteig, the conventional wisdom has been that in Panoptiken settings, the dramatic visual qualities of objects such as moulages did little more than satisfy visitors' less-than-noble desires and urges (*Schaulust*, horror, titillation) and thus had very little to communicate in terms of actual knowledge. Though they note that STD exhibitions used practically the same objects as Panoptikum exhibits, Scholz and Sauerteig maintain that STD exhibitions of moulages' practically identical gruesome visual effects formed the core of an enterprise that deserves to be regarded as having had at least some educational benefit.³³ Such a position dismisses out of hand the statements in Panoptikum guide books and display settings that their aim, particularly with regard to sex and sexuality, was to reveal the effects of "immoral" behaviors, to discourage promiscuity, and to encourage a visit to a doctor if symptoms arise. "We can say with pride," intones the introduction to Carl Gabriel and Emil Eduard Hammer's Anatomical-Ethnological and Natural Science Museum, "that our cabinet has done a great deal of good. After seeing it, many a young man has reversed course on the path he had been heading down, seemingly lost [to vice]."³⁴ A another exhibition guide states, "words of encouragement to those recognizing their venereal disease: may one put aside false shame and go immediately to a doctor (not a quack healer!) in

---

31 Hans Harald Schumacher, *Jugenderinnerungen eines Hamburger Arztes*, unpublished. Quoted in: Gille, *125 Jahre zwischen Wachs und Wirklichkeit*, 35–36.
32 Bertolt Brecht, "Lux in Tenebris," in *Werke* 1, ed. Werner Hecht et al. (Berlin and Frankfurt am Main: Aufbau-Verlag and Suhrkamp, 1989), 293–297.
33 Scholz, "Bekämpfung der Geschlechtskrankheiten," 665. Sauerteig, "Sex in Wachs," 167–170.
34 Carl Gabriel and Emil Eduard Hammer, *Führer durch das anatomisch-ethnologische und naturwissenschaftliche Museum* (Munich: G. Schutz, before 1902), 4.

order to be examined and get better."[35] While these kinds of statements are taken at their word when published by the DGBG, for Scholz and Sauerteig, they can only be read as evidence of a cynical sham, of rhetoric giving middle-class visitors cover for what, Scholz und Sauerteig seem sure, was only ever base amusement.

The fact that Panoptikum anatomical cabinets and STD exhibitions showed objects of comparable workmanship and accuracy sharpens the question of what differentiates the two kinds of exhibition. As Siegfried Mattl, Nick Hopwood, and even Lutz Sauerteig himself observe, Panoptiken medical specimens seem to have differed little from those in collections developed for professional medical settings.[36] Partly responsible for this overlap was the centrality of hyper-realistic visuality for both non-experts and experts alike. Though conventions of medical illustration have since shifted in favor of other media and forms of visualization, medical professionalism of the late-nineteenth and early-twentieth century had little conflict with hyper-realistic visuality. Particularly for moulages, which were especially central in fields such as dermatology and gynecology, hyper-realism had important research functions at a time when no other medium was capable of documenting visible manifestations of disease in ways important for diagnosis and study.[37] "Where particular illnesses changed the normal relief, color, and consistency of the skin, the formation of wax casts suggested itself," writes medical historian Thomas Schnalke, concluding: "Thus, among the whole spectrum of medical fields, dermatology and venerology have been served by moulages most intensely and for the longest period of time."[38] Beyond the one-to-one correspondence of models with disease arising from their being cast directly from patients by highly skilled practitioners, moulages could also be reproduced and circulated to any number of venues, making them useful anywhere display was

---

[35] Emil Eduard Hammer, "Abteilung 'Syphilis, venerische Krankheiten,'" in *Der Mensch: Illustrierter Führer durch Hammer's Original-Ausstellung aus München* (Munich: Hammer, 1914), 11. On the similarities in stated moral aims between STD exhibitions and those in Panoptiken, see also Julia Radtke, "Zwischen Aufklärung und Voyeurismus: die 'Extra-Abteilung,'" in *Blicke! Körper! Sensationen! Ein anatomisches Wachskabinett und die Kunst*, ed. Eva Meyer-Hermann (Göttingen: Wallstein, 2014), 97.

[36] Siegfried Mattl, "Körperspektakel: Ein anatomisches-pathologisches und ethnologisches Museum im fin-de-siecle Wien," *Wiener Zeitschrift zur Geschichte der Neuzeit* 2 (2004): 50–52. Nick Hopwood, "Artist versus Anatomist, Models against Dissection: Paul Zeiller of Munich and the Revolution of 1848," *Medical History* 51 (2007): 279–308. Sauerteig, "Sex in Wachs," 167–170.

[37] See Schnalke, *Diseases in Wax*, 9–13. See also Lawrence Charles Parish and Gretchen Worden, Joseph A. Witkowski, Daniel H. Parish, "Wax Models in Dermatology," *Transactions and Studies of the College of Physicians of Philadelphia* Ser. 5, no. 13 (1991): 29–74.

[38] Schnalke, *Diseases in Wax*, 11.

desired. Well into the twentieth century, their medically useful qualities (accurate color, three-dimensionality) enabled them to remain standard reference objects in research. Even with the advent of high-resolution and color photography, medical journals tended to publish photographs not of dermatological and other conditions, but rather of moulages representing these disorders (See Figure 3).[39]

A contributing factor to the overlap was that many display specimens were produced by the very same modelers and manufacturers who supplied and collaborated with recognized medical researchers. Some professionally trained modelers such as Gustav Zeiller and Emil Eduard Hammer mounted their own Panoptiken even as they supplied medical markets and medical schools.[40] Others such as Adolf Seifert, who built a multi-generational family business producing medical models for pathologist Rudolf Virchow and his successors in Berlin's Charité hospital, trained in the studios of Castan's Panopticum and maintained connections that allowed subsequent generations also to hone their craft there.[41] With that training, modelers could move between the studios of Panoptiken and companies manufacturing medical and scientific teaching materials and medical labs in key research centers such as Berlin, Zurich, Vienna, and Breslau.[42] As Schnalke's recent work on important modelers such as Fritz Kolbow has shown, modern hygiene exhibitions also shared objects and personnel with both professional and popular venues.[43]

The case of Emil Eduard Hammer is particularly helpful for seeing that the skills and experience responsible for Panoptiken success were simultaneously

---

[39] See, for instance, H. Finkelstein, E. Galewsky, L. Halberstaedter, *Hautkrankheiten und Syphilis im Säuglings- und Kindesalter: Ein Atlas* (Berlin: Julius Springer, 1922).

[40] Nike Fakiner, "The Spatial Rhetoric of Gustav Zeiller's Popular Anatomical Museum," *Dynamis* 36, no. 1 (2016): 52–54.

[41] Wilfried Witte, "Vom Diener zum Meister: Der Beruf des Anatomischen Präparators in Berlin von 1852–1959," in *Der zweite Blick: Besondere Objekte aus den historischen Sammlungen der Charité*, ed. Beate Kunst, Thomas Schnalke, and Gottfried Bogusch (Berlin: de Gruyter, 2010), 194–195.

[42] See Schnalke, *Diseases in Wax*, 93–187. Fakiner, "The Spatial Rhetoric," 52–53.

[43] Not everything is known about Fritz Kolbow's work and education, but his path took him through the Charité and apparently also Castan's before becoming a key figure in the workshops involved in manufacturing materials for the hygiene exhibitions. See Thomas Schnalke, "Spuren im Gesicht: Eine Augenmoulage aus Berlin," in *Der zweite Blick: Besondere Objekte aus den historischen Sammlungen der Charité*, ed. Beate Kunst, Thomas Schnalke, and Gottfried Bogusch (Berlin: de Gruyter, 2010), 24–25.

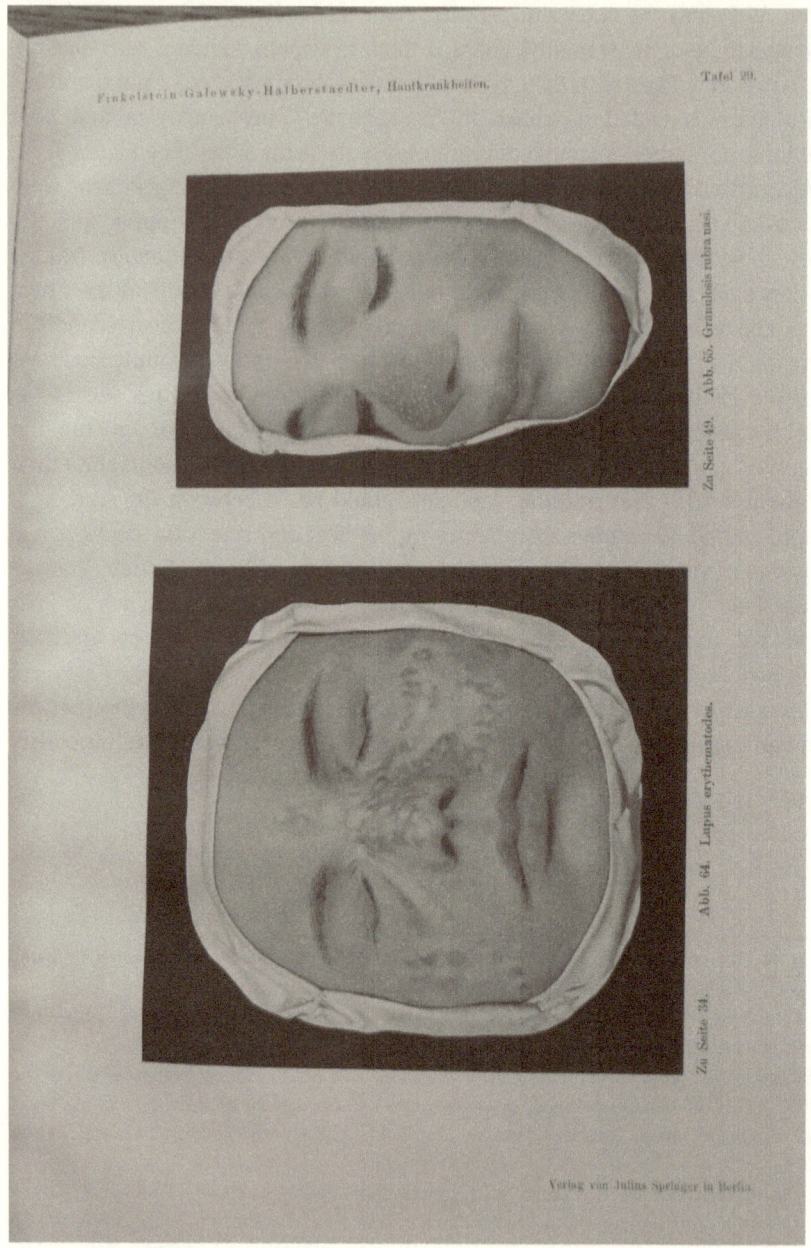

Figure 3: Plate showing the use of moulages as authoritative medical documentation. H. Finkelstein, E. Galewsky, L. Halberstaedter, *Hautkrankheiten und Syphilis im Säuglings- und Kindesalter. Ein Atlas.* Berlin: Julius Springer, 1922, Tafel 29.

valued in professional medical circles.[44] Hammer was the co-founder of Munich's International Trade-Panoptikum, a massive popular offering that, between 1894 and 1902, made Hammer a figure well-known for his entertainment and sculpting acumen. Following the closure of his Panoptikum due to fire in 1902, Hammer is portrayed in many accounts as shifting his exclusive focus to professional medical modeling, eventually gaining the titles of "University Anatomical Modeler" from the medical faculty of the University of Munich in 1913, where he produced large numbers of wax models, moulages, and other specimens in Munich until the early 1930s.[45] Yet already in his formal training at the Bavarian Academy of the Arts in the late 1880s, Hammer worked with anatomist Nikolaus Rüdinger and the physiologist and physical anthropologist Johannes Ranke, recognized authorities well practiced in anatomical modeling. These figures would play important roles in Hammer's later career, with Rüdinger licensing him to produce copies of his famous models and Ranke providing testimonials as to the anthropological and scientific value of Hammer's displays not just in the Panoptiken, but in several subsequent popular anatomy shows.[46] As Munich police records document, Hammer's popular anatomy exhibitions did not cease in 1902, but rather continued with various attempts to stage the Panoptiken in smaller forms. The first appeared in venues outside of Munich, and then as Hammer's "Popular Anatomical

---

44 A version of these arguments regarding Hammer's ear models was published in German in Peter M. McIsaac, "Emil Eduard Hammers anatomische Modelle im kulturellen Kontext," in *Spiegel der Wirklichkeit: Anatomische und dermatologische Modelle in Heidelberg*, ed. Sara Doll and Navena Widulin (Heidelberg: Springer-Verlag, 2019).
45 The German title is "Universitätsplastiker." Bayerisches Hauptstaatsarchiv, MK 11328. Universität München, Titelverleihung "Universitätsplastiker" an Emil Hammer in München. "Emil Eduard Hammer. Zu seinem 70. Geburtstag." *Münchner Zeitung*: 1 October 1935, no page number. Stadtarchiv München, DE-1992-ZA-P-0180-21. "Ein Helfer der Wissenschaft." Münchner Neueste Nachrichten (MNN): 2.10.1935. Philipp Osten, "Zwischen Volksbelehrung und Vergnügungspark." *Deutsches Ärzteblatt* 102, no. 45 (2005): A3086–3087. Lynn K. Nyhart, "Science, Art and Authenticity in Natural History Displays" in *Models: The Third Dimension of Science*, ed. Soraya de Chadarevian and Nick Hopwood (Stanford: Stanford University Press, 2004), 307–338. Hopwood, "Artist versus Anatomist," 307.
46 "Die Pantherdame Mlle. Irma Loustan aus Paris," *Münchner Neueste Nachrichten*: 20.12.1906. 4. Stadtarchiv München, DE-1992-ZA-11322, Schreiben von Hammer an die Polizeidirektion vom 12.4.1906; vom 22.11.1906; and vom 6.6.1916. Stadtarchiv München, Polizeidirektion 1051. Stadtarchiv München, DE-1992-POL-0384, Medizinisches Volksmuseum. Stadtarchiv München, DE-1992-POL-0385, Hammers Anatomische Ausstellungen. Stadtarchiv München, DE-1992-ZS-0158-3, Hammer's anatomische Original-Ausstellung, 1916. Bayerisches Hauptstaatsarchiv. Plakatsammlung, Kultur- und Werbeplakate bis 1945, Ausstellung von Emil Eduard Hammer zu kriegsbedingten Schußverletzungen während des Ersten Weltkrieges in München, 22387.

Museum (Anatomisches Volks-Museum)" in 1906–07. It ran again from 1914–1917 as "Hammer's Original anatomical exhibition 'The Human Being,' with a connected War Museum," and from 1926–1932 again, as the "Anatomical Hygiene Exhibition (AnaHygA)."[47] Alongside his work as a professional anatomical modeler, Hammer never stopped presenting popular anatomy exhibitions that, as the various titles indicate, he adapted to the changing trends in popular display such as the depiction of war wounds during the First World War.[48]

Hammer's skill in creating arresting but accurate models proved crucial for more than his popular shows. Thanks to a collaboration with the otologist Friedrich Bezold, Hammer was also the co-creator of the human ear models most widely used for professional medical education prior to the Nazi era. It was to Hammer that Bezold turned when, in 1906, he was commissioned by Munich's newly founded German Museum of Masterpieces of the Natural Sciences and Technology to create models of the ear especially suited for its popular mandate.[49] As one of the first museums of the present-day, which would also be joined by modern hygiene exhibitions and the German Hygiene Museum in Dresden, the German Museum in Munich sought professional quality display objects that lay audiences could also readily comprehend. Such a conception, as Bezold put it, demanded forms "that are appropriate for audiences comprised of every social class."[50] Despite being one of the world's foremost otologists, however, Bezold knew of no existing model that would work in this fashion, and he struggled to find a solution until tapping into Hammer's particular skill-set.[51] "For the delineation of the physical models," Bezold explained, "we found the appropriate solution in the formally trained sculptor Hammer, who for years now has had experience in the production of anatomical specimens."[52] Long before he received the official recognition as "University Anatomical Modeler" and while he was deeply engaged in producing specimens for popular anatomy, Hammer's objects were capable of crossing into the world of the

---

[47] Stadtarchiv München, DE-1992-ZA-11322, Schreiben von Hammer an die Polizeidirektion, 12.4.1906. Stadtarchiv München, Polizeidirektion, 1051. Bayerisches Hauptstaatsarchiv Plakatsammlung, Kultur- und Werbeplakate bis 1945, Ausstellung von Emil Eduard Hammer zu kriegsbedingten Schußverletzungen während des Ersten Weltkrieges in München, 22387.
[48] On visual depictions of the damage wrought by war, see Byrd's essay in this volume.
[49] Friedrich Bezold, "Drei plastische Modelle des menschlichen Gehörorgans," *Archiv für Ohrenheilkunde* 78 (1908): 262.
[50] Bezold, "Drei plastische Modelle," 262.
[51] Adam Politzer, *Geschichte der Ohrenheilkunde: Band II. Von 1850–1911* (Stuttgart: Verlag von Ferdinand Enke 1913), 271–273. Hans-Heinz Eulner, *Die Entwicklung der medizinischen Spezialfächer an den Universitäten des deutschen Sprachgebietes* (Stuttgart: Enke, 1970).
[52] Bezold, "Drei plastische Modelle," 262.

museums of the present-day, the hygiene exhibition and professional medical collecting.[53]

Indeed, it was Hammer's ability to find "physical expression for the extraordinarily complicated and difficult formal ratios at hand in satisfying manner" that especially pleased Bezold, for it allowed the essential aspects of the ear's anatomy to be immediately comprehended in one overhead glance.[54] This was a crucial demand not least because alternative models involved a lengthy process of removing numerous parts that risked confusing lay audiences, particularly in museum settings. As it turned out, however, these models also ended up being well suited to the purposes of professional medical education. As otologist Otto Wagener's 1929 article reviewing available medical teaching aids noted, the models' success was linked to the modeling solution Bezold had worked out with Hammer.[55] As Wagener put it:

> In producing these three models, a decisive consideration for Bezold was to create representations that, to the greatest extent possible, are capable of providing the viewer with a complete overview of the entire organ in a single glance. For this reason, it was decided not to create a model composed of multiple pieces to be put together in more or less complicated fashion or to be taken apart one piece after the other, which is how other models are constructed.[56]

As surviving exemplars in medical collections of Heidelberg, Münster and other academic medical faculties show, Hammer's models indeed found their professional audience, for the same reasons they were attractive to lay audiences.

---

53 On the complex determinations of scientific models, also see Short's analysis of Blaschka glass models in this volume, which provides a comparable example of scientific, commercial and aesthetic factors co-mingling in visually compelling, three-dimensional objects.

54 Bezold, "Drei plastische Modelle," 262. Questions of how large and small features can be brought into appropriate relationships so as to apprehend fundamental phenomena figures centrally in Hoffmann's examination of scale in the work of Adalbert Stifer, in this volume. In other registers, this problem also resonates with the valorization of the hieroglyph as a symbol capable of rendering invisible phenomena palpable, as Pfannkuchen shows in her essay in this volume.

55 Oskar Wagener, "Unterricht in der Laryngologie, Rhinologie und Otologie: Methoden, Hilfsmittel, Prüfung," in Die Krankheiten der Luftwege und der Mundhöhle, ed. Karl Amersbach et al. (Berlin: Julius Springer, 1929), 1308–1309.

56 Wagener, "Unterricht," 1308–1309.

2 New ways of differentiating popular anatomy exhibitions

The ability of Panoptikum modelers to make objects capable of satisfying non-expert and expert audiences is just one reason to seek new ways of differentiating Panoptiken, STD, and modern hygiene exhibitions. Such an approach remedies the difficulty scholars have had in conceiving of modern hygiene traditions as contingent, experimental, and thus susceptible to error, failure, and improvement. In part because of its massive visitor appeal and critical acclaim, the story of modern hygiene exhibitions has tended to be one of near perfection from the moment the 1911 IHE premiered. Yet as Sibylla Nikolow and Thomas Steller have recently shown, even though the goal of founding a permanent museum really only became central after the success of the IHE, foundational documents written in and after 1912 made a permanent museum seem to have always been Karl August Lingner's aim, even though this was patently not the case.[57] These documents repeatedly portrayed features that ended up proving successful as seemingly always having been part of conceptions that were in fact improvised and experimental. Beyond working to legitimize things achieved by chance by aligning them with a reworked, seemingly visionary past, these efforts amplified the IHE's claim to innovation and seeming sense of genius by obscuring the exhibition's similarities to competing endeavors.

Though IHE organizers were loath to admit it, non-trivial similarities existed between their approach to popular anatomy display and those of competitors during and after their breakthrough years.[58] One reason to focus on these similarities is that contemporaries very clearly perceived them. Representative in this regard were the exhibits on sexually transmitted disease organized by Eugen Galewsky, the point person for STD exhibitions at the 1911 IHE and many other similar exhibitions. In one of the signature moments of the IHE, as already noted, Galewsky's team arrayed moulage after moulage of lesioned and oozing faces, genitals, and extremities, all ruined by syphilis and gonorrhea. For Dresden authorities charged with regulating public exhibitions, Galewsky's displays of moulages were materially and conceptually indistinguishable from

---

57 Nikolow and Steller, "Das lange Echo," 18.
58 As the correspondence from June and July of 1911 indicates, Spalteholz specimens were still being conceived, produced and installed even while the IHE was underway. Sächsisches Staatsarchiv, Hauptstaatsarchiv Dresden, Spalteholz 12/60–61, See R. Seyffarth to Spalteholz, 14 June 1911. Sächsisches Staatsarchiv, Hauptstaatsarchiv Dresden, Spalteholz 12/61–62, J. Ingelfinger to W. Spalteholz, Sächsisches Staatsarchiv, Hauptstaatsarchiv Dresden, Spalteholz 12/64–65, R. Seyffarth to Spalteholz, 25 July 1911.

those shown in Panoptiken, and they forced Galewsky's team to comply with legal and moralistic norms designed to regulate the perceived lewdness of fairground anatomy.[59] Prohibitions such as these first arose in 1850s Britain, in situations where exhibitors promoting quack cures for STDs – medicines prepared by those with no medical training and without scientific basis – benefitted by creating male-only environments that Victorian critics rapidly associated with prurience and illicitness.[60] As I have shown elsewhere, historically, such regulations did not always accompany the public presentation of popular anatomy, with men and women being permitted to view sexually explicit material together before the 1850s in Italy, Austria and Britain without scandal.[61] In Germany, segregation of visitors by gender really only became ubiquitous after the Trade, Commerce and Industry Regulation Act of 1869, which explicitly forbade that sensitive material be available to anyone under 18. Also explicitly forbidden were circumstances that would permit men and women to view that material simultaneously.[62] While scholars have largely dismissed the importance of the strictures, officials in Dresden and other cities saw enough similarity in the displayed objects and display techniques as to require precisely these measures for STD exhibitors, including the 1911 IHE. For DGBG exhibitors, avoiding these sanctions and finding alternative ways of regulating the mix of visitor bodies in exhibition space would become important ways of improving the effectiveness of their installations by ultimately increasing the displayed objects' visual impact.

In accounts of the 1911 IHE as a resounding success, there has been no discussion of the fact that the STD displays only counted as a partial success in the eyes of the DGBG. Looking back at the IHE in its official journal, the DGBG qualified its sense of achievement with awareness of features of the larger IHE environment that compromised its messages. Just outside their displays, which preached abstinence from alcohol, were numerous restaurants imposing minimum purchases of beer or wine.[63] Unfavorable to the DGBG was also what

---

[59] Albert Neisser, "Begrüßungsrede des Vorsitzenden Herrn Geheimrat Neisser zur VIII. Jahresversammlung zu Dresden am 9./10. Juni 1911," *Mitteilungen der Deutschen Gesellschaft zur Bekämpfung der Geschlechtskrankheiten* 9 (1911): 75. See also Scholz, "Bekämpfung der Geschlechtskrankheiten," 664–665. On the similarities in stated moral aims, see Radtke, "Zwischen Aufklärung und Voyeurismus: die 'Extra-Abteilung,'" 97.
[60] McIsaac, "Die medizinische Venus," 323–325.
[61] McIsaac, "Die medizinische Venus," 323–325.
[62] Lang, "Die Einführung des Wandergewerbescheins," 89.
[63] Alcohol consumption was linked at the time to loss of inhibition that could lead to spontaneous sex outside of marriage, and thus a contributor to the spread of STDs. As label text from some Panoptiken groupings shows, these concerns also extended to male drinkers pursuing

critics of the IHE viewed as the "Coney Island funfair atmosphere" arising from officially sanctioned IHE attractions such as *Völkerschauen*, troops of geishas, and belly dancing performed by women in Orientalizing costume – all features to be found in, and popularized by, Panoptiken.[64] Equally detrimental to the desired level of sexual sobriety was the visibility of "prostitutes" and "women of the demi-monde" plying their trade at the exhibition and especially near the special exhibition on STDs.[65] Though sex workers might have conceivably been a target of the Galewsky displays, DGBG leaders seemed most concerned that their presence undermined what male visitors might learn, particularly since banning sex workers from exhibition grounds was not feasible.[66]

To respond to these perceived shortcomings, the DGBG experimented with their exhibition techniques and critical analysis in its official journal.[67] Among the many factors that the group considered as it worked to reach lower- and middle-class German-speaking men and women – the group had cues it believed identified these subgroups – one that underwent the most radical change related to the question of segregating visitors by gender and age. Indeed, one of the more surprising conclusions the group reached was that segregating visitors by gender – i.e., requiring women to visit on days set aside for them, so called *Frauentage* or *Damentage* – was profoundly counterproductive. In looking back at experiences in eight cities between 1911 and 1914, exhibitors in Wiesbaden concluded: "Such a women's only day (*Frauentag*) is actually not absolutely necessary for the kind of exhibition in question, and such arrangements have not been made in all the cities where the exhibition has shown."[68] While *Frauentage* had persisted in some places because some women's groups

---

spontaneous sex with other men. See Eva Meyer-Hermann, ed. *Blicke! Körper! Sensationen! Ein anatomisches Wachskabinett und die Kunst* (Göttingen: Wallstein, 2014). 136–137.

64 The original quotes the English used in the review being discussed. "Unsere Sondergruppe 'Geschlechtskrankheiten' auf der internationalen Dresdner Hygieneausstellung in amerikanischer Beleuchtung." *Mitteilungen der Deutschen Gesellschaft zur Bekämpfung der Geschlechtskrankheiten* 10 (1912): 139.

65 "Unsere Sondergruppe 'Geschlechtskrankheiten,'" 139. Contradictions regarding alcohol would accompany hygiene exhibitions throughout the 1910s and 1920s, as reports from the Association of German Brewers (which welcomed them) and other critical voices attest.

66 "Unsere Sondergruppe 'Geschlechtskrankheiten,'" 139.

67 For most scholars, these accounts have figured primarily as indications that exhibitions represented the most important aspect of the group's public education efforts. See Petra Ellenbrand, *Die Volksbewegung und Volksaufklärung gegen Geschlechtskrankheiten in Kaiserreich und Weimarer Republik* (Marburg: Görich und Weiershäuser, 1999), 136–50. Scholz, "Bekämpfung der Geschlechtskrankheiten," 664–73.

68 *Mitteilungen der Deutschen Gesellschaft zur Bekämpfung der Geschlechtskrankheiten* 12 (1914): 87.

and authorities had requested the possibility of women visiting alone, *Frauentage* were rendered vestigial by making them *optional* for women. As exhibitors wrote in several newspaper articles published in advance of the exhibition, women were encouraged to come on days other than *Frauentage*. "In Wiesbaden, too," one passage reads, "[. . .] young and old, men and women will view the exhibition together, indeed the organizers are assuming that by and large, no separation by gender and by age groups should take place."[69] As leaders also soon reported in the press, their strategy of abandoning *Frauentage* seemed to work: "no one ended up taking offense at the simultaneous visiting of men and women together."[70] Indeed, if sex workers were mingling with the women and men in Wiesbaden (or even waiting outside the exhibition containing such sensitive material, as at the IHE), DGBG was watching and they could not be found. Men also seemed to have acted respectfully toward women and women did not complain of having their sensibilities offended.

Beyond increasing the perceived respectability of the exhibition, such changes to visitor environment also promised to solve the problem of overcrowding, which exhibitors had observed as one of the chief problems facing previous exhibitions and which impaired the impact of their stark visibility.[71] In many exhibitions, jam-packed rooms had prevented visitors from getting good views of the specimens and thus kept the specimens from having maximum impact. Rather than tinker with the objects on display – how they could become more gruesome was not apparent, even to the DGBG – exhibitors explored, with results they deemed better, the abandonment of gender-based restrictions, which helped to ease overcrowding and improve visitors' ability to gaze at objects without interruption.[72] Contrary to what sometimes has been claimed in scholarship with regard to the legitimacy of DGBG shows, greater respectability and visitor impact

---

69 "Vereinsnachrichten," *Mitteilungen der Deutschen Gesellschaft zur Bekämpfung der Geschlechtskrankheiten* 12 (1914): 78. Orthography as in the original.
70 "Vereinsnachrichten," *Mitteilungen der Deutschen Gesellschaft zur Bekämpfung der Geschlechtskrankheiten.* 12 (1914): 80.
71 "Vereinsnachrichten." *Mitteilungen der Deutschen Gesellschaft zur Bekämpfung der Geschlechtskrankheiten* 12 (1914): 80.
72 "It would be in the interest of all visitors," organizers announced to the public, "to arrange your visit so that no overcrowding takes place. Women, for example, can visit at all times the exhibition is open, which many women are also doing." *Mitteilungen der Deutschen Gesellschaft zur Bekämpfung der Geschlechtskrankheiten* 12 (1914): 87. It is important to stress that DGBG exhibitions in this period did not tinker with objects or larger exhibition strategies very much. In the years between 1911 to 1914, DGBG exhibitors continued to strategies of deterrence they had pursued at the IHE, varying visitor regulation instead.

was achieved not by conforming to legal norms designed to deal with lewdness, but in fact by working against such norms.

A brief look at the historical trajectory taken by Panoptiken in relation to segregation of visitors by gender can help sharpen understanding of how these norms affected their efforts. While Panoptiken typically had little choice but to comply with legal norms forcing men and women to visit at separate times and forbidding those under eighteen at all times, there are indications already in the nineteenth century that these strictures often achieved the opposite of their intention. A few impresarios such as Gustav Zeiller avoided legal strictures by not showing any graphic material at all, yet because they seem to have struggled financially, such strictures seem to have been legible in much more successful enterprises as markers ensuring the presence of taboo content.[73] Moreover, if Egon Erwin Kisch's 1926 essay "The Secret Cabinet of the Anatomical Museum" on Berlin's Passage-Panoptikum is any indication, moralistic legal strictures could in fact be tweaked to enhance a sense of allure. In this remarkable text, whose narrative brilliance, historical veracity, and insight lead nearly every Panoptiken scholar to engage with it, Kisch sets up the inner core of the Passagen-Panoptikum's anatomical cabinet as "the most beautiful thing in Berlin" in the 1920s, for reasons that have everything to do with its socially "unspeakable" contents – all that is said about it is a knowing "-pst!" – and the difficulty of gaining access to it.[74] To get even close to "the holiest of holies in the Passage," visitors had to navigate spaces just off the street filled with hawkers, pimps, and same-sex prostitutes (Kisch calls them "Pupen," using the Berlin dialect for "call boys"), followed by a series of wax displays of suggestive content, only eventually to confront the central restriction: "a board, flipped over every fifteen minutes, announcing on one side 'now for gentlemen only,' 'now for ladies only.'"[75] As Kisch makes clear, this reduction of the *Frauentag* – which interestingly enough ended up constraining men's visits as well – to snippets of just fifteen minutes leads to a viewing experience that was not only intensified and ephemeral. It was also eroticized due to a heightened awareness of the fact that many of the models dealing with the female body call to mind exemplars of gender hovering just on the other side of curtain, waiting for

---

[73] Zeiller applied for permission to display his objects with the explicit notice that they would contain no risqué material and thus would not require legal restrictions. Stadtarchiv Dresden Z. 42.VII, Gustav Zeiller: Gesuch um die Eröffnung eines anthropologischen und anatomischen Kabinetts, Dresden, 13 November 1888. See also Fakiner, "The Spatial Rhetoric," 59–70, who neglects to note the impact these approaches had on the bottom line.
[74] Egon Erwin Kisch, "Das Geheimkabinett des anatomischen Museums," *Gesammelte Werke* vol. 5 (Berlin/ Weimar: Aufbau 1974), 170.
[75] Kisch, "Das Geheimkabinett," 170–174.

their turn to inspect "the goods."[76] More than the sight of intimate organs, it is the mental awareness of absent, living bodies that marks this space as exceedingly erotic for Kisch, a condition that measures designed to regulate public morality can be manipulated to produce.

This moment from Kisch is just one example of how the adherence to prevailing moral strictures in Panoptiken produces a starkly different set of visitor outcomes than those the DGBG sought by loosening gender-based prohibitions. Yet, as I hope is clear, attention to exhibition experiments can put our understanding of what differentiates the various traditions of popular anatomy display on much stronger evidential footing than has been possible before. By thinking of exhibition practices in terms of the presence of other, gendered bodies, it becomes possible to identify factors that explain the changing perception of the respective popular anatomy exhibitions. That these changes took hold from the 1910s on is significant for two reasons. First, the changing sense of increasingly eroticized Panoptiken as prurient and lewd surely attracted some visitors such as Kisch, but they also coincided with the historical moment when exhibitors faced economic challenges. During the First World War and the inflation of the early years of the Weimar Republic, Panoptikum exhibitors proved to be most vulnerable.[77] In their drive to appear culturally up-to-date, they were particularly impacted by other media capable of keeping up with the speed of moden life such as film, as contemporary observers clearly noted.[78] These developments produced perceptions of declining cultural value that dominated perceptions of the exhibitions to this day. In contrast, the changing status of STDs and hygiene as ever more suitable for mixed company meshed with narratives that saw these exhibitions gaining increased institutional legitimacy, particularly with the opening of the German Hygiene Museum in Dresden in 1930.

Second, the changes taking hold in the 1910s indicate that particularly for contemporaries, what distinguished the three visually based mass media was far less apparent than previous scholarship has contended. Their significant overlap in material qualities – indeed, the ability for manufacturers of Panoptiken objects to achieve success in the realms of the *Gegenwartsmuseum* and professional medicine, and the demand that early STD and hygiene exhibitions be regulated exactly like Panoptiken all force recognition that the three shows occupied much of

---

76 Kisch, "Das Geheimkabinett," 170–174.
77 One reason for the long period between the founding of the German Hygiene Museum in 1912 and the actual opening of the permanent structure by Wilhelm Kreis was the nearly complete loss of financial reserves caused by the inflation.
78 See Eloesser, "Castan's Ende," 1. Also Joseph Roth, "Philosophie des Panoptikums," *Werke*, vol. 1, ed. Klaus Westermann (Cologne: Kiepenhauer & Witsch, 1956), 939–940.

the same terrain for much longer than has been previously understood. Seen in this light, ample reason exists to revisit this epoch, both to take more seriously the possibility of how learning occurred in Panoptiken and to illuminate where the often problematic notions of sex and race working in Panoptiken might also be operating in STD and modern hygiene exhibitions. To unravel these connections will require a great deal more work than has been possible to examine in this chapter, particularly with regard to conceptions of race, but the framework established here offers new points of access.

Bibliography

Bayerisches Hauptstaatsarchiv, MK 11328. Universität München, Titelverleihung "Universitätsplastiker" an Emil Hammer in München.

Bayerisches Hauptstaatsarchiv, Plakatsammlung. Kultur- und Werbeplakate bis 1945. Ausstellung von Emil Eduard Hammer zu kriegsbedingten Schußverletzungen während des Ersten Weltkrieges in München, 22387.

"Bericht der Ortsgruppe Hirschberg." *Mitteilungen der DGBG* 10 (1912): 80.

Bezold, Friedrich. "Drei plastische Modelle des menschlichen Gehörorgans." *Archiv für Ohrenheilkunde* 78 (1908): 262–264.

Brecht, Bertolt. "Lux in Tenebris." In vol. 1 of *Werke*, edited by Werner Hecht, Jan Knopf, Werner Mittenzwei, and Klaus-Detlef Müller, 291–308. Berlin: Aufbau, 1989.

Dreesbach, Anna. *Gezähmte Wilde: Die Zurschaustellung "exotischer" Menschen in Deutschland 1870–1940*. Frankfurt am Main: Campus, 2005.

Ebenstein, Joanna. *The Anatomical Venus: Wax, God, Death, and the Ecstatic*. London: Thames & Hudson, 2016.

Ellenbrand, Petra. *Die Volksbewegung und Volksaufklärung gegen Geschlechtskrankheiten in Kaiserreich und Weimarer Republik*. Marburg: Görich und Weiershäuser, 1999.

Eloesser, Arthur. "Castan's Ende." *Frankfurter Zeitung*, 26 February 1922, 1.

"Emil Eduard Hammer. Zu seinem 70. Geburtstag." *Münchner Zeitung*, 1 October 1935. no page number. Stadtarchiv München, DE-1992-ZA-P-0180-21

Eulner, Hans-Heinz. *Die Entwicklung der medizinischen Spezialfächer an den Universitäten des deutschen Sprachgebietes*. Stuttgart: Enke, 1970.

Fakiner, Nike. "The Spatial Rhetoric of Gustav Zeiller's Popular Anatomical Museum." *Dynamis* 36, no. 1 (2016): 47–72.

Finkelstein, H., E. Galewsky, and L. Halberstaedter. *Hautkrankheiten und Syphilis im Säuglings- und Kindesalter: Ein Atlas*. Berlin: Julius Springer, 1922.

Fotoalbum mit Fotografien aus der Werkstatt Rudolf Pohl. Archiv des Deutschen Hygiene-Museum Dresden 2012/616.

Friederici, Angelika. *Castan's Panopticum: Ein Medium wird besichtigt*. Berlin: Karl-Robert Schütze, 2009.

Gabriel, Carl, and Emil Eduard Hammer. *Führer durch das anatomisch-ethnologische und naturwissenschaftliche Museum*. Munich: G. Schutz, before 1902.

Galewsky, Eugen, and Friedrich Woithe. "Die Geschlechtskrankheiten und ihre Bekämpfung." Dresden: Deutscher Verlag für Volkswohlfahrt, 1922.

Gille, Klaus. *Panoptikum: 125 Jahre zwischen Wachs und Wirklichkeit; Hamburgs Panoptikum und seine Geschichte.* Hamburg: Panoptikum Gebr. Faerber, 2004.

Hammer, Emil Eduard. "Syphilis, venerische Krankheiten." In *Der Mensch. Illustrierter Führer durch Hammer's Original-Ausstellung aus München*, 11–13. Munich: Hammer, 1914.

"Ein Helfer der Wissenschaft." *Münchner Neueste Nachrichten*, 2 October 1935, 1.

Hoffmann, Kathryn A. "Sleeping Beauties in the Fairground. The Spitzner, Pedley and Chemisé Exhibits." *Early Popular Visual Culture* 4, no. 2 (2006): 139–159

Hopwood, Nick. "Artist versus Anatomist, Models against Dissection: Paul Zeiller of Munich and the Revolution of 1848." *Medical History* 51 (2007): 279–308.

Kisch, Egon Erwin. "Das Geheimkabinett des anatomischen Museums." In vol. 5 of *Gesammelte Werke*, 170–174. Berlin: Aufbau, 1974.

Lang, Johanna. "Die Einführung des Wandergewerbescheins: von reisenden Schaustellern und beanspruchten Wachsmodellen." In *Blicke! Körper! Sensationen! Ein anatomisches Wachskabinett und die Kunst*, edited by Eva Meyer-Hermann, 89. Göttingen: Wallstein, 2014.

Lang, Johanna. "Um 1940: Zerlegt und vorgeführt: das Wachsmodell Eine Figur auf dem Seziertisch liegend." In *Blicke! Körper! Sensationen! Ein anatomisches Wachskabinett und die Kunst*, edited by Eva Meyer-Hermann, 107–108. Göttingen: Wallstein, 2014.

Lingner, Karl August, Arthur Luerssen, and Georg Seiring. *Der Mensch: Ausstellung; Ausgewählte Gruppen aus der Internationalen Hygiene-Ausstellung 1911.* Darmstadt: no publisher, 1912.

Mattl, Siegfried. "Körperspektakel: Ein anatomisches-pathologisches und ethnologisches Museum im fin-de-siecle Wien." *Wiener Zeitschrift zur Geschichte der Neuzeit* 2 (2004): 46–62.

McIsaac, Peter M. "Emil Eduard Hammers anatomische Modelle im kulturellen Kontext." In *Spiegel der Wirklichkeit. Anatomische und dermatologische Modelle in Heidelberg*, edited by Sara Doll and Navena Widulin, 95–112. Heidelberg: Springer, 2019.

McIsaac, Peter M. "Die medizinische Venus. Die performative Basis von anatomischen Zurschaustellungen vor und um 1900." In *Geschlechter Spiel Räume: Dramatik, Theater, Performance und Gender*, edited by Gaby Pailer and Franziska Schößler, 313–328. Amsterdam: Rodopi, 2011.

Meyer-Hermann, Eva, ed. *Blicke! Körper! Sensationen! Ein anatomisches Wachskabinett und die Kunst.* Göttingen: Wallstein, 2014.

Mitteilungen der Deutschen Gesellschaft zur Bekämpfung der Geschlechtskrankheiten 12 (1914): 78–87.

Neisser, Albert. "Begrüßungsrede des Vorsitzenden Herrn Geheimrat Neisser zur VIII. Jahresversammlung zu Dresden am 9./10. Juni 1911." *Mitteilungen der Deutschen Gesellschaft zur Bekämpfung der Geschlechtskrankheiten* 9 (1911): 75.

Nikolow, Sybilla. "'Wissenschaftliche Stillleben' des Körpers im 20. Jahrhundert." In *Erkenne Dich selbst! Strategien der Sichtbarmachung des Körpers im 20. Jahrhundert*, edited by Sybilla Nikolow, 11–46. Cologne: Böhlau, 2015.

Nikolow, Sybilla, and Thomas Steller. "Das lange Echo der 1. Internationalen Hygiene-Ausstellung in der Dresdner Gesundheitsaufklärung." *Dresdner Hefte* 29, no. 4 (2011): 18.

"Number of visitors to the Louvre in Paris from 2007 to 2018 (in millions)." Hamburg: Statista, 2019. https://www.statista.com/statistics/247419/yearly-visitors-to-the-louvre-in-paris/.

Nyhart, Lynn K. "Science, Art and Authenticity in Natural History Displays." In *Models: The Third Dimension of Science*, edited by Soraya de Chadarevian and Nick Hopwood, 307–338. Stanford: Stanford University Press, 2004.

Offizieller Führer durch die Internationale Hygiene-Ausstellung Dresden 1911 und durch Dresden und Umgebung. Berlin: Rudolf Mosse, 1911.

Osten, Philipp. "Zwischen Volksbelehrung und Vergnügungspark." *Deutsches Ärtzeblatt* 102, no. 45 (2005): A 3086–3089.

"Die Pantherdame Mlle. Irma Loustan aus Paris." *Münchner Neueste Nachrichten*, 20 December 1906, 4.

Parish, Lawrence Charles, Gretchen Worden, Joseph A. Witkowski, and Daniel H. Parish. "Wax Models in Dermatology." *Transactions and Studies of the College of Physicians of Philadelphia* 5, no. 13 (1991): 29–74.

Pohl, Rudolf. Geschäftsbuch 1901–1919. Archiv des Deutschen Hygiene-Museums Dresden 2009/657.

Politzer, Adam. *Geschichte der Ohrenheilkunde.* Vol. 2, *Von 1850–1911*, 271–273. Stuttgart: Ferdinand Enke, 1913.

Pudor, Heinrich. "Museumschulen." *Museumskunde* 6 (1910): 248–253.

Radtke, Julia. "Zwischen Aufklärung und Voyeurismus: die 'Extra-Abteilung.'" In *Blicke! Körper! Sensationen! Ein Anatomisches Wachskabinett und die Kunst*, edited by Eva Meyer-Hermann, 97. Göttingen: Wallstein, 2014.

Roth, Joseph. "Philosophie des Panoptikums." In vol. 1 of *Werke*, edited by Klaus Westermann, 939–940. Cologne: Kiepenhauer & Witsch, 1956.

Sauerteig, Lutz. *Krankheit, Sexualität, Gesellschaft: Geschlechtskrankheiten und Gesundheitspolitik in Deutschland im 19. und frühen 20. Jahrhundert.* Stuttgart: Franz Steiner, 1999.

Sauerteig, Lutz. "'Sex in Wachs': Gesundheitswissen, Volksaufklärung und Sinneserregung." In *Blicke! Körper! Sensationen! Ein anatomisches Wachskabinett und die Kunst*, edited by Eva Meyer-Hermann, 169. Göttingen: Wallstein, 2014.

Schnalke, Thomas. *Diseases in Wax: The History of the Medical Moulage.* Chicago: Quintessence, 1995.

Schnalke, Thomas. "Spuren im Gesicht: Eine Augenmoulage aus Berlin." In *Der zweite Blick: Besondere Objekte aus den historischen Sammlungen der Charité*, edited by Beate Kunst, Thomas Schnalke, and Gottfried Bogusch, 19–40. Berlin: de Gruyter, 2010.

Scholz, Albrecht. "Bekämpfung der Geschlechtskrankheiten in verschiedenen politischen Systemen." *Hautarzt* 7 (2003): 664–673.

Schumacher, Hans Harald. *Jugenderinnerungen eines Hamburger Arztes.* Unpublished. Quoted in: Klaus Gille, *Panoptikum: 125 Jahre zwischen Wachs und Wirklichkeit; Hamburgs Panoptikum und seine Geschichte*, 35–36. Hamburg: Panoptikum Gebr. Faerber, 2004.

Stadtarchiv Dresden Z. 42.VII. Gustav Zeiller. Gesuch um die Eröffnung eines anthropologischen und anatomischen Kabinetts. Dresden. 13 November 1888.

Stadtarchiv München. DE-1992-POL-0384. Medizinisches Volksmuseum.

Stadtarchiv München. DE-1992-POL-0385. Hammers Anatomische Ausstellungen.

Stadtarchiv München. DE-1992-ZA-11322. Schreiben von Hammer an die Polizeidirektion vom 12.4.1906.

Stadtarchiv München. DE-1992-ZA-11322. Schreiben von Hammer an die Polizeidirektion vom 6.6.1916.

Stadtarchiv München. DE-1992-ZA-11322. Schreiben von Hammer an die Polizeidirektion vom 22.11.1906.
Stadtarchiv München. DE-1992-ZA-P-0180-21. Hammer, Prof. Emil Eduard, 1929–1939.
Stadtarchiv München. DE-1992-ZS-0158-3. Hammer's anatomische Original-Ausstellung, 1916.
Stadtarchiv München. Polizeidirektion. 1051.
Stein, Claudia. "Organizing the History of Hygiene at the International Hygiene-Ausstellung in Dresden in 1911." *NTM: Zeitschrift für Geschichte der Wissenschaften, Technik und Medizin* 22, no. 1 (2014): 355–387.
te Heesen, Anke. *Theorien des Museums: Zur Einführung*. Hamburg: Junius, 2012.
"Unsere Sondergruppe 'Geschlechtskrankheiten' auf der internationalen Dresdner Hygeineausstellung in amerikanischer Beleuchtung." *Mitteilungen der Deutschen Gesellschaft zur Bekämpfung der Geschlechtskrankheiten* 10 (1912): 139–140.
"Vereinsnachrichten." *Mitteilungen der Deutschen Gesellschaft zur Bekämpfung der Geschlechtskrankheiten* 12 (1914): 78–87.
Wagener, Oskar. "Unterricht in der Laryngologie, Rhinologie und Otologie: Methoden, Hilfsmittel, Prüfung." In *Die Krankheiten der Luftwege und der Mundhöhle*, edited by V. Karl Amersbach et al., 1308–1309. Berlin: Julius Springer, 1929.
Wagner, Cornelia. "Panoptikum: das Wachskabinett als urbane Attraktion." In *Blicke! Körper! Sensationen! Ein anatomisches Wachskabinett und die Kunst*, edited by Eva Meyer-Hermann, 89–90. Göttingen: Wallstein, 2014.
Witte, Wilfried. "Vom Diener zum Meister: Der Beruf des Anatomischen Präparators in Berlin von 1852–1959." In *Der zweite Blick: Besondere Objekte aus den historischen Sammlungen der Charité*, edited by Beate Kunst, Thomas Schnalke, and Gottfried Bogusch, 185–218. Berlin: de Gruyter, 2010.
Zimmerman, Andrew. *Anthropology and Antihumanism in Imperial Germany*. Chicago: University of Chicago Press, 2001.

Part 2: **Materials and Media**

John D. Benjamin
Materials and Media

Following the investigations in the first section above, "Ways of Seeing," which examined the effects of new technologies and social forces on how people saw the world, we now shift our gaze to the objects with which they engaged. Here, we turn to the changes in the nineteenth century resulting from the industrial revolution and the rapid expansion of capitalism that led to new ways materials were procured and shaped into objects. Further, we also grapple with these new objects' concomitant transformation into consumable products – or, as Marx suggested, their commodification into "autonomous figures endowed with a life of their own, which enter into relations both with each other and with the human race."[1] We consider how they were assigned specific values and disseminated; how they were encountered, purchased, read, viewed, heard, touched, and seen; and finally, how these processes were driven by innovations in industrial trade.

This section's four chapters thus expand on the perspectival shifts in the opening section by looking more closely at how artefacts of visual culture interact with new, altered, and reconsidered materials in the nineteenth century. They ask a range of questions: How are these materials repurposed and how do their forms and functions change as a result? How do they reflect the social and technological developments of the era, and what do these renewed and redirected features afford purveyors of specific forms of cultural production? And finally, how do viewers and users interact with these many novel materials constructed as media transmitting meanings that were, more often than not, new?

In the section's opening chapter, "Cut-Ups on the Edges of the Photographic Century," Catriona MacLeod calls for a reassessment of early to mid-nineteenth-century *Scherenschnitte* [papercuts] – domestic artworks created with needlework and embroidery scissors, glue, and paper – of three artists, Luise Duttenhofer, Adele Schopenhauer, and Hans Christian Andersen, arguing that their work both drives and reacts to changes in the availability of artworks in the home and the place of paper in commercial culture. By examining the violation of paper by cutting between authors, genders, and nationalities, she asks the reader to reconsider what visual culture is and what should be understood as art objects – the reduction of such everyday art objects as papercuts to crafts, she argues, is simplistic and marked by bias, especially related to gender.

---

[1] Karl Marx, *Capital* (London: Penguin Classics, 1990), 165.

What MacLeod does with paper, Trevor Brandt finds in prayer in the second chapter, "Printed Pilgrimage: *Spiritual Labyrinths* in the German-American Home." He considers a rare cultural artefact present in German-American Anabaptist homes in the late eighteenth and early nineteenth centuries, the *spiritual labyrinth* broadside, as a medium for prayer and looks at how these products refashion the meanings of the prayers themselves. These curious objects were large pages printed with prayers in varied and often twisting arrangements, intended for interactive but pious domestic religious use. With his focus on the tangible, verbal-visual, and spatial printing of prayers, he enquires about the materiality of these media to ask questions regarding the private sphere. Here, as it does in MacLeod's chapter, gender plays a role in who interacts with these media.

The third and fourth chapters of the section focus even more closely on the effects of trade and the dissemination of objects on people's understanding of the natural and socio-historical worlds respectively. First, J. P. Short's chapter, "Arc of the Anemone: Modeling Nature from the *Wunderkammer* to the *Warenwelt*" examines how shifting trade practices in the latter half of the nineteenth century affected the production of and interaction with Leopold and Rudolf Blaschka's glass marine invertebrates. Short's focus is on the wide range of visual materials on which the Blaschkas based their models that they were able to acquire through the new contexts of trade and commerce in the nineteenth century. These materials represented knowledge from increasingly interconnected global networks of information. But Short does not stop there; he further investigates the similarly intricate and expanding market for the sale of these fragile visual artefacts.

Finally, David Ciarlo concludes the section with "The Traveling Cliché: Circulation and Fixity in Engraved Representations of Ethnic 'Others.'" In the chapter, he considers ethnographic visual representations of the non-European "other," first in how they reduce diverse groups to "types," which are then solidified, popularized, and normalized in the form of primarily wood engravings. He questions here especially the role and power of images in the pervasiveness and longevity of these essentializing and racist clichés throughout the nineteenth century. Further, similarly to how Short looks at the trade of glass marine invertebrates, Ciarlo examines the effects of the distribution and reception of these images around Germany in the nineteenth century.

Bibliography

Marx, Karl. *Capital*. London: Penguin Classics, 1990.

Catriona MacLeod
Cut-Ups on the Edges of the Photographic Century

Let me begin with a quotation from Hans Christian Andersen's late story of 1872, written three years before his death, "Aunty Toothache." "Aunty Toothache" was, in fact, the last story contained in his last published collection. A tale of excruciating dental pain, and one that ends with the loss of teeth that are supposed to last a lifetime as well as the loss of missing manuscript pages, it was also based on Andersen's long and neurotic obsession with his own physical decay. "Where did we get this story? Would you like to know?" asks the narrator, a poetic stand-in for Andersen. He answers his own question as follows, by referring to the paper detritus of the so-called "age of paper,"[1] which is upcycled into the story by a "well-read" grocery boy, for whom, indeed, the smellier and more degraded the paper, the better:

> We got it from the basket that the wastepaper is thrown into.
>
> Many a good and rare book has been taken to the delicatessen and the grocer's, not to be read, but to be used as wrapping paper for starch and coffee beans, for salted herrings, butter, and cheese. Used writing paper has also been found suitable.
>
> Frequently one throws into the wastepaper basket what ought not to go there.
>
> I know a grocer's assistant, the son of a delicatessen owner . . . he is a well-read person, his reading consisting of the printed and written matter to be found on the paper used for wrapping. He has an interesting collection, consisting of several important official documents from the wastepaper baskets of busy and absent-minded officials, a few confidential letters from one lady friend to another – reports of scandal which were not to go further, not to be mentioned by a soul. He is a living salvage institution . . . and . . . has saved many a book, or leaves of a book, well worth reading twice . . . the most valued items of which have come from the delicatessen.[2]

Not only fictional protagonists, but also Romantic authors and visual artists cut, glue, stain, and recycle paper; they generate papercuts, collages, and ink blot poems in profusion and combine these scraps in what are for their time

---

[1] On the "papiernes Zeitalter," see Lothar Müller, *Weisse Magie: Die Epoche des Papiers* (Munich: Carl Hanser, 2012).

[2] Hans Christian Andersen, "Aunty Toothache," in *Hans Christian Andersen: The Complete Stories*, trans. Jean Hersholt (London: The British Library, 2005), 893–894. See also the earlier (1848) tale "The Shirt Collar," in which the aging garment is turned first into a rag and then paper as a punishment for his harassment of objects gendered as feminine, including a pair of scissors that cuts him back in revenge. *The Complete Stories*, 318–319.

striking new hybrid forms such as the picture books of fairy-tale author Hans Christian Andersen (1805–1875) and medical doctor and poet Justinus Kerner (1786–1862). These material acts of cutting and pasting have so far not featured in the scholarship on German Romanticism, put simply, because of the traditional opposition of Romanticism and materiality and the focus of so much of this criticism on the philosophical Jena school. For a Romantic movement that defined itself in terms of reuniting and reintegrating the arts, the suspicion about visual incursions on the printed page is noteworthy.

August Wilhelm Schlegel, writing in 1799 in his early Romantic journal *Athenäum*, stated that words and images should have equal weight in publications, but was vigilant about what he saw as a subservient kind of illustration, such as the narrative vignettes of Daniel Chodowiecki. These types of illustrations he decries as "embryonic births," examples of "the dwarfish and trivial," and to real works of art as sugary children's treats to religious art, "marzipan saints' images."[3] Conversely, the early Romantic fragment, as practiced by the Schlegel brothers or Novalis, does not usually fall under the category of material object – though of course fragments do take material form in the pages of the *Athenäum*, the programmatic publication of Early Romanticism. In one welcome exception to the immaterial tendency in interpreting Jena Romanticism, Anthony Phelan has linked the fragment to the silhouette: he reminds us that Friedrich Schlegel had remarked on its creation as a material process of cutting, in a letter to his brother August Wilhelm in which Friedrich also tellingly comments on excerpting from Caroline Schlegel's letters, as well as on her nose for fragments: "I must also ask Caroline to make do today with my friendliest greetings – but even more to excerpt fragments from her [letters], from yours, from mine, from Hardenberg's, from wherever she likes, from heaven and earth. For even if she can't, i.e., won't make any fragments, it is certain that no one else is better than she is at following the savour of them [auszuschmecken]."[4]

German Romanticism is preoccupied with literary genres that appear small and cryptic: the fragment is one of the most striking and suggestive of these. Friedrich Schlegel declared, in one of his own well-known fragments (*Athenäum* 206), that a fragment "must be entirely isolated from the surrounding world like a little work of art and complete in itself like a hedgehog." This statement,

---

[3] "embryonische Geburten," "das Zwerghafte und Kleinliche," "Heiligenbilder aus Marzipan." August Wilhelm Schlegel, "Über Zeichnungen zu Gedichten und John Flaxmans Umrisse," *Athenäum* 2.2 (1799): 193.

[4] Anthony Phelan, "The Content of Silhouettes," *Paragraph: The Journal of the Modern Critical Theory Group* 21.2 (1998), 162. Original in Friedrich Schlegel, *Kritische Friedrich-Schlegel-Ausgabe*, ed. Ernst Behler, 35 vols (Munich: F. Schöningh, 1958–), 24: 67.

while enigmatic, and even comic (with that delightful surprise word "hedgehog" at the end), claims that the fragment exists in a state of bristly, self-contained separation from the world. Along similar lines, though couched in peaceable, escapist terms, Susan Stewart's recent work on miniature arts more generally characterizes the miniature as a space of order and containment – "a diminutive, and thereby manipulatable, version of experience, a version which is domesticated and protected from contamination."[5] Do these arts, as Stewart suggests further, and as I will challenge, always exist in a non-historical time, "a type of transcendent time which negates change and the flux of lived reality"?[6]

Where Romantic cutting, pasting, and recycling have been conceptualized, it is as "minor" or "salvage" arts or crafts, akin to the work of fairy tale collectors and authors, itself an activity often related to papercutting, for example, in Hans Christian Andersen's or Adele Schopenhauer's dual talents in writing fairy tales and creating papercuts. Thus, unsurprisingly they have also been gendered as feminine and/or primitive. Such a categorization has no doubt also been a factor in the almost complete neglect of German Romantic collage in current scholarship on montage and collage. Hanno Möbius's relatively recent book *Montage und Collage*, for example, contains singularly few references to Romanticism. Möbius does cite E. T. A. Hoffmann's kaleidoscopic 1819 novel *Lebens-Ansichten des Katers Murr*, with its claims to have been composed on waste paper (*Makulatur* – literally, "ein beflecktes Ding").[7] However, he argues that any montage-like moments in the novel are only notionally so, since they do not in his view introduce any genuine "Fremdmaterial" (foreign matter) into the fictional world. Andersen's experiments in papercutting, which I introduce below, are artless, writes Möbius, "ohne . . . Kunstanspruch."[8] Ultimately, collage, for Möbius, is only present before the twentieth century as non-art, in the area of folk and amateur practices such as the pasting of commercially-produced images in albums.[9] Walter Benjamin, to be sure, designates albums as marginal counterparts to books, encouraging children to engage haptically with what are by 1900 pre-cut images manufactured for scrapbooks:

---

5 Susan Stewart, *On Longing: Narratives of the Miniature, the Gigantic, the Souvenir, the Collection* (Durham: Duke University Press, 1993), 69.
6 Stewart, *On Longing*, 65.
7 Hanno Möbius, *Montage und Collage: Literatur, bildende Künste, Film, Fotografie, Musik, Theater bis 1933* (Munich: Wilhelm Fink, 2000), 40–41.
8 Möbius, *Montage and Collage*, 91.
9 Möbius, *Montage and Collage*, 89–90. Although Diane Waldman acknowledges Max Ernst's and Joseph Cornell's debts to Andersen, she, too, differentiates the work of nineteenth-century amateurs and professionals from that of the moderns due to "the special bittersweet quality based in sentiment and nostalgia." Diane Waldman, *Collage, Assemblage, and the Found Object* (New York: Abrams, 1992), 12, 11.

touching, cutting out, gluing.[10] Scholarship on modernist collage and photocollage has repeated quasi-mythical origin stories about the birth of these visual forms in the early twentieth century: whether it be Pablo Picasso attaching a scrap of oilcloth with a *trompe l'oeil* chair-caning pattern to a still life painting in 1912, or Hannah Höch being inspired to create photomontage by a kitschy oleograph of a soldier hanging in a Baltic cottage where she happened to be vacationing in 1918. As Dawn Ades opens her history of collage: "When Pablo Picasso and Georges Braque started gluing bits to their pictures, in 1912, this had nothing to do with long-standing popular past-times like pasting cut out images onto fire screens, and everything to do with art."[11] To sum up the prevalent art-historical account, nineteenth-century collage is neither modern, nor art. In my view, we have long been overdue an attempt to find the right vocabulary for this pre-modernist collage that is commonly to be found in domestic contexts such as albums and as decorative objects.[12]

In what follows I will explore two nineteenth-century strategies for papercutting and gluing, both of which involve intermedial engagements, albeit of very different kinds. The first decades of the nineteenth century witnessed the prolific output of *Scherenschnitte* (papercuts) predominantly by women artists such as Adele Schopenhauer (1797–1849) and Luise Duttenhofer (1776–1829) who take on the medium of sculpture to invert relations of monumentality via an ephemeral art. Unlike these women artists' refined cutting and pasting, which strives for painterly effects, and their employment of luxury papers, Hans Christian Andersen, deploying massive tailor's scissors, uses an apparently crude, primitivist approach to undercut and transform the paper modernity of the newsprint and photographic age. Andersen's scraps, in their juxtaposition of his own freehand papercuts and handwritten text with waste paper, letters, and print and photographic images cannibalized from the press, also introduce craft onto the very site of paper modernity and reproducibility that has helpfully begun to be the focus of photocollage research. The very notion of collage as based in the fragmented, abject, discarded objects of commercial modernity and overproduction is one that obliges us to look at the nineteenth century and collage before

---

10 Walter Benjamin, "Das Pult," in *Berliner Kindheit um 1900*, *Gesammelte Schriften*, ed. Rolf Tiedemann and Hermann Schweppenhäuser, 7 vols (Frankfurt am Main: Suhrkamp, 1974), 4.1: 281. Trevor Brandt also considers the haptic qualities of engagements with paper in his contribution to this volume.
11 Dawn Ades, "Collage: A Brief History," in *About Collage*, ed. Peter Blake (London: Tate Gallery, 2000), 27.
12 For a helpful corrective, see Freya Gowrley, "Collage Before Modernism," in *Cut and Paste: 400 Years of Collage*, ed. Patrick Elliott (Edinburgh: National Galleries of Scotland, 2019), 25–33.

"collage." A brief note on the distinction between the silhouette and the papercut is in order here: in contrast to the silhouette portrait, a forerunner of photography,[13] the *Scherenschnitt* was largely a domestic art, its tool not a technical reproductive device such as the physionotrace, an instrument designed to trace a profile in silhouette, but the fine scissors used for needlework and embroidery. Its production thus required more virtuosity and dexterity than that of the machine-aided and mass-produced silhouette. Nevertheless, with their common focus on physiognomy, they are certainly both precursors to photography.

Schopenhauer, Duttenhofer, Andersen: all three are associated with the salvage art of the fairy tale. All three, crossing boundaries of genre and medium, on the edges of photography, and challenging the scale of monumentality, are in their individual ways, literally at the cutting edge. And, as I have suggested, they reveal certain parallels with avant-garde practices of the early twentieth century such as Picasso's collages and Matisse's papercuts, though their relationship with the public sphere is undoubtedly more tenuous, since their works were, for the most part, destined for domestic contexts such as albums and as decorative objects, or even, in Andersen's case, for the dustbin.

Scissors, whether the delicate embroidery scissors used by Schopenhauer and Duttenhofer, or the hefty tailor's shears favored by Andersen, are always double-edged: at once creative and destructive.[14] What connects the artists who wield them, I argue here, is the artists' double-edged deployment of humble and ephemeral materials (scissors, paper) in order to challenge other, dominant, media of the age, be they sculpture (in the case of Schopenhauer and Duttenhofer) or lithographic reproduction and eventually photography itself (in Andersen's case). Karl Varnhagen von Ense, himself an avid practitioner of papercutting along with his (more talented) sister Rosa Maria von Assing, in his 1814 essay "On Cutting Out" ("Vom Ausschneiden"), a rare Romantic document on the art, introduces *Scherenschnitte* as dwarfish "surrogates" of sculpture. Papercuts are at once too ephemeral, too immaterial, yet at the same time too material. Though they do not possess the solidity of the sculptural medium, which might seem like an advantage to a Romantic thinker, their lightness does

---

13 On this and related media forms on the peripheries of photography, see Katharina Steidl, *Am Rande der Fotografie: Eine Medialitätsgeschichte des Fotogramms im 19. Jahrhundert* (Berlin: De Gruyter, 2018).
14 Wilhelmine Kall's prefatory poem to Adele Schopenhauer's silhouette alphabet, which was published in a well-known *Musenalmanach*, hints albeit playfully at the doubled edge of the papercut. Kall refers to the agency of "das Doppelschwert der Scheere," which even in its lightness multiplies that of the sword. *Beckers Taschenbuch zum geselligen Vergnügen* (1820): 411.

not help them achieve soaring Romantic transcendence. Note the stress throughout this passage on smallness, muteness, and constraint:

> These little arts of sociability, like tiny flying divinities that cannot attain the heaven of art but flutter nicely enough a few feet above the earth, most certainly deserve to be reviewed in the literary section of the morning newspaper. Just as that delicate art [the mouth harmonica] is to music, a bright elfin game of dancing notes, so the art of cutting in paper is to sculpture: as charming in its smallness, just as limited and just as varied, and now we want to speak about this quiet, mutable art, this estimable surrogate of sculpture.[15]

In this discussion of nineteenth-century papercuts I am calling for a reassessment of their status as diminutive, innocuous, self-contained, and nostalgic craft works. On the contrary, they can take the form of social caricature (in the case of Duttenhofer and Schopenhauer) and critically thematize (in the case of Andersen) the proliferation and disposability of paper during the nineteenth century, when the production of images for a mass readership was burgeoning thanks to new print technologies such as lithography.

The critical potency of the *Scherenschnitt* has been rediscovered in contemporary art, as evidenced for example in the 2009 New York Museum of Arts and Design exhibition *Slash: Paper under the Knife*, which featured works by over fifty international artists, both male and female. Probably best known among present-day practitioners of the art form is American artist Kara Walker (b. 1969), who uses its stark black and white to interrogate race alongside gender, sexuality, and violence on a provocatively monumental scale in many room-size installations, playing as well, in smaller individual works, on incongruities of scale and material. Much has been made of Walker's critical – not to say confrontational – appropriation of an apparently trivial art.[16] But that art, despite its seemingly innocuous roots in domestic craft, has always had as its fundamental creative basis a violent

---

15 "Die kleinen Künste der Geselligkeit, gleichsam fliegende Götterchen, die den Himmel der Kunst nicht erschwingen, aber doch artig genug ein Paar Ellen hoch von der Erde aufflattern, verdienen ganz vorzüglich eine Art allgemeiner Literatur-Zeitung am Morgenblatt zu finden . . . . Was diese zarte Kunst [die Mundharmonika] nun der Musik ist, ein helles Zwergenspiel bunter, tanzender Klänge, das ist der Plastik die Kunst in Paper auszuschneiden, eben so reizend in ihrer Kleinheit wie jene, eben so beschränkt, und eben so mannigfaltig; und von dieser im Stillen wandelnden Kunst, diesem trefflichen Surrogat der Bildhauerei, wollen wir jetzt reden." Karl Varnhagen von Ense, "Vom Ausschneiden," in *Werke*, ed. Konrad Feilchenfeldt, 5 vols (Frankfurt am Main: Deutscher Klassiker Verlag, 1990), 4: 384. Later in the essay, a candle adorned with human and animal cut-outs is compared with Trajan's Column, though the former is clearly also a functional, domestic object that is set to be burned and can never exhibit the monumental solidity of the ancient work.
16 See, for example, Anne M. Wagner, "Kara Walker, 'The Black-White Relation,'" in *Kara Walker: Narratives of a Negress*, ed. Ian Berry et al. (Cambridge, MA: MIT Press, 2003), 90–101.

act, the rupture of paper. In Andersen's tale "The Shirt Collar," a pair of scissors being propositioned by a collar (who is captivated by her spread legs) takes her revenge on her suitor: "She cut him so furiously that he never recovered."[17] Papercutting is related to the slashing of the body, or an erasure of corporeality. As David Revere McFadden notes in his introduction to the catalog accompanying the "Slash" exhibition, the very destructiveness of the paper cut-out lends transformative agency to an otherwise banal medium: "through compromising the integrity of the material, paper loses its passivity, its plainness, its neutral passivity."[18]

Contemporary Irish artist Eva Rothschild articulates a similar idea, returning us to Goethe's notion of the void (silhouettes as "sad, half-real representations"), when she describes the silhouette as a "black hole," an "object without information" that the viewer must complete, as he or she is lured and pulled into its center.[19] Along similar lines, discussing eighteenth- and nineteenth-century cut-outs, Juliane Vogel has argued that the works produced by scissors collapse into what she calls presymbolic zones.[20] Consider, for example, Adele Schopenhauer's *Scherenschnitt* alphabet, which appeared in *Beckers Taschenbuch* in 1820 in a section on cryptograms.[21] (Figure 1) Insisting on the opacity of the text-image relationship, Schopenhauer's alphabet is worlds apart from Karl Fröhlich's *ABC für artige Kinder* of 1854, aimed at children, and which in contrast to Schopenhauer's wordless alphabet helpfully explicates each silhouette letter in merry verses.[22] (Figure 2)

The gesture towards a radicalized and resistant passivity has compelling resonance for questions of gender and aesthetics during the period when *Scherenschnitte* came to the fore as a genteel, dilettantish, and diminutive

---

17 Andersen, "The Shirt Collar," 319. The aging shirt collar is turned first into a rag and then paper as a punishment for his harassment of a series of objects gendered as feminine.
18 David Revere McFadden: "Slash: Paper under the Knife," in *Slash: Paper under the Knife*, ed. Martina D'Alton (Milan: 5 continents, 2009), 15.
19 Rothschild is quoted in Marion Ackermann and Helmut Friedel, "Vorwort," in *Schattenrisse: Silhouetten und Cutouts*, ed. Marion Ackermann and Helmut Friedel (Ostfildern-Ruit: Hatje Cantz, 2001), 7; on silhouettes as "traurige[n] halbe[n] Wirklichkeitserscheinungen," Johann Wolfgang Goethe, "Der Sammler und die Seinigen," *Sämtliche Werke: Briefe, Tagebücher und Gespräche*, ed. Dieter Borchmeyer et al., 40 vols (Frankfurt am Main: Deutscher Klassiker Verlag, 1985–), 1.18: 726. Silhouettes, as Goethe's essay would have it, are only worthy of being collected in portfolios, not of decorating wall space.
20 Juliane Vogel, "Schnitt und Linie: Etappen einer Liaison," in *Öffnungen: Zur Theorie und Geschichte der Zeichnung*, ed. Friedrich Teja Bach and Wolfram Pichler (Munich: Wilhelm Fink, 2009), 143.
21 Adele Schopenhauer, *Räthsel-Alphabeth*, *Beckers Taschenbuch zum geselligen Vergnügen* (1820), n.p.
22 Karl Fröhlich, *ABC für artige Kinder in Silhuetten und Reimen* (Cassel: G. E. Vollmann, 1854).

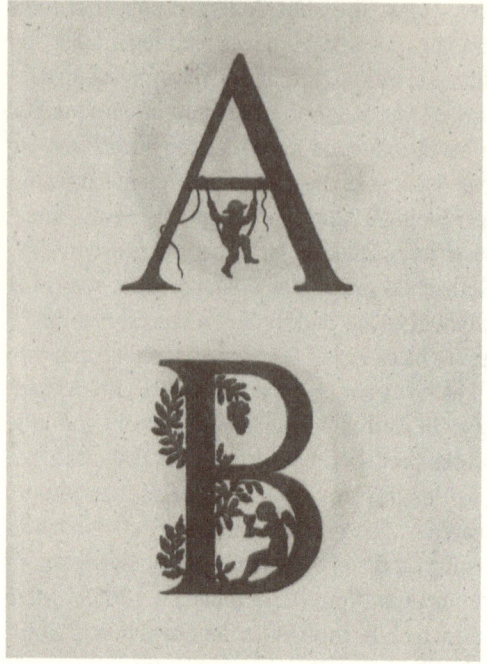

Figure 1: Adele Schopenhauer, Silhouettenalphabet. *Beckers Taschenbuch zum geselligen Vergnügen*, 1820. 12 cm. Rare Book Collection, Kislak Center for Special Collections, Rare Books and Manuscripts, University of Pennsylvania.

feminine art, or as one catalog phrases it in typical terms, a "lovely minor art."[23] In 1979, when the journal of the Deutsches Literaturarchiv Marbach, which houses much of Luise Duttenhofer's archive, devoted a special issue to the artist, the publication was accompanied by a how-to guide offering the reader glossy black paper, pre-traced patterns, and simple instructions, placing Duttenhofer firmly in the craft zone.[24] I turn now to case studies that will, however, reveal scissors' critical potency. I begin with Weimar artist and author Adele Schopenhauer, who was the daughter of the prolific novelist Johanna Schopenhauer, sister of philosopher Arthur Schopenhauer, and an important figure in her own right in the bourgeois salon of her mother.

---

[23] "liebevolle Kleinkunst;" Christa and Claus Weber, *Schwarze Kunst im Buch: Scherenschnitt und Schattenriß als Buchillustration* (Nuremberg: Weber, 1994), 11.
[24] *Marbacher Scherenschnitt-Büchlein*, Beilage zum *Marbacher Magazin* 13 (1979).

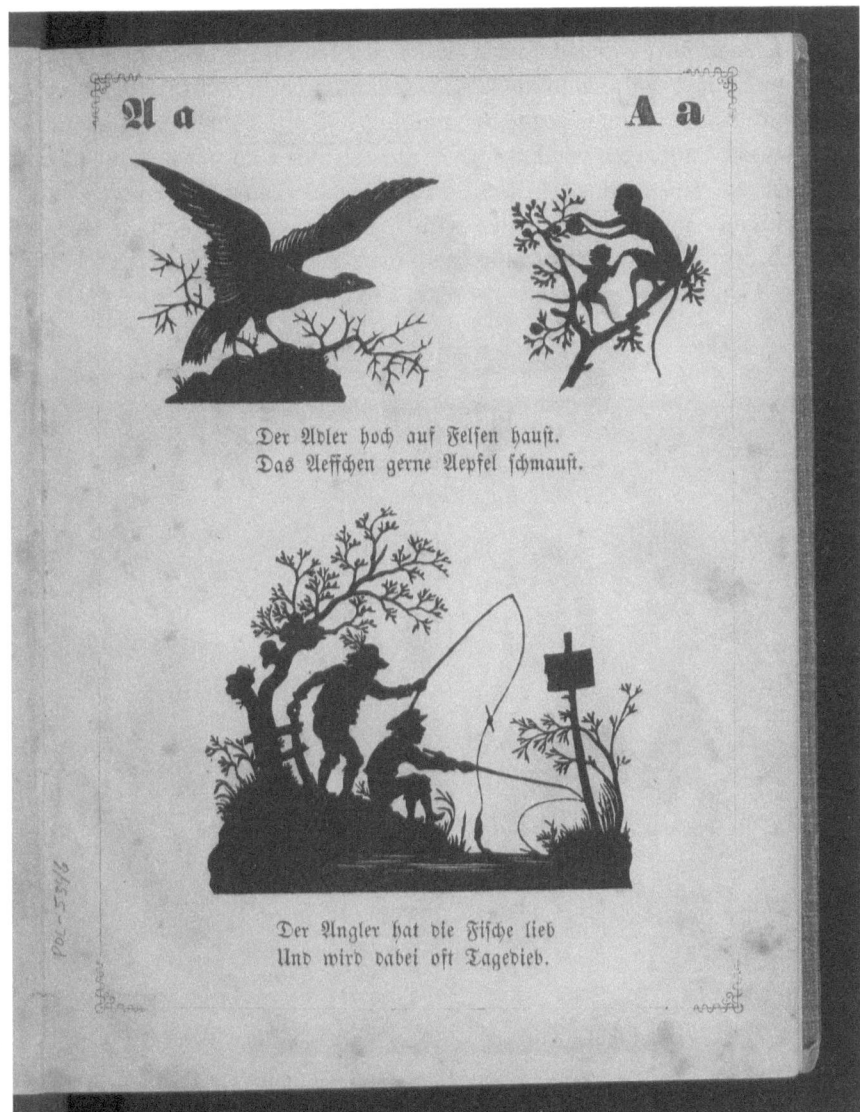

Figure 2: Karl Fröhlich, *ABC für artige Kinder in Silhuetten und Reimen* (Kassel: G.E. Vollmann, 1854). 17 cm. Rare Book Collection, Kislak Center for Special Collections, Rare Books and Manuscripts, University of Pennsylvania.

What does Schopenhauer's insistence on the tiny, on the gossamer, on the precious mean for a woman with a desirous artistic relationship to sculpture? Sculpture is the antithesis to the *Scherenschnitt*, an art requiring considerable economic capital: formal academic training and the resources of a studio. Nevertheless, Varnhagen von Ense is not the only one who saw it as the natural "surrogate" to papercutting.[25] In a rare diary entry referring to her *Scherenschnitte*, Schopenhauer approvingly agrees with a statement by a certain Madame Lutherod, whom she had met in Karlsbad, that, had Schopenhauer been a man, she would have been a sculptor.[26] The diary also reveals that she visited the Berlin

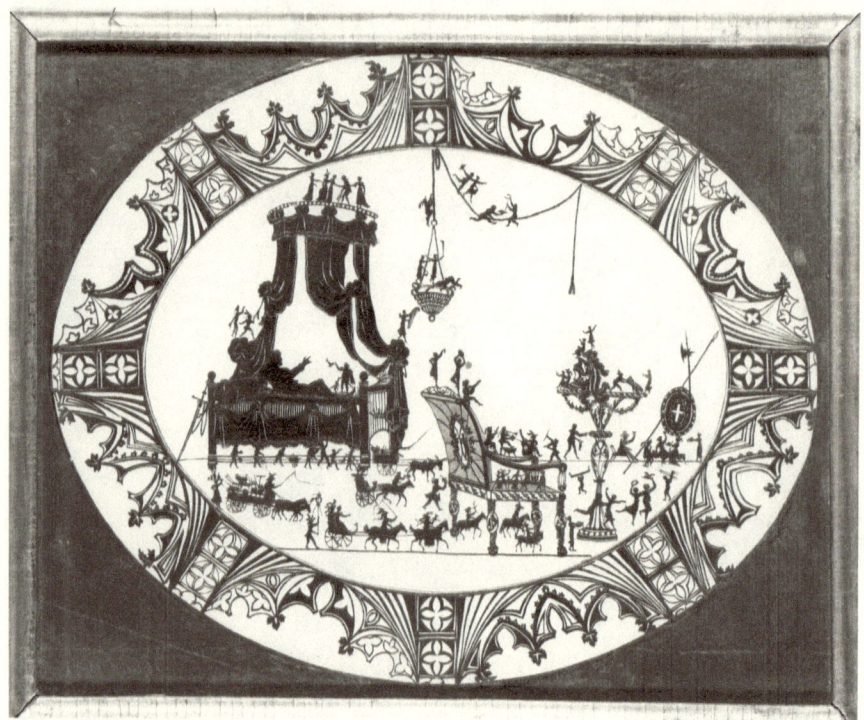

Figure 3: Adele Schopenhauer, "Die Zwergenhochzeit," 1820. 27.5 x 35.5 cm. Klassik Stiftung Weimar.

---

25 Varnhagen von Ense, "Vom Ausschneiden," 384.
26 "[. . .] sie sagte, als sie meine Ausschneiderei sah: 'Sie hätten, wenn Sie ein Mann wären, Bildhauer werden müssen.' Das gefiel mir, denn es ist wahr." Adele Schopenhauer, *Tagebücher*, ed. Kurt Wolff, 2 vols (Leipzig: Insel, 1909), 2: 90.

studios of Christian Daniel Rauch and Christian Friedrich Tieck, the preeminent sculptors of the day, in 1819; she renewed her acquaintance with both artists of the colossal when they came to her home town of Weimar a year later to sculpt Goethe's bust.[27] While the *Scherenschnitt* did permit Schopenhauer fruitful collaboration with the literary colossus of her age, Goethe, in her mother Johanna's literary salon, her art appears at first glance confined within its miniature boundaries and does not make its way, despite some efforts in this direction by her close friend the writer Karl Immermann in 1837, into the emerging mass medium of the century, prints.[28]

The pinnacle of Schopenhauer's creativity with scissors was the supplemental illustration of Goethe's 1804 ballad the "Hochzeitlied," which concerns a count who returns home from war to find a fantastical clan of sweet-natured dwarves – "possierliche[r] kleine[r] Gestalten" – carousing in and laying waste to his castle.[29] Created in 1820, though never published, the *Scherenschnitt* (Figure 3) was a direct response to Goethe's poem and to artistic productions in the salon. Goethe's ballad was published in the *Taschenbuch auf das Jahr 1804*, under the telling rubric "Der Geselligkeit gewidmete Lieder" ("Songs Dedicated to Sociability"), and emerged along with a number of other ballads from the author's own Wednesday salons, with their recreations of medieval courtliness, including sung poetry, in 1801–1802. Schopenhauer attends to the tiniest elements in the composition, achieving refined three-dimensional effects by, for example, scissoring fringes in the bed skirt and canopy and underscoring the neoclassicism of the chair at the center of the image with the addition of grisaille details. Schopenhauer's elves and dwarves are delicate, graceful, and domesticated, far from the grotesque, often malevolent figures that appear in German sagas and fairy tales or Arthurian romances. Yet, in the *Scherenschnitt* they fill the scene with frivolous if not utterly anarchic acts, erupting arabesque-like out of the frame of the restrained neoclassical silhouette with which the chair at the center of the composition is decorated. Indeed, the figural classical silhouettes inset in the chair are interchangeable in size with the dwarves, but are quickly overshadowed by them. Over seventy figures (along with eight horses and a donkey) colonize an aristocratic cultivated world whose long-absent master is now disarmed and confined in bed, to one side of the image. The party is in full swing in every corner of the *Scherenschnitt*: in, on, under, and above the bed (to mention only one piece of the count's furniture). Dwarves brandishing torches swing dangerously from chandeliers while others

---

27 Schopenhauer, *Tagebücher*, 26–27, 60.
28 Houben and Wahl, *Adele Schopenhauer: Gedichte und Scherenschnitte*, II, 5.
29 Goethe, "Hochzeitlied," 115.

perform daring acrobatics using the cables from which the light fixture is suspended; under the count's shield a feast is being consumed; the back of a chair is used as a dance floor as is the count's helmet; on horses and carts dwarves gallop through elegantly-appointed rooms; furniture and other household items are in a constant state of displacement around the theatrically static and massive bed and chair; so many of the figures are playing musical instruments that this is surely a cacophonous festivity and we are returned to the acoustic dimension of the folk ballad (so much for the "quiet mutable art" of which Varnhagen von Ense wrote!). Schopenhauer's overall principle is to counterpose moments of balance with threats to that very balance. We see, for example, a tightrope walker, a woman balancing a tray with dishes, the dwarf king decorously greeting the count from the bed canopy, but these are destabilized by the frenzied kineticism animating the rest of the *Scherenschnitt*: figures propelling themselves into and off every surface, intruding onto the image's very frame. Thus, the miniature world, which is in Susan Stewarts's reading a model of constraint, here serves as a disruptive mechanism of excess and surplus energy. Elsewhere I have pressed the interpretation of Schopenhauer's "Hochzeitlied" cut-out still further, to ask whether that massive count, besieged by the hordes of little people who have invaded his "Local" (locale), as Goethe termed his own scheme for the work's backdrop, might not be a stand-in for the monumental Goethe himself in relation to the middle-class salon of Adele's mother Johanna Schopenhauer, over which he presided.[30]

Luise Duttenhofer's testy relationship with sculptural monumentality is also captured in her *Scherenschnitte*. Stuttgart *Scherenschnitt* artist Duttenhofer, married to the modestly successful engraver Christian Duttenhofer, traveled in circles that included the sculptor Johann Heinrich Dannecker and Martin Wagner, the artist Angelika Kauffmann, and the philosopher F. W. J. Schelling. Gustav Schwab, in an obituary notice, pushed the connection between her thwarted career as a gifted young female artist denied formal training and the art of negation that resulted from it, claiming that this was why even the most cheerful scenes in her work found expression in black.[31] Certainly, one can interpret images such as a Psyche

---

[30] Diary entry of July 27, 1820. *Goethes Werke*, edited im Auftrage der Grossherzogin Sophie von Sachsen, 143 vols. (Weimar: Weidmann, 1887–1909), 3. 7: 201. It is unclear whether Goethe as indicated in the Weimar catalog notes to the *Scherenschnitt* (KSi/11897), actually drew the first sketch for the work. For a more extended reading of Schopenhauer's satirical images of Goethe and Weimar, see Catriona MacLeod, "Cutting up the Salon: Adele Schopenhauer's 'Zwergenhochzeit' and Goethe's 'Hochzeitlied,'" *Deutsche Vierteljahrsschrift für Literatur und Geistesgeschichte* 89.1 (2015): 70–87.

[31] Quoted in *Die Scherenschneiderin Luise Duttenhofer*, ed. Gertrud Fiege, *Marbacher Magazin* 13 (1979), 22.

figure (Duttenhofer returned repeatedly to this motif) submitting to having her wings scissored off as poignant commentaries on female artistic and psych-ic wounding (Figure 4).³² (Schopenhauer also repeats the motif of winged, Psyche-like figures, the gossamer wings serving as visual cues for the scissors that fashioned them.)

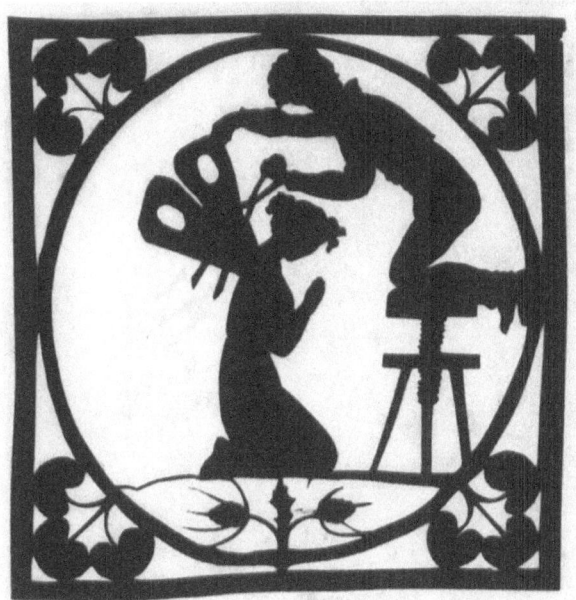

Figure 4: Luise Duttenhofer, Duttenhofer husband and wife, Luise as Psyche. Deutsches Literaturarchiv 1509. 7.3 x 7.1 cm.

---

32 The protagonist of Andersen's gruesome "The Red Shoes" has her feet cut off. Jens Andersen notes that the author seldom traveled without his scissors, a habit that was not without its hazards – on one occasion he sustained serious injuries when he sat on the scissors; "The Man who Wrote with Scissors," in *Cut-Outs and Cut-Ups: Hans Christian Andersen and William Seward Burroughs*, ed. Hendel Teicher (Dublin: Irish Museum of Modern Art, 2008), 142. On Psyche in Duttenhofer, see Christiane Holm, *Amor und Psyche: Die Erfindung eines Mythos in Kunst, Wissenschaft und Alltagskultur (1765–1840)* (Munich: Deutscher Kunstverlag, 2006), 214–217; and Julia Sedda, "Antikenrezeption und christliche Tradition im Scherenschnittwerk der Luise Duttenhofer (1776–1829)," (Ph.D. diss., Eberhard Karls Universität Tübingen, 2012), 143–145.

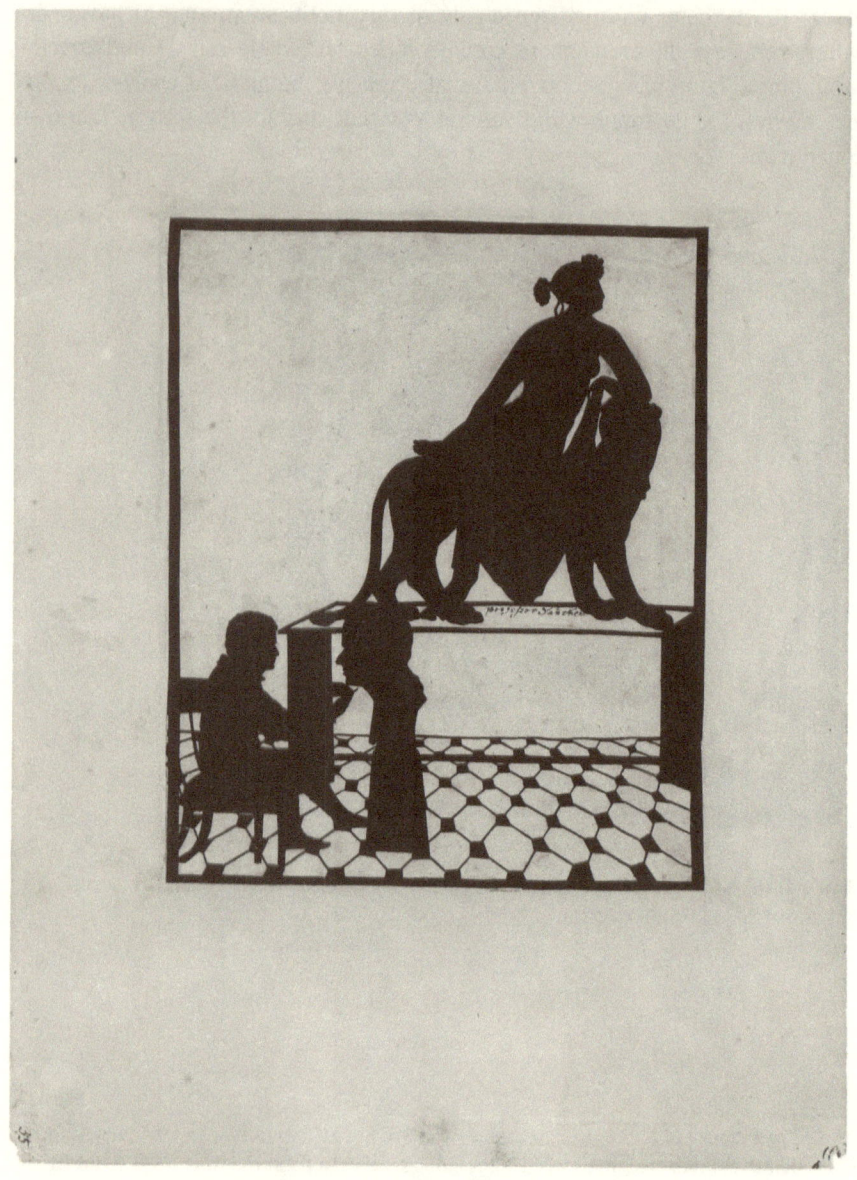

Figure 5: Luise Duttenhofer, Dannecker in his Studio. Deutsches Literaturarchiv 1501. 21 × 17.5 cm.

The case for the scrappy transgressiveness of works by Duttenhofer such as her *Scherenschnitt* of the sculptor Dannecker at work can, however, also readily be made: female figures can trim the appendages of male figures in the mythologically themed images, and in her portrait works of artist circles, akin to caricatures, Duttenhofer makes it her practice to scissor the established male artist down to size. The Dannecker portrait (Figure 5) features an out-of-scale, massive Ariadne statue dwarfing the sculptor Dannecker, whom Duttenhofer has placed doll-like on an oversized chair in the foreground, his feet dangling above the floor, and who is also smaller than the portrait bust of Schiller on which he is working (a work that Dannecker had himself described as "Colossal").[33] Remarkably for an untrained artist, Duttenhofer was able to imbue her paper art with qualities associated with painting and sculpture. She accomplished for the first time the rendering of perspective in what is often held to be a two-dimensional art form, many of her works offering a perspectival representation, as in the Dannecker portrait, of floor tiling or receiving relief-like patterns through embossing. She also lent painterly color to several *Scherenschnitte*, using underlays of more costly, luxury paper tinted yellow, blue, red, golden, or beige. No doubt, however, the ephemerality of the paper art contributes to the irony in representing two of the most colossal sculptural works of the age, Schiller and the Ariadne. Another papercut represents the sculptor Dannecker again, now in the guise of a pastry chef, bowed down under the weight of his sculptural confections, notably of his patron the obese Friedrich I of Württemberg. Many more papercuts take on the weighty personalities and monuments of the age.

Sulpiz Boisserée, for example, the noted champion and collector of medieval art, balances precariously out of scale on the roof of Cologne cathedral, hanging on for grim death to the wings of a stone angel (Figure 6). Sporting a comical Gothic crown on his head, Boisserée looks set to fall off the tower which he himself was still laboring to have rebuilt at the time when Duttenhofer created the *Scherenschnitt* (ca. 1819–27). At the base of the cathedral, to the left, Duttenhofer has placed her husband, Christian, who uses his own sharp etching tool to create engravings for the magnificent 1825 Cotta illustrated book edition devoted to the reconstruction of the edifice and commissioned by Boisserée.[34] Several of these papercuts by Duttenhofer and Schopenhauer, as I have shown, flout the laws of scale and weight and, exceeding the limits of the miniature, stage a gendered

---

33 Quoted in *Friedrich Schiller: Leben, Werk und Wirkung: Eine Ausstellung zum Gedächtnis der 200. Wiederkehr seines Geburtstags* (Marbach: Schiller Nationalmuseum, 1959), 149.
34 Albert Verbeek, "Sulpiz Boisserée auf den Turmspitzen des Kölner Domes: Ein satirischer Scherenschnitt von Luise Duttenhofer," *Kölner Domblatt* 8/9 (1954): 201–203.

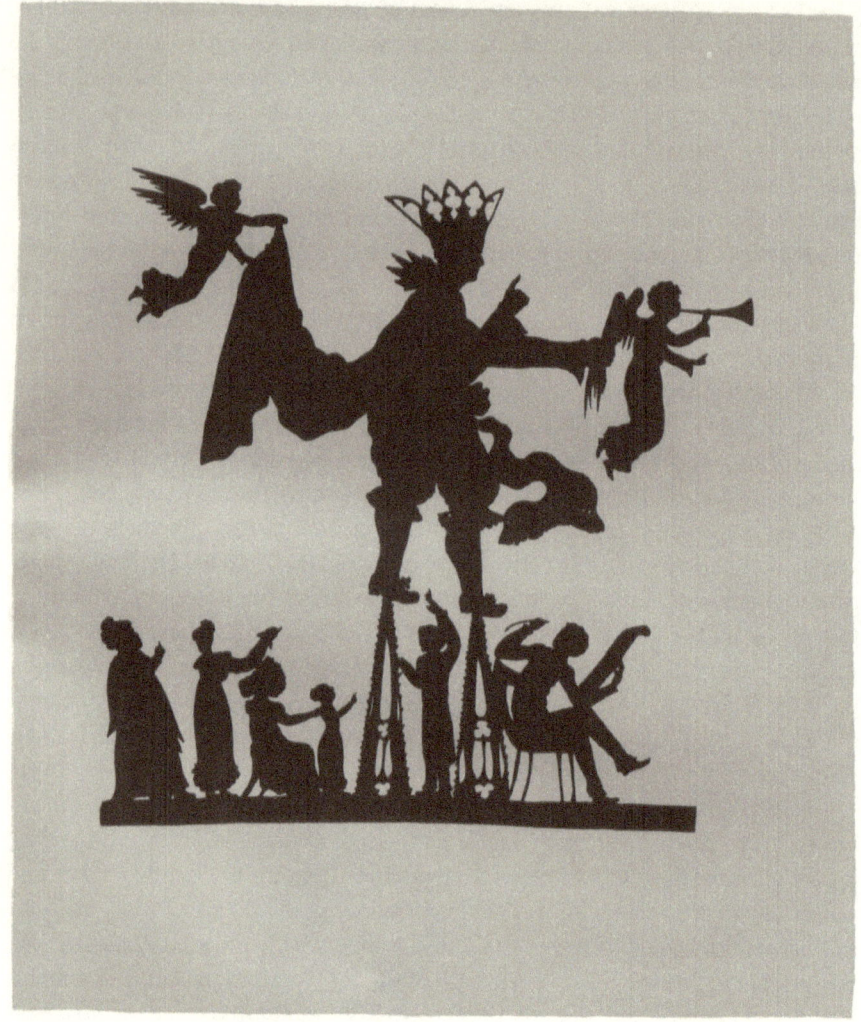

Figure 6: Luise Duttenhofer, Sulpiz Boisserée Balancing on the Spires of Cologne Cathedral. Deutsches Literaturarchiv 5505. 13.6 x 13.6 cm.

intermedial showdown in a manner that can scarcely be said to conform to the winsome and utterly toothless artform described by Varnhagen von Ense.

Hans Christian Andersen represents new departures in Romantic engagements with paper, dealing head on with the matter of paper – unlike the female artists I have discussed who attempt to transcend its limitations. Andersen's strategy in papercutting and collage also differs from that of Schopenhauer and

Duttenhofer in its extreme rejection of pictorial coherence (though it must be added that a good deal of Duttenhofer's work that is not devoted to author or artist portraits remains cryptic in its juxtaposition of Christian, Classical, and Orientalist iconography).[35] Unlike Schopenhauer and Duttenhofer, Andersen departed from exclusive use of luxury papers. The sixteen extant collage albums Andersen created for children, most of which date from the 1850s and 60s, re-use paper scraps in an eclectic, decomposed fashion juxtaposing the mass-produced image with the luxury object, print with handwriting, and including the most intimate personal creations: his own papercuts, handwritten verse, recognizable text fragments from contemporary authors, newspaper and magazine cuttings, advertisements, fashion illustrations, labels, cartoons, lottery tickets, theatre tickets, city maps, train timetables, ribbons, bits of luxury paper. Difficult as it is to identify the precise sources of images, we know that they draw from trade journals, almanacs, catalogs, and mass-produced "picture sheets" (sheets of pictures of categories of objects, animals etc., for pedagogical purposes; in German, *Bilderbogen*).[36]

The lure of waste products recalls Walter Benjamin's account of children's attraction to the detritus of the adult world, which they do not use imitatively, but rather – as they do the waste material of fairy tale, or clothing scraps – in play.[37] For Andersen, papercutting was a way of returning to childhood, to, as Jens Andersen put it, "cut his way back," while also, in the double-edged way I have been describing as characteristic of the *Scherenschnitt*, confronting modernity.[38] (Klaus Müller-Wille points out that Andersen's literary style, in the fairy tales, similarly juxtaposes dissonant registers, from oral quotidian speech to high-flung lyricism.[39]) Thus Andersen was engaging directly with and transforming the vertiginous, disposable, and cheap print culture of the day that had been made

---

[35] In the interests of brevity I am discussing the papercuts, collage albums, and decoupage that preoccupied Andersen throughout his career, though I could also have included literary engagements with shadows that anticipate photography, in particular the story "The Shadow" (1847). On Andersen and photography, see Thomas Smarsly-Fechner, "Der Spiegel und seine Schatten: Abdrücke der frühen Photographie in Texten von Aa. O. Vinje, Henrik Ibsen und H. C. Andersen," in *Zwischen Bild und Text: Zur Funktionalisierung von Bildern in Texten und Kontexten*, ed. Annegret Heitmann and Joachim Schiedermair (Freiburg: Rombach, 2000), 21–42.
[36] Jakob Stougaard-Nielsen, "The Fairy Tale and the Periodical: Hans Christian Andersen's Scrapbooks," *Book History* 16 (2013), 146.
[37] Walter Benjamin, "Old Forgotten Children's Books," in Walter Benjamin, *Selected Writings*, ed. Marcus Bullock and Michael W. Jennings (Cambridge, MA: Harvard UP, 1996), 408.
[38] Andersen, "The Man who Wrote with Scissors," 146.
[39] Klaus Müller-Wille, *Sezierte Bücher: Hans Christian Andersens Materialästhetik* (Paderborn: Wilhelm Fink, 2017), 10–11.

possible by the invention of lithography in 1796 by the German Alois Senefelder.[40] Andersen even made a papercut from newsprint as early as 1830, anticipating by several generations the Dada avant-garde's use of newspaper in collages. The juxtaposition of the folksy/archaic and the modern is encapsulated in this early example in newsprint, which uses a waste product of modernity simultaneously to regenerate an older art form and critique a new reading and viewing experience. Stephen Scobie, writing about avant-garde newspaper collages in Picasso and Braque, stresses the point that these so-called "objets trouvés" are always the representation simultaneously of an object and its materiality, that is, always already a sign of a newspaper, rather than a newspaper,[41] and, indeed, I think Andersen points us in this direction with this early papercut.

This self-reflexive focus on collage's own mediality hints at early twentieth-century notions of avant-garde collage, long held to be a support for "authentic," "found" materials. Möbius, one of the few scholars to seek pre-avant-garde forerunners of collage and montage, notwithstanding his denial that earlier examples display the disruptive potency of Dada or Surrealism, points to the nineteenth-century experience of newspaper reading as registering the sutures and cuts of the page layout.[42] Where in Andersen's last story "Aunty Toothache" we saw luxury paper and printed books degraded as wrapping paper for delicatessen food items, he here works with mass medium paper that is inherently friable, ephemeral, and trashy. Cutting a rather childish, crude outline of a man with a hat, he simultaneously cuts off the legibility of the Brazilian story it transmits. Andersen makes of it a text fragment. Indeed Anke te Heesen, in her work on newspaper cutouts, makes a similar point about Dada uses of newsprint, which force the viewer/reader to toggle between image and text.[43] Where many papercuts, such as those of Duttenhofer, veer in the direction of caricature, the Brazilian figure, sporting a gaucho hat, operates at the more general level of stereotype. Klaus Müller-Wille, the scholar who has done the most for material considerations of Andersen's oeuvre and who has been most attentive to Andersen's self-awareness of cultural techniques [Kulturtechniken], notes

---

40 See also David Ciarlo's contribution to this volume on the circulation and reuse of illustrations.

41 Stephen Scobie, *Earthquakes and Explorations: Language and Painting from Cubism to Concrete Poetry* (Toronto: University of Toronto Press, 1997), 96. The image of the Brazilian newspaper cutout can be seen at: http://andersen.museum.odense.dk/klip/billedvis.asp?billednr=16880&antal=115&language=en

42 Möbius, *Montage und Collage*, 96–99.

43 Anke te Heesen, *Der Zeitungsauschnitt: Ein Papierobjekt der Moderne* (Frankfurt am Main: Fischer, 2006), 189–92.

that even the picture books Andersen created for Agnete Lind, ostensibly addressed to a young child, contain marginal commentaries on contemporary political crises, references to mass communications such as the postal service, and pictures of writing implements, and, therefore, imply a self-reflexively double readership and orientation.[44] Andersen's scraps, in their juxtaposition of his own freehand papercuts and handwritten texts with waste paper, letters, and images cannibalized from the print press (including print silhouettes), layer craft onto the very site of paper modernity and reproducibility.

The album's is a polyvocal, fragmentary, and contingent form, containing what Vivian Liska has distinguished from the writing in books as stuff itself: "particles of reality."[45] Yet, these atoms of the print age are lavishly gathered and bound in book form, as in the Drewsen picture book (Figures 7 and 8), with its heavy handmade paper and leather bindings, held at the Library of Congress – an original scrapbook of colored illustrations made by Andersen and his friend and collaborator A.L. Drewsen for the grandson of the latter, Jonas Drewsen.

Turning now to Andersen's papercuts more generally, I would like to offer some preliminary thoughts about the massive corpus (comprising over 1500 examples in sizes ranging from the minuscule, such as a ship in the harbor of Constantinople measuring 4.5 x 5.5 cm, to the large-scale, such as an arabesque work for Dorothea Melchior measuring 41.9 x 26.5 cm).[46] Most were created in the last two decades of his life and, were, it would appear, motivated by the physically incapacitating rheumatism that made it more difficult for him to handle a pen.[47] The prolific output of cut paper can be divided into three groups: those that he created on the margins of aristocratic salons in a kind of mixed medium theatrical performance accompanying his spinning of tales; papercuts destined for inclusion in the picture books for children and thus for interaction with mass media images; and finally, cut-out/decoupage images, created in the last years of his life for a decoupage folding memory screen and

---

[44] Klaus Müller-Wille, "Hans Christian Andersen und die vielen 19. Jahrhunderte – Eine Einführung," in *Hans Christian Andersen und die Heterogenität der Moderne*, ed. Klaus Müller-Wille (Tübingen: Francke, 2009), 7–8. See also Müller-Wille, *Sezierte* Bücher, esp. the section "Schneiden," 285–333. Müller-Wille places the emphasis on an engagement with modernity's heterogeneity, where I have characterized Andersen's as a double-edged encounter with past and present.
[45] Vivian Liska, "Die Idee des Albums: Zu einer Poetik der Potentialität," in *Album: Organisationsform narrativer* Kohärenz, ed. Anke Kramer and Annegret Pelz (Göttingen: Wallstein, 2013), 37.
[46] See *Hans Christian Andersen: Poet mit Feder und Schere*, ed. Anne Buschhoff and Detlef Stein (Bremen: Wienand, 2018), 154, 173.
[47] Hendel Teicher, "Cuts and Connections," in *Cut-Outs and Cut-Ups*, 13–44; here, 27.

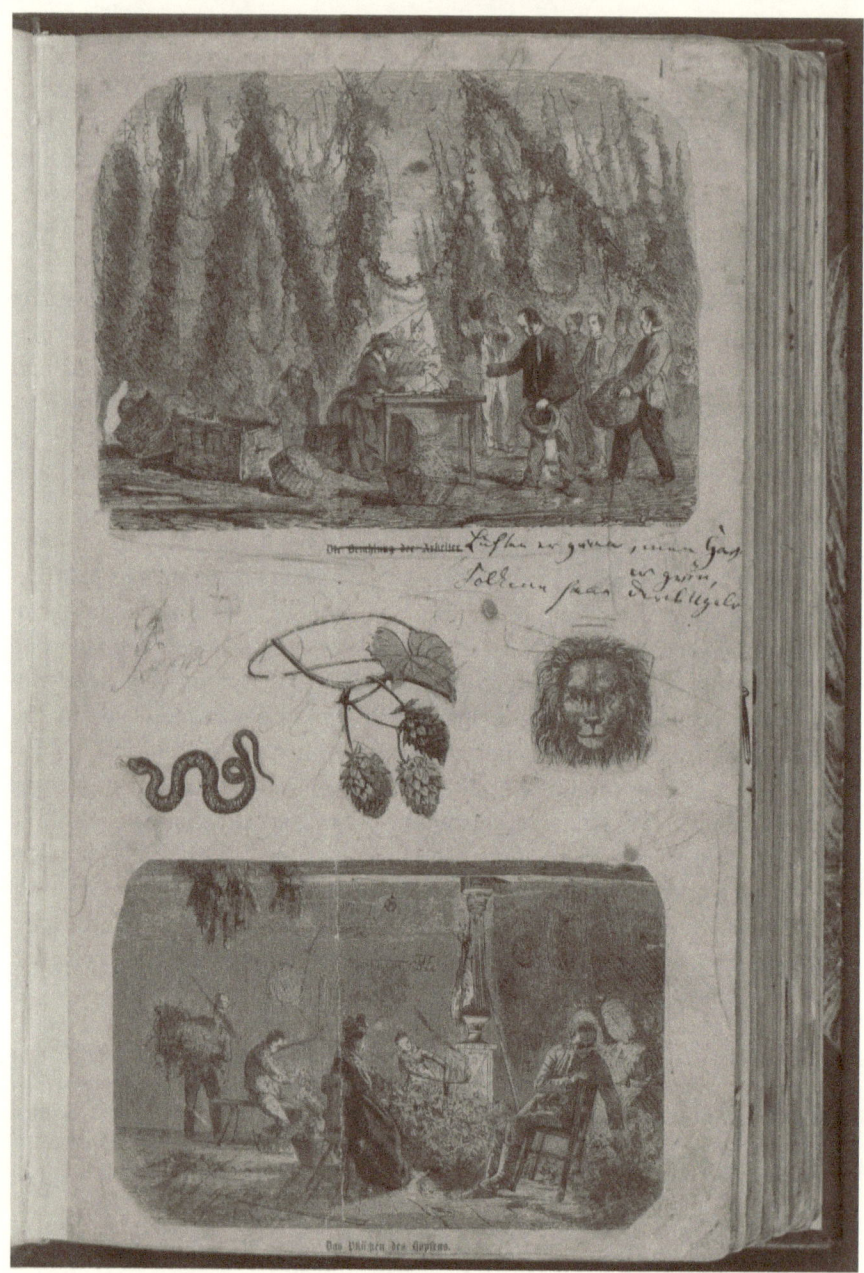

Figure 7: Hans Christian Andersen and Adolf Drewsen, *Billedbog til Jonas Drewsen*, ca. 1862. 140 p. mounted col. illus., ports. 30 cm. Library of Congress.

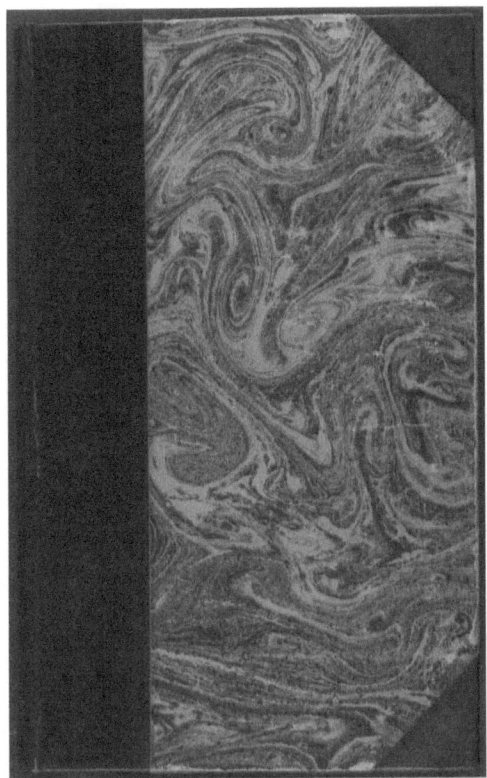

Figure 8: Hans Christian Andersen and Adolf Drewsen, *Billedbog til Jonas Drewsen*, ca. 1862. 140 p. mounted col. illus., ports. 30 cm. Library of Congress.

that are also placed against, below, on top of, modern prints and photographs. Departing from the sharp physiognomic caricature of Luise Duttenhofer, or the elfin irony of Adele Schopenhauer, Andersen's papercuts are on the one hand primitive, if not archaic, grotesques that seem to have little to do with modernity: with those massive scissors, he created gnomes, trolls, hangmen, witches, fertility goddesses, Medusas, paper images which he also partially tore out with his hands. Yet, on the other hand, Andersen's cutting art of refusal, in its repeated allusion to and transformation into refuse, waste, of the burgeoning image culture of nineteenth-century illustrated magazines, and even of photography, deserves to be seen as a distinctly modern preoccupation. Unlike Duttenhofer, Schopenhauer, and Varnhagen von Ense, Andersen cut at the outside margins of sociability: often invited to aristocratic parties, the shoe-maker's son-turned-celebrity removed himself from the card-playing and dancing to make papercuts on demand for children and old people, groups who were situated on the margins of the salon. Unlike Duttenhofer, and perhaps to a lesser extent Schopenhauer, too, who carefully retained copies of their works, Andersen always created already obsolete or *potentially* obsolete works, as Kjeld Heltoft describes the creative process: "Like small, weary elfins, they [the ballet dancers] would lie around on the dining-tables of both the bourgeoisie and the nobility when the evening's entertainment was over. Some ended in the dustpan, a good many were broken in the course of play, and a few were framed and hung on the wall or pasted into an album. Nobody cared much one way or another – he could always make some more next time he came."[48] For Andersen, papercutting became something of a virtuoso performance art, with its magical folding, cutting, and big reveals. Some papercuts emulated sculpture, folded to stand upright. However, disaster-oriented ephemerality is underscored by some of the most typical of Andersen's motifs, which echo in morbid form the out-of-kilter figurations we already encountered in Duttenhofer and Schopenhauer: tightrope walkers, dancers, butterflies, hang men (Figure 9). Further pushing the boundaries of the negation inherent to the papercut, Andersen also worked with the leftover paper: pasting that paper remainder elsewhere on the page, he drew the viewer's attention to the void, to what had been cut away.[49]

In conclusion, let us turn to Andersen's famous so-called "dream screen," a work in which cutting and pasting takes monumental and final encompassing form. It is composed of black and white materials from various sources and including several media – engravings from the Danish publisher Reitzels Forlag, English and Danish illustrated journals, 150 photographs of famous Danes by the court photographer, and an illustration by Vilhelm Pedersen for Andersen's own "Thumbelina," among others. Here, *the* modern medium, photography, itself becomes the object of the scissors' attention. This (dream)screen constituted a virtual, reconfigurable Romantic dreamscape beginning with a panel devoted to childhood and passing through a succession of European countries until the final panel, the Orient (this, and the childhood panel, contain no historical notables or contemporary personalities). Andersen placed the adjustable screen in his bedroom, to view from his sickbed. As Varnhagen von Ense had already noted in his essay "On Cutting Out" cut paper seems to invite nostalgia, to conjure up memories. Visitors to the ailing Andersen's home brought images as gifts and thus the screen also became a collaborative project, echoing his work with Adolph Drewsen and Mathilde Ørsted as well as some children on

---

[48] Kjeld Heltoft, *Hans Christian Andersen as an Artist*, trans. David Hohnen (Copenhagen: Christian Ejler's Forlag, 2005), 134.
[49] Hendel Teicher, "Cuts and Connections," 41–42.

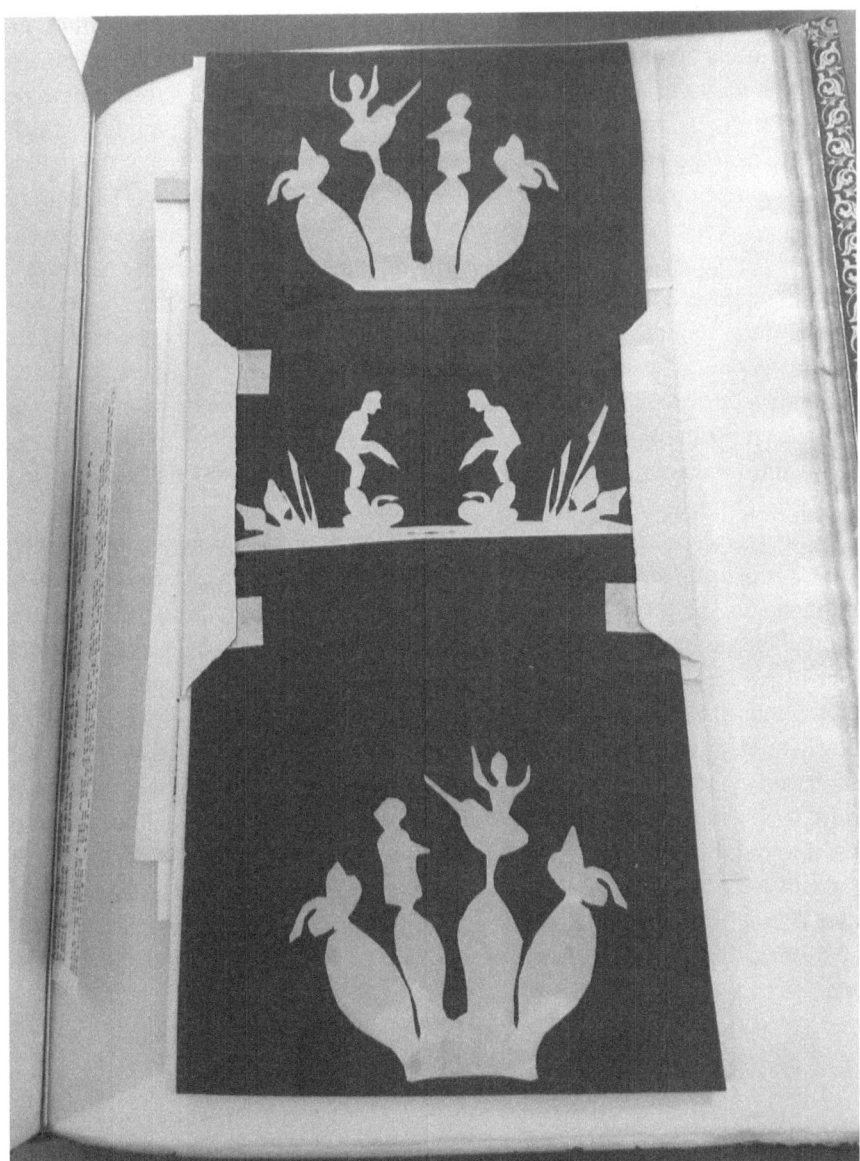

Figure 9: Hans Christian Andersen, Scissor-clipped silhouettes, white paper, mounted on black. 10 ¼ x 4 ¾ inches. The Jean Hersholt Collection of Hans Christian Andersen, Library of Congress.

picture books.[50] Not only was Andersen challenging media boundaries, he also, as in his albums, disrupted the notion of the singular artist or maker. As Andersen wrote in his diary in 1873, having received a small screen prototype from Wanda Danneskiold, he was inspired by her colored pictures, which "merged as if they formed a single picture and yet endlessly many of them gliding into each other, like a strange dream."[51] Each of the eight panels measuring 1.53 x 0.63 meters represents a cultural landscape of famous people from each respective country, aligned vertically from the sovereigns and statesmen at the top, to the poets and scientists in the middle, to the indigent at the bottom, but the borders are still more dream-like, peopled with fabulous creatures. This work was not, as Möbius suggests, using collage as an unreflective means to generate a "painterly effect," but rather, was already fully engaged in reflecting on its own mediality, as it framed the portrait photographs and diverse images sourced from the popular press, including one of the illustrations from his own books, with the fairy tale world of grotesques.[52]

Nineteenth-century cut-outs have appeared to be nostalgic, diminutive craft forms that eschew critique and bracket out modernity and the rising new mass media culture. This is a deceptive and facile reading. While both Duttenhofer and Schopenhauer arguably pay less attention to the materiality of paper than Andersen – with a view to transcending its limitations in a painterly or sculptural direction – both demand critical work of their viewers and cut down to size the work of male cultural giants working in weightier formats. Andersen actively revels in the juxtapositions of the archaic and the contemporary. In view of the sheer range of Andersen's material praxes of cutting and pasting, read in the context of his poetic reflections on the media and print landscape of his time, as well as of the earlier experiments by Schopenhauer and Duttenhofer that had preceded his and that had overtly competed with sculpture, we have to take seriously the idea of scissors as instruments of writing and thought.

---

50 Teicher, 18.
51 Quoted in Heltoft, *Hans Christian Andersen as an Artist*, 207.
52 Möbius, *Montage und Collage*, 103. The screen can be viewed online (with helpful close-up functionality) at: http://andersen.museum.odense.dk/skaerm/index.asp

Bibliography

Ackermann, Marion, and Helmut Friedel. "Vorwort." In *Schattenrisse: Silhouetten und Cutouts*, edited by Marion Ackermann and Helmut Friedel, 6–23. Ostfildern-Ruit: Hatje Cantz, 2001.
Ades, Dawn. "Collage: A Brief History." In *About Collage*, edited by Peter Blake, 37–43. London: Tate Gallery, 2000.
Andersen, Hans Christian. "Aunty Toothache." In *Hans Christian Andersen: The Complete Stories*, translated by Jean Hersholt, 893–902. London: British Library, 2005.
Andersen, Hans Christian. "The Shirt Collar." In *Hans Christian Andersen: The Complete Stories*, translated by Jean Hersholt, 318–319. London: British Library, 2005.
Andersen, Jens. "The Man Who Wrote with Scissors." In *Cut-Outs and Cut-Ups: Hans Christian Andersen and William Seward Burroughs*, edited by Hendel Teicher, 141–148. Dublin: Irish Museum of Modern Art, 2008.
Benjamin, Walter. "Old Forgotten Children's Books." In *Selected Writings*, edited by Marcus Bullock and Michael W. Jennings, 406–413. Cambridge, MA: Harvard University Press, 1996.
Benjamin, Walter. "Das Pult." In *Berliner Kindheit um 1900*, in vol. 4.1 of *Gesammelte Schriften*, edited by Rolf Tiedemann and Hermann Schweppenhäuser, 280–282. Frankfurt am Main: Suhrkamp, 1974.
Bradshaw, Michael. "Hedgehog Theory: How to Read a Romantic Fragment Poem." *Literature Compass* 5, no. 1 (2008): 73–89.
Buschhoff, Anne, and Detlef Stein, eds. *Hans Christian Andersen: Poet mit Feder und Schere*. Bremen: Wienand, 2018.
Fiege, Gertrud, ed. "Die Scherenschneiderin Luise Duttenhofer." Special issue, *Marbacher Magazin* 13 (1979).
Friedrich Schiller: Leben, Werk und Wirkung: Eine Ausstellung zum Gedächtnis der 200. Wiederkehr seines Geburtstags, exhibition catalog. Marbach: Schiller Nationalmuseum, 1959.
Fröhlich, Karl. *A-B-C für artige Kinder in Silhuetten und Reimen*. Cassel: G. E. Vollmann, 1854.
Goethe, Johann Wolfgang. *Goethes Werke*, 143 vols. Weimar: Weidmann, 1887–1909.
Goethe, Johann Wolfgang. "Hochzeitlied." In vol. 1.2 of *Sämtliche Werke: Briefe, Tagebücher und Gespräche*, edited by Dieter Borchmeyer et al., 114–116. Frankfurt am Main: Deutscher Klassiker, 1985–.
Goethe, Johann Wolfgang. "Der Sammler und die Seinigen." In vol. 1.18 of *Sämtliche Werke: Briefe, Tagebücher und Gespräche*, edited by Dieter Borchmeyer et al., 676–733. Frankfurt am Main: Deutscher Klassiker Verlag, 1985–.
Gowrley, Freya. "Collage Before Modernism." In *Cut and Paste: 400 Years of Collage*, edited by Patrick Elliott, 25–33. Edinburgh: National Galleries of Scotland, 2019.
Heltoft, Kjeld. *Hans Christian Andersen as an Artist*. Translated by David Hohnen. Copenhagen: Cristian Ejlers, 2005.
Holm, Christiane. *Amor und Psyche: Die Erfindung eines Mythos in Kunst, Wissenschaft und Alltagskultur (1765–1840)*. Munich: Deutscher Kunstverlag, 2006.
Houben, H. H., and Hans Wahl, eds. *Adele Schopenhauer: Gedichte und Scherenschnitte*. 2 vols. Leipzig: Klinkhardt & Biermann, 1920.

Kall, Wilhelmine. Untitled poem. *Beckers Taschenbuch zum geselligen Vergnügen* (1820): 411–412.
Liska, Vivian. "Die Idee des Albums: Zu einer Poetik der Potentialität." In *Album: Organisationsform narrativer Kohärenz*, edited by Anke Kramer and Annegret Pelz, 35–39. Göttingen: Wallstein, 2013.
MacLeod, Catriona. "Cutting up the Salon: Adele Schopenhauer's 'Zwergenhochzeit' and Goethe's 'Hochzeitlied.'" *Deutsche Vierteljahrsschrift für Literatur und Geistesgeschichte* 89, no. 1 (2015): 70–87.
Marbacher Scherenschnitt-Büchlein, Beilage zum Marbacher Magazin 13 (1979).
McFadden, David Revere. "Slash: Paper under the Knife." In *Slash: Paper under the Knife*, edited by Martina D'Alton, 10–46. Milan: 5 continents, 2009.
Möbius, Hanno. *Montage und Collage: Literatur, bildende Künste, Film, Fotografie, Musik, Theater bis 1933*. Munich: Wilhelm Fink, 2000.
Müller, Lothar. *Weisse Magie: Die Epoche des Papiers*. Munich: Carl Hanser, 2012.
Müller-Wille, Klaus. "Hans Christian Andersen und die vielen 19. Jahrhunderte: Eine Einführung." In *Hans Christian Andersen und die Heterogenität der Moderne*, edited by Klaus Müller-Wille, 1–18. Tübingen: Francke, 2009.
Müller-Wille, Klaus. *Sezierte Bücher: Hans Christian Andersens Materialästhetik*. Paderborn: Wilhelm Fink, 2017.
Phelan, Anthony. "The Content of Silhouettes." *Paragraph: The Journal of the Modern Critical Theory Group* 21, no. 2 (1998): 150–168.
Schlegel, August Wilhelm. "Über Zeichnungen zu Gedichten und John Flaxmans Umrisse." *Athenäum* 2, no. 2 (1799): 193–246.
Schlegel, Friedrich. "Athenaeum Fragments." In *Philosophical Fragments*. Translated by Peter Firchow. Foreword by Rodolphe Gasché. 18–93. Minneapolis: University of Minnesota Press, 1991.
Schopenhauer, Adele. *Räthsel-Alphabeth, Beckers Taschenbuch zum geselligen Vergnügen*. N. p., 1820.
Schopenhauer, Adele. *Tagebücher*. 2 vols. Edited by Kurt Wolff. Leipzig: Insel, 1909.
Scobie, Stephen. *Earthquakes and Explorations: Language and Painting from Cubism to Concrete Poetry*. Toronto: University of Toronto Press, 1997.
Sedda, Julia. "Antikenrezeption und christliche Tradition im Scherenschnittwerk der Luise Duttenhofer (1776–1829)," PhD diss., Eberhard Karls Universität Tübingen, 2012.
Smarsly-Fechner, Thomas. "Der Spiegel und seine Schatten: Abdrücke der frühen Photographie in Texten von Aa. O. Vinje, Henrik Ibsen und H. C. Andersen." In *Zwischen Bild und Text: Zur Funktionalisierung von Bildern in Texten und Kontexten*, edited by Annegret Heitmann and Joachim Schiedermair, 21–42. Freiburg im Breisgau: Rombach, 2000.
Steidl, Katharina. *Am Rande der Fotografie: Eine Medialitätsgeschichte des Fotogramms im 19. Jahrhundert*. Berlin: De Gruyter, 2018.
Stewart, Susan. *On Longing: Narratives of the Miniature, the Gigantic, the Souvenir, the Collection*. Durham, NC: Duke University Press, 1993.
Stougaard-Nielsen, Jakob. "The Fairy Tale and the Periodical: Hans Christian Andersen's Scrapbooks." *Book History* 16 (2013): 132–154.
te Heesen, Anke. *Der Zeitungsauschnitt: Ein Papierobjekt der Moderne*. Frankfurt am Main: Fischer, 2006.

Teicher, Hendel. "Cuts and Connections." In *Cut-Outs and Cut-Ups: Hans Christian Andersen and William Seward Burroughs*, edited by Hendel Teicher, 13–44. Dublin: Irish Museum of Modern Art, 2008.
Varnhagen von Ense, Karl. "Vom Ausschneiden." In vol. 4 of *Werke*, edited by Konrad Feilchenfeldt, 384–390. Frankfurt am Main: Deutscher Klassiker, 1990.
Verbeek, Albert. "Sulpiz Boisserée auf den Turmspitzen des Kölner Domes: Ein satirischer Scherenschnitt von Luise Duttenhofer." *Kölner Domblatt* 8–9 (1954): 201–203.
Vogel, Juliane. "Schnitt und Linie: Etappen einer Liaison." In *Öffnungen: Zur Theorie und Geschichte der Zeichnung*, edited by Friedrich Teja Bach and Wolfram Pichler, 141–159. Munich: Wilhelm Fink, 2009.
Wagner, Anne M. "Kara Walker: 'The Black-White Relation.'" In *Kara Walker: Narratives of a Negress*, edited by Ian Berry et al., 90–101. Cambridge, MA: MIT Press, 2003.
Waldman, Diane. *Collage, Assemblage, and the Found Object*. New York: Abrams, 1992.
Weber, Christa, and Claus Weber. *Schwarze Kunst im Buch: Scherenschnitt und Schattenriß als Buchillustration*. Nuremberg: Weber, 1994.

Trevor Brandt
Printed Pilgrimage: *Spiritual Labyrinths* in the German-American Home

Hanna Schultz embarked upon a strange pilgrimage in 1833 when she was thirteen years old.[1] As a member of the Schwenkfelders, a German-speaking Protestant group that immigrated to southeastern Pennsylvania in the 1730s, Hanna grew up in a church emphasizing an intimate, pietistic relationship with the divine.[2] Hanna's father, a minister in the village of Hereford, sought to encourage Hanna's spiritual education with a new tool for her prayers – a Spiritual Labyrinth (*Geistlicher Irrgarten*) broadside, printed the year before in nearby Allentown.[3] This printed page, measuring twelve inches in width and sixteen in height, set out all the trials and tribulations of the Christian life in a rhyming, interactive format. First printed in the seventeenth century in Europe and later between the eighteenth and twentieth centuries in North America, this genre incorporates a twisting prayer – also printed sideways and upside-down – forming into the image of a labyrinth. While arresting the eye by blending word and image, these Labyrinths engaged other senses as well. The rhyming prayer encouraged verbalization while replicating an underlying feature of labyrinths – bodily movement. To read the prayer, users had to pick up and manipulate the broadside, physically acting out its pilgrimage.

---

1 Reuben Kriebel, *Genealogical Record of the Descendants of the Schwenkfelders, Who Arrived in Pennsylvania in 1733, 1734, 1736, 1737* (Manayunk, PA: Joseph Yeakel, Printer, 1879), 205.
2 The Schwenkfelders were one of many pietist Protestant groups in the early modern period. Pietism is defined as the trends in folk mysticism in seventeenth-century Christianity "emphasiz[ing] the practice of the Christian life" and a general rejection of the mainstream, high ecclesial life seen in organized Catholic and Protestant churches. In this essay, the term "pietist" includes German-Americans of two groups and time periods: the Anabaptists (Amish and Mennonites), who retain elements of pietism even into the present day, and the pre-1850s Lutheran and Reformed German-Americans, whose pietist elements waned during the early-nineteenth century. See Jonathan Strom, ed., *Pietism and Community in Europe and North America, 1650–1850* (Boston: Brill Publishers, 2010), 2.
3 Broadsides, or *Einblattdrucke*, *Flugblätter*, or *Flugschriften*, are "a sheet that is printed on a single sheet on either one or both sides irrespective of its contents." A broadside might contain advertisements, political news, funeral notices, medical advice, hymns, or devotionals. See Herman Wellenreuther, *Citizens in a Strange Land: A Study of German-American Broadsides and Their Meaning for Germans in North America, 1730–1830* (University Park, PA: Pennsylvania State University Press, 2013), 3.

Unlike most owners, Hanna did not simply read her broadside. Rather, she copied the entire labyrinth into manuscript form, replicating every twist and turn and even including the printer's imprint at the bottom (see Figure 1). Hanna's only original contribution was her own imprint, reading: "Composed by Hanna Ye[akel] Schultz, Herfort Township, Berks County. 1833."[4] While writing and illuminating devotional manuscripts were typical elements of Schwenkfelder education intended to develop ties between piety of the hands and heart, Hanna's labyrinth is a rare example of user engagement with these religious texts, combining skills in handwriting with the careful composition of the labyrinth's passages without overlapping the winding lines.[5] Hanna's manuscript highlights the complex, unexpected ways in which owners used these interactive objects within the German-American domestic devotional sphere.[6]

Following Hanna's example, this essay traces the spread of the Spiritual Labyrinth genre throughout North America and examines the physical conditions of ninety-two broadsides to show that these objects reveal two understudied elements of early German-American devotional and visual culture. These are the role of haptic, or tactile, texts in the home and of intertextual reading practices. Unlike other religious broadsides which were often colored and displayed, the Spiritual Labyrinths could not function as prescribed by printers if nailed to a wall or framed as part of a mantle or furniture. Such treatments immobilized the Labyrinths and rendered them unable to be read or performed. By examining these ninety-two broadsides as physical artifacts, this essay shows that early owners did not typically display the Spiritual Labyrinths. Rather, patterns in folding, re-sizing, and paper aging reveal that most were kept within Bibles, from which they could be removed, handled, and read alongside the Bibles from which they were pulled. After focusing on storage and use, this essay then connects the evidenced haptic and cross-textual natures of these broadsides to similar German-American text-objects like the "Perplexing and Winding Way" (*Irr-und Abwegen*)

---

4 "Gedruckt und zu haben bei Gräter und Blumer, Allentaun, Penns. & Vortgsetzt von Hanna YE Schultz. Herfort Taunship, Berks Caunty. 1833. [sic]" *Geistlicher Irrgarten, mit vier Gnadenbrunnen*, 1833 (Hereford, PA), Schwenkfelder Library and Heritage Center, fraktur collection, uncatalogued. See Trevor Brandt, "Perplexion and Pleasure: The *Geistlicher Irrgarten* Broadsides in the German-American Printshop, Home, and Mind," unpublished master's thesis, University of Delaware, 232.
5 Peter C. Erb and W. Kyrel Meschter, "Schwenkfelders and the Preservation of Tradition," in *Schwenkfelders in America*, ed. Peter C. Erb (Pennsburg, PA: the Schwenkfelder Library, 1987), 190.
6 Other manuscript copies include an 1850 text by a sister of Snow Hill, a German Protestant monastery in rural Pennsylvania. This manuscript was sold in 1997 by Horst Auctioneers, lot 367. A circa 1800 example is preserved at the Free Library of Philadelphia, frk00158. The skill needed to create these is highlighted by frk00124, in which the creator appears to have given up after incorrectly crossing two lines.

Printed Pilgrimage: *Spiritual Labyrinths* in the German-American Home —— 159

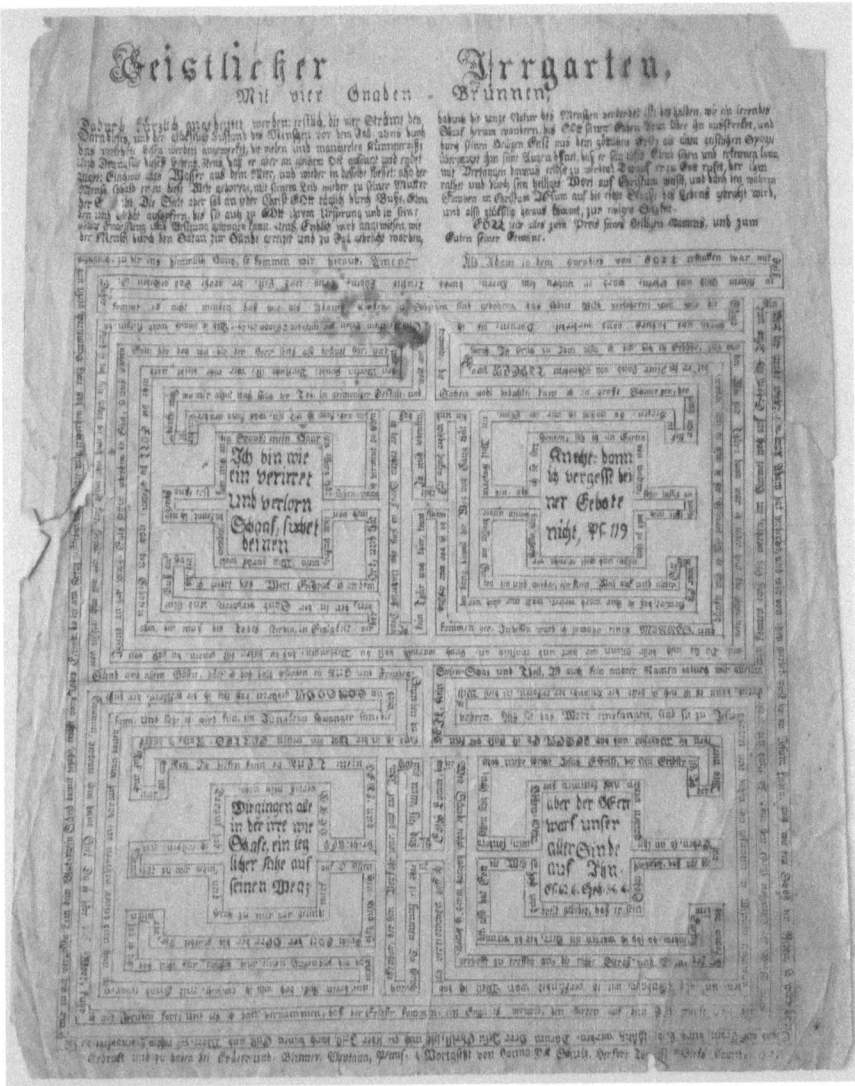

Figure 1: Hanna Schultz's manuscript Labyrinth replicates a broadside printed in 1832 in nearby Allentown. The top panel introduces its purpose in teaching spiritual lessons through the wandering passages. Beginning with "Als Adam in dem Paradies vom GOTT erschaffen war," the text brings the reader through hundreds of turns. At four points, the text passes through the "Springs of Grace." Depending on the edition, these springs –modeled on picnic areas within baroque hedge mazes – included verses, biblical citations corresponding to points in the text, or woodcut images. Courtesy of the Schwenkfelder Heritage Center and Library, fraktur collection, uncatalogued (See Brandt, "Perplexion and Pleasure," 232).

broadsides and the "Pious Lottery or Little Spiritual Treasure Box" (*Der Frommen Lotterie, oder Geistlicher Schatzkästleinen*). These visually confounding texts reveal the role of such objects within the literary, visual, and devotional cultures of German speakers in North America.

German-American broadsides have received considerable attention in recent years due to their value in revealing the political, religious, economic, and social conditions of printers and purchasers, yet many scholars have not recognized their more diverse roles in the household.[7] Informational broadsides such as election calls, funeral notices, and sales advertisements have often been studied at the expense of those perceived as trivial such as broadsides for play, performance, prayer, folk remedies, and even paper clothing. In this same vein, scholars have not typically viewed the Spiritual Labyrinths as serious tools for religious education. While Hermann Wellenreuther speculates on their significance for "meditation and contemplation by the whole family," Don Yoder and Christopher Dolmetsch note their role as "a kind of religious game, where the player enjoyed following the text around and around the sheet," concluding that the objects were novelties, not serious religious tools.[8] Russell and Corinne Earnest focus on the genre's meanings for producers, suggesting that these technically complicated objects allowed printers "to demonstrate their skills [in setting type] and attract[ing] customers."[9] Their research shows the value of examining these labyrinths as physical objects through the lens of material culture, focusing on the technical difficulty of production and their value to printers as evidence of their abilities in typesetting. Rather than viewing these broadsides as primarily literary texts – which is problematic as analysis of the static prayer text suggests immutability both geographically and temporally – the Earnests underline these objects' varying meanings for makers and users.

Scholars of visual culture have come closer to recognizing these objects' complex roles within the household and their ties to interactive Protestant visual culture. David Morgan situates the Spiritual Labyrinths within early Protestant performative and tactile visual culture, underlining their value not as passive texts but rather as objects requiring physical manipulation to be

---

[7] Scholars such as David Luthy, Don Yoder, Hermann Wellenreuther, Russell and Corinne Earnest, and Pat Stuter have advanced scholarship of this topic. See Luthy, David. "Our Amish Devotional Heritage" (Aylmer, ON: Pathway Publishers, 2016); Yoder, Don. *The Pennsylvania German Broadside: A History and Guide*. University Park, PA: The Pennsylvania State University Press, 2005; and Wellenreuther, *Citizens in a Strange Land*, 2013.

[8] Wellenreuther, *Citizens in a Strange Land*, 178; Yoder, *The Pennsylvania German Broadside*, 182.

[9] Russell and Corinne Earnest, *Flying Leaves and One-Sheets: Pennsylvania German Broadsides, Fraktur and Their Printers* (New Castle, DE: Oak Knoll Books, 2005), 280.

read. Morgan connects these interactive labyrinths to a wider Protestant movement in the seventeenth century towards hand-focused piety and multi-sensory prayer.[10] Morgan's focus on these labyrinths as more than novelties and rather as part of a shift in Protestant practiced piety contextualizes them among similarly interactive texts within both German and English Protestant traditions. Likewise, Bret Rothstein's work on puzzles and visually confounding objects provides a framework for situating the Spiritual Labyrinths within conversations about ties between visual difficulty, play, and religious education in the early modern period.[11] Puzzles, labyrinths, and mazes are difficult in their "intertwining of vision with other sense data, especially hearing and touch," heightening the role of the non-visual in solving them. Pleasure, Rothstein notes, is increased by the delay in the satisfaction of solving the puzzle, and the more difficult the puzzle, the greater the eventual pleasure.[12] Similarly, the Spiritual Labyrinths defy users' expectations regarding the primarily visual engagement with a textual object, instead requiring physical manipulation, verbalization, and concentration in ways not necessary when reading a codex or informational broadside. Rothstein also notes early modern connections between difficult play and spiritual education in children.[13] As examined later in this study, the Spiritual Labyrinths were overwhelmingly used by young girls and purchased for them by family members. Rothstein's work draws attention to underlying elements of gendered play and spiritual education in usage of these puzzle-like, visually difficult broadsides.

Research on interactive printmaking by Suzanne Karr Schmidt situates the Spiritual Labyrinths in a nexus of pre-Reformation, multi-sensory paper objects including those intended for consumption (*Schluckbildchen*), visual difficulty (printed triptychs of St. Bridget), or physical movement (rotating paper dials to reveal edifying passages).[14] Karr Schmidt connects these widely available, interactive prints with emerging popular desires in the Renaissance and early modern period for immediate and intimate access to religious experiences formerly controlled by

---

10 David Morgan, *The Embodied Eye: Religious Visual Culture and the Social Life of Feeling* (Berkeley / Los Angeles: University of California Press, 2012), 163.
11 Bret Rothstein, "Visual Difficulty as a Cultural System," *Res: Anthropology and Aesthetics* 65–66 (2014/2015), 332–347; and Bret Rothstein, "Early Modern Play: Three Perspectives," *Renaissance Quarterly* 71 (2018), 1036–1046.
12 Rothstein, "Visual Difficulty as a Cultural System," 333.
13 Rothstein, "Early Modern Play: Three Perspectives," 1043.
14 Suzanne Karr Schmidt, *Interactive and Sculptural Printmaking in the Renaissance* (Leiden: Brill, 2017), 66, 82, 88.

clergy. Karr Schmidt's study also recommends a methodology in examining the physical conditions of paper objects as valuable witnesses to their own histories, emphasizing the role of material analysis in determining patterns of use.[15] This essay expands on Karr Schmidt's work by tracing the relocation of one such interactive genre to America, where it flourished in pietist German-American households into the twentieth century, long after having atrophied in Europe.

This essay identifies editions of the Spiritual Labyrinth broadsides printed in Europe that inspired early American examples, a transatlantic influence not previously recognized by scholars.[16] The earliest-identified Spiritual Labyrinth was printed in 1607 in Stuttgart, though its imprint notes the design's origins in Nuremberg.[17] The genre's appearance in Nuremberg, an epicenter of German publishing in the sixteenth and seventeenth centuries, shows that it emerged at the confluence of the popularity of garden labyrinths, advances in printing technology, and developments in spiritually introspective literature. By the late Renaissance, labyrinths had already functioned for centuries as allegories of pilgrimage in European cathedrals. The sixteenth century witnessed a secular appropriation of these ancient religious constructs – court hedge mazes.[18] With the guidance of texts such as Thomas Hill's *The Gardener's Labyrinth* (1577) or Johann Peschel's *Garten-Ordnung* (1597), architects and dabbling nobles designed mazes for their manors, showcased at palaces such as Versailles, Hampton Court, and Schönbrunn, among others.[19] While such gardens amused the nobility, these constructs also retained subtle religious and educational connotations. Architect Joseph Furttenbach the Elder (1591–1667) notes their value in "rous[ing] good thoughts in the children of walking in Paradise, to practice their Christianity as well as other good, useful, and worthy activities."[20] Notable is the connection between the physical movement of walking through a garden and spiritual contemplation, themes increasingly evident in Protestant visual imagery and print culture throughout the sixteenth century.

Advances in printing technology in the sixteenth century allowed Counter-Reformation authors to develop novel ways of interacting with religious texts.

---

15 Schmidt, *Interactive and Sculptural Printmaking*, 85.
16 Both Yoder and Wellenreuther assume the genre's origins in North America. Yoder, *The Pennsylvania German Broadside*, 182; Wellenreuther, *Citizens in a Strange Land*, 177.
17 *Der Christlich Irrgarten* (1607), composed by Conrad Baur, Nuremberg; printed by Gebhardt Grieb, Stuttgart, Bavarian State Archives, Einblatt XI722.
18 Rubén Wengiel, "Europe's Mazes: On Labyrinthine Thought in Architectural Design," paper presented at the European Forum at the Hebrew University, Jerusalem, 2008.
19 Gailand MacQueen, *The Spirituality of Mazes and Labyrinths* (Kelowna, BC: Wood Lake Publishing Inc., 2005), 48.
20 Joseph Furttenbach the Elder, *Architectura Civilis* (Ulm: Saur, 1628), 30.

Broadsides themselves emerged in the early sixteenth century, enabling the spread of Protestant propaganda and new types of prints that "insisted on an actively personal, tactile, and autodidactive viewership," launching the visual culture of Europe's middle class into a new, interactive phase with printed religious literature.[21] Within this technologically and visually innovative atmosphere, spiritual writers of the Counter-Reformation redirected popular garden and labyrinth imagery to Christian themes of spiritual wandering and pilgrimage. Drawing upon the affective, deeply introspective prayers of Ignatius of Loyola, early Jesuit authors were particularly influential in envisioning Christian worldviews as a labyrinth. Authors such as Georg Stengel (1585–1651), Athanasius Kircher (1602–1680), and Herman Hugo (1588–1629) were fascinated by labyrinths and used them to represent themes of pilgrimage and spiritual disorientation in a tumultuous world.[22] While Jesuit literature moved to focus on Sacred Heart imagery by the late seventeenth century, Protestant spiritual writers had already rushed to develop their own garden-focused literature. Protestant authors such as Johann Arndt (1555–1621), Philipp Jakob Spener (1635–1705), and later Gerhard Tersteegen (1697–1769) were particularly influential in aligning Protestant visual imagery with gardens, labyrinths, and spiritual pilgrimage.[23] For Protestant authors, such imagery came to be "a metaphor for the devotional setting [. . .] as the beloved came to his spouse in the garden, so Christ came to the devout soul in meditation and prayer."[24] These mystical themes became ever more popular with mass printing and distribution networks "enabl[ing] Protestants to flood the market with broadsides, pamphlets, and books [. . .]"[25] It is likely that the Spiritual Labyrinths evolved in this atmosphere, spurred by its novel form of interaction with scripture and reappropriated, popular garden imagery.

The genre appealed to printers and readers throughout Europe and, soon, North America. Editions appeared in Switzerland, France, Holland, and, most commonly,

---

21 Schmidt, *Interactive and Sculptural Printmaking*, 1.
22 Georg Stengel, *Aegyptischer Labyrinth, Oder Geistlicher Irr-Garten der betrieglichen Welt* (Dillingen: Akademische Druckerey, 1629); Athanasius Kircher, *Turris Babel, Sive Archontologia* (Amsterdam, 1679); Herman Hugo, *Pia desideria emblematis elegiis at affectibus* (Antwerp, 1624).
23 David Morgan, *The Forge of Vision: A Visual History of Modern Christianity* (Oakland, CA: University of California Press, 2015), 140.
24 Charles E. Hambrick-Stowe, *The Practice of Piety* (Chapel Hill, NC: University of North Carolina Press, 1982), 28.
25 A. Gregg Roeber, "German and Dutch Books and Printing," in Hugh Amory and David D. Hall, eds., *A History of the Book in America, vol. 1*, (Chapel Hill, NC: University of North Carolina Press, 2010), 300.

the Holy Roman Empire into the early nineteenth century.[26] The Spiritual Labyrinths were especially popular among Swiss-German Anabaptists, a trend continuing in North America and evidenced by several members of these groups carrying the broadsides to the New World.[27] Philadelphia-based printer Henrich Miller (1702–1782) printed the first North American Spiritual Labyrinths in 1762.[28] Miller, better trained and more widely traveled than local competitors, was likely exposed to the genre during his apprenticeship in Switzerland as he modeled his own edition on a broadside printed in Basel.[29] Miller emphasized the genre's uniqueness in North America through a colorful announcement within his newspaper, reading: "([the text] amazingly passes around and through itself!)" and that it was "a quite extraordinary piece" and "quite uplifting!"[30] Through an extended description – twenty-eight lines of valuable advertising space – Miller does not assume that readers are familiar with the interactive genre, suggesting that his edition marked its first appearance in the epicenter of German-speaking North America.

Miller's Spiritual Labyrinths were soon eclipsed by three editions created by the talented printers of the Ephrata Cloister, a semi-monastic Protestant community in the German-speaking hinterland near Lancaster and tied to Philadelphia by commerce and religious interaction.[31] Ephrata's broadsides are

---

26 The Swiss example, by Albrecht Wagner in 1758, is preserved at the Zurich Zentralbibliothek. See *Le Moniteur Judiciaire de Lyon*, 11 October 1769 for a detailed advertisement on the lost L. Buisson French Labyrinth. This French edition was modeled on Wagner's 1758 broadside. A 1705 Dutch edition is in the collection of the Rijksmuseum, RP-P-OB-76.978. The last-identified European Labyrinth was printed by Michael Weiß in Sargemünde and is preserved at the Goshen College Library in Indiana, TBMA 7.1.

27 This influence is evidenced by a broadside printed in 1771 attributed to the von Mechel print-shop in Basel and carried to North America in the bible of a Swiss-Mennonite immigrant. *Geistlicher Irrgarten, Mit vier Gnadenbrunnen*, 1771 (Basel), Mennonite Historical Library at Goshen College, Indiana, TBMA 6.1.

28 *Geistlicher Irrgarten, mit vier Gnadenbrunnen*, 1762 (Philadelphia), Historical Society of Pennsylvania, Ab [1762]-9.

29 See A. Gregg Roeber, *Palatines, Liberty, and Property: German Lutherans in Colonial British America* (Baltimore, MD: Johns Hopkins University Press, 1993), 202, for an account of Miller's life and influence. *Geistlicher Irrgarten, Mit vier Gnadenbrunnen*, 1771 (Basel), Mennonite Historical Library at Goshen College, Indiana, TBMA 6.1.

30 "Durch das verkehrte Lesen (weil es wunderlich durch einander gehet) wird angemerkt die viel und mancherley Kummernussen und Drangsalen dieses Lebens [. . .] Es ist in alten wohlgemeinten Reimen geschrieben, sehr erbaulich, auf einen ganzen Bogen gedruckt, und gewiß ein seltenes Stück." Henrich Miller, "Bey dem Verleger dieser Zeitung ist ganz neulich heraus gekommen . . . " *Der Wöchentliche pennsylvanische Staatsbote*, 18 January 1762. Volume 1, issue 1, page 4, col. 2.

31 The Ephrata Cloister, founded in 1732 and atrophying in the 1790s, was a Protestant Sabbatarian community of eclectic, mystical practices. Ephrata's printshop existed between

remarkable for their highly sophisticated decorations, their number of editions and surviving copies, and, most significantly, their evident popularity among a wide swath of German-American Protestants at the end of the eighteenth century. That Ephrata produced three distinct editions in such a short period suggests that each run sold out, attesting to the genre's popularity within the community's diverse market. Ephrata's printers modeled their 1784 and 1785 editions on Miller's broadside (see Figure 2), and all identified copies from these years were also decorated by the itinerant artist Henrich Otto (fl. 1762–1797), suggesting his influence on the creation and distribution of these editions. Ephrata's printers developed a third, unique edition differing in layout, typesetting, and decoration in 1788, likely through the influence of another itinerant artist, Friedrich Krebs (1749–1815).[32] Provenance and inscriptions on surviving broadsides suggest that peddlers in southeastern Pennsylvania continued to sell Ephrata's labyrinths into the early nineteenth century, attesting to their continued popularity.[33]

The Ephrata Cloister's three editions also allow one to trace the genre's spread across the German-American diaspora and its relative popularity among both church Protestants – i.e., Lutherans and Reformed – and *Sektenleute* – the sect Protestants such as the Anabaptists (Amish and Mennonites) and Schwenkfelders. Tracing the Spiritual Labyrinths across these groups reveals their overwhelming popularity among sect Protestants, especially the Amish and Mennonites. These groups, even as they traveled from Pennsylvania to Canada and the American Midwest in the early nineteenth century, were known to back Ephrata's broadsides onto linen for durability and to carry them along on the journey.[34] The Cloister's three editions also served as models for Mennonite printers from the mid-nineteenth century through the late twentieth century as evidenced by the repetition of compositional

---

1745 and c. 1792. See Jeff Bach, *Voices of the Turtle Doves: The Sacred World of Ephrata* (University Park, PA: Pennsylvania State University Press, 2003).

32 *Geistlicher Irrgarten, mit vier Gnadenbrunnen*, 1788 (Ephrata, PA), the Winterthur Museum, Garden & Library, Winterthur, DE, museum collection 1957.1215.

33 One of Ephrata's broadsides features an inscription on the verso: "Elizabeth Karch / Lebanon [County] / 1826." *Geistlicher Irrgarten, mit vier Gnadenbrunnen*, 1788 (Ephrata, PA), Franklin and Marshall College Library broadside collection, D31. Another broadside was purchased c. 1825, *Geistlicher Irrgarten, mit vier Gnadenbrunnen*, 1784 (Ephrata, PA), the Conrad Grebel University College Library, hist. mss. 23.14.

34 One of Ephrata's 1784 broadsides, backed onto linen, was carried by young Anna Weber from Lancaster, PA to Ontario in 1825. *Geistlicher Irrgarten, mit vier Gnadenbrunnen*, 1784 (Ephrata, PA), the Conrad Grebel University College Library, hist. mss. 23.14.

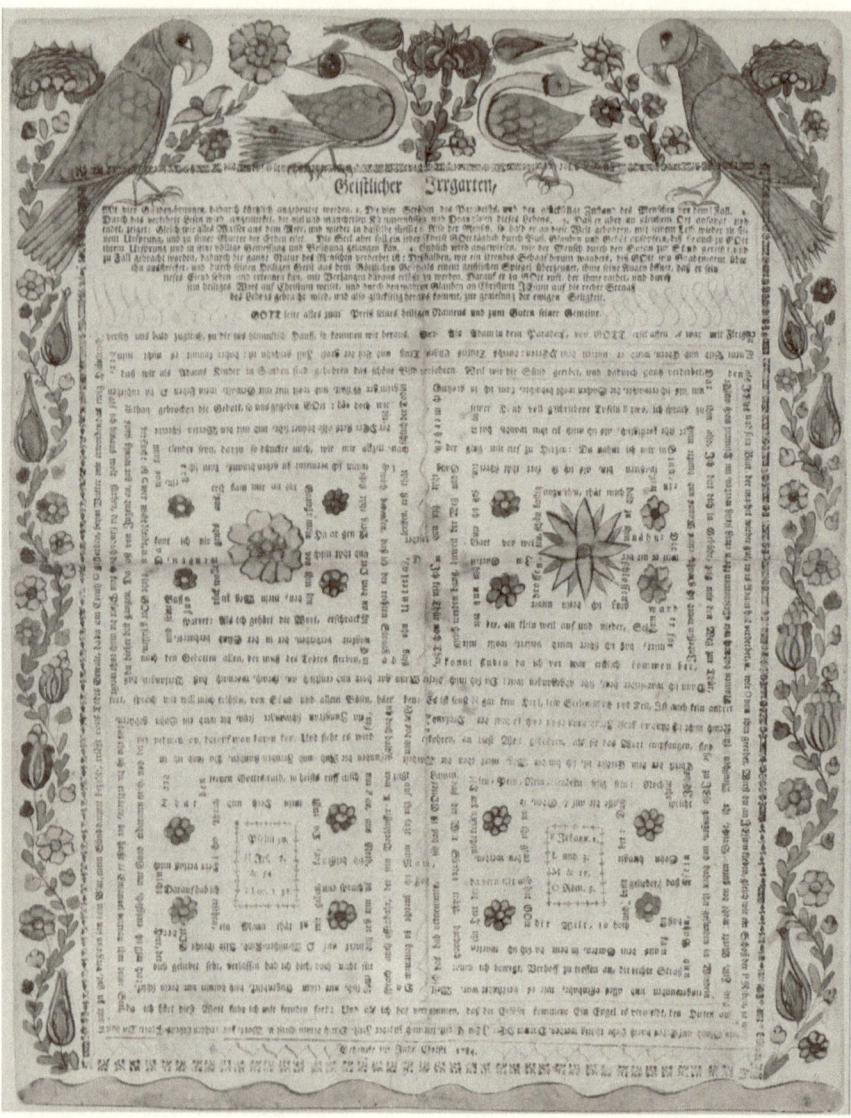

Figure 2: This 1784 Spiritual Labyrinth was the first of Ephrata's three editions. The illuminated parrots and floral borders attribute the edition to scrivener Henrich Otto. Such colorful examples highlight the genre's dual nature – they could be either displayed or didactic. This broadside, on display at the Winterthur Museum, Garden & Library, has evidence of early display (pinholes in the four corners) and storage within a book (stains are mirrored across folded areas). Courtesy of the Winterthur Museum, Garden & Library, 1958.0120.013.

errors and decorative motifs.[35] The genre's popularity among Anabaptists is also evidenced through the longevity of related spiritual garden imagery among these groups. Scholar of Mennonite visual culture, Nancy Patterson, even associates physical Anabaptist gardens with such motifs, noting that "the four-square garden [. . .] was a specific image of the *Paradiesgärtlein*: it reminded the family of the pre-lapsarian Garden of Eden with its four rivers (now paths) and was always placed close to the house where it could be contemplated with pleasure and edification."[36] Such visual imagery, of course, abounded within the Spiritual Labyrinths, themselves representative of a four-square garden used for pleasure and spiritual edification.

German-American printers had more limited success in selling the Spiritual Labyrinths to Lutherans and the Reformed. One such printer was Ambrose Henkel of New Market, Virginia, active in the early nineteenth century. While the large surviving quantities of Henkel's Spiritual Labyrinths suggest his edition's popularity among the Shenandoah Valley's spiritually diverse population, only one broadside is provenanced to a Lutheran purchaser.[37] Wellenreuther notes that devotional broadsides such as the Spiritual Labyrinths found more popularity with church Protestants in rural areas lacking qualified pastors, which is consistent with the genre's appearances on the fringes of German settlement in North America.[38] With the decline of pietism among German-American church Protestants in the early nineteenth century resulting from a rise in organized church life and the wane of German language use in churches, the Spiritual Labyrinths atrophied among Lutherans and the Reformed.[39]

---

35 Mennonite editions inspired by Ephrata include those printed in Elkhart, Indiana; Teeswater and Conestoga, Ontario; Baltic, Ohio; and Gordonville, Pennsylvania. See Brandt, "Perplexion and Pleasure," 154, 168, 171, 173, and 178.
36 Nancy-Lou Patterson, "Imagery of Paradise in Swiss-German Mennonite Folk Art," unpublished paper notes and draft, 1979, the Mennonite Archives of Ontario, hist.mss. 1.197, p. 190.
37 Karr Schmidt estimates that in the sixteenth century, at least 1,000 woodcut images were printed for each surviving example today. Unfortunately, estimates for survivals from the eighteenth and nineteenth centuries do not exist. Karr Schmidt, *Interactive and Sculptural Printmaking*, 2. See also Christopher Dolmetsch, *The German Press of the Shenandoah Valley* (Columbia, SC: Camden House, 1984), 28. This broadside is preserved in the Virginia Historical Society, accession number 1997.71.
38 Wellenreuther, *Citizens in a Strange Land*, 150.
39 A. Gregg Roeber, "Readers and Writers of German," in *A History of the Book in America*, vol. 2, *An Extensive Republic: Print, Culture, and Society in the New Nation, 1790–1840*, ed. Robert Gross and Mary Kelley (Chapel Hill, NC: University of North Carolina Press, 2010), 475.

Throughout their long history in North America, the Spiritual Labyrinths maintained complex and diverse meanings for printers, purchasers, and users. As noted by Russell and Corinne Earnest and in research by the present author, printers often produced the genre to highlight their typesetting abilities and to showcase expensive, newly purchased shipments of letterpress type.[40] The relative obscurity of German-American household devotional life makes user engagement with these objects more difficult to understand, however. This survey has examined ninety-two Spiritual Labyrinths to show the genre's meanings within the household, as revealed by material evidence for display and storage patterns. These examinations reveal that while some labyrinths were displayed as aesthetic pieces like colorful Fraktur manuscripts or other ornamented devotional broadsides, most were stored within Bibles for extended periods and not displayed by early users. Like the glass invertibrate models analyzed by J. P. Short – both scientific models and aesthetic objects – the Spiritual Labyrinths possess evidence of considerable complexity of usage throughout time, especially while these broadsides passed through a family of users.[41]

Scholars have taken for granted that users physically acted out the Spiritual Labyrinths by picking up, turning, and reading them, but such treatment is difficult to prove directly in either the material or written record. No account describes readers performing the labyrinth's prayer and even printers were likely to advertise them as "neatly printed" or "very artfully composed and beautifully printed," highlighting aesthetic more than devotional appeal.[42] Despite such advertisements, a general lack of evidence regarding display in the surveyed broadsides such as punctures from nails, discoloration left by wooden frames, or flyspecking suggests that most users did not display their broadsides. Among the ninety-two surveyed broadsides, only eight possess pin or nail punctures.[43] Of these eight, five also possess flyspecking, suggesting

---

40 Earnest, *Flying Leaves and One-Sheets*, 280; Brandt, "Perplexion and Pleasure," 31–35.

41 See J. P. Short's chapter, "Arc of the Anemone: Modeling Nature from the *Wunderkammer* to the *Warenwelt*," in the present volume.

42 Enos Benner, "Geistlicher Irrgarten," *Der Bauernfreund*, Sumneytown, Pennsylvania, 15 August 1832; Johann Ritter, "Geistlicher Irrgarten," *Der Readinger Adler*, Reading, Pennsylvania, 19 November 1811.

43 These include uncatalogued broadsides in the Aylmer Heritage Library (see Brandt, "Perplexion and Pleasure," 55); *Geistlicher Irrgarten, mit vier Gnadenbrunnen*, c. 1830 (Harrisburg, PA), the Russell and Corinne Earnest Collection, BS #618; *Geistlicher Irrgarten, mit vier Gnadenbrunnen*, 1785 (Ephrata, PA), the Russell and Corinne Earnest Collection, BS #784; *Geistlicher Irrgarten, mit vier Gnadenbrunnen*, c. 1870 (Elkhart, IN), the Franklin and Marshall Library, D114; *Geistlicher Irrgarten, mit vier Gnadenbrunnen*, 1811 (Reading, PA), the Schwenkfelder Library and Heritage Center, uncatalogued (see Brandt, "Perplexion and Pleasure," 194);

that these objects were displayed in common areas of the household for extended periods.[44] Among the three without flyspecking, one was acquired by a collector in the twentieth century from the bedroom of an Amish woman, perhaps a closed space relatively free from pests and potentially explaining its unexpected lack of discoloration.[45]

Framing and backing the Spiritual Labyrinths for display were also uncommon treatments. While illuminated or well-preserved broadsides tend to be framed today, these frames are typically modern additions and not necessarily indicative of treatment during their earlier history. Only six broadsides in this survey possess physical markers of non-modern framing, evidenced by the discoloration resulting from contact with acidic wood or the remnants of pasteboard backing. Despite this evidence of user backing, it is still difficult to determine whether such treatment was contemporaneous with the original purchase. For example, one nineteenth-century broadside is mounted onto an early twentieth century advertisement, suggesting its changing role as an object only later backed and intended for display.[46] Christa Pieska notes that framed and mounted German-American broadsides remained unusual until the 1860s, suggesting that owners in the late nineteenth and twentieth centuries displayed earlier broadsides long after they were created, highlighting their changing roles over time as they passed through a family of users.[47]

While evidence for early user display remains scarce, patterns in folding, paper aging, and staining reveal that owners typically stored the Spiritual Labyrinths in ways that preserved their ability to be picked up, rotated, and read. As mentioned above this storage was often in Bibles. At the end of the

---

Geistlicher Irrgarten, mit vier Gnadenbrunnen, 1784 (Ephrata, PA), the Winterthur Museum, Garden and Library, 1958.120.13.

44 While flyspecking, or the dark stains left by pests, has never been used in material cultural research, it has potential in determining treatment patterns in a paper object's life. An examination by this author of forty-eight German-language almanacs in the Winterthur Library suggests its value. Thirty-eight almanacs have a string tied through a puncture in the upper-left corner, used to hang the almanacs from nails. 90% of almanacs with strings are also flyspecked, suggesting that they were indeed kept exposed on walls. Of the ten calendars without a string, only two possess flyspecking, suggesting that they were kept in less exposed locations such as drawers or desks. See Brandt, "Perplexion and Pleasure," 54.

45 *Geistlicher Irrgarten, mit vier Gnadenbrunnen*, c. 1875 (Berlin, ON), Joseph Schneider Haus Museum, Kitchener, Ontario, 1984.028.347. See Brandt, "Perplexion and Pleasure," 137.

46 *Geistlicher Irrgarten, mit vier Gnadenbrunnen*, c. 1869–1874 (Elkhart, IN), Aylmer Heritage Historical Library, Ontario, GI 2.

47 Christa Pieske, "The European Origins of Four Pennsylvania German Broadside Themes," *Der Reggeboge* 23:1 (1989), 8.

eighteenth century, family Bibles tended to be quarto sized, or about twelve inches tall by nine inches wide.[48] As even the smallest Spiritual Labyrinths measured at least twelve inches wide, folding two or more times was necessary for readers to tip – or to fold and insert – these broadsides within common quarto Bibles. Among the ninety-two surveyed Spiritual Labyrinths, fifty were folded between two and six times, or enough to insert them fully into the quarto Bibles of the early nineteenth century. While an act as anonymous and pervasive as folding does not necessarily reveal early treatment patterns, thirty-one of the fifty folded Spiritual Labyrinths, or a third of the total survey, also exhibit mirrored foxing across folds (see Figure 3). Mirrored foxing, or the "stains, specks, spots, and blotches in paper" from chemical processes associated with paper aging, appear on broadsides within this survey as having been transferred across folded sections.[49] These stains suggest that the folded broadside remained within a location exerting pressure over years, causing the fox-marks to transfer across neighboring folded sections. Such conditions are consistent with tipping inside of large-format books such as Bibles.

The Spiritual Labyrinths' predominant storage within Bibles reveals two features of their use within the pietist German-American household – that they were not displayed, but rather stored so that they could be read in a multi-sensory, performative prayer and that they were evidently used alongside scripture in cross-textual reading. Regarding the former, this genre's use in performed prayer highlights an understudied element of pietist German-American devotional life – the intertwining of the physical and visual, or the haptic and the optic, in meditative household prayer. While literature connecting touch and sight is large, scholars of German-American culture have yet to connect the two as remnants of seventeenth-century Protestant visual cultural and devotional development. Writing on this topic, Morgan draws upon Hegel to note that, "Protestantism has developed an aesthetic that operates on its own terms by sublating space, bodies, and visual imagery," or dethroning the primacy of vision and elevating other senses so that all are attended to and, to use the Hegelian term, synesthized in the user's mind. Morgan's observations suggest that such sublation is at work within the Spiritual Labyrinths, which encourage physical movement through the twisting passages, verbalization through the rhyming prayer, and visual engagement with the printed

---

[48] James N. Green, "The Rise of Book Publishing," in Hugh Amory and David Hall, eds., *A History of the Book in America*, vol. 2 *An Extensive Republic: Print, Culture, and Society in the New Nation, 1790–1840* (Cambridge, UK: The Cambridge University Press, 2000), 83.

[49] Matt T. Roberts and Don Etherington, *Bookbinding and the Conservation of Books: A Dictionary of Descriptive Terminology* (Washington, DC: The Library of Congress), 109.

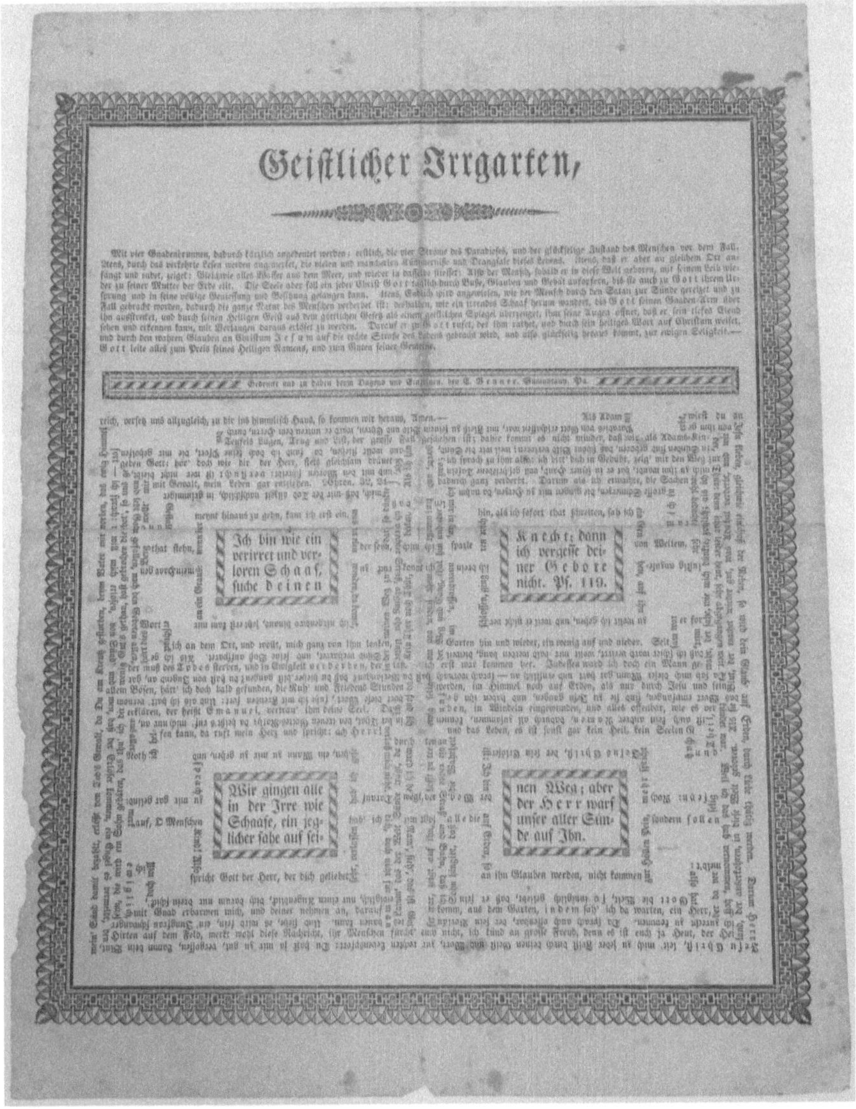

Figure 3: Mirrored stains reveal that in thirty-one surveyed broadsides, enough pressure was applied on the object to transfer discolorations across folded sections, a condition associated with tipping within books. Courtesy of the Franklin and Marshall College Library, D115.

text and often colored decorative embellishments.⁵⁰ In order to solve the labyrinth, readers were forced to allow the broadside to lead them along while working hand, eye, voice, and mind to solve it, emphasizing the devotional text's agency over users and subverting expectations about standard reading practices.

Alongside this synaesthetic prayer experience, the genre also encourages cross-textual engagement with scripture by intermittently ferrying readers between the Bible and broadside and back again. This reading system is most evident in Spiritual Labyrinths printed by the late eighteenth century which feature an intricate system of free-standing letters within the labyrinth that correspond to letters within one of the four "Springs of Grace." At these points, readers follow the letters to one of the four springs, thus interrupting the concentration needed to read the labyrinth. These springs contain both the corresponding letter and a matching biblical verse, encouraging readers to move to the Bible to find the proper passage. Such letter matching mimics Renaissance-era interactive dials which encouraged readers to spin a printed figure of Christ, whose fingers pointed to letters corresponding to edifying scriptural passages.⁵¹ Perhaps most fascinating is that both the printed dials and the Spiritual Labyrinths always begin and end with the most important letters in Christianity – alpha and omega, a designation for Christ in the Book of Revelation. Including these letters was important enough in the Spiritual Labyrinths to remove inconvenient, intervening letters such as "n."⁵² These wayfinding letters were printed in a Latin antiqua typeface and not in the Fraktur typeface of the surrounding labyrinth, which would have caused in the user a "momentary irritation of adjusting to a new typeface push[ing] the reader to switch from what we might call code-related reading (the interpretation of text) to one of context-related reading."⁵³ Editions that appeared by the mid-nineteenth century do not typically reproduce this intricate system, instead quoting Psalm 119 within the springs. Brown notes that this psalm is "perhaps the model for pious reading in Reformation culture" as it focuses on "comprehend[ing] texts as spatial objects."⁵⁴ While these later editions no longer moved readers between Bible and

---

50 Morgan, *The Embodied Eye*, 165.
51 Karr Schmidt, *Interactive and Sculptural Printmaking*, 95–96.
52 Karr Schmidt, *Interactive and Sculptural Printmaking*, 101.
53 The Multigraph Collective, *Interacting with Print: Elements of Reading in the Era of Print Saturation* (Chicago: The University of Chicago Press, 2018), 98.
54 Matthew Brown, *The Pilgrim and the Bee: Reading Rituals and Book Culture in Early New England* (Philadelphia: The University of Pennsylvania Press, 2007), 34.

broadside, inclusion of Psalm 119 does underline the role of these broadsides as a prop within Protestant devotional literary culture.

The Spiritual Labyrinth's role in encouraging intertextual reading between Bible and broadside also explains its predominant use by children, especially young girls. As nearly all provenanced Spiritual Labyrinths were owned by young girls, it is likely that reading the broadside was a devotional activity undertaken as part of gendered household religious education. Such usage is also suggested by a nineteenth-century edition printed on the same sheet as "The Golden ABC" (*Das Goldene ABC Für Jedermann, der gern mit Ehre wollt bestahn*) educational broadside.[55] While no direct evidence proves that these two were sold together, their connection does suggest that the printer assumed a similar market since this manner of printing would have yielded exactly equal numbers of both broadsides. And, while this essay focuses primarily on the use, not creation, of these broadside, Hanna Schultz's manuscript copy (Figure 1) here encourages further inquiry. Hanna's broadside has pinpoints piercing through the paper at the end of each finely delineated line, evidence that she used both a compass and a protractor or straight edge ruler while modeling her labyrinth. Such were the tools of adult male fraktur artists, regional masters who were often also schoolteachers.[56] Just as Catriona MacLeod's essay reassesses terminology surrounding "paper craft" such as *Scherenschnitte*, scholars of Pennsylvania-German folk art must similarly reexamine their understanding of the tools and training available to understudied young female artists and their "religious craft" vis à vis the works of renowned male fraktur artists who might very well have been their schoolteachers.[57] Regardless of whether the young girls were reading or composing the Spiritual Labyrinths, the activity was motivated by belief and religious education. As, for pietist German-American Protestants, the "home is a matrix in which people are first and most enduringly formed as members of a religious community," these broadsides became popular for children and parents in developing proper understanding of the Bible and piety.[58]

While unique in form, the Spiritual Labyrinth was one of several similar multisensory, intertextual objects among German-Americans, suggesting its role

---

55 *Geistlicher Irrgarten, mit vier Gnadenbrunnen / Das Goldene ABC Für Jedermann, der gern mit Ehre wollt bestahn*, c. 1870 (publisher and location unknown, likely Indiana), Mennonite Historical Library at Goshen College, Indiana, TBMA 9.1.1.
56 Dennis K. Moyer, Fraktur Writings and Folk Art Drawings of the Schwenkfelder Library Collection (Kutztown, PA: The Pennsylvania German Society, 1997), 247.
57 See Catriona MacLeod's chapter, "Cut-Ups on the Edges of the Photographic Century," in the present volume.
58 Morgan, *The Forge of Vision*, 60.

within early German-American visual and devotional culture. Notable broadsides include the Winding Way (*Irr- und Abwegen*) broadsides printed in 1819 and 1820 by Joseph Bauman (1789–1862) (see Figure 4). As inheritor of Ephrata's printing press, Bauman's family continued production of the Cloister's mystical theology into the mid-nineteenth century, long after the community's dissolution.[59] As part of this tradition, the Winding Way broadsides incorporate nonlinear text in forming an image of earth, heaven, and a maelstrom in between representing the perils of an un-Christian (or, rather, an un-Ephratan) life. While the Spiritual Labyrinths draw upon the Bible as a companion text, the Winding Way broadsides instead reference the first chapters of *Mystical Theology*, a devotional text by an Ephratan theologian and reprinted by Bauman.[60]

Like readers of the Spiritual Labyrinths, owners of the Winding Way broadsides twisted and turned the page to read its paraphrased passages and cited page numbers alongside a book, in this case, *Mystical Theology*. While the Spiritual Labyrinths were ambiguously aesthetic items with the potential for display, the Winding Way broadsides are more overtly textual. This is evidenced by Bauman printing *Mystical Theology* with the broadside already folded into six sections (transforming the thirteen-by-fifteen-inch broadside into a three-by-four-inch one), small enough to fit within the diminutive (seven-by-four-inch) book.[61] Additionally, Bauman's second edition of the broadside notes that it is "also sold by the sheet," suggesting that most copies were sold as tip-ins, not as single pages.[62]

The *Pious Lottery, or Little Spiritual Treasure Box* (*Der Frommen Lotterie, oder Geistliches Schatzkästlein*), further underlines this complex household visual and devotional culture focused on multi-sensory prayer and engagement with codices. These lotteries, printed by North America's first German-language printer, Christoph Saur (1695–1758), consist of three hundred and eighty-one diminutive cards within a pasteboard box. Each card features passages and page numbers from either the Bible or Gerhard Tersteegen's *Spiritual Garden for Ardent Souls* (*Geistliches Blumengärtlein Inniger Seelen*), the title page of which

---

59 Russell and Corinne Earnest, *Flying Leaves and One-Sheets*, 280.
60 Ezekiel Sangmeister, *Mystische Theologie, oder Wahrer Wegweisser nach unserm Ursprung und Vaterland* (Ephrata, PA: Joseph Bauman, 1819/1820).
61 Franklin and Marshall College Library records that its copy of the Winding Way broadside, m87, was pulled from Bauman's text when catalogued. Two additional broadsides were actually sewn into one copy of *Mystical Theology* as its endpapers.
62 "Auch beym Bogen verkauft," *Ein kleiner Abriss von denen Irr-und Abwegen* (1819/1820), the Winterthur Museum, Garden & Library, DE, manuscript collection 742.

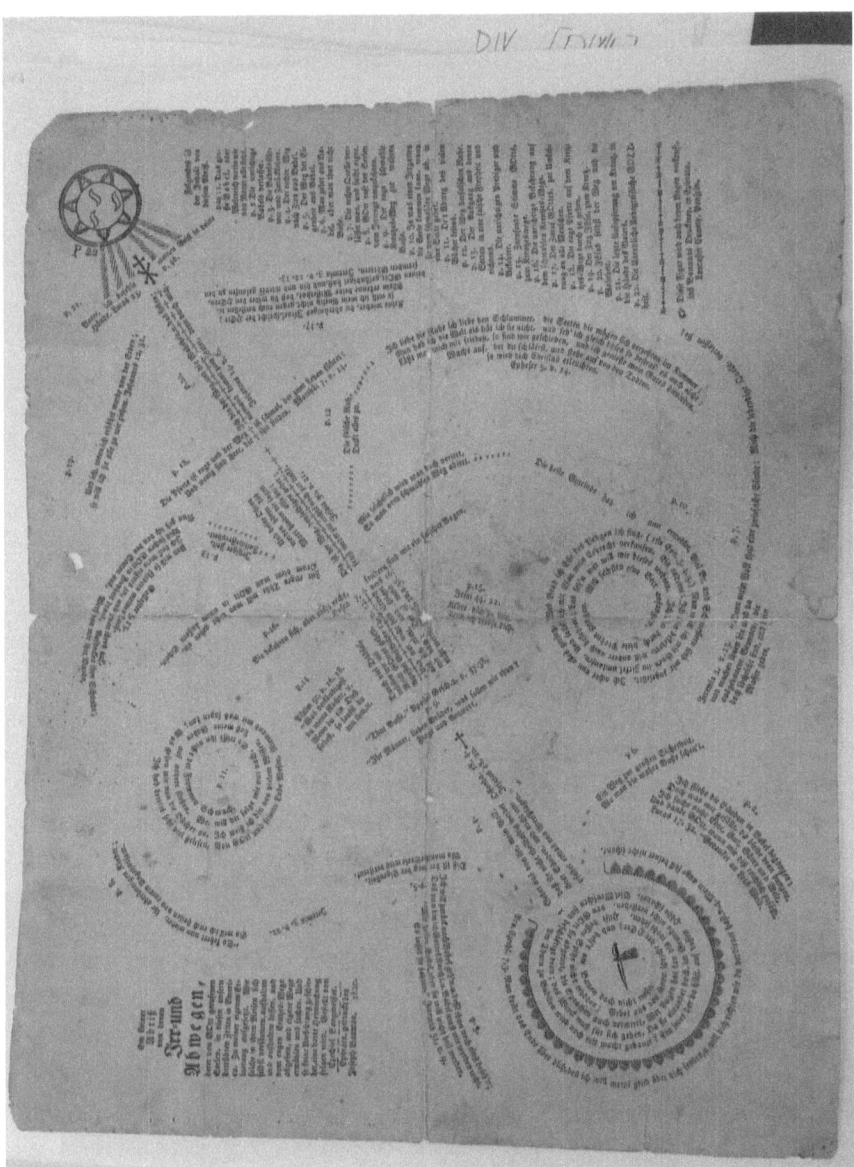

Figure 4: Joseph Bauman's Winding Way (*Irr- und Abwegen*) broadsides were sold either singly or already tipped into the book, *Mystical Theology*, which is referenced within the broadside. Like the Spiritual Labyrinths, they encouraged a performative, cross-referential system of reading as users moved between book and broadside to better comprehend their spiritual teachings. Courtesy of the Schwenkfelder Library and Heritage Center.

notes that it was sold "alongside the Pious Lottery."⁶³ These objects' use within meditative prayer is evident in the devotional practices of Henry Muhlenberg, patriarch of the Lutheran Church in North America. Muhlenberg reveals that he often drew cards out of a similar *Schatzkästlein* by Karl Heinrich von Bogatzky, especially when despondent. Expectant that at "any day or hour a British division will cross over the Schulkiel [sic] [River] to our home," the pastor found comfort in 1777 by "turn[ing] to the light and right of the evangelical covenant of grace; I mean the selected verses of the so-called *Schatzkästlein*, all of which are drawn from the fount of light [. . .]. I pour out my prayer in my chamber and then draw a verse as a reply."⁶⁴ Muhlenberg consults these cards dozens of times throughout his voluminous journals, citing his use of them as often alone but sometimes with family. These objects emphasize the tactile practice of handling the cards, selecting a random passage, and consulting one's copy of Tersteegen's book, heightening the role of the nonvisual and encouraging concentration upon the card and codex. Perhaps objects such as the Spiritual Labyrinths, Winding Way broadsides, and the Pious Lottery even invited divine influence on the devotional practice by destabilizing expectations about reading practices and relinquishing readers' agency to that of the visually-difficult, printed object.

These German-American multisensory, cross-textual objects invite comparisons with other early Protestant reading practices in America, suggesting areas for collaborative research as recommended by Patrick Erben.⁶⁵ The role of these broadsides as an intertextual prop among devotional texts is similar to that described in Brown's study of a three-leaf devotional text common among early New England Puritans which, "accentuates the tactile handling of the codex, its turning of leaves and indexical access [. . .] With its activities of the eye and the hand and its mixture of the linear and the discontinuous, the story of the three-leaf book illuminates the performative nature of literacy in early New England."⁶⁶ The role of this difficult text in sublating the optic and the haptic

---

63 Gerhard Tersteegen, *Geistliches Blumen-Gärtlein inniger Seelen; oder, Kurze Schluss-Reimen, Betrachtungen und Lieder ueber allerhand Wahrheiten des Inwendigen Christenthums, nebst der Frommen Lotterie* (Frankfurt: J. Christoph Böttinger, 1757).
64 Henry Melchior Muhlenberg (Theodore G. Tappert and John W. Doberstein, trans), *The Journals of Henry Melchior Muhlenberg, vol. 3* (Philadelphia: The Evangelical Lutheran Ministerium of Pennsylvania and the Adjacent States and the Muhlenberg Press, 1958), 76–77.
65 Patrick Erben, "(Re)Discovering the German-Language Literature of Colonial America," in *A Peculiar Mixture: German-Language Cultures and Identities in Eighteenth-Century North America*, ed. Jan Stievermann and Oliver Scheiding (University Park, PA: Pennsylvania State University Press, 2013), 119.
66 Brown, *the Pilgrim and the Bee*, 69.

and its indexical engagement with the Bible are, of course, elements of the three German-American objects discussed above. While divided by creed and language, pietist German-Americans and early Anglo-American Protestants shared themes of spiritual pilgrimage. The pious reading of objects such as the Spiritual Labyrinths served to anchor the faithful in a tumultuous world.

Finally, it is important to remember that the Spiritual Labyrinths remained adaptable objects across time, even into the twenty-first century. While a general dearth of provenance makes it impossible to understand detailed histories of individual objects, many in this survey possess evidence of both display and book storage, highlighting their changing roles over time as early users likely appreciated the Spiritual Labyrinths as devotional tools for spiritual education while later owners approached them as aesthetic pieces or heirlooms. Such adaptive use continues to the present day. A letter from 1995 to the Heritage Historical Library in Aylmer, Ontario inquires whether the library sold reproduction Spiritual Labyrinths. Although the inquirer notes that she was "extremely deficient in religious reading," she was fascinated by the genre as she had "never come across anything similar to the Labyrinth before."[67] While raised a Baptist and unfamiliar with German, the writer nonetheless wished to possess the object for her spiritual development. Similar correspondence with a special collections curator in Ohio notes his fascination with a Labyrinth that he has "hung, but in such a way that it can be taken down for the contortions necessary for reading."[68] This curator's sensitivity to the object's dual role as aesthetic and didactic reminds us that while these objects' popularity with religious readers has ebbed and waned over time, their ability to fascinate viewers has remained. As printers used these technically challenging objects as showpieces, it is clear that readers in the pre-photographic and pre-stereotype era understood the immense complication and painstaking detail of composing the lettertype for these objects.[69] Even today, however, Spiritual Labyrinths instill a sense of visual wonder by blending image and text into a single form. This wonder and the ability to change function over time ensures that the Spiritual

---

67 Sarah Plowden, Correspondence with the Aylmer Heritage Historical Library, July 14, 1995, uncatalogued collection, Aylmer Heritage Historical Library, Aylmer, Ontario, Canada.
68 Robert Tibetts, Correspondence with the Aylmer Heritage Historical Library, August 11, 1986, uncatalogued collection, Aylmer Heritage Historical Library, Aylmer, Ontario, Canada.
69 An early copying and text reproduction technology allowing the printer to copy text by using plaster to mould the letter-type used to print. Such technology appeared in the early nineteenth century in the United States, enabling the reproduction of technically challenging objects such as the Spiritual Labyrinths.

Labyrinths continue to move within the home and the heart even after ceasing to move within their user's hands.

Bibliography

Archival sources

Benner, Enos. "Geistlicher Irrgarten," *Der Bauernfreund*. Sumneytown, PA, 15 August 1832.
Der Christlich Irrgarten, 1607 (Gebhardt Grieb, Stuttgart 1607), Bavarian State Archives Germany, Einblatt XI722.
Geistlicher Irrgarten, mit vier Gnadenbrunnen, 1784 (Ephrata, PA), the Winterthur Museum, Garden and Library, Winterthur, DE, 1958.120.13.
Geistlicher Irrgarten, mit vier Gnadenbrunnen, 1784 (Ephrata, PA), the Conrad Grebel University College Library, hist. mss. 23.14.
Geistlicher Irrgarten, mit vier Gnadenbrunnen, 1788 (Ephrata, PA), the Winterthur Museum, Garden & Library, Winterthur, DE, 1957.1215.
Geistlicher Irrgarten, mit vier Gnadenbrunnen, 1811 (Reading, PA), the Schwenkfelder Library and Heritage Center, uncatalogued (see Brandt, "Perplexion and Pleasure," 194)
Geistlicher Irrgarten, mit vier Gnadenbrunnen, c. 1830 (Harrisburg, PA), the Russell and Corinne Earnest Collection, BS #618.
Geistlicher Irrgarten, mit vier Gnadenbrunnen, c. 1830 (Harrisburg, PA), the Earnest Archives and Library, BS #784.
Geistlicher Irrgarten, mit vier Gnadenbrunnen, 1833 (Hereford, PA), Schwenkfelder Library and Heritage Center, fraktur collection, uncatalogued.
Geistlicher Irrgarten, mit vier Gnadenbrunnen, 1869–74 (John Funk and Brother, Elkhart, IN), Aylmer Heritage Historical Library, Ontario, GI 2.
Geistlicher Irrgarten, mit vier Gnadenbrunnen, c. 1875, Joseph Schneider Haus Museum, Kitchener, Ontario; 1984.028.347.
Miller, Henrich. "Bey dem Verleger dieser Zeitung ist ganz neulich heraus gekommen . . .," *Der Wöchentliche pennsylvanische Staatsbote*, 18 January 1762.
Plowden, Sarah. Correspondence with the Aylmer Heritage Historical Library, 14 July 1995. Uncatalogued collection, Aylmer Heritage Historical Library, Aylmer, ON.
Ritter, Johann. "Geistlicher Irrgarten," *Der Readinger Adler*, Reading, PA, 19 November 1811.
Tibbets, Robert. Correspondence with the Aylmer Heritage Historical Library, 11 August 1986. Uncatalogued collection. Aylmer Heritage Historical Library, Aylmer, ON.

Primary and secondary sources

Bach, Jeff. *Voices of the Turtledoves: The Sacred World of Ephrata*. University Park: Pennsylvania State University Press, 2003.
Brandt, Trevor. "Perplexion and Pleasure: The *Geistlicher Irrgarten* Broadsides in the German-American Printshop, Home, and Mind." MA thesis, The University of Delaware, 2017. The

University of Delaware Library (1015314042). http://udspace.udel.edu/handle/19716/21797.

Brown, Matthew. *The Pilgrim and the Bee: Reading Rituals and Book Culture in Early New England*. Philadelphia: University of Pennsylvania Press, 2007.

Dolmetsch, Christopher L. *The German Press of the Shenandoah Valley*. Columbia, SC: Camden House, 1984.

Earnest, Russell, and Corinne Earnest. *Flying Leaves and One-Sheets: Pennsylvania German Broadsides, Fraktur, and Their Printers*. New Castle, DE: Oak Knoll Books, 2005.

Earnest, Russell, and Corinne Earnest. *God Bless This House: The Printed House Blessings (Haus-Segen) of the Pennsylvania Germans, 1780–1921*. Clayton, DE: Russell D. Earnest, 2015.

Earnest, Russell, and Corinne Earnest. *Papers for Birth Dayes: Guide to the Fraktur Artists and Scriveners*. Albuquerque: Russell D. Earnest, 1989.

Erb, Peter C., and W. Kyrel Meschter. "Schwenkfelders and the Preservation of Tradition." In *Schwenkfelders in America*, edited by Peter C. Erb, 189–201. Pennsburg, PA: Schwenkfelder Library, 1987.

Erben, Patrick. "(Re)Discovering the German-Language Literature of Colonial America." In *A Peculiar Mixture: German-Language Cultures and Identities in Eighteenth-Century North America*, edited by Jan Stievermann and Oliver Scheiding, 117–149. University Park: Pennsylvania State University Press, 2013.

Furttenbach the Elder, Joseph. *Architectura Civilis*. Ulm: Saur, 1628.

Good, E. Reginald. *Anna's Art: The Fraktur Art of Anna Weber, a Waterloo County Mennonite Artist, 1814–1888*. Kitchener, ON: Pochauna, 1976.

Green, James N. "The Rise of Book Publishing." In *An Extensive Republic; Print, Culture, and Society in the New Nation, 1790–1840*. Vol. 2 of *A History of the Book in America*, edited by Hugh Amory and David Hall, 75–127. Cambridge: Cambridge University Press, 2000.

Hambrick-Stowe, Charles E. *The Practice of Piety: Puritan Devotional Disciplines in Seventeenth-Century New England*. Chapel Hill: University of North Carolina Press, 1982.

Hill, Thomas. *The Gardener's Labyrinth*. London: Adam Islip, 1594.

Hugo, Herman. *Pia desideria emblematis elegiis at affectibus*. Antwerp: Henrik Aertssens, 1624.

Karr Schmidt, *Interactive and Sculptural Printmaking in the Renaissance*. Leiden: Brill, 2017.

Kircher, Athanasius. *Turris Babel, Sive Archontologia*. Amsterdam: Janssonio-Waesbergianna, 1679.

Kriebel, Reuben. *Genealogical Record of the Descendants of the Schwenkfelders, Who Arrived in Pennsylvania in 1733, 1734, 1736, 1737*. Manayunk, PA: Joseph Yeakel, 1879.

Lineweaver Paul, Bonnie. *Shenandoah Valley Folk Art Fraktur (1774–1850)*. Dayton, VA: Harrisonburg-Rockingham County Historical Society, 2011.

Luthy, David. *Our Amish Devotional Heritage*. Aylmer, ON: Pathway, 2016.

Luthy, David. "The Spiritual Labyrinth: An Unusual Devotional Form." *Pathway Publishers: The Family Life Magazine* 17, no. 3 (1984): 18–21.

MacQueen, Gailand. *The Spirituality of Mazes and Labyrinths*. Kelowna, BC: Wood Lake, 2005.

Morgan, David. *The Embodied Eye: Religious Visual Culture and the Social Life of Feeling*. Berkeley: University of California Press, 2012.

Morgan, David. *The Forge of Vision: A Visual History of Modern Christianity*. Oakland: University of California Press, 2015.

Moyer, Dennis K. *Fraktur Writings and Folk Art Drawings of the Schwenkfelder Library Collection*. Kutztown: Pennsylvania German Society, 1997.

Muhlenberg, Henry Melchior. *The Journals of Henry Melchior Muhlenberg*. Vol. 3. Translated by Theodore G. Tappert and John W. Doberstein. Philadelphia: Evangelical Lutheran Ministerium of Pennsylvania and the Adjacent States, 1958.

The Multigraph Collective. *Interacting with Print: Elements of Reading in the Era of Print Saturation*. Chicago: University of Chicago Press, 2018.

Patterson, Nancy-Lou. "Imagery of Paradise in Swiss-German Mennonite Folk Art," unpublished paper notes and manuscript draft, c. 1979. Conrad Grebel University College Archives. Hist. mss. 1.197.

Patterson, Nancy-Lou. *The Language of Paradise: Folk Art from Mennonite and Other Anabaptist Communities of Ontario*. London, ON: London Regional Art Gallery, 1985.

Peschel, Johann. *Garten-Ordnung*. Leipzig: Henning Große, 1597.

Pieske, Christa. "The European Origins of Four Pennsylvania German Broadside Themes." *Der Reggeboge* 23, no. 1 (1989): 7–10.

Roberts, Matt T., and Don Etherington. *Bookbinding and the Conservation of Books: A Dictionary of Descriptive Terminology*. Washington, DC: Library of Congress, 1981.

Roeber, A. Gregg. "German and Dutch Books and Printing." In *A History of the Book in America*. Vol. 1, *The Colonial Book in the Atlantic World*, edited by Hugh Amory and David D. Hall, 298–313. Chapel Hill: University of North Carolina Press, 2010.

Roeber, A. Gregg. *Palatines, Liberty, and Property: German Lutherans in Colonial British America*. Baltimore: Johns Hopkins University Press, 1993.

Roeber, A. Gregg. "Readers and Writers of German." In *A History of the Book in America*. Vol. 2, *An Extensive Republic: Print, Culture, and Society in the New Nation, 1790–1840*, edited by Robert Gross and Mary Kelley, 471–482. Chapel Hill: University of North Carolina Press, 2010.

Rothstein, Bret. "Early Modern Play: Three Perspectives." *Renaissance Quarterly* 71 (2018): 1036–1046.

Rothstein, Bret. "Visual Difficulty as a Cultural System." *Res: Anthropology and Aesthetics* 65–66 (2014–2015): 332–347.

Sangmeister, Ezekiel. *Mystische Theologie; oder, Wahrer Wegweisser nach unserm Ursprung und Vaterland*. Ephrata, PA: Joseph Bauman, 1819–1820.

Stengel, Georg. *Aegyptischer Labyrinth, Oder Geistlicher Irr-Garten der betrieglichen Welt*. Dillingen: Akademische Druckerey, 1629.

Strom, Jonathan, ed. *Pietism and Community in Europe and North America, 1650–1850*. Boston: Brill, 2010.

Tersteegen, Gerhard. *Geistliches Blumen-Gärtlein inniger Seelen; oder, Kurze Schluss-Reimen, Betrachtungen und Lieder ueber allerhand Wahrheiten des Inwendigen Christenthums, nebst der Frommen Lotterie*. Frankfurt am Main: J. Christoph Böttinger, 1757.

Wellenreuther, Hermann. *Citizens in a Strange Land: A Study of German-American Broadsides and Their Meaning for Germans in North America, 1730–1830*. University Park: Pennsylvania State University Press, 2013.

Wengiel, Rubén. "Europe's Mazes: On Labyrinthine Thought in Architectural Design." Paper presented at the European Forum at the Hebrew University, Jerusalem, 2008.

Yoder, Don. *The Pennsylvania German Broadside: A History and Guide*. University Park: Pennsylvania State University Press, 2005.

J. P. Short
Arc of the Anemone: Modeling Nature from the *Wunderkammer* to the *Warenwelt*

The glassmaker Rudolf Blaschka (1857–1939) was, like his father Leopold (1822–1895), Bohemian-born, but insisted he was a true "Dresden boy" – otherwise, he said, he would be neither fish nor fowl.[1] He lived in the city beginning in 1863, where, rather like a fish, he was surrounded by sea anemones. From the time that Rudolf was six or seven years old, in the mid-1860s, his father made extraordinary glass models of marine invertebrate animals that he sold around the world. Leopold began this work with an expanding series of sea anemones (see Figures 1–2). He had already been a maker of glass eyes and, in the tradition of his family, of costume jewelry and fancy pieces for chandeliers, but he was increasingly a maker of (mostly) cnidarians: "Models"--according to his business card--"of delicate sea creatures, anemones, jellyfish, mollusks, etc."[2] Leopold did not stick with the sort of glasswork for which family tradition and early apprenticeship had prepared him. Rather, he bent and shaped his skills to serve natural history and, more strikingly, its submarine forms. His exact "imitations of invertebrates," as he later described them in an 1885 catalogue, would supply not only "object lessons for museums, but also serve as means of instruction" in marine zoology. His pedagogical models, he could boast, had been "universally pronounced to be strikingly true to nature."[3]

But what nature was that? The models were known for their uncanny power of resemblance, but to what truth did the fantastic details correspond? The Blaschkas' submarine world must have been almost entirely made of lithographic and then glass representations, at least at first. Leopold and his son would have to have traveled a great distance down the Elbe, beyond Saxony, through the great port at Hamburg, until they finally reached the North Sea, before they could have observed true sea anemones. Barring that, Rudolf might

---

[1] Rudolf Blaschka, Hosterwitz to George Lincoln Goodale, Harvard University, draft, n. d. Leopold and Rudolf Blaschka Collection (LRBC), MS 0013, Box 21, Folder 51. The Rakow Research Library (RRL), The Corning Museum of Glass (CMoG), Corning, New York.
[2] Leopold Blaschka's business card, n. d. LRBC, MS 0013, Box 22. RRL, CMoG, Corning, New York.
[3] Leopold Blaschka, Preface, Katalog über Blaschka's Modelle von wirbellosen Thieren dargestellt von Leopold Blaschka in Dresden (Dresden: Leopold Blaschka, 1885)."

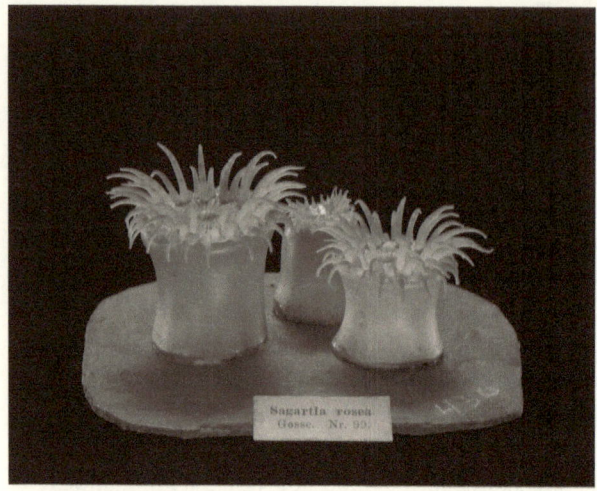

Figure 1: *Sagartia rosea*. Blaschka model no. 99. 1885. Flameworked glass, paint, metal wire and resin. From the Cornell University Blaschka Collection, photo courtesy of the Corning Museum of Glass, Corning, New York.

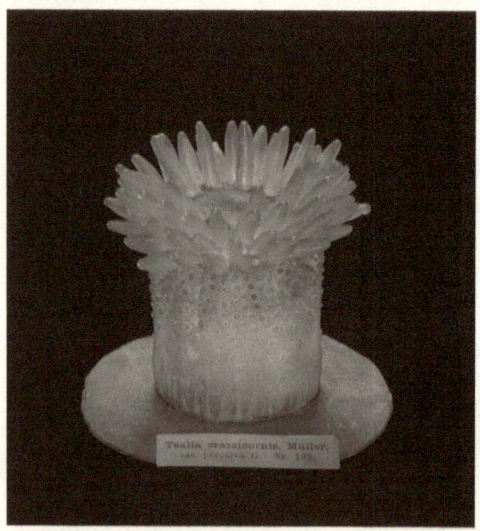

Figure 2: *Tealia crassicornis*, var. *purpurea*. Blaschka model no. 109. 1885. Flameworked glass, paint, metal wire and resin. From the Cornell University Blaschka Collection, photo courtesy of the Corning Museum of Glass, Corning, New York.

gaze at the vivid, luminous phantasmagoria of his father's growing inventory, a sort of undersea grotto at home. Making marine models was a striking direction for Leopold Blaschka to choose, the affinities of glass and these delicate invertebrates notwithstanding, and the powerful effect of the models depends in part on the very strangeness of the unknown nature they perfectly reproduce, even as they are emblematic of a world of man and nature set in motion – and a new proximity – by a vast global circulation of goods in the nineteenth century. These are scientific models, specimens; and they are wonders of nature and of representation, too; and, indeed, aesthetic objects. But these several aspects do not exhaust their meaning, which lies also in their status as merchandise, as goods traded around the world, but above all in the compounding and bonding of all of these strands.

Leopold Blaschka and his son Rudolf are singular examples of a nineteenth-century convergence of skilled labor, commerce, art and autodidact science operating in global circuits of trade and knowledge. Their models are special cases of the natural history object: composite forms that were at once crystallizations of "nature," scientific tools, exotica, curiosities, collections, and goods. Examples of a large series of naturalia shipped by sail, steam and railroad worldwide, they mediated a growing sense of the global as at once commercial network and zoogeography, reflecting the first modern globalization from mid-century to about 1914. Over about sixty years up to the First World War, commodities of many kinds circulated internationally at unprecedented levels, following expanding flows of credit, capital, and labor. Price convergence revealed emergent global markets. In the same period, an enlarged and institutionalized natural history produced nature in a form commensurate with the projected industrialization of the earth. Collections, associations, academic programs, museums, publications and dealers multiplied in profusion. Especially the largest museums, housed in monumental new buildings from Hamburg to London and New York to Berlin, aspired to global reach through their expeditions, massive collections, and scientific networks. Natural history became a system of world representation – the exploration of the poles figuring significantly here, and also of the submarine globe – so that ultimately the whole of the earth was encompassed.

Animals played a special role in this system of representation as the emblematic forms of a world zoogeography. They were accumulated through commercial transaction: circulation and exchange, conversion into freight and inventory – in a word, transformation into commodities. The natural-history business accomplished the transposition of the world of animals into the animal world (*Tierwelt*), a total representation that ultimately exceeded its object as living diversity was diminished in favor of what Marx called the *Warenwelt*, the world of goods. The Blaschka models are examples of this process. They stand out as dialectic objects in conjuring organic life in lifeless glass; fusing disinterested science and commercial interest; and crystallizing natural beauty as artificial ornament. They belong to a constellation with fossils and zoophytes, petrifaction and taxidermy: expressions of the ambiguity and tension in the commercial animal-object generally, which found reflection in contemporary discourse about fetishized exchange value and the animate commodity form. That these were representations of marine animals in particular, fragile figures from an unknown world just then being annexed by globalizing science, underlines their significance as materializations of a new natural cosmology.

You did not have to be a Bohemian glassmaker to be ignorant of the sea in the 1860s. Most undersea life was mysterious or unknown even to science and sailors. The popular science and fiction that would open it up as an imaginative terrain were in their early development. Naturalists still depended on dredging, in relatively shallow waters, and combing beaches and tidal pools, for their zoological specimens.[4] The celebrated *Challenger* expedition for oceanographic exploration, which assembled an international scientific network to analyze the oceans on an unprecedented scale, was undertaken only in 1872, wrapping up four years later.[5] Jules Michelet's (1798–1874) natural history work *The Sea* (1861) conjures "a world of obscurity," where below a certain depth "one is quickly deprived of light and enters a twilight where only a single color persists – a sinister red." Beyond that, "total darkness." "We are just now," he says, "beginning to learn for certain about what we imagine is a prodigious world, filled with life, war, love."[6] The English naturalist Philip Henry Gosse (1810–1888), whose work would come to play a powerful role in the visual imagination of Leopold Blaschka, reflects on a "certain indefiniteness and mystery" attached to the sea. *The Ocean* (1845), one of his many volumes of natural history, confines itself noticeably to the shore, the coast, the island, the surface. The sea is disorienting, elusive. "At times," he writes, on being out at sea, "in peculiar states of the atmosphere, the boundary of the horizon becomes undistinguishable [. . .] and we seem alone in infinite space." While at other times, "particularly in the clear waters of the tropical seas, we look downward unmeasured fathoms [. . .] but still find no boundary; the sight is lost in one uniform transparent blueness. Mailed and glittering creatures of strange forms suddenly

---

[4] Helen M. Rozwadowski, *Fathoming the Ocean: The Discovery and Exploration of the Deep Sea* (Cambridge, MA: Harvard University Press, 2005), 34–35.
[5] Doug Macdougal, *Endless Novelties of Extraordinary Interest: The Voyage of the H. M. S. Challenger and the Birth of Modern Oceanography* (New Haven: Yale University Press, 2019).
[6] Jules Michelet, *The Sea* (Los Angeles: Green Integer, 2012), 17, 22.

appear, play a moment in our sight, and with the velocity of a thought have vanished in the boundless depths."[7] In 1870, the longing to know the sea found expression in Jules Verne's (1828–1905) fantastical, encyclopedic *20,000 Leagues under the Sea*. Subtitled a "submarine tour of the world," it was a compendium of the latest science, speculative writing and fantasy. Illustrated periodicals and books as well as rudimentary museum collections began both to reflect and to fuel the new fascination, as they would for Leopold Blaschka.

Blaschka first made his own journey in 1853 from Bohemia to the sea, via Bremen, and then crossed the Atlantic. It was on this trip to the United States that the primal scene of his marine naturalism unfolded. The ship was becalmed and from its deck he began to observe marine organisms for the first time. Some thirty years later, speaking on hydromedusae – or jellyfish – to the members of the Natural Science Society ISIS, in Dresden, Rudolf Blaschka read from his father's description of "a beautiful May night" on the still ocean:

> We peer hopefully into the darkness of the glassy sea: a flashing illumination develops [. . .] all around us, as from thousands of sparks, which form veritable bursts of fire and other brightly glowing points, like the reflection of the surrounding stars. And there appears right in front of us a small speck of bright greenish light, which gets bigger and bigger and finally forms a brightly shining sun-like shape. Their delicate rays seem to dance in the sea of sparks; a second forms, then a third; ten, a hundred such suns shine [. . .], brightly glowing rings form strangely shaped figures, and in between them spots of glowing light – making for an indescribably beautiful show. [. . .] Then one sun after the other becomes smaller, until just tiny glowing disks and finally only small sparks are visible. Trailing long shafts of sparks, they slowly sink ever deeper down, now and then resting motionless, and become by turns slowly bigger and smaller, until suddenly they disappear entirely from our sight [. . .] as if they wanted to lure the delighted observer into a fairy kingdom.[8]

The abstraction and estrangement of Leopold's language – the ISIS rapporteur helpfully suggests that the "sun-, spark- and star-like luminous figures derive from scyphozoans, while infusoria, worm larvae, salps, pyrosomes, siphonophores and other invertebrate animals contributed to the full effect of the show" – indicate

---

[7] Philip Henry Gosse, *The Ocean* (London: Society for Promoting Christian Knowledge, 1846), 2. Alain Corbin argues that the sea frightened and repelled Europeans until the mid-eighteenth century, after which an "irresistible awakening of a collective desire for the shore" gradually occurred. Alain Corbin, *The Lure of the Sea: The Discovery of the Seaside in the Western World, 1750–1840* (Berkeley: University of California Press, 1994). On discovering the subaqueous world, see Rozwadowski, *Fathoming the Ocean* and Glyn Williams, *Naturalists at Sea: Scientific Travelers from Dampier to Darwin* (New Haven: Yale University Press, 2013).
[8] Sitzungsberichte der naturwissenschaftlichen Gesellschaft ISIS in Dresden, 1880 (Dresden, 1881), 48.

how unfamiliar and enigmatic the sea was to him.[9] But the luminous abstraction is also powerfully visual, rendering a vivid scene of form, light and color in the darkness of the ocean, a prefiguration of the strange jellyfish forms or the dazzling geometries of radiolarians that the Blaschkas would later create. The sense of wonder here intermingles with recognition as Leopold perceives a suggestion of glass, of the visual play of light and glass, in these delicately translucent, even transparent, sometimes phosphorescent forms. As his son much later told it, Leopold "was interested in the glass-like appearance of these animals, which he had known before only from illustrations in Nat. History books and here he first got the idea that these forms could be imitated in glass."[10]

Even with this actual personal experience, it was a book that prompted Leopold to make sea anemones: the exact, powerfully descriptive work *Actinologia Britannica: A History of the British Sea-Anemones and Corals* that Philip Henry Gosse had published just a few years before, in 1860.[11] The Dresden naturalist Ludwig Reichenbach (1793–1879), director of the Royal Museum of Natural History, who had been impressed by some botanical models Leopold had made, was lent Gosse's book by a resident Englishman, and Leopold agreed to attempt some anemones.[12] Here, in Gosse's dense description and his overcrowded, otherworldly lithographic anemone scenes, Leopold returned to the phantasmagoria of marine life. The debossed cover with its gilt coral ornament opened to a richly appointed cabinet of wonders: marigold wartlets, walled corklets, gem pimplets; forms variously globose or ovate, distended or flaccid, with colored warts and corrugations. The *Aiptasia couchii* in Gosse's work, for example (eventually number thirty-four in the Blaschka catalogue), suggests the fascination these ambiguous, otherworldly "animal-plants" exerted on observers who spared no effort to picture them, through language as much as illustration, down to the finest details. The anemone's column – in "substance pulpy,"[13] the "surface corrugated, adhesive, but without distinct suckers"[14]– is "slender above the base, enlarging upwards, dilating at the summit into a wide hemispheric cup or trumpet-shaped disk,"[15] in color a "warm orange-buff, richer at base, blending into a bluish-black hue where

---

9 Sitzungsberichte, 49.
10 Rudolf Blaschka, Hosterwitz to Professor George Lincoln Goodale, Cambridge, 6 January 1896 (photocopy). LRBC, MS 0013, Box 21, Folder 12. RRL, CMoG, Corning, New York.
11 Philip Henry Gosse, *Actinologia Britannica: A History of the British Sea-Anemones and Corals* (London: Van Voorst, 1860).
12 Rudolf Blaschka, Hosterwitz to Professor George Lincoln Goodale, Cambridge, 6 January 1896 (photocopy). LRBC, MS 0013, Box 21, Folder 12. RRL, CMoG, Corning, New York.
13 Gosse, *Actinologia Britannica*, 152.
14 Gosse, *Actinologia Britannica*, 151.
15 Gosse, *Actinologia Britannica*, 152.

it expands into the cup-like disk,"[16] which, "membranous" and "concave,"[17] is in turn a "dark iron-gray, becoming ashy toward the center, each radius bounded by lines of pale grayish blue."[18] The tentacles run in "several rows, long, lax, irregularly flexuous, perforate at the tip,"[19] their color "sepia brown; but [. . .] under a low magnifying power [. . .] a warm umber" that "usually softens into white at the extreme tip."[20] Even the accompanying lithographs struggle to compete with the concentrated prose of observation. While their stylized, crowded forms might appear to betray in illustration the sober precision of the microscopist, in fact a kind of ecstasy of the concrete in language is already at work. Metaphor is essentially absent here, from images and descriptions alike, but language, as preparatory sketch, teems and pulsates – and finds semblance in line and color. Readers not only of Gosse but of many marine naturalists, the Blaschkas copied out extracts of such language into their notebooks.

Philip Gosse spent much of 1858 and 1859, especially the summers, "on the shore, tramping along the pebbled terraces of the beach, clambering over the great blocks of fallen conglomerate [. . .] or, finally, bending over those shallow tidal pools in the limestone rocks which were our proper hunting ground." So Edmund Gosse (1849–1928), then ten years old, later remembered the makings of his father's *Actinologia Britannica* on the Devonshire coast. The

> rocks between tide and tide were submarine gardens of a beauty that seemed often to be fabulous, and was positively delusive, since, if we delicately lifted the weed-curtains of a windless pool, though we might for a moment see its sides and floor paven with living blossoms, ivory-white, rosy-red, orange and amethyst, yet all that panoply would melt away, furled into the hollow rock, if we so much as dropped a pebble in to disturb the magic dream.[21]

This fantastic scene stood in stark contrast to the extreme austerity of the Calvinist Gosse household: days and nights of quiet, solitary contemplation and prayer; Gosse "forever in his study, writing, drawing, dissecting; sitting [. . .] absolutely motionless, with his eye glued to the microscope, for twenty minutes at a time."[22] Few worldly pleasures were tolerated there, no fiction, not even once a trip to a natural history museum or zoo. "We used to be seated, my Father at his

---

16 Gosse, *Actinologia Britannica*, 153.
17 Gosse, *Actinologia Britannica*, 151.
18 Gosse, *Actinologia Britannica*, 153.
19 Gosse, *Actinologia Britannica*, 151.
20 Gosse, *Actinologia Britannica*, 153.
21 Edmund Gosse, *Father and Son: A Study in Two Temperaments* (London: Penguin, 1989), 124.
22 Gosse, *Father and Son*, 41.

microscope, I with my map or book. [...] There would be a hush around us in which you could hear a sea-anemone sigh."[23]

It seems as if, for Gosse, all sensuous life was sublimated into his art, the varieties of anemones herded into stylized, teeming scenes like overstuffed Victorian drawing rooms (see Figure 3). "Sometimes," he tells us, the *Aiptasia couchii* "lies utterly flaccid and withered" and then, "especially at night, it swells up," and when, "in full vigor it towers up, and with its ever-twisting tentacles and semipellucid tapering column, it is a very elegant object."[24] The drawings are all tumescent, snaky, waving vigor, impossible constellations of weird forms and vivid colors. The image of nature was fixed through the mediations of his intent descriptive gaze, the microscopic lens, the compressorium, the aquarium and finally, "numerous water-color drawings of minute and even of microscopic forms of life," which, Edmund remembered, "he executed in the manner of miniature, with an amazing fidelity of form and with a brilliancy of color."[25] Philip Gosse compares his book favorably to those others that "bear evidence in every page of being the produce of the museum and the closet, not of the aquarium and the shore." "I have resorted to nature itself," he insisted; "I have studied the living animals" – along the coasts of South and North Devon, Dorset, South Wales – "and, have moreover [...] had poured into my aquaria the productions of almost every other part of our coasts."[26] Leopold Blaschka enjoyed no proximity to the coast. But no matter; it was the nineteenth century, and sea anemones could travel by railroad.

Indeed, Gosse's emphasis on unmediated experience conceals the prodigious role of technology in shaping access to nature, from the railroad or print capitalism down to the microscope. The boy Edmund in South Devon, like young Rudolf in Saxony, was surrounded by living anemones, and he soon began – "a fervent imitator" of his father's work – to copy it, though he lamented that "the multitude of my designs and my descriptions have left me helplessly ignorant of the anatomy of a sea-anemone."[27] Leopold would, of course, have better luck over time. Here began the chain of practices, techniques, and devices that produced the iconography of the anemone: specimen, compressorium, microscope, sketch, lithograph, model – but above all the aquarium (see Figure 4).[28] Edmund

---

23 Gosse, *Father and Son*, 139.
24 Gosse, *Actinologia Britannica*, 156.
25 Gosse, *Father and Son*, 135.
26 Gosse, *Actinologia Britannica*, vi.
27 Gosse, *Father and Son*, 135, 148–149.
28 For more on the transnational chains of technology, commerce, and remediation that shaped the dynamic circulation of images in the nineteenth century, see especially the contributions in *Before Photography* by Vance Byrd and David Ciarlo.

Arc of the Anemone: Modeling Nature from the *Wunderkammer* to the *Warenwelt* — 189

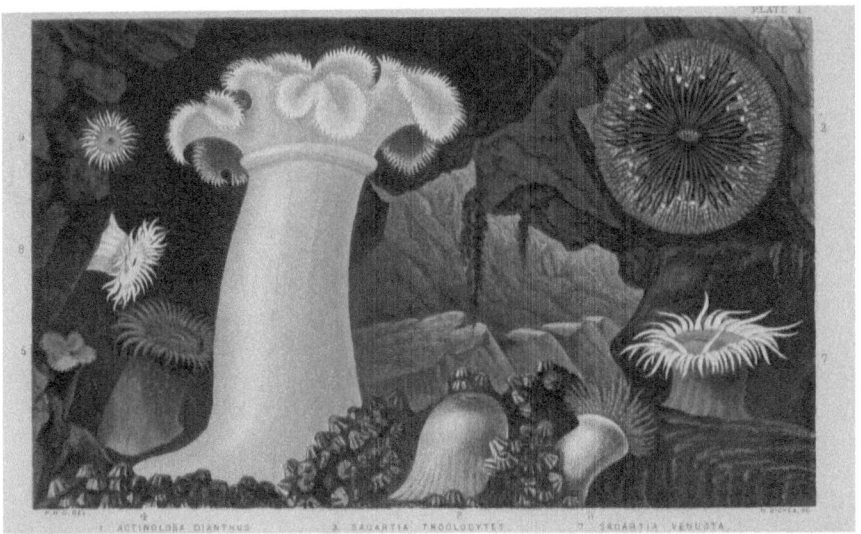

Figure 3: Philip Henry Gosse, lithograph, Plate I, *Actinologia Britannica: A History of the British Sea-Anemones and Corals*, 1860.

Gosse remembered how in 1857 "the newly-invented marine aquarium was the fashionable toy of the moment."[29] His father was perhaps its greatest popularizer, publishing in 1854 *The Aquarium: An Unveiling of the Wonders of the Deep Sea*, and then *A Handbook to the Marine Aquarium* the following year. The aquarium, he says, "bids fair to [. . .] make us acquainted with the strange creatures of the sea, without diving to gaze on them."[30] Among the surviving books from the Blaschkas' house outside of Dresden is an 1866 volume of *Das Buch der Welt*, an illustrated popular-science journal, that includes an article instructing readers on keeping a saltwater aquarium at home. "The first occupants should be the perennial varieties of the sea anemone." Among them, "the *Actinia mesembryanthemum* is found in plenty on the coasts. Closed it resembles a ripe strawberry," but unfolded "one sees a circle of bright blue tubercles in the middle and numerous tentacles or coral-like fingers spread out from the center on all sides. [. . .] They do

---

[29] Gosse, *Father and Son*, 82–83. On the history of the aquarium see Bernd Brunner, *The Ocean at Home: An Illustrated History of the Aquarium* (New York: Princeton Architectural Press, 2005) and Mareike Vennen, *Das Aquarium: Praktiken, Techniken und Medien der Wissensproduktion (1840–1910)* (Göttingen: Wallstein, 2018).
[30] Philip Henry Gosse, *The Aquarium: An Unveiling of the Wonders of the Deep Sea*, 2nd ed., rev. and enl. (London: John Van Voorst, 1856), v–vi.

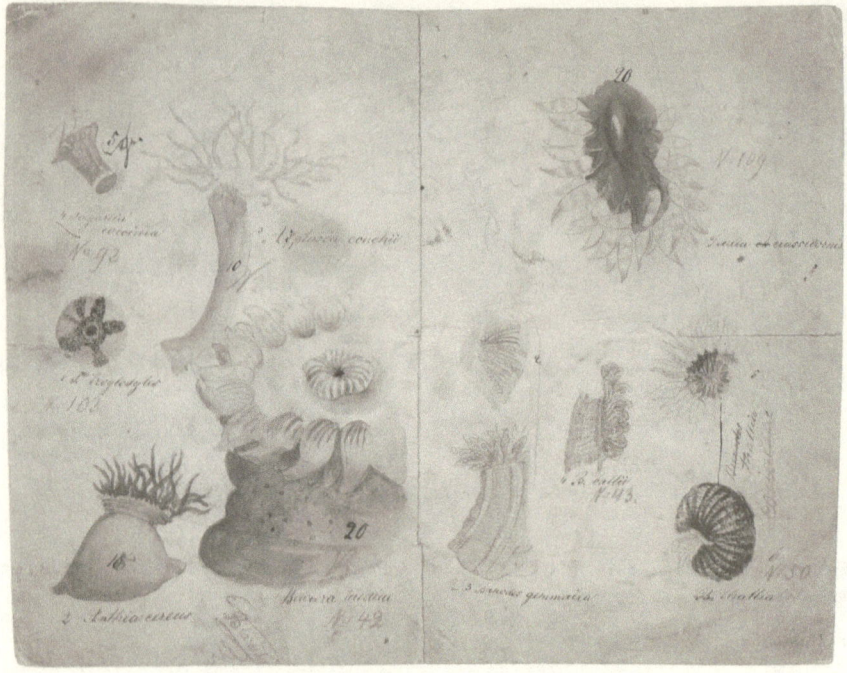

Figure 4: Rudolf Blaschka, sketch of sea anemone anatomy (including *Sagartia troglodytes*, *Anthea cereus*, *Tealia crassicornis* and *Aiptasia couchii*). Ink, watercolor, colored pencil and pencil on paper. BIB 121327, The Rakow Research Library, The Corning Museum of Glass, Corning, New York.

very beautifully in the aquarium"[31] (see Figure 5). Philip Gosse thought the *Aiptasia* made for "an interesting occupant of the aquarium," especially the way "it marches from stone to stone, and around the walls of the tank, frequently creeping to the top of the water."[32]

The Blaschkas eventually had a room in their house in Dresden "filled with sea-water-tanks with living animals, sent to us partly by the Imper. Austrian Zoolog. station of Triest partly from England and the Northern coasts."[33] These latter came from an anemone dealer in Weymouth, R. T. Smith. Right through

---

[31] "Aquarium," *Das Buch der Welt* (1866), 360. LRBC, MS 0013, Box 13. RRL, CMoG, Corning, New York.
[32] Gosse, *Actinologia Britannica*, 156.
[33] Rudolf Blaschka, Hosterwitz to Professor George Lincoln Goodale, Cambridge, 6 January 1896 (photocopy). LRBC, MS 0013, Box 21, Folder 12. RRL, CMoG, Corning, New York.

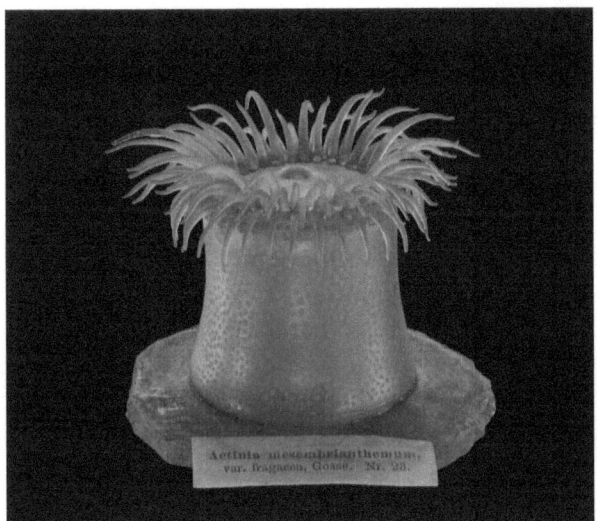

Figure 5: *Actinia mesembrianthemum*. Blaschka model no. 23. 1885. Flameworked glass, paint, metal wire and resin. From the Cornell University Blaschka Collection, photo courtesy of the Corning Museum of Glass, Corning, New York.

the 1880s, long after his first encounter with Gosse's remarkable images, Leopold carried on an urgent, pleading, variously grateful or exasperated correspondence with Smith, coaxing small shipments of anemones. Leopold was a savvy customer with international connections. He knew what he wanted, how it should be packed and by what means shipped. "As I like to complete my collection of British sea anemones in my Aquarium," he wrote in March 1886,

> I beg to request you, that you be as good as to furnish me as soon as possible with a consignment of anemones [. . .]. Upon the whole I leave the selection to your convenience as all species are welcome, except Actinoloba dianthus, Tealia crassicornis and Anthea cereus. Especially I should like to get several Bunodes gemmacea, about a dozen Act. mesembryanthemum, Strawberry red, and other varieties, several large B. ballii, S. viduata, and some S. troglodytes, bellis and miniata, if possible. I request for as different varieties as possible.[34]

By the end of the month he had "received the parcel with anemones" and determined that the "manner of forwarding is excellent practically as I get the sample one day sooner than with the parcelpost, wanting 2½ days only from Weymouth to

---

[34] Leopold Blaschka, Dresden, to R. T. Smith, Weymouth, draft, 1 March (1886?), notebook, 1886–1887. LRBC, MS 0013, Box 23. RRL, CMoG, Corning, New York.

Dresden," although "a certain feebleness of the anemones was to be observed [. . .] and 4 specimens did not revive, which is perhaps a consequence of the very bad weather these days, I think they have got a night frost on the railway."[35] He ordered only "when the weather will be most favorable for anemone fishing and forwarding" – neither too hot nor too cold – mindful of the stresses of travel by rail.[36] This was the European traffic in sea anemones.

The aquarium brought the sea to upper Saxony, into the domestic interior, making it possible for the skilled artisan to observe very closely the organisms he would reproduce. If, for Walter Benjamin – looking back on his Berlin boyhood – the stereoscopic images of the *Kaiserpanorama* were "aquariums of the faraway and the past," then for the Blaschkas we may reverse the metaphor: the aquarium was a like a stereoscope, perfectly reproducing the submarine world in three dimensions.[37] As Gosse had put it, reflecting on his own experience, "I could mark with leisure and precision the manners of the creatures that were living *at home*, yet constantly under my eye."[38] The aquarium enhanced the illusion of an unmediated nature prized by Gosse even as it transformed marine animals into decorative objects. But also, exactly as the aquarium mediated the undersea, domesticated and interiorized it, so it shaped the initial reception of the glass models, the sense of their value and their use. Looking back, Ludwig Reichenbach remembered that "anemones and jellyfish were first attempted and given to lovers of marine aquariums," even offering "the advantage, over living specimens, that when one approaches them they do not contract."[39] Late in 1863, speaking "on the nature and distribution of anemones" to the members of the Natural Science Society ISIS in Dresden, Reichenbach had observed that museum "conservation is up to now not yet successful, while propagating them in marine aquariums presents great difficulties." He presented, as a solution,

> an arrangement of a number of anemone species, exhibited in glass basins filled with water, which are made from colored glass by the glass artist, here today as our speaker, Herr Blaschka. These are such lifelike imitations, and look so particularly splendid in the

---

35 Leopold Blaschka, Dresden, to R. T. Smith, Weymouth, draft, n. d. (late March 1886?), notebook, 1886–1887. LRBC, MS 0013, Box 23. RRL, CMoG, Corning, New York.
36 Leopold Blaschka, Dresden, to R. T. Smith, Weymouth, draft, 25 December 1882, notebook of draft correspondence, 1880–1885. LRBC, MS 0013, Box 23. RRL, CMoG, Corning, New York.
37 Walter Benjamin, *Berliner Kindheit um neunzehnhundert* (Frankfurt/M.: Suhrkamp, 2000), 18.
38 Gosse, *The Aquarium*, 4.
39 Ludwig Reichenbach, notice, catalogue of Leopold Blaschka ("Wenig bekannte Seethiere"), n. d. DF ZOO/200/1/169, Library and Archives, Natural History Museum, London (NHML). See also Florian Huber, "Spiegelbilder vom Meeresgrund: Leopold Blaschka's Marine Aquarien," *Berichte zur Wissenschaftsgeschichte* 36 (2013), 83–84.

water, in which the otherwise disturbing glare of the glass disappears, that they excite to a high degree the amazement of all present.⁴⁰

The bizarre spectacle of a glass aquarium filled with glass organisms was repeated when, as Rudolf later recounted it, a

> number of water-tanks filled with artificial sea-anemones made by my father after Gosse's drawings were exhibited in the Museum. Reichenbach invited the king and the Haute-Volée and Scientific world, whereupon the minister of public instruction permitted the purchase of all the original work of my father in marine Zoology for the Natural History Museum. . . . He had to work very assiduously at home in our lodging as he got plenty orders for artificial aquariums.⁴¹

Here we observe the extraordinary reciprocal play of media forms, the chain of remediation in which the glass aquarium, privileged as a direct portal into undersea life, produces the glass model as perfect imitation of its life forms, only for the model to in turn produce an imitation of the aquarium, confirming *it* as the ground of truth, the scene of nature, precisely by the underlying logic of representation according to which the more perfect the model the more it is a reflection of the *real*.

Constituting the scene of nature on different scales – local, regional, global – became the essential task of natural history in the later nineteenth century. Leopold's work coincided with the rapidly accelerating proliferation of natural history museums in Central Europe, but this was only a variant of a global phenomenon and the Blaschkas were from the beginning linked into transnational scientific and commercial networks and museum markets.⁴² In 1866 Leopold shipped a complete anemone collection to the natural history museum in Liverpool and another to the Stockholm museum and began selling to the Museum of Natural History in

---

40 Sitzungsberichte, 1863 (Dresden, 1864), 170.
41 Rudolf Blaschka, Hosterwitz to Professor George Lincoln Goodale, Cambridge, 6 January 1896 (photocopy). LRBC, MS 0013, Box 21, Folder 12. RRL, CMoG, Corning, New York.
42 The Blaschkas sold to big museums in Berlin and Vienna, among many others. See Sabine Hackethal, "Kunstwerke für die Wissenschaft--Glasmodelle wirbelloser Tiere aus dem Atelier von Leopold und Rudolf Blaschka," in *Klasse, Ordnung, Art: 200 Jahre Museum für Naturkunde*, ed. Ferdinand Damaschun, et al. (Rangsdorf: Basilisken-Presse, 2010), 169; Christa Riedl-Dorn, *Das Haus der Wunder: Zur Geschichte des Naturhistorichen Museums in Wien* (Vienna: Holzhausen, 1998), 200. On the development of natural history museums in Central Europe see Damaschun, et al., ed., *Klasse, Ordnung, Art*; Susanne Köstering, *Natur zum Anschauen: Das Naturkundemuseum des deutschen Kaiserreichs 1871–1914* (Cologne: Böhlau, 2003) and *Ein Musem für Weltnatur: Die Geschichte des Naturhistorischen Museums in Hamburg* (Munich: Dölling & Galitz, 2018); Riedl-Dorn, *Das Haus der Wunder*.

South Kensington.[43] The following year he was sending anemones to the Oxford Museum of Natural History and a "suite of anemones" to the German *Naturalienhändler* Schaufuß. By the winter of 1868 at the latest, the large Prague dealer Václav Frič (1839–1916) began to place orders, becoming a regular and substantial customer.[44] His purchases grew in the early 1870s, in 1872 and 1873 amounting to around ten percent of Blaschka's total sales of both glass eyes and organisms – and signifying the distribution of anemones across Habsburg Central Europe.[45] By the 1880s, Frič's forty-three-page catalogue of naturalia – reptiles, amphibians, fishes, crustaceans, insects, birds, mammals and more – included the Blaschkas' holothurians, corals, medusae and, of course, sea anemones, many familiar from the original encounter with Gosse. It advertised "glass imitations of sea creatures" in "natural colors, remarkably convincing." "Only in this way can one give a clear idea of these wonderful creatures in inland schools."[46] The models entered the market and became – as intended – objects of exchange. They began to appear as series, catalogue numbers, inventories, orders, prices, insured goods and invoices.

The visual experience of these submarine wonders exceeded their use-values as scientific specimens and pedagogical tools. They were startling curiosities, both as fantastical organisms and uncanny representations, but also as highly-wrought objects concealing the traces of their manufacture and thus appearing to bear secrets. They were, equally, aesthetic objects. Philip Gosse's own experience suggests thinking about the reception of the models in a mode of wonder. "There are more ways than one of studying natural history," he wrote, among them "the poet's way; who looks at nature through a glass peculiarly his own; the aesthetic aspect, which deals, not with statistics, but with the emotions of the human mind, – surprise, wonder, terror, revulsion."[47] In the market these

---

43 C. Giles Miller and Miranda Lowe, "The Natural History Museum Blaschka Collections," *Historical Biology* 20, no. 1 (March 2008), 51.
44 Adreß und Preisverzeichniß, 1866–72. LRBC, MS 0013, Box 24. RRL, CMoG, Corning, New York.
45 Notizbüchel für 1869–1870, 1869–71. LRBC, MS 0013, Box 24; Jahres-Rechnung 1872 and Geschäfts-Uebersicht 1873, in Geschäfts-Anmerkungen, 1872–1887. LRBC, MS 0013, Box 23, Folder 64. RRL, CMoG, Corning, New York.
46 Catalogue of Vaclav Frič, n. d. (1886?), Zoological Department, Letters January-June 1886, 29/139, Library and Archives, Natural History Museum, London (NHML). On the relationship with Frič, see also Henri Reiling, "Glass Models of Soft Bodied Animals: The Relation Between Blaschka, Frič and the National Museum," *Časopis Národního muzea, Rada prírodovedná* 117 (2002), 81–84.
47 Philip Henry Gosse, *The Romance of Natural History*, 7th ed. (London: James Nisbet, 1866), v–vi.

emotions resolved into the aesthetics of the decorative and the collectible. The live sea anemone in the tidal pool became interior décor first in the form of aquariums: as Gosse put it, "those imitations of such rock-pools, which we make in glass tanks and china pans for our drawing-rooms."[48] And then in object form, as model. The origins of the Blaschkas' scientific models bear traces of ornament and luxury good. Perhaps even vestiges of the Blaschka family experience of making glass costume jewelry.[49] The models appeared in Leopold's first catalogue "both as decoration for elegant rooms and, appropriately, for instruction in scientific institutes and museums" – fusing science and ornament and instantiating natural history as the global circulation of values.[50] The glass anemones, both in their crystalline form and as exchange values, literalize, in a sense, Marx's metaphorical image of money as a "crystal" (*Geldkristall*) formed "by the exchange process in which different products of labor are effectively equated to one another and thereby in effect transformed into commodities."[51]

The Blaschka models must be read in the context of the traffic in naturalia as much as in scientific or aesthetic terms. Indeed, these categories are inseparable if we perceive in natural history its aspect as a market. For much of the nineteenth century, commerce was the dynamic center of the European science of natural history. The British East India Company's India Museum in London, established in 1801 and soon trafficking in natural history, was an early example of the intertwining of globalizing science and trade.[52] In Germany, Johan Cesar Godeffroy (1813–1885), Hamburg merchant-king and patron of science, set the standard. He was deeply invested in the *Südseegeschäft*, with outposts and agents across Polynesia, Australia, and what became the Bismarck Archipelago. By 1861, he had, as one journalist described it, looking back,

> devised a plan to establish a [. . .] museum [. . .] and to accumulate [. . .] natural science collections [. . .] at his own cost [. . .]. [T]ravelers were employed to research in different countries, particularly Australia and the South Seas and his ships' captains given instructions to collect natural science specimens as well as their observations and experiences and to report on them. In [. . .] the first decade the museum had already collected such

---

48 Gosse, *Actinologia Britannica*, 52.
49 Lorraine Daston, "The Glass Flowers," in *Things That Talk: Object Lessons from Art and Science*, ed. Lorraine Daston (New York: Zone, 2004), 223–254, here 237.
50 Catalogue of Leopold Blaschka ("Wenig bekannte Seethiere"), n. d. DF ZOO/200/1/169, Library and Archives, NHML.
51 Karl Marx, *Das Kapital: Kritik der politischen Ökonomie*, vol. 1 (Berlin: Karl Dietz, 1962), 101–102.
52 Jessica Ratcliff, "The East India Company, the Company's Museum, and the Political Economy of Natural History in the Early Nineteenth Century," *Isis* 107, no. 3 (2016): 504.

magnificent material that it had become [. . .] by far the best, indeed almost the only source of our knowledge of the South Seas.[53]

Godeffroy was celebrated as a businessman who also, unusually, advanced science. "More even than the enterprising spirit of this man as a great merchant, his quality as a friend and patron of science emerges foremost in the public interest."[54] His trade in mother-of-pearl, coconut oil, tortoise shell and trepang – that is, sea cucumbers, taken in the South Seas, boiled, dried, smoked and shipped to China for soup or aphrodisiac – seems barely distinguishable from his traffic in naturalia.[55]

An 1866 catalogue advertised specimens – jellyfish, hydroids, siphonophores, gorgonians, madrepore corals – gathered by Eduard Graeffe in Samoa and Fiji, by Amalie Dietrich in Queensland, and generally by "Godeffroy & Son ships' captains instructed and equipped for the collection of naturalia."[56] Three years later, a 139-page catalogue offered hundreds and hundreds of specimens from the South Seas, Australia, and the Americas, including fish, crustaceans, cephalopods, echinoderms and fifty-eight different medusae from New Holland, Fiji, Samoa, Madeira, Singapore, and Tasmania.[57] The bulk and range and pricing suggested an extraordinary new stability in wildlife inventory amassed on the far side of the earth. Where once such naturalia would have counted as rarities, as curiosities, with emblematic or symbolic meaning to be illuminated in the idiosyncratic collection of the *Wunderkammer*, or curiosity cabinet, now it moved through systematic collection, classification, preparation and shipment.[58] In the 1860s, the Godeffroy Museum offered the Museum of Natural History in Berlin

---

[53] A. Woldt, "Zur Kenntnis der Südsee," *Westermanns Illustrierte Deutsche Monatshefte* 60 (April–September 1886): 329.

[54] Woldt, "Zur Kenntnis," 328.

[55] Helene Kranz, *Das Museum Godeffroy, 1861–1881: Naturkunde und Ethnographie der Südsee* (Hamburg: Altonaer Museum, 2005), 14. See also Birgit Scheps, *Das verkaufte Museum: Die Südsee-Unternehmungen des Handelshauses Joh. Ces. Godeffroy & Sohn, Hamburg, und die Sammlungen "Museum Godeffroy"* (Keltern-Weiler: Goecke & Evers, 2005).

[56] Museum Godeffroy, Catalog III der zum Verkauf stehenden Doubletten aus den naturhistorischen Expeditionen der Herren Joh. Ces. Godeffroy & Sohn (Hamburg, 1866). Library and Archives, NHML.

[57] Museum Godeffroy, Catalog IV (Hamburg, 1869), 125–126. Library and Archives, NHML.

[58] On early modern collecting and the *Wunderkammer* or curiosity cabinet, see Paula Findlen, *Possessing Nature: Museums, Collecting and Scientific Culture in Early Modern Italy* (Berkeley: University of California Press, 1994); Krzysztof Pomian, *Collectors and Curiosities: Paris and Venice, 1500–1800* (Cambridge: Polity, 1990).

specimens from Bangkok, Canton, Penang, Siam, Samoa and elsewhere.[59] By the 1870s, it was in the business of building a South Seas collection for the Museum of Natural History in London.[60] Henry Ward (1834–1906), the biggest North American dealer in naturalia – and the Blaschkas' agent there – described "beautiful coral-polyps and other zoophytes, [. . .] pyrosomes, salpidæ, ascidians, holothurians" and many others preserved in alcohol in the Museum Godeffroy – that "vast storehouse of material available for the cabinets and laboratories of working naturalists," a "Zoological Comptoir" without compare.[61] Many of these were, as Ludwig Reichenbach had lamented, in recommending Leopold Blaschka's work, exactly "those delicate sea [. . .] animals which, preserved in spirits or by other means, entirely lose form and color and close up until they are no longer recognizable."[62] This was exactly the problem Leopold Blaschka was solving with his models; he had found a market niche. At just the same moment, in 1876, he began selling to the august London museum himself.

By then a young carpenter on one of Godeffroy's ships, Johann Umlauff (1833–1889), who would become a celebrated dealer in naturalia in the later nineteenth century, had made his own start in the business.[63] Like Godeffroy, Umlauff got his objects at first rather haphazardly, from travelers, sea captains or naturalists arriving in Hamburg from overseas. By 1868, he founded his own firm, which would develop into a commercial "Welt-Museum," selling "extensive collections of natural-history and ethnographic objects from all parts of the world" to a spectrum of collectors, and developing dense relations with the scientific community (see Figure 6).[64] His son Johannes (1874–1951) later remembered how, through his father's connections with captains and crew, there came entire shiploads of seashells as ballast. The captain of one ship brought

---

59 Correspondence, J. D. E. Schmeltz, Godeffroy Museum, Hamburg to Museum für Naturkunde, Berlin. 1863–69. Museum für Naturkunde der Humboldt-Universität zu Berlin (MfNB), Historische Bild- und Schriftgutsammlungen (HBS). Bestand: Zool. Mus. Signatur: S I Godeffroy Museum.
60 DF ZOO/200/9/231–231e, 232–232h; Schmeltz, Museum Godeffroy, Hamburg to Günther, Library and Archives, NHML, 1876, 1878–79. DF ZOO/200/10/379–385, 387–88, 395–398, 400–403, Library and Archives, NHML.
61 Henry A. Ward, "Museum Godeffroy," *Popular Science Monthly* 8 (1876), 701.
62 Ludwig Reichenbach, notice, Leopold Blaschka, catalogue ("Wenig bekannte Seethiere"), n. d. DF ZOO/200/1/169, Library and Archives, NHML.
63 Hilke Thode-Arora, "Die Familie Umlauff und ihre Firmen--Ethnographica-Händler in Hamburg," *Mitteilungen aus dem Museum für Völkerkunde Hamburg* 22 (1992), 143.
64 H. Benrath, *Hamburg und Umgebungen* (Berlin: Albert Goldschmidt, 1895), 41; Britta Lange, "1892: Die Firma J. F. G. Umlauff präsentiert 'anthropologisch-zoologische Prachtgruppen,'" in *Mit Deutschland um die Welt: Eine Kultrurgeschichte des Fremden in der Kolonialzeit*, ed. Alexander Honold and Klaus R. Scherpe (Stuttgart: J. B. Metzler, 2004), 152.

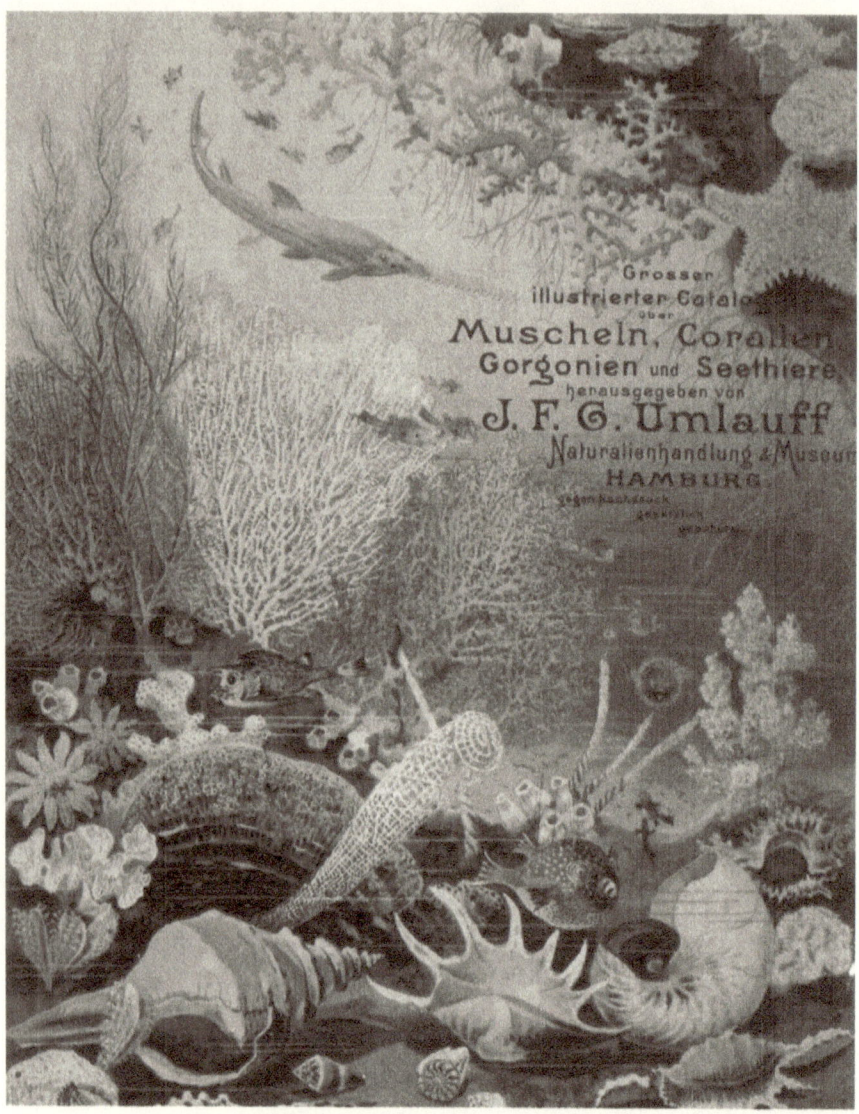

Figure 6: J. F. G. Umlauff, Hamburg. Frontispiece, Large Illustrated Catalogue of Shells, Corals, Gorgonians and Sea Creatures. Circa 1890. Archiv des Zoologischen Museums, Hamburg.

from the South Seas "vast amounts of shells and corals. Every available free spot on the ship was filled, with not just shells but every sort of rarity."[65]

In the 1890s Johannes succeeded his father and expanded the firm in many directions. Over two decades of dealings with the Museum of Natural History in Berlin, he supplied objects for the collection, proposed exchanges, solicited expertise, traded information about objects, collectors and expeditions, demonstrating the reciprocity of business and science.[66] In the late 1890s, he turned his attention to expanding his aquarium business, in particular the novel trade in exotic fish from faraway seas.[67] One of his sea captain collaborators, he recounted, told him "what wonderful sea creatures and fish lived on the sea bottom at Tampico." Yes, he went on, "someone has got to bring that to Hamburg someday, for our aquarium in the zoo." Umlauff, seeing an opportunity, suggested an onboard water tank of wood, with a pump for fresh seawater, and months later received a detailed letter from the ship's paymaster: "basin built, caught with your net the most beautiful fish and crabs and other sea creatures." There would turn out to be "parrot fish, and big bass and two small sharks among them. It was wonderful, our first haul . . . . The steamer was sighted already from Cuxhaven and I prepared everyone for an immediate reception. The professor from the Hamburg Aquarium would not believe it" and "was speechless at what he saw. But he had taken too long to think about the purchase. I had sold everything to Amsterdam and the large vats with all of the fish and other sea creatures would be sent express."[68] Gradually, live specimens of rare and exotic marine life would be introduced onto a global market shaped by the improvisations and innovations of such zoological entrepreneurs. The unknown seas were opened to investigation; coral reefs and broad stretches of ocean to both scientific collection and commodity exchange.

Together these "Sammlungen naturhistorischer [. . .] Gegenstände" – these collections of natural history objects for study and sale – mark the threshold where nature is reconfigured in what Marx in the 1840s called the *gegenständliche Welt*, the world of objects.[69] This is the *Warenwelt*, the world of commodities,

---

[65] Johannes Umlauff, unpublished memoir, no date, 3, Tierpark Carl Hagenbeck, Archive, Hamburg-Stellingen.
[66] J. F. G. Umlauff to Paul Matschie, Museum für Naturkunde, 1895–1913. MfNB, HBS. Bestand: Zool. Mus. Signatur: S III Umlauff J. F. G.
[67] On the development of commercial traffic in live tropical fish, see Brunner, *The Ocean at Home*, 78–85.
[68] Umlauff, unpublished memoir, 20, 21–23.
[69] Karl Marx, *The Economic and Philosophic Manuscripts of 1844* (New York: International Publishers, 1964), 113.

where, like the naturalia they imitate, the glass models manifest as *Geldkristall*. The fugitive form – undulate, pellucid, delicate – crystallized as exchange value in the models. The exquisite fragility of these glass marine invertebrates – the anemones, but also jellyfish, cephalopods and other creatures – effaces the global commercial trajectories in which they moved. Even as models – made permanent, still, fixed for viewing,

They seem to bear the vanishing, translucent qualities of their submarine originals. They had faithfully to depict the ephemeral, shape-shifting invertebrate life of distant seas, which in its watery evanescence eluded adequate representation, by freezing it, objectifying it – by crystalizing it. The glass models were ready for shipment, for science, for pedagogy – for sale. As such, they formed part of a substantial, expanding world of natural history models made of wax, plaster, glass or celluloid: representations of life forms that seemed to expose the limits of lithography.[70] Models and lithographs together moved in a growing stream of naturalia – fossils, shells, mammals, reptiles, butterflies – circulating around the world in the nineteenth century.

The Blaschkas' anemones, these impossibly fragile creations, outlasted the marine profusion that inspired them. Edmund Gosse depicts a melancholy scene of a coastline denuded of anemones already in the late nineteenth century. "All this is long over, and done with," he writes of the diverse and plentiful marine life his father had studied and painted.

> The ring of living beauty drawn about our shores was a very thin and fragile one. It had existed all those centuries solely in consequence of the indifference, the blissful ignorance of man. These rock-basins, fringed by corallines, filled with still water almost as pellucid as the upper air itself, thronged with beautiful sensitive forms of life, – they exist no longer, they are all profaned, and emptied, and vulgarized. An army of "collectors" has passed over them and ravaged every corner of them. [. . .] No one will see again on the shore of England what I saw in my early childhood, the submarine vision of dark rocks, speckled and starred with an infinite variety of color, and streamed over by silken flags of royal crimson and purple.[71]

The object world expanded in proportion to the depletion of the natural world it imitated and, finally, frantically ransacked.

---

[70] On models as visual form and object lesson, as well as on their public reception, see Peter McIsaac's chapter on visual cultures of popular anatomy exhibitions.
[71] Gosse, *Father and Son*, 123–125.

Bibliography

Adreß und Preisverzeichniß, 1866–1872. LRBC, MS 0013, Box 24. RRL, CMoG, Corning, New York.
"Aquarium," *Das Buch der Welt* (1866), 360. LRBC, MS 0013, Box 13. RRL, CMoG, Corning, New York.
Benjamin, Walter. *Berliner Kindheit um neunzehnhundert*. Frankfurt am Main.: Suhrkamp, 2000.
Benrath, H. *Hamburg und Umgebungen*. Berlin: Albert Goldschmidt, 1895.
Blaschka, Leopold. Business card, n. d. LRBC, MS 0013, Box 22. RRL, CMoG, Corning, New York.
Blaschka, Leopold. Catalogue ("Wenig bekannte Seethiere"), n. d. DF ZOO/200/1/169, Library and Archives, NHML.
Blaschka, Leopold. Preface, Katalog über Blaschka's Modelle von wirbellosen Thieren dargestellt von Leopold Blaschka in Dresden. Dresden: Leopold Blaschka, 1885.
Blaschka, Leopold to R. T. Smith, Weymouth, draft, 25 December 1882, notebook of draft correspondence, 1880–1885. LRBC, MS 0013, Box 23. RRL, CMoG, Corning, NY.
Blaschka, Leopold to R. T. Smith, Weymouth, draft, 1 March (1886?), notebook, 1886–87. LRBC, MS 0013, Box 23. RRL, CMoG, Corning, NY.
Blaschka, Leopold to R. T. Smith, Weymouth, draft, n. d. (late March 1886?), notebook, 1886–87. LRBC, MS 0013, Box 23. RRL, CMoG, Corning, NY.
Blaschka, Rudolf. Hosterwitz to George Lincoln Goodale, Harvard University, draft, n. d. LRBC, MS 0013, Box 21, Folder 51. RRL, CMoG, Corning, NY.
Blaschka, Rudolf. Hosterwitz to Professor George Lincoln Goodale, Cambridge, 6 January 1896 (photocopy). LRBC, MS 0013, Box 21, Folder 12. RRL, CMoG, Corning, NY.
Brunner, Bernd. *The Ocean at Home: An Illustrated History of the Aquarium*. New York: Princeton Architectural Press, 2003.
Corbin, Alain. *The Lure of the Sea: The Discovery of the Seaside in the Western World, 1750–1840*. Berkeley: University of California Press, 1994.
Daston, Lorraine. "The Glass Flowers." In *Things That Talk: Object Lessons from Art and Science*, edited by Lorraine Daston, 223–254. New York: Zone, 2004.
Findlen, Paula. *Possessing Nature: Museums, Collecting and Scientific Culture in Early Modern Italy*. Berkeley: University of California Press, 1994.
Frič, Vaclav. Catalogue. n.d. (1886?). Zoological Department. Letters January–June 1886, 29/139. Library and Archives. NHML.
Gosse, Edmund. *Father and Son: A Study of Two Temperaments*. London: Penguin, 1989.
Gosse, Philip Henry. *Actinologia Britannica: A History of the British Sea-Anemones and Corals*. London: Van Voorst, 1860.
Gosse, Philip Henry. *The Aquarium: An Unveiling of the Wonders of the Deep Sea*. 2nd ed. London: John Van Voorst, 1856.
Gosse, Philip Henry. *A Naturalist's Rambles on the Devonshire Coast*. London: John Van Voorst, 1853.
Gosse, Philip Henry. *The Ocean*. London: Society for Promoting Christian Knowledge, 1846.
Gosse, Philip Henry. *The Romance of Natural History*. 7th ed. London: James Nisbet, 1866.
Hackethal, Sabine. "Kunstwerke für die Wissenschaft – Glasmodelle wirbelloser Tiere aus dem Atelier von Leopold und Rudolf Blaschka." In *Art, Ordnung, Klasse: 200 Jahre Museum für Naturkunde*, edited by Ferdinand Damaschun et al. Rangsdorf: Basilisken, 2010.

Huber, Florian. "Spiegelbilder vom Meeresgrund: Leopold Blaschkas marine Aquarien." *Berichte zur Wissenschaftsgeschichte* 36 (2013): 172–186.

Jahres-Rechnung 1872 and Geschäfts-Uebersicht 1873, in Geschäfts-Anmerkungen, 1872–1887. LRBC, MS 0013, Box 23, Folder 64. RRL, CMoG, Corning, New York.

Köstering, Susanne. *Ein Museum für Weltnatur: Die Geschichte des Naturhistorishcen Museums in Hamburg*. Munich: Dölling & Galitz, 2018.

Köstering, Susanne. *Natur zum Anschauen: Das Naturkundemuseum des deutschen Kaiserreichs, 1871–1914*. Cologne: Böhlau, 2003.

Kranz, Helene. *Das Museum Godeffroy, 1861–1881: Naturkunde und Ethnographie der Südsee*. Hamburg: Altonaer Museum, 2005.

Lange, Britta. "1892: Die Firma J. F. G. Umlauff präsentiert 'anthropologisch-zoologische Prachtgruppen.'" In *Mit Deutschland um die Welt: Eine Kulturgeschichte des Fremden in der Kolonialzeit*, edited by Alexander Honold and Klaus R. Scherpe, 152–162. Stuttgart: J. B. Metzler, 2004.

Macdougall, Doug. *Endless Novelties of Extraordinary Interest: The Voyages of H. M. S. Challenger and the Birth of Modern Oceanography*. New Haven: Yale University Press, 2019.

Marx, Karl. *The Economic and Philosophic Manuscripts of 1844*. New York: International Publishers, 1964.

Marx, Karl. *Das Kapital: Kritik der politischen Ökonomie*. Vol. 1. Berlin: Karl Dietz, 1962.

Michelet, Jules. *The Sea*. Copenhagen: Green Integer, 2012.

Museum Godeffroy. Catalog III der zum Verkauf stehenden Doubletten aus den naturhistorischen Expeditionen der Herren Joh. Ces. Godeffroy & Sohn. Hamburg, 1866. Library and Archives, NHML.

Museum Godeffroy. Catalog IV. Hamburg, 1869. Library and Archives, NHML.

Notizbüchel für 1869–1870, 1869–1871. LRBC, MS 0013, Box 24. RRL, CMoG, Corning, New York.

Pomian, Krzysztof. *Collectors and Curiosities: Paris and Venice, 1500–1800*. Cambridge: Polity, 1990.

Ratcliff, Jessica. "The East India Company, the Company's Museum, and the Political Economy of Natural History in the Early Nineteenth Century." *Isis* 107 (2016): 495–517.

Reichenbach, Ludwig. Notice, catalogue of Leopold Blaschka ("Wenig bekannte Seethiere"), n. d. DF ZOO/200/1/169, Library and Archives, NHML.

Reiling, Henri. "Glass Models of Soft Bodied Animals: The Relation Between Blaschka, Frič and the National Museum." *Časopis Národního muzea, Rada přírodovědná* [Journal of the national museum, scientific council] 171 (2002): 81–84.

Riedl-Dorn, Christa. *Das Haus der Wunder: Zur Geschichte des Naturhistorischen Museums in Wien*. Vienna: Holzhausen, 1998.

Rozwadowski, Helen M. *Fathoming the Ocean: The Discovery and Exploration of the Deep Sea*. Cambridge, MA: Harvard University Press, 2005.

Scheps, Birgit. *Das verkaufte Museum: Die Südsee-Unternehmungen des Handelshauses Joh. Ces. Godeffroy & Sohn, Hamburg und die Sammlungen "Museum Godeffroy."* Keltern-Weiler: Goecke & Evers, 2005.

Schmeltz, J. D. E. Godeffroy Museum to MfNB. 1863–1869. MfNB, HBS. Bestand: Zool. Mus. Signatur: S I Godeffroy Museum.

Schmeltz, J. D. E. Museum Godeffroy to Günther, MfNB. 1876, 1878–1879. Library and Archives, NHML. DF ZOO/200/10/379–385, 387–88, 395–398, 400–403, Library and Archives, NHML.

Sitzungsberichte der naturwissenschaftlichen Gesellschaft ISIS in Dresden, 1880. Dresden, 1881.
Sitzungsberichte der naturwissenschaftlichen Gesellschaft ISIS zu Dresden, 1863. Dresden, 1864.
Thode-Arora, Hilke. "Die Familie Umlauff und ihre Firmen – Ethnographica-Händler in Hamburg." *Mitteilungen aus dem Museum für Völkerkunde Hamburg* 22 (1992): 143–158.
Umlauff, Johannes. J. F. G. Umlauff to Paul Matschie, MfNB, 1895–1913. MfNB, HBS. Bestand: Zool. Mus. Signatur: S III Umlauff J. F. G.
Umlauff, Johannes. Unpublished memoir. Hagenbeck Archive, Tierpark Carl Hagenbeck, Hamburg-Stellingen, n. d.
Vennen, Mareike. *Das Aquarium: Praktiken, Techniken und Medien der Wissensproduktion (1840–1910)*. Göttingen: Wallstein, 2018.
Ward, Henry A. "Museum Godeffroy." *Popular Science Monthly* 8 (1876): 699–702.
Williams, Glyn. *Naturalists at Sea: Scientific Travelers from Dampier to Darwin*. New Haven: Yale University Press, 2013.
Woldt, A. "Zur Kenntnis der Südsee." *Westermanns Illustrierte Deutsche Monatshefte* 60 (April–September 1886): 326–344, 455–474.

David Ciarlo
The Traveling Cliché: Circulation and Fixity in Engraved Representations of Ethnographic "Others"

Over the last several decades, scholars have reflected on how often Europeans dealt in clichéd views of non-European "others." Savage African chiefs, sensual Polynesian women, inscrutable Chinese, and sage-like American Indians pepper both the literary and visual culture of Europe in the nineteenth century. In whatever medium or cultural form, such clichéd representations all too often seem to reduce non-European "others" to basic characteristics or even to a singular attribute: in the process, such figures were thereby essentialized as "types."[1] Some have argued that representing peoples as types reflects a peculiarly European way of thought, one that is bound up with Enlightenment modes of categorization.[2] Others have argued equally persuasively that, in the midst of an increasingly interconnected and globalizing world, representing "others" in familiar patterns was not only a comforting way to comprehend complexity, but in fact became a fundamental cornerstone of Europeans' self-identity *as European*.[3] Either way, there seems to be a curious *sameness* even among different types of non-European "others," whether savage Africans or primitive Aboriginals. "Primitives in the age of discovery," Christopher Steiner writes, "appeared to be identical throughout the globe because, wherever they were encountered, they were portrayed and represented by the same people – European

---

[1] A broad, accessible overview can be found in Ewen and Ewen, *Typecasting: On the Arts and Sciences of Human Inequality* (New York: Seven Stories Press, 2006).
[2] The literature on the Enlightenment *vis-à-vis* the categorization of non-Europeans is vast. See particularly George Mosse, *Toward the Final Solution: A History of European Racism* (New York: Howard Fertig, 1978) and more recently, Hans-Jürgen Lüsebrink, ed., *Das Europa der Aufklärung und die außereuropäische koloniale Welt* (Göttingen: Wallstein, 2006).
[3] Scholarship on "otherness" and European identity is equally vast: most recently, see Lara Day and Oliver Haag, eds., *The Persistence of Race: Continuity and Change in Germany from the Wilhelmine Empire to National Socialism* (New York: Berghahn, 2018). For a broad look at "otherness" in Western visual culture as background for this essay, see especially Jan Nederveen Pieterse, *White on Black: Images of Africa and Blacks in Western Popular Culture* (New Haven: Yale University Press, 1992).

https://doi.org/10.1515/9783110696448-011

observers who reduced them to a metaphor of Otherness that served only to confirm European expectations of the exotic."[4]

Germany was no exception to this European habit of representation. As scholars have delved more deeply into the visual history of Germany in recent years, this repetition – this "sameness" of "otherness" – has become ever more clear.[5] In the mid- and late nineteenth century, the savage ferocity of Africans or the erotic beauty of South Sea Islanders appeared again and again in an increasingly broad array of German publications, from entertainment journals to books of travel writing, scholarly treatises, scientific tomes, and children's books. In the process of repetition, such images took on a certain fixity, becoming trite clichés as they collectively constructed an increasingly familiar vision of "otherness."[6]

What is often not recognized, however, is the degree to which the images themselves were not only clichéd, but were *literally* clichés: that is, these images of "others" – like all images circulating through German and European printed visual culture – were engraved wood blocks set alongside the moveable type of the text, or copper or steel engraving plates placed between pages of text. The word "cliché" in fact began as a technical term for an engraved illustration-block in France around 1800, and only later took on its larger meaning – namely, a phrase or idea that has become unoriginal through overuse.[7] The German term is *Klischee* (though other technical terms were also common in German printing) and it too

---

[4] Christopher Steiner, "Travel Engravings and the Construction of the Primitive," in *Prehistories of the Future: The Primitivist Project and the Culture of Modernism*, ed. Elazar Barkan and Ronald Bush (Stanford: Stanford University Press, 1995), 203.

[5] See Joachim Zeller, *Weiße Blicke – Schwarze Körper: Afrikaner im Spiegel westlicher Alltagskultur* (Erfurt: Sutton Verlag, 2010); and Rosemarie Beier-de-Haan and Jan Werquet, eds., *Fremde? Bilder von den "Anderen" in Deutschland und Frankreich seit 1871* (Dresden: Deutsches Historisches Museum, 2009). Illustrations of "otherness" can be found in John Phillip Short, *Magic Lantern Empire: Colonialism and Society in Germany* (Ithaca: Cornell University Press, 2012); Michael Perraudin and Jürgen Zimmerer, eds., *German Colonialism and National Identity* (New York: Routledge, 2010); Joachim Zeller, *Bilderschule der Herrenmenschen: Koloniale Reklamesammelbilder* (Berlin: Ch Links, 2008); Jeff Bowersox, *Raising Germans in the Age of Empire: Youth and Colonial Culture, 1871–1914* (Oxford: Oxford University Press, 2013); and Alexander Honold and Klaus R. Scherpe, *Mit Deutschland um die Welt: Eine Kulturgeschichte des Fremden in der Kolonialzeit* (Stuttgart: J. B. Metzler, 2004), among many other catalogs and monographs.

[6] For other paths and processes by which various modes of imagery could become "standardized," but which I do not discuss in this essay, see David Ciarlo, *Advertising Empire: Race and Visual Culture in Imperial Germany* (Cambridge: Harvard University Press, 2011). These processes include the practices of allegory in tobacco labels (68–69, 72–75), the "visual logic" of colonial power in advertising inserts (192–203), and the racial stereotypification of mass-produced commercial imagery (291–303).

[7] See "cliché" *OED Online*. Oxford University Press, December 2019.

connotes a sense of unoriginality.⁸ The metaphorical meaning emerged out of everyday printing practices. Using the same engraved block in different publications meant that the same image was seen over and over again – and a cliché thereby became *cliché*. Of course, the context for reused illustrations could change dramatically because the same image could fulfill a very different function in a news report than in a scientific treatise or entertaining magazine article. But the "sameness" of the image, especially when attached to different kinds of texts, which could have vastly different stylistic structures, narrative arcs, audiences, and goals, could only intensify the sense of fixity of this otherness. One of the reasons that Germans and Europeans seem to have seen non-Germans and non-Europeans as fixed and unchanging types, I argue here, is that they were, in fact, seeing *the same images* over and over again (whether they realized it or not).

The backdrop for my analysis is the rapid expansion of image reproduction. Over the second half of the nineteenth century, new technologies and practices made image reproduction easier and cheaper. Rotation presses churned out ever-greater quantities of printed matter; paper prices dropped; literacy rose; and new distribution networks (such as the railway) emerged to collectively expand the circulation of print.⁹ New business practices, such as the birth of modern advertising and growing consolidation within the publishing industry, made the printing of text and images less and less expensive.¹⁰ As the scale and scope of print expanded dramatically, the role of illustration took on new importance: images became commercially *necessary* to capture attention and to compete with rival publications.¹¹

---

8 In addition to *Klischee*, the terms *Druckstock, Stereotypie, Galvano* and *Galvanoplastik* were commonly used in German printing between 1850 and 1930. This differing terminology conveyed the distinct technical processes by which the block was made, copied, or even circulated.
9 See Corey Ross, *Media and the Making of Modern Germany* (Oxford: Oxford University Press, 2008), 11–33; Kirsten Belgum, "Unifying a Nation of Readers," in *Popularizing the Nation: Audience, Representation, and the Production of Identity in Die Gartenlaube, 1853–1900* (Lincoln: University of Nebraska Press, 1998), 1–27; and Sibylle Obenaus, *Literarische und politische Zeitschriften, 1848–1880* (Stuttgart: J. B. Metzler, 1987).
10 On advertising, see Dirk Reinhardt, *Von der Reklame zum Marketing: Geschichte der Wirtschaftswerbung in Deutschland* (Berlin: Akademie, 1993). On consolidation in the publishing industry, see Kurt Koszyk, *Deutsche Presse im 19. Jahrhundert, Teil II* (Berlin: Colloquium, 1966).
11 Patricia Anderson, *The Printed Image and the Transformation of Popular Culture, 1790–1860* (Oxford: Clarendon, 1991); and especially Kirsten Belgum, "Visualizing the World in *Meyer's Universum*," *Colloquia Germanica* 49, no. 2/3 (2016 [2018]): 235–258.

In the nineteenth century illustration usually meant engraving.[12] Engraving required tremendous skill, which made it both time-consuming and expensive. For high-end publications, such as luxury editions of books, publishers could afford to commission original copperplate or steel engravings, and they had the luxury of time to wait for completion. (The plates could be interspersed among pages of set type.) For lower-cost magazines or journals that were geared towards a larger public and driven by the need to be both topical and timely, such expensive and slow production of illustrations was not feasible. Wood blocks were quicker and therefore less expensive to engrave than metal. But woodblocks still required great skill to carve, and so were far from *in*expensive. Yet images were needed. The solution for most journals was simple: re-use cliché blocks from elsewhere. Engravings could be used many times: blocks or plates could be loaned out, rented out, or even sold (to recoup costs), while electrotyping could be used to make inexpensive copies of a cliché block.

It only took a bit of creative writing to "re-cast" any image that was available, that is, to narrate the borrowed image into a new role. Indeed, textual re-inscription of previously used and/or borrowed images was one of the mechanisms that made the world of illustration accessible to broader segments of society. The first cheap illustrated journal to appear in Germany, for example, was Johann Jakob Weber's *Pfennig-Magazin* of 1833: its cheap wood engravings were borrowed from a British source, the successful *Penny Magazine* of London.[13] Only the text was set in Germany, as stories were "written around" images that had been carved earlier in London. This cost-savings allowed the *Pfennig-Magazin* a low price, which meant it could orient towards the working classes and reach a circulation of 100,000.[14] Yet the final product was of dubious quality and its

---

[12] Even though planographic printing (lithography) emerged in Germany as early as the 1840s and found its way into offset printing after the 1880s, most illustration through 1910 or so involved relief and intaglio methods. Intaglio persisted in commercial publishing even into the 1930s. For an overview of different types of printed imagery, see Richard Benson, ed., *The Printed Picture* (New York: Museum of Modern Art, 2008).

[13] Charles Knight's *Penny Magazine* appeared in London in 1832 and quickly found a circulation of 200,000 copies per week, but escalating costs of the images brought its demise by 1845. See Richard Altick, *The English Common Reader: A Social History of the Mass Reading Public, 1800–1900*, 2nd ed. (Columbus: Ohio State University Press, 1998), 332–334, 335, and 337; Anderson, *The Printed Image*, 50–83.

[14] In fact, Weber's *Pfennig-Magazin* actually acquired the cliché blocks *third*-hand: the *Pfennig-Magazin* purchased all of its woodcuts from the *Magasin Pittoresque* in Paris, and the Paris publication purchased the clichés from the *Penny Magazine*. Hermann Diez, *Das Zeitungswesen* (Leipzig: Teubner, 1910), 57; and Joachim Kirchner, *Das deutsche Zeitschriftwesen*, vol. II (Wiesbaden: Otto Harrassowitz, 1962), 140. See also Obenaus, *Zeitschriften, 1830–1848* (Stuttgart:

success short lived. Jakob Weber would go on to found the *Illustrirte Zeitung* a decade later in 1843, with a much higher price, and which could therefore commission more original engravings. But the illustrated German press that emerged after the 1850s still frequently used engravings from London or Paris. For example, Hermann Meyer's popular geography magazine *Globus*, started in 1862, reused images from the French travel magazine *Le Tour du Monde*, founded two years prior. Kirsten Belgum has shown how text could re-narrate the re-used image (and, in the process, further fictionalize, intensify, and sensationalize it).[15] The birth of the mass media in Germany was thereby more transnational and more pan-European than we have realized.

As engraved cliché blocks physically crossed national borders, the figurative clichés of the exotic crossed with them. After the 1850s, illustrated entertainment magazines like Leipzig's *Illustrirte Zeitung*, *Die Gartenlaube*, or *Über Land und Meer* became primary fonts of imagery for the German reading public. Each of these bourgeois journals sought to offer surveys of distant lands as a way to interlace edifying content with a bit of fascinating exoticism. *Die Gartenlaube* ["the Arbor"], the most successful and acclaimed of these magazines, was first published in 1853 and attained the unheard-of circulation of 382,000 at its peak in 1875.[16] It was instrumental in building a national community of readers, and even in mapping the contours of "Germanness" before there was a Germany, as Kirsten Belgum has so persuasively argued.[17] Meanwhile, magazines such as the *Illustrirte Zeitung*, *Über Land und Meer*, and *Globus*, tended to focus even more on images of exotic lands.[18] In this purveying of overseas exoticism, the visual imagery of all of these magazines borrowed heavily from the British or French commercial press.

One example of image-borrowing can be found in the *Gartenlaube*, in Ernst von Weber's essay "The Zulus and the Looming Threat of Race War in South Africa" of April 1879. The sensationalistic title – with the idea of "race war" (*Racenkrieg*) so prominent – was a bit unusual for the rather refined, genteel

---

J. B. Metzler, 1986). For a glimpse of this "borrowing" across all three magazines, see Nicola Kaminski and Jens Ruchatz, "Journalliteratur – ein Avertissement" *Pfennig-Magazin zur Journalliteratur* 1 (2017): 23–25. (My thanks to Kirsten Belgum for this source!)

15 Kirsten Belgum, "Popularizing the World: Karl Andree's *Globus*," *Colloquia Germanica* 46, no. 3 (2013 [2016]): 245–265, esp. 255, 256, 258.
16 Obenaus, *Zeitschriften 1848–1880*, 22, 31–33 and 47–48.
17 See especially Belgum, *Popularizing the Nation*, 28–54.
18 See, for instance, Antje Harnisch, "Der Harem in Familienblättern des 19. Jahrhunderts: Koloniale Phantasien und Nationale Identität," *German Life and Letters* 51, no. 3 (1998): 325–341; Belgum "Popularizing the World," esp. 245, 252.

pages of the *Gartenlaube*.¹⁹ But the war between the British and the Zulu that began in January of that year had made for gripping news, particularly after the British disaster at Isandlwana, where a British column was annihilated by a Zulu army. Colonial warfare held a particularly strong appeal for German newspapers and magazines, in that it blended the topicality of current events with the thrill of martial exploits and the stakes of global imperial positioning, all under a fascinating aura of exoticism lent by far-away locales.²⁰ Weber's article begins in the more established mode of a travelogue, offering evocative descriptions of the landscape of southern Africa, a short history of its discovery by European explorers, and a bit on the purported ethnographic peculiarities of the natives there. It then turns to a description of the Natal colony, before finally arriving at the promised topic of race war: the "great mass of blacks [*Schwarzen*]" in Natal colony, Weber relates, vastly outnumber the whites there (with 20,000 whites and 350,000 blacks), and since "seventy percent" of these blacks are of the "powerful and able-bodied race (*Race*)" of the Zulu, they might well obey their "ancestral leaders" in Zululand. Britain's war with the Zulu King Ketschwayo (Cetewayo), Weber concludes, could escalate into a massive uprising of blacks all across Natal, and produce a force of 200,000 *Kafirs* (sic), that could easily drive all whites out of the colony entirely.²¹ This dramatic, violent imagery was odds with the usually more high-minded and restrained tone found in the *Gartenlaube*. At the end of the short essay, Weber plugs his book, *Four Years in Africa* [*Vier Jahre in Afrika*].

The only illustration in Weber's short essay, however, is *not* one that shows Natal, either its landscape or its social conditions or even racial tensions there. It is instead an illustration of three "Types in the Army of the Zulu King Cetshwayo" from neighboring Zululand: a married warrior, an unmarried warrior, and in the center, a member of the royal bodyguard (see Figure 1). This royal bodyguard, with high-feathered headdress and steely gaze, stands with particular prominence. As Weber describes the figure: "A streak of otter skin and a mighty plume adorn his head; a fur blanket of white cow-tails clads his torso. A mighty oval shield of oxhide and a short lance are his traditional weapons [. . .]." Weber assures us that these engravings of Zulu warriors were made "from original

---

19 Ernst von Weber, "Die Zulus und der drohende Racenkrieg in Südafrika," *Die Gartenlaube: Illustrirtes Familienblatt*, Heft 12 (1879): 205–208. Weber uses the Anglicized "Race" instead of the related German term "Rasse" throughout the article.
20 See Ciarlo, *Advertising Empire*, 161–173. On the empire of Great Britain as an alluring theme prevalent in German commercial culture before Germany acquired colonies in 1885, see Ciarlo, *Advertising Empire*, 13, 28, 30–31, 108–114, and 135–137.
21 Weber, *Die Gartenlaube*, Heft 12 (1879): 207.

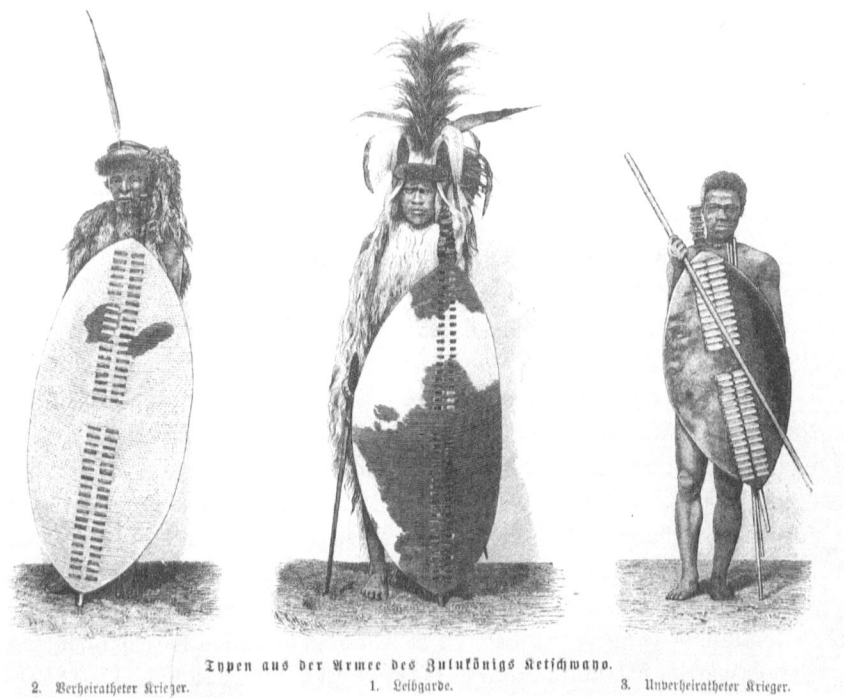

Figure 1: "Types in the Army of the Zulu King Cetshwayo – Married Warrior – Royal Bodyguard – Unmarried Warrior." Note the pattern on the central figure's shield. *Die Gartenlaube* Heft 12 (1879): 205.

photographs." While the illustrations are explicitly captioned as being "types" in the Zulu army, Weber's text seems to contradict the illustration, conceding that "in recent years most of the army has been armed with European rifles."[22] The three illustrated types are perhaps not so typical after all! But the larger question here is why *this* illustration was included in the first place. Weber talks very little about the actual Anglo-Zulu war. Instead, most of his essay is fundamentally about the Natal colony. Why not illustrate this essay with a more relevant image?

As it turns out, the image was likely derived from a British periodical. The *Illustrated London News*, the premier illustrated paper in the world, devoted

---

22 *Die Gartenlaube*, Heft 12 (1879): 208. For an insightful look into Zulu military culture and masculinity – and sporadic use of rifles – see John Laband, *Zulu Warriors: The Battle for the South African Frontier* (New Haven: Yale University Press, 2014), esp. 10–11, 216–217.

most of its 22 February 1879 issue to the Anglo-Zulu war, seeking to feed news and images to a British public hungry for both. The cover illustration of the issue featured an eye-catching image of a massive, brooding, bare-chested King Cetewayo.[23] And the issue features a number of other dramatic illustrations as well, from a vista of the landscape around Rourke's Drift (the site of one of the war's dramatic battles) to vivid engravings of British artillery crews and cavalry in action. Finally, at the end of the issue there appears a supplemental illustration – a collage of "Zulus and Kaffirs of South Africa," drawn and arrayed in ethnographic style (see Figure 2).

Given the recent British defeat at Isandlwana, the *Illustrated London News* article was particularly keen to convey the determination and ferocity of the Zulu. "The Zulu is one of two great nations of Kaffirs [. . .]. Its absolute despotic constitution and singular military organization, with the determined character of its ruler, make it the most formidable of all Native Africa Powers [. . .]." Later, the essay emphasizes, "The Zulu has an innate love of fighting, and firmly believes in his own invincibility."[24] The appended collage of "Zulus and Kaffirs of South Africa" in the *Illustrated London News*, then, visually underscored this narrative by providing fearsome pictures of Zulu warriors alongside the rain makers and witch-doctors who urged them on to fearlessness in battle. The inclusion of "Pondo warriors" is a bit more puzzling. Certainly, as Sadiah Qureshi reflects, lumping the Pondo in with the Zulu and the Xhosa reflected the blurred distinctions of larger "chains of association": in Britain, one black warrior-tribe in southern Africa blurred easily into another.[25] But the depictions of Pondo with the Zulu might also suggest that the engraving of the illustration predated the outbreak of the war with the Zulu. The colonial war in southern Africa made images of Zulus apt and irresistible, and the Pondo figures were left in the collage to avoid having to rework it. In fact, the ethnographic collage was borrowed or duplicated and printed in other magazines, appearing in *Harper's Weekly* in March of 1879, for instance.[26]

---

[23] "Zulu War," *Illustrated London News* LXXIV, no. 2071 (22 Feb. 1879): 165. I abbreviate the *Illustrated London News* as *ILN* throughout the rest of this chapter.
[24] *ILN* LXXIV, no. 2071 (22 Feb. 1879): 168 and 170.
[25] Sadiah Qureshi, *Peoples on Parade: Exhibitions, Empire, and Anthropology in Nineteenth-Century Britain* (Chicago: University of Chicago Press, 2011), 73–76.
[26] *Harper's Weekly*, Supplement, March 29 (1879): 208. *Harper's* engraving might have been an electrotype reproduction: see Marianne Van Remoortel, "Women Editors and the Rise of the Illustrated Fashion Press in the Nineteenth Century," *Nineteenth-Century Contexts* 39:4 (2017): 278–279.

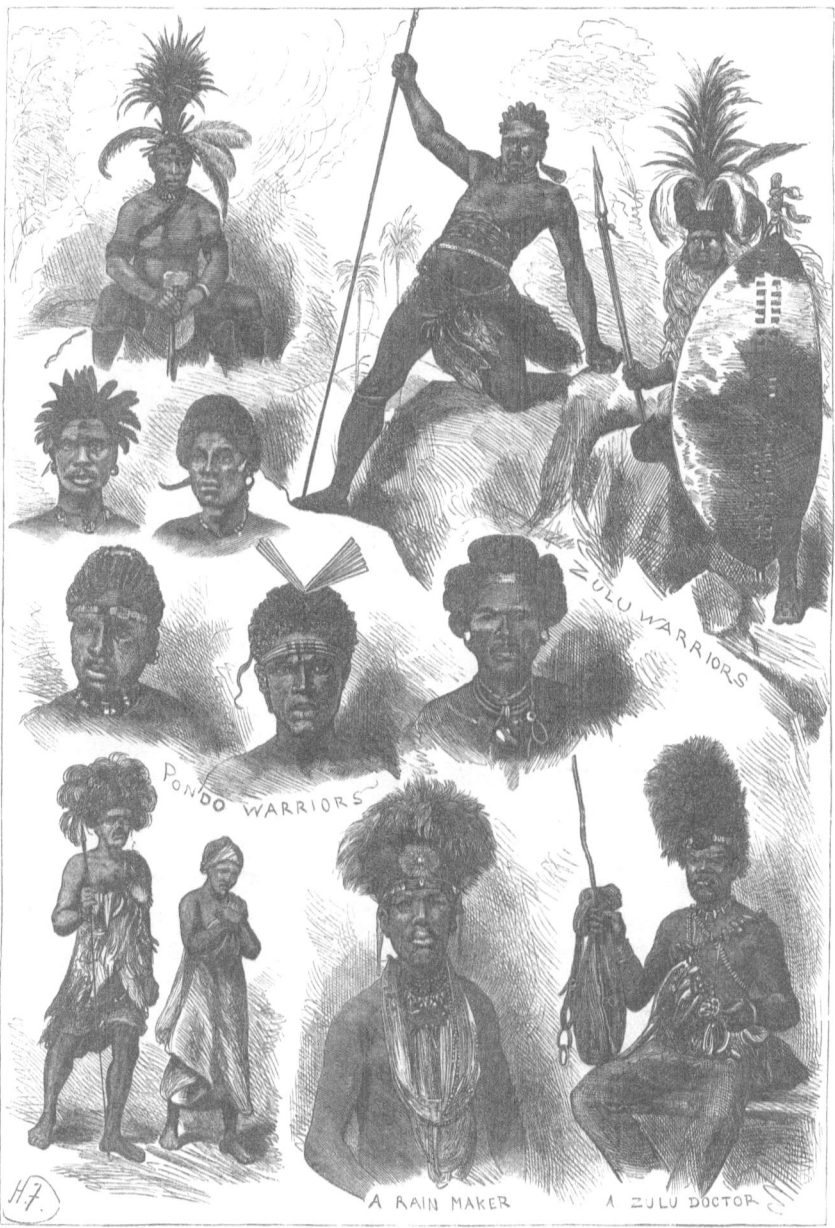

Figure 2: "Zulus and Kaffirs of South Africa." Note again the pattern on the shield of the upper-right figure. *Illustrated London News* LXXIV (22 Feb. 1879): supplement following p. 180.

Evidence of this borrowing is seen in the Zulu warrior in the upper right corner. His head is adorned with a mighty plume, and his torso clad in a fur blanket of white cow-tails. His mighty oval shield of oxhide and a short lance stand at the ready. Yes, it is the same figure that appears in the *Gartenlaube* six months later. It is not the same cliché block, however: the London engraver (initials H.F.) has taken the artistic liberty of perching his Zulu warrior on a rock, ready to spring forth into combat. Moreover, the *Illustrated London News* figure looks to the left (while the *Gartenlaube* figure looks straight on, more befitting a "type") and the white cow-tails in the *Illustrated London News* are in a bit more of disarray. The cowhide shield, however, is mottled in an identical pattern in both illustrations, which reveals a common origin for both images. In fact, we are informed, at the end of the *Illustrated London News* article, that "the page of Illustrations of Zulu and Kaffir people in their native costumes is supplied by the photographs of Mr. Kisch, of Durban."[27] It is possible that multiple copies of a photograph served as the inspiration for both the *Illustrated London News* in London and *Die Gartenlaube* in Leipzig. If so, then the differences between the two engravings show the artistic license that artists could deploy when engraving "from" a photograph. But it is also entirely possible that the *Gartenlaube*'s engravers used the *Illustrated London News* image itself as their model (especially given the difficulty of reproducing photographs in this era).

Illustrated magazines in Britain and Germany took the lead in generating and circulating illustrations to the public across Europe. The reach of the images they produced, moreover, extended far beyond what we commonly recognize today. As the prevalence of imagery grew steadily in the second half of the nineteenth century, other kinds of publications – from travel-writing to fiction – scrambled to find images to "illustrate" *their* writing. And these other publications borrowed or copied images from the periodicals. Even scientific tomes borrowed images from popular magazines. For instance, the Zulu warrior that appears in the *Gartenlaube* (and was likely copied from the *Illustrated London News*) found its way into the geographer Friedrich Ratzel's magisterial tome of ethnography, *Völkerkunde*, six years later (see Figure 3).

(Another of the illustrations from the ethnographic collage – the seated warrior with feathered headdress and tomahawk – appears in Ratzel's book as well,

---

[27] *ILN* LXXIV, no. 2071 (22 Feb. 1879): 170. The note continues, "Our Special Artist, Mr. Melton Prior, who went through the last Kaffir War, is now on his voyage to South Africa for the service of this Journal." The initialed signatures in the corners suggest that the engraver of the ethnographic collage in the supplement is different from the other engravers in the same *ILN* issue.

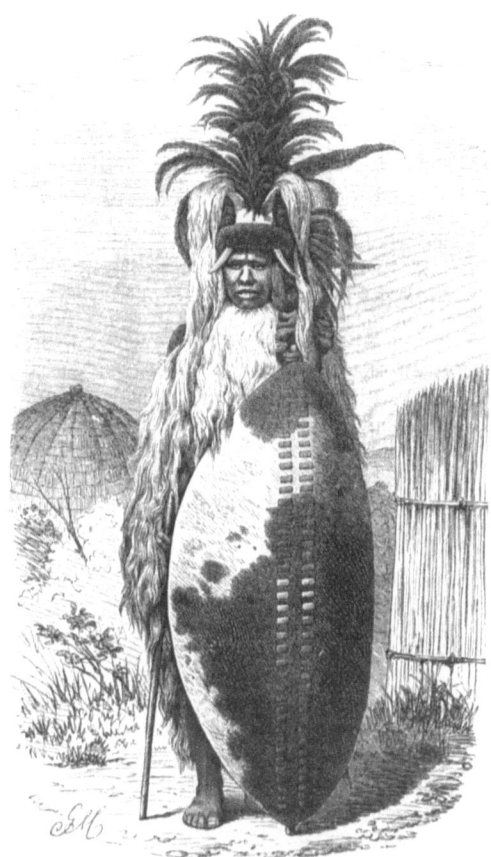

Ein Zuluhäuptling im Kriegsschmucke (nach Photographie im Besitze des Missionsdirektors Herrn Dr. Wangemann in Berlin).

Figure 3: "A Zulu Chieftain in War Costume." Note the pattern on the shield. Friedrich Ratzel, *Völkerkunde: Erster Band. Die Naturvölker Afrikas* (Leipzig: Bibliographisches Institut, 1885), 159.

but re-captioned as a Zulu magician – *Zauberer*.[28]) Ratzel had been a journalist and popularizer of Darwin before joining the faculty at the Technical University of Munich; he moved to Leipzig – where the *Gartenlaube* was published – joining

---

28 Friedrich Ratzel, *Völkerkunde: Erster Band. Die Naturvölker Afrikas* (Leipzig: Bibliographisches Institut, 1885), 268. This is a different engraving, with Ratzel's figure facing a different direction and grass and clouds added in the background among many other changes; it is signed both "G. M." and "Z. A. v. K. Jahrmarg" (certainly Gustav Mützel and Karl Jahrmargt).

the Leipzig University faculty in 1886.²⁹ The first volume of *Völkerkunde* appeared in 1885, and it contains several hundred engraved illustrations. Many of these illustrations were borrowed from prior publications. The Zulu warrior (Figure 3) appears in the section "Allgemeines über die Neger," although differences in detail and the signature of the engraver reveal that it is not the same cliché-block as that of the *Gartenlaube*. Moreover, the figure is no longer a member of the royal bodyguard, but is now re-captioned as a Zulu *chieftain* (*Zuluhäuptling*).

The section-title of Ratzel's tome in which this image appears – "Allgemeines über die Neger" or "General Observations about the *Neger*" – is significant. While the term *Neger* is recognized today as an offensive term laden with racist connotations,³⁰ it first came into more common currency in German in the late eighteenth century as an ostensibly scientific word to replace "Mohr" (Moor), which had romanticized associations.³¹ By the middle of the nineteenth century, the term *Neger* had become a fixture in both German ethnological discourse (as a taxonomic descriptor) and in the popularization of race-theory.³² By the 1880s, it had also become a pivotal concept for German colonialists, where the complexity of a vast range of African cultures and polities were simplified into a single, typified "Neger."³³

---

29 On Ratzel, see especially Andrew Zimmerman, *Anthropology and Antihumanism in Imperial Germany* (Chicago: University of Chicago Press, 2001), 204–207, as well as Woodruff D. Smith, *Politics and the Sciences of Culture in Germany, 1840–1920* (New York: Oxford University Press, 1991), 140–154.
30 See Georg Stötzel and Martin Wengeler, *Kontroverse Begriffe: Geschichte des öffentlichen Sprachgebrauchs in der Bundesrepublik Deutschland* (Berlin: Walter de Gruyter, 1995), 707; Susan Arndt and Antje Hornscheidt, eds., *Afrika und die deutsche Sprache. Ein kritisches Nachschlagewerk* (Münster: Unrast, 2004), 184–189.
31 Peter Martin, *Schwarze Teufel, edle Mohren. Afrikaner in Bewußtsein und Geschichte der Deutschen* (Hamburg: Junius, 1993), especially 81–88 and 195–204.
32 The literature on German racial thinking vis-à-vis Africa and blackness is truly vast. See Zimmerman, *Anthropology and Antihumanism*; George Mosse, *Toward the Final Solution: A History of European Racism* (New York: Howard Fertig, 1978); Zeller, *Weiße Blicke – Schwarze Körper*; Richard T. Gray, *About Face: German Physiognomic Thought from Lavater to Auschwitz* (Detroit: Wayne State University Press, 2004), among many others.
33 For some of the different articulations of race vis-à-vis "Neger" in colonialist discourse, see Frank Becker, ed. *Rassenmischehen – Mischlinge – Rassentrennung. Zur Politik der Rasse im deutschen Kolonialreich* (Stuttgart: Steiner 2004); Birthe Kundrus, *Moderne Imperialisten: das Kaiserreich im Spiegel seiner Kolonien* (Köln: Böhlau, 2003), 219–261; Renate Hücking and Ekkehard Launer, *Aus Menschen Neger machen. Wie sich das Handelshaus Woermann an Afrika entwickelt hat.* (Hamburg: Galgenberg, 1986); and Sebastian Conrad, *Globalization and the Nation in Imperial Germany* (Cambridge: Cambridge University Press, 2014), 77–143.

Borrowed imagery played a role in this larger process of typification and simplification, which ultimately fed into popular racism. In his chapter, "General Observations about the *Neger*," Ratzel makes many broad claims, including that "der Neger" tends naturally towards despotism, and so tribal chiefs must play the part.[34] Ratzel continues, "the arrogance and vanity of the *Neger* chiefs (*Negerfürsten*), so often annoying to the Europeans, is therefore only natural."[35] African chiefs *must* puff themselves up, for (given the "natural" tendency of the *Neger* towards despotism) such puffery and dramatic appearance is a crucial element of the chief's political power. As an example, Ratzel offers a mocking description from the famous explorer Henry Morton Stanley, who talks of a Manjema chief who "struts around his village, holding a staff in his hand as if it were a royal scepter, dressed in a large mass of plaited grass (that could be measured at 20 square meters in size) twined around his waist in double folds, decorated with trinkets and fringes, his skin painted with different colors, bronze and black, white and yellow, and on his head, a headdress of feathers." This Manjema chief, Ratzel adds knowingly, "is a type that, in all of its grotesque ridiculousness, is just so familiar."[36] Here, I emphasize that this Zulu chieftain (Figure 3) does not appear in Ratzel's large section on the Zulu.[37] Instead, in his section on "General Observations about the *Neger*," Ratzel wants to give us a visual illustration of the puffery, vanity, and arrogance he describes. Ratzel thus promotes the figure from warrior to chieftain to better fit the text he was trying to illustrate. The rather striking image of a fearsome royal bodyguard from the *Gartenlaube* has now been recast as an image of the ridiculousness of African leaders more generally.

An even more unsettling dynamic may well be at play here. Perhaps the image came first. Ratzel began with this available engraving (or original photograph) and desired to incorporate such a dramatic exotic image. Ratzel might well have crafted the text about puffery, vanity, arrogance, and ridiculousness *in order to fit the image*, based on what he imagined his readers would see in it (or describing what he himself saw). Indeed, in this era before extensive

---

34 Friedrich Ratzel, *Völkerkunde: Erster Band. Die Naturvölker Afrikas* (Leipzig: Bibliographisches Institut, 1885), 157.
35 Ratzel, *Völkerkunde: Erster Band*, 158. The following sentence goes on to describe another "trait" (*Eigenschaft*) of the *Negercharakter*.
36 "[. . .] ist bei aller grotesken Lächerlichekeit nur ein Typus für viele ähnliche." Ratzel, *Völkerkunde: Erster Band*, 158, 159.
37 In Ratzel's section on the Zulu, *Völkerkunde: Erster Band*, 239–270, there is an image of a "Zuluzauberer" – a Zulu "magician" – that is identical to that in the upper left of the *Illustrated London News*. See Ratzel, *Völkerkunde: Erster Band*, 268; *ILN* LXXIV, no. 2071 (22 Feb. 1879): 170 and footnote 27.

fieldwork, when ethnography itself was largely an "armchair" phenomenon of the metropole, anthropologists were dependent upon such sources as travel narratives, ethnographic shows (*Völkerschauen*), and museum collections for their information.[38] Perhaps recycled engravings should be added to this list of sources. In this situation, Stanley's quotation about strutting Manjema chieftains would have been dug up and inserted to bolster the point he was making based upon the image. We have no way of knowing, but it does raise questions about the actual focal point of Ratzel's ethnographic gaze. Regardless of which came first – the text or the image – the disjunction between this image and the text around it only becomes apparent once we recognize the ways in which the image was used previously to show different things. With this in mind, Ratzel's caption that the image is "drawn from photographs in the possession of the mission-director Dr. Wangemann in Berlin"[39] might not only be recognized as a reassurance that the image is authentic (and not invented from whole cloth), but also seen as Ratzel's desperate insistence that *his* usage of this often-used image – his interpretation of it – is the most legitimate one.

Thus, in a few short years, this image of a Zulu warrior made quite the journey from London to Leipzig and possibly also via Durban and Berlin, if captions about photographic origins are to be taken at face value. But a journey took place in meaning as well: in London, the figure was the image of a fierce and determined opponent, a member of an ethnic group whose innate love of fighting requires that the British take them seriously. Two months later in Leipzig, the image was now an ethnographic "type," standing in to represent the larger racial threat posed by the more numerous blacks to the paltry whites in southern Africa. Finally, six years later, the image is presented by a popularizing geographer as a "racial type," as a typical African leader, who puffs himself up with feathers and beads, a costume that appears ridiculous to knowing Europeans, but is "only natural" given the *Neger's* racial inclination towards despotic authority. The arc of the figure's meaning, then, moves from deadly serious, to just deadly, to neither deadly nor serious, but instead naturally ridiculous.

---

[38] See Zimmerman, *Anthropology and Antihumanism*, 15, 217–218.

[39] This is surely Theodor Wangemann, the director of the Berliner Missionsgesellschaft from 1865 to his death in 1894, and son of the famous missionary in southern Africa, Hermann Wangemann. I have not yet successfully located any photographs of Wangemann's that may have survived, however. Ratzel also credits his Zulu "magician" (see footnote 32) as "nach Photographie im Besitze des Missionsdirecktors Herrn Dr. Wangemann in Berlin." Ratzel, *Völkerkunde: Erster Band*, 268.

In this dawning era of illustration, images themselves were in short supply, and so they were reused or copied across publications that had radically different goals. The more heavily-illustrated the book, it seems, the more likely its illustrations had appeared elsewhere earlier. Meanwhile, the trade in clichés had become, by the second half of the nineteenth century, a thriving side-business of established publishing houses. Publishers would regularly gather their cliché blocks to print booklets of clichés for sale to other publishers, printers, and (after the 1880s) even to advertisers. Some of these cliché offerings were meant to be convenient and timely, namely, offering publishers a ready-made illustration that, with re-captioning and agile writing, could capitalize on current news and events. As one example, the Cliché-Katalog of the Verlag Leonhard Simion printed in 1885 included a cliché of the "Zulufürst Cetewayo"[40] (see Figure 4).

Even after the defeat of the Zulu by the British at Ulundi in 1879, the Zulu remained in the news. Cetewayo came to London in 1882, and this leader featured prominently in the visual culture of the British capital, in illustrated dailies and humorous caricature, but also in photography and even high-art portraiture.[41] But the cliché of Cetewayo that the German publishing house of Simion offered for sale seems a bit odd. It was not the famous, dramatic illustration of a "savage" Cetewayo, bare-chested, in feathered headdress that featured on the front page of the *Illustrated London News* in February of 1879.[42] Neither was it Carl Sohn's oil painting of the Zulu celebrity from 1882, which presented a sympathetic portrait (while featuring an exotic tiger-tooth necklace). Nor was it Alexander Bassano's photograph of a westernized Cetewayo wearing a three-piece suit.[43] Instead, they offered an older image – a stranger image, an engraving with Anglicized features for the Zulu king, who sports a very odd, cone-style hat topped with feathers (compare Figure 4). As it turns out, Simion borrowed the cliché itself from the London weekly illustrated *The Graphic* of February of 1879.[44] Indeed, although Simion's image is truncated (cropping off Cetewayo's legs as well as the throne-like chair on which he sits), and though there are other modifications (such as larger eyes), Simion's "Zulufürst" seems to be the same block as that from *The Graphic*, since the print reveals identical engraving cut-marks (see Figure 5). The *Graphic*'s engraving of Cetewayo (with the conical hat), it turns out, was

---

40 *Cliché-Katalog* (Berlin: Verlag Leonhard Simion, 1885), Nr. 112.
41 Catherine E. Anderson, "A Zulu King in Victorian London: Race, Royalty and Imperialist Aesthetics in Late Nineteenth-Century Britain," *Visual Resources* 24, no. 3 (2008): 299–319.
42 *ILN* LXXIV, no. 2071 (22 Feb. 1879), cover.
43 Anderson, "A Zulu King," 309, 309, and especially the juxtaposition of the two in the caricature on p. 312.
44 *The Graphic*, 22 February (1879): 185.

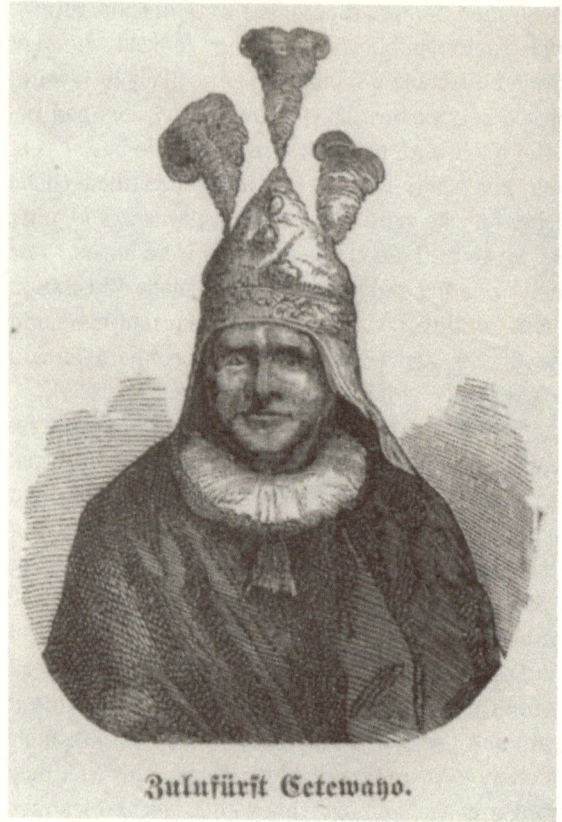

Figure 4: "Zulu Ruler Cetewayo," purchase-able cliché. Cliché-Katalog of the Verlag Leonhard Simion (Berlin, 1885), Nr. 112.

widely shared: it appeared in later publications on the Zulu War, such as in James Grant's popular series on British battles in 1894.[45]

Where did the *Graphic* get the original image for *their* engraving? They seem to have crafted it from an older engraving of Cetewayo's coronation in 1873 (attended by the South African Secretary for Native Affairs, Theophilus Shepstone). This coronation engraving, featuring a larger scene with many European and

---

[45] James Grant, *British Battles on Land and Sea,* Vol. IV (London/Paris/Melbourne: Cassell Petter & Galpin, 1880). The printed image appears here even more worn; but it is clearly the same block as the *Graphic's*, as the cut-marks are identical.

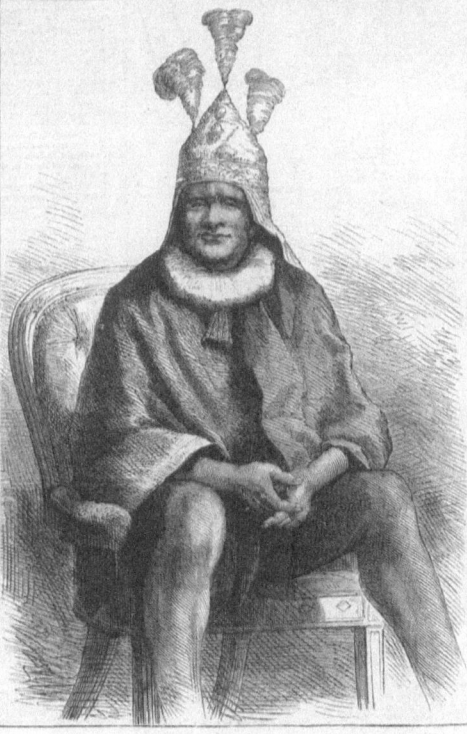

Figure 5: "Cetewayo, King of the Zulus." *The Graphic* (22 February, 1879), 185. (Also in James Grant, *British Battles on Land and Sea*, Vol. IV, Cassell Petter & Galpin, 1880).

Africans posing together, can be found in the monthly reader's digest *Sunshine* of 1883 (see Figure 6).[46]

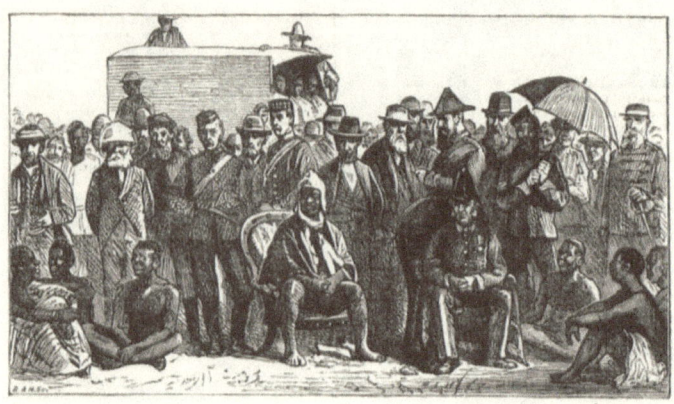

Figure 6: "The Coronation of Cetewayo." Engraving based upon a photograph from 1873. W. Meynell Whittemore, ed., *Sunshine for 1883: for the Home, the School, and the World* (London: George Stoneman, 1883), 160.

Sunshine certainly did not carve it themselves, as *Sunshine* was a religious penny-magazine, edited by the Reverend William Meynell Whittemore, that compiled and reprinted serialized stories and religious poetry, as well as pictures collected from other sources. I have not yet found the original source from which *Sunshine* reprinted. It must be a different cliché block than that in *The Graphic* since the conical hat, for one thing, has no feathers.

As it turns out, all of these images can be traced to the same original source: a photograph from 1873, which has survived.[47] Both the engraving in *Sunshine* and that in *The Graphic* turn out to be rather artistic interpretations when compared

---

46 See W. Meynell Whittemore, ed., *Sunshine for 1883: for the Home, the School, and the World* (London: George Stoneman, 1883), 160.
47 The photograph is reproduced in Ken Gillings, *Discovering the Battlefields of the Anglo-Zulu War* (Pinetown, South Africa: 30 Degrees South publishers, 2014), 16. It is credited as from the author's personal collection.

to the actual photograph. The engraver of the image that ended up in *Sunshine*, for instance, clarified the blurry and indistinct figures in the photograph – and in the process, visually differentiated the black figures from the white figures to a much greater degree. (In the blurry photo, it is not easy to distinguish the black and white participants from each other.) Meanwhile, the *Graphic*'s engraver, focusing on Cetewayo, invented a number of details – most notably, the three feathers on the conical hat. The hat, it turns out, may even have survived in a Welsh museum.[48] In both processes of engraving, then, we can immediately see the tremendous liberties engravers took in rendering a "faithful" reproduction.[49]

In short, Simion's cliché, offered for sale to German magazines and advertisers, stood at the tail-end of a long line of borrowings from British publishers. Borrowed or copied from *The Graphic*, it was what Simion had available, even though (a decade out of date) it had been superseded by almost countless other images of the Zulu king. In nineteenth-century publishing, an available image was a potentially useful one. Still, the engravings, borrowed and copied over a decade, ended up radically different from the original photograph, given the artistic re-interpretations and copying of copies at every step along the way. By the 1880s, of course, the cliché trade in Germany was big business: all significant publishing houses had a cliché section, which would regularly rent out their blocks to other publishers (often for a fee, of course). But even well into the 1880s, the original font for many German commercial images remained the illustrated weeklies of London. Borrowed images thereby helped to illustrate (and make "visual") a whole range of commercial texts.

---

[48] I say "may have survived," because the "crown of Cetewayo" which was "presented to him by Sir Theophilus Shepstone" is on display at the Regimental Museum of the Royal Welsh in Brecon (see Gillings, *Battlefields*, 16), but looks nothing like the cone-shaped hat in the photograph *or* the feathered cone-hats in the various engravings. Richard Davies, the Curator of the Regimental Museum of The Royal Welsh, relates that "The Museum purchased [the headdress] from a man named James Hooper in March 1950. Mr. Hooper ran a museum in Croxley Green, Hertfordshire, but he bought and sold ethnographical material from Africa, Asia and the Pacific region. I cannot verify the story of it having been presented to King Cetshwayo. This may have been provided to Mr. Gillings (himself now deceased), by a former curator of this museum . . . Mr. Hooper felt the headdress was brought back to Britain by a member of the 24th Regiment who fought against the Zulu nation in 1879." Richard Davies (curator, Regimental Museum of The Royal Welsh) email correspondence with the author, January, 2020.
[49] For a revealing example of an engraver's altering of a photograph to clarify its meaning in a colonialist frame, see "Treaty Making in East Africa," in James Ryan, *Picturing Empire. Photography and the Visualization of the British Empire* (London: Reaktion, 1997), 221.

Personal connections, moreover, played a role in securing borrowed images. An example from an unexpected quarter is Rudolf Cronau's *The Book of Advertising* [*Das Buch der Reklame*] published in Leipzig in 1887, which was effectively the first book on advertising in the German language.[50] Despite its title and status, the book is less a handbook for advertising professionals than a bricolage of travel writing and erudite conjecture; it describes the long history of advertising as innate to human society, and deploys dramatic images to showcase important moments in this long history.[51] Indeed, Cronau's tome is heavily illustrated, with literally hundreds of engraved woodcuts: it thereby offers us not only a glimpse into early advertising but a panorama of the nineteenth-century visual world. We see fantastic street scenes of New York and illustrations of scorpion-eating and cheek-piercing Dervishes of the Orient. We see centuries-old Albrecht Dürer prints reproduced alongside the most modern Pears Soap ads. We see bedraggled sandwich-board carriers from the streets of London in the same section as a Basuto Rain-Maker from an African tribal village and a mask-wearing Lama from the remote Himalayas. Such an overabundance of imagery is rather startling in a popular and inexpensive publication from the 1880s: indeed, the cost would have been prohibitive – except that a close look reveals that the vast majority of images were borrowed.

As it turns out, Rudolf Cronau had worked for the *Gartenlaube* in the 1880s, as a travel-writer and journalist, and also as an illustrator and engraver of considerable talent. In 1879, he engraved a striking illustration of the new *Germania* statue for the *Gartenlaube*, for instance, as well as a romantic landscape on the Coast of Cameroon, that depicted the new German colony as a tropical paradise even though Cronau had never been to West Africa.[52] He became widely-known in Germany from his article-series in the *Gartenlaube* "Um die Erde" that evocatively narrated his travels to New York and from there into the interior of the American west.[53] Cronau cashed in on this renown, giving talks as an "expert"

---

[50] Rudolf Cronau, *Das Buch der Reklame: Geschichte, Wesen und Praxis der Reklame* (Ulm: Wohler'schen, 1887). Technically, J. H. Wehle's *Die Reclame, ihre Theorie und Praxis* (Vienna: A. Hartleben, 1880) was the first book on advertising in the German language, but it received far less attention in Germany.

[51] See also Ciarlo, *Advertising Empire*, 108–109, 112–114, 120–125, 146.

[52] See *Die Gartenlaube*, Heft 25 (1879): 413, *Die Gartenlaube*, Heft 40 (1884): 665, and especially Belgum, *Popularizing the Nation*, 165–167.

[53] This series began with "Um die Erde: Erste Brief: Aus den Straßen New-Yorks," *Die Gartenlaube*, Heft 31 (1881): 508–510, and concluded with "Um die Erde: Zwölfter Brief: Tchanopa-o-kä, das Heiligthum der rothen Rasse." *Die Gartenlaube*, Heft 5 (1883): 83–87. See especially H. Glenn Penny, *Kindred by Choice: Germans and American Indians since 1800* (Chapel Hill: University of North Carolina Press, 2013), 98–100. Engravings from this trip are

on America and on Native Americans (especially the Sioux), and publishing a number of books as well.[54] Indeed, in 1886, he even accompanied a *Völkerschau* of Sioux that traveled through Europe.[55] Cronau, in short, became a master at purveying the exotic to German audiences. He would eventually emigrate to the United States, where his artistic renderings of Native Americans and western landscapes became well known.[56]

Crucially, Cronau was deeply familiar with the world of images from his work as an illustrator with *Die Gartenlaube*. Though a talented artist himself, the hundreds of illustrations in *The Book of Advertising* were not his own; that would have been impracticable. Cronau instead accessed the *Gartenlaube*'s cliché collection, and he also borrowed innumerable clichés from other publications as well. Some of these "borrowings" are attributed in captions: Cronau's illustration of a merchants' street in Canton, which features the hanging merchant signs in exotic-looking Chinese characters, is attributed to "Hubner, *Ein Spaziergang um die Welt* [A Stroll Around the World]."[57] Most of the borrowings are *not* attributed, however. Cronau's ode to P.T. Barnum (the greatest huckster of them all), for instance, includes an engraving of Barnum's special advertising coach ("*Ankündigungswagen*"), which shows a train coach vividly decorated with paintings of exotic animals, such as bison, bears, lions, elephants, all framing a bust of Barnum himself. (In the engraving, appreciative onlookers tip their hats or otherwise hail the vividly-painted train car.)[58] The original, uncredited illustration can be found in *Frank Leslie's Illustrated Newspaper* of 1878.[59] The

---

reproduced in Gerold Wunderlich, *Rudolf Cronau, 1855–1939: Topographical Views of America* (New York: Gerold Wunderlich & Co., 1993).

54 Rudolf Cronau, *Fahrten im Lande der Sioux* (1886). On Cronau's view of and relationship to American Indians, see the thoughtful and thorough chapter in Penny, 96–126. Cronau's heavily illustrated publications on Native Americans, "the Wild West," and the discovery of America include *Von Wunderland zu Wunderland* (1886/87); *Im Wilden Westen* (1890); *Amerika: Die Geschichte seiner Entdeckung* (1892).

55 *Über Land und Meer* 28, no. 56 (1886): 1074. The article describes the show as "unter Führung des genial Landschaftmalers Rudolf Cronau." Glenn Penny, however, argues that it is more likely that Cronau, already on the lecture circuit for his tales of the Sioux, was simply asked by Fred Harvey to accompany the show. Penny, 113–114.

56 See the biographical sketch of Cronau at the Museum of Nebraska Art, https://mona.unk.edu/mona/rudolf-cronau/

57 See Cronau, *Reklame*, Part I, 19. This is Alexander Freiherrn von Hübner, *Ein Spaziergang um die Welt. Mit 324 Abbildungen* (Leipzig: Schmidt & Günther, 1889), 423.

58 Cronau, *Reklame*, Part VI, 211.

59 *Frank Leslie's Illustrated Newspaper* XLVI, no. 1,191 (27 July 1878), supplement p. 361. The block might even predate 1878 by a decade and a half, as Leslie himself was an engraver for P. T. Barnum's short-lived *Illustrated News* of 1853.

engravings are identical, though small imperfections in Cronau's version reveal some wear-and-tear of the block. It is clear that Cronau borrowed this now decade-old cliché block from Frank Leslie. In another case, while looking at advertising in New York City, Cronau borrowed a number of clichés from a *Scribner's* special essay on advertising a half-decade earlier, in 1880. Cronau's illustrations of "Sandwichmen" (sign-board carriers) and a wagon advertising dumb-bells, for instance, are the same cliché blocks as those in the Scribner's essay.[60] Backtracing the visual abundance in *The Book of Advertising*, then, gives us a glimpse of how heavily book publishers borrowed clichés from illustrated magazines.

The borrowing of imagery had particularly significant implications for meaning when the figures were of exotic "others" from distant lands. As we have seen, images of non-Europeans –and especially, of primitive or savage peoples – were particularly desired, in that their exoticism drew readers. This exotic allure flowed from a *lack* of familiarity, of course: while a European reader might personally encounter a sandwich-board carrier in the city, for instance, they would never encounter a Zulu witch-doctor. It is not surprising, then, that images of exotic "others" became so common in magazines, popular scholarship, and even books of advertising. (Despite the fact that the *text* of *The Book of Advertising* is mostly about European and American advertising, the bulk of the illustrations are exotic and/or ethnographic, which certainly brought Cronau's book a great deal of attention.[61]) At the same time, images of exotic "others" could be imagined as showing a more complete "truth" about the "type" being depicted. Personal encounters with familiar figures, such as sandwich-board carriers, would immediately erode any claim that any single printed image of a sandwichman might accurately represent them all. But exotic "others" were not encountered in the everyday, so that an illustration of a Zulu warrior could more easily be seen as distilling some larger truth about the Zulu as a type. Finally, the constant reuse of these exotic clichés, I argue, lent the imagery of exotic others a visual fixity that fit well with the ideologies of typologies, typecasting, and racial differentiation. (And indeed, the fixity of these images fed into popular racism as well.) An image of an African savage, for instance, would seem all the more "typical" if the same image appeared in different sorts of publications, to different sorts of readers, who would all share (if unknowingly) a visual memory of the image.

An additional example is provided by Cronau's image of "A Rainmaker and Sorcerer of the Basuto" (see Figure 7). The illustration appears in the chapter

---

[60] Cronau *Reklame*, Part I, 31 and 44; *Scribner's Monthly (The Century Magazine)* 20, no. 4 (1880): 607 and 608.
[61] On this point, see Ciarlo, *Advertising Empire*, 116–125.

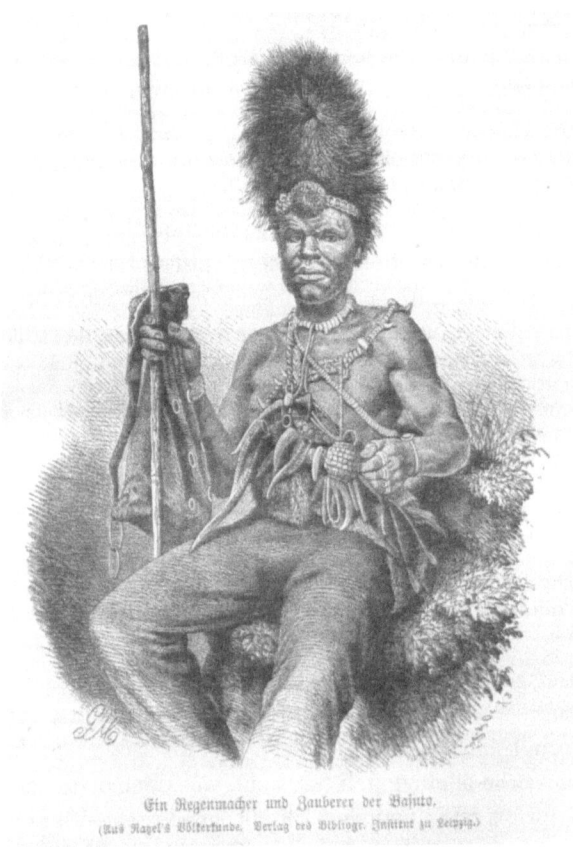

Ein Regenmacher und Zauberer der Basuto.
(Aus Ratzel's Völkerkunde. Verlag des Bibliogr. Instituts zu Leipzig.)

Figure 7: "A Rainmaker and Sorcerer of the Basuto. (From Ratzel's Völkerkunde.)" Compare to Figure 2, bottom left. Rudolf Cronau, *Das Buch der Reklame: Geschichte, Wesen und Praxis der Reklame* (Ulm: Wohler'schen, 1887) Part II, 15.

"Of Magicians, Shamans, Medicine-Men, and Rain-makers," which Cronau starts off by averring, "The members of the lower rungs of the primitives (*Naturvölker*) do not know how to explain and interpret everyday natural phenomena and their effects [. . .] Their *fear*, which is the source of all religion, drives them [. . .] to humble pleading and supplication (prayer) or to offer gifts (sacrifices) to gain favor."[62] While rain-makers might seem to stray far afield from the book's ostensible topic, Cronau's text does wind back around to advertising: *all* cultures, from the most primitive to the most modern, create

---

62 Cronau, *Reklame*, Part II, 1–2. Italics added.

"advertising" that offers products that promise magical results. However, Cronau concludes at the end of his section, one cannot *excuse* the sorcerers by claiming they believe in their own magical powers; they "deserve no other name than *worthless fraudster* and *unconscionable advertiser*."[63] Cronau's sharp critique of sorcerers who take advantage of superstition, also becomes a not-so-subtle jab at false promises by unscrupulous modern advertisers. By using the "primitives" to make this point, he can do so more subtly and also more sensationally.

Cronau borrows most of his images of exotic "others," just as he borrowed most of the hundred-odd illustrations in his book. He credits the illustration of the Basuto Rainmaker to Friedrich Ratzel (who had published the first volume of his *Völkerkunde* in 1885, two years prior). Cronau clearly borrowed an enormous number of cliché blocks from Ratzel's publisher, the Bibliographisches Institut. The Bibliographisches Institut, as Kirsten Belgum has shown us, was an early pioneer of both producing and borrowing engraved imagery. This firm published many illustrated works of geography, from the series *Meyer's Universum* (1833–1860) to the inexpensive *Die fünf Weltteile* in the 1850s.[64] With Cronau's *The Book of Advertising*, personal connections with Ratzel certainly played a role in the borrowing: several of Cronau's own illustrations, such as a luxurious color lithograph of a Sioux War-Dance, appear in the second volume of Ratzel's *Völkerkunde* which was then in progress.[65] Cronau and Ratzel, in short, traded pictures.

Cronau's rainmaker and sorcerer illustration appears in Ratzel's first volume on Africa as a *Basutozauberer* – a Basuto sorcerer – in his section on the Bechuana (Tswana) people.[66] The engraving, it turns out, was done by the artist Gustav Mützel, famous for his bird engravings, who created many of the illustrations in Ratzel's scholarly tome. Ratzel's intention for the image was quite different than Cronau's, though: Ratzel, as a geographer and popular ethnographer, was seeking to delineate and typologize ethnographic groups across Africa and the world, in pop-scientific fashion. Ratzel uses the "Basuto sorcerer" specifically to describe and illustrate the contours of primitive religion. He does so in a rather patronizing and dismissive way: "It is impossible to understand their many superstitious customs without understanding their belief in supreme powers. The savages' (*Wilden*) lack of logic goes a long way, but not

---

63 Cronau, *Reklame*, Part II, 23. Italics added.
64 Belgum, "Visualizing the World," especially 237–238, 240, and 249.
65 "Sioux Beim Kriegestanz. Nach der Natur von Rudolf Cronau," in Friedrich Ratzel, *Völkerkunde: Zweiter Band. Die Naturvölker Ozeaniens, Amerikas, und Asiens* (Leipzig: Bibliographisches Institut, 1886), 638.
66 Ratzel, *Völkerkunde: Erster Band*, 301.

so far that they would pray (*erflehen*), and sacrifice all sorts of things, for nothing." Ratzel's text then describes the power of the tribal rainmaker in the dry African climate: his authority could exceed even that of the chief, able to issue all sorts of strict commands and injunctions to villagers. And a rainmaker could even claim that he could turn the villages of an enemy into desert wastelands by directing the clouds themselves.[67] "All of this is taken as pure truth," Ratzel assures us. But prevarication comes with a price: "It is a noteworthy fact that no rainmaker ever dies of natural causes. There is no tribe whose people have not dipped their hands into the blood of these deceivers, who they first adore, then curse, and then, ultimately, kill."[68] Ratzel's and Cronau's texts on "religion" echo each other: but where Cronau writes about commonality (between African and European beliefs; between trickster-rainmakers and unscrupulous advertisers) with some sympathy, Ratzel seeks to underscore the racial difference (of the natural primitives) with mockery.

Ultimately, the legitimacy of Ratzel's musings depends both upon his authority as a scholar and on the sources he can draw upon and present. The illustration of the Basuto sorcerer, then, is both visual flair for the book – an illustration of his text – and a building-block of his scholarly authority in its own right. The engraving of the Basuto sorcerer, Ratzel claims, is drawn from photographs in the possession of the mission director Dr. Wangemann in Berlin.[69] And yet Ratzel's "Basuto" sorcerer can be seen in that same collage of "Zulus" from the *Illustrated London News* of 1879 and reprinted in *Harper's* (Figure 2).[70] What are we to make of this claim, that the engraving is from an original photograph in Berlin, when we can see that the illustration was published six years earlier in London?

One thing we do know is that the image also appeared in other sources before Ratzel's book. The illustration is found in Robert Brown's *Peoples of the World*, published in 1882, and captioned as a "Zulu 'Doctor'" (with the word Doctor in quotation marks) (see Figure 8).[71] Interestingly, Brown's illustration is neither Mützel's version reproduced in Ratzel's and Cronau's books, nor a cut-out from the collage of the *Illustrated London News* and *Harper's*; the engraved markings on the bag, the delineation of musculature, and the "native"

---

67 Ratzel, *Völkerkunde: Erster Band*, 300.
68 Ratzel, *Völkerkunde: Erster Band*, 303.
69 See footnote 39, above, on Theodor Wangemann.
70 *Harper's Weekly*, Supplement, March 29 (1879): 208. See also Figures 7, 8, and 9 below.
71 Robert Brown, *Peoples of the World Being a Popular Description of the Characteristics, Manners, and Customs of the Human Family*, Volume 2 (London: Cassell, Petter, Galpin & Co., 1882), 240.

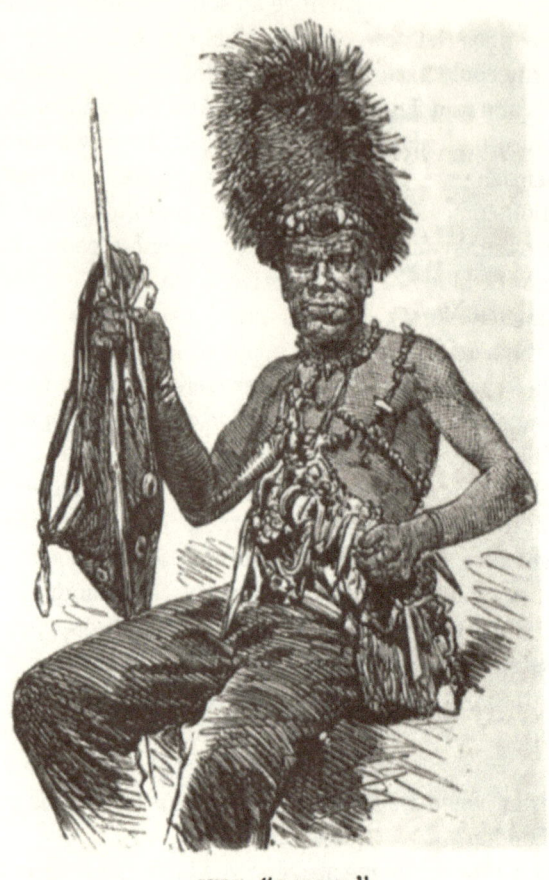

ZULU "DOCTOR."

Figure 8: "Zulu 'Doctor.'" Robert Brown, *Peoples of the World Being a Popular Description of the Characteristics, Manners, and Customs of the Human Family*, vol. 2 (London: Cassell, Petter, Galpin & Co., 1882), 240.

amulets and necklaces are all quite different from both.[72] In Brown's *Peoples of the World*, the Zulu Doctor illustration is nestled in a section on marriage and dowries. Curiously, there is absolutely no reference to the image itself in the text

---

72 Based on the shoddier execution of the engraving in Brown's *Peoples of the World*, it was either carved by a less-skilled artist or by one working from a poor original – perhaps from the print in the *London Illustrated News*.

at all. The illustration may have been a last-minute insert, simply to provide eye-catching exoticism.⁷³ Indeed, Brown's book barely mentions the Zulu, even though it reprints a half-dozen illustrations of Zulu, including a number borrowed from the *Illustrated London News*. The role of these Zulu images in Brown's *Peoples of the World* seems to provide visual flair. Given the media interest in the Zulu War in the few years before, images of Zulus were likely among the most readily available and widely circulating images of exotic others. Consider: this same version of the Zulu "Doctor" appears a year later in the Rev. John Mackenzie's *Day-Dawn in Dark Places: A Story of Wanderings and Work in Bechwanaland*. The book is a missionary's account of his travels and missionary work in southern Africa between 1858 and 1882, replete with stories of natural wonders, crippling fevers, and confrontations with suspicious African chiefs and stubborn African superstition. The figure appears in a section that describes the growing tension between the Bechuana's "heathen" ways and the Christianity preached by the missionaries and their converts; the heathens, MacKenzie relates, believed in witchcraft and feared that by converting to Christianity they would lose all protection from hostile spells. The illustration follows several pages later and is captioned, simply, "A Sorcerer."⁷⁴ It is clear that Cassel, the publisher of both this missionary account and Brown's popular ethnography, was simply repurposing their cliché block for both of these books. Another illustration from MacKenzie's book, however, is of a "Rain-Maker." This is a different version of the Rain Maker in the bottom of the Zulu collage in Figure 2. It is clear that Cassell had their own engraver simply copy some of the figures from *Illustrated London News* several years earlier.⁷⁵

This is not the end of the Zulu doctor/sorcerer/rainmaker. Almost three decades later, in the late 1920s, the figure appears again, this time in a book oriented towards children, as a more generic "African witch-doctor (*Zauberdoktor*)" (see Figure 9). Wilhelm Fintel's, *Shaka the Great Zulu King* (1928) offers a romanticized story of the dramatic rise of Shaka Zulu.⁷⁶ The engraving here is, in fact, a *fourth* version; one can tell by the number of circles visible on the figure's bag, and the different position of rings on the figure's fingers, for

---

73 Brown's earlier book, *The Races of Mankind*, published before the Anglo-Zulu war, does not include this Zulu "Doctor," which suggests the image was not yet widely available to copy. See Robert Brown, *The Races of Mankind* (London: Cassell, Petter, Galpin & Co., 1873–1876).
74 Rev. John Mackenzie, *Day-Dawn in Dark Places: A Story of Wanderings and Work in Bechwanaland* (London: Cassel, 1883), 229–238, see illustration on 240.
75 MacKenzie, *Dark Places*, 37.
76 Wilhelm von Fintel, *Tschaka der große Zulukönig* (Hermannsburg: Verlag der Missionshandlung, 1928), 32.

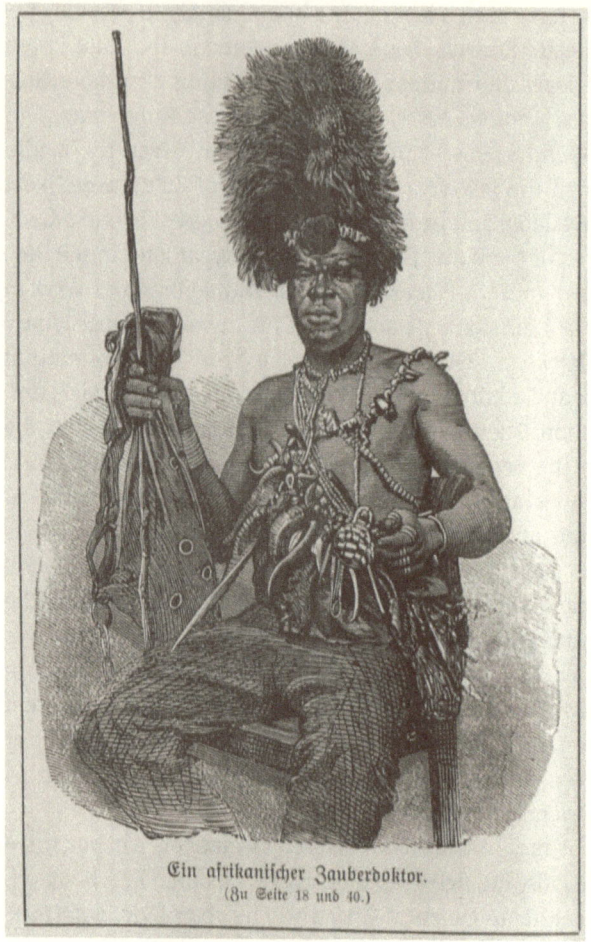

Figure 9: "An African Witch-Doctor (for pages 18 and 40)." Wilhelm von Fintel, *Tschaka der große Zulukönig* (Hermannsburg: Verlag der Missionshandlung, 1928), 32.

instance. The illustration, one of only a handful in the book, adds both exotic and "authentic" visual flavoring. It also provides grist for the invention of detail. The author, Fintel, vividly describes a scene from early in Shaka's rise to power: on a hot January morning of 1812, a mighty Zulu army assembled, and out strode "a doctor, painted in war-colors, carrying a mat in which was a sharp axe, a knife, a magic bag made out of a gnu's tail, and medicine was carefully wrapped up."⁷⁷ This must be pure invention, as records of Shaka's early life are incredibly sparse.⁷⁸ But the fictional scene seems sparked and guided by the inclusion of the "witch-doctor" illustration itself. Image availability, in short, inspired historical invention.

The Zulu/Basuto witch-doctor/rainmaker made one last appearance in print. In 1969, when the State Library of Pretoria reprinted Hermann Wangemann's missionary memoir *Biographical Sketches from South Africa* (originally published in 1876), they featured this image on the cover – an engraved version, and yet one still different from *all* of the versions discussed thus far.⁷⁹ As a cover-illustration for a reprint, it is an odd choice, for it does not at all "fit" with Wangemann's original illustrations. The 1876 edition included engravings of southern African landscapes and romanticized sketches of African individuals such as Josef Kathedi. For the cover of the 1969 reprint edition, either a photograph found in one of Wangemann's archival papers or a copy of one of the earlier engravings served as the source. By whatever means it came to the publisher by the late 1960s, the "Basuto/Zulu/Bechuana Rainmaker-Sorcerer-Witch-Doctor" had taken on such visual momentum that it must have *seemed* the "right" cover choice for the State Library of Pretoria's reprint. In truth, the cover is anachronistic, deviating wildly from the visual style seen in the original memoir.

Clichés of exotic others, then, were something more than the simple pictorialization of ideological constructions. They instead possess a history in their own right, involving a complex web of visual imitation that ranged from the simple borrowing of cliché blocks, to the re-engraving of plates or recutting into woodblocks, to the artistic interpretation of photographs. German ethnographers copied illustrations of Zulu warriors from Leipzig entertainment magazines – illustrations that German magazine editors likely first saw in London illustrated journals. German publishers offered clichés of Zulu kings for sale, borrowing the actual blocks from British tabloids, that in turn had copied them from other engravings, engravings which were already very loose interpretations of original photographs. And German popular writers borrowed clichés

---

77 Fintel, *Tschaka*,18.
78 See Carolyn Hamilton, *Terrific Majesty: The Powers of Shaka Zulu and the Limits of Historical Invention* (Cambridge: Harvard, 1998), 36–71.
79 Hermann Wangemann, *Lebensbilder aus Südafrika: Ein Beitrag zur Kirchen- und Culturgeschichte des neunzehnten Jahrhunderts*, 3ʳᵈ edition (Berlin: Verlag des Berliner Missionshauses, 1876). Hermann Wangemann was the father of Theodor. See also Kirsten Rüther and Angelika Schaser, *Gender and Conversion Narratives in the Nineteenth Century: German Mission at Home and Abroad* (Farnham, England: Ashgate, 2019): 105–148.

from German ethnographers, who borrowed from British tabloids or were inspired by them. Moreover, these traveling clichés were *durable*. These illustrations could end up in a children's book a half a century later or adorn the cover of a reprint almost one hundred years later.

All too often, the implications of these traveling clichés for the study of visual culture is overlooked. Scholars often see the illustrations in a journal or book that they are researching, and assume that the image was created *for* that publication and thereby also assuming that the illustration reflects or connects to authorial "perspective." Yet, as we have seen, many images have origins elsewhere. Indeed, for any *inexpensive* illustrated publication from the 1850s through 1900, odds are high that some or most of the images were crafted earlier for a different publication elsewhere and may have crossed national boundaries or even an ocean. The images one finds, then, often have little to do with national culture or even the perspective in the author's text. Instead they were simply images that happened to be on hand.

Authors often wrote "around" images, shaping much more fungible text to "fit" whatever images happened to be readily available. In the process, Zulu warriors were promoted to African chiefs, and martial valor was thereby transformed into ridiculous posturing. African leaders, like Cetewayo, became a literal cliché to be sold in a series of copyings and borrowings, even as the image veered wildly from the original photographic record. Zulu doctors became Basuto sorcerers who became Basuto rain-makers who became African witchdoctors. The fact that these images were used over and over again, interchangeably, erased these images' specificity, and, I would suggest, this helped to erode the individuality of the subjects – the *people* – being depicted. In this way, the constant repetition of images of Zulu warriors or the constant repatterning of African chieftains lent itself to their fixity as *types*, and thereby, reveals one more avenue in the visual reification of racial difference.

The driving force behind this re-circulation, re-usage, and re-patterning of images was neither philosophical nor ideological. It was commercial. For the image-lender (such as the illustrated magazines), selling or renting their engravings was an opportunity to recoup some of the high costs of production. For the image-borrower, repurposing an already existing image allowed one to compete economically in the visual world. Certainly, images in publications collectively constructed images of "Others" and of "selves" in Germany. But at least some portion of this construction stemmed from commercial practices rather than from deliberate or ideologically-driven self-stylings. We see the same *types* of images over and over in the German visual world, because they are clichés: they *are* the same images.

Bibliography

Altick, Richard. *The English Common Reader: A Social History of the Mass Reading Public, 1800–1900*. 2nd ed. Columbus: Ohio State University Press, 1998.
Anderson, Catherine E. "A Zulu King in Victorian London: Race, Royalty and Imperialist Aesthetics in Late Nineteenth-Century Britain." *Visual Resources* 24, no. 3 (2008): 299–319.
Anderson, Patricia. *The Printed Image and the Transformation of Popular Culture, 1790–1860*. Oxford: Clarendon, 1991.
Arndt, Susan, and Antje Hornscheidt, eds. *Afrika und die deutsche Sprache: Ein kritisches Nachschlagewerk*. Münster: Unrast, 2004.
Becker, Frank. ed. *Rassenmischehen – Mischlinge – Rassentrennung: Zur Politik der Rasse im deutschen Kolonialreich*. Stuttgart: Steiner, 2004.
Beier-de-Haan, Rosemarie, and Jan Werquet, eds. *Fremde? Bilder von den "Anderen" in Deutschland und Frankreich seit 1871*. Dresden: Deutsches Historisches Museum, 2009.
Belgum, Kirsten. *Popularizing the Nation: Audience, Representation, and the Production of Identity in "Die Gartenlaube," 1853–1900*. Lincoln: University of Nebraska Press, 1998.
Belgum, Kirsten. "Popularizing the World: Karl Andree's *Globus*." *Colloquia Germanica* 46, no. 3 (2013 [2016]): 245–265.
Belgum, Kirsten. "Visualizing the World in *Meyer's Universum*." *Colloquia Germanica* 49, nos. 2–3 (2016 [November 2018]): 235–258.
Benson, Richard, ed. *The Printed Picture*. New York: Museum of Modern Art, 2008.
Bowersox, Jeff. *Raising Germans in the Age of Empire: Youth and Colonial Culture, 1871–1914*. Oxford: Oxford University Press, 2013.
Brown, Robert. *Peoples of the World Being a Popular Description of the Characteristics, Manners, and Customs of the Human Family*. Vol. 2. London: Cassell, Petter & Galpin, 1882.
Brown, Robert. *The Races of Mankind*. London: Cassell, Petter & Galpin, 1873–1876.
Ciarlo, David. *Advertising Empire: Race and Visual Culture in Imperial Germany*. Cambridge, MA: Harvard University Press, 2011.
Cliché-Katalog. Berlin: Leonhard Simion, 1885.
Conrad, Sebastian. *Globalization and the Nation in Imperial Germany*. Cambridge: Cambridge University Press, 2014.
Cronau, Rudolf. *Das Buch der Reklame: Geschichte, Wesen und Praxis der Reklame*. Ulm: Wohler'schen, 1887.
Cronau, Rudolf. *Fahrten im Lande der Sioux*. Leipzig: Weigel, 1886.
Day, Lara, and Oliver Haag, eds. *The Persistence of Race: Continuity and Change in Germany from the Wilhelmine Empire to National Socialism*. New York: Berghahn, 2018.
Diez, Hermann. *Das Zeitungswesen*. Leipzig: Teubner, 1910.
Ewen, Elizabeth. *Typecasting: On the Arts and Sciences of Human Inequality*. New York: Seven Stories, 2006.
Fintel, Wilhelm von. *Tschaka der große Zulukönig*. Hermannsburg: Missionshandlung, 1928.
Frank Leslie's Illustrated Newspaper. New York: Frank Leslie, 1878.
Die Gartenlaube: Illustrirtes Familienblatt. Leipzig: Ernst Keil, 1853–1884.
Gillings, Ken. *Discovering the Battlefields of the Anglo-Zulu War 30*. Pinetown, South Africa: 30 Degrees South, 2014.

Grant, James. *British Battles on Land and Sea*. Vol. 4. London: Cassell Petter & Galpin, 1880.
The Graphic. London: Illustrated Newspapers, 1879.
Gray, Richard T. *About Face: German Physiognomic Thought from Lavater to Auschwitz*. Detroit: Wayne State University Press, 2004.
Harnisch, Antje. "Der Harem in Familienblättern des 19. Jahrhunderts: Koloniale Phantasien und Nationale Identität." *German Life and Letters* 51, no. 3 (1998): 325–341
Hamilton, Carolyn. *Terrific Majesty: The Powers of Shaka Zulu and the Limits of Historical Invention*. Cambridge, MA: Harvard University Press, 1998.
Harper's Weekly. New York: Harper & Brothers, 1879.
Honold, Alexander, and Klaus R. Scherpe. *Mit Deutschland um die Welt: Eine Kulturgeschichte des Fremden in der Kolonialzeit*. Stuttgart: J. B. Metzler, 2004.
Hübner, Alexander Freiherr von. *Ein Spaziergang um die Welt*. Leipzig: Schmidt & Günther, 1889.
Illustrated London News. London: Illustrated London News & Sketch, 1842.
Kaminski, Nicola, and Jens Ruchatz. "Journalliteratur – ein Avertissement." *Pfennig-Magazin zur Journalliteratur* 1 (2017): 23–25.
Kirchner, Joachim. *Das deutsche Zeitschriftwesen*, Vol. 2. Wiesbaden: Otto Harrassowitz, 1962.
Koszyk, Kurt. *Deutsche Presse im 19. Jahrhundert*. Part 2. Berlin: Colloquium, 1966.
Kundrus, Birthe. *Moderne Imperialisten: das Kaiserreich im Spiegel seiner Kolonien*. Cologne: Böhlau, 2003.
Laband, John. *Zulu Warriors: The Battle for the South African Frontier*. New Haven: Yale University Press, 2014.
Lüsebrink, Hans-Jürgen, ed. *Das Europa der Aufklärung und die außereuropäische koloniale Welt*. Göttingen: Wallstein, 2006.
Mackenzie, Rev. John. *Day-Dawn in Dark Places: A Story of Wanderings and Work in Bechwanaland*. London: Cassel, 1883.
Martin, Peter. *Schwarze Teufel, edle Mohren: Afrikaner in Bewußtsein und Geschichte der Deutschen*. Hamburg: Junius, 1993.
Mosse, George. *Toward the Final Solution: A History of European Racism*. New York: Howard Fertig, 1978.
Obenaus, Sibylle. *Literarische und politische Zeitschriften, 1830–1848*. Stuttgart: J. B. Metzler, 1986.
Obenaus, Sibylle. *Literarische und politische Zeitschriften, 1848–1880*. Stuttgart: J. B. Metzler, 1987.
Penny, H. Glenn. *Kindred by Choice: Germans and American Indians since 1800*. Chapel Hill: University of North Carolina Press, 2013.
Perraudin, Michael, and Jürgen Zimmerer, eds. *German Colonialism and National Identity*. New York: Routledge, 2010.
Pieterse, Jan Nederveen. *White on Black: Images of Africa and Blacks in Western Popular Culture*. New Haven: Yale University Press, 1992.
Qureshi, Sadiah. *Peoples on Parade: Exhibitions, Empire, and Anthropology in Nineteenth-Century Britain*. Chicago: University of Chicago Press, 2011.
Ratzel, Friedrich. *Völkerkunde: Erster Band; Die Naturvölker Afrikas*. Leipzig: Bibliographisches Institut, 1885.
Ratzel, Friedrich. *Völkerkunde: Zweiter Band; Die Naturvölker Ozeaniens, Amerikas, und Asiens*. Leipzig: Bibliographisches Institut, 1886.

Reinhardt, Dirk. *Von der Reklame zum Marketing: Geschichte der Wirtschaftswerbung in Deutschland*. Berlin: Akademie, 1993.
Ross, Corey. *Media and the Making of Modern Germany*. Oxford: Oxford University Press, 2008.
Rüther, Kirsten, and Angelika Schaser. *Gender and Conversion Narratives in the Nineteenth Century: German Mission at Home and Abroad*. Farnham, England: Ashgate, 2019.
Ryan, James. *Picturing Empire: Photography and the Visualization of the British Empire*. London: Reaktion, 1997.
Scribner's Monthly: The Century Magazine. New York: Scribner & Co., 1880.
Short, John Phillip. *Magic Lantern Empire: Colonialism and Society in Germany*. Ithaca, NY: Cornell University Press, 2012.
Smith, Woodruff D. *Politics and the Sciences of Culture in Germany, 1840–1920*. New York: Oxford University Press, 1991.
Steiner, Christopher. "Travel Engravings and the Construction of the Primitive." In *Prehistories of the Future: The Primitivist Project and the Culture of Modernism*, edited by Elazar Barkan and Ronald Bush, 202–225. Stanford: Stanford University Press, 1995.
Stötzel, Georg, and Martin Wengeler. *Kontroverse Begriffe: Geschichte des öffentlichen Sprachgebrauchs in der Bundesrepublik Deutschland*. Berlin: Walter de Gruyter, 1995.
Van Remoortel, Marianne. "Women Editors and the Rise of the Illustrated Fashion Press in the Nineteenth Century." *Nineteenth-Century Contexts* 39, no. 4 (2017): 278–279.
Wangemann, Hermann. *Lebensbilder aus Südafrika: Ein Beitrag zur Kirchen- und Culturgeschichte des neunzehnten Jahrhunderts*. 3rd ed. Berlin: Berliner Missionshaus, 1876.
Whittemore, W. Meynell, ed. *Sunshine for 1883: for the Home, the School, and the World* London: George Stoneman, 1883.
Wunderlich, Gerold. *Rudolf Cronau, 1855–1939: Topographical Views of America*. New York: Gerold Wunderlich & Co., 1993.
Zeller, Joachim, *Bilderschule der Herrenmenschen: Koloniale Reklamesammelbilder*. Berlin: Ch. Links, 2008.
Zeller, Joachim. *Weiße Blicke – Schwarze Körper: Afrikaner im Spiegel westlicher Alltagskultur*. Erfurt: Sutton, 2010.
Zimmerman, Andrew. *Anthropology and Antihumanism in Imperial Germany*. Chicago: University of Chicago Press, 2001.

Part 3: **Image and Text**

John D. Benjamin
Image and Text

The previous sections, "Ways of Seeing" and "Materials and Media," considered how people in the nineteenth century came to see and interact with new materials in novel ways in a period of significant changes in trade and education. Along with rapid industrialization came an increase in literacy as well as in consumable materials disseminated to be viewed *and* read. This final section now turns to the affordances of two central modes of meaning construction[1]– the visual and the verbal; image and text – and the changes that occurred in the relationship between them in the period before photography. It considers what happens to Gotthold Ephraim Lessing's claim that "the passage of time is the domain of the poet, just as space is the domain of the painter"[2] when time and space no longer behave and relate as they once did. This phenomenon is further complicated when we recall the topics of this volume's first two sections, that is, the changes in materials creators used and the audiences who interacted with their work.

Visual culture studies can look to many prior examples of this type of inquiry, including early German works such as Alexander Gottlieb Baumgarten's *Aesthetica* (1750), Johann Joachim Winckelmann's *Thoughts on the Imitation of Greek Works in Painting and Sculpture* (1755), and Lessing's *Laocöon* (1766) or those by more recent figures from fields like semiotics, Roland Barthes and Umberto Eco, and multimodality studies, Gunther Kress and Theo van Leeuwen. This final section contributes to this tradition with three chapters investigating how images and words, the visual and the verbal, interact in the period before photography.

Antje Pfannkuchen's chapter, "Image, Language, Science: Hieroglyphs and the Romantic Quest for Primordial Truth," opens the section by questioning how best to understand the roles of the verbal and the visual in the figure of the hieroglyph in eighteenth- and nineteenth-century German culture. Brief histories of the hieroglyph in ancient Egypt and its incorporation into eighteenth-century scientific writing preface how German Romantics appropriated its sacred linguistic form for their own purposes. Using the work of Novalis, among others, Pfannkuchen shows how the authors were able to make the formerly invisible speak to an audience

---

[1] For a useful overview of discussions of image-text relations as well as a metalanguage for discussing the meaning potentialities of modes of meaning, see Gunther Kress and Theo van Leeuwen, Reading Images: The Grammar of Visual Design (London: Routledge, 2006).
[2] "[D]ie Zeitfolge ist das Gebiete des Dichters; so wie der Raum das Gebiete des Malers." Gotthold Ephraim Lessing, *Laokoon* (Stuttgart: Reclam, 1964), 123. [translation mine]

through the visual symbol of the hieroglyph. Her chapter culminates in a look at aural and visual experiments conducted by the physicists Georg Christoph Lichtenberg and Ernst Florens Friedrich Chladni at the close of the eighteenth century to make sound and electricity visible, much as the Romantics did with hieroglyphs.

The remaining chapters each consider a well-known author in light of the visual images juxtaposed with their literary work. Agnes Hoffmann's contribution, "A Poetics of Scaling: Adalbert Stifter and the Measures of Nature Around 1850," focuses on scalar changes to visual observation in the work of Adalbert Stifter. She first examines the perspectival shifts in the preface to his *Many-Colored Stones*, an 1853 volume of short stories. Hoffmann then discusses how Stifter's *Indian Summer* (1857), a *Bildungsroman* bearing many characteristics of the Biedermeier period, addresses issues of scale in its verbal descriptions of the visual – here focused on the natural world. In so doing, like Pfannkuchen, she connects the world of science to literature. Finally, she considers how this verbal description of the visual can be read together with and in light of Stifter's own art critical writings and painterly work.

In the final chapter, "Adventure from Concentrate: Visual Interventions in German Youth Adaptations of James Fenimore Cooper's *Leatherstocking Tales*," Matthew O. Anderson discusses the diversity of editions published for youth and adult readers in Germany during the 1840s–1850s of works by Cooper, including *Leatherstocking Tales*, a five-volume series of his frontier novels. Anderson further considers the concurrent phenomenon in Germany of Cooper himself, a cultural figure whose fame was shipped across national lines much like the objects in the preceding chapters by Byrd, Ciarlo, and Short, among others. For Anderson, the readings of these diverse editions are contingent on the varied uses of images in these editions and the resulting relationships of the visual to the verbal. In his analysis, he investigates the ways words themselves take on new meanings in the context of the accompanying visual images on both sides of the Atlantic.

Bibliography

Kress, Gunther, and Theo van Leeuwen. *Reading Images: The Grammar of Visual Design*. London: Routledge, 2006.
Lessing, Gotthold Ephraim. *Laokoon*. Stuttgart: Reclam, 1964.

Antje Pfannkuchen
Image, Language, Science: Hieroglyphs and the Romantic Quest for Primordial Truth

Novalis (1772–1801), poet and scientist of early German Romanticism, opens his novel fragment *Die Lehrlinge zu Sais* [translated as *The Apprentices* or *The Novices at Sais*], a meditation on the relationship of human knowledge and natural wisdom, with the description of a world composed of visual cues:

> Mankind travels along manifold pathways. He who pursues and compares them will perceive the emergence of certain strange figures; figures that appear to be inscribed in that massive tome composed in cipher that one beholds everywhere and in everything: on wings, eggshells, in clouds, in the snow, in crystalline and stone formations, in freezing waters, on the skins and in the bowels of mountain-ranges, of plants, beasts, people, in the stars of the heavens, in affected and stroked discs of pitch and glass, in the clustering of iron filings around the magnet, in the extraordinary ebb and flow of contingency. In these one may glimpse an intimation of the key to this wondrous text, its very grammar-book [. . .].[1]

Strange figures inviting decipherment reappear throughout Novalis's text, which he wrote between 1798 and 1799 at least in part as a reaction to Friedrich Schiller's 1795 poem "The Veiled Image at Sais" ["Das verschleierte Bild zu Sais"].

---

1 "Mannigfache Wege gehen die Menschen. Wer sie verfolgt und vergleicht, wird wunderliche Figuren entstehen sehn; Figuren, die zu jener großen Chiffernschrift zu gehören scheinen, die man überall, auf Flügeln, Eierschalen, in Wolken, im Schnee, in Kristallen und in Steinbildungen, auf gefrierenden Wassern, im Innern und Äußern der Gebirge, der Pflanzen, der Tiere, der Menschen, in den Lichtern des Himmels, auf berührten und gestrichenen Scheiben von Pech und Glas, in den Feilspänen um den Magnet her, und sonderbaren Konjunkturen des Zufalls, erblickt. In ihnen ahndet man den Schlüssel dieser Wunderschrift, die Sprachlehre derselben [. . .]." Novalis, *Schriften: Die Werke Friedrich von Hardenbergs*, ed. Paul Kluckhohn, R. H. Samuel, and Hans Joachim Mähl, 2., nach den Handschriften erg., erw. und vergrösserte Aufl., vol. I (Stuttgart: W. Kohlhammer, 1960), 79. Volume I, 79. Translations from Novalis's *Die Lehrlinge zu Sais* are mostly my own, in part adapted from http://shirty sleeves.blogspot.com/2007/11/translation-of-die-lehrlinge-zu-sais-by.html.

Note: The following paper attempts to uncover the roots of a Romantic fascination with hieroglyphs that I began to explore in "A Science of Hieroglyphs, or the Test of *Bildung*," in *The Technological Introject: Friedrich Kittler between Implementation and the Incalculable*, ed. Jeffrey Champlin and Antje Pfannkuchen (New York: Fordham UP, 2018), 84–92. The earlier text takes the Romantic concept of hieroglyphs as its starting point and relates it to contemporary science with the goal of diversifying Friedrich Kittler's analysis of Romantic reading. My project in the present chapter is to decipher the origins of the Romantic understanding of hieroglyphics and to show the centrality of this concept for early German Romanticism.

https://doi.org/10.1515/9783110696448-013

Both verses invoke the mythical city of Sais in Ancient Egypt, where, if we believe the legend, priests guarded wisdom symbolized in a cloaked statue of Isis representing ultimate knowledge and truth. Lifting the veil was strictly forbidden. Schiller and Novalis show us different outcomes to the transgression against this interdiction. In both parables a young man in search of insight arrives after a long journey at the shrouded figure. Schiller's protagonist, driven by a "hot thirst" for knowledge, "des Wissens heißer Durst,"[2] ignores all warnings and approaches the statue in the dead of night. Despite the threat of dire consequences, he lifts the veil and is found the next morning pale and senseless, "besinnungslos und bleich;"[3] falling subsequently into a deep depression that results in an early death.

Novalis in contrast tells his story within multiple frames. Not unlike other Romantic works, *The Apprentices at Sais* contains several stories within the story and also a fairy tale that appears to be separated from the rest of the novel but crystallizes some central ideas. In the tale, young Hyacinth leaves behind his beloved Rose to go out into the world in search of Isis, who is here a figure combining polar opposites, "the mother of all things, the veiled virgin."[4] When Hyacinth reaches the designated location he falls asleep knowing that only a dream can take him to the holiest place for which he longs. In contrast to Schiller's rather straightforwardly told story, Novalis's version stages the encounter with the veiled virgin within a dream within a fairy tale. When Hyacinth lifts the shroud, his true love Rose sinks into his arms. It is no surprise that for a Romantic writer ultimate truth is found in love. But it is also important to understand the Romantic conviction that truth cannot be accessed without mediation, something Schiller's youth tried to accomplish. The veil that is lifted successfully in Novalis's version has previously been supplanted by the shrouding and blurring of dream and fairy tale. In the same way, the truth to be found in nature is depicted in the beginning of *The Apprentices at Sais* as open for everyone to see in ubiquitous and strange figures, even if it is simultaneously obscured by their unreadability without the "grammar book" that is needed for decipherment.

In the same novel fragment, Novalis offers a second path to acquiring knowledge and understanding nature's secrets. This alternative route touches on an overarching topic of his writing and points out to us a way in which to grasp the meaning of the ciphers in the passage cited above. These figures, unlike Isis in the fairy tale, refuse to disclose their secrets through the powers of Romantic love alone. Nonetheless, as Novalis assures us, they will become

---

[2] Quoted in Jan Assmann, *Das verschleierte Bild zu Sais: Schillers Ballade und ihre griechischen und ägyptischen Hintergründe* (Stuttgart/Leipzig: Teubner, 1999), 69.
[3] Quoted in Assmann, *Das verschleierte Bild zu Sais*, 71.
[4] Novalis, *Schriften*, I, 93.

decipherable in the intimate and necessary collaboration of science and poetry. In their shared language, these two ways of approaching nature combined create a holistic understanding that each individually fails to achieve. Beneath the hands of the dissecting scientist, in Novalis's account, "the companionable Nature of old has expired, leaving behind only her lifeless, twitching remains." The poet, by contrast, "endowed her with new life; he has given ear to her divinely animate fancies and exalted her above the level of quotidian existence, he has ascended to heaven, danced and prophesied, welcomed every guest, and squandered the treasures of her joyous spirit."[5] For Novalis, wisdom and truth have to be comprehended in their diverse and wide-ranging dimensions and any attempt at removing these facets will only leave destruction in its wake. Poetry needs science as an anchor, but science without poetry devastates and ultimately kills nature and the world. Science may be able to dissect and analyze the details of nature, but "he who wishes properly to understand [nature's] temperament must seek her in the company of the poet, for when she is with him, she unabashedly dispenses the wondrous effusions of her heart."[6]

Novalis lived this intimate relationship of poetry and science in his double existence as a Romantic writer and a mining engineer. He also performed it in his writing on countless occasions. The Romantics' interaction with science has been neglected in the context of what Catriona McLeod describes above as "the traditional opposition of Romanticism and materiality and the focus of so much of this criticism on the philosophical Jena school"[7] which has only slowly been expanded to acknowledge the foundational role the engagement with science has played in it. Novalis, though, spells out clearly (if poetically) the equitable relationship of science and poetry that will be our guide to reading the visual setting of the opening scene. In this passage, the Romantic turn in the visual culture around 1800 toward a poetic science is on full display. Instead of Schiller's protagonist suddenly attempting to pull away truth's cover, Novalis invites the reader to decode the signs he finds on the surface to access the wisdom lying beyond it.

By exploring the cultural past and future of Novalis's opening scene, this paper investigates some connected questions about Romantic visuality: Why did the Romantics begin to see patterns on wings, eggshells, crystals, and their like as symbols of a potentially readable language? What kind of truth were they trying to find and promote in their attempt to translate these images found in nature or, as we will see, in natural science into legible characters? And how do these

---

5 Novalis, *Schriften*, I, 84.
6 Novalis, *Schriften*, I, 84.
7 See Catriona MacLeod's chapter in this volume.

images that were at once scientifically material and poetically ephemeral come to represent a kernel of what it meant to be an Early Romantic who did not just show an interest in the newest science but actually practiced and shaped it?

The place to which the title of Novalis's novel fragment refers shall be our starting point for answering the first of these questions: In the Ancient Egyptian city of Sais the suggestive visual imagery everyone could see when looking around would have been hieroglyphs.[8] These ancient signs had been brought to the European attention where they were perceived as highly evocative though mostly impenetrable symbols during Novalis's lifetime. Recent expeditions had created mounting excitement over hieroglyphics and attempts at decipherment were under way but had yet to be successful. Hieroglyphs do not appear verbatim in *The Apprentices at Sais*, but they are found in one of Novalis' fragments that is also concerned with the understanding of something seemingly incomprehensible. There he writes: "Formerly every apparition was revelation. Now we don't see anything but lifeless repetition we don't understand. The meaning of the hieroglyph is missing."[9] Novalis mourns the lost comprehension of literal or metaphorical hieroglyphs[10] that appear to have been infinitely meaningful in another time. The distant time of Ancient Egypt had become quite present in the years leading up to 1800 when an increasing number of European forays to the Middle East brought back more and more reports, drawings, and artifacts that were welcomed with great enthusiasm.[11] Novalis was impressed enough to plan an

---

8 In terms of the linguistic usage, hieroglyph refers to an individual character, the plural to multiples and hieroglyphics to the system of writing in hieroglyphs.

9 Novalis, *Schriften*, II, 545.

10 As Astrid Keiner noted in her study of Romanticism and hieroglyphics: "Wer sich heute mit dem Terminus *Hieroglyphe* beschäftigt, bekommt es scheinbar mit zwei Gegenständen zu tun: Einerseits interessieren sich Literaturwissenschaft und Kunstgeschichte für einen ästhetisch-poetologischen Begriff [. . .]; andererseits referiert dieser Begriff aber auf die *ägyptischen Hieroglyphen*, deren Entzifferung im Jahr 1822 die Ägyptologie begründete." According to Keiner, this separation long implied, "daß die literarische Figur *Hieroglyphe* eben nur metaphorisch aufzufassen sei und nicht mehr als den Namen mit den ägyptischen Schriftzeichen gemein habe." In her thorough study, however, Keiner countered this strict separation of Egyptian and literary hieroglyph and argued that it describes only the situation after the deciphering of the Ancient script. In her view, the scientific study of Egyptian hieroglyphics as it was conducted before the modern decoding relied on the same forms of imagination that can be found in the literary uses of the term and "deren Inhalt allein aus Projektionen zusammengesetzt ist." Astrid Keiner, *Hieroglyphenromantik: zur Genese und Destruktion eines Bilderschriftmodells und zu seiner Überforderung in Friedrich Schlegels Spätphilosophie* (Würzburg: Königshausen & Neumann, 2003), 9–10.

11 Egyptologist Jan Assmann reminds us that "die 90er Jahre des 18. Jahrhunderts den Höhepunkt der europäischen Ägyptenbegeisterung bilden – ich erinnere nur an die überall in

epic poem about the French expedition.[12] These developments not only spawned the birth of Egyptology, they also made the word "hieroglyph" highly fashionable. As a result, the frequency of the word "hieroglyphics" in English, as much as in German printed matter, increased dramatically after 1750 with a peak between 1800 and 1850.[13]

We know today that Ancient Egyptians used hieroglyphics for at least 3,000 years.[14] During these millennia various systems of writing were employed at different times and also simultaneously for distinct purposes. The most recent hieroglyphs would be inscribed in the fourth century CE. Concurrently, beginning in the second century, one Egyptian dialect known as Coptic was also written in Greek letters. Coptic remained in use until the sixteenth century, but the knowledge that this was originally Egyptian fell into oblivion. The hieroglyphic signs appeared to be all that endured of the Egyptian language.[15] Athanasius Kircher (1602–1680) seems to have been the first and possibly only hieroglyphic researcher before Jean-François Champollion (1790–1832) to recognize Coptic as an Egyptian remnant that was still readable because of the use of the Greek alphabet. Nevertheless, Kircher was ultimately unsuccessful in his deciphering attempts; only much later, in 1822, did Champollion use, among other things, his knowledge of the Coptic language successfully to present the widely accepted decoding of the Rosetta Stone.[16]

Before that translation, in the course of almost 1500 years since their active use, the old Egyptian symbols had become a surface for innumerable projections. The Greeks gave them their name composed of *hieros* = sacred, and *gluphē* = carving, a characterization that marked them as non-secular writing, suggesting a

---

dieser Zeit entstehenden Parkanlagen mit Pyramiden und Obelisken, Sphingen und Isisstatuen, an die Zauberflöte, die in diesen Jahren ihren Siegeszug durch Deutschland antrat, und an die napoleonische Expedition nach Ägypten." Jan Assmann, *Das verschleierte Bild zu Sais, Schillers Ballade und ihre griechischen und ägyptischen Hintergründe*, 12.

12 See Novalis, *Schriften*, I, 432.
13 This increased usage is suggested by the "Wortverlaufskurve" [word usage curve] in the entry Hieroglyphe of the DWDS "DWDS – Digitales Wörterbuch der deutschen Sprache." ("Hieroglyphe," <https://www.dwds.de/wb/Hieroglyphe>, accessed 5 February 2019.) as well as by Google's Ngram Viewer https://books.google.com/ngrams when searched for "hieroglyphic" and "hieroglyphics."
14 Here is neither time nor space to fully acknowledge the many and fascinating dimensions of Egyptian hieroglyphics. I will focus on some very basic aspects relevant for the study of Romanticism's use of the notion. Please see for further reference: Aleida Assmann and Jan Assmann, *Hieroglyphen: Stationen einer anderen abendländischen Grammatologie* (Munich: Wilhelm Fink, 2003) and Keiner, *Hieroglyphenromantik*.
15 See Keiner, *Hieroglyphenromantik*, 22–24.
16 Keiner, *Hieroglyphenromantik*, 77.

significance beyond everyday use. The concept of hieroglyphs as "symbolic images with a secret meaning" came to be widely accepted after Horapollo's books of late antiquity, rediscovered in 1419, seemed to offer the key to reading hieroglyphics.[17] It appears that one of Champollion's greatest achievements was his questioning of the established concept of hieroglyphs as highly emblematic signs. Only this new perspective created a void that invited the modern deciphering.[18]

The Romantic imagination though was fed by several pre-1800 interpretations of hieroglyphs of which those of Johann Gottfried Herder (1744–1803) and, somewhat indirectly, Giambattista Vico (1668–1744) were the two most relevant. Even before increased travel to the Middle East, references to hieroglyphs had seen a renaissance in eighteenth-century debates regarding the nature and origin of language and new theories alluded "to the derivation of alphabetical [writing] from original hieroglyphic systems of writing."[19]

Vico was one of the first to detach his understanding of hieroglyphics from an Egyptian context. He used the word in a number of different circumstances and meanings. The initial edition of his major work *Principj di Scienza Nuova* was published in 1725. As in many books of its time, here the historian of science Martin Rudwick reminds us, "the only illustration was a single frontispiece, which for this reason always deserves especially close historical scrutiny, since it functioned as a visual summary of what the author and/or the publisher considered most important about the book."[20] In addition to the singularity of the image, Vico begins his book with an "Explanation of the Picture Placed as Frontispiece to Serve as Introduction to the Work"[21] in which he describes the engraving in great detail, pointing out the arrangement of the depicted objects (see Figure 1). It is here that he introduces the notion of the "hieroglyph" and uses it more or less synonymously with "symbol."

---

17 Assmann and Assmann, *Hieroglyphen*, 9.
18 Assmann and Assmann, *Hieroglyphen*, 10.
19 Tom Jones, "Theories of Language in the Eighteenth Century," 5 October 2015. See Gregory Sharpe who mused in 1751: "The first character, as being the most natural, must have been a representation, or rude draught of the object: And such were the *Hieroglyphics* of the *Ægyptians*, and the characters of the *Chinese*." Gregory Sharpe, *Two Dissertations: I. Upon the Origin, Construction, Division, and Relation of Language: II. Upon the Original Powers of Letters; Wherein Is Proved from the Analogy of Alphabets, and the Proportion of Letters, That the Hebrew Ought to Be Read Without Points. To Which Is Added, the Second Edition, Enlarged, of a Hebrew Grammar and Lexicon, Without Points* (John Millan, 1751), 56–57.
20 Martin J. S. Rudwick, "The Emergence of a Visual Language for Geology, 1760–1840," *History of Science* 14 (1976): 154.
21 Giambattista Vico, *The New Science*, trans. Max Harold Fisch and Thomas Goddard Bergin (Ithaca, NY: Cornell University Press, 1948), 3.

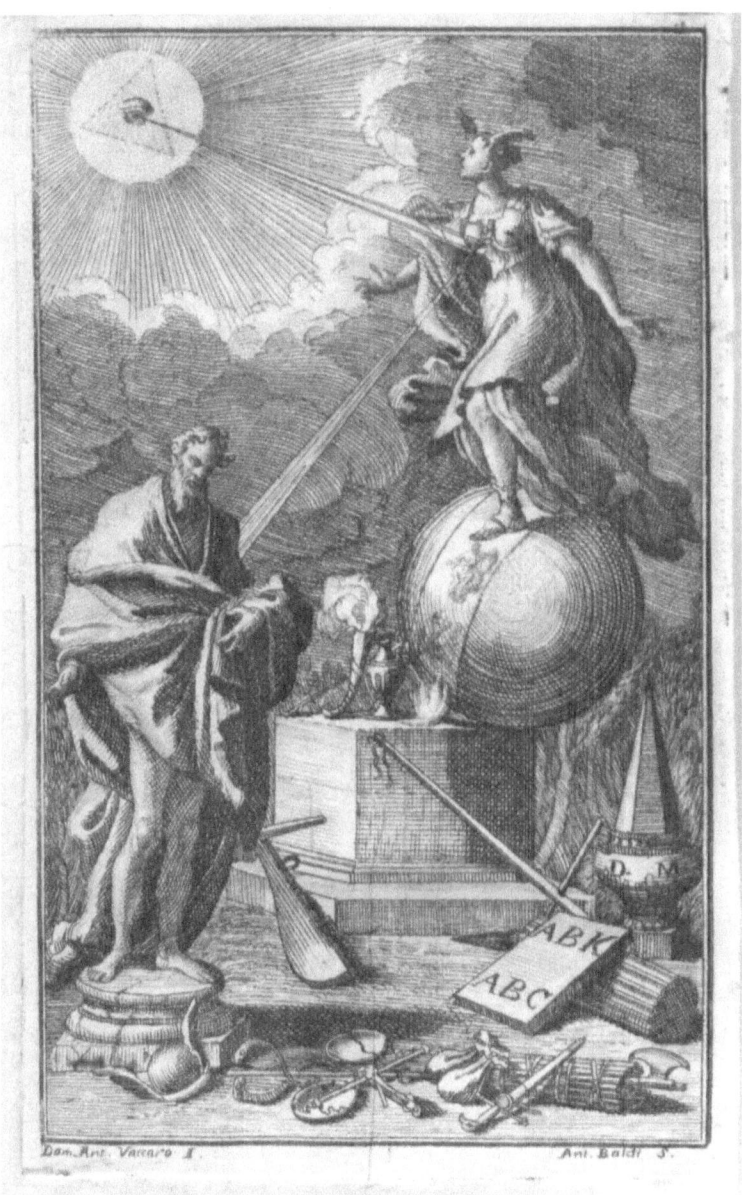

Figure 1: Vico Frontispiece. Giambattista Vico, *Principj d'una Scienza Nuova* (Napoli: Nella Stamperia Muziana, 1744) n.p. Digitized by Münchener Digitalisierungszentrum der Bayerischen Staatsbibliothek from signature Rar. 1735.

Vico first highlights the female figure wearing a winged helmet which he declares to be "metaphysic" who "contemplates in God the world of human minds, which is the metaphysical world, in order to show His providence in the world of human spirits, which is the civil world or world of nations."[22] This civil world, so Vico, is formed by all the elements represented as hieroglyphs in the lower half of the print. The hieroglyphs depict a globe balancing on the edge of an altar, a tablet with alphabetic letters, and a number of other tools and scientific instruments. Vico specifies that these "hieroglyphs [. . .] represent the principles [of this world of nations], known until now only by the[ir] effects."[23] In other words, foundational laws and theories of the world are only knowable through hieroglyphic images which are their manifestations in the world. This consideration of hieroglyphic appearances as signs or codes for larger principles is one of Vico's major influences on the Romantics.

But Vico also introduces another reading of hieroglyphics. His *Scienza Nuova* sets out to study three periods in world history: the ages of the gods, the heroes, and men that for Vico corresponded with three ages and three types of languages known from the history of Egypt. "The first [age was] hieroglyphic, with sacred characters; the second symbolic, with heroic characters; the third epistolary, with characters agreed on by the people."[24] In contrast to his use of hieroglyphics to describe elements of what he calls the civil human world, Vico here declares the hieroglyphic language best "suited to the uses of religion, which it is more important to attend to than to talk about." For Vico, this first "hieroglyphic or sacred or secret language" was the language of the Gods and it operated "by means of mute acts." In that sense, it was a language that connected acts directly with writing without recourse to the spoken voice, a writing that preceded any spoken language. In Vico's reading, hieroglyphics were an indication that despite the fact "[. . .] that philologists have believed that among the nations languages first came into being and then letters" the case was rather that "letters and languages were born twins and proceeded apace through all their three stages."[25] Vico here makes the claim that his book is about to show "all nations began to speak by writing, since all were originally mute."[26] In this concept,

---

22 Vico, *The New Science*, 3.
23 Vico, *The New Science*, 6.
24 Vico, *The New Science*, 31.
25 Vico, *The New Science*, 19.
26 Vico, *The New Science*, 124–125.

hieroglyphs become a kind of originary writing, expressing "mute acts" for which no spoken words exist.[27]

Despite connecting the visual symbols on some level to a sacred language, similarly to the Greeks, Vico simultaneously secularized the understanding of hieroglyphics. For him, hieroglyphs were an ancient, less-developed form of notation that had a direct relationship to the acts and objects they represented. He mentions uses of hieroglyphics from the "Mexicans of the New World" to the Chinese of his time "who still write in hieroglyphics" and employs these contemporary examples in his attempt to dispel the myth about the existence of any kind of "esoteric wisdom under hieroglyphics."[28] Hieroglyphs are thus seen as a more direct and less abstracted form of writing and, in that sense, at once superior in their immediacy and inferior in their range of expressions compared to later alphabets.

The strongest influence on Romanticism's understanding of hieroglyphics came undoubtedly via Johann Gottfried Herder. Herder appears to have followed the distinction of hieroglyphics as a kind of writing that is not unequivocally connected to spoken language and wrote an early *Treatise on the Origin of Language* [*Abhandlung über den Ursprung der Sprache*] in 1772 without any recourse to hieroglyphs. He studied them subsequently and in detail, however, in his *Oldest Document of the Human Race* [*Älteste Urkunde des Menschengeschlechts*], published between 1774 and 1776, in which he traces the origin of writing back to hieroglyphics and calls the latter the oldest picture writing or pictographic script, "älteste Bilderschrift."[29] Herder imagined how a true understanding of just *one* genuine ancient hieroglyph, "eine wirklich ächte alte Hieroglyphe," would allow the formation of an *Urbild*, a primary image or concept containing the root not only of all human writing and symbolism but also of all arts and sciences. In other words, compared to Vico, Herder expands the possible meaning of a hieroglyph in two significant ways: First, from being a representation of one act or one principle, a hieroglyph is now turned into a symbol and metaphor for an entire world. Secondly, a predominantly visual concept of what a hieroglyph is becomes a fairly expansive metaphorical category. Herder's example for both of

---

27 This argument reminds of Derrida's insistence on a writing that does not conceive of itself as a "derivative, auxiliary form of language," and, on the contrary, appears as "pure" writing that never pretends to have a "linguistic sign before writing." Jacques Derrida, *Of Grammatology* (Baltimore: Johns Hopkins University Press, 1976), 7 and 14.
28 Vico, *The New Science*, 128–129.
29 Johann Gottfried Herder, *Älteste Urkunde des Menschengeschlechts* (Tübingen: Cotta, 1806), 126.

these expansions was his reading of the beginning of the Bible, in which he found the hieroglyphic origin of the world.[30]

The history of writing, as Herder recorded it, partially resembled Vico's account. For Herder, hieroglyphs also constituted some of the earliest instances of script: "The beginning of writing [Buchstabenschrift] could not have been other than by images, runes, hieroglyphs."[31] In contrast to Vico, however, Herder proliferates the myth perhaps best known from Plato's *Phaedrus* of the Egyptian ibis-headed god, "Theut, Thot, Thaaut [...] who gave the gift of the Gods – Letters!"[32] as secondary to spoken language. Herder devotes a significant portion of his book to Egypt. The second part of the *Urkunde* is subtitled "Key to the Sacred Sciences of the Egyptians" in which he makes his disapproval of much of contemporary research concerning Egypt known by referring to Egypt as "fashionable country for the latest oriental figments"[33] before setting out to present his own reading of what he declares to be the first letter, the first symbol of Egyptian writing. He calls this first hieroglyph "the image of Ibis" ("das Ibisbild,")[34] as derived from the Egyptian names for Thoth and ibis.[35] According to Herder, this ibis image can take a number of forms but seems to have one dominant representation as shown in the excerpt from his text in Figure 2.

The form of this symbol allows us to trace a direct visual line from Herder's hieroglyphs to their reappearance in Romanticism, namely in Johann Wilhelm Ritter's texts, as Jocelyn Holland has shown in detail in a recent article.[36] So let's meet Ritter (1776–1810) who is still one of the lesser-known Romantics before returning to Herder. Ritter was a close friend of Novalis's and probably the most actively engaged scientist of the early Romantic circle in Jena. His work and life have attracted increased attention in recent years not only from scholars[37] but

---

30 See Herder, *Älteste Urkunde*, 128–130.
31 Herder, *Älteste Urkunde*, 137.
32 Herder, *Älteste Urkunde*, 201–202.
33 Herder, *Älteste Urkunde*, 194.
34 Herder, *Älteste Urkunde*, 202.
35 "The name of the god Thoth, [...], Tehuti, appears to be derived from the supposed oldest name of the ibis in Egypt, i.e., tehu, to which the termination it has been added, with the idea of indicating that the king called Tehuti possessed the qualities and attributes of the ibis." E. A. Wallis Budge, *The Gods of the Egyptians; or, Studies in Egyptian Mythology*, vol. 1 (London: Methuen & Co., 1904), 402.
36 See Jocelyn Holland's discussion of Herder's hieroglyph. Jocelyn Holland, "The Silence of Ritter's Symbol ⊗," *The Germanic Review: Literature, Culture, Theory* 92, no. 4 (2017): 347–348.
37 Jocelyn Holland, *German Romanticism and Science: The Procreative Poetics of Goethe, Novalis, and Ritter*. Routledge Studies in Romanticism (New York: Routledge, 2009) and Klaus

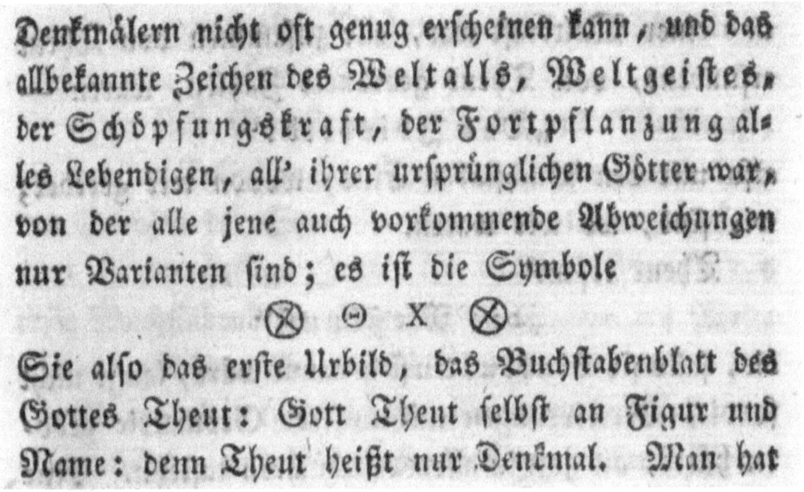

> Denkmälern nicht oft genug erscheinen kann, und das
> allbekannte Zeichen des Weltalls, Weltgeistes,
> der Schöpfungskraft, der Fortpflanzung al-
> les Lebendigen, all' ihrer ursprünglichen Götter war,
> von der alle jene auch vorkommende Abweichungen
> nur Varianten sind; es ist die Symbole
>   ⊗   ⊙   X   ⊗
> Sie also das erste Urbild, das Buchstabenblatt des
> Gottes Theut: Gott Theut selbst an Figur und
> Name: denn Theut heißt nur Denkmal. Man hat

Figure 2: Johann Gottfried Herder, *Älteste Urkunde des Menschengeschlechts* (Tübingen: Cotta, 1806), 203. Digitized by Münchener Digitalisierungszentrum der Bayerischen Staatsbibliothek from signature Opp. 493–29.

also from writers of historical fiction.[38] Ritter himself already intertwined these two genres artfully. The Prologue to his *Fragments from the Estate of a Young Physicist* [*Fragmente aus dem Nachlass eines jungen Physikers*], a volume he published just before his death, is a semi-fictional autobiography, written in the third person. He names Herder and Novalis as the only two friends and influences in his otherwise reclusive and outright lonely life.[39] According to this account, Novalis showed up at Ritter's house one day, and they "understood each other at first sight; for the former there was not the slightest strangeness in their meeting; for the latter it was virtually as if he could for once speak aloud with himself."[40] This intense friendship was cut short by Novalis's untimely death. But only a short time later "a chance event, itself completely innocuous, led [Ritter] to

---

Richter, *Das Leben des Physikers Johann Wilhelm Ritter: Ein Schicksal in der Zeit der Romantik* (Weimar: H. Böhlaus Nachfolger, 2003).

38 Thea Dorn, *Die Unglückseligen* (Munich: Albrecht Knaus Verlag, 2017).

39 "He lived at that time in the greatest isolation in a secluded alley, in a meagerly furnished room, which he often did not leave during four weeks on end; because he did not know why he should and moreover whom it would be worth the effort to visit." Johann Wilhelm Ritter and Jocelyn Holland, *Key Texts of Johann Wilhelm Ritter (1776–1810) on the Science and Art of Nature*. History of Science and Medicine Library (Leiden/Boston: Brill, 2010), 37. (Holland's invaluable collection and translation of some of Ritter's important writings cannot be commended enough.)

40 Ritter and Holland, *Key Texts*, 37.

Herder." Seeing Herder regularly "became to a certain extent the complement to the visits by Novalis, the age of the worthy man comprised almost the only difference, which meanwhile was completely advantageous."[41] Ritter had not yet read any of Herder's writings when he first met the man more than three decades his senior but from the "close contact with Herder onward is dated an enormous number of new things in his mind. [. . .] In this time he had read little, yet deeply: the most important work for him then was the *Oldest Document of the Human Race*, – whereby he enjoyed the distinctive advantage of having the author himself as commentator for those passages which were more difficult for him to understand."[42] As if to illustrate what he had learned from that reading, Ritter describes Herder in "his entire being, his eye, his countenance and existence" as "the living hieroglyph of the word for which the tongue was no longer the sufficient organ." Instead of just listening to him, "one had to see Herder speak in order even to listen and understand him; thus one had to have *heard* him – and *seen him be silent* – in order to say, one were reading him."[43] Only a multimedia combination of listening and observing allows for a total reading experience that promises any comprehension. Ritter's transference of the concept of hieroglyphics onto the reading of signs, symbols, persons, and other appearances in the world was clearly learned from Herder himself. As Holland reminds us, "through Herder, the physicist understands that there is a symbolic language connecting natural, divine, and human phenomena."[44]

While Ritter had not read any Herder before meeting him, Novalis was familiar with the elder's writings.[45] Thus, independently, Herder became an influence and guiding force for both. His attempt to declare the hieroglyph an *Urbild* appealed to them in its universality and unifying power. One decisive shift they initiated was to turn Herder's *Urbild* into an *Urschrift* that did not just symbolize a secret meaning but implied its own readability.[46] This shift foreshadows the application of the concept of the readable hieroglyph to other observations and experiences, particularly in the sciences in which both Ritter and Novalis were deeply engaged.

The centrality of hieroglyphics for Romanticism was underscored by Novalis when he explored the "I" in his Fichte studies. In a note "Remarks on

---

41 Ritter and Holland, *Key Texts*, 49. A four-year age difference made Novalis and Ritter contemporary equals while the much older Herder became more of a mentor and father figure.
42 Ritter and Holland, *Key Texts*, 51.
43 Ritter and Holland, *Key Texts*, 51–53.
44 Holland, "The Silence of Ritter's Symbol ⊗," 349.
45 See Novalis, *Schriften*, I, 431; II, 578 and elsewhere.
46 Friedrich Kittler's study is one of the best-known examples showing this shift. See Friedrich Kittler, *Aufschreibesysteme 1800/1900* (Munich: Wilhelm Fink, 1985), 107–111.

Consciousness" ["Bemerkungen über das Bewußtsein"] he answers the question "What do we think of as the I?" or "How do we understand the I?" ("Was verstehn wir unter Ich?") by ascribing to the I a hieroglyphic, or, in a seemingly invented neologism, a hieroglyphistic power: "Das Ich hat eine hieroglyphystische Kraft."[47] Novalis returns to hieroglyphs as a desirable attribute in a different context and in this case elaborates further which aids our decoding of the Romantic concept of hieroglyphics. Criticizing the lack of hieroglyphic power of the Enlightenment thinker Gotthold Ephraim Lessing (1729–1781) – "Lessings Prosa fehlts oft an hieroglyphischem Zusatz" – Novalis clarifies: "Lessing scrutinized too sharply and lost the sense for the ambiguous whole, the magical perception of things in relation to one another in manifold illuminations and darknesses."[48] For Novalis, Lessing shone his enlightened beam too harshly onto the world which to the Romantic resulted in a similar effacement as the scientific dissection eschewing poetry he had criticized in *The Apprentices at Sais*. The multilayered opacity, holistically composed of different forms of light and darkness which lay at the center of Romanticism could not be recognized under the glare of the Enlightenment. The hieroglyphic "Zusatz," the supplement that Lessing was missing, appears to have been central to what separated Romanticism from the Enlightenment. As August Wilhelm Schlegel writes in the Athenaeum Fragment 173: "There's nothing ornamental about the style of the real poet: everything is a necessary hieroglyph."[49] The necessity of hieroglyphics for "real," that is, Romantic, poetry points to a similar activity as the act of romanticizing ("romantisiren"), in Novalis's famous demand: "The world must be romanticized."[50] Only in the act of romanticizing can an original meaning be found again. And, indeed, immediately leading up to his call to romanticize, we find the previously quoted passage in which Novalis mourns the loss

---

47 Novalis, *Schriften*, II, 107.
48 Novalis, *Schriften*, II, 537.
49 Friedrich Schlegel, "Athenaeum Fragments," *Philosophical Fragments*. Translated by Peter Firchow. Foreword by Rodolphe Gasché. (Minneapolis: University of Minnesota Press, 1991), 40.
50 "Die Welt muß romantisirt werden. So findet man den urspr[ünglichen] Sinn wieder. Romantisiren ist nichts, als eine qualit[ative] Potenzirung. Das niedre Selbst wird mit einem bessern Selbst in dieser Operation identificirt. So wie wir selbst eine solche qualit[ative] Potenzreihe sind. Diese Operation ist noch ganz unbekannt. Indem ich dem Gemeinen einen hohen Sinn, dem Gewöhnlichen ein geheimnißvolles Ansehn, dem Bekannten die Würde des Unbekannten, dem Endlichen einen unendlichen Schein gebe so romantisire ich es – Umgekehrt ist die Operation für das Höhere, Unbekannte, Mystische, Unendliche – dies wird durch diese Verknüpfung logarythmisirt – Es bekommt einen geläufigen Ausdruck. . .. Wechselerhöhung und Erniedrigung." Novalis, *Schriften*, II, 545.

of understanding of the hieroglyph[51] which now appears as a ghostly and spiritual remnant, as a dead symbol referring to a formerly lively and now near magical past. The hieroglyph promises knowledge and understanding which is veiled and cannot be accessed directly. The remedy for this incomprehension of the hieroglyph is to romanticize the world in ways described in *The Apprentices at Sais*: a close collaboration of science and poetry will lead to wisdom and truth. As such, the hieroglyph becomes a symbol that represents the core of what it means to be a Romantic.

In this Romantic metaphor, the hieroglyph has entirely lost the connection to its Egyptian heritage. Instead, the readings we found in Vico and Herder are supplanted by an understanding of nature that Friedrich Schelling expressed in his lectures "On University Studies" ["Vorlesungen über die Methode des akademischen Studiums"], delivered in 1802 at Jena University. Many of the early Romantics were among the audience. Schelling contemplated, not unlike Novalis, how it could be possible "to recognize the living spirit in a discourse that has become dead to us" and equates this linguistic endeavor with the work of the natural scientist: "the relation is no different from that of the scientist to nature. Nature for us is an ancient author who wrote in hieroglyphs."[52] These hieroglyphs authored by nature take us back to Novalis's cipher code at the beginning of *Sais*,[53] to the figures he found on any number of natural surfaces and attempted to read. What makes Novalis's enumeration both unusual for Romanticism as it is often understood and representative of this early version as it was conducted specifically by Ritter and Novalis is his skillful combination of highly imaginative poetry with very well-grounded empirical science. Among the clouds and eggshells, Novalis included a kind of nature writing that is only rarely recognized by readers. This writing appeared in experimental setups Novalis and Ritter created both individually and together to investigate the latest advancements in science.[54] Taking a closer look at these scientific innovations will enable us to recognize their traces and imprints on what we know as Novalis's poetic work and to understand subsequently the effect of the poetic musings on the development of science. The linking element was a reading of visually observable signs on a surface as symbols for knowledge and wisdom lying beyond it.

---

51 Novalis, *Schriften*, II, 545.
52 Friedrich Wilhelm Joseph von Schelling, *Vorlesungen über die Methode (Lehrart) des akademischen Studiums: Auf der Grundlage des Textes der Ausgabe von Otto Weiss*. Edited by Melchior Meyr, Vol. 2, Philosophische Bibliothek (Hamburg: Meiner, 1990), 40.
53 Novalis, *Schriften*, I, 79.
54 See Novalis, *Schriften*, III, 595–563.

One of the newest[55] and seemingly most magical physical forces at the time was electricity and both Ritter and Novalis inquired into its powers, partly by repeating the latest experiments in the field. The "affected discs of pitch" or resin ("berührten [. . .] Scheiben von Pech")[56] in Novalis's text refer to some of these experiments that had been made famous by Georg Christoph Lichtenberg (1742–1799) just around the time when Herder published his *Oldest Document* in the late 1770s. Lichtenberg had met Herder in 1772 and followed his publications even though he did not seem to have had any further relationship to him.[57] Lichtenberg, who is today known primarily as the first German aphorist, was in his main occupation a professor of physics and a practicing experimenter at the University of Göttingen. His most successful lecture topic on the state of electrical research included demonstrations that became so popular "people, even students, came to physics lectures expecting to be entertained."[58] The latest and most advanced device for electrical research was the electrophore, alternately referred to as the electrophorus. It consisted of a circular base – often called a "cake" – and a fitted metal cover. The cake was constructed of poured resin that, after hardening, needed to be planed and polished to make a smooth surface. The typical size seems to have been around fifty centimeters,[59] but Lichtenberg had an extra-large example manufactured for his laboratory with a diameter of some six feet ("sechs Pariser Fuß"[60]), or about two meters. After experiments with electrical sparks on smaller devices, he had found visual remnants on the surface and hoped to magnify these on the larger apparatus.[61] He wanted to be able to investigate the properties of electricity at close range.

---

55 Static electricity had, of course, been known for a long time in the form of rubbed amber and lightning bolts, but research by the two Italians Luigi Galvani and Alessandro Volta reshaped and reinvigorated the field of electrical research in the late eighteenth century significantly.
56 Novalis, *Schriften*, I, 79.
57 Georg Christoph Lichtenberg, *Aus Lichtenbergs Nachlass: Aufsätze, Gedichte, Tagebuchblätter, Briefe: zur hundertsten Wiederkehr seines Todestages (24. Februar 1799)*. H. Böhlau Nachfolger, 1899, 153–154.
58 Quoted in J. L. Heilbron, *Electricity in the 17th and 18th Centuries: A Study of Early Modern Physics* (Berkeley: University of California Press, 1979), 16.
59 Lichtenberg mentions "18 Zoll," i.e. 18 inches which would be almost 50 cm. Georg Christoph Lichtenberg, *Observationes: Die lateinischen Schriften*, ed. Dag Nikolaus Hasse (Göttingen: Wallstein, 1997), 145.
60 Lichtenberg, *Observationes*, 147.
61 "Denn Versuche mit großen Instrumenten durchzuführen ist dasselbe, wie die auftretenden Erscheinungen unter das Mikroskop zu bringen." Lichtenberg, *Observationes*, 145.

Almost as soon as the new electrophorus was completed it showed "appearances formerly completely unknown to me,"[62] thereby mirroring the experience of earlier experimenters with the microscope which did not just magnify known phenomena but revealed an entirely new world.[63] Lichtenberg's novel appearances showed an unfamiliar visual dimension of electricity that seems to have surprised the scientist (Figure 3). He begins his description by relaying an annoyance with the resin dust that had covered his lab since the polishing of the electrophorus. Lichtenberg then details how at one point the dust fell on the "cake" where it began to form starry configurations and this sight makes the otherwise rather sober scholar nearly break into Romantic poetry:

> In the beginning they were only faint and difficult to see; but when I purposefully sprinkled more dust on the surface, they became clear and beautiful and appeared embossed. At times countless stars, milky ways and larger suns became visible. The arcs on their concave side were plain, on their convex side they were adorned with manifold spouts. Exquisite little branches developed, similar to those the frost creates on windows, also clouds, impressive in their manifold shapes and differing degrees of shadows.[64]

The metaphors Lichtenberg uses to describe the formations recall Novalis's catalog of figures belonging to the great cipher code; some of the images even overlap directly: clouds, frost, and lights of the heavens.

Despite his poetic language, Lichtenberg's interest in the figures was of a practical nature. Before Lichtenberg, electricity could mainly be studied by observing sparks and their immediate effects. These electrical sparks disappeared as quickly as they flared up. Lichtenberg's figures, as they were soon called in his honor, now brought a new lasting and thus observable visual dimension to the field of electrical research. The figures conserved an electrical spark in an image: formerly invisible and as unknowable as the thoughts of Ancient Egyptians,

---

62 Lichtenberg, *Observationes*, 147.
63 See in particular Robert Hooke, *Micrographia: Or, Some Physiological Descriptions of Minute Bodies Made by Magnifying Glasses, with Observations and Inquiries Thereupon 1665* (Lincolnwood: Science Heritage Ltd., 1987).
64 Lichtenberg, *Observationes*, 151. See Short's article in this volume for a comparable instance of a first encounter with "unfamiliar and enigmatic" natural forms resulting in a vivid and imaginative narrative, curiously describing sparks, bursts of fire and stars when gazing into the depths of the sea. For an expanded study of Lichtenberg's approach to visuality in science and elsewhere see my own "A Matter of Visibility – Georg Christoph Lichtenberg's Art and Science of Observation." Configurations 24 no. 4 (2016), 375–400.

electricity suddenly left a trace that could be preserved and examined. Lichtenberg even managed to "print" the dust stars directly onto sticky paper.⁶⁵

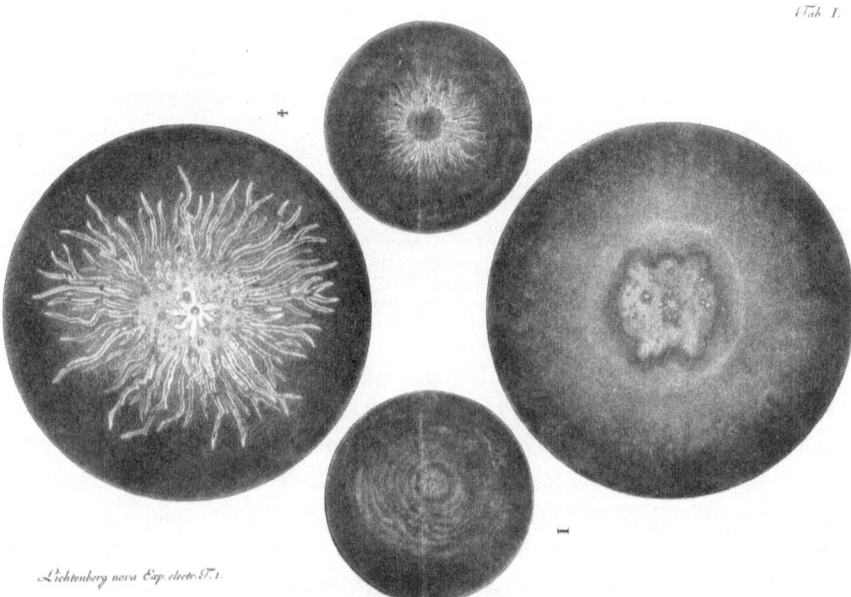

Figure 3: Lichtenberg's illustration showing some of the different electrical figures he found. Georg Christoph Lichtenberg, "De nova methodo naturam ac motum fluidi electrici investigandi. Pars posterior," in Commentationes Societatis Regiae Scientiarum Gottingensis recentiores (Gottingae: Dieterich, 1779), pp. 65–79, image insert following p. 79. Digitized by SUB Göttingen from signature 4 PHYS MATH IV 356.

A few years later the founder of modern acoustics, Ernst Florens Friedrich Chladni, introduced sound figures (*Klangfiguren*)⁶⁶ and declared them inspired

---

65 While Lichtenberg's own prints do not seem to have survived, the versions produced by his contemporary and correspondent Adolf Traugott von Gersdorff (1744–1807) can be admired at the *Kulturhistorisches Museum* in Görlitz, Germany. See also Ernst-Heinz Lemper, *Adolf Traugott von Gersdorf (1744–1807): Naturforschung und soziale Reformen im Dienste der Humanität* (Berlin: VEB Deutscher Verlag der Wissenschaften, 1974).
66 Ernst Florens Friedrich Chladni, *Entdeckungen über die Theorie des Klanges* (Leipzig: Bey Weidmanns Erben und Reich, 1787).

by Lichtenberg's electrical dust figures.[67] His technique, though, was completely different from anything Lichtenberg ever did. Chladni drew a violin bow over the edge of a glass or metal plate, the "stroked discs of [. . .] glass" Novalis mentioned, that he had sprinkled with sand. Once the plate began to vibrate the sand was thrown off the parts that were in motion. The images Chladni published with his text appear schematized; in contrast to Lichtenberg, he could not preserve the figures directly since they only existed in motion. Interestingly enough, the first collections of patterns Chladni presented resemble Lichtenberg's starry sun and moon galaxies even though such patterns materialize rarely through sound (Figure 4).[68] The distinct connection between these two kinds of figures is created in the presumption that an invisible and in many ways inaccessible natural force causes visual images to emerge and thereby reveals information about itself. Lichtenberg and Chladni were interested in understanding physical laws, first those governing electricity, then sound.

For the Romantics Ritter and Novalis, who were practicing scientists[69] and trained by Herder's example to read the world as hieroglyphs, Lichtenberg's and Chladni's figures became only the latest incarnation of nature's visual manifestations asking to be deciphered. Just as we saw in Vico's and Herder's treatment of the Egyptian hieroglyphs, electrical and sound figures now become ciphers referring to a deeper invisible meaning encrypted in the signs on the surface. These signs formed a new kind of Romantic alphabet in the merging of scientific investigation and poetic comprehension of nature. In analogy to Herder's derivation of the first letters from the earliest hieroglyphs, Ritter declares letters to have directly evolved from naturally written sound figures: "So organized into the infinite as word, tone, must the letter also be portrayed. Crystal affords a good example here, then the organic images, etc. Each letter is sound-figure."[70] Novalis had mused a bit more tentatively: "Could the letters have been originally acoustical

---

[67] Ernst Florens Friedrich Chladni, *Die Akustik: Mit 12 Kupfertafeln* (Leipzig: Breitkopf & Härtel, 1802), XVII.

[68] This can be observed in a multitude of YouTube videos when searching for "Chladni figures."

[69] See Jürgen Daiber, *Experimentalphysik des Geistes: Novalis und das romantische Experiment* (Göttingen: Vandenhoeck & Ruprecht, 2001); Erk F. Hansen, *Wissenschaftswahrnehmung und - Umsetzung im Kontext der deutschen Frühromantik: Zeitgenössische Naturwissenschaft und Philosophie im Werk Friedrich von Hardenbergs (Novalis)* (Frankfurt am Main/New York: P. Lang, 1992); Holland, *German Romanticism and Science*; Stuart Walker Strickland, "Circumscribing Science: Johann Wilhelm Ritter and the Physics of Sidereal Man," (Dissertation, Harvard University, 1992); Walter Dominic Wetzels, *Johann Wilhelm Ritter: Physik im Wirkungsfeld der deutschen Romantik* (Berlin/New York: Walter de Gruyter, 1973).

[70] Ritter and Holland, *Key Texts*, 484.

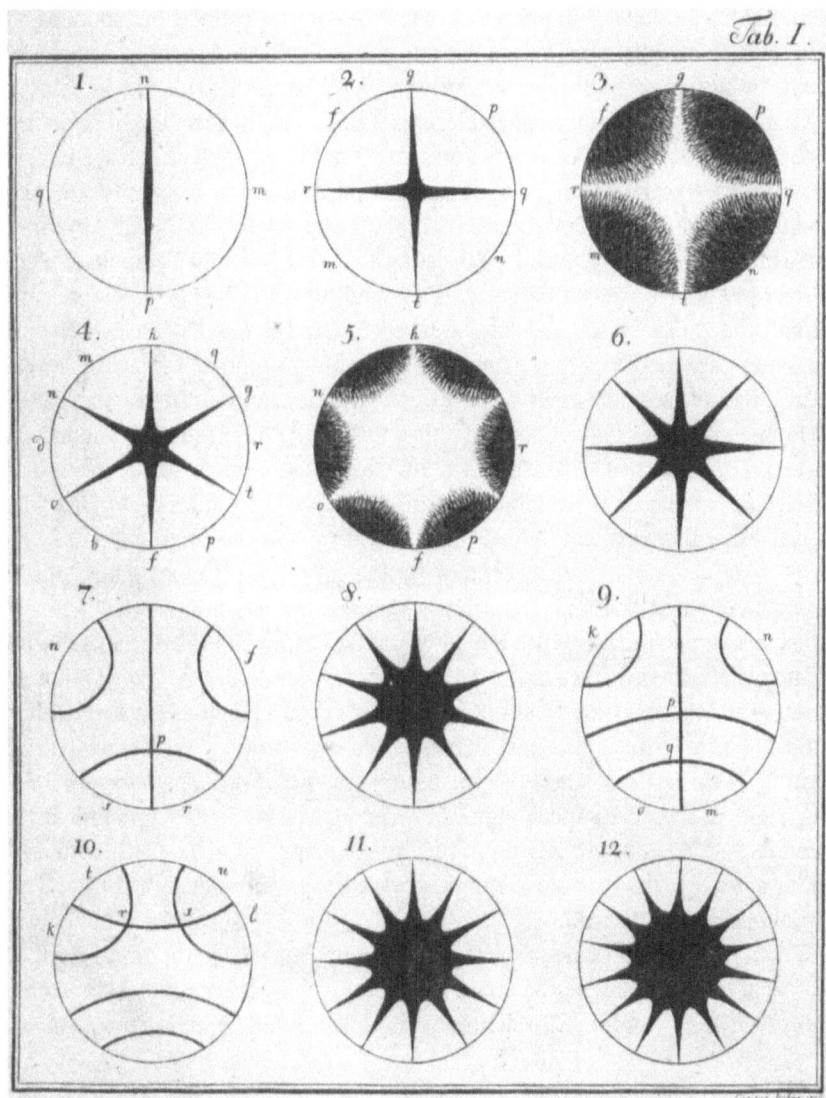

Figure 4: Chladni figures. Ernst Florens Friedrich Chladni, *Entdeckungen über die Theorie des Klanges* (Leipzig: Weidmanns Erben und Reich, 1787), insert after p. 77. Digitized by Münchener Digitalisierungszentrum der Bayerischen Staatsbibliothek from signature Res/4 Phys.sp. 52.

figures. Letters a priori?"⁷¹ In neither case is this assumed connection meant to be understood as simplistic as letters having been inscribed by spoken language. Instead, these figures represent, similarly to Vico's description of hieroglyphs, a more immediate and less specialized form of expression. In this case, it is not an ancient people but nature that is expressing itself in hieroglyphs. Novalis and Ritter both extend the image of the figures beyond sound or electricity. Novalis contemplates color images as figures of light, "Farben*bilder* sind Lichtfiguren,"⁷² whereas Ritter combines the two by insisting that "every sound-figure is an electric [figure], and every electric [figure] is a sound figure. *Lichtenberg's* figures are nothing other than the regular appearance of sound-figures."⁷³ Following that logic, letters are preconfigured as much by Chladni's sound as by Lichtenberg's electrical figures, both of which are first of all scientific images. The symbol Ritter took from Herder (see Figure 2), exemplifies this strong association of poetic language with hard science. As Holland skillfully analyzed, Ritter's was a "gesture of layering" with the goal of reaching an equilibrium. She continues that his choice to replace the mathematical "−" with a circle, or "O" in the combination of "+" and "−" was made due to the needs of "graphical representation" since "the + and − signs" when "directly superimposed, [. . .] become indistinguishable."⁷⁴ Against this simple practical reasoning I would like to argue: the more substantial motivation for Ritter's choice of symbolism was the form of Lichtenberg's figures. Lichtenberg described two distinctly different types of figures he found that convinced him of the existence of two kinds of electricity that cancel each other out.⁷⁵ He portrays the positive figures as suns and little stars and assigns them the mathematical sign "+". The negative figures, on the other hand, are described as consisting of the "finest rings, as well as elliptical and circular spots in which at close range more ellipses and concentric rings can be recognized (cf. Figure 3)."⁷⁶

When Ritter declares his plan to continue the search for the origin of language in a new experimental manner, he devises the identification of the hieroglyph taken from Herder with Lichtenberg's science. He explains in a letter to

---

71 Novalis, *Schriften*, III, 305.
72 Novalis, *Schriften*, III, 305.
73 Ritter and Holland, *Key Texts*, 475 (translation slightly adjusted).
74 Holland, "The Silence of Ritter's Symbol ⊗," 344.
75 One of his main insights was, "daß die positive Elektrizität andere Figuren erzeugt als die negative" which seemed to suggest "irgendeine innere Beziehung zwischen der positiven und der negativen Elektrizität," a fact that was anything but settled at this point. Lichtenberg, *Observationes*, 185.
76 Lichtenberg, *Observationes*, 161.

his Danish friend and collaborator Hans Christian Ørsted (1777–1851) how the first and last letters of the oldest alphabets are Lichtenberg figures in their most basic version (Figure 5). By combining the simplified visible forms of positive and negative Lichtenberg figures (see Figure 3), Ritter turns a rudimentary star and circle into exactly the symbol Herder had declared the first hieroglyph (see Figure 2) and calls it a cipher of a *"primal-* or *nature-writing* by way of electricity."[77]

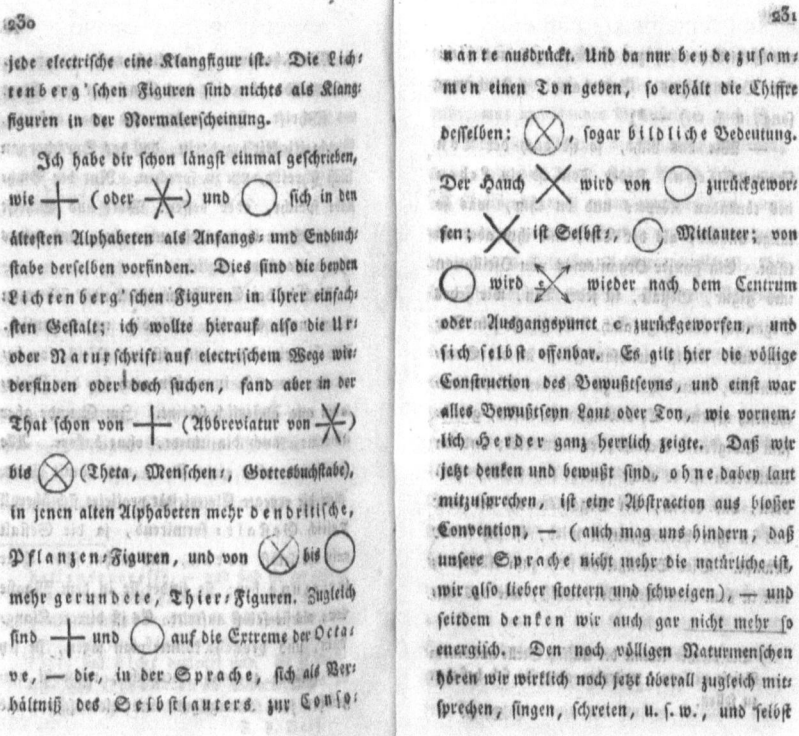

Figure 5: Excerpt from Ritter's letter to his friend Hans Christian Ørsted as printed in: Johann Wilhelm Ritter, *Fragmente aus dem Nachlass eines jungen Physikers. Ein Taschenbuch für Freunde der Natur. Zweites Bändchen.* (Heidelberg: Mohr und Zimmer, 1810), 230–231. Digitized by Münchener Digitalisierungszentrum der Bayerischen Staatsbibliothek from signature Phys.g. 379-2.

In this way, Ritter constructs a direct correlation, if not identity, between his electrical *Ur-* and *Naturschrift* and the oldest, that is, hieroglyphic alphabets by

---

77 Ritter and Holland, *Key Texts*, 475.

way of the same sign that constituted the primordial written character for Herder. The hieroglyphics of an ancient culture and the figures of nature are merged into one and the same visual object by following Novalis's dictum that only the intimate collaboration of poetry and science will show the path to wisdom and truth. This Romantic hieroglyph symbolizes and represents in its multiple layers the pivotal role and simultaneously the disguise of science in early Romanticism. As in the patterns on eggshells, the hieroglyphs in Sais, and the dust figures on the electrophorus, "the great secret is lying open for everyone to see but remains eternally unfathomable,"[78] except that this Romantic eternity also has a historical time.

Hieroglyphs, even if only as long as they were not deciphered yet, provided the ideal visual representation for a genre of perceived secrets that were at once omnipresent and unknowable in their depths. Novalis and Ritter did not live to see the decipherment. As Keiner noted, image and metaphor were one during these days of the earliest Romanticism which allowed the two Romantic scientists to approach their scientific images metaphorically and poetically as signs and symbols of a language of nature that should be read. This poetic method in natural science allowed them to see connections that others could not. The most far-reaching was probably the discovery of electromagnetism, i.e., the close relationship of electricity and magnetism that Ritter had implied in many ways and his colleague Hans Christian Ørsted proved experimentally.[79] The visual correlation of dust figures on "affected disks," i.e., traces of electricity on the electrophore and "the clustering of iron filings around the magnet" had already been an integral part of Novalis's catalog of readable natural hieroglyphs.

The hieroglyph comes to symbolize not just the Romantic search for primordial truth but even more so the intimate union of poetry and science necessary to recognize this truth. And while the Romantic hieroglyph has many metaphorical dimensions, it epitomizes the observable visual phenomena that root Romantic transcendency in the material and visible world.

---

[78] Novalis, *Schriften*, I, 312. "Das große Geheimnis ist allen offenbart, und bleibt ewig unergründlich."

[79] See Brain, Robert Michael, R. S. Cohen, and Ole Knudsen. *Hans Christian Ørsted and the Romantic Legacy in Science: Ideas, Disciplines, Practices* (Boston Studies in the Philosophy of Science. Dordrecht: Springer, 2007).

Bibliography

Assmann, Aleida, and Jan Assmann. *Hieroglyphen: Stationen einer anderen abendländischen Grammatologie*. Munich: Wilhelm Fink, 2003.
Assmann, Jan. *Das verschleierte Bild zu Sais, Schillers Ballade und ihre griechischen und ägyptischen Hintergründe*. Stuttgart: Teubner, 1999.
Brain, Robert Michael, R. S. Cohen, and Ole Knudsen. *Hans Christian Ørsted and the Romantic Legacy in Science: Ideas, Disciplines, Practices*. Boston Studies in the Philosophy of Science. Dordrecht: Springer, 2007.
Budge, E. A. Wallis (Ernest Alfred Wallis). *The Gods of the Egyptians; or, Studies in Egyptian Mythology*. Vol. 1. London: Methuen, 1904.
Chladni, Ernst Florens Friedrich. *Die Akustik: Mit 12 Kupfertafeln*. Leipzig: Breitkopf & Härtel, 1802.
Chladni, Ernst Florens Friedrich. *Entdeckungen über die Theorie des Klanges*. Leipzig: Bey Weidmanns Erben und Reich, 1787.
Daiber, Jürgen. *Experimentalphysik des Geistes: Novalis und das romantische Experiment*. Göttingen: Vandenhoeck & Ruprecht, 2001.
Derrida, Jacques. *Of Grammatology*. Translated by Gayatri Chakravorty Spivak. Baltimore: Johns Hopkins University Press, 1976.
Dorn, Thea. *Die Unglückseligen*. Munich: Albrecht Knaus, 2017.
"DWDS – Digitales Wörterbuch der deutschen Sprache." https://www.dwds.de/wb/Hieroglyphe. Accessed 5 February 2019.
Hansen, Erk F. *Wissenschaftswahrnehmung und -umsetzung im Kontext der deutschen Frühromantik: Zeitgenössische Naturwissenschaft und Philosophie im Werk Friedrich von Hardenbergs (Novalis)*. Frankfurt am Main: Peter Lang, 1992.
Heilbron, J. L. *Electricity in the 17th and 18th Centuries: A Study of Early Modern Physics*. Berkeley: University of California Press, 1979.
Herder, Johann Gottfried. *Älteste Urkunde des Menschengeschlechts*. Tübingen: Cotta, 1806.
Holland, Jocelyn. *German Romanticism and Science: The Procreative Poetics of Goethe, Novalis, and Ritter*. Routledge Studies in Romanticism. New York: Routledge, 2009.
Holland, Jocelyn. "The Silence of Ritter's Symbol ⊗." *The Germanic Review: Literature, Culture, Theory* 92, no. 4 (2017): 340–354.
Hooke, Robert. *Micrographia; or, Some Physiological Descriptions of Minute Bodies Made by Magnifying Glasses, with Observations and Inquiries Thereupon 1665*. Lincolnwood, IL: Science Heritage, 1987.
Jones, Tom. "Theories of Language in the Eighteenth Century." *Oxford Handbooks Online*. 5 October 2015. https://doi.org/10.1093/oxfordhb/9780199935338.013.100.
Keiner, Astrid. *Hieroglyphenromantik: Zur Genese und Destruktion eines Bilderschriftmodells und zu seiner Überforderung in Friedrich Schlegels Spätphilosophie*. Würzburg: Königshausen & Neumann, 2003.
Kittler, Friedrich. *Aufschreibesysteme 1800–1900*. Munich: Wilhelm Fink, 1985.
Lemper, Ernst-Heinz. *Adolf Traugott von Gersdorf (1744–1807): Naturforschung und soziale Reformen im Dienste der Humanität*. Berlin: VEB Deutscher Verlag der Wissenschaften, 1974.
Lichtenberg, Georg Christoph. *Aus Lichtenbergs Nachlass: Aufsätze, Gedichte, Tagebuchblätter, Briefe: zur hundertsten Wiederkehr seines Todestages (24. Februar 1799)*. Edited by Albert Leitzmann. Weimar: H. Böhlaus Nachfolger, 1899.

Lichtenberg, Georg Christoph. *Observationes: Die lateinischen Schriften*. Edited by Dag Nikolaus Hasse. Göttingen: Wallstein, 1997.

Novalis. *Schriften: Die Werke Friedrich von Hardenbergs*. Edited by Paul Kluckhohn, R. H. Samuel, and Hans Joachim Mähl. 2nd ed. Stuttgart: W. Kohlhammer, 1960.

Pfannkuchen, Antje. "A Matter of Visibility – Georg Christoph Lichtenberg's Art and Science of Observation." *Configurations* 24, no. 4 (2016): 375–400.

Pfannkuchen, Antje. "A Science of Hieroglyphs, or the Test of *Bildung*." In *The Technological Introject: Friedrich Kittler between Implementation and the Incalculable*, edited by Jeffrey Champlin and Antje Pfannkuchen, 84–92. New York: Fordham University Press, 2018.

Richter, Klaus. *Das Leben des Physikers Johann Wilhelm Ritter: Ein Schicksal in der Zeit der Romantik*. Weimar: H. Böhlaus Nachfolger, 2003.

Ritter, Johann Wilhelm, and Jocelyn Holland. *Key Texts of Johann Wilhelm Ritter (1776–1810) on the Science and Art of Nature*. History of Science and Medicine Library. Leiden: Brill, 2010.

Rudwick, Martin J. S. "The Emergence of a Visual Language for Geology, 1760–1840." *History of Science* 14 (1976): 149–195.

Schelling, Friedrich Wilhelm Joseph. *Vorlesungen über die Methode (Lehrart) des akademischen Studiums: Auf der Grundlage des Textes der Ausgabe von Otto Weiss*. Edited by Melchior Meyr. Vol. 2. Philosophische Bibliothek. Hamburg: Meiner, 1990.

Schlegel, Friedrich. "Athenaeum Fragments." In *Philosophical Fragments*. Translated by Peter Firchow. Foreword by Rodolphe Gasché. 18–93. Minneapolis: University of Minnesota Press, 1991.

Sharpe, Gregory. *Two Dissertations: I. Upon the Origin, Construction, Division, and Relation of Language; II. Upon the Original Powers of Letters; Wherein Is Proved from the Analogy of Alphabets, and the Proportion of Letters, That the Hebrew Ought to Be Read Without Points. To Which Is Added, the Second Edition, Enlarged, of a Hebrew Grammar and Lexicon, Without Points*. London: John Millan, 1751.

Strickland, Stuart Walker. "Circumscribing Science: Johann Wilhelm Ritter and the Physics of Sidereal Man." PhD diss., Harvard University, 1992.

Vico, Giambattista. *The New Science*. Translated by Max Harold Fisch and Thomas Goddard Bergin. Ithaca, NY: Cornell University Press, 1948. http://archive.org/details/newscienceofgiam030174mbp.

Wetzels, Walter Dominic. *Johann Wilhelm Ritter: Physik im Wirkungsfeld der deutschen Romantik*. Berlin: Walter de Gruyter, 1973.

Agnes Hoffmann
A Poetics of Scaling: Adalbert Stifter and the Measures of Nature Around 1850

"Großes ist mir klein, Kleines ist mir groß"[1]– what may sound like the experience of a perceptive disorder[2] or the impossible view through both the right and the wrong ends of binoculars actually describes the transformative learning process depicted in Adalbert Stifter's (1805–1868) novel *Indian Summer: A Tale* [*Der Nachsommer: Eine Erzählung*, 1857]. The underlying idea occurs throughout his work as a leitmotif. In his literary, poetological, and art critical writings, Stifter calls for a new perspective on the proportions of nature, emphasizing the equality and interrelatedness of the small and great in it. But if the paradoxical phrase quoted above is not just a logical or naïve mistake ["Irrtum"] as Walter Benjamin remarked in an essay on Stifter,[3] questions arise: What kind of experience is Stifter describing here? From which standpoint do the scales of nature become interchangeable? And where does this idea lead in aesthetic and poetic terms, in an œuvre so deeply concerned with questions of the observation and artistic representation of nature?

Stifter's concern with scales and scaling is related to new models of scientific observation and artistic representation of nature that emerged around 1850. On the one hand, Stifter's adjustment of conventional categories of great and small used for understanding nature corresponded to new inductive sciences that flourished in the Habsburg Empire at the middle of the century. New disciplines

---

1 Adalbert Stifter, *Der Nachsommer. Eine Erzählung. Erster Band*, vol. 4.1 of *Werke und Briefe. Historisch-kritische Gesamtausgabe*, ed. Wolfgang Frühwald and Walter Hettche (Stuttgart/Berlin/Köln: Verlag W. Kohlhammer, 1997), 217. In the following, all German quotations from Stifter's texts will be cited from the *Historisch-kritische Gesamtausgabe*, as *HKG* plus volume, and page number parenthetically; for example: (*HKG* 4.1: 217). The English quotations from *Indian Summer* are cited after the translation by Wendell Frye. Adalbert Stifter, *Indian Summer*, trans. Wendell Frye. (New York: Peter Lang, 1985), hereafter as *"Indian Summer"* plus page number.
2 On the distortion of scales caused by perceptive disorder, the so-called "Alice in Wonderland Syndrome," and on literary concepts of scale disorder in postmodern literature, see Mirjam Steiner, "Inseparably United: Big and Small in Literary Settings," in *Too Big To Scale – On Scaling Space, Numbers, Time, and Energy*, ed. Florian Dombois and Julie Harboe (Zurich: Verlag Scheidegger & Spiess AG, 2017), 113–128.
3 Walter Benjamin criticized Stifter's idea of a radical equality or relativity of scales as a naïve mistake; see Walter Benjamin, "Stifter," in *Gesammelte Schriften*, vol. II. 2, ed. Rolf Tiedemann and Hermann Schweppenhäuser (Frankfurt a. M.: Suhrkamp, 1991), 608–610, 608.

such as climatology, geology, and statistics systematically examined qualitative interrelations between small data and greater developments in nature. Stifter had been familiar with this scientific paradigm shift since his school days in the abbey of Kremsmünster.[4] On the other hand, the relation between minute detail and the big picture of nature became crucial in the field of the verbal and visual arts, particularly in theories of literary Realism and landscape painting, and in debates surrounding the advent of photography, which discussed the role of singular aspects in the representations of nature.[5]

These two dimensions are intertwined in Stifter's work: Throughout his writings, this new perspective on nature stands for both epistemic and aesthetic progress, an aspect that is often overlooked in research dealing with the perception of nature in Stifter.[6] This chapter proposes to close this gap by conducting a comparative study of exemplary passages from *Indian Summer* as well as

---

[4] Christian Begemann, "Metaphysik und Empirie: Konkurrierende Naturkonzepte im Werk Adalbert Stifters," in *Wissen in Literatur im 19. Jahrhundert*, ed. Lutz Danneberg and Friedrich Vollhardt (Tübingen: Max Niemeyer, 2002), 92–126, esp. 93–105; Deborah R. Coen, *Climate in Motion: Science, Empire, and the Question of Style* (Chicago: University of Chicago Press, 2018), 67–68.

[5] For more on the aesthetic controversies on detail see below.

[6] The fundamental ties between Stifter's aesthetics and the natural sciences have been subject to extensive research since the groundbreaking study by Martin Selge, *Poesie aus dem Geist der Naturwissenschaft* (Stuttgart: Kohlhammer, 1976), which focused on patterns of verification and falsification in Stifter's descriptions of nature. More recent studies have emphasized the importance of the historical context of Habsburgian Science, that is, of scientific disciplines like climatology or geology, which was reflected in Stifter's aesthetics during his lifetime; see Christian Begemann, "Metaphysik und Empirie"; Petra Gehring, *Zwischen unsicherem Wissen und sicherem Unwissen. Erzählte Wissensformation im realistischen Roman: Stifters 'Der Nachsommer' und Vischers 'Auch Einer'* (Bielefeld: Aisthesis, 2014), 101–173; or Michael Gamper, "Literarische Meteorologie am Beispiel von Stifters 'Das Haidedorf,'" in *Wind und Wetter. Kultur–Wissen–Ästhetik*, ed. Georg Braungart and Urs Büttner (Paderborn: Wilhelm Fink, 2018), 219–232. While all these studies discuss the relation between Stifter's literary aesthetics and natural sciences, they do not explicitly address questions of perspective and vision in science and art, neither do they discuss the aspect of measurement and proportion. Coen's aforementioned study *Climate in Motion* is an exception here, although she, too, does not mention relations to contemporary discussions on scales and perspective in literary theory and aesthetics. Juliane Vogel has analyzed the correlation between vision and poetics in Stifter but misses the connection to epistemological questions. See Vogel, "Stifters Gitter: Poetologische Dimensionen einer Grenzfigur," in *Die Dinge und die Zeichen: Dimensionen des Realistischen in der Erzählliteratur des 19. Jahrhunderts* ed. Barbara Hunfeld and Sabine Schneider (Würzburg: Königshausen & Neumann, 2008), 43–58. Elisabeth Strowick's excellent study on perspective and poetics in Stifter discusses Stifter's poetics of vision in the context of contemporary theories of physiology and motion, but is not interested in the link to contemporary discussions on measurements and flexible scales, but focuses on the aspect of individual vision in movement.

other poetological and art critical texts. The first part discusses ideas of scaling in Stifter's poetological preface to his volume *Many-Colored Stones* [*Bunte Steine*, 1853], focusing on ties to both contemporary debates on meteorology and the discourse on literary realism. The next section takes a look at Stifter's idea of painterly representation of the great and small in nature in the novel *Indian Summer*, focusing on auxiliary techniques (like naturalist sketching of detail or the use of perspectival instruments) that help his characters to adjust their perception of nature. Finally, the chapter examines some aesthetic problems resulting from the effort to establish relations between nature's proportions and the artistic work, with reference to Stifter's work as an art critic and painter.

1 Adjusting the focus: The preface to *Many-Colored Stones*

Questions of scaling play a significant role in Stifter's poetics of literary representation. In the famous preface to his volume of short stories *Many-Colored Stones* (1853), he presents his theory of literary mimesis as a readjustment of habitual views of nature.[7] As in the quotation at the outset of this chapter, here he pleads for a new attitude which seeks nature's greatness in small things: True interest in nature must not be directed towards the spectacular and the sensational, but towards the seemingly small and ordinary details – the growth of grass and flowers, the flow of waters, the clouds in the sky – in which the elementary laws of all existence manifest themselves, determining nature and society.[8] Contemporaries had previously sharply criticized Stifter's work for its attention to the small and particular, but this preface responds to their accusations with a call for the new perspective on nature he seeks to embody in his writings. To illustrate how minute individual data can be indicative of elementary forces of nature when accurately observed, Stifter describes an experimental setting common to the natural sciences:

> Let us elucidate what has been said with an example. If a man were to observe a magnetic needle, whose one end always points north, day after day at fixed times and were to write

---

See Strowick, "Poetological-Technical Operations: Representation of Motion in Adalbert Stifter," *Configurations* 18 [2010]: 273–289.
7 Stifter, *HKG* 2.2: 9–20.
8 Stifter, *HKG* 2.2: 10.

in a book the changes as the needle points north now more clearly, now less, certainly an ignorant person would look upon this activity as something small and frivolous; but how awesome does this small thing become and how inspiring this frivolity when we learn that these observations are really being made all over the world [. . .], that the whole surface of the earth, as it were, feels a magnetic shiver all the time.[9]

Like the conscientious observer of the magnetic needle, every "true observer"[10] ("Forscher"[11]) of nature – and thus also the literary author, whose idea of imitating nature the text seeks to demonstrate – should strive to recognize the underlying elementary laws, which govern natural processes, small and large. Any superficial interest in the sensational and spectacular aspects of nature may thus be exchanged for a deeper look into general, even universal principles. Since the division of phenomena into categories of "large" or "small" is subject to the constant change in judgments of taste ("As in the history of nature the attitudes towards greatness have continually changed, so it is in the moral history of mankind"[12]), for Stifter, the "eye of science"[13] is clearly superior to the changeability and inaccuracy of human perception of nature:

> If we had a sensory organ for electricity and the magnetism emanating from it, such as we have eyes for the light, what a great world, what an abundance of immense phenomena would be open to us. But if we do not have this physical eye, we have the mental eye of science, and this teaches us that the electrical and magnetic force acts upon a huge scene, that it is spread over the whole earth and through the whole sky, that it flows around everything and manifests itself in gentle and incessant transmutation, by forming shapes and generating life.[14]

The preface here describes science as a teacher of perception, the "mental eye of science" enabling human eyes to see the artwork of creation: the effect of earth's magnetism may not be perceived directly as a visual effect in nature, but can nonetheless be seen as "creative and life-giving" ("bildend und lebenerzeugend"[15]), with man enjoying this sublime spectacle like a theater spectator once his eyes have been opened accordingly.

---

9 The English quotations from *Many-Colored Stones* are cited from the translation by Jeffrey L. Sammons, Adalbert Stifter, "Preface to 'Many-Colored Stones,'" in *German Novellas of Realism*, vol. 1, ed. and trans. Jeffrey L. Sammons (New York: Continuum, 1989), 1–6, here 2. Quoted in the following as "Preface" with page numbers.
10 Stifter, "Preface," 2 and 4.
11 Stifter, *HKG* 2.2: 10.
12 Stifter, "Preface," 2.
13 Stifter, "Preface," 2.
14 Stifter, "Preface," 2.
15 Stifter, *HKG* 2.2: 11.

Using the analogy of the scientific (i.e., geomagnetic) measuring method, Stifter thus introduces the idea of a perspective from which small things appear large and large things small: the magnetic waves are indicative of a "huge scene," that is, a universal theater or drama of creation, which in turn can be observed in the form of simple measured values and their recording. This idea can be specifically placed in a context of the history of knowledge and media. First, Stifter appears to be an insider to contemporary theories of geomagnetism and its measurement,[16] as well as to the idea of knowledge gained by collecting individual data and noting minimal differences with its clear proximity to the advent of statistical methods.[17] Second, the relationality of "great" and "small" he uses in the preface has a clear parallel in natural-philosophical and meteorological writings of the time, in the emerging landscape of scientific culture in Habsburg Empire.

It is evident that the inductive conclusion of the large from the small and curiosity about the change of scales occupied the minds of scientists working during the Habsburg Empire. In fact, the topos of re-scaling circumstances, redirecting one's view to the miniscule or searching for the small in the large, can be found in contemporary discourse in surprising abundance, as the extensive study by historian of science Deborah R. Coen has recently shown.[18] In addition to academic institutions, the latest findings about discoveries, expeditions, and inventions were circulated in various circles of friends, such as the Society of Friends of Natural Science [*Verein der Freunde der Naturwissenschaften*], which was equally open to professionals and interested laymen, one of whose founding members was Stifter's acquaintance, the alpine researcher Friedrich

---

[16] The first systematic research on earth magnetism was carried out in the 1830s. In a publication of the so-called "Magnetische Gesellschaft" in 1836, its founder Carl Friedrich Gauss described the use of a "small apparatus for measuring earth magnetism to an absolute measure for travellers," which was intended to allow the uncomplicated collection of measurement data "from the entire surface of the earth." *Resultate aus den Beobachtungen des Magnetischen Vereins im Jahre 1836*, ed. Carl Friedrich Gauss and Wilhelm Weber (Göttingen: Dietrichische Buchhandlung, 1837), 63–64. In crediting science with the ability to guide the artistic perception of nature, Stifter's preface differs notably from the romantic ideal of a "poetic science" one generation earlier, that Antje Pfannkuchen discusses in her chapter on romantic hieroglyphs in this volume. In Stifter, poetry and science still share a common ground (i.e., the observation of nature), but for him, the advanced contemporary sciences are clearly superior in their ability to guide and educate the human "eye" and, in this, provide a model for the arts.
[17] Paul Fleming, *Exemplarity and Mediocrity: The Art of the Average from Bourgeois Tragedy to Realism* (Stanford: Stanford University Press, 2009), 132–138.
[18] The question of scaling in Habsburgian scientific culture and the extension of categories of measurement on abstract subjects like "nature," "society," or "nation" is the main focus in Deborah R. Coen, *Climate in Motion*.

Simony (1813–1896).[19] Compare for example the following quote by the physicist Andreas von Baumgartner from his article "The Great and the Small in Nature" ("Das Große und das Kleine in der Natur"), published in the popular Austrian *Volks- und Wirtschaftskalender* from 1860, that illustrates how the figural and metaphorical language found in Stifter's writings were common to the scientific field between 1840 and 1860. Baumgartner's concern could well have been part of Stifter's preface and its prevailing metaphysical framework, including a theatrical metaphor of nature's drama, when he demands "that in observing the great and the small we do not want to confine ourselves to what is long, wide and high, but also to draw attention to what, though physically small, plays an important role in the great drama of nature."[20]

Regarding these historical parallels, the focus on the scaling of nature, the demand for attention to small details and phenomena, and the resulting adaptation of perceptual habits in Stifter's preface can be justified in epistemological terms. But there is also a tie to contemporary debates on literary realism, which, interestingly enough, also revolved around proportions, an interdiscursive connection in Stifter's work that has so far received little attention.[21] In his preface

---

[19] The analogy applies in particular to Stifter's transference of the idea of a general lawfulness that can be found in natural circumstances as well as in social and political systems at the end of his preface. This was a common trope during the upswing of Habsburg scientific culture, where it was supposed to have a calming and identity-building effect in post-revolutionary times: In many publications of the time, e.g., also in the founding speech of the above-mentioned association, one finds the idea that society and state are organized according to laws just like nature, so that the natural sciences can contribute to their understanding and stabilize them. See *Bericht über die Mittheilungen von Freunden der Naturwissenschaft in Wien*, vol. IV, 2, ed. Wilhelm Haidinger (Vienna: Wilhelm Braumüller, 1848), 272–273; Coen, *Climate in Motion*, 89–91. On the association, see Coen, *Climate in Motion*, 100–103. Regarding its institutional politics, see the association's constitution and founding speech in Haidinger, ed., *Bericht*, 278–287.

[20] Andreas Baumgartner, "Das Große und Kleine in der Natur," *Österreichischer Volks- und Wirtschafts-Kalender für das Jahr 1860* (Vienna: Prandel & Ewald, 1860), 3–11, here 7 [my translation; A.H.]. Baumgartner's article is also mentioned in Hannes Etzlstorfer, "'Die Wolken, ihre Bildung [. . .] waren mir wunderbare Erscheinungen' ("Nachsommer"): Bemerkungen zu Adalbert Stifters Motivrepertoire als Landschaftsmaler," in *Sanfte Sensationen: Stifter 200: Beiträge zum 200. Geburtstag Adalbert Stifters*, ed. Johann Lachinger, Regina Pintar, Christian Schachreiter, and Martin Sturm (Linz: StifterHaus, 2005), 60–74, 65.

[21] Werner Michler has emphasized the common interest in regulations and order in Stifter's work and the journal *Die Grenzboten*, where leading theories of literary realism developed; see Michler, "Adalbert Stifter und die Ordnungen der Gattung. Generische Veredelung und die Arbeit am 'Habitus,'" in *Stifter und Stifterforschung im 21. Jahrhundert: Biographie – Wissenschaft – Poetik*, ed. Hartmut Laufhütte, Alfred Doppler, Johannes John, and Johann Lachinger (Tübingen: Max Niemeyer, 2007), 182–200, here 184.

Stifter defends himself against contemporary criticism of the descriptive, detailed style of his poetry. Friedrich Hebbel (1813–1863), for example, judged Stifter's early *Studien* (1844–1850) as showing too little interest in the great whole of nature, being devoted merely to "beetles" and "buttercups."[22] Later criticism would echo Hebbel's claim. Contemporary critics raised concerns about the writer's inappropriate tendency – from his narratives to his last novel *Witiko* (1865) – to distort things by describing his subjects "much too minutely" and in "endless detail."[23] One even warned against the "dangers that are only too common to this poet with the microscope. [. . .] In his writings, everything is a 'small painting,' a drawing in detail, which makes of the most insignificant things the most extensively studied matter."[24]

Optical instruments had been a topic in literary poetics since Aristotle as symbols for artistic perception of nature, especially during the Baroque period, in which poetological writings frequently referred to telescopes, magnifying glasses, or microscopes.[25] Around 1800, one generation before Stifter, the microscope in particular was still more than popular in German literature and poetics. Goethe, Jean Paul, and E. T. A. Hoffmann regarded the microscopic view of nature as a creative and astonishing extension of the human sensorium and the literary perspective.[26] Around 1850, however, this changed. In apparent

---

22 See Friedrich Hebbel's poem "Die alten Naturdichter und die neuen," in Hebbel, *Gedichte, Erzählungen, Schriften*, vol. 3, *Werke*, 3, ed. Gerhard Fricke, Werner Keller, and Karl Pörnbacher (Munich: Hanser, 1965), 122.
23 "viel zu minutiös" in "unendlicher Detaillierung." In a critical review by F. Th. Bratanek, "Adalbert Stifter. Eine literarhistorische Skizze," *Österreichische Revue* 6 (1863): 62–76 [my translation, A.H.].
24 "[. . .] Gefahren, die diesem Dichter mit dem Mikroskop naheliegen. [. . .] Es ist alles bei ihm 'Kleinmalerei', ein Zeichnen ins Detail, welches das Unwesentliche zur ausführlich auseinandergesetzten Hauptsache macht." Anonymous review of Stifter's *Witiko* in *Europa: Chronik der gebildeten Welt. Wochenchronik* 31 (1865): 497–499, here 498 [my translation, A.H.].
25 On Baroque poetics and its interest in enhancing the human perception of nature, see Ralph Köhnen, *Das optische Wissen, Mediologische Studien zu einer Geschichte des Sehens* (Paderborn/München: Wilhelm Fink, 2009), 213–236; Ulrich Stadler, *Der technisierte Blick: Optische Instrumente und der Status von Literatur: Ein kulturhistorisches Museum* (Würzburg: Königshausen und Neumann, 2003), 59–68; Nicola Gess, "Instruments of Wonder – Wondrous Instruments: Optical Devices of the Marvelous of Fontenelle, Rist, Breitinger, and Hoffmann," *German Quarterly* 90:4 (2017): 407–422.
26 Gerhard Neumann. "Fernrohr, Mikroskop, Luftballon. Wahrnehmungstechnik und Literatur in der Goethezeit," in *Spektakuläre Experimente. Praktiken der Evidenzproduktion im 17. Jahrhundert*, ed. Helmar Schramm, Ludger Schwarte, and Jan Lazardzig (Berlin/New York: De Gruyter 2006), 345–377; Janina Wellmann, "Bewegung an der Wand. Zur Aufführung von Organismen mit dem Sonnenmikroskop," in *Belebungskünste: Praktiken lebendiger Darstellung in Literatur, Kunst und Wissenschaft um 1800*, ed. Nicola Gess, Agnes Hoffmann, and Annette

contradiction to Stifter's detail-rich prose, theories of literary realism that evolved, e.g., in the context of the *Die Grenzboten* [*The Border Messengers*] (1841–1922), called for the unity of form and the reduction of details in the literary text.[27] This was not just a question of taste. Julian Schmidt (1818–1886), one of the editors of *Die Grenzboten*, considered Stifter's particular style to be a hindrance to the development of any large-scale literary composition: "Anyone who is so absorbed in detail as Stifter is in these early works will not be able to execute a painting of large dimensions such that a certain overall impression prevails."[28]

In view of the prevailing literary poetics of the time, Stifter's interest in details made him seem guilty of following an anti-realist agenda on the level of content and form. The counterargument he articulates in the preface to *Many-Colored Stones* seems to be all the more important in this context: Following Stifter and his analogy of a seismograph, literature actually cannot proceed too detailed or "with a microscope,"[29] since even in the most minute and banal of details, it would always detect and represent the laws of sublime nature. Within his framework of scientific observation, Stifter simply avoids questioning the choice of subject or the coherence of the resulting composition. Just as the magnetic needle allows empirical conclusions to be drawn about the laws of nature, the literary work of the "true observer"[30] already achieves its goal in the "collection" of the observed "cases,"[31] as Stifter states in the end of the

---

Kappeler (Paderborn: Wilhelm Fink, 2019), 227–245. The literary interest in optical instruments around 1800 corresponds to a general curiosity regarding the aesthetics of vision and its affective and cognitive dimensions, which could also include technologies that were not optical instruments at all, as Kathrin Maurer has shown in her chapter on Jean Paul and ballooning in this volume.

27 Claudia Stockinger, *Das 19. Jahrhundert: Zeitalter des Realismus* (Berlin: Akademie-Verlag, 2010), 55–56; Veronika Thanner, Joseph Vogl, and Dorothea Walzer, "Die Wirklichkeit des Realismus. Einleitung," in *Die Wirklichkeit des Realismus*, ed. Veronika Thanner, Joseph Vogl, and Dorothea Walzer (Paderborn: Wilhelm Fink, 2018), 9–10.

28 "Wer so ganz in das Detail aufgeht wie Stifter in jenen ersten Werken, wird nicht im Stande sein, ein Gemälde von großen Dimensionen so auszuführen, daß ein bestimmter Gesammteindruck vorherrscht." Julian Schmidt, *Geschichte der deutschen Literatur nach Lessings Tod*, vol. 3 (Leipzig: Friedrich Ludwig Herbig, 1856), 370–381, here 372 [my translation, A.H.].

29 Anonymous review of Stifter's *Witiko*, 498.

30 Stifter, "Preface," 2 and 4.

31 Stifter, "Preface," 6; German original "[. . .] so sei es mir auch erlaubt zu sagen, daß ich in der Geschichte des menschlichen Geschlechtes manche Erfahrungen zu sammeln bemüht gewesen bin, und daß ich einzelnes aus diesen Erfahrungen zu dichtenden Versuchen zusammengestellt habe" (*HKG* 2.2: 16).

preface. To address the great by way of the small detail thus not only connects Stifter's work to contemporary thought in Habsburgian scientific culture. The readjustment of conventional scalar frames also provides Stifter with an alternative way for thinking about how literature could represent nature. While some critics argued for a literary realism that excluded the "insignificant"[32] in favor of "large dimensions" (Schmidt), Stifter insisted on the arbitrariness of such attributions while directing the attention of his readers to the epistemic importance of consciously defining the measures according to which humans perceive nature.

2 Picturing nature in *Indian Summer*

While Stifter's preface addresses correspondences between natural phenomena and the adjustments of perspective that result from this insight, it does not say much about the visual perception of nature. This changes in the novel *Indian Summer*, in which a perceptual shift towards the true scale of natural relations is once again a central theme, combined in this instance with a strong interest in questions of visuality. The novel shows the maturation of its protagonist, Heinrich von Drendorf, from adolescence to adulthood and his education in the natural sciences and art. Heinrich finds guidance on the farm of the landlord Baron von Risach, a collector and naturalist with many interests, who introduces him to various scientific fields, mechanical skills, and ethical ways to conduct life. As the novel advances, the hero's education in natural history, geology, and the arts unfolds as a conscientious training of his observational skills. Over the course of seven years, he literally learns to see nature and art objects in a new way.[33] In accordance with the principles set out in the 1853 preface, Heinrich begins to understand his surroundings within the framework of superordinate contexts. Small details become signs for elemental forces, for example, when he learns to read individual stones as an expression of the history of the earth, or when he starts to understand the behavior of plants and insects as indications of meteorological developments.[34] The statement quoted

---

[32] Like the anonymous reviewer in *Europa* (1865).
[33] This is why the phrase "Schule der Wahrnehmung" (schooling of perception) is often used to describe Stifter's studies on *Indian Summer*. For an overview, see Florian Welle, *Der irdische Blick durch das Fernrohr: Literarische Wahrnehmungsexperimente vom 17. bis zum 20. Jahrhundert* (Würzburg: Königshausen & Neumann, 2009), 62.
[34] Stifter, *HKG* 4.2: 28–32.

at the beginning of this chapter thus summarizes the general motto of Heinrich's education in the novel – great and small are literally one and the same thing to him, as his learning success consists in understanding that elemental forces become manifest in the smallest details. Again, the necessary adjustment of perspective has an epistemic as well as an aesthetic dimension to it: The novel not only refers to contemporary scientific debates about climatology and geology, but presents possible consequences for an aesthetics of painting.

In accordance with his new awareness of nature's true scales and dimensions, Heinrich develops new perspectives on the natural world and its beauty. Early in the novel, he starts drawing natural objects, such as plants and stones, as an auxiliary skill that, as the novel reflects time and again, promotes closer study and aids their morphological and topological systematization. Compare for instance the following passage, in which Heinrich describes his drawing of a stone formation in a cliff:

> From the lake I observed the cliff stratification. What is called foliation with crystals was evident here on a larger scale. In some spots the slope was one way, in other places it was another. Are these gigantic leaves that fell down at one time, have they been elevated, is the process still going on? I sketched many stratifications in their beautiful compositions and in their slope towards the horizontal.[35]

The protagonist observes a morphological analogy between the cliff and the foliation of crystals, which makes him wonder about the forces that created the stratifications he sees in front of him: Were those stone formations static, or did they develop over time, similar to a process of crystallization? Again, his observational interest is based on the discovery of correlations. The fact that the stratifications remind him of the foliation of crystals only "on a larger scale" triggers his curiosity. While his attention is directed towards greater geohistorical developments, he is also aware of the aesthetic beauty that lies in the "compositions" of these stratifications. As in the preface to *Many-Colored Stones*, here, too, the discovery of a correlation of phenomena on a smaller and greater scale enables movement back and forth between particular details and superordinate circumstances without ignoring their overall aesthetic value. Heinrich's drawings extend this twofold perspective in capturing the stratification of the stone in general and its "beautiful compositions" in particular.[36]

---

[35] Adalbert Stifter, *Indian Summer*, 191.
[36] Drawing after nature was an integral part of contemporary science culture, especially in the field of botany and geology, and it was taught in both elementary schools and art schools. On drawing and geography see Petra Mayer, *Zwischen unsicherem Wissen und sicherem Unwissen*, 140–157. On Stifter's own art education in Kremsmünster, see Lothar Schultes,

Once he masters sketching, Heinrich moves on to landscape painting. Instead of focusing only on specific parts of nature in his sketches, here he wants to depict the natural surroundings of the Alps as a whole ("im Ganzen"[37]). Again, the correlation between the small and the great plays a significant role in the process of representation. But at first, he has to realize that his perception of nature needs further training in order to create a convincing artistic representation. Baron von Risach and the art-minded carpenter Eustach, to whom he presents his first attempts at painting, reach the same conclusion:

> Their judgment was unanimous: the natural scientific aspects had been much more successful than the artistic. I had expressed the stones in the foregrounds [sic], the plants around them, a piece of old wood lying there, parts of boulders toward the foreground, even waters in the immediate field of view, faithfully and with their distinctive characteristics. The distance, the large areas of shadows and light on entire mountain bodies, the receding and fading of the sky weren't done successfully.[38]

While his representation of objects in the foreground is successful, he failed to capture the mountains in the background effectively. Von Risach and Eustach explain this failure by referring to his amateurish handling of colors and proportions. Heinrich learns that he delivered the coloring too boldly and made the distant objects too large, because he was working more in accordance with his cognitive assumptions than from his visual impressions of the mountains ("as a result of using my knowledge of distant parts and not my eye"[39]). This had distorting effects on the composition as a whole: "through both, the clarity of color and the enlargement of distant things, I had brought [the Alps] closer, robbing them of the splendor they possessed in reality."[40] Ultimately, he failed to deliver the spatial dimensions of the mountain scenery convincingly on canvas, as the relationship between near and far, between the concrete objects in the foreground (stones, pieces of wood, boulders) and the sublime Alps in the background became inconsistent. His mentors attribute this failure to Heinrich's untrained attention: In his desire to depict the mountains as important objects, he had made them too prominent – a judgment that recalls Baron von Risach's

---

"Adalbert Stifter als Zeichner und Maler," *Jahrbuch des Oberösterreichischen Musealvereines: Gesellschaft für Landeskunde* 152 (2007): 237–300, especially 241–243.
37 Stifter, *HKG* 4.2: 20.
38 Stifter, *Indian Summer*, 194.
39 Stifter, *Indian Summer*, 194–195.
40 Stifter, *Indian Summer*, 194.

later remarks about the medieval perspective of meaning, which established the size of objects in painting based on their significance.[41]

Is a successful painting of the Alps therefore only a matter of applying the rules of perspective correctly? The narrator himself on the other hand diagnoses an error at the level of practice and knowledge. His training in scientific drawing, he explains, had taught him to pay attention exclusively to the "characteristics"[42] ("Merkmale"[43]) of his objects, to thus reproduce the colors and outlines of foreground and background with equal emphasis. Either way, there is a need for an instrument that will reliably correlate foreground and distance, that is, the small details and the greatness of the Alps. Such an instrument would compensate for the uncertainty and unreliability of human vision, fulfilling the same function that Stifter had assigned to the seismograph in the 1853 preface.

In *Indian Summer*, the instrument in question is a semi-transparent glass plate, which is meant to facilitate the two-dimensional recording of spatial relations on a canvas:

> Eustach advised me to cover a glass plate with Canadian balsam to make it somewhat coarser so colors would adhere to it without losing its transparency; then with a brush I should draw things in the distance bordered by objects closer at hand; I would see how small the largest and most extensive mountains in the distance should be depicted and how large the closer but infinitely smaller objects. However, he only recommended this method to become convinced of relationships, not as a means of making artistic drawings of landscapes since through such a method one loses the heart and soul of Art, artistic freedom and facility. The eye should only be practiced and trained; the soul must create, the eye should serve it.[44]

The glass plate coated with Canadian wax seems to be an invention of Stifter.[45] As an auxiliary technique, it is supposed to support the untrained eye and offer orientation by simplifying the representation of both close and distant objects. Comparable techniques of placing glass plates or lucid paper sheets between

---

[41] When contemplating a newly restored medieval altar in the seventh chapter ("The Meeting") Eustach and Baron von Risach introduce Heinrich to the logic of representational perspective, according to which the medieval artist represented objects in proportion to their salvation-historical significance (the figures of the saints are much larger in scale than other objects like houses or a dragon). Stifter, *Indian Summer*, chapter 7, 134–178.
[42] Stifter, *Indian Summer*, 194.
[43] Stifter, *HKG* 4.2: 37.
[44] Stifter, *Indian Summer*, 195. (*HKG* 4.2: 36–37)
[45] Not the only one: on inventions in Stifter's work, see: Monika Ritzer, "Von Suppenwürfeln, Induktionsstrom und der Äquivalenz der Kräfte: Zum Kulturwert der Naturwissenschaft am Beispiel von Adalbert Stifters Novelle 'Abdias,'" *Kulturpoetik. Journal for Cultural Poetics* 2.1 (2002): 44–67.

object and eye have a long tradition in classical theories of perspective, as formulated, for example, by Leonardo da Vinci or Albrecht Dürer, or in modern theories of practical geometry in Stifter's time, as in the book *Malerische Perspektive* (1854) by Guido Schreiber, a professor of geometry in Karlsruhe.[46]

The difficulty of finding the right scale for the pictorial representation of nature was at the same time a central theme in discourses on painting, triggered by the rise of photography and its technical possibilities of, among other things, representing nature in detail.[47] Similar to Eustach in the passage just quoted, the art critic John Ruskin (1819–1900) referred to the sheer technical challenge of capturing a scene from nature in minute detail in his *Modern Painters* (1843).[48] Other critics defended the art of painting against the exactness of the new medium of photography, like Charles Baudelaire (1821–1867), who praised painting for its ability to eliminate unimportant details.[49] For Stifter, the decision about what should be painted and how becomes a matter of training and technical support of human sight: The painting scene from *Indian Summer* emphasizes the importance of being accurate in detail, but there is also a clear skepticism towards the ability of the eye to simply see a natural scene in a way that allows its reproduction on canvas. For Stifter, the painter's task is to pay attention to the details, particularly in their relationship to that which is distant – if necessary, with the help of a tool that correlates

---

[46] Guido Schreiber, *Malerische Perspektive: Mit einem Anhang über den Gebrauch geometrischer Grundrisse* (Karlsruhe: Herder, 1854), 22–24 (§13–15).

[47] On the detail as a core problem in debates on painting and photography around 1850 and after, see Wolfgang Kemp, "Fotografie als Kunst," in *Theorie der Fotografie, 1839–1912*, ed. Wolfgang Kemp (Munich: Schirmer/Mosel, 1980), 13–45; Peter Geimer, "Blow Up," in *"Der liebe Gott steckt im Detail". Mikrostrukturen des Wissens*, ed. Wolfgang Schäffner, Sigrid Weigel, and Thomas Macho (Munich: Wilhelm Fink, 2003), 187–202.

[48] See John Ruskin in *Modern Painters*, who focuses on the challenge to find artistic solutions to the problem: "We have seen that a literal fac-simile [of a mountain scenery] is impossible, just as a literal fac-simile of the carving of an entire cathedral front is impossible. But it is as vain to endeavor to give any conception of an Alpine cliff without minuteness of detail, and by mere breadth of effect, as it would be to give a conception of the façades of Rouen or Rheims, without indicating any statues or foliation." John Ruskin, *Mountain Beauty*, vol. IV, 5, *Modern Painters* (London: Smith, Elder and Co., 1856), 267. Ruskin himself was also much interested in the empirical foundations of perception, but his argument here holds on to the idea of the possibilities of the artistic representation of nature, not – like the protagonist of *Indian Summer* – for example to the question of the (atmospheric) conditions of nature as source of its aesthetic appearance.

[49] Charles Baudelaire, "Salon de 1848," in *Curiosités esthétiques*, vol. 2, *Œuvres complètes de Charles Baudelaire* (Paris: Calmann-Lévy, 1868), 77–198, here 90.

what is near with what is far away, "to become convinced of relationships"[50] among the elements in nature.

Once the spatial conditions are fixed on the canvas thanks to the waxed plate, the task of the painter, Heinrich learns, is to pay more attention to atmospheric values such as light and air, which he had ignored as "obstacles to observation,"[51] although they define the visual impression of the scene significantly: "The objects gained a different appearance through air, light, haze, clouds, through other bodies close to them; I had to ascertain this and make it a part of my studies just as I had previously done with the features which almost literally jumped into the eye."[52]

It is not surprising that Heinrich would want to practice the observation of the atmosphere as a systematic science, because, as has been shown, Stifter refers to contemporary discoveries on the atmosphere here, which also placed an emphasis on the visual qualities of atmospheric phenomena.[53] In this way, the "eye of science"[54] again guides the artistic view in *Indian Summer*, because pictorial representation of nature remains bound to models of scientific observation, although the novel also articulates problems from contemporary debates about the treatment of details in art. For Stifter, the aesthetic choice to render natural details in an artwork so vigorously discussed by his contemporaries must be anchored in scientific reason. This notion differs significantly from some recent studies on sight and visuality in Stifter which have pointed out the autonomy of vision in his writings, as well as Stifter's interest in experimenting with it, and the proximity of both to the discourse of physiological optics and body-related vision around 1850.[55] With regard to the poetological preface from

---

50 Stifter, *Indian Summer*, 195.
51 Stifter, *Indian Summer*, 195.
52 Stifter, *Indian Summer*, 195.
53 See Franz Pichler, "Andreas Baumgartner und sein Werk zur Naturlehre," in *Stifter und Stifterforschung im 21. Jahrhundert*, ed. Hartmut Laufhütte et al., 117–126, here 120–122; Kathrin Maurer, "Adalbert Stifter's Poetic of Clouds and Nineteenth-century Meteorology," *Oxford German Studies* 45 no. 4 (2016): 421–433, here 424–430.
54 Stifter, "Preface," 2.
55 See Elisabeth Strowick, "Poetological-Technical Operations: Representation of Motion in Adalbert Stifter," *Configurations* 18 (2010): 273–289; Kathrin Maurer, "'Ich hatte dieses Ding nie so gesehen wie heute.' Zur Verunsicherung der Wahrnehmung in Adalbert Stifters 'Eisgeschichte,'" *Colloquia Germanica* 92.1/2 (2013): 35–48; Silke Brodersen, "Phänomenale Wirklichkeit und Naturgesetz in Hermann von Helmholtz' populärwissenschaftlichen Schriften und in Adalbert Stifters 'Sanftem Gesetz,'" in *Turns und Trends der Literaturwissenschaft zwischen Nachmärz und Jahrhundertwende im Blickfeld aktueller Theoriebildung*, ed. Christian Meierhofer and Eric Scheufler (Zurich: germanistik.ch, 2011), 205–221. Florian Welle, *Der irdische Blick durch das*

1853 as well as to the theme of painting in *Indian Summer*, it is rather the subordination of vision to the "eye of science,"[56] and the idea of its education and training for the sake of art. The systematic observation of stone foliations or atmospheric phenomena in *Indian Summer* thus becomes the solid base from which the "true observer"[57] can develop his artistic vision of nature, similar to the preface from 1853 and its reference to the study of geomagnetic forces.

3 The risk of incompletion: Scaling the artistic process

In Stifter's lifelong practical preoccupation with the visual arts, the problem of the right perspective on natural scenes is front and center time and again. His search for correlations between small and great details, concrete and unseizable aspects of nature stands also at the core of his art criticism and his own painterly work. When Stifter reviewed the annual exhibition of the Upper Austrian Art Association in 1860, he gave some remarks on contemporary landscape painting. His thoughts on the painting *Landscape at the River Isar* [*Gegend an der Isar*, 1860], by the Munich-based painter August Albert Zimmermann (1808–1888),[58] sounds familiar: the question of the great and small in nature and the aesthetic value of their correspondence. By referring to contemporary alpine painting, which had become popular during Romanticism, Stifter first examines his contemporaries' interest in the subject of the Alps. While he considers the sublime object itself worthy of a picture, he complains about the shortcomings in its execution that contemporaries had frequently observed:

> If the artist could paint the magnificence of the alpine world in the precise extent in which the eye captures it from a good vantagepoint, these pictures would far surpass in artistic effect those which, for example, show a simpler rural picture within smaller boundaries, just like the tragedy, when completed, is far more powerful than the elegy or idyll. But it is in the tragedy and the Alpine landscape that perfection is the most difficult thing, and that is the angle around which the whole thing revolves. Rarely has this difficulty been overcome, which is why great artists approach these subjects with caution.

Fernrohr emphasizes the experimental character of Stifter's narrative explorations of vision; id. 145–181.
56 Stifter, "Preface," 2.
57 Stifter, "Preface," 2 and 4.
58 Adalbert Stifter, "Ausstellung des oberösterreichischen Kunstvereins (1860)," in *HKG* 8.4: 281–295.

> The older landscape artists [like Claude or Ruysdael] almost never chose the Alps, although they could not have been unfamiliar with them. [. . .] Young artists or weaker ones choose large subjects, and begin with the tragedy[,] the Alpine landscape.[59]

Just as in the preface to *Many-Colored Stones*, Stifter expresses doubts about artistic depictions of "large" or spectacular materials in this art review. In terms of taste, his views are in keeping with the landscape art of the Austrian Biedermeier period, which preferred realistic portraits of tangible places in the native Alpine landscape or more distant regions of the Habsburg Empire to romantically sublime landscapes.[60] Nevertheless, Stifter is concerned with the representation of great subjects rather than style. He explicitly valorizes the Alps as a subject of painting by relating it to the art of classical tragedy – an analogy which is motivated here by the category of the sublime, as this refers to both the philosophical sublime, associated with alpine mountains since the eighteenth century, and the noble or sublime style of classical tragedy.[61] But in contrast to the rendering of a subject in tragedy, the alpine painting poses great challenges because its subject is even more difficult to render:

> The reason doesn't seem very far away. Great subjects always have very prominent features. It is these that the artist's eye sees and knows how to render, while the more subtle inherent relations of the sublime subject, which actually constitute its aesthetic greatness and completion, escape his attention, and generate the incompletion of the work. [. . .] But the deep and great artist sees the many delicate relations and nuances also in the small fabric, and from this he creates richness and seeks to express it.[62]

This argument, too, is by now familiar: there is danger in falling for great and eye-catching subjects; for their aesthetic greatness does not lie in their most spectacular "features,"[63] but is precisely defined by immanent and hardly visible "delicate relations."[64] The seemingly small is the great, the great the small – and once again, Stifter maintains, this is due to virtue of the artist's capacity to adjust the perspective accordingly, and to "see"[65] the "many delicate relationships and

---

[59] Stifter, *HKG* 8.4: 283 [my translation, A. H.].
[60] Stifter's own artistic practice can be seen in the context of Biedermeier landscape art. See Lothar Schultes, "Adalbert Stifter als Zeichner und Maler," 289–296.
[61] Elisabeth Häge in her monograph on the aesthetics of the sublime in Stifter does not mention his art criticism at all, although this might be one of the seldom references to the philosophy of the sublime in Stifter. See Elisabeth Häge, *Dimensionen des Erhabenen bei Adalbert Stifter* (Berlin/Boston: De Gruyter, 2018).
[62] Stifter, *HKG* 8.4, 283–284.
[63] Stifter, *HKG* 8.4, 283.
[64] Stifter, *HKG* 8.4, 284.
[65] Stifter, *HKG* 8.4, 283.

gradations"[66] in the "small fabric."[67] The painting of Zimmermann mentioned above offers an example of such a "deep"[68] art in Stifter's sense. It shows a hardly spectacular object – a wide plane and rocks on the banks of the Isar river in the summer heat – depicted with great care and in a manner of painting apparently trained in nature study. Stifter concludes his extensive ekphrasis of the painting with a great deal of praise for the artist, who succeeded in portraying all the pictorial objects "in their most poetically hidden characteristics [. . .], which again and again provoke contemplation."[69] While the review does not elaborate on Zimmermann's painterly technique in detail, it praises his sensitivity to nature and underscores that it must be the result of meticulous study: "At the same time [the paintings] are so true as one would hardly see in the most celebrated images of former and contemporary times. The artist [. . .] must have made very detailed studies over years in order to be able to represent the work as he portrayed it."[70]

Stifter obviously spoke from his own experience. Several studies and drawings based on nature survived his habit of destroying and burning what he deemed imperfect,[71] and we know from letters and friends that he spent great amounts of time preparing larger works by way of sketching details like stones or plants beforehand.[72] This is especially true for the large, unfinished art project Stifter pursued from 1854 until his death in 1868: In February 1854, Stifter planned a series of eight canvases representing individual landscape settings, each meant to embody an abstract quality or principle of nature (e.g. *Calmness* [*Die Ruhe*]; *Serenity* [*Die Heiterkeit*], *Movement* [*Die Bewegung*]; *Solitude* [*Die Einsamkeit*]) in subject, tone, and execution.[73] Until then, Stifter's painterly

---

66 Stifter, *HKG* 8.4, 284.
67 Stifter, *HKG* 8.4, 284.
68 Stifter, *HKG* 8.4, 284.
69 Stifter, *HKG* 8.4, 285.
70 Stifter, *HKG* 8.4, 283–284.
71 See Stefan Schmitt, "Adalbert Stifter als Zeichner," in *Adalbert Stifter*, ed. Hartmut Laufhütte et al., 261–308, here 266–264.
72 Stefan Schmitt, "Adalbert Stifter als Zeichner," 264–267.
73 On the series, see Fritz Novotny, *Adalbert Stifter als Maler* (Wien: Schroll & Co, 1941), 101–104, 110; Karl Möseneder, "Stimmung und Erdleben. Adalbert Stifters Ikonologie der Landschaftsmalerei," in Hartmut Laufhütte and Möseneder, *Adalbert Stifter, Dichter und Maler, Denkmalpfleger und Schulmann: Neue Zugänge zu seinem Werk* (Tübingen: Niemeyer, 1996), 18–57; Martina Wedekind, *Wiederholen – Beharren – Auslöschen: Zur Prosa Adalbert Stifters* (Heidelberg: Winter, 2005), 141–164.

work comprised mainly landscape paintings that followed the aforementioned manner of the Austrian Biedermeier period in motif and composition.[74] The idea of iterating an abstract principle throughout different subjects, execution, as well as the project's cyclic structure, were new to his œuvre. Although he would spend much time and effort on the proposed project in the fourteen years before his death in the winter of 1868, the only tangible outcome was two unfinished canvases, several preparatory oil sketches and drawings, and a diary documenting the working process during that time. From what is left we can hardly imagine what the paintings would have looked like, even if the subtitles roughly indicate what they were supposed to depict. The two exceptions which were partially executed, *Serenity* and *Movement*, show an ideal landscape with Greek temple ruins and a stream bed with stones in a rocky landscape, respectively.

The preparatory drawings and sketches show that Stifter approached painting in the same way he assumed Zimmermann had in 1860, that is, in "very detailed studies over years." But this extended work process left other traces, which strengthens the argument that Stifter's own painterly work was based on the same assumptions as his poetics and art criticism: He apparently worked hard to find a correlation between small details of nature and greater aspects of atmospheric and elemental forces, in a way that subordinated the painterly process to the observational practices of the naturalist. First, letters sent to family, friends, and colleagues testify to Stifter's frequent use of instruments for meteorological observation when he painted. During a retreat to Kirchschlag near Linz in the winter and spring of 1865–1866, which he undertook to strengthen his health and to focus on painting, Stifter wrote about using binoculars to look at the distant mountains, but he frequently mentions observing a barometer and a thermometer to predict weather conditions several times a day – that is, to see if and when light and atmosphere would allow him to continue his work.[75] Another more famous trace confirms that he organized the artistic

---

74 The most elaborate of these examples exhibit a precise rendering of detail and a sensitivity for atmospheric conditions that resulted in careful handling of sky and clouds. For parallels to Biedermeier taste in landscape art see Lothar Schultes, "Adalbert Stifter als Zeichner und Maler," 289–296.

75 See the references in Adalbert Stifter, *Briefe. Dritter Band*, vol. 3 of *Briefe*, ed. Johannes Aprent (Pest: Gustav Heckenast, 1869); on Stifter's meteorological observations during the painting process see Stifter, *Briefe*, 235–298, especially 263–265, 278–280, 285–286, 289–290, 291, 293–294.

process in analogy to the practice of meteorological observation; from the moment he started the project in 1854, the notorious list-keeper recorded in a special diary when, what, and how long exactly he worked on the individual paintings of the cycle (see Figure 1). In columns filled with hundreds upon hundreds of entries in neat and clear handwriting, it records the data framework of Stifter's painting activity: the date and the time he began and ended, the subject chosen on that day, and the duration spent on it, summed up in regular intervals. Though none of the paintings were ever completed, we have a register of the working process that recorded duration and focus; a strictly formalized chronicle, its rich details serve as a counterpoint to the absence and incomplete nature of the eight paintings.

The diary's odd bureaucratic form has attracted some hermeneutic attention.[76] As a textual object, it has often been interpreted with regard to Stifter's late literary writings and some of their peculiar anomalies, such as the predominance of repetitive and serial structures,[77] as well as to how it relates to his interest in the economization and at times obsessive ritualization of everyday phenomena.[78] It has also been noted on more than one occasion that the diary resembles a commercial balance sheet rather than an artist's notebook.[79] Either way, Stifter's meticulous effort in protocoling the way he worked over decades stands in stark contrast to the actual fragmentary character of the series. In the

---

[76] A variety of meanings have been read into the pages; it was characterized as a mirror of the artist's obsessive and tautological self-affirmation by Helena Ragg-Kirkby in *Adalbert Stifter's Late Prose: The Mania for Moderation* (Rochester: Camden House, 2000), 3; as an instrument of economization and temporalization of the artistic process in the medium of writing in Elisabeth Strowick, *Gespenster des Realismus: Zur literarischen Wahrnehmung von Wirklichkeit* (Paderborn: Wilhelm Fink, 2019), 95–100; and as an expression of antinomies typical for Stifter's concept of mimesis and the artwork in his later years in Johannes John, "'Übermalungen' – Transkription, Emendation, Interpretation: Zur 17. Manuskriptseite von Adalbert Stifters 'Nachkommenschaften,'" in *Text – Material – Medium: Zur Relevanz editorischer Dokumentationen für die literaturwissenschaftliche Forschung*, ed. Wolfgang Lukas, Rüdiger Nutt-Kofoth, and Madleen Podewski (Berlin/Boston: De Gruyter, 2014), 107–122, here 119–121.
[77] See the focus on textual practices in Wedekind, *Wiederholen – Beharren – Auslöschen*; Strowick, *Gespenster*.
[78] Stefan Willer, "Grenzenlose Zeit, schlingernder Grund. Genealogische Ordnungen in Stifters 'Nachkommenschaften,'" in *Figuren der Übertragung*, ed. Michael Gamper and Karl Wagner (Zurich: Chronos, 2009), 45–62, note 13.
[79] Even in the case of contemporaries using bookkeeping notation practices, such as Friedrich Gauermann or Carl Gustav Carus, notebooks contained personal details and descriptive annotations. For more on Gauermann, see Schultes, "Adalbert Stifter als Zeichner und Maler," 263. With regard to Carus, see Wedekind, *Wiederholen – Beharren – Auslöschen*, 160.

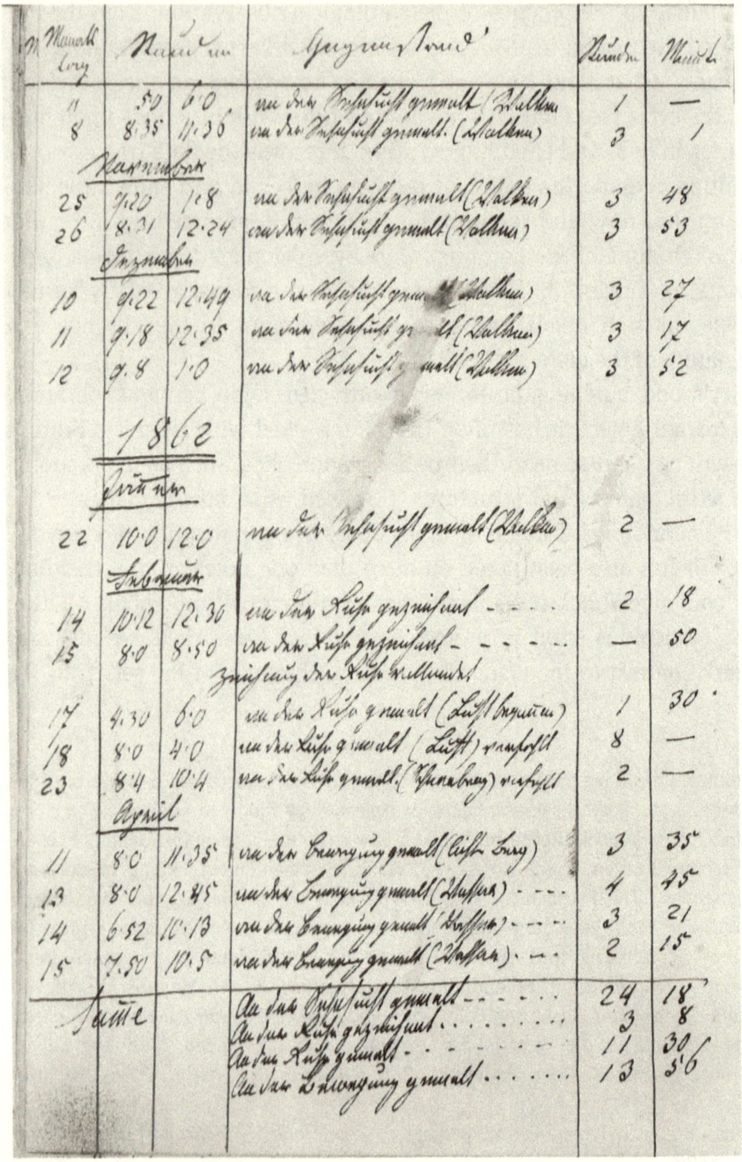

Figure 1: Page 16 (28/29) from Adalbert Stifter: *Diary of Painting* – started on 5 February 1854 [*Tagebuch über Malereiarbeiten / am 5. Februar 1854 begonnen*]. Stifter Archive in the National Library of the Czech Republic, Prague, StA-Nr. 238. Reproduction with permission of the National Library of the Czech Republic.

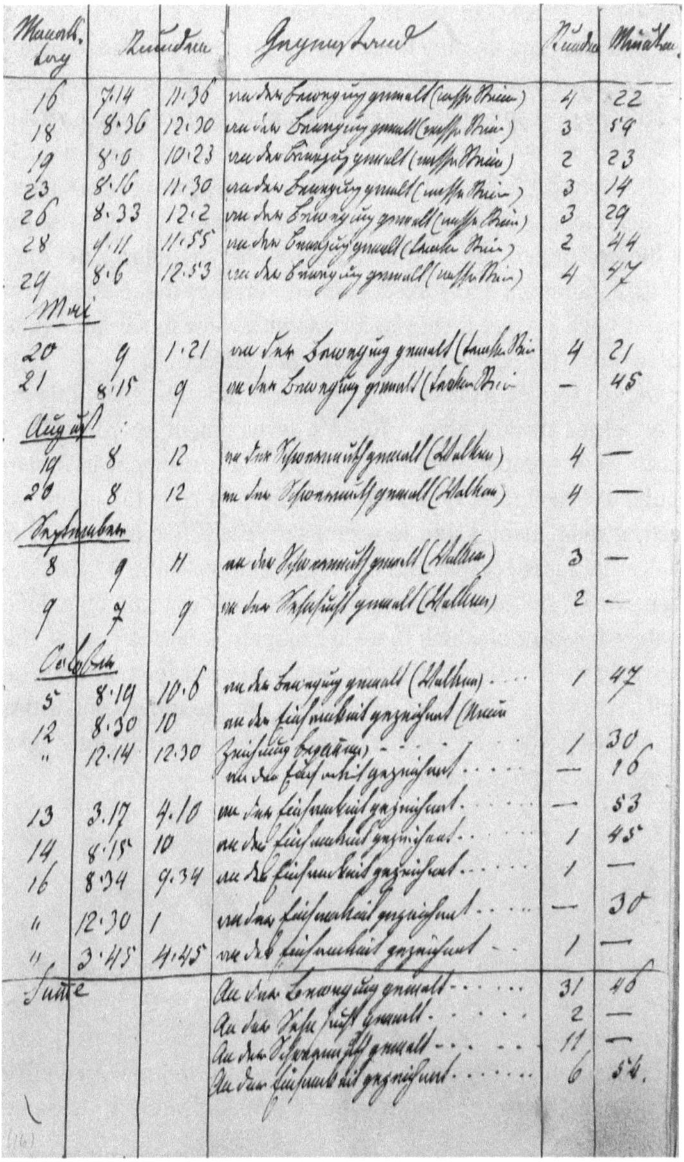

Figure 1 (continued)

end, the list indicates an artistic concept that was apparently too grand, and a work process that over the time became lost in preliminary sketches, overpaintings, and partially executed canvases. However, the tabular notation exemplifies a practice to protocol the persisting parameters of a painting process which itself was, after all, difficult to oversee and unreliable in its course. Just like a statistically reliable weather forecast is based on the regular measurement of temperature, air pressure, and clouds, the register of the diary provided a framework for Stifter to control the artistic process. In this sense, the diary visualizes not only the sheer facts of date, duration, and subject painted; it makes the relations and proportions between them visible. It shows, for example, how much more time Stifter spent on *Movement* [*Die Bewegung*] than on other subjects.[80]

Since Stifter worked for years on several pictures at the same time, this instrument certainly helped track a given project's development by keeping its various elements in view. Comparable to the perspective instrument in *Indian Summer*, the tabular list facilitates our understanding of a complex effort "to become convinced of relationships and to establish a scale" ("damit man zur Überzeugung der Verhältnisse komme und einen Maßstab gewinne").[81] But the transition between micro- and macrostructure did not work out this time. Like an erroneous weather forecast, of which there are so many in Stifter's work, the listed data did not lead their author to the atmospheric landscape paintings he envisioned.[82] Instead, what is left visualizes nothing but the inner regularities of the artistic process itself; the failure of the overall project is documented by a plurality of individual data and achievements.

4 Conclusion

As this comparative examination has shown, Stifter considered a focus on small details of nature and their "delicate relationships"[83] to be the most effective way to create artworks – be they literary texts or paintings – that truly represent the greatness of nature. His ideas were in line with the new inductive sciences flourishing in the Habsburg Empire around 1850 and were, at the same

---

[80] Wedekind, *Wiederholen – Beharren – Auslöschen*, 160–162.
[81] See Stifter, *Indian Summer*, 195 (*HKG* 4.2: 37).
[82] Oliver Grill, "Das meteorologische Kalkül Stifters," in *Die Wetterseiten der Literatur: Poetologische Konstellationen und meteorologische Kontexte im 19. Jahrhundert* (Paderborn: Wilhelm Fink, 2019), 137–212.
[83] Stifter, *HKG* 8.4, 284.

time, also connected to contemporary debates in the field of literature and the arts, where the question of details and their artistic representation was central to emerging theories of realism.

The foregoing discussion has made clear that there is a strong nexus between human vision and its education or training guided by scientific practices and knowledge. For Stifter, a naïve understanding of nature and natural phenomena was (re-)oriented by practices underpinned by scientific reason. Systematic observation, the sketching of details that show the "small fabric"[84] of nature, and the use of instruments like waxed plates or meteorological equipment were central to this shift. Stifter's texts transfer these ideas to the field of artistic production and, at the same time, make apparent the limits of such an approach. In *Indian Summer*, the readjustment of perception is shown as a result of trial and error, which is accompanied by the fact that the unreliability of individual perception must be reflected and corrected by the social environment (i.e., Eustach and the Baron) before the painting will be successful. Stifter's art criticism and practice also testify to the fact that the "small fabric"[85] of the relations between small and large are ultimately hardly accessible; they remain "poetically hidden characteristics,"[86] and even their empirical monitoring (via lists) led Stifter's own large-scale project to what he himself referred to as "incompletion."[87] Nevertheless, the writer's desire for a perfect correlation of the small and great was a remarkable impulse. Stifter's poetics of scaling responds to contemporary epistemic practices and offers alternatives to theories of Realism that, around 1850, have begun to set definite standards of composition for artistic creation, like formal unity or perspective coherence. For Stifter, on the contrary, the mimetic capability of an artwork – be it literature or painting – does not depend on ideal principles of composition, but first and foremost on the reliable understanding of nature and its proportions.

---

84 Stifter, *HKG* 8.4, 284.
85 Stifter, *HKG* 8.4, 284.
86 Stifter, *HKG* 8.4, 285.
87 Stifter, *HKG* 8.4, 283–284.

Bibliography

Anonymous. Review of *Witiko*, by Adalbert Stifter. *Europa: Chronik der gebildeten Welt* 31 (1865): 497–499.
Baudelaire, Charles. "Salon de 1848." In *Curiosités esthétiques*. Vol. 2 of *Œuvres complètes de Charles Baudelaire*, 77–198. Paris: Calmann-Lévy, 1868.
Baumgartner, Andreas. "Das Große und Kleine in der Natur." In *Österreichischer Volks- und Wirtschafts-Kalender für das Jahr 1860*, 3–11. Vienna: Prandel & Ewald, 1860.
Begemann, Christian. "Metaphysik und Empirie: Konkurrierende Naturkonzepte im Werk Adalbert Stifters." In *Wissen in Literatur im 19. Jahrhundert*, edited by Lutz Danneberg and Friedrich Vollhardt, 92–126. Tübingen: Max Niemeyer, 2002.
Benjamin, Walter. "Stifter." In vol. 2.2 of *Gesammelte Schriften*, edited by Rolf Tiedemann and Hermann Schweppenhäuser, 608–610. Frankfurt am Main: Suhrkamp, 1991.
Bericht über die Mittheilungen von Freunden der Naturwissenschaft in Wien 6, no. 2, edited by Wilhelm Haidinger. Vienna: Wilhelm Braumüller, 1848.
Bratanek, Friedrich Theodor. "Adalbert Stifter: Eine literarhistorische Skizze." *Österreichische Revue* 6 (1863): 62–76.
Brodersen, Silke. "Phänomenale Wirklichkeit und Naturgesetz in Hermann von Helmholtz' populärwissenschaftlichen Schriften und in Adalbert Stifters 'Sanftem Gesetz.'" In *Turns und Trends der Literaturwissenschaft zwischen Nachmärz und Jahrhundertwende im Blickfeld aktueller Theoriebildung*, edited by Christian Meierhofer and Eric Scheufler, 205–221. Zurich: germanistik.ch, 2011.
Coen, Deborah R. *Climate in Motion: Science, Empire, and the Question of Style*. Chicago: University of Chicago Press, 2018.
Etzlstorfer, Hannes. "'Die Wolken, ihre Bildung [. . .] waren mir wunderbare Erscheinungen' (*Nachsommer*): Bemerkungen zu Adalbert Stifters Motivrepertoire als Landschaftsmaler." In *Sanfte Sensationen: Stifter 2005; Beiträge zum 200. Geburtstag Adalbert Stifters*, edited by Johann Lachinger, Regina Pintar, Christian Schachreiter, and Martin Sturm, 60–74. Linz: StifterHaus, 2005.
Fleming, Paul. *Exemplarity and Mediocrity: The Art of the Average from Bourgeois Tragedy to Realism*. Stanford: Stanford University Press, 2009.
Gamper, Michael. "Literarische Meteorologie am Beispiel von Stifters 'Das Haidedorf.'" In *Wind und Wetter: Kultur–Wissen–Ästhetik*, edited by Georg Braungart and Urs Büttner, 219–232. Paderborn: Wilhelm Fink, 2018.
Geimer, Peter. "Blow Up." In *"Der liebe Gott steckt im Detail": Mikrostrukturen des Wissens*, edited by Wolfgang Schäffner, Sigrid Weigel, and Thomas Macho, 187–202. Munich: Wilhelm Fink, 2003.
Gess, Nicola. "Instruments of Wonder – Wondrous Instruments: Optical Devices of the Marvelous of Fontenelle, Rist, Breitinger, and Hoffmann." *The German Quarterly* 90, no. 4 (2017): 407–422.
Grill, Oliver. *Die Wetterseiten der Literatur: Poetologische Konstellationen und meteorologische Kontexte im 19. Jahrhundert*. Paderborn: Wilhelm Fink, 2019.
Hebbel, Friedrich. *Gedichte, Erzählungen, Schriften*. Vol. 3 of *Werke*. Edited by Gerhard Fricke, Werner Keller, and Karl Pörnbacher. Munich: Hanser, 1965.
John, Johannes. "'Übermalungen' – Transkription, Emendation, Interpretation: Zur 17. Manuskriptseite von Adalbert Stifters 'Nachkommenschaften.'" In *Text – Material –*

Medium: Zur Relevanz editorischer Dokumentationen für die literaturwissenschaftliche Forschung, edited by Wolfgang Lukas, Rüdiger Nutt-Kofoth, and Madleen Podewski, 107–122. Berlin: De Gruyter, 2014.

Kemp, Wolfgang. "Fotografie als Kunst." In *Theorie der Fotografie, 1839–1912*, edited by Wolfgang Kemp, 13–45. Munich: Schirmer/Mosel, 1980.

Köhnen, Ralph. *Das optische Wissen: Mediologische Studien zu einer Geschichte des Sehens*. Paderborn: Wilhelm Fink, 2009.

Maurer, Kathrin. "Adalbert Stifter's Poetics of Clouds and Nineteenth-Century Meteorology." *Oxford German Studies* 45, no. 4 (2016): 421–433.

Maurer, Kathrin. "'Ich hatte dieses Ding nie so gesehen wie heute': Zur Verunsicherung der Wahrnehmung in Adalbert Stifters 'Eisgeschichte.'" *Colloquia Germanica* 92, nos. 1–2 (2013): 35–48.

Mayer, Petra. *Zwischen unsicherem Wissen und sicherem Unwissen: Erzählte Wissensformation im realistischen Roman: Stifters "Der Nachsommer" und Vischers "Auch Einer."* Bielefeld: Aisthesis, 2014.

Michler, Werner. "Adalbert Stifter und die Ordnungen der Gattung: Generische Veredelung und die Arbeit am 'Habitus.'" In *Stifter und Stifterforschung im 21. Jahrhundert: Biographie – Wissenschaft – Poetik*, edited by Hartmut Laufhütte, Alfred Doppler, Johannes John, and Johann Lachinger, 182–200. Tübingen: Max Niemeyer, 2007.

Möseneder, Karl. "Stimmung und Erdleben: Adalbert Stifters Ikonologie der Landschaftsmalerei." In *Adalbert Stifter, Dichter und Maler, Denkmalpfleger und Schulmann: Neue Zugänge zu seinem Werk*, edited by Hartmut Laufhütte and Karl Möseneder, 18–57. Tübingen: Niemeyer, 1996.

Neumann, Gerhard. "Fernrohr, Mikroskop, Luftballon: Wahrnehmungstechnik und Literatur in der Goethezeit." In *Spektakuläre Experimente: Praktiken der Evidenzproduktion im 17. Jahrhundert*, edited by Helmar Schramm, Ludger Schwarte, and Jan Lazardzig, 345–377. Berlin: De Gruyter, 2006.

Novotny, Fritz. *Adalbert Stifter als Maler*. Vienna: Schroll, 1941.

Pichler, Franz. "Andreas Baumgartner und sein Werk zur Naturlehre." In *Stifter und Stifterforschung im 21. Jahrhundert*, edited by Hartmut Laufhütte, Alfred Doppler, Johannes John, and Johann Lachinger, 117–126. Tübingen: Max Niemeyer, 2007.

Ragg-Kirkby, Helena. *Adalbert Stifter's Late Prose: The Mania for Moderation*. Rochester, NY: Camden House, 2000.

Resultate aus den Beobachtungen des Magnetischen Vereins im Jahre 1836. Edited by Carl Friedrich Gauss and Wilhelm Weber. Göttingen: Dietrichische Buchhandlung, 1837.

Ritzer, Monika. "Von Suppenwürfeln, Induktionsstrom und der Äquivalenz der Kräfte: Zum Kulturwert der Naturwissenschaft am Beispiel von Adalbert Stifters Novelle 'Abdias.'" *Kulturpoetik: Journal for Cultural Poetics* 2, no. 1 (2002): 44–67.

Ruskin, John. *Mountain Beauty*. Vol. 4 of *Modern Painters*. London: Smith, Elder, 1856.

Schmidt, Julian. *Geschichte der deutschen Literatur nach Lessings Tod*. Vol. 3. Leipzig: Friedrich Ludwig Herbig, 1856.

Schmitt, Stefan. "Adalbert Stifter als Zeichner." In *Adalbert Stifter, Dichter und Maler, Denkmalpfleger und Schulmann: Neue Zugänge zu seinem Werk*, edited by Hartmut Laufhütte and Karl Möseneder, 261–308. Tübingen: Niemeyer, 1996.

Schreiber, Guido. *Malerische Perspektive: Mit einem Anhang über den Gebrauch geometrischer Grundrisse*. Karlsruhe: Herder, 1854.

Schultes, Lothar. "Adalbert Stifter als Zeichner und Maler." *Jahrbuch des Oberösterreichischen Musealvereines: Gesellschaft für Landeskunde* 152 (2007): 237–300.

Selge, Martin. *Poesie aus dem Geist der Naturwissenschaft*. Stuttgart: Kohlhammer, 1976.

Stadler, Ulrich. *Der technisierte Blick: Optische Instrumente und der Status von Literatur: Ein kulturhistorisches Museum*. Würzburg: Königshausen und Neumann, 2003.

Steiner, Mirjam. "Inseparably United: Big and Small in Literary Settings." In *Too Big to Scale: On Scaling Space, Numbers, Time, and Energy*, edited by Florian Dombois and Julie Harboe, 113–28. Zurich: Scheidegger & Spiess, 2017.

Stifter, Adalbert. *Briefe*. Vol. 3. Edited by Johannes Aprent. Pest: Gustav Heckenast, 1869.

Stifter, Adalbert. *Indian Summer*. Translated by Wendell Frye. New York: Peter Lang, 1985.

Stifter, Adalbert. "Preface to 'Many-Colored Stones.'" In vol. 1 of *German Novellas of Realism*, edited and translated by Jeffrey L. Sammons, 1–6. New York: Continuum, 1989.

Stifter, Adalbert. *Werke und Briefe: Historisch-kritische Gesamtausgabe*. Edited by Alfred Doppler, Wolfgang Frühwald et al. Stuttgart: W. Kohlhammer, 1978.

Stockinger, Claudia. *Das 19. Jahrhundert: Zeitalter des Realismus*. Berlin: Akademie, 2010.

Strowick, Elisabeth. *Gespenster des Realismus: Zur literarischen Wahrnehmung von Wirklichkeit*. Paderborn: Wilhelm Fink, 2019.

Strowick, Elisabeth. "Poetological-Technical Operations: Representation of Motion in Adalbert Stifter." *Configurations* 18 (2010): 273–289.

Thanner, Veronika, Joseph Vogl, and Dorothea Walzer, eds. *Die Wirklichkeit des Realismus*. Paderborn: Wilhelm Fink, 2018.

Vogel, Juliane. "Stifters Gitter: Poetologische Dimensionen einer Grenzfigur." In *Die Dinge und die Zeichen: Dimensionen des Realistischen in der Erzählliteratur des 19. Jahrhunderts*, edited by Barbara Hunfeld and Sabine Schneider, 43–58. Würzburg: Königshausen & Neumann, 2008.

Wedekind, Martina. *Wiederholen – Beharren – Auslöschen: Zur Prosa Adalbert Stifters*. Heidelberg: Winter, 2005, 141–164.

Wellmann, Janina. "Bewegung an der Wand: Zur Aufführung von Organismen mit dem Sonnenmikroskop." In *Belebungskünste: Praktiken lebendiger Darstellung in Literatur, Kunst und Wissenschaft um 1800*, edited by Nicola Gess, Agnes Hoffmann, and Annette Kappeler, 227–245. Paderborn: Wilhelm Fink, 2019.

Willer, Stefan. "Grenzenlose Zeit, schlingernder Grund: Genealogische Ordnungen in Stifters 'Nachkommenschaften.'" In *Figuren der Übertragung*, edited by Michael Gamper and Karl Wagner, 45–62. Zurich: Chronos, 2009.

Matthew O. Anderson
Adventure from Concentrate: Visual Interventions in German Youth Adaptations of James Fenimore Cooper's *Leatherstocking Tales*

James Fenimore Cooper's (1789–1851) *Leatherstocking Tales*, a five-volume collection of the American author's successful frontier novels, dominated the nineteenth-century German literary market. The individual works comprising the *Leatherstocking Tales* – *The Pioneers* (1823), *The Last of the Mohicans* (1826), *The Prairie* (1827), *The Pathfinder* (1840), and *The Deerslayer* (1841) – had already established an enduring, elegiac image of North America and its natives that captured the world's attention since their initial publication. Their re-release as the collected *Leatherstocking Tales* in the 1840s and 1850s further cemented the author's legacy and inspired subsequent generations of German readers and writers to follow him into the mythic space of the North American frontier.

Cooper is often considered a canonical author of youth literature, but he did not intentionally write any of the individual *Leatherstocking Tales* for a juvenile readership.[1] Biographers note that the author's primary concern was literary legitimacy: Cooper was inspired by the international success of national-historical novelist Sir Walter Scott and sought to bring similar literary acclaim home to the United States.[2] Beyond his own fame, Cooper was concerned with legitimizing American literature in the eyes of European literary critics. As such, his prose is rich in allusions to Milton, Shakespeare, and the King James Bible. However, despite the highbrow associations that he so actively sought, much of Cooper's international literary legacy today is tied to his works' long-term success as youth literature. Like many of his works, the collected *Leatherstocking Tales* were

---

[1] *Intentional children's literature* is a category of literary production defined by its *intended* child readership. Hans-Heino Ewers defines the term as the "totality of texts or works that are aimed at children and young people as addressees." Cooper's original texts are not *intentional* children's literature, but youth adaptations by German authors explicitly target this reading demographic. Hans-Heino Ewers, *Fundamental Concepts of Children's Literature Research: Literary and Sociological Approaches*, trans. William J. McCann (New York: Routledge, 2009), 18.

[2] Wayne Franklin, *James Fenimore Cooper: The Later Years*. (New Haven/London: Yale University Press, 2017), xiv.

subsequently adapted for juvenile readers between the ages of eleven and sixteen.[3] In Germany, youth adaptations of *Leatherstocking Tales* continue to be regarded as canonical works of juvenile literature to this day. Irmgard Egger observes that German editions of Cooper's *Leatherstocking Tales* "have been considered among the most beloved German youth books for generations," even though they had also been deemed respectable world literature for adult readers throughout the nineteenth century.[4]

Few Cooper scholars have focused on the visual interpretations of his work, yet illustrations feature prominently in the first two adaptations of *Leatherstocking Tales* for young German readers. Extensive visual and paratextual components in Hoffmann's and Stein's juvenile editions suggest that German adaptations of the *Leatherstocking Tales* used illustrations to frame Cooper's tales as appropriate reading material for older German youths. As Gérard Genette has noted, paratexts operate in an "undefined zone" at the "fringe" of the narrative text and yet act as a "commentary that is authorial or more or less legitimated by the author."[5] Illustrations frequently act as potent paratexts that operate in this space between and off-text. In this essay, I explore how the visual paratexts in these German Cooper editions had a significant impact on their interpretation and presentation of adventure stories and why they merit further study as *multimodal* works. Applying the lens of multimodality to these illustrated books broadens my engagement with visual-verbal interactions beyond the predefined, hierarchical roles that

---

[3] While twenty-first-century scholarship is right to criticize antiquated models of "age-appropriate reading material," these models remained prominent well into the middle of the twentieth century. In the German context, "heroic literature" – including *Indianerliteratur* – is often recommended as appropriate reading material for pre-teen to teenage boys. In "Das Märchen und die Phantasie des Kindes," C. Bühler identifies ages thirteen to fifteen as the "Heldenalter" (cited in Lichtenberger, Sigrid. "Lesealter." *Lexikon der Kinder- und Jugendliteratur. Zweiter Band: I-O.* Ed. Klaus Doderer. [Weinheim: Beltz Verlag, 1977], 346–349, here 346). In "Der Mensch als Leser. Entwicklungsverlauf der literarischen Erlebnisfähigkeit," E. Lippert claims that boys ages eleven to thirteen are in the middle of an "apsychological, sense-driven reading phase" ("apsychologisch-sensationsgesteuerte Lesephase") defined by the "predominance of the heroic" ("Vorherrschaft des Heldenhaften") (cited in Lichtenberger, Sigrid. "Lesealter." *Lexikon der Kinder- und Jugendliteratur. Zweiter Band: I-O.* Ed. Klaus Doderer. [Weinheim: Beltz Verlag, 1977], 346–349, here 348). Both scholars mark the "heroic" protagonist as the pivotal figure in process of literary maturation for the majority of male German readers.

[4] Irmgard Egger, "Lederstrumpf: ein deutsches Jugendbuch: Untersuchung zu den Bedingungen und Strukturen literarischer Transformation" (PhD dissertation, University of Vienna, 1991), 2. All translations that appear in this chapter are my own unless otherwise noted.

[5] Gérard Genette, *Paratexts: Thresholds of Interpretation* (Cambridge: Cambridge University Press, 1997), 2.

monomodal perspectives often assume *must* be at work.[6] Building on these observations, I argue that the illustrated youth editions of Cooper's adventure novels provide new insights into the complex and often personal ways in which (nascent) national and international publishing trends were connected to printing technologies and transnational visual conventions. Like the other objects explored in this volume, illustrated youth books can and should be read as important participants in the pre-photographic, visual culture of nineteenth-century Germany.

1 Coopermania: James Fenimore Cooper in the nineteenth century

James Fenimore Cooper's literary career coincided with growing European interest in the people, places, and politics of the young United States of America, and both the style and substance of his novels resonated with American and European audiences alike. Reflecting on his earlier career, Cooper noted that his works had attained a special status abroad: "In Europe, the books which embody [Natty Bumppo's] adventures are read with an interest which no other productions of American literature excite; and in our own country he not only charms the fresh imagination of boyhood, but gratifies the severer tastes of manhood."[7] While Cooper's American readers may have yearned for a national story set in North America as a means to literary self-legitimization, his European readership, in Wayne Franklin's assessment, "reinforced this imperative by their hunger for those same settings," which appeared to them as "fresh and exotic."[8] In both geographical contexts, Cooper's skill at depicting wild landscapes and peoples in a vivid, visual manner appears to have been the key to his popularity.

---

[6] Gunther Kress and Theo van Leeuwen's notion that common semiotic principles operate in and across different modes moves analysis beyond the presumed subservience of illustrations to their textual bases. By bracketing monomodal assumptions, their framework of *multimodality* opens productive pathways to reconsidering how image and text operate together as intertwined semiotic modes in the illustrated book. Gunther Kress and Theo van Leeuwen, *Multimodal Discourse: The Modes and Media of Contemporary Communication* (London: Arnold, 2001), 1–2.
[7] James Fenimore Cooper, *Stories of the Woods* (New York: James G. Gregory, 1863), 9.
[8] Wayne Franklin, "James Fenimore Cooper, 1789–1851: A Brief Biography," in *A Historical Guide to James Fenimore Cooper* (Oxford/New York: Oxford University Press, 2007), 45.

Cooper's interest in developing the visuality of his prose was inspired, in part, by his connections to prominent American Romantics. Through associations such as the "Bread and Cheese Club" that Cooper himself hosted, the author became acquainted with a variety of writers, artists, and intellectuals in New York interested in a Romantic vision of America.[9] Cooper was especially close to a group of landscape painters who came to be known as the Hudson River School and became friends with Thomas Cole (1801–1848), who painted three scenes for *The Last of the Mohicans*. John P. McWilliams notes that Cooper and Cole's artistic exchanges were reciprocal:

> as in many a Hudson River School painting, Cooper's novels repeatedly set up a character as the feeling observer of a landscape that is described in detail, either by the character or the narrator. Cooper's words thus provide a stationary, framed painting within which natural details are forever in motion.[10]

This latter analogy evokes a second, closely related factor – Cooper was frequently lauded for his painterly qualities, or what Leland S. Person calls his *scenic*, or *cinematic*, imagination.[11] In both instances, Cooper's visual prose is closely associated with the ponderous, primordial vistas common to Romantic landscape painting.

Early nineteenth-century visualizations of Cooper's work also often reflect aesthetic priorities common to painterly Romanticism, such as favoring landscape over action. For example, the oil paintings that Thomas Cole created after reading *The Last of the Mohicans* (1826) are so landscape dominant that foreground to midground figures are nearly indistinguishable from their surroundings. By contrast, early literary reviews highlighted Cooper's strengths as a painter of motion; his scenic imagination not only created expansive settings but also captured the individual human conflicts that unfolded within them. For example, in his 1826 review of Cooper's *The Spy* for *The North American Review*, W. H. Gardiner observed that

> The particular talent of our author seems to lie in describing action and hitting off the humors of low life. Wherever there is something to be done, he sets about doing it with his whole soul; the reader's attention is chained to the event; every other interest is absorbed in the deed, which is exhibited with a boldness of outline and vividness of coloring, proportioned to its importance in itself, or in its results. The flight, the hot pursuit,

---

[9] Martin Barker and Roger Sabin, *The Lasting of the Mohicans: History of an American Myth* (Jackson, MS: University Press of Mississippi, 1995), 18.
[10] John P. McWilliams, *The Last of the Mohicans: Civil Savagery and Savage Civility* (New York: Twayne, 1995), 29.
[11] Leland S. Person, "Introduction: Fenimore Cooper's Literary Achievements," in *A Historical Guide to James Fenimore Cooper*, ed. Leland S. Person (Oxford/New York: Oxford University Press, 2007), 1–26, here 8.

the charge, the victory, pass before you with the rapidity, and the distinctness too, of forked lightning which plays in the summer cloud; and the reader, not less than the writer, is irresistibly borne on by the subject.[12]

In many of Cooper's novels, bold and vivid flashes of violence punctuate the melancholic landscape of a receding wilderness. This combination may not have pleased all of his readers, but its lasting impact on the Western novel has been considerable.[13] However, the visual qualities of his prose were not always mirrored in the visual presentation of his texts. The majority of early German-language editions for an adult, bourgeois readership were either unillustrated or used steel engravings to reproduce the principle scenes in each novel. Given the limitations of that medium, most images were constrained to close-up or mid-range perspectives that compelled the artist to highlight either Cooper's brooding landscapes or his climactic action scenes. This connection will be explored in greater detail below.

2 Frontier illustrated

Contemporary German readers of Cooper's *Leatherstocking Tales* may be familiar with abundance of sensational action scenes depicting European trappers locked in deadly struggles with Native-American antagonists (see Figure 1). These range from "native-on-native" action scenes pitting recognizably "noble savages" against their irredeemable, savage counterparts to even more violent imaginings of native attacks that tap into a deeper reservoir of European racial anxieties.[14] However, they generally present a violent encounter with a terrifying and bloodthirsty exotic "other." Rather than accentuating racial terror, another common strategy is portraying a calm, confident European settler-explorer in a friendlier light, rendered in color but using softer, less garish hues. Both strategies visually asserted Eurocentric, ethnic hierarchies.

---

12 W. H. Gardiner, cited in Leland S. Person, *A Historical Guide to James Fenimore Cooper* (Oxford/New York: Oxford University Press, 2007), 276.
13 For example, Person claims that "even a quick survey of Cooper's fiction reveals a remarkable number of scenes whose basic structures and elements we take for granted and seem deeply embedded as a kind of deep structure in our imaginations." Person, "Introduction," 9. In a similar vein, Franklin notes that the full impact of Cooper's literary work is often underestimated: "To later generations familiar with the western as a literary and cinematic form, Cooper's innovations may be less apparent than they were at the time." Franklin, "James Fenimore Cooper," 38.
14 For more on the clichéd fixity of such ethnographic "types," see David Ciarlo's contribution to this volume.

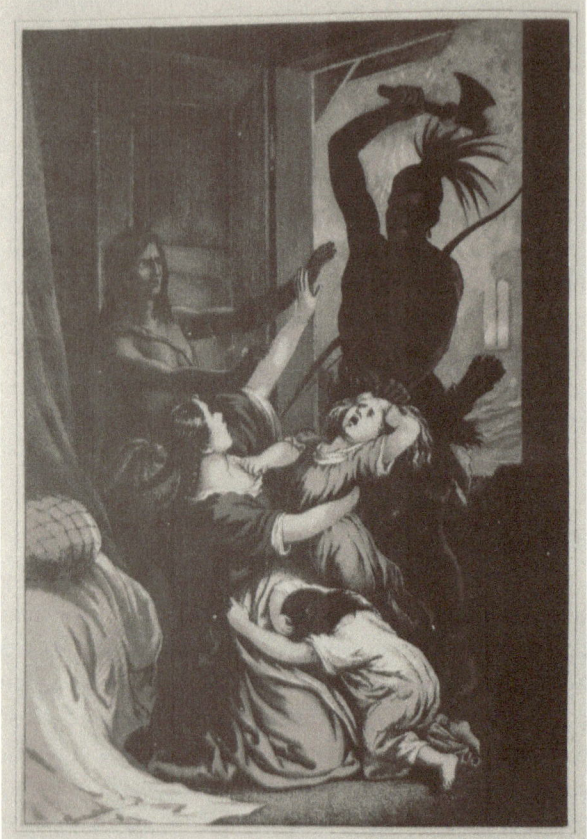

Figure 1: Frontispiece for *Conanchet, der Indianerhäuptling. Conanchet, der Indianerhäuptling. Eine Erzählung für die reifere Jugend. Nach dem Englischen des J. F. Cooper bearbeitet von Franz Hoffmann.* 6th ed. Stuttgart: K. Thienemanns Verlag, 1886.

The earliest German youth editions of Cooper's novels are not exempt from problematic issues of racial representation.[15] They often evoked the familiar imagery of an industrious Robinson Crusoe taming the wilderness against depictions

---

15 Scholars on both sides of the Atlantic have observed that Cooper's *Leatherstocking Tales* popularized an incredibly biased view of Native Americans, one that would remain prominent in Germany for decades to come. For example, Klaus-Ulrich Pech notes that ideological image construction and a series of interchangeable elements from the larger, European reservoir of exotic iconography contributed to the creation of a racist perception of Native Americans that came to be viewed as self-evident ("[ein] als selbstverständlich wahrgenommenen Rassismus.") Klaus-Ulrich

of violent native cannibals. While only a small portion of a broader European visual lexicon of depicting ethnic alterity, such visual tropes became particularly associated with the Wild West, Western, or Native American novel.[16] The use of these tropes continues well into the 1900s for Cooper editions around the world, and the author's legacy is inextricably linked to these problematic colonial images.[17]

Even within the first few decades of their publication alone, juvenile editions of the *Leatherstocking Tales* were packaged with a diverse set of visual interpretations. Part of this is due to major shifts in the book industry during this time – Cooper's novels spanned a period of publishing history marked by overlapping illustration techniques and stylistic trends. Yet there is surprisingly little scholarship on the illustrations created for Cooper editions intended for juvenile readers. In her brief treatment of Cooper illustrations, Irmgard Egger observes that they vacillate between excitement and exoticism and "naïve familiarity" (*biedere Vertrautheit*), a description that emphasizes the insular nature of the bourgeois family sphere vis-à-vis larger social and political concerns.[18] In her view, this tension signals "the foundational structure of evasive-identificational reading." It remains "historical and yet still up-to-date; foreign and adventurous and nevertheless not too remote or dangerous."[19] For example, in a later edition of Springer's *Leatherstocking Tales* (1862), Egger observes two major thematic clusters: depictions of the domestic and familiar (*Heimatlich-Vertrauliches*) and reflective-affective (*Beschaulich-Ergreifendes*).[20] She also notes that the "vibrancy and starkness of the illustrations" serve to amplify the youth reader's attention to foreign and familial contexts.[21]

In her project, Egger reads manuscript organization, presentation, form, illustration, and publisher/author commentary as interrelated signals to potential buyers and readers. For her, each of these signals fosters specific class, gender, age, and genre identifications and associations – features that she acknowledges are interlinked, but whose specific constellation(s) she does *not* investigate further. Precisely

---

Pech, "Vom Biedermeier zum Realismus," *Geschichte der deutschen Kinder- und Jugendliteratur*, ed. Reiner Wild, 3rd ed. (J. B. Metzler: Stuttgart, 2008), 131–170, here 157.
16 For an extensive exploration of European ethnographic clichés, see David Ciarlo's contribution to this volume.
17 For a survey of nineteenth-century representational trends across oil painters in the United States, see Francis Flavin, "The Adventurer-Artists of the Nineteenth Century and the Image of the American Indian," *Indiana Magazine of History* 98.1 (2002), pp. 1–29.
18 Egger, *Lederstrumpf: ein deutsches Jugendbuch*, 199.
19 Egger, *Lederstrumpf: ein deutsches Jugendbuch*, 200.
20 Egger, *Lederstrumpf: ein deutsches Jugendbuch*, 200.
21 Egger, *Lederstrumpf: ein deutsches Jugendbuch*, 200–201, 202.

that question, the relationship between the visual and textual "signals" that Egger fleetingly describes, will be the focus of the following analyses.

2.1 *Leatherstockings* aus Stuttgart: Respectable adult collections in conversation with Franz Hoffmann's *Leatherstocking Tales by Cooper* (1845)

The following outline of the formal and familial links connecting the various editions will help to contextualize the different editions of *Leatherstocking Tales* produced in Stuttgart during the 1840s and 1850s. The first adaptation of *Leatherstocking Tales* for juvenile German readers, Franz Hoffmann's *Leatherstocking Tales by Cooper*, was published in 1845 by the Verlag von Schmidt & Spring. Stuttgart is particularly noteworthy because Schmidt & Spring was a pioneer in the commercial publication of intentional works of youth and children's literature.[22] Like many other children's publishers, Schmidt & Spring began as an offshoot of an established literary publishing enterprise: Carl Hoffmann's Hoffmann'sche Verlagsbuchhandlung. It is no coincidence that, following the success of Schmidt & Spring's youth edition, the Hoffmann'sche Verlags-Buchhandlung also published a series for adults entitled *J. F. Coopers American Novels*, nearly a decade later in 1853/54.

Franz Hoffmann's *Leatherstocking Tales by Cooper* was not the first Cooper publication to bring financial success to the Hoffmann publishing family. By the time Schmidt & Spring's *Leatherstocking Tales* were released in 1845, Franz's older brother Carl Hoffmann had already established a sprawling publishing empire in Stuttgart that was indirectly connected to Cooper.[23] The success of Franz Hoffmann's youth adaptations was due in no small part to the strength of his brother's publishing enterprise(s). Through family connections and publishing alliances, Carl had the advantage of printing, illustrating, and binding books in

---

[22] J. H. Campe's Schulbuchhandlung (later Vieweg) in Braunschweig had existed for much longer, but its adaptation and publication philosophies were guided by its founder's much stricter pedagogical principles. Cooper, it appears, did not pass muster as an appropriate work of juvenile literature, though Vieweg did publish a translation of *The Last of the Mohicans* in 1827.

[23] Hoffmann's former employee Friedrich Franckh had secured an exclusive publishing contract with Cooper for this regional market before passing on his collection to his apprentice. Kurt Hoffmann, "Hoffmann, Carl," in *Neue Deutsche Biographie* 9 (1972), 432, <https://www.deutsche-biographie.de/pnd116974036.html#ndbcontent>.

house for a range of buyer demographics.[24] The Hoffmann family's publishing empire was in a position to issue a major, illustrated Cooper compilation for young readers followed by an illustrated collected works for adults in less than a decade. In sum, the Hoffmanns occupied a powerful position within the Stuttgart publishing trade, and this allowed the Hoffmann'sche Verlags-Buchhandlung and subsidiaries like Schmidt & Spring to dominate the local literary market for youths.

Given his regional prominence and the early success of his juvenile literary adaptations, Carl Hoffmann's publishing enterprises had a significant impact on James Fenimore Cooper's German reception *as* juvenile literature. The following two sections will compare Schmidt & Spring's youth editions – Franz Hoffmann's initial *Leatherstocking Tales by Cooper* (1845) and its later guises – to the Hoffmann'sche Verlag's principal adult-literary edition – *J. F. Cooper's American Novels* [*Amerikanische Romane*, 1853–1854]. To better understand the interplay between each work's abridged or unabridged narrative and its visual presentation, I will pay particular attention to illustrations and their interplay with the accompanying narrative.

2.2 *J. F. Cooper's American Novels* (1853–1854)

In Stuttgart, Franz Hoffmann's *Leatherstocking Tales by Cooper* (1845) preceded a comparable adult compilation of Cooper's complete works by nearly a decade. Despite this substantial temporal gap, it will be useful to take this typical adult *Lederstrumpf* collection as a baseline for comparison to (earlier) youth adaptations. This section explores the paratextual and the visual elements that frame and present *J. F. Cooper's American Novels* (1853–1854).

The Hoffmann'sche Verlags-Buchhandlung released *J. F. Cooper's American Novels*, its version of Cooper's collected works, as an octavo-sized set in thirty volumes between 1853 and 1854. The publication occurred two years after the author's death and the release of his revised edition(s) in 1851, which had made minor

---

24 Hoffmann owned or was in close partnership with his own Hoffmann'sche Verlags-Buchhandlung, Weise and Stoppani – a subsidiary created from the Julius Weise publishing catalogue, then split into Julius Weise and A. Stoppani Verlag; and the Verlag von Schmidt & Spring – a formal separation of the Hoffmann'schen Jugendschriften from the parent company under the control of Carl August Schmidt (Hoffmann's brother-in-law) and Louis Spring. Schmidt, Rudolf. "Übersichtstafel der abgezweigten Firmen aus der von Carl Hoffmann in Stuttgart 1826 begründeten Buchhandlung," in *Deutsche Buchhändler: Deutsche Buchdrucker*, vol. 3 (Berlin/Eberswalde: Contumax GmbH & Co. KG., 1905), 482.

modifications to each of the texts and framed them as one, coherent collection of *Leatherstocking Tales* for an Anglophone readership. The German translations incorporate Cooper's revised front matter, but the content of each book was not significantly altered for the collection. The volumes range in length from 187 pages (vol. 4, *Der Bravo, Theil* I) to 707 pages (vol. 12, *Der Wildtöter*), though most remain close to 500 pages. Attributed to Eduard Mauch, Dr. Leonhard Tafel, and Dr. Carl Kolb, the translations hew very closely to the language of their source materials. In brief, the Hoffmann'sche set presented James Fenimore Cooper not merely as the author of the *Leatherstocking Tales*, but as a wide-ranging novelist attuned to the particular social and aesthetic sensibilities of his bourgeois audience.

The collection is visually unremarkable except that each volume is introduced by a single, steel-engraved frontispiece from the Carl Mayer's Kunst-Anstalt in Nuremberg.[25] When considering the thirty frontispiece engravings of the Hoffmann edition as a group, the unnamed artist's thematic preference for non-violent, subdued scenes is striking given the level of violence presented throughout the volumes. This applies both to the scene-selection process and to the artist's interpretation of those scenes. Frequently, the illustration corresponds to one of the pivotal moments in the narrative, and they capture this scene with a sense of reserved, visual decorum. For example, the engraving for *The Pathfinder* portrays the climactic death scene near the novel's end, when Mabel Dunham's dying father gives Natty Bumppo permission to marry his daughter. The illustrator omits the cause of the father's injury – the previous battle scene at the fort, where Sgt. Dunham was wounded – but chooses instead to accentuate the mortally wounded man's emotional farewell. The eponymous hero, Chingachgook, Jasper Western, and Mabel Dunham are all shown gathered around Sgt. Dunham's deathbed in the fort. The wounded man and his daughter both have hands folded and faces uplifted in an attitude of prayer, Western is overcome with grief, and Natty and Chingachgook stand and observe stoically. These two characters are clearly affected but not disproportionately so: respectful and subdued grief is here coded as the appropriate response.

Other selections similarly defuse the sensational elements of frontier encounters or emphasize class-bound propriety in completely unadventurous circumstances. Perhaps the most charged scene, the moment of Deerslayer's binding in *The Deerslayer* (see Figure 2), depicts all the characters in a calm,

---

[25] The decision to feature engravings from an unaffiliated institute is most likely an economic one – thirty steel engravings may have been cheaper to produce than comparably sized lithographs in house, especially if the plates had been previously used. For more on the cost-differences between media up to this time, see Anthony Griffiths, *The Print Before Photography: An Introduction to European Printmaking, 1550–1820* (London: British Museum Press, 2016).

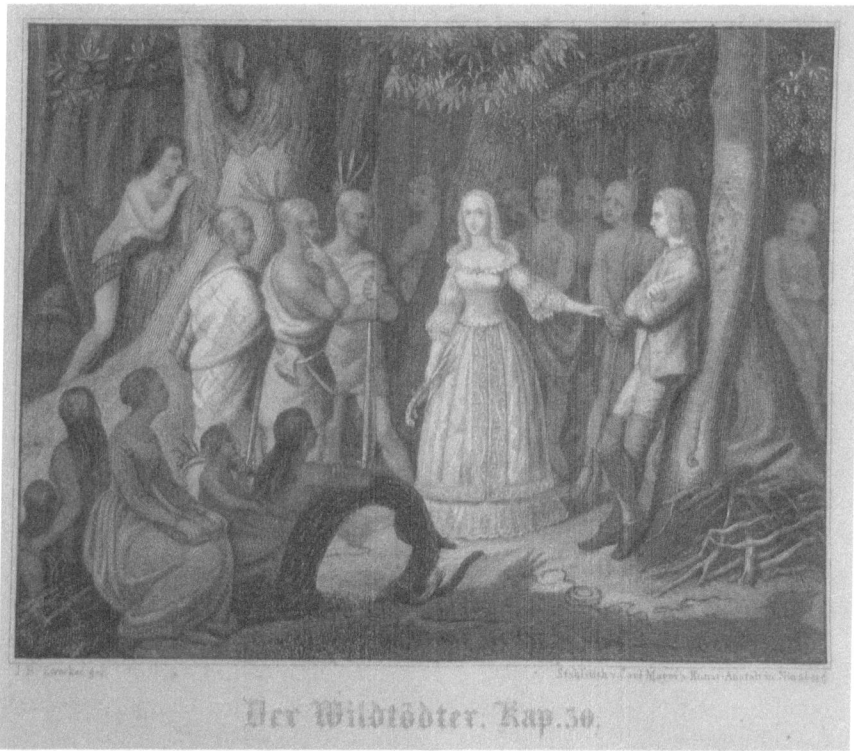

Figure 2: Steel engraving for *Der Wildtödter. J. F. Cooper's Amerikanische Romane, neu aus dem Englischen übertragen von Dr. C. Kolb. Zwölfter Band. Der Wildtödter.* 4th ed. Stuttgart: Hoffmann'sche Verlags-Buchhandlung, 1853.

conciliatory state. This choice is certainly defensible: in the moment depicted, Judith is attempting to negotiate Deerslayer's release from his Huron captors. She fails, though she and he are both rescued moments later when the English soldiers arrive. However, as will soon become clear in the case of children's editions, the selection of this moment – and its rendition that depicts *every* figure in an attitude of polite, disaffected ease – stands in stark contrast to the illustrations of tomahawks flying at the prisoner's head. Similarly, the frontispiece to *The Oak-Openings; or The Bee-Hunter* (1848) features a strategic conference between Europeans and Native Americans *before* they drive out the bees – not, as subsequent artists would depict, the chaotic consequences of doing so. If these images defuse danger, others avoid it completely. For example, the frontispieces for Cooper's most overtly moralizing bourgeois novel, the two-part *Afloat and Ashore: or The Adventures of Miles Wallingford. A Sea Tale* and its sequel, *Afloat and Ashore 2*, also titled *Lucy Hardinge: A Second Series of Afloat and Ashore*, which Hoffmann published in 1844, reproduce the very domestic idylls the hero tries to recover in both novels.

In each case, scenes of familial bliss ease the reader into the comfortable and decorous realm of the story. The peaceful scenes depicted in the collection's frontispieces do not correspond to the frequent moments of violence throughout Cooper's novels. Uniformly titled and bound in green leather, this set appears intended for a respectable readership interested in displaying their cultural capital on the bookshelf. When opened, small, steel-engraved frontispieces mirror each volume's exterior modesty. The frontispiece illustrations are ornamental; they capture emotional moments without impelling the reader toward any form of engagement beyond modest appreciation. The volumes include translations of all of the prefatory matter from Cooper's English-language originals, including updated introductions to revised editions, and each title page prominently advertises the respective translator's credentials. Each volume also includes the highbrow literary quotations (especially Milton and Shakespeare) that Cooper often used as chapter or section prefaces in his original works. In this and the other respects mentioned above, every work in *J. F. Cooper's American Novels* appears to have been treated with the appreciation, care, and reverence one may expect to be accorded to an epoch-defining author. In short, it promised to be an ideal addition to any bourgeois reader's literary collection.

2.3 Franz Hoffmann's *Leatherstocking Tales by Cooper* (1845)

J. F. Cooper's American Novels (1853–1854) appears to be the first publication of Cooper's collected works marketed to adults on the Swabian literary market, but it was not the first repackaging of the *Leatherstocking Tales* to come from Stuttgart. In 1845, the Verlag von Schmidt & Spring published the *Leatherstocking Tales by Cooper*, a juvenile abridgement presenting all five novels in a two-volume set by the *Vielschreiber* and *Verlagsautor* (house author), Franz Hoffmann. The first edition totaled 666 pages and was released in two parts that included twenty unattributed steel engravings. Though it was released twenty-two years after the first *Leatherstocking* tale, *The Pioneers*, had appeared in the United States, Hoffmann's German-language adaptation for juvenile readers preceded the first English-language adaptation of any of his works for juvenile readers by five years.

Franz Hoffmann's influence as an editor and translator is immediately apparent due to the extreme brevity of his adaptations. Compared to the originals, the individual episodes in this abridgment are all very short – consider, for example, that the 666 page-long youth compilation does not even equal the 707 page-length of Hoffmann'sche's *Deerslayer* [*Wildtödter*], only *one* of the five source novels. Such extreme truncation has been previously documented as a trend spanning youth adaptations of Cooper's work. For example, Malte Dahrendorf observes that most adaptations reduce the original text's length by 50% or more – in some extreme cases, as much as 90% of the source material is left out.[26] Cooper's historical-topographical descriptions account for a majority of the cuts; Hans Eich notes that most youth adaptations completely eliminate Cooper's "depictions of nature."[27] In his adaptations, Franz Hoffmann omits many of the side plots, characters, and episodes that give the unabridged texts their great depth and realism. Unlike early sets of collected works, such as the aforementioned *J. F. Cooper's American Novels* or Cooper's own *Leatherstocking Tales* (1850–1851), Franz Hoffmann does not provide *any* sort of series introduction or preface to contextualize the author, his work, or the interpretive choices made by the translator.[28] The abridged novels are rearranged from their initial publication order into chronological order according to the narrated events: *Wildtödter* (*The Deerslayer;* set in 1740) is followed by *Der letzte Mohikaner* (*The Last of the Mohicans;* set in 1757), then *Der Pfadfinder* (*The Pathfinder;* set in "the second half of the previous century"), *Lederstrumpf* (*The Pioneers;* set in 1793), and finally *Der Wildsteller* (*The Prairie;* set in 1804). Additionally, the last two *Leatherstocking Tales* have been renamed to reflect the hero's changing titles: *The Pioneers,* previously translated as *Die Ansiedler,* becomes *Lederstrumpf* (*Leatherstocking*); while *The Prairie,* frequently rendered in adult editions as *Die Steppe* or *Die Prärie,* becomes *Der Wildsteller.* By changing the titles and severely reducing the content, Hoffmann reframes the *Leatherstocking Tales* as Natty Bumppo's *individual* frontier narrative. As noted above, Hoffmann opens without explanation – the first story, *Wildtödter,* dives directly into some "part of the endless forest which stretches east of the Mississippi" – and the author rarely pauses for contextualization or reflection of any kind, leaving the reader to sort out the details as they come.[29] The text is left to speak for itself; it has little time for anything but adventure.

---

26 Malte Dahrendorf, "Lederstrumpf," in *Lexikon der Kinder- und Jugendliteratur. Zweiter Band: I-O,* ed. Klaus Doderer (Beltz Verlag, Weinheim, 1977), 328.
27 Hans Eich, "Bearbeitung von Texten für Kinder und Jugendliche." *Lexikon der Kinder- und Jugendliteratur. Erster Band: A-H.* Ed. Klaus Doderer, (Beltz Verlag, Weinheim, 1975): 119–120, here 120.
28 One may well speculate that this is a way of distracting from, rather than highlighting, Hoffmann's hand in shaping the adaptation. As has been discussed previously, his name was – especially in critical circles – not an effective endorsement.
29 Franz Hoffmann, *Lederstrumpf-Erzählungen von Cooper. Für die Jugend bearbeitet von Franz Hoffmann. Erster Band. Mit 8 Stahlstichen* (Stuttgart: Verlag von Schmidt & Spring, 1845), 3.

German Cooper scholars have enumerated the many weaknesses in Franz Hoffmann's adaptation – and they are right to do so.[30] Yet whatever it lacks in narrative form or substance, this first Hoffmann edition offers a unique and dynamic illustration style. As Hoffmann makes no textual or paratextual attempts of any kind to explain or situate narrative events for a youth audience, these unattributed images are particularly vital in framing the juvenile reader's engagement with the *Leatherstocking Tales*.

Each of the two volumes' eighteen steel engravings is designed in a similar fashion: a prominent central "panel" framed by trees, bamboo, or other natural borders displays the focal image, while small rectangular segments above and below this area – roughly in the space where a supertitle or subtitle (caption) would normally be placed – display small scenes that ostensibly take place before (above) and after (below) the main event in the center. This *collage scene*[31] introduces a temporal continuity between the separate "cells" that suggests a more dynamic, parallel visual narrative than that of its contemporaries. Illustrations of this style engage the reader in a much more active and frequent manner than those in *J. F. Cooper's American Novels*, bringing established reader expectations, past knowledge, and visual foreshadowing into conversation with the putative main event in the central panel. Seeing the three moments in succession creates a sense of progress, a forward motion that encourages more immediate reader engagement with the narrative.[32]

This format focuses the reader's attention on particular continuities, ambiguities, and the disparity between what the reader sees and what (presumably) he has learned from the written narrative. Figure 3, taken from *Wildtödter*, provides a telling example. The collage scene's central segment, about two-thirds of the engraving, depicts a bound Deerslayer, surrounded by his captors and a pleading Judith, awaiting his death at the stake.[33] Each figure is drawn in a simple, straightforward manner and expresses an unambiguous attitude: Judith

---

30 See especially Malte Dahrendorf, "Lederstrumpf," 328.

31 This term is borrowed from Tom Gretton, who uses it to describe composite images in the early periodical press. This is the only instance where I have seen it appear as part of a bound collection, however. For more on this type of image, see Tom Gretton, "The Pragmatics of Page Design in Nineteenth-Century General-Interest Magazines in London and Paris," *Art History* 33 (2010): 680–709.

32 This also plays into reader identification. For more extensive studies on juvenile (male) reader psychology, see Egger, *Lederstrumpf: ein deutsches Jugendbuch*; or Anneliese Hölder, *Das Abenteuerbuch im Spiegel der männlichen Reifezeit. Die Entwicklung des literarischen Interesses beim männlichen Jugendlichen* (Ratingen: A. Henn Verlag, 1967).

33 Though later German translations may colloquially use the term *Marterpfahl* (stake) for this scene, it is clearly a tree in this illustration.

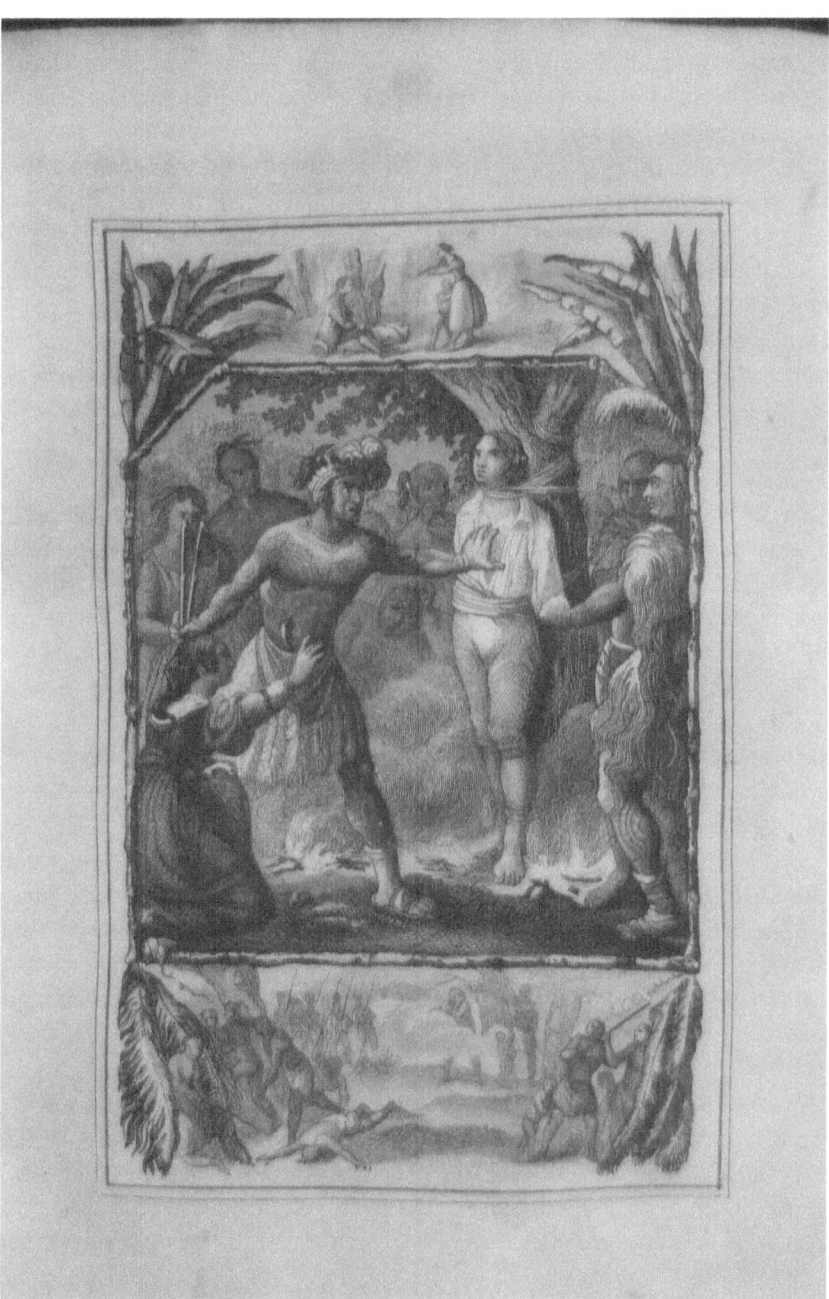

Figure 3: Steel engraving for *Wildtödter. Lederstrumpf-Erzählungen von Cooper. Für die Jugend bearbeitet von Franz Hoffmann. Erster Band.* Stuttgart: Verlag von Schmidt & Spring, 1845.

pleads on her knees for mercy, the Huron torturer feels for the hero's heart with one hand and brandishes his weapons in the other, and the remaining Huron spectators lurk in the background, all while the Deerslayer maintains a look of steadfast resolve. This scene, which is frequently replicated in other German editions and taps into the reservoir of existing ethnographic "types" that David Ciarlo mentions in his contribution, presents the climax of Deerslayer's trial, the moment of maximum narrative tension.[34] However, the reader *also* sees both the before and after of Deerslayer's ordeal at the hands of the Huron, Judith's conversation with the captive hero above, and the arrival of the English troops that results in their escape below. This does little to lessen the overall tension in the image, as neither Deerslayer nor Judith is depicted in the scene below, leaving their fate a mystery. Instead, seeing related scenes refocuses the reader-viewer's attention on the most immediate question: what happens next? Here, the individual collage components work together with the text to amplify the reader-viewer's focus on the experience of this narrative climax. In other words, by replicating the reader's experience of narrative temporality visually, the collage scene creates a powerful, direct connection between seeing and reading the event portrayed.

Individual compositions do not always direct the reader/viewer's focus "inward" toward the main segment, but can also lead "outward" (e.g., *beyond* the frame) toward the bottom scene of the collage. One example of this can be seen in the final scene from *Der Wildsteller*, in which the ultimate fate of the hunters and their buffalo quarry remains visually unresolved – the collage scene does not provide narrative closure. In other cases, the visual focus is more evenly distributed across segments that are very close together in narrative time, as in the iconic clash between the mounted Sioux and Pawnee warriors in the same novel (see Figure 4). In this instance, the small group of settlers surveys the Sioux and Pawnee forces as they prepare for the battle (above), which opens with a duel (middle) and continues below. This duel appears frequently in German illustrated editions of *The Prairie*, but almost always as a fight between two riders against an unanchored, blank background.[35] In this rendition, the smaller settlers and combatants are spectators to this clash.

In each of the examples above, the steel-engraved collage scenes reinforce the immediacy of the *Leatherstocking Tales*, drawing the reader closer to the emotional, psychological, and sensory experiences of its protagonists. This experimental visual presentation makes the overwhelming sense of propriety in Hoffmann's *J. F. Cooper's American Novels* seem quaint by comparison. In an

---

34 See, for example, Figure 5.
35 See Figure 6.

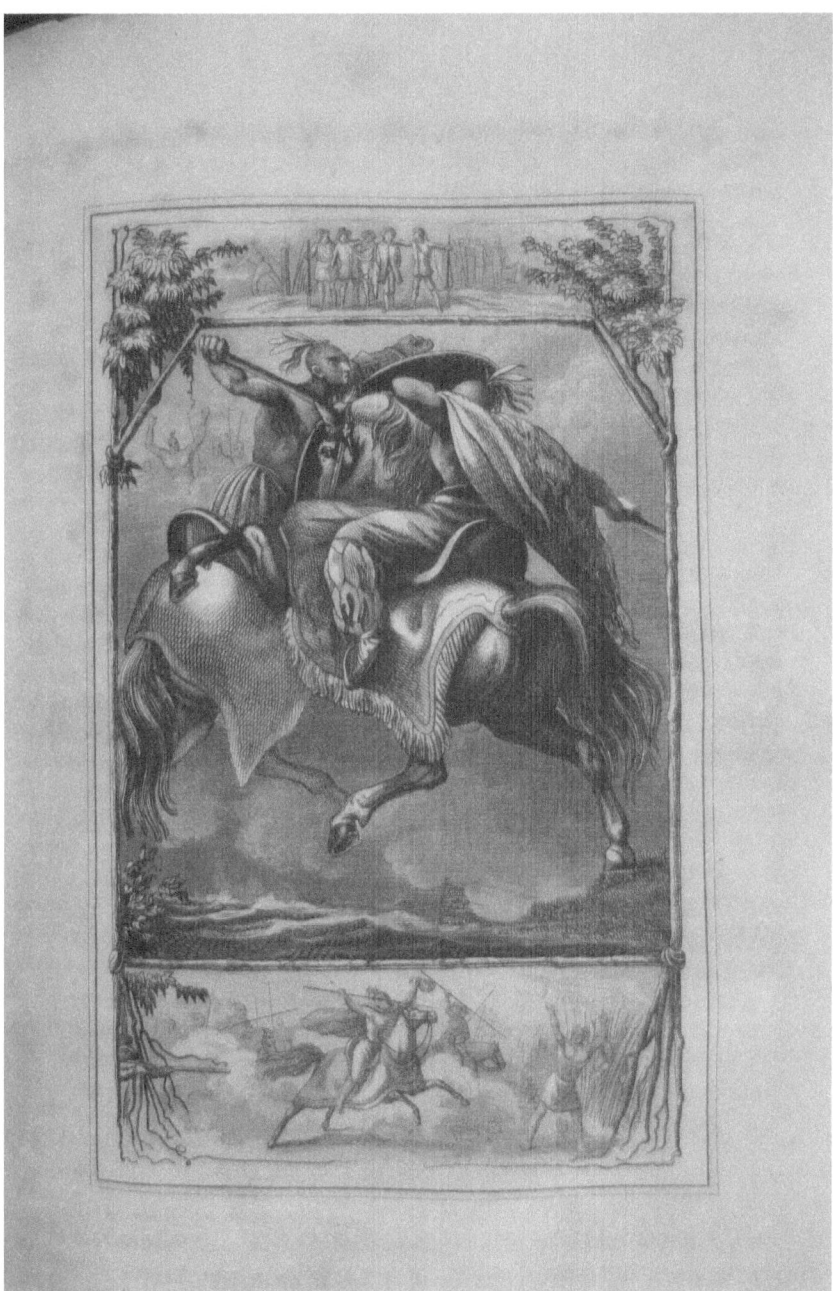

Figure 4: Steel engraving for *Der Wildsteller. Lederstrumpf-Erzählungen von Cooper. Für die Jugend bearbeitet von Franz Hoffmann. Band 2.* Stuttgart: Verlag von Schmidt & Spring, 1845.

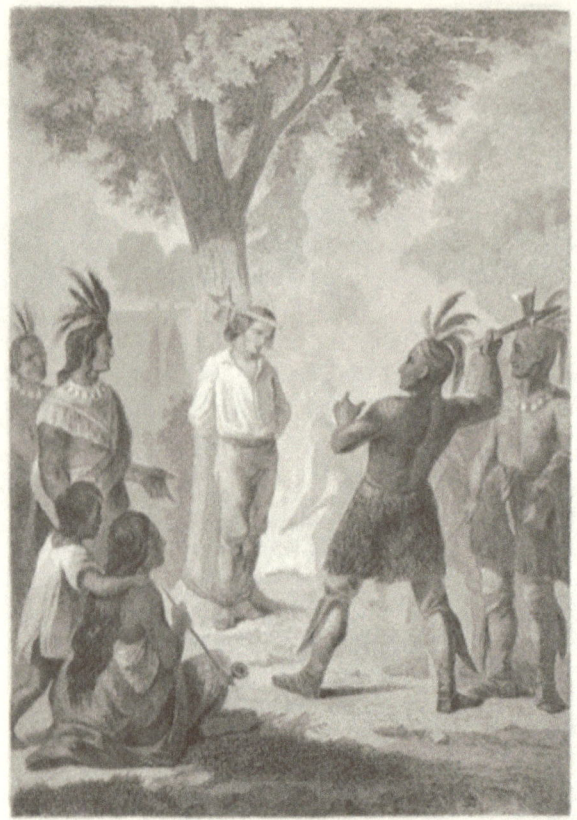

Figure 5: Steel engraving for *Wildtödter. Lederstrumpf-Erzählungen von Cooper. Für die Jugend bearbeitet von Franz Hoffmann. 6th unaltered ed.* Stuttgart: Verlag von Schmidt & Spring, 1867.

often quite literal sense, the main difference is between sanguine and sanguinary: if the illustrations for *J. F. Cooper's American Novels* present scenes of peace and tranquility, the engravings for Hoffmann's *Leatherstocking Tales* highlight violence and conflict. Perhaps unsurprisingly, this trend toward violence and sensationalism was not curtailed, but amplified in later editions, many of which also came from Stuttgart.

The first edition of Franz Hoffmann's *Leatherstocking Tales* appears to have been a financial success. The Schmidt & Spring publication alone reached eleven editions by 1883. The first edition's unique *collage scene* format was eventually replaced by more conventional formats in later editions during this time and did not return in either adult or youth collections. Despite this, the selection,

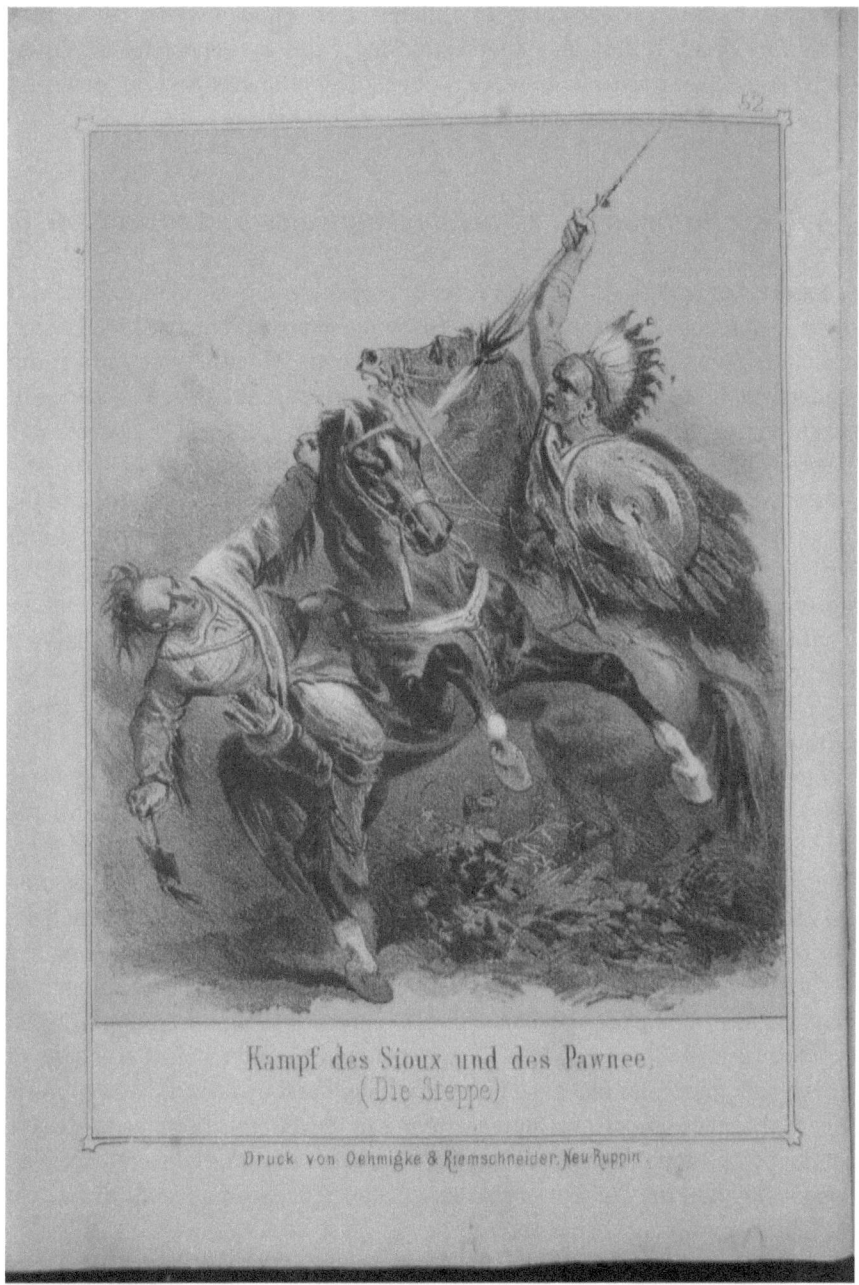

Figure 6: Kampf des Sioux und des Pawnee. *Cooper's Lederstrumpf-Erzählungen für die Jugend bearbeitet von Adam Stein.* 5th ed. Neu-Ruppin: Verlag von Alfred Oehmigke, 1869.

composition, and specific contents of many of the *collage scenes* in the 1845 edition of Franz Hoffmann's *Leatherstocking Tales by Cooper* clearly influenced subsequent visualizations of the text. The following section moves on to the 1860s, the next phase of this edition's visual history.

2.4 Franz Hoffmann's *Leatherstocking Tales by Cooper* (1867)

Schmidt & Spring's *Leatherstocking Tales by Cooper* was already in its sixth edition by 1867. Not much of the text had changed in the intervening years. At 656 pages, it remained one of the longer *Leatherstocking* collections adapted for a youth readership, though the individual works – on average 131.2 pages – were still substantially shorter than their source materials: *Wildtödter* (*The Deerslayer*) covered 160 pages, *Der letzte Mohikaner* (*The Last of the Mohicans*) 116, *Der Pfadfinder* (*The Pathfinder*) only 100, *Lederstrumpf* (*The Pioneers*) 114, and the longest, *Der Wildsteller* (*The Prairie*), only 166 pages. This same brevity is replicated on a chapter level. Editor and translator Franz Hoffmann divides the stories into digestible chunks of between five and twenty pages (the average length across the entire volume is 10.4 pages per chapter) and establishes a predictable pace to the narrative(s). Like the first edition, the language in this iteration of *Leatherstocking* emphasized the hero at the expense of the depth, setting, and mood.

Beginning with the fourth edition (1861), Franz Hoffmann's *Leatherstocking Tales by Cooper* abandoned its unusual and complex visual format for a more conventional approach. The Verlag von Schmidt & Spring commissioned Ernst Dertinger, a local Stuttgart artist and engraver, to produce sixteen steel engravings for this edition. Following the prevailing youth-literary trend at the time, Dertinger featured mid-ground and close-up perspectives of the primary figures in each scene and used clarity and simplicity of form to present their identities and attitudes. The artist also balanced his scene selection, vacillating between exciting moments of action (five), moments showing non-violent meetings or transitions (four), and reflective moments of deliberation (seven). While the action in the narrative can be quite terrifying in its content, Dertinger's stylistic simplicity and tonal softness frequently combine to blunt the overall sense of danger. In sum, the illustrations strike a balance between adventurous action and child-appropriate visual decorum.

Dertinger's illustrations reveal a growing consensus around which scenes from the *Leatherstocking Tales* should be accorded visual attention, and how this is to be achieved. Many of his illustrations reproduce individual segments from *collage scenes* in the first four editions as stand-alone images, with only minor modifications in content details.

Several of Dertinger's designs appear directly indebted to his unnamed predecessor at Schmidt & Spring. In particular, the duel between the Sioux and Pawnee warriors in *Der Wildsteller* appears to borrow directly from compositions in Franz Hoffmann's 1845 edition. Minor details in dress, background landscape, and framing have been altered, but the relative position of the combatants remains intact. Another example, the scene of Deerslayer bound to the tree (Figure 5), recalls most of the particulars in the first edition (Figure 3), but the scene has shifted in perspective to a more embodied view. In other words, the perspective chosen by the illustrator places the reader-viewer much closer to the action, as though the reader-viewer were a direct participant in the scene rather than a detached audience member viewing the scene from a distance. Exactly whose perspective it is remains unclear. Is Dertinger trying to bring the reader-viewer into closer perspectival alignment with the tomahawk-wielding Huron through an "over-the-shoulder" third-person view, or is the reader meant to share the absent Judith's (embodied) perspective? In both of these instances, the reader-viewer's distance to the action is close but detached – the figures do not gaze out of the frame in the same way that Deerslayer defiantly does in Figure 3.

Most of the other illustrations portray the dangers of the North American frontier from a similarly safe space. This tendency reflects larger trends between adult and juvenile illustrations. On the one hand, visual paratexts for a respectable adult readership attempt to dress up or downplay scenes of conflict. They consistently evoke a clean, bourgeois vision of security and harmony, visually uniting all of Cooper's novels under that theme. On the other hand, youth illustrations balance decorum with danger, pitting the familiar Robinsonade and their noble savage proxies against a new set of nonetheless familiar, foreign foes. How this presentational balancing act is played out again in new guises in the publishing centers of Berlin (Neu-Ruppin) and Leipzig is the subject of the following section.

3 Adam Stein & *Cooper's Leatherstocking Tales* (1868)

While Franz Hoffmann experimented with several visual formats before settling on one convention in *Leatherstocking Tales by Cooper*, Adam Stein maintained the same format for his *Cooper's Leatherstocking Tales* across multiple editions and publishers. The collection first appeared with the Julius Springer Verlag in Berlin in 1863 and was also published by Alfred Oehmigke in both Leipzig & Neu-Ruppin during the latter half of that decade.[36] Both editions feature six lithographs created by Wilhelm Schäfer from paintings by Gustav Bartsch, a successful portraitist and genre painter from Dresden. Bartsch's illustrations and this version of the text were featured for at least seventeen editions through 1883.

Most of the same textual criticisms leveled at the Hoffmann adaptation apply here as well, with one important difference: both translators omit significant portions of the source material, but Stein does *not* alter or substitute the resulting texts to the degree that Hoffmann does.[37] This is borne out in both the total length of the work – 380 pages – and the length of its individual components: *Der Wildtödter auf dem Kriegspfade* (*The Deerslayer*) is 87 pages long, *Der Kundschafter am Binnensee* (*The Pathfinder*) a paltry 56, *Der Letzte der Mohikaner* (*The Last of the Mohicans*) 70, *Die Ansiedler von Newyork* (*The Pioneers*) 90, and *Die Steppe* (*The Prairie*) 76 pages. Like Hoffmann's adaptation, the chapters are consequently fewer and shorter – about five or six per story with an average length of fourteen pages each. The volume is also printed in octavo format, but with substantially fewer lines per page: thirty-two compared to Hoffmann's forty-seven, most likely to increase readability.

This same concern for readability appears to have influenced other aspects of this adaptation. Like Hoffmann's *Leatherstocking Tales by Cooper*, Stein's abridgment dispenses with a series introduction, though it is marginally better at providing historical context. Hoffmann's series starts *in medias res*; Stein's version of *Der Wildtödter* opens with a paragraph sketching the political landscape and its primary players – the French, the English, and the Native Americans – in upstate New York during the "last half of the previous century."[38] Subsequent stories receive similarly perfunctory introductions.

The only other preparation given to the reader comes in the form of the frontispiece, which features another rendition of the Sioux-Pawnee duel (see Figure 6). The selection of this image as the frontispiece sets the tone for the rest of the volume. Bartsch borrows the body positioning of Dertinger's combatants – one (the Sioux chief and villain, Mahtoree) charges at full tilt, bearing down on

---

[36] It is unclear when Stein's *Cooper's Lederstrumpf-Erzählungen* first appeared with Oehmigke. The Prussian State Library in Berlin has copies from as early as 1870, which are listed as the seventh edition.
[37] Egger, *Lederstrumpf: ein deutsches Jugendbuch*, 318.
[38] Adam Stein, *Cooper's Lederstrumpf-Erzählungen für die Jugend bearbeitet von Adam Stein. Mit 6 Bildern von G. Bartsch*. 5th ed. (Neu-Ruppin: Verlag von Alfred Oehmigke, 1869), 3.

his foe (the Pawnee hero Hard-Heart) with poised lance, while the other is atop a rearing horse, his shield raised to deflect the blow – but presents the two figures from a new angle. Whereas the previous image (Figure 4) views the clash from behind one of the warriors (the one with the shield) allowing us to face his charging opponent head-on with him, Bartsch presents them from a perspective that is not clearly focalized through a character.[39] While the lance-wielding native is still in the background, the encounter is shown from a sidelong, perpendicular angle. Here too, the horse rears as the defender moves to ward off the coming blow, but this time it appears to fall away from the contact and to the left of the image. The reader is detached from the moment – a neutral, rather than active, observer of the events.

Bartsch's other illustrations convey a similar sense of strategic distance, further accentuated by their subtitles. For example, the illustration for *The Last of the Mohicans* presents one of the most comical scenes in the *Leatherstocking Tales* – the rescue of Alice Munro (rendered here as Alix) from the Huron camp by Heyward (dressed as a Huron) and Hawkeye (dressed as a bear) – again from a non-embodied perspective. The reader-viewer is in on the joke and joins the leftmost Huron observer in his skeptical appraisal of the pair. While the tension (i.e., the fear of discovery) is present, so is the inherent ridiculousness of the plan. The caption reads "Heyward entführt Alix" (*Heyward abducts Alix/Alice*) – a further play on Heyward's resemblance to the same Huron captors who had first kidnapped the girl.

Through these lithographs, the reader-viewer is encouraged to feel *for* – but not *with* – the protagonists. They may laugh or cheer as Heyward and Hawkeye save Alice, but the image does not accentuate the character's internal fears or anxieties (indeed, Bartsch provides no visible external threat); they may gasp as Hard-Heart and Mahtoree collide on the plain, but they do not share a stake in that fight. The closest Bartsch allows his reader-viewers to get to the action is in his other illustration for *Die Steppe,* entitled "Mahtoree im Lager der Auswanderer" (*Mahtoree in the settler's camp*). In this image, the Sioux warrior stoops over a prone settler, dagger held tightly in hand. However, as the narrative will soon confirm, the threat is fleeting, and the dreamer escapes unscathed. It is almost as though the lithograph itself – with its clean lines, gentle shapes, and bright colors – is the product of that prone dreamer, a

---

39 In other words, the visual presentation of the narrative information does not appear to be selected or restricted relative to the experience of any of the narrative figures. To apply Genette's term to this context, the image is not "focalized." Gérard Genette, *Narrative Discourse: An Essay on Method* (Oxford: Blackwell, 1980), 188–189.

youthful fantasy that has the power to imagine the individual elements of an untimely demise but lacks the experience to accurately fill in all of the details.

Later nineteenth-century editions would capture these details in vivid color and detail. The scenes often remained the same, but the emphasis shifted dramatically. Some illustrations appear to completely abandon bourgeois taste in favor of sensational violence. Unlike their predecessors in 1845, these editions not only had to vie with works by successful competitors within the field of respectable youth literature, they also experienced a second phase of growing pains as they were repackaged for more popular audiences.[40] Though they do not mention it specifically, the sensationalized violence is one of the unshakeable associations – the visual baggage – that (in)visibly drags down youth adaptations in the eyes of twentieth-century literary critics.[41] Bloodstained, bloodthirsty braves stalk innocent white maidens; heroic trapper-hunters face down rabid herds of rampaging bison; noble savages meet their menacing cousins on the open plain. These and many similar scenes, all part of Cooper's work, have become a central component of that author's German legacy, the visual shorthand that has come to stand for the whole. Much like his larger legacy, Cooper's *Leatherstocking Tales* are remembered today less as epochal literary works, but as foundational visualizations of the American frontier.

4 Conclusion

Cooper's historical-mythical vision of a vanishing frontier may have been novel to an audience of adult Germans from the 1820s to the 1840s, but adaptations for young readers consistently alluded to the same images from early juvenile editions from the mid-1840s. Both Franz Hoffmann's and Adam Stein's illustrated youth editions of the *Leatherstocking Tales* lean on familiar visual and generic conventions to blunt the force of their violent content and recast a

---

40 Some have called this next generation of sensational, colonial adventure novels – stories in which the idealistic and poetic elements are jettisoned in favor of gripping action and bloodcurdling terror – a reprehensible "bang-bang-bang literature" ("Piff-paff-puff-Literatur") in which the "gunning down redskins" ("Niederschießen der Rothäute") had become an acceptable leisure activity. Göhring, quoted in Gisela Wilkending, "Vom letzten Drittel des 19. Jahrhunderts bis zum Ersten Weltkrieg," in *Geschichte der deutschen Kinder- und Jugendliteratur*, ed. Reiner Wild, 3rd ed. (J. B. Metzler: Stuttgart, 2008), 171–240, here 219.

41 For the most extreme example of this argument, see Wolfgang Hochbruck, "Leatherstockings and River Pirates: The Adventure Novels of Friedrich Gerstäcker," *The Arkansas Historical Quarterly* 73, no. 1 (2014): 42–55, here 43.

literary novelty in an acceptable manner for their intended audience. The youth images, especially those accompanying the first Hoffmann edition, are brimming with impetuous immediacy. Images of the most action-packed moments grab the reader-viewer's attention and encourage vicarious, visual identification with the exhilarating experience of danger and suspense on the frontier. In these editions, the text and image work together to help the viewer-reader to clearly identify positive and negative role models in each episode.

By contrast, the engravings for the thirty-volume set, *J. F. Cooper's American Novels*, preserve and uphold specific textual moments that seem to be selected more for their suitability for a bourgeois bookshelf than their centrality to the narrative they accompany (or, as frontispieces, precede). Rather than amplifying the reader-viewer's engagement with the experience of the text, they tend to transport him or her away from it. The fine detail of their compositions adds cultural caché to the volumes without pushing the boundaries of the medium. In other words, the illustrations in/for the adult edition behave less as frontier portals than as images whose primary value is disconnected from their depicted content.

My analysis of visual-material presentations of German youth and adult editions of Cooper's *Leatherstocking Tales* reveals two distinct histories driven by diverging sets of priorities. In Cooper scholarship, the difference in literary status between adult-literary and youth-literary editions histories often impedes productive engagement with the author's reception. However, both adult and youth Coopers have an important story to tell. In their expansive survey of multimedia Cooper adaptations, *The Lasting of the Mohicans: History of an American Myth*, Martin Barker and Roger Sabin provide a useful way of rethinking "classic" works of literature:

> the most important thing about classics is not their content at all. It is their name. To be a "classic" is to be assigned a place in the calendar of saints [. . .]. The most important thing about classics therefore is the way they are announced, they announce themselves, to us. What most needs study is their look, their feel, their publicity, and their manner of distribution.[42]

When considered from this perspective, the transformation of Cooper's *Leatherstocking Tales* from international adult bestseller to German youth classic is a fascinating story of comprehensive visual rebranding. The publishing history outlined above is only a small part of larger literary and visual-cultural histories that happened to cross in 1845 when Franz Hoffmann's *Leatherstocking*

---

42 Martin Barker and Roger Sabin, *The Lasting of the Mohicans: History of an American Myth* (Jackson, MS: University Press of Mississippi, 1995), 50–51.

Tales by Cooper first began entertaining young readers in Stuttgart. Many other youth editions followed suit, and this particular weaving of Cooper's stories about the enterprising trapper and frontiersman Natty Bumppo became the most popular German adventure story of the nineteenth century.[43] James Fenimore Cooper's *Leatherstocking Tales* has a long and rich history as an illustrated classic of German youth literature. This story is an indelible part of the author's legacy, one that, as I have demonstrated here, cannot be seen without acknowledging the vital role of visual culture in nineteenth-century publishing.

Bibliography

Barker, Martin, and Roger Sabin. *The Lasting of the Mohicans: History of an American Myth*. Jackson: University Press of Mississippi, 1995.

Cooper, James Fenimore. *J. F. Cooper's Amerikanische Romane, neu aus dem Englischen übertragen: Zweiter Band; Der Pfadfinder oder das Binnenmeer*. 4th ed. Translated by Dr. C. Kolb. Stuttgart: Hoffmann'sche Verlags-Buchhandlung, 1853.

Cooper, James Fenimore. *J. F. Cooper's Amerikanische Romane, neu aus dem Englischen übertragen: Zwölfter Band; Der Wildtödter*. 4th ed. Stuttgart: Hoffmann'sche Verlags-Buchhandlung, 1853.

Cooper, James Fenimore. *J. F. Cooper's Amerikanische Romane, neu aus dem Englischen übertragen: Achtzehnter Band; Miles Wallingfords Abenteuer zu Land und zur See*. 2nd ed. Translated by Eduard Mauch. Stuttgart: Hoffmann'sche Verlags-Buchhandlung, 1853.

Cooper, James Fenimore. *J. F. Cooper's Amerikanische Romane, neu aus dem Englischen übertragen: Neunzehnter Band; Lucy Hardinge, oder Miles Wallingfords Abenteuer zu Land und zur See, Zweiter Theil*. 2nd ed. Translated by Dr. Carl Kolb. Stuttgart: Hoffmann'sche Verlags-Buchhandlung, 1853.

Cooper, James Fenimore. *J. F. Cooper's Amerikanische Romane, neu aus dem Englischen übertragen: Dreißigster Band; Der Bienenjäger, oder die Eichen-Lichtungen*. Stuttgart: Hoffmann'sche Verlags-Buchhandlung, 1854.

Dahrendorf, Malte. "Lederstrumpf." In *Lexikon der Kinder- und Jugendliteratur: Zweiter Band; I-O*, edited by Klaus Doderer, 327–328. Weinheim: Beltz, 1977.

Doderer, Klaus, and Peter Aley, eds. *Klassische Kinder- und Jugendbücher: Kritische Betrachtungen*. Weinheim: Beltz, 1969.

Egger, Irmgard. "Lederstrumpf: ein deutsches Jugendbuch: Untersuchung zu den Bedingungen und Strukturen literarischer Transformation." PhD diss., University of Vienna, 1991.

Eich, Hans. "Bearbeitung von Texten für Kinder und Jugendliche." In *Lexikon der Kinder- und Jugendliteratur: Erster Band; A-H*, edited by Klaus Doderer, 119–120. Weinheim: Beltz, 1975.

Ewers, Hans-Heino. *Fundamental Concepts of Children's Literature Research: Literary and Sociological Approaches*. Translated by William J. McCann. New York: Routledge, 2009.

---

43 Pech, "Vom Biedermeier zum Realismus," 156.

Flavin, Francis. "The Adventurer-Artists of the Nineteenth Century and the Image of the American Indian." *Indiana Magazine of History* 98, no. 1 (2002): 1–29.

Franklin, Wayne. "James Fenimore Cooper, 1789–1851: A Brief Biography." In *A Historical Guide to James Fenimore Cooper*, edited by Leland S. Person, 27–60. Oxford: Oxford University Press, 2007.

Franklin, Wayne. *James Fenimore Cooper: The Early Years*. New Haven: Yale University Press, 2007.

Franklin, Wayne. *James Fenimore Cooper: The Later Years*. New Haven: Yale University Press, 2017.

Genette, Gérard. *Narrative Discourse: An Essay on Method*. Oxford: Blackwell, 1980.

Genette, Gérard. *Paratexts: Thresholds of Interpretation*. Cambridge: Cambridge University Press, 1997.

Gretton, Tom. "The Pragmatics of Page Design in Nineteenth-Century General-Interest Magazines in London and Paris." *Art History* 33 (2010): 680–709.

Griffiths, Anthony. *The Print Before Photography: An Introduction to European Printmaking, 1550–1820*. London: British Museum, 2016.

Hoffmann, Franz. *Conanchet, der Indianerhäuptling: Eine Erzählung für die reifere Jugend; Nach dem Englischen des J. F. Cooper bearbeitet von Franz Hoffmann; Mit 6 Bildern in Farbendruck nach Aquarellen von J. Simmler*. 6th ed. Stuttgart: K. Thienemanns, 1886.

Hoffmann, Franz. *Lederstrumpf-Erzählungen von Cooper: Für die Jugend bearbeitet von Franz Hoffmann; Erster Band; Mit 8 Stahlstichen*. Stuttgart: Schmidt & Spring, 1845.

Hoffmann, Franz. *Lederstrumpf-Erzählungen von Cooper: Für die Jugend bearbeitet von Franz Hoffmann; Zweiter Band; Mit 12 Stahlstichen*. Stuttgart: Schmidt & Spring, 1845.

Hoffmann, Franz. *Lederstrumpf-Erzählungen von Cooper: Für die Jugend bearbeitet von Franz Hoffmann; Mit sechzehn Stahlstichen*. 6th ed. Stuttgart: Schmidt & Spring, 1867.

Hoffmann, Kurt. "Hoffmann, Carl." *Neue Deutsche Biographie* 9 (1972): 432, https://www.deutsche-biographie.de/pnd116974036.html#ndbcontent.

Kress, Gunther, and Theo van Leeuwen. *Multimodal Discourse: The Modes and Media of Contemporary Communication*. London: Arnold, 2001.

Lichtenberger, Sigrid. "Lesealter." In *Lexikon der Kinder- und Jugendliteratur: Zweiter Band; I-O*, edited by Klaus Doderer, 346–349. Weinheim: Beltz, 1977.

McWilliams, John P. *The Last of the Mohicans: Civil Savagery and Savage Civility*. New York: Twayne, 1995.

Melville, Hermann. *Memorial of James Fenimore Cooper*. New York: G. P. Putnam, 1852.

Mensch, G. *Der Bienenjäger: Eine Erzählung für die reifere Jugend; Frei nach Cooper bearbeitet von G. Mensch; Mit sechs Bildern in Farbendruck nach Zeichnungen von H. Leutemann lithographiert von W. Schäfer*. 2nd ed. Leipzig: Alfred Oehmigke, 1876.

Pech, Klaus-Ulrich, "Vom Biedermeier zum Realismus." In *Geschichte der deutschen Kinder- und Jugendliteratur*, edited by Reiner Wild. 3rd ed., 131–170. Stuttgart: J. B. Metzler, 2008.

Penny, H. Glenn. "Elusive Authenticity: The Quest for the Authentic Indian in German Public Culture." *Comparative Studies in Society and History* 48, no. 4 (2006): 798–819.

Person, Leland S. "Introduction: Fenimore Cooper's Literary Achievements." In *A Historical Guide to James Fenimore Cooper*, edited by Leland S. Person, 1–26. Oxford: Oxford University Press, 2007.

Rossbacher, Karlheinz. *Lederstrumpf in Deutschland: Zur Rezeption James Fenimore Coopers beim Leser der Restaurationszeit*. Munich: Wilhelm Fink, 1972.

Schmidt, Rudolf. "Übersichtstafel der abgezweigten Firmen aus der von Carl Hoffmann in Stuttgart 1826 begründeten Buchhandlung." In vol. 3 of *Deutsche Buchhändler: Deutsche Buchdrucker*, 482. Berlin: Contumax, 1905.

Stein, Adam. *Cooper's Lederstrumpf-Erzählungen für die Jugend bearbeitet von Adam Stein: Mit sechs Bildern von G. Bartsch*. 5th ed. Neu-Ruppin: Alfred Oehmigke, 1869.

Stein, Adam. *Cooper's Lederstrumpf-Erzählungen für die Jugend bearbeitet von Adam Stein: Mit sechs Bildern in Farbendruck von W. Schäfer*. 17th ed. Leipzig: Alfred Oehmigke, 1883.

Stein, Adam. *Cooper's Seegemälde: Für die Jugend bearbeitet von Adam Stein; Mit sechs Bildern in Farbendruck nach Zeichnungen von G. Bartsch*. 2nd ed. Leipzig: Alfred Oehmigke, 1865.

Wasserman, Renata R. Mautner. *Exotic Nations: Literature and Cultural Identity in the United States and Brazil, 1830–1930*. Ithaca, NY: Cornell University Press, 1994.

Wilkending, Gisela. "Vom letzten Drittel des 19. Jahrhunderts bis zum Ersten Weltkrieg." In *Geschichte der deutschen Kinder- und Jugendliteratur*, edited by Reiner Wild, 3rd ed., 171–240. Stuttgart: J. B. Metzler, 2008.

Wolff, Mark. "Western Novels as Children's Literature in Nineteenth-Century France." *Mosaic: An Interdisciplinary Critical Journal* 34, no. 2 (2001): 87–102.

Epilogue

Kirsten Belgum
Scans, Databases, and Apps: Using Twenty-First-Century Technology to Study Nineteenth-Century Visual Culture

Compared to the previous chapters in this volume, this final contribution takes a radically different approach to thinking about nineteenth-century visual culture. It concludes this examination of pre-photographic visual culture by looking not directly at exemplars of that period or at contemporary mechanisms of producing such visual objects or at their distribution and circulation. Rather it discusses some digital applications that have emerged in the twenty-first century that enable scholars to gain access to that culture and study it in new ways. In other words, this final chapter considers innovations in recent decades for investigating nineteenth-century pre-photographic visual culture and insights that can be gained from newly available tools. In doing so, it also reminds us that visual culture, like other forms of expression, is not static or fixed for all time. Rather it is a resource that can continue to reveal aspects about the society in which it emerged, including elements that were not apparent to those who were the originally intended recipients of it. Indeed, this chapter points to the ways in which initial consumers and users of nineteenth-century print might have interacted with these visual culture objects in ways quite different from how we can now.

To be sure, it is difficult for twenty-first-century scholars to reconstruct the impact that the quickly expanding encounter with visual culture might have had on contemporaries of the pre-photographic era. We see those artefacts from the vantage point of our own context of visual saturation.[1] Today, visual imagery is pervasive thanks to the prevalence of photography, film, electronic media, and, most recently, digital media. We not only see new images all the time and enjoy almost simultaneous transmission of sights from around the world, we also have seemingly unlimited access to visual representations of older images as well. And those same technological advances that today provide us with an immense and seemingly endless supply of visual information are also relevant for our study of

---

1 "Visual saturation" is, of course, a relative concept. As the essays in this volume reveal, the nineteenth century in Europe was a time of increased "saturation" of visual material. Vanessa Meikle Schulman has used the word to describe the number of images about industry and technological production present in mid-nineteenth-century American periodicals. Vanessa Meikle Schulman, *Work Sights: The Visual Culture of Industry in Nineteenth-Century America* (Amherst, MA: University of Massachusetts Press, 2015), 3.

https://doi.org/10.1515/9783110696448-016

nineteenth-century visual culture. New technologies, tools, applications, and resources, that seem quite removed from the original processes of print, for example, give scholars and historians unparalleled access to earlier forms, as I will show in the following case study by focusing on the domain with which I am most familiar, print images, a subject that resonates with several of the previous chapters.[2] This chapter specifically discusses the popular early nineteenth-century illustrated serial, *Meyer's Universum* to reveal what insights into pre-photographic visual culture recent tools can provide.

From the beginning, my interest in *Meyer's Universum* has been related to my research on nineteenth-century geographical imagination. The success of the work and the diversity of locations it depicted suggested that it might provide important insights into the rapidly expanding ability of Europeans to view the world. The more I investigated the serial's place in contemporary networks of landscape drawing, reproduction, and publishing, however, the more complicated and puzzling its development became. I began to wonder how, beginning in the 1830s, the work's publisher was able to assemble such a vast and varied archive of images so quickly.

This chapter describes my attempt to understand the story of *Meyer's Universum* and to provide some suggestions about new ways to study nineteenth-century visual culture. It addresses the impact of digital technology on issues of availability and access across multiple collections, and thus on the ability to locate and to compare examples of visual culture over time and across sources. Much of this has to do with the massive amount of nineteenth-century print culture that has now been digitally scanned, archived in on-line collections, and made publicly accessible.[3] This project also relies on digital search engines that

---

[2] David Ciarlo's chapter follows the reuse and recycling of one image in particular through a wide variety of venues and contexts. Vance Byrd's contribution explores the symbiotic relationship between the monumental visual work of a panorama and the handheld medium of the periodical press. And Matt Anderson's analysis of illustrations in Cooper editions shows the way in which visual images impacted a work in different contexts. Scholars working on other visual materials, such as painting, papercuts, glass-blown objects, wax models, would likely bring additional insights to bear on new ways of seeing and researching nineteenth-century visual culture.

[3] In October 2019 Google Books stated it had digitized almost 40 million books. Haimin Lee, "15 years of Google Books," 17 October 2019, https://www.blog.google/products/search/15-years-google-books/ <accessed 2 April 2020>. Many of these, however, are under copyright protection and thus not accessible to public. See James Somers, "Torching the Modern-Day Library of Alexandria," *The Atlantic*, 20 April 2017. https://www.theatlantic.com/technology/archive/2017/04/the-tragedy-of-google-books/523320/ <accessed 2 April 2020>. Hathitrust, which participates in a partnership with Google Books, states that it "preserves and provides

can reveal aspects of the development, expansion, and borrowing across sources and national boundaries of visual images in print that were previously unrecognized and unrecognizable. In presenting this one example, I hope to show what new technologies offer us as researchers. But I also describe the limitations of digital tools and ways these limitations can be addressed. Digital technology presents us with a myriad of new insights, but it cannot replace a continued engagement with the material visual objects that were produced, sold, encountered, manipulated, and observed in the nineteenth century.

First, a bit of background. As an illustrated serial work, *Meyer's Universum* was remarkably successful. It was launched in 1833 by (Carl) Joseph Meyer (1796–1856) and his relatively young publishing house the Bibliographisches Institut located in the small provincial city of Hildburghausen (as of 1828 part of the Duchy of Saxe-Meiningen; today part of Thuringia). The serial's popularity and claim to fame lay in the striking illustrations it offered its readers. Each monthly installment (or "part") presented four steel engraved plates of notable landscapes, vedute (or cityscapes), or architectural works from around the world. A short text (anywhere from a long paragraph to a few pages in length) accompanied each plate. If subscribers combined twelve installments into a bound volume, which they often did, the number of pages of letterpress averaged 140 per volume.[4] Two aspects of the engraved plates strike a modern reader and must have impressed contemporary consumers as well; on the one hand, as illustrations, they contain amazing detail and spatial accuracy about the places and objects they depict (such as Edinburgh, the Parthenon, or the Taj Mahal), and, on the other hand, taken together, within each part, but especially within any single annual volume, they present viewers with a striking variety of sites and geographical range.

Both aspects probably played a key role in the work's success. Within two decades of publication of the first part, the publisher and editor Meyer, who would later become most well-known for his encyclopedia, *Meyer's Conversations-Lexikon*, claimed that his *Universum* had a circulation of 50,000 and had been translated into every language of Europe, claims that may or may not have been colored by

---

lawful access to the seventeen million digitized items." "Welcome to HathiTrust!" https://www.hathitrust.org/about <accessed 2 April 2020>. Books and periodicals in these databases that were published in the nineteenth century are typically publicly accessible since works published before 1923 are now in the public domain.
4 The number of pages per volume was lower in the first two years of publication (180 for vol. 1 and 112 for vol. 2), but stabilized at average of 140 over the next six volumes (148 for vol. 3, 140 for vol. 4, 136 for vol. 5, 130 for vol. 6, 152 for vol. 7, and 134 for vol. 8).

self-congratulatory overstatement.⁵ *Meyer's Universum* began publication in 1833 just as another highly successful illustrated periodical genre, the penny magazine, was beginning to proliferate in Britain, France, and Germany. Unlike in those periodicals, however, in which the wood engraved illustrations were quite rough and considered supplemental embellishments to the text, in *Meyer's Universum* the high-quality steel engraved prints that revealed amazing detail were the focus of the work (see Figure 1).

The intaglio print process of steel engraving, unlike the relief process for wood engraving, also required that the prints be impressed on sheets of paper separately from the accompanying text or letterpress printed sheets.⁶ The paper used for these steel engraved prints was also thicker and more durable than the paper used for the pages of letterpress printing in the rest of the work. These

---

5 Herrmann J. Meyer, Joseph's son, touted this in a prospectus mailed in 1852 to "agents and postmasters" in North America, i.e., distributors of an English-language edition to promote its sale: "This edition of the 'Universum,' which enjoys a circulation of fifty thousand copies on the other side of the Atlantic, will be generally welcomed in the United States and British America, and I trust that your exertions bestowed upon it, will meet with a remunerative success." Bifolium, folded quarto leaflet used as self-mailer available for sale by an antiquarian bookdealer, accessed here: https://www.abebooks.com/Prospectus-Meyers-Universum-Meyer-Herrmann-J/30343037976/bd#&gid=1&pid=2 <accessed 27 December 2019>. Confirming this, Angelika Marsch, who compiled a complete index of the images from *Meyer's Universum* in the 1970s, points out that some copies seemed to have been made from heavily worn plates suggesting a very large number of impressions had been made from them. Angelika Marsch, *Meyer's Universum: Ein Beitrag zur Geschichte des Stahlstiches und des Verlagswesens im 19. Jahrhundert* (Lüneburg: Nordostdeutsches Kulturwerk, 1972), 45.

6 Relief printing involves inking the top of a surface and then placing a piece of paper on the wet ink, applying pressure, and thereby pulling the ink off the plate and onto the paper. This is the principle behind letterpress printing where the individual pieces of type present a flat and level surface for inking. As a consequence, relief blocks that have been carved with images can be set onto the bed of a printing press alongside or surrounded by letter type to print pages that contain both text and images. By contrast, in intaglio printing the image that one intends to print is engraved into the plate (copper or steel). When the plate is inked, the ink flows into in the cut or carved lines on the plate. The top surface of the plate is cleaned of ink before printing, but ink remains in the recessed groves. The printing process involves pushing the paper onto the plate with enough pressure to pull that ink out of the tiny crevasses to make the image or "impression." Rather than the image coming from what is not cut away (as in relief printing), it comes from the marks that have been made into the plate's surface. For a more detailed discussion of the difference between relief and intaglio printing see Bamber Gascoigne, *How to Identify Prints: A complete guide to manual and mechanical process from woodcut to inkjet*. 2nd ed. (London: Thames & Hudson, 2014): sections 1a–1b; and Basil Hunnisett, *Engraved on Steel: The History of Picture Production using Steel Plates* (Aldershot: Ashgate, 1998), 220.

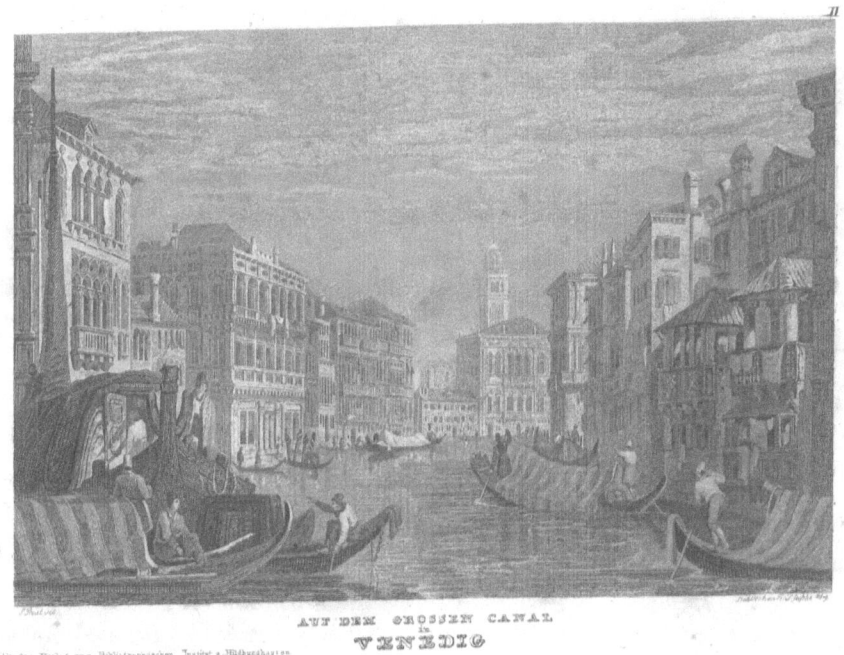

Figure 1: "On the Grand Canal in Venice" ["Auf dem Grossen Canal in Venedig"]. *Meyer's Universum* vol. 1 (1833), plate II.

two facts, that the engravings were printed separately and on better quality paper, meant that *Meyer's Universum* also had value as an item for display. The individual pages with visual images printed from steel engraved plates could be and often were removed from their respective monthly part for framing and hanging on walls. This was not just an activity done by contemporaries. The large number of prints from various volumes of *Meyer's Universum* currently available for sale on antiquarian book sites (see Figure 2) as well as on consumer-to-consumer e-commerce sites such as eBay (see Figure 3) attest to the longevity of this practice. In addition, the continuing market for prints from *Meyer's Universum* will, as we shall see, also be one of the digital resources for my historical investigation.

The quality of these prints was the first aspect to pique my curiosity about how Joseph Meyer came to be able to publish them, but the quantity of them also raised questions. If each monthly part contained four distinct engravings, then each volume included on average forty-eight of them. At the time of Joseph Meyer's death in 1856 the firm had published seventeen volumes of *Meyer's*

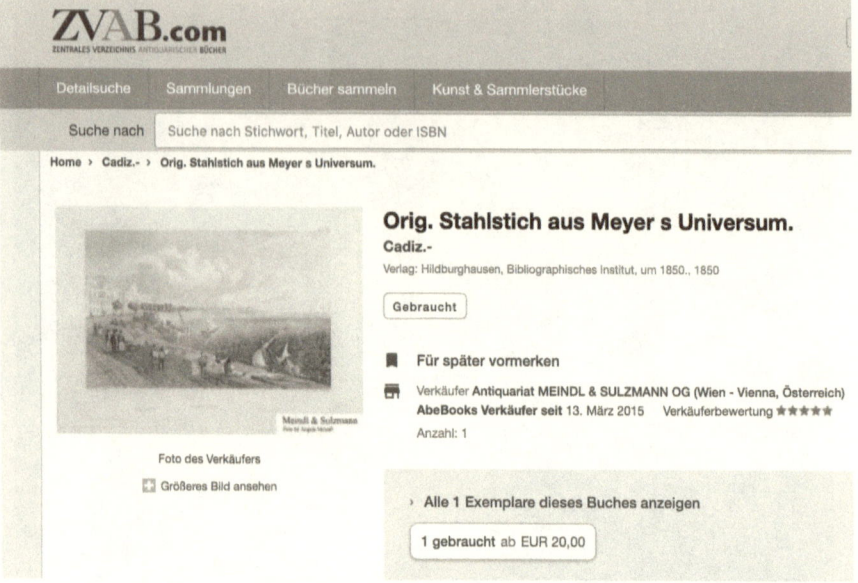

Figure 2: Original steel engraving "Cadiz" from *Meyer's Universum* offered for sale via the web site of the Zentrales Verzeichnis Antiquarischer Bücher (ZVAB). https://www.zvab.com/Orig-Stahlstich-Meyer-Universum-Cadiz.–Hildburghausen/15565976374/bd. Accessed 30 January 2019.

Universum, or over 700 distinct steel engravings.[7] In the hands of Joseph's son, Herrmann, the publishing house issued four more volumes in the original oblong quarto format, and then proceeded to amplify the impact of this serial in new formats: a slightly smaller and vertically oriented octavo "people's edition" (Volksbuchausgabe) that appeared from 1858 to 1863 in sixteen volumes and a yearbook edition (Jahrbuch, also called a Prachtausgabe) that appeared in three volumes between 1862 and 1864. In this same timeframe, the Bibliographisches Institut also re-used some of these engravings in its illustrated encyclopedias (the *Conversations-Lexikon* and the *Neues Conversations-Lexikon*).[8] Angelika Marsch places the number of distinct engravings the publishing house produced for this serial alone by the mid-1860s at more than 1200.[9] Her index of the engravings according to the location of the depicted scene highlights the geographical range they covered; over 300 were of venues in the German lands; over 600 from the rest

---

[7] Peter Kaiser, *Der Pläneschmied: Das außergewöhnliche Leben des Verlegers Carl Joseph Meyer* (Leipzig: Salier Verlag, 2007), 134.
[8] Marsch, *Meyer's Universum*, 65–67.
[9] Marsch, *Meyer's Universum*, 6.

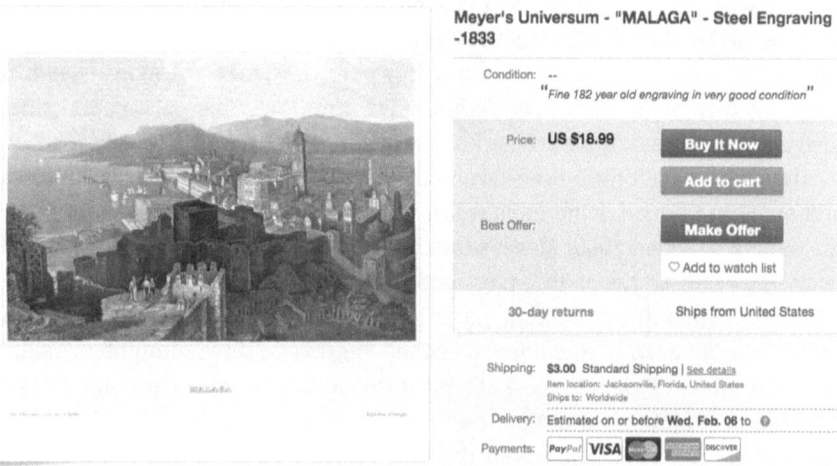

Figure 3: Steel engraving "Malaga" from *Meyer's Universum* offered for sale on eBay. https://www.ebay.com/itm/Meyers-Universum-MALAGA-Steel-Engraving-1833-/171630502200. Accessed 30 January 2019.

of Europe; forty-two from Africa, eighty-two from Asia, two from Australia, twenty-four from Latin America, and 145 from North America. In other words, Meyer truly aspired to depict much of the whole world, or the "Universum."[10]

The global variety, but also the detail and realism of these steel engravings clearly suggest that they were based on eye-witness views drawn or painted on site. This raises the question: how did a publisher and editor like Joseph Meyer, located in provincial Hildburghausen and who, aside from several years early in life as a merchant intern in London, rarely traveled outside of his home duchy, access such a treasure trove of images from across the world? This question led me first to consult scholarship on Meyer's firm and on steel engravings in general, but I did not find satisfying answers in such locations. Historians of the Bibliographisches Institut gloss over the issue of where these images came from. Armin Human, the first biographer of Carl Joseph Meyer and his publishing house, writing in 1898 focuses primarily on the written contributions of Meyer to the *Universum*, noting his "Byronic" style. Human only laconically mentions that "splendid English steel engravings illustrated the text in an

---

10 Because she is writing in the late twentieth century Marsch includes Bohemia/Moravia and Austria as parts of Europe that were not in Germany. Publishing prior to the founding of the North German Confederation, Meyer would most likely not have done so. Marsch, *Meyer's Universum*, 68–109.

extensive manner" ("prächtige englische Stahlstiche [illustrierten] den Text in eingehendster Weise").[11] Johannes Hohlfeld notes only that the *Universum* eventually included 1252 steel engravings over the years.[12] A more recent in-house history by Heinz Sarkowski provides even fewer insights, commenting instead that the serial was most known in the 1970s not for Meyer's text, but for the plates which have been taken out of it and framed, sometimes colorized, and hung on German living room walls.[13] Sarkowski recites the same information that others provided about Meyer's firm, namely that by the early 1830s it had already grown to be the sixth largest publishing house in Germany and included what was called at the time an "artistic" or "graphic institute" (artistische or graphische Anstalt) that employed sixteen engravers, three draughtsmen, and twelve printers of visual images.[14] But if this ability to produce visual images suggests that Meyer had the plates engraved in Germany, how did his engravers gain access to the images in the first place? Even a recent biographer of Meyer, Peter Kaiser, comes to the conclusion that "the vast majority of the illustrations came from the workshop of the publisher."[15] And the pre-eminent historian of steel engraving, Basil Hunnisett, notes only that a few of the engravings include names of British engravers.[16]

Marsch, who, as mentioned above, compiled an exhaustive index of the images that appeared in *Meyer's Universum* (in all of its diverse incarnations), comes the closest to understanding Meyer's process. But even she, conducting her research in the 1970s without the benefit of the digital technologies and tools of today, could not gain a comprehensive overview of that process. She does point out that some of the images from *Meyer's Universum* are very similar

---

11 Armin Human, *Carl Joseph Meyer und das Bibliographische Institut von Hilburghausen-Leipzig: Eine kulturhistorische Studie* (Hildburghausen: Printed by F. W. Gadow & Wohn, 1896), 16.
12 Johannes Hohlfeld, *Das Bibliographische Institut: Festschrift zu seiner Jahrhundertfeier* (Leipzig: Bibliographisches Institut, 1926), 95. There is one quote from an elderly former employee of Meyer who mentions in passing in his reminiscence that "the plates were engraved in England," but Hohlfeld produces no further evidence for that claim or an indication from which engravers in England these plates had been supplied. Hohlfeld, *Das Bibliographische Institut*, 68.
13 Heinz Sarkowski, *Das Bibliographische Institut: Verlagsgeschichte und Bibliographie, 1826–1976* (Mannheim: Bibliographisches Institut, 1976), 48.
14 Sarkowski, *Das Bibliographische Institut*, 30.
15 "Die überwiegende Mehrzahl der Illustrationen aber stammte aus den Werkstätten des Instituts," Kaiser, *Der Pläneschmied*, 136.
16 Hunnisett, *Engraved on Steel*, 244–248.

to those in two works, *Heath's Picturesque annual for 1832* and *Illustrations of the Life and Works of Lord Byron*,[17] that appeared just a year earlier.[18] And, yet, without the mass of evidence that I have been able to assemble using digital tools, she hesitates to draw any conclusion about Meyer's method from this knowledge, even surmising that Meyer in some cases may have received the plates from British publishers (with permission to use them).[19] She also suggests that British publishers would not have minded if Meyer made copies of their work, since they had already "flooded" Germany with copies of them.[20] This conclusion, however, is at odds with her own admitted inability to find British landscape annuals in German library collections or for sale by antiquarian book dealers.[21] Marsch points out that Meyer's work itself was "imitated" by other publishers in Germany, but this does not lead her to suspect Meyer himself of untoward copying practices.[22]

Other historians also do not extrapolate from Meyer's other publishing practices to the *Universum*. Some acknowledge Meyer's anthologizing propensity, the system he established at the beginning of his career of borrowing existing material, repackaging it, and selling it as his own product in an era that lacked international copyright agreements. With regard to illustrations, however, Hohlfeld mentions only an "unfortunate" event of Meyer's work *Views of the Danube* (*Donau-Ansichten*) (1839–1840) not being successful because there was a "disagreement" about the source of the images.[23] Indeed, in this instance, Meyer had copied images from another illustrated work, but this time one published in Germany. Georg Lange, who had an established engraving institute in Darmstadt, charged Meyer with the unauthorized reproduction of

---

17 Marsch, *Meyer's Universum*, 39.
18 Marsch, *Meyer's Universum*, 43.
19 She writes, implying this may be been the case with Meyer, that the bankruptcy of publishers meant that their valuable engraved plates might have become available for purchase. Marsch, *Meyer's Universum*, 35.
20 Marsch, *Meyer's Universum*, 39.
21 Marsch, *Meyer's Universum*, 39.
22 She lists two examples: first, *Payne's Universum* that followed the same format and pricing as *Meyer's Universum* and was published in eight volumes from 1843 to 1850 first by Theodor Thomas publishers and then by Brain and Payne in Leipzig. Unlike *Meyer's Universum*, the texts in this work had no political tendency and the images were not limited to landscape and city scapes; and second, *Das kleine Universum der Erd-, Länder- und Völkerkunde* edited by A. Schiffner and published by the art publisher J. Scheible in Stuttgart in twelve installments per year with twelve engravings each, but in a much smaller 16mo format (approx. 4" x 6," as opposed to the octavo format of *Meyer's Universum* that was 10.5" x 7.5") and in four volumes only (1840–43). Marsch, *Meyer's Universum*, 47–48.
23 Hohlfeld, *Das Bibliographische Institut*, 100.

engravings from his work *Original Views of the Most Notable Cities of Germany (Original-Ansichten der vornehmsten Städte Deutschlands)* a serial that had begun publication in the early 1830s.[24]

Despite these details, none of the historians of Meyer or his firm draws the logical conclusion regarding the plates of *Meyer's Universum*, that from the outset they were almost exclusively copies of other works.[25] Even Hunnisett, who surely was familiar with the sources that Meyer used, British landscape annuals illustrated with steel engravings, only notes in a remarkable understatement: "not all the views were original."[26] Again, at the time these scholars were writing their histories, it would have been nearly impossible to track down these sources. Now, however, in the twenty-first century, ready access to digital copies of *Meyer's Universum* and to other illustrated works of the nineteenth century makes establishing the provenance of Meyer's steel engravings a puzzle that can be solved.

There are several main pieces to this puzzle and its solution. The first involves the extensive access to older works provided in recent decades by digital technology. The ability of academics to read nineteenth-century publications from their own computer desktops frees them from the need to travel to a range of collections in libraries or archives in order to view and study images in illustrated published works. Already in 2012 James Mussell pointed out that the large number of newspapers and periodicals to which scholars had access via the internet in archives hosted by Google Books and Hathitrust among others was altering the way scholars work in the field of periodical studies.[27] Mark Turner has elaborated on this idea pointing out that: "we are 'in touch' with the material base of nineteenth-century serial culture more than at any time since the nineteenth century, and perhaps even more than the nineteenth century itself ever actually was."[28]

---

[24] A notice published in the *Literarischer Anzeiger (Beilage zu den Blättern für literarische Unterhaltung)* in early 1840 asserted that all of Meyer's engravings were copied. As a result, Meyer had to halt the publication after 12 installments. Christine Milde, "Carl Joseph Meyers "Universum:" Ein Beitrag zur Geschichte der Publizistik des deutschen Vormärz" (PhD Dissertation, University of Leipzig, 1990), 177.

[25] Sarkowski says little about the plates of *Meyer's Universum* and nothing about where he thinks Meyer may have acquired the images to engrave. Sarkowski, *Das Bibliographische Institut*, 44–45.

[26] Hunnisett, *Engraved on Steel*, 245.

[27] Mussell argues that "the sheer amount of material that is now available to be read electronically alters the profile of the press in scholarly research and teaching." James Mussell, *The Nineteenth-Century Press in the Digital Age* (New York: Palgrave Macmillan, 2012), 28.

[28] Mark W. Turner, "The Unruliness of Serials in the Nineteenth Century (and in the Digital Age)," in *Serialization in Popular Culture*, ed. Rob Allen and Thijs van den Berg (London: Routledge, 2014), 12. This does not mean, however, that access is universal or even; holdings of

This phenomenon also allows for side-by-side comparison of works that a scholar might otherwise not be able to view at the same time due to their location in collections that are geographically far apart. An additional problem that traditionally has complicated the comparison of images is that, in some cases, the illustrations, in particular high-quality intaglio prints that were printed on separate pages within a work, have been removed from individual copies by previous users. Now the availability on-line of scans of copies from multiple holdings increases the likelihood that a scholar can gain access to a full set of images from any given work, even if some images are missing from the copy in one collection. On-line access can thus help fill in the common gaps in holdings in any one library collection. In other words, digital access to the holdings of multiple libraries significantly increases the ability to compare texts and images across time. For my investigation of the models for the engravings in *Meyer's Universum*, that advantage presents a fundamental change to research that has proven crucial.

A caveat is in order here, however: While the text in such scanned versions is generally readable, images often suffer from being scanned at a resolution so low that it prevents a detailed analysis of them. This is particularly problematic for scholars hoping to study elements that can reveal information about the production or the provenance of illustrations. The attributions on scans of *Meyer's Universum* from Google Books or Hathitrust, for example, are typically so blurry as to be very difficult to decipher (see Figure 4). The images show little detail when magnified; lines in the scans are faint, fuzzy, and run together and sometimes the pixilation produces a color pattern on the digitized image that was not in the original. It is often impossible to decipher the large captions let alone the much smaller text containing attributions for artist and engraver (see Figure 5).

---

digitized versions differ from one database to another, as does the percentage of a volume's scan that a user can see. Google Books, for example, provides access to the first volume of the Pfennig-Magazine (from May 1833) under https://books.google.com/books?id=QxAiAQAAMAAJ <accessed 21 December 2019>. Archive.org provides access to the first five issues of the first volume from 1843 of the *Illustrirte Zeitung* but without the volume (cover) and editor's foreword: https://archive.org/details/IllustrirteZeitung184301 <accessed 10 January 2020>. That volume was added on 6 January 2018. The catalog of Hathitrust indicates that that database provides access to scans from various libraries including the University of Chicago, the University of Michigan, the Ohio State University, and the University of Minnesota. The copies from the University of Minnesota, however, are available for "limited search only" and of the volumes originally published before 1878, only one volume (1861) is available for such limited searching: https://catalog.hathitrust.org/Record/000059400 <accessed 10 January 2020>. Scans of copies from the Pennsylvania State University holdings exist for some years in the twentieth century, but are also available for "limited search only." https://catalog.hathitrust.org/Record/012272518 <accessed 10 January 2020>.

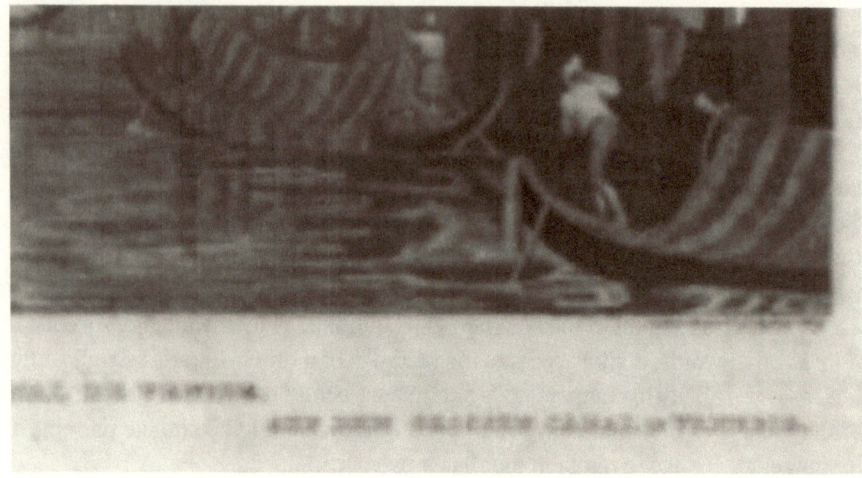

Figure 4: Poor visual quality of the scan makes it difficult to decipher the caption and attribution detials from "Auf dem Grossen Canal in Venedig," *Meyer's Universum*, vol. 1 (5th printing, 1834), plate II. Original in University of California Library. https://babel.hathitrust.org/cgi/pt?id=uc1.c3128882&view=1up&seq=17&size=175 Accessed 30 January 2019.

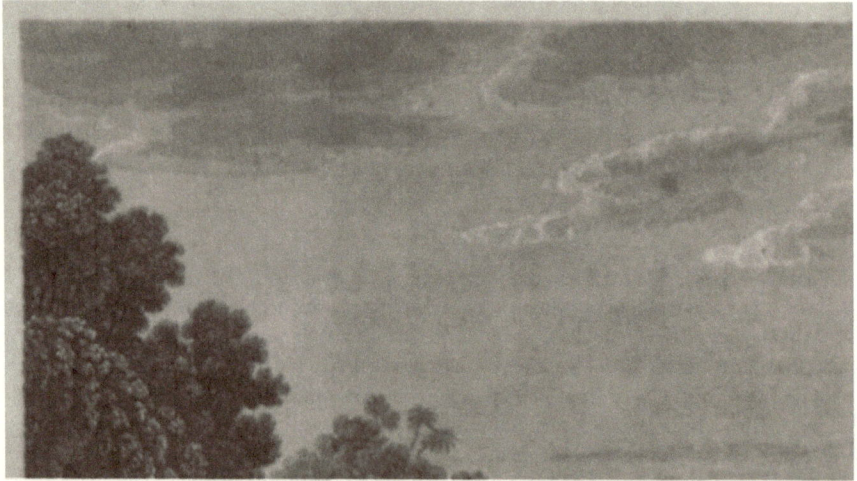

Figure 5: Low resolution makes it difficult to analyze (and thus compare) engraving techniques in digital scans such as this detail from "Die Seil Brücke (sic) bey Tiri," *Meyer's Universum*, vol. 2 (6th printing, 1835), plate L. Original in Princeton University Library. https://babel.hathitrust.org/cgi/pt?id=njp.32101064246513&view=1up&seq=6/ Accessed 30 January 2019.

In recent years, however, scans at much higher resolution and with much more consistent quality have become available at the websites of German academic institutions, such as the Münchner DigitalisierungsZentrum: Digitale Bibliothek of the Bayrische Staatsbibliothek digital and the Österreichische Nationalbibliothek.[29] These scans, typically made at a resolution of 300 dpi,[30] are clear enough for important parts of the research process. Yet, despite this clarity, for some key aspects of the analysis and comparison I conducted even they were not sufficient. Recourse to original print editions thus remains essential as I will discuss at the end of this argument.[31]

With extensive access to digital images of the steel engravings in *Meyer's Universum* available from on-line archives, I can (unlike Hohlfeld, Sarkowski, or Marsch) take advantage of another digital tool to search for sources: namely a "reverse image search engine." Such on-line search engines conduct rapid searches of enormous collections of images that have been uploaded onto the internet and are available for viewing by both human users and digital applications. Using visual algorithms, the reverse image search engine can compare a given image (that a user uploads into it) to the vast dataset of images on-line, looking for similarities in shapes, relative dimensions, and compositional elements (forms and lines) to find what it then will term a "match," an image that is highly similar. Given the

---

29 Digipress, the newspaper portal of the Münchner DigitalisierungsZentrum (Digitale Bibliothek) of the Bavarian State Library has color scans of the *Illustrirte Zeitung* beginning with the first issue: https://reader.digitale-sammlungen.de/de/fs1/object/display/bsb10498693_00009.html <accessed 10 January 2020>. The resolution is at least 300 dpi, presuming it is adhering to the minimal standards for scanning resolution established by the German Research Community (DFG), to which it provides a link (https://www.dfg.de/formulare/12_151/12_151_de.pdf). It does not, however, list an easily traceable record of details for the *Illustrirte Zeitung* scans. The Austrian National Library offers in its collection ANNO, Historische österreichische Zeitungen und Zeitschriften, access to high quality digital scans (that are not in full color, however) that are organized and accessible according to the date of each weekly issue. For example, the first issue is available at: http://anno.onb.ac.at/cgi-content/anno?aid=izl&datum=18430701&zoom=33. See also the discussion of these resources in Vance Byrd and Sean Franzel, "Introduction: Periodical Literature in the Nineteenth Century," *Colloquia Germanica* 49, nos. 2–3 (2016 [November 2018]): 106–107.
30 Email communication from Flora Dörögdy, Division of Digital Services. Austrian National Library, 16 January 2020.
31 As Ryan Cordell also reminds us, digitized copies are different objects from the three-dimensional works that were originally printed on paper. They are, indeed, new, distinct editions. Cordell's work, like that of others conducting word searches and data-mining, is particularly impacted by errors made during the optical character recognition (OCR) of scanned objects. While the project I am describing here does not include such searches, it is still important to "avoid the myth of surrogacy proffered by page images." Ryan Cordell, "'Q i-Jtb the Raven': Taking Dirty OCR Seriously," *Book History* 20 (2017): 188–225, here 190 and 193.

ready availability of the aforementioned high resolution digitized copies of *Meyer's Universum*, I had access to good quality scans of many of the work's steel engraved illustrations, from which I could create individual digital copies.[32] As long as each digital image was a relatively clean copy, i.e., one with the right proportions and appropriate alignment and that had not been scanned at odd angles or with any distortion from movement during the scanning process, for example, my copies would be reasonable approximations to use in a search for matches. I named each file to link it to the respective volume of *Meyer's Universum* in which it appeared, to its plate number, and to its title before uploading them one at a time into a reverse image search engine to look for matches.

It is important to note that some reverse image search engines are more useful and powerful in finding matches than others.[33] In the context of finding similar images, Google's reverse image search platform was not useful. First, it limits the types of file formats it accepts; it does not accept pdf files. Second, for the files I submitted (even those in accepted formats) it returned numerous inaccurate and misleading "matches." A search of an image of Eaton Hall in Cheshire from volume I of *Meyer's Universum*, for example, yielded the following only vaguely similar "hits" on "images.google.com" (see Figure 6).

By contrast, the application TinEye proved highly effective at finding eleven very close matches for the same image file (see Figure 7). The volume and processing speed of the two applications also vary. On 20 February 2020 TinEye boasted the ability to scan 39.7 billion images in 2.9 seconds in order to find those matches, whereas the Google reverse image search application scanned 4.7 billion images in .51 seconds.[34]

---

32 For the purpose of creating a digital copy of each illustration to upload into a reserve image search engine, it sufficed to take a cropped screen shot of the image as it was visible on the screen of my computer.

33 The website beebom.com (which is not secure) provides a ranking of the best reverse image search engines at https://beebom.com/reverse-image-search-engines-apps-uses/ <accessed 23 February 2020>. As will be apparent from the discussion below and for the research purpose described here, I consider TinEye to be the best.

34 There are numerous other commercial and scholarly uses of TinEye. For a few examples see Jason B. Jones, "Image Citation and Reverse Search with TinEye," *Chronicle of Higher Education*, 18 March 2011, https://www.chronicle.com/blogs/profhacker/image-citation-and-reverse-search-with-tineye/32013 <accessed 14 February 2018>. The software engineer John Resig has used TinEye's MatchEngine to analyze images of anonymous Italian art works and to correct merged photo databases in the photo archive (that contains over 1.2 million photos) of the Frick Art Reference Library. John Resig, "Using computer vision to increase the research potential of photo archives," a blog hosted on the TinEye website: https://services.tineye.com/solutions/JohnResigComputerVisionResearchPaperMatchEngine. <accessed 14 February 2018>.

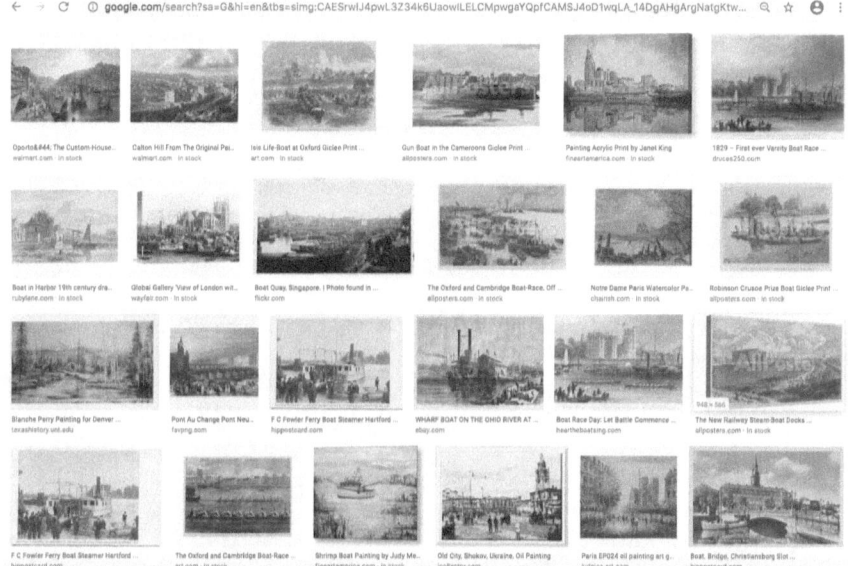

Figure 6: Screen shot of a search on Google Images for images comparable to a scan of the engraving "Eaton Hall" from *Meyer's Universum*, vol. 1 (1833), plate XX. Accessed 20 February 2020.

The success of such searches using TinEye, of course, depends on the presence of matches on the internet, i.e., on the extent to which others have uploaded well-scanned copies of images to publicly accessible websites. And, of course, not all of these "matches" will be helpful. Indeed, in conducting searches I have found that many, sometimes all, matches for one particular image file will be scans of images from *Meyer's Universum* itself. Due to the popular practice of subscribers of *Meyer's Universum* of separating the plates from their original textual context of the monthly part or annual volume, individual prints have long existed as items for display and distribution. Apparently, they were available for inheritance, gifting, and resale across the almost two centuries since they were originally published. Furthermore, the large number of copies originally printed by Meyer has ensured that many have survived into the twenty-first century.[35] As we

---

[35] Human, whose father worked for Joseph Meyer, writes that the serial had 80,000 subscribers without providing evidence for the claim. Human, *Carl Joseph Meyer*, 18. Marsch, however, as mentioned above, argues that prints, especially in early volumes, that reveal highly worn plates are evidence for an immense number of impressions having been made. Marsch, *Meyer's Universum*, 45.

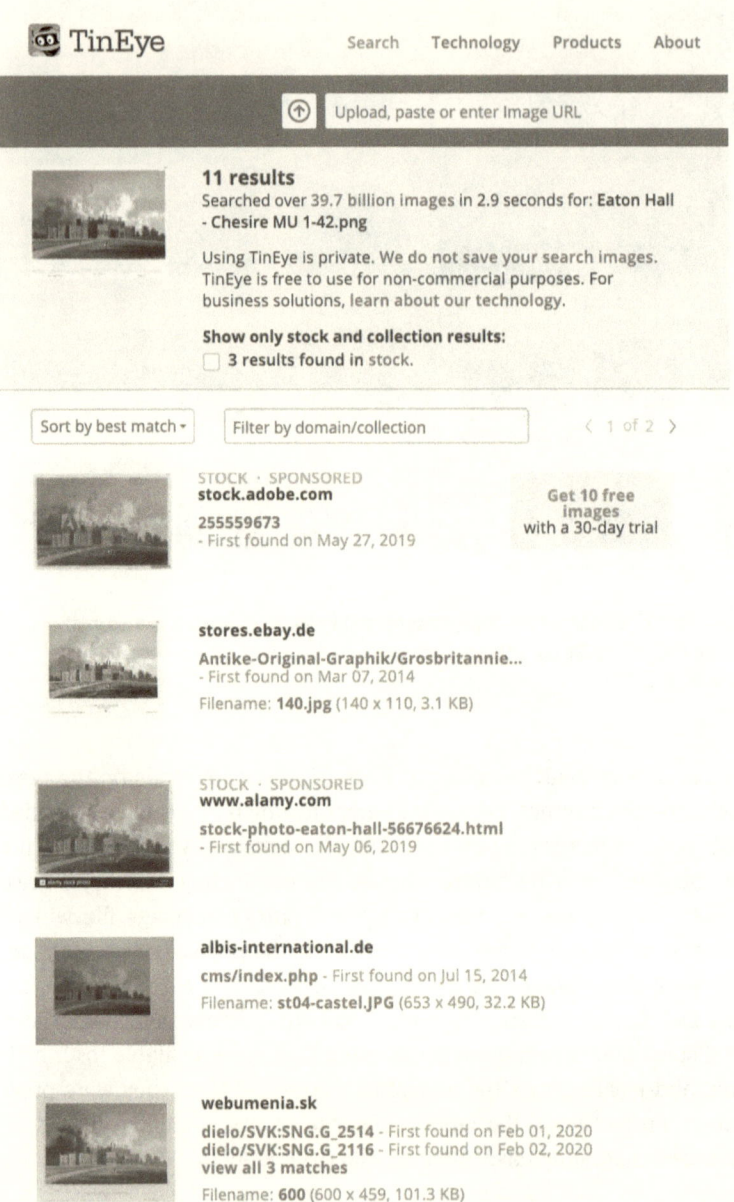

Figure 7: Screen shot of a search on TinEye for images comparable to a scan of the engraving "Eaton Hall" from *Meyer's Universum*, vol. 1 (1833), plate XX. Accessed 20 February 2020.

have already seen, the market for such images exists to the present day and the existence of internet sales platforms for private sellers (such as eBay) as well as for antiquarian art and book dealers means that copies have been digitized for the purpose of advertising their availability for purchase.

Of course, finding a matching image is only one step in the process of establishing what "source" Meyer might have used. The provenance of that match is crucial, especially any information regarding the date and place the matching image would have been originally produced and printed. TinEye provides a link to the URL where it finds each matching image. Sometimes, however, the link is no longer active, such as when the URL for the image (that might end in .png) leads to a file that was at one time on a seller's site but is no longer present there. Active links, by contrast, often lead to images that are still visible on the internet and that might be accompanied by descriptive information about the source site. Following a given link sometimes yields further information regarding the origins of the scanned image. But even then, in some instances, that information is limited, vague, or unreliable. In other cases a link to a site that is no longer maintained also leads to a dead end.

This long-lived market of nineteenth-century steel engravings was fascinating to discover, but when the "matches" that TinEye identified were simply other scans of plates from *Meyer's Universum*, my search led me in a circle, confirming that a scan of a plate from *Meyer's Universum* matched a scan from another copy of that same volume (or a later re-use of the same image in another work published by the Bibliographisches Institut), that was now for sale. The breakthrough came, however, in those rarer "matches" that contained provenance information related neither to *Meyer's Universum* itself nor to the Bibliographisches Institut in general.

Soon after I began my searching, I started to find, amid the profusion of *Meyer's Universum* "matches," and often lower down in the list of them, occasional images that were not connected to Meyer's own products, but rather to other sources. For example, the "match" for the "Natürliche Brücke in Virginien" (Natural Bridge in Virginia) (*Meyer's Universum* vol. 1, plate XXXV) led to a website that specializes in the sale of antique prints.[36] In such cases, the most useful descriptive information would include specific bibliographic details that could lead me directly to the original book in which the same image appeared. In the case of the "Natural Bridge in Virginia" the webpage includes the following information: "Antique Steel Engraving Published 1830–32 by Hinton, Simpkin & Marshall, London for *'The History and*

---

36 https://www.albion-prints.com/hinton-usa-1832-antique-print-natural-bridge-virginia-264024-p.asp <accessed 10 February 2019>.

Topography of the United States of America' by John H. Hinton." If the publication date of that book, as it was in this case (1830–1832), precedes the date in which the image was included in *Meyer's Universum* (in this case 1833), then I can be certain I have found the source for Meyer's engraving.

More often, however, especially when the relevant website is not from a professional art or book dealer, bibliographic details are scarce. This was the case, for example, when I uploaded a copy of the image "Havre" from *Meyer's Universum* vol. 4, plate CLII into TinEye. The application identified a match and the link to that image led me to the site of the Tate art museum in London.[37] While no book in which this engraving might have been published was listed there, the Tate page did provide the attribution to an artist, J. M. W. Turner, and an engraver, R. Wallis.[38] In such instances, additional searching for biographical information or collaborations of such persons can lead me to a title of a book with works by that artist or engraver. In the case of "Havre" it was a book entitled *Wanderings by the Seine* by Leitch Ritchie (1834), also known as *Turner's Annual Tour*.[39] I could establish the earliest date of publication using such on-line databases as WorldCat (OCLC) and library catalogues.

If it so happened that the published work in question had also (like *Meyer's Universum*) been digitized and included in open access holdings such as Google Books, Hathitrust or a major research library, then I was often able to visually confirm the precise location of the illustration in a volume that predated *Meyer's Universum*.[40] In most cases, I could also see a list of all plates of engravings included in the volume and look for image titles that seemed similar to those of other images that appeared in volumes of *Meyer's Universum*. A visual comparison of the respective prints in scanned versions of the source text and in the relevant volume of *Meyer's Universum* could confirm additional instances of borrowing that might not be found using TinEye. Using this process of beginning with digitally scanned sources, creating digital image files, then consulting an on-line search engine, websites, databases, and again

---

[37] See http://www.tate.org.uk/art/images/work/T/T05/T05728_8.jpg <accessed 24 April 2016>.
[38] https://www.tate.org.uk/art/artworks/turner-havre-tower-of-francis-i-engraved-by-r-wallis-t06223 <accessed 24 April 2016>.
[39] Leitch Ritchie, *Wanderings by the Seine*, with twenty engravings from drawings by J. M. W. Turner (London: Longman, Rees, Orme, Brown, Green, and Longman, 1834).
[40] This is not always possible. For example, the engravings are missing from the sole digitized copy of Ritchie's *Wanderings by the Seine*, mentioned above, available via Hathitrust: https://babel.hathitrust.org/cgi/pt?id=nyp.33433066647367&view=image&seq=7&q1=17 <accessed 21 December 2018>.

perusing digitally scanned sources, I was able to confirm the original versions of almost all 200 illustrations that appeared in the first four volumes of *Meyer's Universum*.[41]

What were these sources? My sleuthing discovered that, to a work, they were all published in England and consisted of three kinds of publications. The main type was landscape annuals that focused on one particular region of Britain or a tour of other regions of Europe, typically following the route of a river (such as the Seine or the Rhine), or presenting a specific area (such as Northern Italy).[42] Another kind of source, in this case for images of North America, was a topographical survey of the United States.[43] A third kind that included images from southern Europe, the Middle East, and northern Africa was a set of illustrations meant to accompany a complete edition of the works of Lord Byron or volumes presenting images from India or China.[44]

What can we learn from this? As I have argued elsewhere, the fact that England was one of the few places in Europe in which Meyer did not attempt to market his *Universum*, suggests not, as Marsch and others have argued, that Meyer had permission or at a minimum encountered no objections from English publishers in reproducing their images.[45] Rather it indicates that he wisely chose not to distribute his work in the country where all of the images were originally produced and included in published works. A comparison of the plates also reveals that Meyer systematically removed attributions for the artist who made the on-site sketch and the engraver who first transformed

---

41 In a different context I have elaborated in detail on the small, but important differences between the "originals" and the engraved illustrations as they appeared in *Meyer's Universum* that prove that the images were re-engraved, and not printed from purchased or rented plates as Marsch and others have suggested. Kirsten Belgum, "Serialized Landscapes: Joseph Meyer and the Transnational Print Market, 1833–1856," a paper presented at a symposium entitled "Romantic Prints on the Move," at the Philadelphia Museum of Art, 2 February 2019.
42 Just three examples of British landscape annuals from which *Meyer's Universum* reproduced steel engravings that had appeared in the years before it began are: *Great Britain Illustrated: A Series of Original Views* from Drawings by William Westall, A.R.A. engraved by, and under the direction of, Edward Finden, with descriptions by Thomas Moule (London: Charles Tilt, 1830); *Travelling sketches in the North of Italy, the Tyrol, and on the Rhine*, with twenty-six beautifully finished engravings from drawings by Clarkson Stanfield, Esq., by Leitch Ritchie, Esq. (London: Longman, Rees, Orme, Brown, and Green, 1832); and *Tombleson's Views of the Rhine*, ed. W. G. Fearnside (London: W. Tombleson & Co., 1832).
43 John Howard Hinton, ed., *The History and Topography of the United States of America*, 2 vols. (London: Jennings & Chaplin & I. T. Hinton, 1830–1832).
44 *Finden's Landscape Illustrations to Mr. Murray's First Complete and Uniform Edition of the Life and Works of Lord Byron*, vol. 1, [in parts] (London: John Murray, 1832).
45 Belgum, "Serialized Landscapes."

that drawing onto a printable plate, attributions that were present in the earlier English publications.

But here we come to instances in which the scholar of nineteenth-century printed illustrations encounters the limits of digital tools. A detailed examination of original paper copies of the works discussed here reveals differences between the illustrations in the British works and those in *Meyer's Universum* that is not always apparent from a comparison of digital copies. For one thing, it is easier (sometimes with the aid of magnification of the originals) to see not only the omission or replacement of attributions when compared to the British prints, but also changes in the images themselves. Magnification of the printed originals can reveal relevant information about Meyer's production process. For example, it shows that each of Meyer's images included a significant amount of etching in addition to some engraving.

In engraving, sharp and very fine metal tools called burins are pushed along the surface of the steel plate to remove each line that should eventually appear in printing (during the inking process ink was left in those minute grooves to be transferred to the paper under the pressure of printing). This work is difficult, laborious, and time consuming. In the etching process, by contrast, a thin film was applied to the metal plate and then removed with fine metal tools. After the desired lines of the film were removed the plate was immersed in an acid bath that etched those same lines into the plate chemically. Etching was, as a result, a much faster and thus more economical process of creating or finishing the steel plate.[46] There is a perceptible difference between engraved lines (that have pointed ends due to the onset and conclusion of pressure from the burin) and etched lines (that have duller or more rounded ends due to the use of acid to make the indentation in the plate).[47] But this difference can only be seen on originals and usually under significant magnification (6x or higher). This distinction is lost in digitally scanned copies.

In addition to being limited by scanning resolution quality, digital copies provide no detailed information about the dimensions of an image or the size of the original metal plate from which images were printed (even if detailed bibliographic information available on the digital site provides the approximate dimensions of the work as a whole). Engagement with the printed copy, by contrast, allows for comparisons such as of the identification of plate marks, the slight indentation in the paper left by the edges of the metal plate during printing. These can be visually perceived or sometimes felt by touch on the

---

[46] Hunnisett, *Engraved on Steel*, 190.
[47] Gascoigne, *How to Identify Prints*, section 12b.

paper surface. A comparison of such dimensions (between copies of the British landscape annuals or topographical works and *Meyer's Universum*) reveals an important piece in the answer to my initial puzzle. Different plate dimensions prove that Meyer did not borrow or purchase plates from British publishers. Rather Meyer must have had the images from the previous work re-engraved, most likely without any permission from the original publisher.

In sum, the use of numerous twenty-first century tools is essential to tracking down the sources that Joseph Meyer used to create his highly successful illustrated serial *Meyer's Universum*. Without them it would be nearly impossible to locate and to access the range of images he and his son printed across three decades, like hunting for needles in a haystack. Scans, a reverse search engine, the plethora of images loaded up onto the internet from commercial, private, and professional users, and databases that confirm bibliographic information all enabled me to sleuth backwards to locate the sources for Meyer's images. This digital research has exposed Meyer's strategic attempt to monetize existing images of places from around the world, to remove them from their original regional context, to shuffle them into an ostensibly global ("universal") project, and then to profit from the reproduction of an eclectic assemblage of images first published in England.[48] His process of using the visual work of others was not acknowledged and probably not authorized. The extent of his debt to others was possibly something his customers might not have even thought about, and surely something they could not have known. Powerful digital tools and resources from the twenty-first century can help us to uncover previously unrecognized aspects of the visual world that nineteenth-century readers and viewers experienced. But it is important to keep in mind that even with their help a definitive statement about Meyer's visual borrowing could not be completed without the historical works themselves, a true blending of twenty-first-century and nineteenth-century scholarship.

---

48 For some of the results of this research, see Kirsten Belgum, "Visualizing the World in *Meyer's Universum*," *Colloquia Germanica* 49, nos. 2–3 (2016 [November 2018]): 235–257.

Bibliography

Belgum, Kirsten. "Serialized Landscapes: Joseph Meyer and the Transnational Print Market, 1833–1856." Paper presented at a symposium entitled "Romantic Prints on the Move" at the Philadelphia Museum of Art, 2 February 2019.

Belgum, Kirsten. "Visualizing the World in *Meyer's Universum*." *Colloquia Germanica* 49, nos. 2–3 (2016 [November 2018]): 235–258.

Byrd, Vance, and Sean Franzel. "Introduction: Periodical Literature in the Nineteenth Century." *Colloquia Germanica* 49, nos. 2–3 (2016 [November 2018]): 105–118.

Cordell, Ryan. "'Q i-Jtb the Raven': Taking Dirty OCR Seriously." *Book History* 20 (2017): 188–225.

Dörögdy, Flora. Email communication on 16 January 2020. Division of Digital Services. Austrian National Library.

Finden's Landscape Illustrations to Mr. Murray's First Complete and Uniform Edition of the Life and Works of Lord Byron. Vol. 1. [in parts] London: John Murray, 1832.

Gascoigne, Bamber. *How to Identify Prints: A Complete Guide to Manual and Mechanical Process from Woodcut to Inkjet*. London: Thames & Hudson, 2014.

Great Britain Illustrated: A Series of Original Views from Drawings by William Westall, A.R.A. engraved by, and under the direction of, Edward Finden, with descriptions by Thomas Moule. London: Charles Tilt, 1830.

Hinton, John Howard, ed. *The History and Topography of the United States of America*. 2 vols. London: Jennings & Chaplin & I.T. Hinton, 1830–1832.

Hohlfeld, Johannes. *Das Bibliographische Institut: Festschrift zu seiner Jahrhundertfeier*. Leipzig: Bibliographisches Institut, 1926.

Human, Armin. *Carl Joseph Meyer und das Bibliographische Institut von Hilburghausen-Leipzig: Eine kulturhistorische Studie*. Hildburghausen: F. W. Gadow & Wohn, 1896.

Hunnisett, Basil. *Engraved on Steel: The History of Picture Production using Steel Plates*. Aldershot: Ashgate, 1998.

Jones, Jason B. "Image Citation and Reverse Search with TinEye." *Chronicle of Higher Education*. 18 March 2011. https://www.chronicle.com/blogs/profhacker/image-citation-and-reverse-search-with-tineye/32013. Accessed 19 December 2019.

Kaiser, Peter. *Der Pläneschmied: Das außergewöhnliche Leben des Verlegers Carl Joseph Meyer*. Leipzig: Salier, 2007.

Lee, Haimin. "15 Years of Google Books." 17 October 2019. https://www.blog.google/products/search/15-years-google-books/. Accessed 2 April 2020.

Marsch, Angelika. *Meyer's Universum: Ein Beitrag zur Geschichte des Stahlstiches und des Verlagswesens im 19. Jahrhundert*. Lüneburg: Nordostdeutsches Kulturwerk, 1972.

Meyer's Universum; oder, Abbildung und Beschreibung des Sehenswerthesten und Merkwürdigsten der Natur und Kunst auf der ganzen Erde. Hildburghausen: Bibliographisches Institut, 1833–1860.

Milde, Christine. "Carl Joseph Meyers 'Universum': Ein Beitrag zur Geschichte der Publizistik des deutschen Vormärz." PhD Diss., University of Leipzig, 1990.

Mussell, James. *The Nineteenth-Century Press in the Digital Age*. New York: Palgrave Macmillan, 2012.

Payne's Universum: Darstellung und Beschreibung der schönsten Gegenden, Städte und merkwürdigsten Baudenkmale auf der ganzen Erde, von Portraits ausgezeichneter Personen, volkstümlicher Scenen und Genrebildern. Leipzig: A. H. Payne, 1843.

Resig, John. "Using Computer Vision to Increase the Research Potential of Photo Archives." *TinEye*. https://services.tineye.com/solutions/JohnResigComputerVisionResearchPaperMatchEngine. Accessed 14 February 2018.

Ritchie, Leitch. *Wanderings by the Seine*, with twenty engravings from drawings by J. M. W. Turner. London: Longman, Rees, Orme, Brown, Green, and Longman, 1834.

Sarkowski, Heinz. *Das Bibliographische Institut: Verlagsgeschichte und Bibliographie, 1826–1976.* Mannheim: Bibliographisches Institut, 1976.

Schulman, Vanessa Meikle. *Work Sights: The Visual Culture of Industry in Nineteenth-Century America.* Amherst: University of Massachusetts Press, 2015.

Somers, James. "Torching the Modern-Day Library of Alexandria." *The Atlantic*. 20 April 2017. https://www.theatlantic.com/technology/archive/2017/04/the-tragedy-of-google-books/523320/. Accessed 2 April 2020.

Tombleson's Views of the Rhine. Edited by W. G. Fearnside. London: W. Tombleson, 1832.

Travelling Sketches in the North of Italy, the Tyrol, and on the Rhine, with twenty-six beautifully finished engravings from drawings by Clarkson Stanfield, Esq., by Leitch Ritchie, Esq. London: Longman, Rees, Orme, Brown, and Green, 1832.

Turner, Mark W. "The Unruliness of Serials in the Nineteenth Century (and in the Digital Age)." In *Serialization in Popular Culture*, edited by Rob Allen and Thijs van den Berg, 11–32. London: Routledge, 2014.

"Welcome to HathiTrust!" https://www.hathitrust.org/about. Accessed 2 April 2020.

Contributors

Matthew O. Anderson (andersmo227@gmail.com) is Visiting Instructor of German in the Department of Modern Languages, Literatures, and Linguistics at Luther College. His dissertation, "Bildung and Bilder? *Text, Illustration, and Adventure in Popular German Children's Books of the Early Nineteenth Century*," explores the intermedial and international nexes of visuality, genre formation, and reading practice in historical German youth adventure literature. Further academic interests include processes of genre creation, adaptation, and consumption; illustration and identity formation in children's and popular literature; and visual culture in Germany and Scandinavia.

Christian A. Bachmann (cb@edition-bachmann.de) is Research Associate (Wissenschaftlicher Mitarbeiter) in the research unit "Journal Literature" focusing on German humorous-satirical publications and US newspaper comic strips. His previous research has dealt with the materiality and mediality of comics, graphic novels, and artists' books, as well as German and American Literature from the nineteenth to the twenty-first century.

Kirsten Belgum (belgum@austin.utexas.edu) is Associate Professor in the Department of Germanic Studies at the University of Texas at Austin. Her research focuses on nineteenth-century German realism, popular culture, travel writing, gender studies, children's literature, transatlantic cultural transfer, and the history of the book. She is the author of *Interior Meaning: Design of the Bourgeois Home in the Realist Novel* and *Popularizing the Nation: Audience, Representation, and the Production of Identity in Die Gartenlaube, 1853–1900*. Her recent work examines the connection between text and illustration and the issue of transnational borrowing of visual images in *Globus* and *Meyer's Universum*.

John D. Benjamin (john.benjamin@westpoint.edu) is Assistant Professor of German in the Department of Foreign Languages at the United States Military Academy. His research focuses on second language multimodal reading practices, German comics, visual culture studies, and the Texas Polish language variety. Recent publications include "Relocating the Text: *Mosaik* and the Invention of a German East German Comics Tradition," which appeared in *The German Quarterly*, and "'Is' nicht egal': Guided Multimodal Reading of a Music Video Advertisement" in *Die Unterrichtspraxis*.

Trevor Brandt (tbrandt@uchicago.edu) is a Ph.D. student in art history at the University of Chicago as a Neubauer Family Distinguished Doctoral Fellow. Prior to this, he was the curator of the American Swedish Historical Museum in Philadelphia. In this role, he planned exhibitions on Nordic folk textiles, contemporary fine arts and climate change, orienteering and traditional Swedish navigation, and midcentury-modern Swedish glass. He received his MA from the Winterthur Museum's program in American Material Culture.

Vance Byrd (byrdvl@grinnell.edu) is Frank and Roberta Furbush Scholar and Associate Professor of German Studies at Grinnell College. His research investigates how literary and print history intersect with the history of visual media. Beyond his first book, *A Pedagogy of Observation: Nineteenth-Century Panoramas, German Literature, and Reading Culture*, Byrd co-edited *Market Strategies and German Literature*, and co-edited a journal issue on approaches to the first-publication of literature in periodicals. His articles have appeared in *German Studies Review*, *The German Quarterly*, *Seminar*, *The Germanic Review*, and *The Journal of Austrian Studies*. His second monograph, *Listening to Panoramas: Sonic and Visual Cultures of Commemoration*, is in preparation.

David Ciarlo (david.ciarlo@colorado.edu) is Associate Professor of Modern European History at the University of Colorado at Boulder. His first book, *Advertising Empire: Race and Visual Culture in Imperial Germany* explores the imagery of colonial rule and of racial difference in German visual culture between 1880 and 1910. His new project, *Selling War*, looks at advertising and propaganda from 1910 through 1923, tracing the visual and commercial roots of the fascist aesthetic.

Agnes Hoffmann (agnes.hoffmann@unibas.ch) is Postdoctoral Assistant in the German Department at the University of Basel. Her first book, *Landschaft im Nachbild*, focuses on landscape aesthetics in the literature of Henry James and Hugo von Hofmannsthal, visual arts, and anthropology around 1900. She is currently working on a monograph on drama and collective affects from the baroque to the present. Other publications include co-edited volumes on theatricality and revolt (*Theatrale Revolten*, with Annette Kappeler) and on "Darstellung" around 1800 in literature, science, and the visual arts (*Belebungskünste: Praktiken lebendiger Darstellung um 1800*, with Annette Kappeler and Nicola Gess).

Catriona MacLeod (cmacleod@uchicago.edu) is Frank Curtis Springer and Gertrude Melcher Springer Professor in the Department of Germanic Studies at the University of Chicago, where she is also affiliated with History of Art. Her research considers word and image studies and material culture in the context of German Classicism and Romanticism. In addition to her current book in progress, *Romantic Scraps: Cutouts, Collages, and Inkblots*, she has published *Embodying Ambiguity: Androgyny and Aesthetics from Winckelmann to Keller* and *Fugitive Objects: Lterature and Sculpture in the German Nineteenth Century*. Since 2011, she has been senior editor of the journal *Word & Image*.

Kathrin Maurer (kamau@sdu.dk) is Professor for Humanities and Technology at the University of Southern Denmark. Her research areas include art about surveillance, drone technology, visual culture, and nineteenth-century German literature. She has published *Visualizing War: Emotions, Technology, Communities*; *Visualizing History: The Power of the Image in German Historicism*; and *Discursive Interaction: Literary Realism and Academic Historiography in Nineteenth-century Germany*. She has published articles on drone warfare, culture, and art and the aerial perspective in nineteenth-century culture. She leads the research cluster *Drone Imaginaries and Communities* and the network *Drones and Aesthetics* (sponsored by the Danish Research Council).

Peter M. McIsaac (pmcisaac@umich.edu) is Associate Professor of German Studies und Museum Studies at the University of Michigan. His research focuses on the intersections of literature and museums, the cultural history of popular anatomical exhibitions, and digital analyses of German-speaking monthly magazines. He has authored *Museums of the Mind: German Modernity and the Dynamics of Collecting* and co-edited *Exhibiting the German Past: Museums, Film, and Musealization* (with Gabriele Müller). His articles have appeared in

German Studies Review, The German Quarterly, Seminar, Monatshefte, Literatur für Leser, German Life and Letters, and *The International Journal of Cultural Policy*.

Antje Pfannkuchen (pfannkua@dickinson.edu) is Associate Professor in the Department of German at Dickinson College in Pennsylvania and a 2020–2021 Burkhardt Fellow at Johns Hopkins University. She studies the relationships of media-technology, science, literature, and art, especially in the late eighteenth and early nineteenth centuries. She has published on Georg Christoph Lichtenberg, Johann Kaspar Lavater, Johann Wilhelm Ritter and on German approaches to cultural and media histories. Most recently she co-edited "The Technological Introject: Friedrich Kittler between Implementation and the Incalculable." She is working on a book manuscript tracing the connections between Romanticism and the invention of photography.

J. P. Short (jshort@uga.edu) is Associate Professor of modern European history at the University of Georgia. He specializes in the cultural and social history of nineteenth- and twentieth-century Germany and continental Europe, as well as modern European imperialism. He is author of articles on the social, cultural, and visual history of German imperialism and the book *Magic Lantern Empire: Colonialism and Society in Germany*. He is currently at work on the history of global consciousness in nineteenth- and early twentieth-century Europe.

Bibliography

Ackermann, Marion, and Helmut Friedel. "Vorwort." In *Schattenrisse: Silhouetten und Cutouts*, edited by Marion Ackermann and Helmut Friedel, 6–23. Ostfildern-Ruit: Hatje Cantz, 2001.
Ades, Dawn. "Collage: A Brief History." In *About Collage*, edited by Peter Blake, 37–43. London: Tate Gallery, 2000.
Adey, Peter. *Aerial Life: Spaces, Mobilities, Affects*. Chichester: John Wiley & Sons, 2010.
Adreß und Preisverzeichniß, 1866–1872. LRBC, MS 0013, Box 24. RRL, CMoG, Corning, New York.
Ahmed, Sara. *Queer Phenomenology: Orientations, Objects, Others*. Durham, NC: Duke University Press, 2006.
Alpers, Svetlana, Emily Apter, Carol Armstrong, Susan Buck-Morss, Tom Conley, Jonathan Crary, Thomas Crow et al. "Visual Culture Questionnaire." *October* 77 (Summer 1996): 25–70.
Altick, Richard. *The English Common Reader: A Social History of the Mass Reading Public, 1800–1900*. 2nd ed. Columbus: Ohio State University Press, 1998.
Andersen, Hans Christian. "Aunty Toothache." In *Hans Christian Andersen: The Complete Stories*, translated by Jean Hersholt, 893–902. London: British Library, 2005.
Andersen, Hans Christian. "The Shirt Collar." In *Hans Christian Andersen: The Complete Stories*, translated by Jean Hersholt, 318–319. London: British Library, 2005.
Andersen, Jens. "The Man Who Wrote with Scissors." In *Cut-Outs and Cut-Ups: Hans Christian Andersen and William Seward Burroughs*, edited by Hendel Teicher, 141–148. Dublin: Irish Museum of Modern Art, 2008.
Anderson, Catherine E. "A Zulu King in Victorian London: Race, Royalty and Imperialist Aesthetics in Late Nineteenth-Century Britain." *Visual Resources* 24, no. 3 (2008): 299–319.
Anderson, Matthew O. "Bildung and Bilder? Text, Illustration, and Adventure in Popular German Children's Books of the Early Nineteenth Century." PhD diss., University of Texas at Austin, 2019.
Anderson, Patricia. *The Printed Image and the Transformation of Popular Culture, 1790–1860*. Oxford: Clarendon, 1991.
Anonymous. "Laterna magica-Bilder mit Citatenaufguß." *Die Glühlichter* 3, no. 68 (25 June 1892): 4.
Anonymous. "Locus Sigilli." *Kladderadatsch* 28, no. 18 (18 April 1875): title page.
Anonymous. "Mikroskopische Studien." *Figaro* 16, nos. 52–53 (16 November 1872): 209.
Anonymous. Review of *Witiko*, by Adalbert Stifter. *Europa: Chronik der gebildeten Welt* 31 (1865): 497–499.
"Aquarium," *Das Buch der Welt* (1866), 360. LRBC, MS 0013, Box 13. RRL, CMoG, Corning, New York.
Arndt, Susan, and Antje Hornscheidt, eds. *Afrika und die deutsche Sprache: Ein kritisches Nachschlagewerk*. Münster: Unrast, 2004.
Assmann, Aleida, and Jan Assmann. *Hieroglyphen: Stationen einer anderen abendländischen Grammatologie*. Munich: Wilhelm Fink, 2003.
Assmann, Jan. *Das verschleierte Bild zu Sais, Schillers Ballade und ihre griechischen und ägyptischen Hintergründe*. Stuttgart: Teubner, 1999.

Bach, Jeff. *Voices of the Turtledoves: The Sacred World of Ephrata*. University Park: Pennsylvania State University Press, 2003.

Bachmann. Christian A. *Bilder/Rahmen: Rahmungen in visueller Satire, Bildergeschichte und Comic um 1900*. Hanover: Wehrhahn, 2018.

Bachmann, Christian A. *Macht der Musik: Musik in Karikatur, Bildergeschichte und Comic, 1830–1930*. Berlin: Ch. A. Bachmann, 2017.

Baldwin, Thomas. *Airopaidia*. London: J. Flechter, 1786.

Bär, Gerald. "Poetische Perspektiven aus dem (Fessel) Ballon: Das Jahrhundertereignis als Eventcharakter und seine Fiktionalisierung." In *Transit oder Transformation? Sprachliche und Literarische Grenzerfahrungen: Yearbook of the German Studies Association in Ireland*, edited by Sabine Egger, 29–48. Konstanz: Hartung-Gorre, 2016.

Barker, Martin, and Roger Sabin. *The Lasting of the Mohicans: History of an American Myth*. Jackson: University Press of Mississippi, 1995.

Baudelaire, Charles. "Salon de 1848." In *Curiosités esthétiques*. Vol. 2 of *Œuvres complètes de Charles Baudelaire*, 77–198. Paris: Calmann-Lévy, 1868.

Baumgartner, Andreas. "Das Große und Kleine in der Natur." In *Österreichischer Volks- und Wirtschafts-Kalender für das Jahr 1860*, 3–11. Vienna: Prandel & Ewald, 1860.

Bayerisches Hauptstaatsarchiv, MK 11328. Universität München, Titelverleihung "Universitätsplastiker" an Emil Hammer in München.

Bayerisches Hauptstaatsarchiv, Plakatsammlung. Kultur- und Werbeplakate bis 1945. Ausstellung von Emil Eduard Hammer zu kriegsbedingten Schußverletzungen während des Ersten Weltkrieges in München, 22387.

Becker, Frank. ed. *Rassenmischehen – Mischlinge – Rassentrennung: Zur Politik der Rasse im deutschen Kolonialreich*. Stuttgart: Steiner, 2004.

Begemann, Christian. "Metaphysik und Empirie: Konkurrierende Naturkonzepte im Werk Adalbert Stifters." In *Wissen in Literatur im 19. Jahrhundert*, edited by Lutz Danneberg and Friedrich Vollhardt, 92–126. Tübingen: Max Niemeyer, 2002.

Begley, Adam. *The Great Nadar: The Man behind the Camera*. New York: Tim Duggan Books, 2017.

Behler, Ernst. *Ironie und Literarische Moderne*. Paderborn: Ferdinand Schöningh, 1997.

Behringer, Wolfgang, and Constance Ott-Koptschalijski. *Der Traum vom Fliegen: Zwischen Mythos und Technik*. Frankfurt am Main: Fischer, 1991.

Beier-de-Haan, Rosemarie, and Jan Werquet, eds. *Fremde? Bilder von den "Anderen" in Deutschland und Frankreich seit 1871*. Dresden: Deutsches Historisches Museum, 2009.

Belgum, Kirsten. *Popularizing the Nation: Audience, Representation, and the Production of Identity in "Die Gartenlaube," 1853–1900*. Lincoln: University of Nebraska Press, 1998.

Belgum, Kirsten. "Popularizing the World: Karl Andree's *Globus*." *Colloquia Germanica* 46, no. 3 (2013 [2016]): 245–265.

Belgum, Kirsten. "Serialized Landscapes: Joseph Meyer and the Transnational Print Market, 1833–1856." Paper presented at a symposium entitled "Romantic Prints on the Move" at the Philadelphia Museum of Art, 2 February 2019.

Belgum, Kirsten. "Visualizing the World in *Meyer's Universum*." *Colloquia Germanica* 49, nos. 2–3 (2016 [November 2018]): 235–258.

Benjamin, John D. "Reading the German Graphic Novel: Understanding Learners' Readings of Multimodal Literary Comics." PhD diss., University of Texas at Austin, 2019.

Benjamin, John D. "Relocating the Text: *Mosaik* and the Invention of a German East German Comics Tradition." *The German Quarterly* 92, no. 2 (Spring 2019): 148–165.

Benjamin, Walter. *Berliner Kindheit um neunzehnhundert*. Frankfurt am Main: Suhrkamp, 2000.
Benjamin, Walter. "Old Forgotten Children's Books." In *Selected Writings*, edited by Marcus Bullock and Michael W. Jennings, 406–413. Cambridge, MA: Harvard University Press, 1996.
Benjamin, Walter. "Das Pult." In *Berliner Kindheit um 1900*, in vol. 4.1 of *Gesammelte Schriften*, edited by Rolf Tiedemann and Hermann Schweppenhäuser, 280–282. Frankfurt am Main: Suhrkamp, 1974.
Benjamin, Walter. "Stifter." In vol. 2.2 of *Gesammelte Schriften*, edited by Rolf Tiedemann and Hermann Schweppenhäuser, 608–610. Frankfurt am Main: Suhrkamp, 1991.
Benjamin, Walter. "The Work of Art in the Age of Mechanical Reproduction." In *Illuminations: Essays and Reflections*, edited by Hannah Arendt and translated by Harry Zohn, 217–251. New York: Schocken Books, 1968.
Benner, Enos. "Geistlicher Irrgarten," *Der Bauernfreund*. Sumneytown, PA, 15 August 1832.
Benrath, H. *Hamburg und Umgebungen*. Berlin: Albert Goldschmidt, 1895.
Benson, Richard, ed. *The Printed Picture*. New York: Museum of Modern Art, 2008.
Berger, Gustav A. "Conservation of the Atlanta Cyclorama." In *Conservation within Historic Buildings*, 155–161. London: International Institute for Conservation, 1980.
Berger, John. *Ways of Seeing*. London: Penguin, 1972.
"Bericht der Ortsgruppe Hirschberg." *Mitteilungen der DGBG* 10 (1912): 80.
Bericht über die Mittheilungen von Freunden der Naturwissenschaft in Wien 6, no. 2, edited by Wilhelm Haidinger. Vienna: Wilhelm Braumüller, 1848.
"Berichtigung." *Deutsche Kolonialzeitung* 3, no. 8 (1886): 254–255.
Bezold, Friedrich. "Drei plastische Modelle des menschlichen Gehörorgans." *Archiv für Ohrenheilkunde* 78 (1908): 262–264.
Blaschka, Leopold. Business card, n. d. LRBC, MS 0013, Box 22. RRL, CMoG, Corning, New York.
Blaschka, Leopold. Catalogue ("Wenig bekannte Seethiere"), n. d. DF ZOO/200/1/169, Library and Archives, NHML.
Blaschka, Leopold. Preface, Katalog über Blaschka's Modelle von wirbellosen Thieren dargestellt von Leopold Blaschka in Dresden. Dresden: Leopold Blaschka, 1885.
Blaschka, Leopold to R. T. Smith, Weymouth, draft, 25 December 1882, notebook of draft correspondence, 1880–1885. LRBC, MS 0013, Box 23. RRL, CMoG, Corning, NY.
Blaschka, Leopold to R. T. Smith, Weymouth, draft, 1 March (1886?), notebook, 1886–87. LRBC, MS 0013, Box 23. RRL, CMoG, Corning, NY.
Blaschka, Leopold to R. T. Smith, Weymouth, draft, n. d. (late March 1886?), notebook, 1886–87. LRBC, MS 0013, Box 23. RRL, CMoG, Corning, NY.
Blaschka, Rudolf. Hosterwitz to George Lincoln Goodale, Harvard University, draft, n. d. LRBC, MS 0013, Box 21, Folder 51. RRL), CMoG, Corning, NY.
Blaschka, Rudolf. Hosterwitz to Professor George Lincoln Goodale, Cambridge, 6 January 1896 (photocopy). LRBC, MS 0013, Box 21, Folder 12. RRL, CMoG, Corning, NY.
The BLOCK Reader in Visual Culture. New York: Routledge, 1996.
Böhme, Hartmut. *Natur und Figur: Goethe im Kontext*. Paderborn: Wilhelm Fink, 2016.
Bowersox, Jeff. *Raising Germans in the Age of Empire: Youth and Colonial Culture, 1871–1914*. Oxford: Oxford University Press, 2013.
Bradshaw, Michael. "Hedgehog Theory: How to Read a Romantic Fragment Poem." *Literature Compass* 5, no. 1 (2008): 73–89.

Brain, Robert Michael, R. S. Cohen, and Ole Knudsen. *Hans Christian Ørsted and the Romantic Legacy in Science: Ideas, Disciplines, Practices*. Boston Studies in the Philosophy of Science. Dordrecht: Springer, 2007.

Brandt, Trevor. "Perplexion and Pleasure: The *Geistlicher Irrgarten* Broadsides in the German-American Printshop, Home, and Mind." MA thesis, The University of Delaware, 2017. The University of Delaware Library (1015314042). http://udspace.udel.edu/handle/19716/21797.

Bratanek, Friedrich Theodor. "Adalbert Stifter: Eine literarhistorische Skizze." *Österreichische Revue* 6 (1863): 62–76.

Brecht, Bertolt. "Lux in Tenebris." In vol. 1 of *Werke*, edited by Werner Hecht, Jan Knopf, Werner Mittenzwei, and Klaus-Detlef Müller, 291–308. Berlin: Aufbau, 1989.

Brodersen, Silke. "Phänomenale Wirklichkeit und Naturgesetz in Hermann von Helmholtz' populärwissenschaftlichen Schriften und in Adalbert Stifters 'Sanftem Gesetz.'" In *Turns und Trends der Literaturwissenschaft zwischen Nachmärz und Jahrhundertwende im Blickfeld aktueller Theoriebildung*, edited by Christian Meierhofer and Eric Scheufler, 205–221. Zurich: germanistik.ch, 2011.

Brown, Matthew. *The Pilgrim and the Bee: Reading Rituals and Book Culture in Early New England*. Philadelphia: University of Pennsylvania Press, 2007.

Brown, Robert. *Peoples of the World Being a Popular Description of the Characteristics, Manners, and Customs of the Human Family*. Vol. 2. London: Cassell, Petter & Galpin, 1882.

Brown, Robert. *The Races of Mankind*. London: Cassell, Petter & Galpin, 1873–1876.

Brüggemann, Heinz. "Luftbilder eines kleinstädtischen Jahrhunderts: Ekstase und imaginäre Topographie in Jean Paul: 'Des Luftschiffers Giannozzo Seebuch.'" In *Die Stadt in der europäischen Romantik*, edited by Gerhard von Graevenitz, 127–182. Würzburg: Königshausen & Neumann, 2000.

Brunner, Bernd. *The Ocean at Home: An Illustrated History of the Aquarium*. New York: Princeton Architectural Press, 2003.

Buddemeier, Heinz. *Panorama, Diorama, Photographie*. Munich: Wilhelm Fink, 1970.

Budge, E. A. Wallis (Ernest Alfred Wallis). *The Gods of the Egyptians; or, Studies in Egyptian Mythology*. Vol. 1. London: Methuen, 1904.

Burke, Edmund. *A Philosophical Enquiry into the Origin of our Ideas of the Sublime and the Beautiful*. Cambridge: Cambridge University Press, 2014.

Buschhoff, Anne, and Detlef Stein, eds. *Hans Christian Andersen: Poet mit Feder und Schere*. Bremen: Wienand, 2018.

Byrd, Vance. "Covering the Wound: Panorama Exhibitions and Handmade History." *Seminar* 51, no. 1 (2015): 10–27.

Byrd, Vance. *A Pedagogy of Observation: Nineteenth-Century Panoramas, German Literature, and Reading Culture*. Lewisburg, PA: Bucknell University Press, 2017.

Byrd, Vance, and Sean Franzel. "Introduction: Periodical Literature in the Nineteenth Century." *Colloquia Germanica* 49, nos. 2–3 (2016 [November 2018]): 105–118.

Campe, Rüdiger. "Die Schreibszene: Schreiben." In *Paradoxien, Dissonanzen, Zusammenbrüche: Situationen offener Epistemologie*, edited by Hans Ulrich Gumbrecht and Ludwig Pfeiffer, 759–772. Frankfurt am Main: Suhrkamp, 1991.

Champion, Erik, and Bharat Dave. "Dialing up the Past." In *Theorizing Digital Cultural Heritage*, edited by Fiona Cameron and Sarah Kenderine, 333–347. Cambridge, MA: MIT Press, 2007.

Chladni, Ernst Florens Friedrich. *Die Akustik: Mit 12 Kupfertafeln.* Leipzig: Breitkopf & Härtel, 1802.
Chladni, Ernst Florens Friedrich. *Entdeckungen über die Theorie des Klanges.* Leipzig: Bey Weidmanns Erben und Reich, 1787.
Der Christlich Irrgarten, 1607 (Gebhardt Grieb, Stuttgart 1607), Bavarian State Archives Germany, Einblatt XI722.
Chute, Hillary. *Disaster Drawn: Visual Witness, Comics, and Documentary Form.* Cambridge, MA: Belknap, 2016.
Ciarlo, David. *Advertising Empire: Race and Visual Culture in Imperial Germany.* Cambridge, MA: Harvard University Press, 2011.
Cliché-Katalog. Berlin: Leonhard Simion, 1885.
Coen, Deborah R. *Climate in Motion: Science, Empire, and the Question of Style.* Chicago: University of Chicago Press, 2018.
Comment, Bernard. *The Panorama*. Translated by Anne-Marie Glasheen. London: Reaktion Books, 1999.
Conrad, Sebastian. *Globalisierung und Nation im Deutschen Kaiserreich.* Munich: Beck, 2006.
Conrad, Sebastian. *Globalization and the Nation in Imperial Germany.* Cambridge: Cambridge University Press, 2014.
Conrad, Sebastian. *What Is Global History?* Princeton: Princeton University Press, 2016.
Conrad, Sebastian, and Jürgen Osterhammel, eds. *Das Kaiserreich transnational: Deutschland in der Welt, 1871–1914.* Göttingen: Vandenhoeck & Ruprecht, 2004.
Cooper, James Fenimore. *J. F. Cooper's Amerikanische Romane, neu aus dem Englischen übertragen: Zweiter Band; Der Pfadfinder oder das Binnenmeer.* 4th ed. Translated by Dr. C. Kolb. Stuttgart: Hoffmann'sche Verlags-Buchhandlung, 1853.
Cooper, James Fenimore. *J. F. Cooper's Amerikanische Romane, neu aus dem Englischen übertragen: Zwölfter Band; Der Wildtödter.* 4th ed. Stuttgart: Hoffmann'sche Verlags-Buchhandlung, 1853.
Cooper, James Fenimore. *J. F. Cooper's Amerikanische Romane, neu aus dem Englischen übertragen: Achtzehnter Band; Miles Wallingfords Abenteuer zu Land und zur See.* 2nd ed. Translated by Eduard Mauch. Stuttgart: Hoffmann'sche Verlags-Buchhandlung, 1853.
Cooper, James Fenimore. *J. F. Cooper's Amerikanische Romane, neu aus dem Englischen übertragen: Neunzehnter Band; Lucy Hardinge, oder Miles Wallingfords Abenteuer zu Land und zur See, Zweiter Theil.* 2nd ed. Translated by Dr. Carl Kolb. Stuttgart: Hoffmann'sche Verlags-Buchhandlung, 1853.
Cooper, James Fenimore. *J. F. Cooper's Amerikanische Romane, neu aus dem Englischen übertragen: Dreißigster Band; Der Bienenjäger, oder die Eichen-Lichtungen.* Stuttgart: Hoffmann'sche Verlags-Buchhandlung, 1854.
Corbin, Alain. *The Lure of the Sea: The Discovery of the Seaside in the Western World, 1750–1840.* Berkeley: University of California Press, 1994.
Cordell, Ryan. "'Q i-Jtb the Raven': Taking Dirty OCR Seriously." *Book History* 20 (2017): 188–225.
Cosgrove, Daniel. *Apollo's Eye: A Cartographic Genealogy of the Earth in the Western Imagination.* Baltimore: John Hopkins University Press, 2001.
Crary, Jonathan. *Techniques of the Observer: On Vision and Modernity in the Nineteenth Century.* Cambridge, MA: MIT Press, 2012.
Cronau, Rudolf. *Das Buch der Reklame: Geschichte, Wesen und Praxis der Reklame.* Ulm: Wohler'schen, 1887.

Cronau, Rudolf. *Fahrten im Lande der Sioux*. Leipzig: Weigel, 1886.
Dahrendorf, Malte. "Lederstrumpf." In *Lexikon der Kinder- und Jugendliteratur: Zweiter Band; I-O*, edited by Klaus Doderer, 327–328. Weinheim: Beltz, 1977.
Daiber, Jürgen. *Experimentalphysik des Geistes: Novalis und das romantische Experiment*. Göttingen: Vandenhoeck & Ruprecht, 2001.
Darstellung der Anfertigung eines Schlachtenpanoramas. Photographic paper on canvas. 38 x 43 cm (15 x 17 in.). Stadtgeschichtliches Museum Leipzig. Inventar-Nr. f/7/2003.
Daston, Lorraine. "The Glass Flowers." In *Things That Talk: Object Lessons from Art and Science*, edited by Lorraine Daston, 223–254. New York: Zone, 2004.
Davis, Theodore R. "How a Battle Is Sketched." *St. Nicholas: An Illustrated Magazine for Young Folks* 16, no. 9 (1889): 661–668.
Davis, Theodore R. "How a Great Battle Panorama Is Made." *St. Nicholas: An Illustrated Magazine for Young Folks* 14, no. 2 (1886): 99–112.
Day, Lara, and Oliver Haag, eds. *The Persistence of Race: Continuity and Change in Germany from the Wilhelmine Empire to National Socialism*. New York: Berghahn, 2018.
Deleuze, Gilles, and Félix Guattari. *A Thousand Plateaus*. Translated by Brian Massumi. Minneapolis: University of Minnesota Press, 1993.
Derrida, Jacques. *Of Grammatology*. Translated by Gayatri Chakravorty Spivak. Baltimore: Johns Hopkins University Press, 1976.
Diez, Hermann. *Das Zeitungswesen*. Leipzig: Teubner, 1910.
Dikovitskaya, Margaret. "Major Theoretical Frameworks in Visual Culture." In *The Handbook of Visual Culture*, edited by Ian Heywood and Barry Sandywell, 68–89. New York: Berg, 2012.
Dikovitskaya, Margaret. *Visual Culture: The Study of the Visual after the Cultural Turn*. Cambridge, MA: MIT Press, 2006.
Doderer, Klaus, and Peter Aley, eds. *Klassische Kinder- und Jugendbücher: Kritische Betrachtungen*. Weinheim: Beltz, 1969.
Dolmetsch, Christopher L. *The German Press of the Shenandoah Valley*. Columbia, SC: Camden House, 1984.
Doré, Gustave. *Dés-agréments d'un voyage d'agrément*. Paris: Féchoz & Letouzey, n.d.
Dorn, Thea. *Die Unglückseligen*. Munich: Albrecht Knaus, 2017.
Dörögdy, Flora. Email communication on 16 January 2020. Division of Digital Services. Austrian National Library.
Dorrian, Mark. "The Aerial View: Notes for a Cultural History." *Strates* 13 (2007): 1–17.
Dreesbach, Anna. *Gezähmte Wilde: Die Zurschaustellung "exotischer" Menschen in Deutschland 1870–1940*. Frankfurt am Main: Campus, 2005.
Dubbini, Renzo. *Geography of the Gaze in Early Modern Europe*. Chicago: University of Chicago Press, 2002.
"DWDS – Digitales Wörterbuch der deutschen Sprache." https://www.dwds.de/wb/Hieroglyphe. Accessed 5 February 2019.
Early Popular Visual Culture. 2003–present.
Earnest, Russell, and Corinne Earnest. *Flying Leaves and One-Sheets: Pennsylvania German Broadsides, Fraktur, and Their Printers*. New Castle, DE: Oak Knoll Books, 2005.
Earnest, Russell, and Corinne Earnest. *God Bless This House: The Printed House Blessings (Haus-Segen) of the Pennsylvania Germans, 1780–1921*. Clayton, DE: Russell D. Earnest, 2015.

Earnest, Russell, and Corinne Earnest. *Papers for Birth Dayes: Guide to the Fraktur Artists and Scriveners*. Albuquerque: Russell D. Earnest, 1989.
Ebenstein, Joanna. *The Anatomical Venus: Wax, God, Death, and the Ecstatic*. London: Thames & Hudson, 2016.
Eckert, Alfred. "Zur Geschichte der Ballonfahrt." In *Leichter als Luft: Zur Geschichte der Ballonfahrt*, edited by Bernard Korzus and Gisela Noehles, 13–128. Münster: Westfälisches Landesmuseum für Kunst und Kulturgeschichte, 1978.
Egger, Irmgard. "Lederstrumpf: ein deutsches Jugendbuch: Untersuchung zu den Bedingungen und Strukturen literarischer Transformation." PhD diss., University of Vienna, 1991.
Eich, Hans. "Bearbeitung von Texten für Kinder und Jugendliche." In *Lexikon der Kinder- und Jugendliteratur: Erster Band; A-H*, edited by Klaus Doderer, 119–120. Weinheim: Beltz, 1975.
Eickenrodt, Sabine. *Augen-spiel: Jean Pauls optische Metaphorik der Unsterblichkeit*. Göttingen: Wallstein, 2013.
Elkins, James. *Visual Studies: A Skeptical Introduction*. New York: Routledge, 2003.
Elkins, James, Sunil Manghani, and Gustav Frank, eds. *Farewell to Visual Studies*. University Park: Pennsylvania State University Press, 2015.
Ellenbrand, Petra. *Die Volksbewegung und Volksaufklärung gegen Geschlechtskrankheiten in Kaiserreich und Weimarer Republik*. Marburg: Görich und Weiershäuser, 1999.
Eloesser, Arthur. "Castan's Ende." *Frankfurter Zeitung*, 26 February 1922, 1.
"Emil Eduard Hammer. Zu seinem 70. Geburtstag." *Münchner Zeitung*, 1 October 1935. no page number. Stadtarchiv München, DE-1992-ZA-P-0180-21
Erb, Peter C., and W. Kyrel Meschter. "Schwenkfelders and the Preservation of Tradition." In *Schwenkfelders in America*, edited by Peter C. Erb, 189–201. Pennsburg, PA: Schwenkfelder Library, 1987.
Erben, Patrick. "(Re)Discovering the German-Language Literature of Colonial America." In *A Peculiar Mixture: German-Language Cultures and Identities in Eighteenth-Century North America*, edited by Jan Stievermann and Oliver Scheiding, 117–149. University Park: Pennsylvania State University Press, 2013.
Etzlstorfer, Hannes. "'Die Wolken, ihre Bildung [. . .] waren mir wunderbare Erscheinungen' (*Nachsommer*): Bemerkungen zu Adalbert Stifters Motivrepertoire als Landschaftsmaler." In *Sanfte Sensationen: Stifter 2005; Beiträge zum 200. Geburtstag Adalbert Stifters*, edited by Johann Lachinger, Regina Pintar, Christian Schachreiter, and Martin Sturm, 60–74. Linz: StifterHaus, 2005.
Eulner, Hans-Heinz. *Die Entwicklung der medizinischen Spezialfächer an den Universitäten des deutschen Sprachgebietes*. Stuttgart: Enke, 1970.
Evans, Jessica, and Stuart Hall. "What is Visual Culture?" In *Visual Culture: The Reader*, edited by Jessica Evans and Stuart Hall, 1–7. Thousand Oaks: Sage, 1999.
Ewen, Elizabeth. *Typecasting: On the Arts and Sciences of Human Inequality*. New York: Seven Stories, 2006.
Ewers, Hans-Heino. *Fundamental Concepts of Children's Literature Research: Literary and Sociological Approaches*. Translated by William J. McCann. New York: Routledge, 2009.
Fakiner, Nike. "The Spatial Rhetoric of Gustav Zeiller's Popular Anatomical Museum." *Dynamis* 36, no. 1 (2016): 47–72.
Fiege, Gertrud, ed. "Die Scherenschneiderin Luise Duttenhofer." Special issue, *Marbacher Magazin* 13 (1979).

Finden's Landscape Illustrations to Mr. Murray's First Complete and Uniform Edition of the Life and Works of Lord Byron. Vol. 1. [in parts] London: John Murray, 1832.
Findlen, Paula. *Possessing Nature: Museums, Collecting and Scientific Culture in Early Modern Italy.* Berkeley: University of California Press, 1994.
Finkelstein, H., E. Galewsky, and L. Halberstaedter. *Hautkrankheiten und Syphilis im Säuglings- und Kindesalter: Ein Atlas.* Berlin: Julius Springer, 1922.
Fintel, Wilhelm von. *Tschaka der große Zulukönig.* Hermannsburg: Missionshandlung, 1928.
Flavin, Francis. "The Adventurer-Artists of the Nineteenth Century and the Image of the American Indian." *Indiana Magazine of History* 98, no. 1 (2002): 1–29.
Fleming, Paul. *Exemplarity and Mediocrity: The Art of the Average from Bourgeois Tragedy to Realism.* Stanford: Stanford University Press, 2009.
Fleming, Paul. *The Pleasures of Abandonment: Jean Paul and the Life of Humor.* Würzburg: Königshausen & Neumann, 2006.
Fotoalbum mit Fotographien aus der Werkstatt Rudolf Pohl. Archiv des Deutschen Hygiene-Museum Dresden 2012/616.
Frank Leslie's Illustrated Newspaper. New York: Frank Leslie, 1878.
Frank, Gustav, Madleen Podewski, and Stefan Scherer. "Kultur – Zeit – Schrift." *Internationales Archiv für Sozialgeschichte der deutschen Literatur* 34, no. 2 (2009): 1–45.
Franklin, Wayne. "James Fenimore Cooper, 1789–1851: A Brief Biography." In *A Historical Guide to James Fenimore Cooper*, edited by Leland S. Person, 27–60. Oxford: Oxford University Press, 2007.
Franklin, Wayne. *James Fenimore Cooper: The Early Years.* New Haven: Yale University Press, 2007.
Franklin, Wayne. *James Fenimore Cooper: The Later Years.* New Haven: Yale University Press, 2017.
Frič, Vaclav. Catalogue. n.d. (1886?). Zoological Department. Letters January–June 1886, 29/139. Library and Archives. NHML.
Friederici, Angelika. *Castan's Panopticum: Ein Medium wird besichtigt.* Berlin: Karl-Robert Schütze, 2009.
Friedrich Schiller: Leben, Werk und Wirkung: Eine Ausstellung zum Gedächtnis der 200. Wiederkehr seines Geburtstags, exhibition catalog. Marbach: Schiller Nationalmuseum, 1959.
Fröhlich, Karl. *A-B-C für artige Kinder in Silhuetten und Reimen.* Cassel: G. E. Vollmann, 1854.
Furttenbach the Elder, Joseph. *Architectura Civilis.* Ulm: Saur, 1628.
Gabriel, Carl, and Emil Eduard Hammer. *Führer durch das anatomisch-ethnologische und naturwissenschaftliche Museum.* Munich: G. Schutz, before 1902.
Galassi, Peter. *Corot in Italy: Open-Air Painting and the Classical-Landscape Tradition.* New Haven: Yale University Press, 1991.
Galewsky, Eugen, and Friedrich Woithe. "Die Geschlechtskrankheiten und ihre Bekämpfung." Dresden: Deutscher Verlag für Volkswohlfahrt, 1922.
Gamper, Michael. "Literarische Meteorologie am Beispiel von Stifters 'Das Haidedorf.'" In *Wind und Wetter: Kultur–Wissen–Ästhetik*, edited by Georg Braungart and Urs Büttner, 219–232. Paderborn: Wilhelm Fink, 2018.
Gannon, Susan R. "'The Best Magazine for Children of All Ages': Cross-Editing *St. Nicholas Magazine* (1873–1905)." *Children's Literature* 25 (1997): 153–180.
Die Gartenlaube: Illustrirtes Familienblatt. Leipzig: Ernst Keil, 1853–1884.

Gascoigne, Bamber. *How to Identify Prints: A Complete Guide to Manual and Mechanical Process from Woodcut to Inkjet.* London: Thames & Hudson, 2014.
Geimer, Peter. "Blow Up." In *"Der liebe Gott steckt im Detail": Mikrostrukturen des Wissens,* edited by Wolfgang Schäffner, Sigrid Weigel, and Thomas Macho, 187–202. Munich: Wilhelm Fink, 2003.
Geistlicher Irrgarten, mit vier Gnadenbrunnen, 1784 (Ephrata, PA), the Winterthur Museum, Garden and Library, Winterthur, DE, 1958.120.13.
Geistlicher Irrgarten, mit vier Gnadenbrunnen, 1784 (Ephrata, PA), the Conrad Grebel University College Library, hist. mss. 23.14.
Geistlicher Irrgarten, mit vier Gnadenbrunnen, 1788 (Ephrata, PA), the Winterthur Museum, Garden & Library, Winterthur, DE, 1957.1215.
Geistlicher Irrgarten, mit vier Gnadenbrunnen, 1811 (Reading, PA), the Schwenkfelder Library and Heritage Center, uncatalogued (see Brandt, "Perplexion and Pleasure," 194)
Geistlicher Irrgarten, mit vier Gnadenbrunnen, c. 1830 (Harrisburg, PA), the Russell and Corinne Earnest Collection, BS #618.
Geistlicher Irrgarten, mit vier Gnadenbrunnen, c. 1830 (Harrisburg, PA), the Earnest Archives and Library, BS #784.
Geistlicher Irrgarten, mit vier Gnadenbrunnen, 1833 (Hereford, PA), Schwenkfelder Library and Heritage Center, fraktur collection, uncatalogued.
Geistlicher Irrgarten, mit vier Gnadenbrunnen, 1869–74 (John Funk and Brother, Elkhart, IN), Aylmer Heritage Historical Library, Ontario, GI 2.
Geistlicher Irrgarten, mit vier Gnadenbrunnen, c. 1875, Joseph Schneider Haus Museum, Kitchener, Ontario; 1984.028.347.
Genette, Gérard. *Narrative Discourse: An Essay on Method.* Oxford: Blackwell, 1980.
Genette, Gérard. *Paratexts: Thresholds of Interpretation.* Cambridge: Cambridge University Press, 1997.
Gess, Nicola. "Instruments of Wonder – Wondrous Instruments: Optical Devices of the Marvelous of Fontenelle, Rist, Breitinger, and Hoffmann." *The German Quarterly* 90, no. 4 (2017): 407–422.
Gille, Klaus. *Panoptikum: 125 Jahre zwischen Wachs und Wirklichkeit; Hamburgs Panoptikum und seine Geschichte.* Hamburg: Panoptikum Gebr. Faerber, 2004.
Gillings, Ken. *Discovering the Battlefields of the Anglo-Zulu War 30.* Pinetown, South Africa: 30 Degrees South, 2014.
Goethe, Johann Wolfgang. *Goethes Werke,* 143 vols. Weimar: Weidmann, 1887–1909.
Goethe, Johann Wolfgang. "Hochzeitlied." In vol. 1.2 of *Sämtliche Werke: Briefe, Tagebücher und Gespräche,* edited by Dieter Borchmeyer et al., 114–116. Frankfurt am Main: Deutscher Klassiker, 1985–.
Goethe, Johann Wolfgang. "Der Sammler und die Seinigen." In vol. 1.18 of *Sämtliche Werke: Briefe, Tagebücher und Gespräche,* edited by Dieter Borchmeyer et al., 676–733. Frankfurt am Main: Deutscher Klassiker Verlag, 1985–.
Gombrich, E. H. "The Cartoonist's Armory." In *Meditations on a Hobby Horse and Other Essays on the Theory of Art,* 2nd ed., 127–142. London: Phaidon, 1971.
Good, E. Reginald. *Anna's Art: The Fraktur Art of Anna Weber, a Waterloo County Mennonite Artist, 1814–1888.* Kitchener, ON: Pochauna, 1976.
Gosse, Edmund. *Father and Son: A Study of Two Temperaments.* London: Penguin, 1989.
Gosse, Philip Henry. *Actinologia Britannica: A History of the British Sea-Anemones and Corals.* London: Van Voorst, 1860.

Gosse, Philip Henry. *The Aquarium: An Unveiling of the Wonders of the Deep Sea*. 2nd ed. London: John Van Voorst, 1856.
Gosse, Philip Henry. *A Naturalist's Rambles on the Devonshire Coast*. London: John Van Voorst, 1853.
Gosse, Philip Henry. *The Ocean*. London: Society for Promoting Christian Knowledge, 1846.
Gosse, Philip Henry. *The Romance of Natural History*. 7th ed. London: James Nisbet, 1866.
Gowrley, Freya. "Collage Before Modernism." In *Cut and Paste: 400 Years of Collage*, edited by Patrick Elliott, 25–33. Edinburgh: National Galleries of Scotland, 2019.
Grant, James. *British Battles on Land and Sea*. Vol. 4. London: Cassell, Petter & Galpin, 1880.
The Graphic. London: Illustrated Newspapers, 1879.
Gray, Richard T. *About Face: German Physiognomic Thought from Lavater to Auschwitz*. Detroit: Wayne State University Press, 2004.
Great Britain Illustrated: A Series of Original Views from Drawings by William Westall, A.R.A. engraved by, and under the direction of, Edward Finden, with descriptions by Thomas Moule. London: Charles Tilt, 1830.
Green, James N. "The Rise of Book Publishing." In *An Extensive Republic; Print, Culture, and Society in the New Nation, 1790–1840*. Vol. 2 of *A History of the Book in America*, edited by Hugh Amory and David Hall, 75–127. Cambridge: Cambridge University Press, 2000.
Gretton, Tom. "The Pragmatics of Page Design in Nineteenth-Century General-Interest Magazines in London and Paris." *Art History* 33 (2010): 680–709.
Gretz, Daniela. "Archen in der Papierflut der Gegenwart: Zur medialen Selbstinszenierung von Zeitschriften als Archiven in der 'Bildungspresse' des 19. Jahrhunderts." *Sprache und Literatur* 45, no. 2 (2014): 89–107.
Griffiths, Anthony. *The Print Before Photography: An Introduction to European Printmaking, 1550–1820*. London: British Museum, 2016.
Grill, Oliver. *Die Wetterseiten der Literatur: Poetologische Konstellationen und meteorologische Kontexte im 19. Jahrhundert*. Paderborn: Wilhelm Fink, 2019.
Gunning, Tom. "What's the Point of an Index? or, Faking Photographs." *Nordicom Review* 41, no. 2 (2004): 39–49.
Hackethal, Sabine. "Kunstwerke für die Wissenschaft – Glasmodelle wirbelloser Tiere aus dem Atelier von Leopold und Rudolf Blaschka." In *Art, Ordnung, Klasse: 200 Jahre Museum für Naturkunde*, edited by Ferdinand Damaschun et al. Rangsdorf: Basilisken, 2010.
Hambrick-Stowe, Charles E. *The Practice of Piety: Puritan Devotional Disciplines in Seventeenth-Century New England*. Chapel Hill: University of North Carolina Press, 1982.
Hamilton, Carolyn. *Terrific Majesty: The Powers of Shaka Zulu and the Limits of Historical Invention*. Cambridge, MA: Harvard University Press, 1998.
Hammer, Emil Eduard. "Syphilis, venerische Krankheiten." In *Der Mensch. Illustrierter Führer durch Hammer's Original-Ausstellung aus München*, 11–13. Munich: Hammer, 1914.
Handbuch Literatur & Visuelle Kultur. Edited by Claudia Benthien and Brigitte Weingart. Berlin: De Gruyter, 2014.
Hansen, Erk F. *Wissenschaftswahrnehmung und -umsetzung im Kontext der deutschen Frühromantik: Zeitgenössische Naturwissenschaft und Philosophie im Werk Friedrich von Hardenbergs (Novalis)*. Frankfurt am Main: Peter Lang, 1992.
Harnisch, Antje. "Der Harem in Familienblättern des 19. Jahrhunderts: Koloniale Phantasien und Nationale Identität." *German Life and Letters* 51, no. 3 (1998): 325–341
Harper's Weekly. New York: Harper & Brothers, 1879.

Haschemi Yekani, Minu, and Ulrike Schaper. "Pictures, Postcards, Points of Contact: New Approaches to Cultural Histories of German Colonialism." *German History* 35, no. 4 (December 2017): 603–623, https://doi.org/10.1093/gerhis/ghx106.
Hayles, Katherine. *Writing Machines*. Cambridge, MA: MIT Press, 2002.
Hebbel, Friedrich. *Gedichte, Erzählungen, Schriften*. Vol. 3 of *Werke*. Edited by Gerhard Fricke, Werner Keller, and Karl Pörnbacher. Munich: Hanser, 1965.
Heilbron, J. L. *Electricity in the 17th and 18th Centuries: A Study of Early Modern Physics*. Berkeley: University of California Press, 1979.
"Ein Helfer der Wissenschaft." *Münchner Neueste Nachrichten*, 2 October 1935, 1.
Heltoft, Kjeld. *Hans Christian Andersen as an Artist*. Translated by David Hohnen. Copenhagen: Cristian Ejlers, 2005.
Herder, Johann Gottfried. *Älteste Urkunde des Menschengeschlechts*. Tübingen: Cotta, 1806.
Hill, Thomas. *The Gardener's Labyrinth*. London: Adam Islip, 1594.
Hinton, John Howard, ed. *The History and Topography of the United States of America*. 2 vols. London: Jennings & Chaplin & I.T. Hinton, 1830–1832.
"Histories: Anglo-American Visual Studies, 1989–1999." In *Farewell to Visual Studies*, edited by James Elkins, Sunil Manghani, and Gustav Frank, 43–55. University Park: Pennsylvania State University Press, 2015.
Hobsbawm, Eric. "Introduction: Inventing Traditions." In *The Invention of Tradition*, edited by E. J. Hobsbawm and T. O. Ranger, 1–14. Cambridge: Cambridge University Press, 2012.
Hoffmann, Agnes. *Landschaft im Nachbild: Imaginationen von Natur in der Literatur um 1900 bei Henry James und Hugo von Hofmannsthal*. Rombach Litterae 245. Baden-Baden: Rombach, 2020.
Hoffmann, E. T. A. *Master Flea*. In vol. 2 of *Specimens of German romance: Selected and Translated from Various Authors*. Translated by George Soane. London: Geo. B. Whittaker, 1826.
Hoffmann, E. T. A. *Meister Floh: Ein Märchen in sieben Abenteuern zweier Freunde*. In *Sämtliche Werke in sechs Bänden*, edited by Hartmut Steinecke and Wulf Segebrecht. Vol. 6, *Späte Prosa, Briefe, Tagebücher und Aufzeichnungen: Juristische Schriften: Werke 1814–1822*, edited by Gerhard Allroggen et al., 303–467. Frankfurt am Main: Deutscher Klassiker, 2004.
Hoffmann, Franz. *Conanchet, der Indianerhäuptling: Eine Erzählung für die reifere Jugend; Nach dem Englischen des J. F. Cooper bearbeitet von Franz Hoffmann; Mit 6 Bildern in Farbendruck nach Aquarellen von J. Simmler*. 6th ed. Stuttgart: K. Thienemanns, 1886.
Hoffmann, Franz. *Lederstrumpf-Erzählungen von Cooper: Für die Jugend bearbeitet von Franz Hoffmann; Erster Band; Mit 8 Stahlstichen*. Stuttgart: Schmidt & Spring, 1845.
Hoffmann, Franz. *Lederstrumpf-Erzählungen von Cooper: Für die Jugend bearbeitet von Franz Hoffmann; Zweiter Band; Mit 12 Stahlstichen*. Stuttgart: Schmidt & Spring, 1845.
Hoffmann, Franz. *Lederstrumpf-Erzählungen von Cooper: Für die Jugend bearbeitet von Franz Hoffmann; Mit sechzehn Stahlstichen*. 6th ed. Stuttgart: Schmidt & Spring, 1867.
Hoffmann, Kathryn A. "Sleeping Beauties in the Fairground. The Spitzner, Pedley and Chemisé Exhibits." *Early Popular Visual Culture* 4, no. 2 (2006): 139–159
Hoffmann, Kurt. "Hoffmann, Carl." *Neue Deutsche Biographie* 9 (1972): 432, https://www.deutsche-biographie.de/pnd116974036.html#ndbcontent.
Hohlfeld, Johannes. *Das Bibliographische Institut: Festschrift zu seiner Jahrhundertfeier*. Leipzig: Bibliographisches Institut, 1926.

Holland, Jocelyn. *German Romanticism and Science: The Procreative Poetics of Goethe, Novalis, and Ritter*. Routledge Studies in Romanticism. New York: Routledge, 2009.

Holland, Jocelyn. "The Silence of Ritter's Symbol ⊗." *The Germanic Review: Literature, Culture, Theory* 92, no. 4 (2017): 340–354.

Holm, Christiane. *Amor und Psyche: Die Erfindung eines Mythos in Kunst, Wissenschaft und Alltagskultur (1765–1840)*. Munich: Deutscher Kunstverlag, 2006.

Honold, Alexander, and Klaus R. Scherpe. *Mit Deutschland um die Welt: Eine Kulturgeschichte des Fremden in der Kolonialzeit*. Stuttgart: J. B. Metzler, 2004.

Hooke, Robert. *Micrographia; or, Some Physiological Descriptions of Minute Bodies Made by Magnifying Glasses with Observations and Inquiries Thereupon*. London: Martin & Allesty, 1665.

Hooke, Robert. *Micrographia; or, Some Physiological Descriptions of Minute Bodies Made by Magnifying Glasses, with Observations and Inquiries Thereupon 1665*. Lincolnwood, IL: Science Heritage, 1987.

Hopwood, Nick. "Artist versus Anatomist, Models against Dissection: Paul Zeiller of Munich and the Revolution of 1848." *Medical History* 51 (2007): 279–308.

Hoser, Paul. *Das Bayerische Vaterland*. In *Historisches Lexikon Bayerns*. http://www.historisches-lexikon-bayerns.de/Lexikon/Das Bayerische Vaterland. 3 July 2006. Accessed 22 Januar 2019.

Houben, H. H., and Hans Wahl, eds. *Adele Schopenhauer: Gedichte und Scherenschnitte*. 2 vols. Leipzig: Klinkhardt & Biermann, 1920.

Huber, Florian. "Spiegelbilder vom Meeresgrund: Leopold Blaschkas marine Aquarien." *Berichte zur Wissenschaftsgeschichte* 36 (2013): 172–186.

Hübner, Alexander Freiherr von. *Ein Spaziergang um die Welt*. Leipzig: Schmidt & Günther, 1889.

Hugo, Herman. *Pia desideria emblematis elegiis at affectibus*. Antwerp: Henrik Aertssens, 1624.

Human, Armin. *Carl Joseph Meyer und das Bibliographische Institut von Hilburghausen-Leipzig: Eine kulturhistorische Studie*. Hildburghausen: F. W. Gadow & Wohn, 1896.

Hunnisett, Basil. *Engraved on Steel: The History of Picture Production using Steel Plates*. Aldershot: Ashgate, 1998.

Illustrated London News. London: Illustrated London News & Sketch, 1842.

Jahres-Rechnung 1872 and Geschäfts-Uebersicht 1873, in Geschäfts-Anmerkungen, 1872–1887. LRBC, MS 0013, Box 23, Folder 64. RRL, CMoG, Corning, New York.

Jay, Martin. *Downcast Eyes: The Denigration of Vision in Twentieth-Century French Thought*. Berkeley: University of California Press, 1993.

Jenks, Chris, ed. *Visual Culture*. New York: Routledge, 1995.

John, Johannes. "'Übermalungen' – Transkription, Emendation, Interpretation: Zur 17. Manuskriptseite von Adalbert Stifters 'Nachkommenschaften.'" In *Text – Material – Medium: Zur Relevanz editorischer Dokumentationen für die literaturwissenschaftliche Forschung*, edited by Wolfgang Lukas, Rüdiger Nutt-Kofoth, and Madleen Podewski, 107–122. Berlin: De Gruyter, 2014.

Jones, Jason B. "Image Citation and Reverse Search with TinEye." *Chronicle of Higher Education*. 18 March 2011. https://www.chronicle.com/blogs/profhacker/image-citation-and-reverse-search-with-tineye/32013. Accessed 19 December 2019.

Jones, Tom. "Theories of Language in the Eighteenth Century." *Oxford Handbooks Online*. 5 October 2015. https://doi.org/10.1093/oxfordhb/9780199935338.013.100.

Journal of Visual Culture. 2002–present.
Jüttner, Franz. "Bakteriologische Untersuchungen." *Kladderadatsch* 55, no. 36 (4 September 1892): n.p.
Kaiser, Peter. *Der Pläneschmied: Das außergewöhnliche Leben des Verlegers Carl Joseph Meyer.* Leipzig: Salier, 2007.
Kall, Wilhelmine. Untitled poem. *Beckers Taschenbuch zum geselligen Vergnügen* (1820): 411–412.
Kaminski, Nicola, and Jens Ruchatz. "Journalliteratur – ein Avertissement." *Pfennig-Magazin zur Journalliteratur* 1 (2017): 23–25.
Kamphoefner, Walter D., and Wolfgang Helbich. "Introduction." In *Germans in the Civil War: The Letters They Wrote Home*, edited by Walter D. Kamphoefner and Wolfgang Helbich, 1–34. Chapel Hill: University of North Carolina Press, 2006.
Kamphoefner, Walter D., Wolfgang Helbich, and Ulrike Sommer. "Introduction." In *News from the Land of Freedom: German Immigrants Write Home*, edited by Walter D. Kamphoefner, Wolfgang Helbich, and Ulrike Sommer, 1–50. Ithaca, NY: Cornell University Press, 1988.
Kant, Immanuel. *Kritik der Urteilskraft.* Edited by Karl Vorländer. Hamburg: Felix Meiner, 1990.
Kaplan, Caren. "The Balloon Prospect: Aerostatic Observation and the Emergence of Militarized Aeromobility." In *From Above: War, Violence, and Verticality*, edited by Caren Kaplan and Lisa Parks, 19–40. New York: Oxford University Press, 2014.
Karr Schmidt, Suzanne. *Interactive and Sculptural Printmaking in the Renaissance.* Leiden: Brill, 2017.
Keiner, Astrid. *Hieroglyphenromantik: Zur Genese und Destruktion eines Bilderschriftmodells und zu seiner Überforderung in Friedrich Schlegels Spätphilosophie.* Würzburg: Königshausen & Neumann, 2003.
Kemp, Wolfgang. "Fotografie als Kunst." In *Theorie der Fotografie, 1839–1912*, edited by Wolfgang Kemp, 13–45. Munich: Schirmer/Mosel, 1980.
Kircher, Athanasius. *Turris Babel, Sive Archontologia.* Amsterdam: Janssonio-Waesbergianna, 1679.
Kirchner, Joachim. *Das deutsche Zeitschriftwesen*, Vol. 2. Wiesbaden: Otto Harrassowitz, 1962.
Kisch, Egon Erwin. "Das Geheimkabinett des anatomischen Museums." In vol. 5 of *Gesammelte Werke*, 170–174. Berlin: Aufbau, 1974.
Kittler, Friedrich. *Aufschreibesysteme 1800–1900.* Munich: Wilhelm Fink, 1985.
Kittler, Friedrich. *Aufschreibesysteme 1800–1900.* Munich: Wilhelm Fink, 2003.
Kocur, Zoya. *Global Visual Culture: An Anthology.* Oxford: Wiley-Blackwell, 2011.
Köhnen, Ralph. *Das optische Wissen: Mediologische Studien zu einer Geschichte des Sehens.* Paderborn: Wilhelm Fink, 2009.
Koller, Gabriele. "The European Origins of Milwaukee Panorama Painting." *Milwaukee County History* 1, nos. 1–2 (2010): 3–12.
Koller, Gabrielle. "Panoramen als Orte bürgerlicher Schaulust und Bildung im deutschen Kaiserreich." In *Kunst, Nation und Repräsentation*, edited by Brigitte Buberl, 87–100. Bönen: Kettler, 2007.
Koselleck, Reinhart. "Geschichte: Historie." In vol. 2 of *Geschichtliche Grundbegriffe: Historisches Lexikon zur politisch-sozialen Sprache in Deutschland*, edited by Otto Brunner, Werner Conze, and Reinhart Koselleck, 647–652. Stuttgart: Klett, 1972.
Köstering, Susanne. *Ein Museum für Weltnatur: Die Geschichte des Naturhistorishcen Museums in Hamburg.* Munich: Dölling & Galitz, 2018.
Köstering, Susanne. *Natur zum Anschauen: Das Naturkundemuseum des deutschen Kaiserreichs, 1871–1914.* Cologne: Böhlau, 2003.
Koszyk, Kurt. *Deutsche Presse im 19. Jahrhundert.* Part 2. Berlin: Colloquium, 1966.

Kranz, Helene. *Das Museum Godeffroy, 1861–1881: Naturkunde und Ethnographie der Südsee*. Hamburg: Altonaer Museum, 2005.

Krauss, Rosalind. "Grids." *October 9* (1979): 50–64.

Kress, Gunther, and Theo van Leeuwen. *Multimodal Discourse: The Modes and Media of Contemporary Communication*. London: Arnold, 2001.

Kress, Gunther, and Theo van Leeuwen. *Reading Images: The Grammar of Visual Design*. London: Routledge, 2006.

Kriebel, Reuben. *Genealogical Record of the Descendants of the Schwenkfelders, Who Arrived in Pennsylvania in 1733, 1734, 1736, 1737*. Manayunk, PA: Joseph Yeakel, 1879.

Kundrus, Birthe. *Moderne Imperialisten: das Kaiserreich im Spiegel seiner Kolonien*. Cologne: Böhlau, 2003.

Kunzle, David. *The History of the Comic Strip*. Vol. 2, *The Nineteenth Century*. Berkeley: University of California Press, 1990.

Laband, John. *Zulu Warriors: The Battle for the South African Frontier*. New Haven: Yale University Press, 2014.

Lang, Johanna. "Die Einführung des Wandergewerbescheins: von reisenden Schaustellern und beanspruchten Wachsmodellen." In *Blicke! Körper! Sensationen! Ein anatomisches Wachskabinett und die Kunst*, edited by Eva Meyer-Hermann, 89. Göttingen: Wallstein, 2014.

Lang, Johanna. "Um 1940: Zerlegt und vorgeführt: das Wachsmodell Eine Figur auf dem Seziertisch liegend." In *Blicke! Körper! Sensationen! Ein anatomisches Wachskabinett und die Kunst*, edited by Eva Meyer-Hermann, 107–108. Göttingen: Wallstein, 2014.

Lange, Britta. "1892: Die Firma J. F. G. Umlauff präsentiert 'anthropologisch-zoologische Prachtgruppen.'" In *Mit Deutschland um die Welt: Eine Kulturgeschichte des Fremden in der Kolonialzeit*, edited by Alexander Honold and Klaus R. Scherpe, 152–162. Stuttgart: J. B. Metzler, 2004.

Lee, Anthony W. "The Image of War." In *On Alexander Gardner's Photographic Sketch Book of the Civil War*, 8–51. Berkeley: University of California Press, 2007.

Lee, Haimin. "15 Years of Google Books." 17 October 2019. https://www.blog.google/products/search/15-years-google-books/. Accessed 2 April 2020.

Lefebvre, Niki. "'The Rebels' Last Device': Theodore R. Davis and Faithful Representations of Black Soldiers During the Civil War." In *So Conceived and So Dedicated: Intellectual Life in the Civil War-Era North*, edited by Lorien Foote and Kanisorn Wongsrichanalai, 153–173. New York: Fordham University Press, 2015.

Lemper, Ernst-Heinz. *Adolf Traugott von Gersdorf (1744–1807): Naturforschung und soziale Reformen im Dienste der Humanität*. Berlin: VEB Deutscher Verlag der Wissenschaften, 1974.

Lessing, Gotthold Ephraim. *Laokoon*. Stuttgart: Reclam, 1964.

Lichtenberg, Georg Christoph. *Aus Lichtenbergs Nachlass: Aufsätze, Gedichte, Tagebuchblätter, Briefe: zur hundertsten Wiederkehr seines Todestages (24. Februar 1799)*. Edited by Albert Leitzmann. Weimar: H. Böhlaus Nachfolger, 1899.

Lichtenberg, Georg Christoph. *Observationes: Die lateinischen Schriften*. Edited by Dag Nikolaus Hasse. Göttingen: Wallstein, 1997.

Lichtenberger, Sigrid. "Lesealter." In *Lexikon der Kinder- und Jugendliteratur: Zweiter Band; I-O*, edited by Klaus Doderer, 346–349. Weinheim: Beltz, 1977.

Lidtke, Tom. "Panorama Painting in Milwaukee." *Milwaukee County History* 1, nos. 1–2 (2010): 13–23.

Lineweaver Paul, Bonnie. *Shenandoah Valley Folk Art Fraktur (1774–1850)*. Dayton, VA: Harrisonburg-Rockingham County Historical Society, 2011.
Lingner, Karl August, Arthur Luerssen, and Georg Seiring. *Der Mensch: Ausstellung; Ausgewählte Gruppen aus der Internationalen Hygiene-Ausstellung 1911*. Darmstadt: no publisher, 1912.
Link, Jürgen. "Literaturanalyse als Interdiskursanalyse: Am Beispiel des Ursprungs literarischer Symbolik in der Kollektivsymbolik." In *Diskurstheorien und Literaturwissenschaft*, edited by Harro Müller and Gerhard von Graevenitz, 284–307. Frankfurt am Main: Suhrkamp, 1988.
Liska, Vivian. "Die Idee des Albums: Zu einer Poetik der Potentialität." In *Album: Organisationsform narrativer Kohärenz*, edited by Anke Kramer and Annegret Pelz, 35–39. Göttingen: Wallstein, 2013.
Locher, Walter. "Zur militärischen Nutzung des Ballons." In *Leichter als Luft: Zur Geschichte der Ballonfahrt*, edited by Bernd Korzus, 238–250. Münster: Landesverband Westfalen-Lippe, 1985.
Lüsebrink, Hans-Jürgen, ed. *Das Europa der Aufklärung und die außereuropäische koloniale Welt*. Göttingen: Wallstein, 2006.
Luthy, David. *Our Amish Devotional Heritage*. Aylmer, ON: Pathway, 2016.
Luthy, David. "The Spiritual Labyrinth: An Unusual Devotional Form." *Pathway Publishers: The Family Life Magazine* 17, no. 3 (1984): 18–21.
Macdougall, Doug. *Endless Novelties of Extraordinary Interest: The Voyages of H. M. S. Challenger and the Birth of Modern Oceanography*. New Haven: Yale University Press, 2019.
Mackenzie, Rev. John. *Day-Dawn in Dark Places: A Story of Wanderings and Work in Bechwanaland*. London: Cassel, 1883.
MacLeod, Catriona. "Cutting up the Salon: Adele Schopenhauer's 'Zwergenhochzeit' and Goethe's 'Hochzeitlied.'" *Deutsche Vierteljahrsschrift für Literatur und Geistesgeschichte* 89, no. 1 (2015): 70–87.
MacLeod, Catriona. *Fugitive Objects: Sculpture and Literature in the German Nineteenth Century*. Evanston, IL: Northwestern University Press, 2011.
MacQueen, Gailand. *The Spirituality of Mazes and Labyrinths*. Kelowna, BC: Wood Lake, 2005.
Marbacher Scherenschnitt-Büchlein, Beilage zum *Marbacher Magazin* 13 (1979).
Marsch, Angelika. *Meyer's Universum: Ein Beitrag zur Geschichte des Stahlstiches und des Verlagswesens im 19. Jahrhundert*. Lüneburg: Nordostdeutsches Kulturwerk, 1972.
Martin, Peter. *Schwarze Teufel, edle Mohren: Afrikaner in Bewußtsein und Geschichte der Deutschen*. Hamburg: Junius, 1993.
Marx, Karl. *Capital*. London: Penguin Classics, 1990.
Marx, Karl. *The Economic and Philosophic Manuscripts of 1844*. New York: International Publishers, 1964.
Marx, Karl. *Das Kapital: Kritik der politischen Ökonomie*. Vol. 1. Berlin: Karl Dietz, 1962.
Massumi, Brian. *Parables for the Virtual: Movement, Affect, Sensation*. Durham, NC: Duke University Press, 2007.
Mattl, Siegfried. "Körperspektakel: Ein anatomisches-pathologisches und ethnologisches Museum im fin-de-siecle Wien." *Wiener Zeitschrift zur Geschichte der Neuzeit* 2 (2004): 46–62.
Maurer, Kathrin. "Adalbert Stifter's Poetics of Clouds and Nineteenth-Century Meteorology." *Oxford German Studies* 45, no. 4 (2016): 421–433.

Maurer, Kathrin. "'Ich hatte dieses Ding nie so gesehen wie heute': Zur Verunsicherung der Wahrnehmung in Adalbert Stifters 'Eisgeschichte.'" *Colloquia Germanica* 92, nos. 1–2 (2013): 35–48.

Maurer, Kathrin. *Visualizing the Past: The Power of the Image in Nineteenth-Century Historicism*. Berlin: De Gruyter, 2013.

Mayer, Petra. *Zwischen unsicherem Wissen und sicherem Unwissen: Erzählte Wissensformation im realistischen Roman: Stifters "Der Nachsommer" und Vischers "Auch Einer."* Bielefeld: Aisthesis, 2014.

McFadden, David Revere. "Slash: Paper under the Knife." In *Slash: Paper under the Knife*, edited by Martina D'Alton, 10–46. Milan: 5 continents, 2009.

McIsaac, Peter M. "Emil Eduard Hammers anatomische Modelle im kulturellen Kontext." In *Spiegel der Wirklichkeit. Anatomische und dermatologische Modelle in Heidelberg*, edited by Sara Doll and Navena Widulin, 95–112. Heidelberg: Springer, 2019.

McIsaac, Peter M. "Die medizinische Venus. Die performative Basis von anatomischen Zurschaustellungen vor und um 1900." In *Geschlechter Spiel Räume: Dramatik, Theater, Performance und Gender*, edited by Gaby Pailer and Franziska Schößler, 313–328. Amsterdam: Rodopi, 2011.

McIsaac, Peter M. *Museums of the Mind: German Modernity and the Dynamics of Collecting*. University Park: Pennsylvania State University Press, 2007.

McWilliams, John P. *The Last of the Mohicans: Civil Savagery and Savage Civility*. New York: Twayne, 1995.

Melville, Hermann. *Memorial of James Fenimore Cooper*. New York: G. P. Putnam, 1852.

Mensch, G. *Der Bienenjäger: Eine Erzählung für die reifere Jugend; Frei nach Cooper bearbeitet von G. Mensch; Mit sechs Bildern in Farbendruck nach Zeichnungen von H. Leutemann lithographiert von W. Schäfer*. 2nd ed. Leipzig: Alfred Oehmigke, 1876.

Metz, Christian. *The Imaginary Signifier: Psychoanalysis and the Cinema*. Translated by Celia Britton. Bloomington: Indiana University Press, 1983.

Meyer-Hermann, Eva, ed. *Blicke! Körper! Sensationen! Ein anatomisches Wachskabinett und die Kunst*. Göttingen: Wallstein, 2014.

Meyer's Universum; oder, Abbildung und Beschreibung des Sehenswerthesten und Merkwürdigsten der Natur und Kunst auf der ganzen Erde. Hildburghausen: Bibliographisches Institut, 1833–1860.

Michelet, Jules. *The Sea*. Copenhagen: Green Integer, 2012.

Michler, Werner. "Adalbert Stifter und die Ordnungen der Gattung: Generische Veredelung und die Arbeit am 'Habitus.'" In *Stifter und Stifterforschung im 21. Jahrhundert: Biographie – Wissenschaft – Poetik*, edited by Hartmut Laufhütte, Alfred Doppler, Johannes John, and Johann Lachinger, 182–200. Tübingen: Max Niemeyer, 2007.

Milde, Christine. "Carl Joseph Meyers 'Universum': Ein Beitrag zur Geschichte der Publizistik des deutschen Vormärz." PhD Diss., University of Leipzig, 1990.

Miller, Henrich. "Bey dem Verleger dieser Zeitung ist ganz neulich heraus gekommen . . .," *Der Wöchentliche pennsylvanische Staatsbote*, 18 January 1762.

Milton, John. *Paradise Lost: A Poem in Ten Books*. London: Simmons, 1668.

Mirzoeff, Nicholas. *An Introduction to Visual Culture*. New York: Routledge, 1999.

Mirzoeff, Nicholas. *The Right to Look: A Counterhistory of Visuality*. Durham, NC: Duke University Press, 2011.

Mirzoeff, Nicholas. "The Subject of Visual Culture." In *The Visual Culture Reader*, edited by Nicholas Mirzoeff, 2nd ed., 3–23. New York: Routledge, 2002.

Mirzoeff, Nicholas, ed. *The Visual Culture Reader*. New York: Routledge, 1998.
Mitteilungen der Deutschen Gesellschaft zur Bekämpfung der Geschlechtskrankheiten 12 (1914): 78–87.
Möbius, Hanno. *Montage und Collage: Literatur, bildende Künste, Film, Fotografie, Musik, Theater bis 1933*. Munich: Wilhelm Fink, 2000.
Morgan, David. *The Embodied Eye: Religious Visual Culture and the Social Life of Feeling*. Berkeley: University of California Press, 2012.
Morgan, David. *The Forge of Vision: A Visual History of Modern Christianity*. Oakland: University of California Press, 2015.
Möseneder, Karl. "Stimmung und Erdleben: Adalbert Stifters Ikonologie der Landschaftsmalerei." In *Adalbert Stifter, Dichter und Maler, Denkmalpfleger und Schulmann: Neue Zugänge zu seinem Werk*, edited by Hartmut Laufhütte and Karl Möseneder, 18–57. Tübingen: Niemeyer, 1996.
Mosse, George. *Toward the Final Solution: A History of European Racism*. New York: Howard Fertig, 1978.
Moyer, Dennis K. *Fraktur Writings and Folk Art Drawings of the Schwenkfelder Library Collection*. Kutztown: Pennsylvania German Society, 1997.
Muhlenberg, Henry Melchior. *The Journals of Henry Melchior Muhlenberg*. Vol. 3. Translated by Theodore G. Tappert and John W. Doberstein. Philadelphia: Evangelical Lutheran Ministerium of Pennsylvania and the Adjacent States, 1958.
Müller, Lothar. *Weisse Magie: Die Epoche des Papiers*. Munich: Carl Hanser, 2012.
Müller-Wille, Klaus. "Hans Christian Andersen und die vielen 19. Jahrhunderte: Eine Einführung." In *Hans Christian Andersen und die Heterogenität der Moderne*, edited by Klaus Müller-Wille, 1–18. Tübingen: Francke, 2009
Müller-Wille, Klaus. *Sezierte Bücher: Hans Christian Andersens Materialästhetik*. Paderborn: Wilhelm Fink, 2017.
The Multigraph Collective. *Interacting with Print: Elements of Reading in the Era of Print Saturation*. Chicago: University of Chicago Press, 2018.
Museum Godeffroy. Catalog III der zum Verkauf stehenden Doubletten aus den naturhistorischen Expeditionen der Herren Joh. Ces. Godeffroy & Sohn. Hamburg, 1866. Library and Archives, NHML.
Museum Godeffroy. Catalog IV. Hamburg, 1869. Library and Archives, NHML.
Mussell, James. *The Nineteenth-Century Press in the Digital Age*. New York: Palgrave Macmillan, 2012.
Neisser, Albert. "Begrüßungsrede des Vorsitzenden Herrn Geheimrat Neisser zur VIII. Jahresversammlung zu Dresden am 9./10. Juni 1911." *Mitteilungen der Deutschen Gesellschaft zur Bekämpfung der Geschlechtskrankheiten* 9 (1911): 75.
Neri, Janice. "Between Observation and Image: Representations of Insects in Robert Hooke's 'Micrographia.'" *Studies in the History of Art* 69 (2008), *Symposium Papers XLVI: The Art of Natural History: Illustrated Treatises and Botanical Paintings, 1400–1850*: 82–107.
Neumann, Gerhard. "Fernrohr, Mikroskop, Luftballon: Wahrnehmungstechnik und Literatur in der Goethezeit." In *Spektakuläre Experimente: Praktiken der Evidenzproduktion im 17. Jahrhundert*, edited by Helmar Schramm, Ludger Schwarte, and Jan Lazardzig, 345–377. Berlin: De Gruyter, 2006.
Niehle, Victoria. "Die ästhetische Funktion des Raumes: Jean Pauls 'Des Luftschiffer Giannozzo Seebuch.'" In *Raumlektüren: Der Spatial Turn und die Literatur der Moderne*, edited by Tim Mehigan and Alan Corkhill, 69–85. Bielefeld: transcript, 2013.

Nikolow, Sybilla. "'Wissenschaftliche Stillleben' des Körpers im 20. Jahrhundert." In *Erkenne Dich selbst! Strategien der Sichtbarmachung des Körpers im 20. Jahrhundert*, edited by Sybilla Nikolow, 11–46. Cologne: Böhlau, 2015.

Nikolow, Sybilla, and Thomas Steller. "Das lange Echo der 1. Internationalen Hygiene-Ausstellung in der Dresdner Gesundheitsaufklärung." *Dresdner Hefte* 29, no. 4 (2011): 18.

Notizbüchel für 1869–1870, 1869–1871. LRBC, MS 0013, Box 24. RRL, CMoG, Corning, New York.

Novalis. *Schriften: Die Werke Friedrich von Hardenbergs*. Edited by Paul Kluckhohn, R. H. Samuel, and Hans Joachim Mähl. 2nd ed. Stuttgart: W. Kohlhammer, 1960.

Novotny, Fritz. *Adalbert Stifter als Maler*. Vienna: Schroll, 1941.

"Number of visitors to the Louvre in Paris from 2007 to 2018 (in millions)." Hamburg: Statista, 2019. https://www.statista.com/statistics/247419/yearly-visitors-to-the-louvre-in-paris/.

Nyhart. Lynn K. "Science, Art and Authenticity in Natural History Displays." In *Models: The Third Dimension of Science*, edited by Soraya de Chadarevian and Nick Hopwood, 307–38. Stanford: Stanford University Press, 2004.

Obenaus, Sibylle. *Literarische und politische Zeitschriften, 1830–1848*. Stuttgart: J. B. Metzler, 1986.

Obenaus, Sibylle. *Literarische und politische Zeitschriften, 1848–1880*. Stuttgart: J. B. Metzler, 1987.

Oettermann, Stephan. *The Panorama: History of a Mass Medium*. Translated by Deborah Lucas Schneider. New York: Zone Books, 1997.

Offizieller Führer durch die Internationale Hygiene-Ausstellung Dresden 1911 und durch Dresden und Umgebung. Berlin: Rudolf Mosse, 1911.

Olson, Roberta J. M. *The Florentine Tondo*. Oxford: Oxford University Press, 2000.

Onnes-Fruitema, Evelyn, and Ron Rombout. "The Origin of the Panorama Phenomenon." In *Panorama Phenomenon*, 11–28. The Hague: Uitgeverij P/F Kunstbeeld, 2006.

Osten, Philipp. "Zwischen Volksbelehrung und Vergnügungspark." *Deutsches Ärzteblatt* 102, no. 45 (2005): A 3086–3089.

Osterhammel, Jürgen. *Die Verwandlung der Welt: Eine Geschichte des 19. Jahrhunderts*. Munich: Beck, 2010.

"Die Pantherdame Mlle. Irma Loustan aus Paris." *Münchner Neueste Nachrichten*, 20 December 1906, 4.

Parish, Lawrence Charles, Gretchen Worden, Joseph A. Witkowski, and Daniel H. Parish. "Wax Models in Dermatology." *Transactions and Studies of the College of Physicians of Philadelphia* 5, no. 13 (1991): 29–74.

Patterson, Nancy-Lou. "Imagery of Paradise in Swiss-German Mennonite Folk Art," unpublished paper notes and manuscript draft, c. 1979. Conrad Grebel University College Archives. Hist. mss. 1.197.

Patterson, Nancy-Lou. *The Language of Paradise: Folk Art from Mennonite and Other Anabaptist Communities of Ontario*. London, ON: London Regional Art Gallery, 1985.

Paul, Gerhard. *Das visuelle Zeitlater: Punkt und Pixel*. Göttingen: Wallstein, 2016.

Paul, Jean. "Des Luftschiffers Giannozzo Seebuch." In vol. 3 of *Jean Paul: Sämtliche Werke*, edited by Norbert Miller, 925–1010. Darmstadt: Wissenschaftliche Buchgesellschaft, 2000.

Payne's Universum: Darstellung und Beschreibung der schönsten Gegenden, Städte und merkwürdigsten Baudenkmale auf der ganzen Erde, von Portraits ausgezeichneter Personen, volkstümlicher Scenen und Genrebildern. Leipzig: A. H. Payne, 1843.

Pech, Klaus-Ulrich, "Vom Biedermeier zum Realismus." In *Geschichte der deutschen Kinder- und Jugendliteratur*, edited by Reiner Wild. 3rd ed., 131–170. Stuttgart: J. B. Metzler, 2008.

Penny, H. Glenn. "Elusive Authenticity: The Quest for the Authentic Indian in German Public Culture." *Comparative Studies in Society and History* 48, no. 4 (2006): 798–819.

Penny, H. Glenn. *Kindred by Choice: Germans and American Indians since 1800*. Chapel Hill: University of North Carolina Press, 2013.

Perraudin, Michael, and Jürgen Zimmerer, eds. *German Colonialism and National Identity*. New York: Routledge, 2010.

Person, Leland S. "Introduction: Fenimore Cooper's Literary Achievements." In *A Historical Guide to James Fenimore Cooper*, edited by Leland S. Person, 1–26. Oxford: Oxford University Press, 2007.

Peschel, Johann. *Garten-Ordnung*. Leipzig: Henning Große, 1597.

Pfannkuchen, Antje. "A Matter of Visibility – Georg Christoph Lichtenberg's Art and Science of Observation." *Configurations* 24, no. 4 (2016): 375–400.

Pfannkuchen, Antje. "A Science of Hieroglyphs, or the Test of *Bildung*." In *The Technological Introject: Friedrich Kittler between Implementation and the Incalculable*, edited by Jeffrey Champlin and Antje Pfannkuchen, 84–92. New York: Fordham University Press, 2018.

Pfannkuchen, Antje. "When Nature Begins to Write Herself – German Romantics Read the Electrophore." PhD diss., New York University, 2010.

Phelan, Anthony. "The Content of Silhouettes." *Paragraph: The Journal of the Modern Critical Theory Group* 21, no. 2 (1998): 150–168.

Pichler, Franz. "Andreas Baumgartner und sein Werk zur Naturlehre." In *Stifter und Stifterforschung im 21. Jahrhundert*, edited by Hartmut Laufhütte, Alfred Doppler, Johannes John, and Johann Lachinger, 117–126. Tübingen: Max Niemeyer, 2007.

Pieske, Christa. "The European Origins of Four Pennsylvania German Broadside Themes." *Der Reggeboge* 23, no. 1 (1989): 7–10.

Pieterse, Jan Nederveen. *White on Black: Images of Africa and Blacks in Western Popular Culture*. New Haven: Yale University Press, 1992.

Plowden, Sarah. Correspondence with the Aylmer Heritage Historical Library, 14 July 1995. Uncatalogued collection, Aylmer Heritage Historical Library, Aylmer, ON.

Pohl, Rudolf. Geschäftsbuch 1901–1919. Archiv des Deutschen Hygiene-Museums Dresden 2009/657.

Politzer, Adam. *Geschichte der Ohrenheilkunde*. Vol. 2, *Von 1850–1911*, 271–273. Stuttgart: Ferdinand Enke, 1913.

Pomian, Krzysztof. *Collectors and Curiosities: Paris and Venice, 1500–1800*. Cambridge: Polity, 1990.

Pudor, Heinrich. "Museumschulen." *Museumskunde* 6 (1910): 248–253.

Qureshi, Sadiah. *Peoples on Parade: Exhibitions, Empire, and Anthropology in Nineteenth-Century Britain*. Chicago: University of Chicago Press, 2011.

Radtke, Julia. "Zwischen Aufklärung und Voyeurismus: die 'Extra-Abteilung.'" In *Blicke! Körper! Sensationen! Ein Anatomisches Wachskabinett und die Kunst*, edited by Eva Meyer-Hermann, 97. Göttingen: Wallstein, 2014.

Ragg-Kirkby, Helena. *Adalbert Stifter's Late Prose: The Mania for Moderation*. Rochester, NY: Camden House, 2000.

Ratcliff, Jessica. "The East India Company, the Company's Museum, and the Political Economy of Natural History in the Early Nineteenth Century." *Isis* 107 (2016): 495–517.

Ratzel, Friedrich. *Völkerkunde: Erster Band; Die Naturvölker Afrikas*. Leipzig: Bibliographisches Institut, 1885.

Ratzel, Friedrich. *Völkerkunde: Zweiter Band; Die Naturvölker Ozeaniens, Amerikas, und Asiens*. Leipzig: Bibliographisches Institut, 1886.

Reichenbach, Ludwig. Notice, catalogue of Leopold Blaschka ("Wenig bekannte Seethiere"), n. d. DF ZOO/200/1/169, Library and Archives, NHML.

Reiling, Henri. "Glass Models of Soft Bodied Animals: The Relation Between Blaschka, Frič and the National Museum." *Časopis Národního muzea, Rada prírodovedná* [Journal of the national museum, scientific council] 171 (2002): 81–84.

Reinhardt, Dirk. *Von der Reklame zum Marketing: Geschichte der Wirtschaftswerbung in Deutschland*. Berlin: Akademie, 1993.

Resig, John. "Using Computer Vision to Increase the Research Potential of Photo Archives." *TinEye*. https://services.tineye.com/solutions/JohnResigComputerVisionResearchPaperMatchEngine. Accessed 14 February 2018.

Resultate aus den Beobachtungen des Magnetischen Vereins im Jahre 1836. Edited by Carl Friedrich Gauss and Wilhelm Weber. Göttingen: Dietrichische Buchhandlung, 1837.

Richter, Klaus. *Das Leben des Physikers Johann Wilhelm Ritter: Ein Schicksal in der Zeit der Romantik*. Weimar: H. Böhlaus Nachfolger, 2003.

Riedl-Dorn, Christa. *Das Haus der Wunder: Zur Geschichte des Naturhistorischen Museums in Wien*. Vienna: Holzhausen, 1998.

Rimmele, Marius, and Bernd Stiegler. *Visuelle Kulturen/Visual Culture*. Hamburg: Junius, 2012.

Ritchie, Leitch. *Wanderings by the Seine*, with twenty engravings from drawings by J. M. W. Turner. London: Longman, Rees, Orme, Brown, Green, and Longman, 1834.

Ritter, Johann. "Geistlicher Irrgarten," *Der Readinger Adler*, Reading, PA, 19 November 1811.

Ritter, Johann Wilhelm, and Jocelyn Holland. *Key Texts of Johann Wilhelm Ritter (1776–1810) on the Science and Art of Nature*. History of Science and Medicine Library. Leiden: Brill, 2010.

Ritzer, Monika. "Von Suppenwürfeln, Induktionsstrom und der Äquivalenz der Kräfte: Zum Kulturwert der Naturwissenschaft am Beispiel von Adalbert Stifters Novelle 'Abdias.'" *Kulturpoetik: Journal for Cultural Poetics* 2, no. 1 (2002): 44–67.

Roberts, Matt T., and Don Etherington. *Bookbinding and the Conservation of Books: A Dictionary of Descriptive Terminology*. Washington, DC: Library of Congress, 1981.

Roeber, A. Gregg. "German and Dutch Books and Printing." In *A History of the Book in America*. Vol. 1, *The Colonial Book in the Atlantic World*, edited by Hugh Amory and David D. Hall, 298–313. Chapel Hill: University of North Carolina Press, 2010.

Roeber, A. Gregg. *Palatines, Liberty, and Property: German Lutherans in Colonial British America*. Baltimore: Johns Hopkins University Press, 1993.

Roeber, A. Gregg. "Readers and Writers of German." In *A History of the Book in America*. Vol. 2, *An Extensive Republic: Print, Culture, and Society in the New Nation, 1790–1840*, edited by Robert Gross and Mary Kelley, 471–482. Chapel Hill: University of North Carolina Press, 2010.

Ross, Corey. *Media and the Making of Modern Germany*. Oxford: Oxford University Press, 2008.

Rossbacher, Karlheinz. *Lederstrumpf in Deutschland: Zur Rezeption James Fenimore Coopers beim Leser der Restaurationszeit*. Munich: Wilhelm Fink, 1972.

Roth, Joseph. "Philosophie des Panoptikums." In vol. 1 of *Werke*, edited by Klaus Westermann, 939–940. Cologne: Kiepenhauer & Witsch, 1956.

Rothstein, Bret. "Early Modern Play: Three Perspectives." *Renaissance Quarterly* 71 (2018): 1036–1046.
Rothstein, Bret. "Visual Difficulty as a Cultural System." *Res: Anthropology and Aesthetics* 65–66 (2014–2015): 332–347.
Rozwadowski, Helen M. *Fathoming the Ocean: The Discovery and Exploration of the Deep Sea.* Cambridge, MA: Harvard University Press, 2005.
Rudwick, Martin J. S. "The Emergence of a Visual Language for Geology, 1760–1840." *History of Science* 14 (1976): 149–195.
Ruskin, John. *Mountain Beauty.* Vol. 4 of *Modern Painters.* London: Smith, Elder, 1856.
Rüther, Kirsten, and Angelika Schaser. *Gender and Conversion Narratives in the Nineteenth Century: German Mission at Home and Abroad.* Farnham, England: Ashgate, 2019.
Ryan, James. *Picturing Empire: Photography and the Visualization of the British Empire.* London: Reaktion, 1997.
Sandywell, Barry, and Ian Heywood. "Critical Approaches to the Study of Visual Culture: An Introduction to the Handbook." In *The Handbook of Visual Culture*, edited by Barry Sandywell and Ian Heywood, 1–56. New York: Berg, 2012.
Sangmeister, Ezekiel. *Mystische Theologie; oder, Wahrer Wegweisser nach unserm Ursprung und Vaterland.* Ephrata, PA: Joseph Bauman, 1819–1820.
Sarkowski, Heinz. *Das Bibliographische Institut: Verlagsgeschichte und Bibliographie, 1826–1976.* Mannheim: Bibliographisches Institut, 1976.
Sauerteig, Lutz. *Krankheit, Sexualität, Gesellschaft: Geschlechtskrankheiten und Gesundheitspolitik in Deutschland im 19. und frühen 20. Jahrhundert.* Stuttgart: Franz Steiner, 1999.
Sauerteig, Lutz. "'Sex in Wachs': Gesundheitswissen, Volksaufklärung und Sinneserregung." In *Blicke! Körper! Sensationen! Ein anatomisches Wachskabinett und die Kunst*, edited by Eva Meyer-Hermann, 169. Göttingen: Wallstein, 2014.
Savage, Kirk. *Standing Soldiers, Kneeling Slaves: Race, War, and Monument in Nineteenth-Century America.* Princeton: Princeton University Press, 2018.
Schelling, Friedrich Wilhelm Joseph. *Vorlesungen über die Methode (Lehrart) des akademischen Studiums: Auf der Grundlage des Textes der Ausgabe von Otto Weiss.* Edited by Melchior Meyr. Vol. 2. Philosophische Bibliothek. Hamburg: Meiner, 1990.
Scheps, Birgit. *Das verkaufte Museum: Die Südsee-Unternehmungen des Handelshauses Joh. Ces. Godeffroy & Sohn, Hamburg und die Sammlungen "Museum Godeffroy."* Keltern-Weiler: Goecke & Evers, 2005.
Schinkel, Eckhard. "Der Ballon in der Literatur." In *Leichter als Luft: Zur Geschichte der Ballonfahrt*, edited by Bernard Korzus and Gisela Noehles, 200–236. Münster: Westfälisches Landesmuseum für Kunst und Kulturgeschichte, 1978.
"Schlachtenbummler." In *Das deutsche Wörterbuch*, edited by Jacob Grimm and Wilhelm Grimm. Leipzig: S. Hirzel, 1854–1961. http://dwb.uni-trier.de/de/, here http://www.woerterbuchnetz.de/DWB?lemma=schlachtenbummler.
Schlegel, August Wilhelm. "Über Zeichnungen zu Gedichten und John Flaxmans Umrisse." *Athenäum* 2, no. 2 (1799): 193–246.
Schlegel, Friedrich. "Athenaeum Fragments." In *Philosophical Fragments*. Translated by Peter Firchow. Foreword by Rodolphe Gasché. 18–93. Minneapolis: University of Minnesota Press, 1991.
Schlegel, Friedrich. *Kritische Friedrich-Schlegel-Ausgabe.* 35 vols. Edited by Ernst Behler. Munich: F. Schöningh, 1958–.

Schmeltz, J. D. E. Godeffroy Museum to MfNB. 1863–1869. MfNB, HBS. Bestand: Zool. Mus. Signatur: S I Godeffroy Museum.

Schmeltz, J. D. E. Museum Godeffroy to Günther, MfNB. 1876, 1878–1879. Library and Archives, NHML. DF ZOO/200/10/379–385, 387–88, 395–398, 400–403, Library and Archives, NHML.

Schmidt, Julian. *Geschichte der deutschen Literatur nach Lessings Tod*. Vol. 3. Leipzig: Friedrich Ludwig Herbig, 1856.

Schmidt, Rudolf. "Übersichtstafel der abgezweigten Firmen aus der von Carl Hoffmann in Stuttgart 1826 begründeten Buchhandlung." In vol. 3 of *Deutsche Buchhändler: Deutsche Buchdrucker*, 482. Berlin: Contumax, 1905.

Schmitt, Stefan. "Adalbert Stifter als Zeichner." In *Adalbert Stifter, Dichter und Maler, Denkmalpfleger und Schulmann: Neue Zugänge zu seinem Werk*, edited by Hartmut Laufhütte and Karl Möseneder, 261–308. Tübingen: Niemeyer, 1996.

Schmitz-Emans, Monika. "Über Bilder und die bildene Kunst bei Jean Paul." In *Jean Paul und die Bilder: Bildkünstlerische Auseinandersetzungen mit seinem Werk; 1783–2013*, edited by Monika Schmitz-Emans and Wolfram Benda, 19–64. Würzburg: Königshausen & Neumann, 2013.

Schnalke, Thomas. *Diseases in Wax: The History of the Medical Moulage*. Chicago: Quintessence, 1995.

Schnalke, Thomas. "Spuren im Gesicht: Eine Augenmoulage aus Berlin." In *Der zweite Blick: Besondere Objekte aus den historischen Sammlungen der Charité*, edited by Beate Kunst, Thomas Schnalke, and Gottfried Bogusch, 19–40. Berlin: de Gruyter, 2010.

Scholz, Albrecht. "Bekämpfung der Geschlechtskrankheiten in verschiedenen politischen Systemen." *Hautarzt* 7 (2003): 664–673.

Scholz, Wilhelm. "Soldat und Diplomat: Dissolving-views aus dem schleswig-holsteinischen Feldzuge." *Kladderadatsch* 17, nos. 44–45 (25 September 1864): n.p.

Scholz, Wilhelm. "Ein Wassertropfen aus der Spree." *Kladderadatsch* 6, no. 2 (13 March 1853): n.p.

Schopenhauer, Adele. *Räthsel-Alphabeth*, Beckers Taschenbuch zum geselligen Vergnügen. N. p., 1820.

Schopenhauer, Adele. *Tagebücher*. 2 vols. Edited by Kurt Wolff. Leipzig: Insel, 1909.

Schreiber, Guido. *Malerische Perspektive: Mit einem Anhang über den Gebrauch geometrischer Grundrisse*. Karlsruhe: Herder, 1854.

Schulman, Vanessa Meikle. *Work Sights: The Visual Culture of Industry in Nineteenth-Century America*. Amherst: University of Massachusetts Press, 2015.

Schultes, Lothar. "Adalbert Stifter als Zeichner und Maler." *Jahrbuch des Oberösterreichischen Musealvereines: Gesellschaft für Landeskunde* 152 (2007): 237–300.

Schumacher, Hans Harald. *Jugenderinnerungen eines Hamburger Arztes*. Unpublished. Quoted in: Klaus Gille, *Panoptikum: 125 Jahre zwischen Wachs und Wirklichkeit; Hamburgs Panoptikum und seine Geschichte*, 35–36. Hamburg: Panoptikum Gebr. Faerber, 2004.

Schwartz, Vanessa R., and Jeannene M. Przyblyski, eds. *The Nineteenth-Century Visual Culture Reader*. New York: Routledge, 2004.

Scobie, Stephen. *Earthquakes and Explorations: Language and Painting from Cubism to Concrete Poetry*. Toronto: University of Toronto Press, 1997.

Scribner's Monthly: The Century Magazine. New York: Scribner & Co., 1880.

Sedda, Julia. "Antikenrezeption und christliche Tradition im Scherenschnittwerk der Luise Duttenhofer (1776–1829)," PhD diss., Eberhard Karls Universität Tübingen, 2012.
Selge, Martin. *Poesie aus dem Geist der Naturwissenschaft*. Stuttgart: Kohlhammer, 1976.
Sharpe, Gregory. *Two Dissertations: I. Upon the Origin, Construction, Division, and Relation of Language; II. Upon the Original Powers of Letters; Wherein Is Proved from the Analogy of Alphabets, and the Proportion of Letters, That the Hebrew Ought to Be Read Without Points. To Which Is Added, the Second Edition, Enlarged, of a Hebrew Grammar and Lexicon, Without Points*. London: John Millan, 1751.
Short, John Phillip. *Magic Lantern Empire: Colonialism and Society in Germany*. Ithaca, NY: Cornell University Press, 2012.
Siegert, Bernhard. *Cultural Techniques: Grids, Filters, Doors, and Other Articulations of the Real*. Translated by Geoffrey Winthrop-Young. New York: Fordham University Press, 2015.
Sitzungsberichte der naturwissenschaftlichen Gesellschaft ISIS in Dresden, 1880. Dresden, 1881.
Sitzungsberichte der naturwissenschaftlichen Gesellschaft ISIS zu Dresden, 1863. Dresden, 1864.
Sloterdijk, Peter, Amy Patton, and Steve Corcoran. *Terror from the Air*. Los Angeles: Semiotext(e), 2009.
Smarsly-Fechner, Thomas. "Der Spiegel und seine Schatten: Abdrücke der frühen Photographie in Texten von Aa. O. Vinje, Henrik Ibsen und H. C. Andersen." In *Zwischen Bild und Text: Zur Funktionalisierung von Bildern in Texten und Kontexten*, edited by Annegret Heitmann and Joachim Schiedermair, 21–42. Freiburg im Breisgau: Rombach, 2000.
Smith, Woodruff D. *Politics and the Sciences of Culture in Germany, 1840–1920*. New York: Oxford University Press, 1991.
Smolderen, Thierry. *The Origins of Comics: From William Hogarth to Winsor McCay*. Translated by Bart Beaty and Nick Nguyen. Jackson: University Press of Mississippi, 2014.
Somers, James. "Torching the Modern-Day Library of Alexandria." *The Atlantic*. 20 April 2017. https://www.theatlantic.com/technology/archive/2017/04/the-tragedy-of-google-books/523320/. Accessed 2 April 2020.
Sontag, Susan. *Regarding the Pain of Others*. London: Penguin Books, 2003.
Stadler, Ulrich. *Der technisierte Blick: Optische Instrumente und der Status von Literatur: Ein kulturhistorisches Museum*. Würzburg: Königshausen und Neumann, 2003.
Stadtarchiv Dresden Z. 42.VII. Gustav Zeiller. Gesuch um die Eröffnung eines anthropologischen und anatomischen Kabinetts. Dresden. 13 November 1888.
Stadtarchiv München. DE-1992-POL-0384. Medizinisches Volksmuseum.
Stadtarchiv München. DE-1992-POL-0385. Hammers Anatomische Ausstellungen.
Stadtarchiv München. DE-1992-ZA-11322. Schreiben von Hammer an die Polizeidirektion vom 12.4.1906.
Stadtarchiv München. DE-1992-ZA-11322. Schreiben von Hammer an die Polizeidirektion vom 6.6.1916.
Stadtarchiv München. DE-1992-ZA-11322. Schreiben von Hammer an die Polizeidirektion vom 22.11.1906.
Stadtarchiv München. DE-1992-ZA-P-0180-21. Hammer, Prof. Emil Eduard, 1929–1939.
Stadtarchiv München. DE-1992-ZS-0158-3. Hammer's anatomische Original-Ausstellung, 1916.
Stadtarchiv München. Polizeidirektion. 1051.

Starke, Holger. "Der Empfang der sächsischen Truppen in Dresden am 11. Juli 1871." In *Sachsen in Deutschland: Politik, Kultur und Gesellschaft 1830–1918*, edited by James N. Retallack, 143–159. Bielefeld: Verlag für Regionalgeschichte, 2000.

Steidl, Katharina. *Am Rande der Fotografie: Eine Medialitätsgeschichte des Fotogramms im 19. Jahrhundert*. Berlin: De Gruyter, 2018.

Stein, Adam. *Cooper's Lederstrumpf-Erzählungen für die Jugend bearbeitet von Adam Stein: Mit sechs Bildern von G. Bartsch*. 5th ed. Neu-Ruppin: Alfred Oehmigke, 1869.

Stein, Adam. *Cooper's Lederstrumpf-Erzählungen für die Jugend bearbeitet von Adam Stein: Mit sechs Bildern in Farbendruck von W. Schäfer*. 17th ed. Leipzig: Alfred Oehmigke, 1883.

Stein, Adam. *Cooper's Seegemälde: Für die Jugend bearbeitet von Adam Stein; Mit sechs Bildern in Farbendruck nach Zeichnungen von G. Bartsch*. 2nd ed. Leipzig: Alfred Oehmigke, 1865.

Stein, Claudia. "Organizing the History of Hygiene at the International Hygiene-Ausstellung in Dresden in 1911." *NTM: Zeitschrift für Geschichte der Wissenschaften, Technik und Medizin* 22, no. 1 (2014): 355–387.

Steiner, Christopher. "Travel Engravings and the Construction of the Primitive." In *Prehistories of the Future: The Primitivist Project and the Culture of Modernism*, edited by Elazar Barkan and Ronald Bush, 202–225. Stanford: Stanford University Press, 1995.

Steiner, Mirjam. "Inseparably United: Big and Small in Literary Settings." In *Too Big to Scale: On Scaling Space, Numbers, Time, and Energy*, edited by Florian Dombois and Julie Harboe, 113–28. Zurich: Scheidegger & Spiess, 2017.

Stengel, Georg. *Aegyptischer Labyrinth, Oder Geistlicher Irr-Garten der betrieglichen Welt*. Dillingen: Akademische Druckerey, 1629.

Stewart, Susan. *On Longing: Narratives of the Miniature, the Gigantic, the Souvenir, the Collection*. Durham, NC: Duke University Press, 1993.

Stifter, Adalbert. *Briefe*. Vol. 3. Edited by Johannes Aprent. Pest: Gustav Heckenast, 1869.

Stifter, Adalbert. *Indian Summer*. Translated by Wendell Frye. New York: Peter Lang, 1985.

Stifter, Adalbert. "Preface to 'Many-Colored Stones.'" In vol. 1 of *German Novellas of Realism*, edited and translated by Jeffrey L. Sammons, 1–6. New York: Continuum, 1989.

Stifter, Adalbert. *Werke und Briefe: Historisch-kritische Gesamtausgabe*. Edited by Alfred Doppler, Wolfgang Frühwald et al. Stuttgart: W. Kohlhammer, 1978.

Stockinger, Claudia. *Das 19. Jahrhundert: Zeitalter des Realismus*. Berlin: Akademie, 2010.

Stockinger, Claudia. *An den Ursprüngen populärer Serialität: Das Familienblatt "Die Gartenlaube."* Göttingen: Wallstein, 2018.

Stötzel, Georg, and Martin Wengeler. *Kontroverse Begriffe: Geschichte des öffentlichen Sprachgebrauchs in der Bundesrepublik Deutschland*. Berlin: Walter de Gruyter, 1995.

Stougaard-Nielsen, Jakob. "The Fairy Tale and the Periodical: Hans Christian Andersen's Scrapbooks." *Book History* 16 (2013): 132–154.

Strickland, Stuart Walker. "Circumscribing Science: Johann Wilhelm Ritter and the Physics of Sidereal Man." PhD diss., Harvard University, 1992.

Strom, Jonathan, ed. *Pietism and Community in Europe and North America, 1650–1850*. Boston: Brill, 2010.

Strowick, Elisabeth. *Gespenster des Realismus: Zur literarischen Wahrnehmung von Wirklichkeit*. Paderborn: Wilhelm Fink, 2019.

Strowick, Elisabeth. "Poetological-Technical Operations: Representation of Motion in Adalbert Stifter." *Configurations* 18 (2010): 273–289.

te Heesen, Anke. *Theorien des Museums: Zur Einführung*. Hamburg: Junius, 2012.

te Heesen, Anke. *Der Zeitungsauschnitt: Ein Papierobjekt der Moderne*. Frankfurt am Main: Fischer, 2006.
Teicher, Hendel. "Cuts and Connections." In *Cut-Outs and Cut-Ups: Hans Christian Andersen and William Seward Burroughs*, edited by Hendel Teicher, 13–44. Dublin: Irish Museum of Modern Art, 2008.
Tersteegen, Gerhard. *Geistliches Blumen-Gärtlein inniger Seelen; oder, Kurze Schluss-Reimen, Betrachtungen und Lieder ueber allerhand Wahrheiten des Inwendigen Christenthums, nebst der Frommen Lotterie*. Frankfurt am Main: J. Christoph Böttinger, 1757.
Thanner, Veronika, Joseph Vogl, and Dorothea Walzer, eds. *Die Wirklichkeit des Realismus*. Paderborn: Wilhelm Fink, 2018.
Thode-Arora, Hilke. "Die Familie Umlauff und ihre Firmen – Ethnographica-Händler in Hamburg." *Mitteilungen aus dem Museum für Völkerkunde Hamburg* 22 (1992): 143–158.
Tibbets, Robert. Correspondence with the Aylmer Heritage Historical Library, 11 August 1986. Uncatalogued collection. Aylmer Heritage Historical Library, Aylmer, ON.
Tombleson's Views of the Rhine. Edited by W. G. Fearnside. London: W. Tombleson, 1832.
Travelling Sketches in the North of Italy, the Tyrol, and on the Rhine, with twenty-six beautifully finished engravings from drawings by Clarkson Stanfield, Esq., by Leitch Ritchie, Esq. London: Longman, Rees, Orme, Brown, and Green, 1832.
Turner, Mark W. "The Unruliness of Serials in the Nineteenth Century (and in the Digital Age)." In *Serialization in Popular Culture*, edited by Rob Allen and Thijs van den Berg, 11–32. London: Routledge, 2014.
Umlauff, Johannes. J. F. G. Umlauff to Paul Matschie, MfNB, 1895–1913. MfNB, HBS. Bestand: Zool. Mus. Signatur: S III Umlauff J. F. G.
Umlauff, Johannes. Unpublished memoir. Hagenbeck Archive, Tierpark Carl Hagenbeck, Hamburg-Stellingen, n. d.
"Unsere Sondergruppe 'Geschlechtskrankheiten' auf der internationalen Dresdner Hygeineausstellung in amerikanischer Beleuchtung." *Mitteilungen der Deutschen Gesellschaft zur Bekämpfung der Geschlechtskrankheiten* 10 (1912): 139–140.
Van Remoortel, Marianne. "Women Editors and the Rise of the Illustrated Fashion Press in the Nineteenth Century." *Nineteenth-Century Contexts* 39, no. 4 (2017): 278–279.
Varnhagen von Ense, Karl. "Vom Ausschneiden." In vol. 4 of *Werke*, edited by Konrad Feilchenfeldt, 384–390. Frankfurt am Main: Deutscher Klassiker, 1990.
Vennen, Mareike. *Das Aquarium: Praktiken, Techniken und Medien der Wissensproduktion (1840–1910)*. Göttingen: Wallstein, 2018.
Verbeek, Albert. "Sulpiz Boisserée auf den Turmspitzen des Kölner Domes: Ein satirischer Scherenschnitt von Luise Duttenhofer." *Kölner Domblatt* 8–9 (1954): 201–203.
"Vereinsnachrichten." *Mitteilungen der Deutschen Gesellschaft zur Bekämpfung der Geschlechtskrankheiten* 12 (1914): 78–87.
Vico, Giambattista. *The New Science*. Translated by Max Harold Fisch and Thomas Goddard Bergin. Ithaca, NY: Cornell University Press, 1948. http://archive.org/details/newscienceofgiam030174mbp.
Vigus, James. *Shandean Humour in English and German Literature and Philosophy*. London: Taylor and Francis, 2017.
Vogel, Juliane. "Schnitt und Linie: Etappen einer Liaison." In *Öffnungen: Zur Theorie und Geschichte der Zeichnung*, edited by Friedrich Teja Bach and Wolfram Pichler, 141–159. Munich: Wilhelm Fink, 2009.

Vogel, Juliane. "Stifters Gitter: Poetologische Dimensionen einer Grenzfigur." In *Die Dinge und die Zeichen: Dimensionen des Realistischen in der Erzählliteratur des 19. Jahrhunderts*, edited by Barbara Hunfeld and Sabine Schneider, 43–58. Würzburg: Königshausen & Neumann, 2008.

Wagener, Oskar. "Unterricht in der Laryngologie, Rhinologie und Otologie: Methoden, Hilfsmittel, Prüfung." In *Die Krankheiten der Luftwege und der Mundhöhle*, edited by V. Karl Amersbach et al., 1308–1309. Berlin: Julius Springer, 1929.

Wagner, Anne M. "Kara Walker: 'The Black-White Relation.'" In *Kara Walker: Narratives of a Negress*, edited by Ian Berry et al., 90–101. Cambridge, MA: MIT Press, 2003.

Wagner, Cornelia. "Panoptikum: das Wachskabinett als urbane Attraktion." In *Blicke! Körper! Sensationen! Ein anatomisches Wachskabinett und die Kunst*, edited by Eva Meyer-Hermann, 89–90. Göttingen: Wallstein, 2014.

Waldman, Diane. *Collage, Assemblage, and the Found Object*. New York: Abrams, 1992.

Walker, John A., and Sarah Chaplin. "Production, Distribution, and Consumption Model." In *Visual Culture: An Introduction*, 65–80. Manchester: Manchester University Press, 1997.

Wangemann, Hermann. *Lebensbilder aus Südafrika: Ein Beitrag zur Kirchen- und Culturgeschichte des neunzehnten Jahrhunderts*. 3rd ed. Berlin: Berliner Missionshaus, 1876.

Ward, Henry A. "Museum Godeffroy." *Popular Science Monthly* 8 (1876): 699–702.

Wasserman, Renata R. Mautner. *Exotic Nations: Literature and Cultural Identity in the United States and Brazil, 1830–1930*. Ithaca, NY: Cornell University Press, 1994.

Weber, Christa, and Claus Weber. *Schwarze Kunst im Buch: Scherenschnitt und Schattenriß als Buchillustration*. Nuremberg: Weber, 1994.

Wedekind, Martina. *Wiederholen – Beharren – Auslöschen: Zur Prosa Adalbert Stifters*. Heidelberg: Winter, 2005, 141–164.

Weizman, Eyal. *Forensic Architecture: Violence at the Threshold of Detectability*. New York: Zone Books, 2017.

"Welcome to HathiTrust!" https://www.hathitrust.org/about. Accessed 2 April 2020.

Welle, Florian. *Der irdische Blick durch das Fernrohr: Literarische Wahrnehmungsexperimente vom 17. bis zum 20. Jahrhundert*. Würzburg: Königshausen und Neumann, 2009.

Wellenreuther, Hermann. *Citizens in a Strange Land: A Study of German-American Broadsides and Their Meaning for Germans in North America, 1730–1830*. University Park: Pennsylvania State University Press, 2013.

Wellmann, Janina. "Bewegung an der Wand: Zur Aufführung von Organismen mit dem Sonnenmikroskop." In *Belebungskünste: Praktiken lebendiger Darstellung in Literatur, Kunst und Wissenschaft um 1800*, edited by Nicola Gess, Agnes Hoffmann, and Annette Kappeler, 227–245. Paderborn: Wilhelm Fink, 2019.

Wengiel, Rubén. "Europe's Mazes: On Labyrinthine Thought in Architectural Design." Paper presented at the European Forum at the Hebrew University, Jerusalem, 2008.

West, Peter. "Introduction to American Panoramas." In *Panoramas, 1787–1900: Texts and Contexts*, edited by Laurie Garrison, Anne Anderson, Sibylle Erle, Verity Hunt, Peter West, and Phoebe Putnam. Vol. 5, *American Panoramas*, edited by Peter West, vii–xxiv. London: Routledge, 2012.

Wetzels, Walter Dominic. *Johann Wilhelm Ritter: Physik im Wirkungsfeld der deutschen Romantik*. Berlin: Walter de Gruyter, 1973.

Whittemore, W. Meynell, ed. *Sunshine for 1883: for the Home, the School, and the World* London: George Stoneman, 1883.

Wilcox, Scott Barnes. "The Panorama and Related Exhibitions in London." M. Litt. thesis, University of Edinburgh, 1976.
Wilkending, Gisela. "Vom letzten Drittel des 19. Jahrhunderts bis zum Ersten Weltkrieg." In *Geschichte der deutschen Kinder- und Jugendliteratur*, edited by Reiner Wild, 3rd ed., 171–240. Stuttgart: J. B. Metzler, 2008.
Willer, Stefan. "Grenzenlose Zeit, schlingernder Grund: Genealogische Ordnungen in Stifters 'Nachkommenschaften.'" In *Figuren der Übertragung*, edited by Michael Gamper and Karl Wagner, 45–62. Zurich: Chronos, 2009.
Williams, Glyn. *Naturalists at Sea: Scientific Travelers from Dampier to Darwin*. New Haven: Yale University Press, 2013.
Witte, Wilfried. "Vom Diener zum Meister: Der Beruf des Anatomischen Präparators in Berlin von 1852–1959." In *Der zweite Blick: Besondere Objekte aus den historischen Sammlungen der Charité*, edited by Beate Kunst, Thomas Schnalke, and Gottfried Bogusch, 185–218. Berlin: de Gruyter, 2010.
Woldt, A. "Zur Kenntnis der Südsee." *Westermanns Illustrierte Deutsche Monatshefte* 60 (April–September 1886): 326–344, 455–474.
Wolff, Mark. "Western Novels as Children's Literature in Nineteenth-Century France." *Mosaic: An Interdisciplinary Critical Journal* 34, no. 2 (2001): 87–102.
Wunderlich, Gerold. *Rudolf Cronau, 1855–1939: Topographical Views of America*. New York: Gerold Wunderlich & Co., 1993.
Yoder, Don. *The Pennsylvania German Broadside: A History and Guide*. University Park: Pennsylvania State University Press, 2005.
Zeller, Joachim, *Bilderschule der Herrenmenschen: Koloniale Reklamesammelbilder*. Berlin: Ch. Links, 2008.
Zeller, Joachim. *Weiße Blicke – Schwarze Körper: Afrikaner im Spiegel westlicher Alltagskultur*. Erfurt: Sutton, 2010.
Zimmerman, Andrew. *Anthropology and Antihumanism in Imperial Germany*. Chicago: University of Chicago Press, 2001.

Index

Adaptation 242, 272, 293–294, 300–301, 304–306, 314, 316–317, 347
Adria (exhibition) 104
Advertisements and advertising 4, 11, 99, 145, 157, 160, 164, 168, 206–207, 210, 224–228, 235, 339, 348
Aeolian wind harp [*Äolsschlauch*] 32
Aeropetomanie 20
Africa 4, 75, 205–206, 209–210, 212–214, 216–218, 220, 222–224, 228–229, 231, 233–236, 329, 341
Ahmed, Sara 90
Albert of Saxe-Coburg and Gotha 43
Album 131–133, 145, 147, 150, 152, 154
Ally Sloper's Half Holiday 39
Alphabet 133n14, 135, 247–248, 250, 251, 260, 263, 266
America 4–5, 90–91, 93, 157–158, 160, 162–164, 167–168, 170, 174, 176, 179–180, 196, 225, 237, 293, 295–296, 323, 326, 329, 340–341, 344–345
American Panorama Company 65–66, 78, 80–81, 84, 88–91
Amish 157, 160n7, 165, 169
Anabaptist 128, 157n2, 164–165, 167
Anatomical models 16, 95, 97–102, 107–108, 111–112
– Anatomical Venus 95–96
Andersen, Hans Christian 127–153
– "Aunty Toothache," 129, 146
– "The Shirt Collar," 129n2, 135
Anderson, Benedict 90
Application (software application) 323–324, 335–336, 340
Aquarium 101, 188–193, 195, 199
Arabesque 139, 147
Archive 65, 84, 136, 324, 332, 335, 336n34
Arndt, Johann 163
Assemblage 29–31, 35, 343
Athenäum 130
Authenticity 69, 87

Baldwin, Thomas 19, 27
– *Airopaidia* 19

Ballooning, hot air balloon 2, 15–16, 17–38, 73, 83
Barker, Robert 78
Barnum, P.T. 225
Bartsch, Gustav 314–315
Basuto 224, 226–229, 233–234
Battle Between the Merrimac and Monitor (panorama) 80
Battle of Atlanta 81, 86–87
Battle of Atlanta (panorama) 90
Battle of Lookout Mountain (panorama) 81
Battle of Sedan 65, 69, 79–80
Battle of Sedan (panorama) 89
Battlefields 66–67, 69, 70, 74, 80, 82–84, 89
Bauman, Joseph 174–175
Baumgarten, Alexander Gottlieb 241
– *Aesthetica* 241
Benjamin, Walter 29, 36, 131, 145, 153, 192, 201, 267
Bezold, Friedrich 112–113
Bibliographisches Institut 228, 325, 328–330, 339
Bildungsroman 21, 242
Binoculars 26–28, 267, 284
Blanchard, Jean-Pierre 19
Blaschka, Leopold and Rudolf 128, 181–200
Blaschko, Alfred 104
Boisserée, Sulpiz 143–144
Bombe 39
Boner, Ulrich 42
– *Der Edelstein* 42
Botticelli, Sandro 43
– *Madonna of the Magnificat* 43
Bourgeois, bourgeoisie 19, 21, 74, 79, 136, 150, 209, 297, 299, 302–304, 313, 316–317
Braun, Kaspar 39
Braun, Louis 79–80
Brecht, Bertolt 107
– *Lux in tenebris* 107
Britain 17, 115, 210, 212, 214, 223n48, 326, 341
Broadside(s) 5–6, 8, 128, 157–178

Burke, Edmund 22
Busch, Wilhelm 40

Callot, Jacques 67n2
Camera obscura 29
Cameroon 80, 224
Carlsbad Decrees 39
Cartographic representation 27, 86
Castan, Louis and Gustav 96, 101
Castan's Panopticum 96, 98–102, 106–109, 111, 114, 118, 119
Catalogues 102, 105, 135–136, 145, 181, 186, 194–198
Centennial Cotton Exhibition 80
Cetewayo 210, 212, 219–223, 234
Chattanooga Times 82
Children's literature 5, 206, 234, 294n1, 300, 303
Chladni, Ernst Florens Friedrich 242, 259–262
Cinema 1–2, 41, 296, 297n13
Cipher(s) 243–244, 256, 258, 260, 263
Civil War (American) 65–67, 69n7, 78, 80–82, 84, 86, 89–90
Civilization 72
Cliché (blocks and stereotypes) 128, 205-209, 214, 216, 219–220, 222, 223, 225–226, 228, 231, 233–234
Close-Up 152n52, 297, 312
Cole, Thomas 296
Collage 129, 131–133, 144–146, 152, 212, 214, 229, 231, 306, 308, 310, 312–313
Colonialism 4, 8, 41, 72, 79–80, 97, 206n5-6, 210, 212, 216, 223n49, 299, 316n40
Comic Cuts 39
Comics 5, 9–11, 16, 40–41, 55, 57, 62–63, 67, 92, 347
Commemorative culture 65, 81, 84, 91
Conrad, Sebastian 3, 65, 92, 216n33, 235
Cooper, James Fenimore
– *The Deerslayer* 293, 302–308, 312–314
– *The Last of the Mohicans* 293, 296, 300n22, 305, 312–315
– *Leatherstocking Tales* 242, 293–294, 297–302, 304–306, 308, 310, 312–318
– *The Pathfinder* 293, 302, 305, 312, 314
– *The Pioneers* 293, 304–305, 312, 314
– *The Prairie* 293, 305, 308, 312, 314
Coptic 247
Copy, copying 177n69, 223, 234, 331–333, 336, 339, 340, 342
Crafts 127, 131–132, 134, 136, 147, 152, 173
Crary, Jonathan 18, 28–29, 35
Cronau, Rudolf 224–229
Cruikshank, Isaac 39
Cultural techniques [*Kulturtechniken*, Bernhard Siegert] 86, 146
Cut-out 134n15, 135, 140, 147, 152, 229
Cutting 4, 57, 127, 130–134, 140–152

Dada 146
Dannecker, Johann Heinrich 140, 142–143
Database 324–325n3, 325, 332–333n28, 336n34, 340, 343
Daumier, Honoré 39
Davis, Theodore R. 65–66, 78, 81–88
Deball, C. 57, 60
Decipher, decipherment 75, 77, 243–248, 264, 333–334
Decoupage 145n35, 147
Denis, Michael 20
Dermatology 98, 104, 108
De Rozier, Jean-François Pilâtre 26
Dertinger, Ernst 312–314
Deutsches Museum [German Museum in Munich] 100, 112
Devotional culture 157n3, 158, 160, 163, 167–168, 170, 172–174, 176–177
Digital media 1, 3, 10, 52, 323–343
Dirks, Rudolph 40
– *The Katzenjammer Kids* 40
Dissemination 2, 7, 9–10, 101, 128
Donau-Ansichten [*Views of the Danube*] 331
Doré, Gustave 39, 57
Draner (Jules Jean Georges Renard) 39
Dreams 18, 21, 32, 150, 152, 187, 244, 315

Duttenhofer, Luise 127, 132–134, 136, 140–146, 149–150, 152

Ecstasy 18, 20–23, 187
Edition(s) 8, 143, 159, 162–167, 172–174, 208, 233, 242, 248, 294–295, 297–306, 308, 310, 312–314, 316–318, 324, 326n5, 328, 335, 341, 347
Education 5, 7, 8, 16, 21, 95, 98, 100–101, 103n17, 107, 109n43, 112–113, 116n67, 157–158, 160–162, 173, 177, 241, 275–276, 281, 289
Electrical, electricity 242, 257–260, 262–264, 270
Electrophore, electrophorus 257–258, 264
Electrotype 82, 212n26
Eloesser, Arthur 101
Engraving 2, 49, 52, 68–69, 77, 81–82, 83, 91, 128, 140, 143, 150, 205–234, 248, 297, 302–304, 306–307, 309–310, 312, 317, 325–343
Engraving from a photograph 211, 214, 218, 222–223, 229, 233-4
Enlightenment 22, 30, 34, 101, 106, 205, 255
Entertainment 5, 19, 79, 90–91n51, 111, 150, 206, 209, 233
Ephemerality 118, 132–133, 143, 146, 150, 200, 246
Ephrata 164–169, 174
Etching 143, 342
Ethnography 128, 197, 210, 212, 214–215, 218, 223n48, 226, 228, 230–231, 233–234, 308
Eulenspiegel 39
Exhibitions 2, 8–9, 16, 78–80, 87, 91, 95, 97–109, 111–117, 119–120, 134–135, 281
Eye 19, 23–26, 28–31, 33–35, 49, 55, 57, 70, 77, 83, 157, 161, 172, 176, 181, 187, 192, 194, 219, 254, 270, 271n16, 277–282

Fairy tale(s) 130, 131, 133, 139, 145, 152, 154, 244
Figaro 39, 52, 57, 61
Film 1n2, 2n4, 3, 10, 52, 57, 106, 119, 131, 323, 342
Fliegende Blätter 39, 43–44
Flyspecking (paper condition) 168–169

Fontana, Felice 95
Foxing (paper condition) 170
Fragment, fragmentary 33, 130–132, 145–147, 243–244, 246, 253, 255, 285
Franco-Prussian War 65, 67, 69, 78–79, 90
Frederick II (the Great) 21, 30
French Revolution 18
Frič, Václav 194
Fröhlich, Karl 135, 137
 – *ABC für artige Kinder* 135, 137
Frontier (North American) 242, 293, 297, 302, 305, 313, 316–317
Frontispiece 248–249, 298, 302–304, 314, 317
Furttenbach the Elder, Joseph 162

Gabriel, Carl 107
Galewsky, Eugen 104, 114, 116
Galilei, Galileo 41, 49
 – *Sidereus Nuncius* 41, 49
Gardener, Thomas 80
Die Gartenlaube: Illustrirtes Familienblatt [*The Garden Arbor: Illustrated Family Paper*] 67–78, 209–217, 224–225
Garten-Ordnung 162
Gaze 25, 30, 34–35, 86n42, 117, 127, 183, 188–189, 210, 218, 313
Gegenwartsmuseum [Museum of the Present Day] 98–99n6, 103n18, 119
Gender 8, 9, 16, 20, 100, 105, 115–119, 127–128, 129n2, 131, 134–135, 143, 161, 173, 233, 237, 299
Genette, Gérard 294, 315n39
German City Exhibition 99
German Confederation 39–40, 329n10
German Hygiene Museum 99, 104, 112, 119
German Museum [Deutsches Museum] 100, 112
German Society to Combat Venereal Disease [Deutsche Gesellschaft für die Bekämpfung der Geschlechtskrankheiten, DGBG] 98
German-Americans 5, 128, 157–63, 165, 167–171, 173–177
German-Danish War 79
Gillray, James 39
Glass works 7–8

Global 3, 11, 65, 80n17, 92, 128, 183–184, 193, 195, 199–200, 205, 210, 329, 343
Globus 209
Godeffroy, John Cesar 195–197
Godeffroy Museum 196
Goethe, Johann Wolfgang 14, 20, 135, 139–140, 273
– "Hochzeitlied," 139–140
Gombrich, E.H. 62
Google Books 324n3, 332–333, 340
Gosse, Edmund 187–189, 200, 201
Gosse, Philip Henry 184, 186–192, 194–195, 201
Goya y Lucientes, Francisco José 28, 67, 74–75
– *The Balloon* 28
– *Los Desatres de la Guerra* 74
The Graphic 219–223
Grandville (Jean Ignace Isidore Gérard) 39
Great Exhibition of 1926 for Healthcare, Social Welfare, and Sports and Exercise, 103
Die Grenzboten [*The Border Messengers*] 272n21, 274
Grids 84, 86, 87, 93
Grimm, Jacob and Wilhelm 44, 69, 69–70n8
Günderrode, Karoline von 15, 20
Guys, Constantin 67n2
Gynecology 108

Hammer, Emil Eduard 107–109, 111, 121
Haptic 5, 131, 132, 158, 170, 176
Harper's Weekly 81, 212
Hathitrust 324–325-n3, 332-334, 340
Heath, William 50–51, 55
Hegel, Georg Wilhelm Friedrich 170
Heine, Friedrich Wilhelm 65–91
Herder, Johann Gottfried 248, 251–254, 256–257, 260, 262–264
– *Älteste Urkunde des Menschengeschlechts* [*Oldest Document of the Human Race*] 251, 254, 257
Hergé (Georges Prosper Remi) 57

Hieroglyph(s), hieroglyphics 8, 113n54, 241–243, 246–248, 250–252, 254–256, 260–264, 271
Hill, Thomas 162, 179
Hoffmann, E.T.A. 49, 50n16, 131, 273
– *Meister Floh* [*Master Flea*] 49–50, 62
Hoffmann'sche Verlagsbuchhandlung 300, 301–303, 305
Hoffmann, Franz 298, 300–301, 304–305, 306–313, 316–317
Hogarth, William 39, 57–58
Hohlfeld, Johannes 330–331, 335
Hooke, Robert 49, 54, 63, 258n63, 265
– *Micrographia* 49, 52, 54–55
Hudson River School 296
Hugo, Herman 163, 179
Human, Armin 344
Hygiene exhibition(s) 2, 8, 98–103, 109, 112, 114, 116n65, 119–120
Hyper-realism 98, 108

Ibis 252
Illusionism 78, 89
The Illustrated London News 211–214, 217n37, 219, 229, 230n72, 231
Illustration 4, 5, 8, 16, 27, 40, 41, 42, 44, 52, 55, 57, 59, 65–91, 108, 130, 139, 145–147, 149–150, 152, 185–187, 189, 205–234, 248, 259, 269, 294–295, 297, 299–304, 306, 308, 310, 312–318, 324–326, 328–333, 336, 340, 341–343
Illustrations of the Life and Works of Lord Byron 331
Imagination 8, 17, 18–19, 23, 28, 32, 34, 36, 55, 65, 70, 72–75, 77, 82, 86–88, 90–91, 97, 184, 217, 226, 246n10, 248, 251, 256, 258n64, 295–297, 316, 324
Immediacy 68–69, 251, 308, 317
Immigration, immigrant groups 4, 5, 40, 69n7, 81–82, 93, 164n27
Installment publication 48, 68–69, 325, 331n22, 332n24
Intaglio print 208n12, 326, 333
International Hygiene Exhibition 99, 102–103

Isis (natural science society) 185, 192, 195, 202–203, 244

Jean Paul (Johann Paul Friedrich Richter) 8, 15, 17–36, 273
– *Des Luftschiffers Giannozzo Seebuch* [*Aeronaut Giannozzo's Voyage Diary*] 15, 17–36
– *Titan* 20–21
Juvenile literature [*Jugendliteratur*] 5, 293–294, 299, 300–301, 304, 306, 313, 316

Kant, Immanuel 22, 30
Katzen-Musik 39
Keil, Ernst 67–69
Kikeriki 39, 44–45
Kircher, Athanasius 163, 247
Kisch, Egon Erwin 118–19
– "The Secret Cabinet of the Anatomical Museum," 118
Kittler, Friedrich 35, 37
Kladderadatsch 39, 43–44, 46–48, 52–53, 55–56
Kleist, Heinrich von 15, 20
Knigge, Adolph Freiherr von 20
Koch, Max 79
Kress, Gunther 241, 241n1, 295n6
Kunzle, David 40, 63

Landscape(s) 5, 27, 46, 73, 79, 86–87, 92, 152, 210, 212, 224–225, 233, 268, 271, 277–278, 281–284, 288, 295–297, 313–314, 324–325, 331–332, 341, 343
Landscape aesthetics 5, 86
Laterna magica 16, 46, 48
Leeuwen, Theo van 241, 241n1, 295n6
Leipziger Illustrirte Zeitung [*Leipzig Illustrated Newspaper*] 67
Lens 24, 46, 50–52, 55, 57, 188, 294
Lessing, Gotthold Ephraim 241, 255
– *Laocöon* (*Laokoon, oder über die Grenzen der Mahlerey und Poesie* [*Laocöon, or the Limitations of Painting and Poetry*]) 241
Letterpress 168, 325–326
Lindenpassage (Friedrichstaße) 101
Lingner, Karl August 98–99, 114
Lithography 2, 133–134, 146, 181, 186–189, 200, 208n12, 228, 302n25, 314–315
Louis Philippe I 39, 41

Magasin Pittoresque 208n14
Magazine(s) 6, 8, 16, 39–40, 83, 149, 208–210, 212, 214, 222, 223, 226, 233–234, 326, 332–333n28
Magnification 2, 55, 342
March Revolution 39
Marx, Karl 127, 183, 195, 199, 202
Mass media 119, 147, 152, 209
Material culture 5, 160, 169n44
Materiality 5–6, 128, 130, 146, 152, 245
Mennonite 157n2, 164–165, 167
"Der Mensch" ["The Human Being"] (exhibition) 103–105, 108
Meteorology 269, 271, 275, 284–285, 289, 291
Meyer, Carl Joseph 325, 329
– *Meyer's Universum* 228, 324–330, 331n22, 332–343,
Michelet, Jules 184
Microscope 16, 26, 39, 49–51, 55, 59, 187–188, 258, 273–274
Military 28, 35–36, 43, 49, 66, 68–70, 73, 75, 78–80, 83, 86, 104, 211–212
Miller, Henrich 164, 165
Milton, John 50–51, 293, 304
– *Paradise Lost* 50–51, 63
Miniature(s) 27, 41, 131, 139–140, 143, 154, 188
Minor art 136
Mirzoeff, Nicholas 1n1, 1n2, 6n15, 83
Mitchell, W.J.T. 1n1
Montgolfier Brothers 18
Monumentality 132–133, 134, 140, 150, 183, 324
Moulages 97–98, 104, 106–111, 114
Muhlenberg, Henry Melchior 176
Multimodality 241, 294–295, 295n6

Münchener Punsch 39
Münchner DigitalisierungsZentrum [Munich DigitiZation Center] 335
Museum(s) 4–5, 7–8, 80, 97n3, 99–100, 103–104, 107–109, 112–114, 118-120, 134, 181, 183, 185–188, 192–197, 199, 218, 223, 225, 340
Museum of Human Beings [Menschenmuseum, ethnologisches-anthropologisches Museum] 97
Museum Studies 4–5, 8, 100
Music 5, 134, 140

Nadar, Félix 19
Napoleonic Wars 28
Nast, Thomas 40
Nation 3–4, 16, 28, 65, 67–69, 72, 75, 79, 80, 84, 90, 127, 167, 170, 179–180, 209, 212, 216, 223–224, 234, 242, 250, 271n18, 295, 325
Native Americans 225, 297, 298n15, 299, 303, 314
Natural sciences 185, 192, 195, 245, 264, 268n6, 269, 272n19, 275
Neisser, Albert 104
The New York Times 82
Newspapers 19, 40, 65–68, 80, 82, 83, 117, 134, 145–146, 164, 210, 236, 332, 335n29
Noble savage(s) 297, 313, 316
Northwestern Panorama Company 81
Novalis (Georg Philipp Friedrich von Hardenberg) 130, 241, 243–247, 252–258, 260, 262
– *Die Lehrlinge zu Sais* [*The Apprentices at Sais*] 243–244, 246, 255–258

Observers 8, 26, 28–29, 32, 100, 105–106, 119, 185–186, 206, 270, 274, 281, 296, 315
Ochs, Adolph Simon 82
Oehmigke, Alfred 314
Ørsted, Hans Christian 263–264
Original Views of the Most Notable Cities of Germany [*Original-Ansichten der vornehmsten Städte Deutschlands*] 332

Page format 70
Painting 7, 8, 16, 19, 24–25, 28, 43, 65, 70, 72, 79, 86–87, 89, 92, 132, 143, 219, 225, 241, 268, 273–274, 276–289, 296, 314, 324n2
Panel 57, 150, 152, 159, 306
Panoptikum (Louis and Gustav Castan) 96, 98–102, 106–109, 111, 114, 118, 119
Panorama of the War 80
Panoramic point of view 24, 33, 73–74, 83, 87, 88
Paper 6, 7, 8, 18, 82, 84, 127-128, 129–152, 158, 160–162, 169–170, 173, 207, 259, 278, 324, 326–327, 335n31, 342–343
Papercuts [*Scherenschnitte*] 6–8, 127, 129, 131–152
Paratexts 294, 301, 306, 313
Paris 69, 73–74, 99n8, 196, 202, 208n14, 209
Passage-Panoptikum 101, 118
Pasting 130–132, 150, 152
Perception 15, 17–18, 27, 29–31, 34, 100, 119, 255, 268–271, 273, 275, 277, 279n48, 289
Performance 10, 91, 97, 147, 150, 160
Pergamon Panorama 79
Periodicals (serials) 2, 5, 16, 39–40, 42–43, 65–69, 77–78, 81–82, 88, 90–91, 185, 211, 214, 306n31, 323n1, 324–325, 328, 332, 335, 337n35, 341n41, 343
Peschel, Johann 162
Das Pfennig-Magazin 208–209
Pfister, Albrecht 42
Photography 1, 2n4, 3–4, 7–10, 15–16, 29, 41, 52, 57, 62, 66, 74n11, 82, 84, 86, 91, 98, 102, 109, 127, 132–133, 145n35, 149, 150, 152, 177, 211, 214, 217, 218–219, 222–223, 229, 233, 234, 241, 268, 279, 295, 323–324
Physiognomy 133, 149
Picasso, Pablo 132–133, 146
Picture book 130, 147, 152
Pietism 157n2, 167
Pilgrimage (broadside) 128, 157–178
Pohl, Rudolf 102
Poiesis 31–32
Pondo 212

Printing technology 8–9, 42–43, 68, 88, 90, 128, 145, 162–163, 172–174, 206–208, 295, 300, 324, 326, 326n6, 334, 342
Prostitutes (sex workers) 116–118
Psyche (Greek mythology) 140–141
Puck 40
Pudor, Heinrich 103
Punch, the London Charivari 39, 42–43, 57, 59

Race, racism, racist thought 50, 72, 90, 93, 97, 101, 120, 127–128, 134, 205–206, 209–210, 216–217, 219, 231, 236, 298
Ratzel, Friedrich 214–218, 227–229
Reader(s), readership 8–9, 16, 43, 57, 59, 62, 66–70, 72–74, 77, 82–84, 90, 134, 147, 163–164, 168, 170, 172, 174, 176–177, 187, 189, 209, 217, 226, 242, 256, 275, 293–295, 297, 299–302, 304, 312–313, 316–318, 325
Realism 90, 98, 108, 268–275, 289, 305, 329, 343
Redon, Odilion 24–25
– The Eye like a strange Balloon mounts towards Infinity 24–25
Reenactment 66, 84, 90
Reichard, Wilhelmine 19
Reichenbach, Ludwig 186, 192–193, 197
Révénant 32, 49
Reverse image search 335–336, 343
Ritchie, Leitch 340–341
Ritter, Johann Wilhelm 252, 253n39, 263
Romanticism 130–131, 243–264, 281, 296
Rosetta Stone 247
Rowlandson, Thomas 39
Ruskin, John 279

Salon 136, 139–140, 147, 150
Salvage 129, 131, 133
Sandwichman 226
Satire 16, 21, 39–62
Scans 323–343
Schelling, Friedrich 266
Scherenschnitte [papercuts] 6–8, 127, 129, 131–152
Schiller, Friedrich 30, 48, 143, 243–245, 246–247n11

– "Das verschleierte Bild zu Sais" ["The Veiled Image at Sais"] 243
Schlegel, August Wilhelm 130, 154, 255
Schlegel, Friedrich 130, 154, 266
Schmidt & Spring 300–301, 304–305, 307, 309–310, 312–313
Scholz, Albrecht 105, 107, 122
Scholz, Wilhelm 46–48, 52–53, 57
Schopenhauer, Adele 127, 131–152
Schopenhauer, Arthur 20, 136
Schultz, Anna 157–158, 173
Schwenkfelder 157–159, 165, 168, 173, 175
Scientific images 262, 264
Scissors 127, 129n2, 132–133, 135–136, 139, 141, 143, 145, 149–152
Scrap 129, 132, 145, 147
Scrapbooks 131, 145, 147
Screen (computer or surface for display) 1n2, 336–338
Screen (partition) 132, 147, 150, 152
Screening (performance or show) 46
Sculpture 5, 7, 70, 89, 132–134, 138, 143, 150, 152, 241, 348
Search engine 324, 335–336, 340, 343
Second Schleswig War 46–47
Sedan Day 79
Sedan Panorama 80, 89
Sensorium (human) 17–18, 20, 23, 29–30, 36, 273
Seriality 9, 78, 222, 285
Serial(s) 2, 5, 16, 39–40, 42–43, 65–69, 77–78, 81–82, 88, 90–91, 185, 211, 214, 306n31, 323n1, 324–325, 328, 332, 335, 337n35, 341n41, 343
Sex workers (prostitutes) 116–118
Sexually transmitted disease 96, 98, 103, 106, 114
Shaka (Zulu king) 231–233
Silhouette 57, 130, 133, 135–136, 139, 147, 151
Sioux 225, 228, 308, 311, 313–315
Sketch(es), sketching 65, 67–70, 75, 77–79, 81–91, 140n30, 187–188, 190f4, 233, 269, 277, 283–284, 288–289, 341
Slavery 79
Sloterdijk, Peter 25, 35
Smith, George Albert 55
– As Seen Through A Telescope 57

– *Grandmother's Reading Glass* 55–56
Smolderen, Thierry 40–41
Soap bubbles 44–46
Social media 1
Salomon, Ernst von 107
– *Kadetten* 107
Sorcerer 226–229, 231, 233–234
Spiritual labyrinth 128, 157–177
Spiritual pilgrimage 128, 157–177
St. Nicholas: An Illustrated Magazine for Young Folks 82–84, 90–91
Steel engraving 2, 206, 208, 297, 302–307, 309–312, 326–330, 332, 335, 339, 341n42
Stein, Adam 313–317
Sterne, Laurence 21
– *Tristram Shandy* 21
Stereoscope 28–29, 35, 41, 192
Stereotype (illustration technique) 82, 146, 177
Stewart, Susan 131, 140
Stifter, Adalbert 8, 15, 242, 267–289
– *Bunte Steine* [*Many Colored Stones*] 242, 269–276, 282
– *Der Condor* [*The Condor*] 20
– *Der Nachsommer: Eine Erzählung* [*Indian Summer A Tale*] 267
– *Tagebuch über Malereiarbeiten* [*Diary of Painting*] 284–288
The Storming of Missionary Ridge (panorama) 66, 81
Sublime 19, 22, 34, 270, 274, 277, 281–282

te Heesen, Anke 104n19, 123, 146, 154
Telescope 16, 27, 39, 41, 49, 52, 57, 59, 273
Tersteegen, Gerhard 163, 174, 176
– *Geistliches Blumengärtlein Inniger Seelen* [*Spiritual Garden for Ardent Souls*] 174
Der Teutsche Merkur 20
Theut 252
Thot 252
TinEye 336–340
Tondo(s) (round frames) 40–48, 51, 57, 59, 62
Transnational 3–4, 9, 16, 188, 193, 209, 295, 341n41
Truth 29, 68–70, 74, 88–90, 181, 193, 226, 229, 233, 241, 243–245, 256, 264

Über Land und Meer 67, 209, 225
Umlauff, Johann(es) 197–199
Urbild 251, 254
Urschrift 254, 263

Varnhagen von Ense, Karl 133, 138, 140, 144, 149–150
– "Vom Ausschneiden" ["Cutting Out"] 133
Veil, veiled 243–244, 256
Venerology 108
Verne, Jules 185
Versailles 18, 69, 78, 162
Vico, Giambattista 248–249
– *Principj di Scienza Nuova* 248–249
Violence 67, 70, 72, 74–75, 78, 90, 134, 297, 302, 304, 310, 316
Virchow, Rudolf 109
Vision 6, 17n2, 18, 20, 26–31, 34–36, 59, 73, 83, 161, 170, 200, 206, 268n6, 273–274n26, 278, 280–281, 289, 296, 313, 316
Visual culture 1–12, 15–16, 18–20, 41, 59, 80, 83, 127, 158, 160–161, 163, 167, 205–206, 219, 234, 241, 245, 295, 318, 323–343
Visual history 67, 206, 312
Visual narrative 41, 306
Visuality 6, 36, 83, 99–100, 104, 108, 245, 258n64, 275, 280, 296
Völkerschau (ethnological exhibition) 97, 116, 218, 225
Voyeurism 57, 70

Wagener, Otto 113
Walker, Kara 134
Wangemann, Hermann 218, 229, 233
War, warfare 25, 35, 66–68, 78, 210, 348
War journalism 65–69, 77–78, 81–83
Ward, Henry 197
Waste 41, 131–132, 139, 145-147, 149
Weber, Ernst von 209–211
Wehner, William 80–81
Werner, Anton von 79–80
Westward expansion 79
Wieland, Christoph Martin 19, 22
Winckelmann, Johann Joachim 241

– *Gedanken über die Nachahmung der griechischen Werke in der Malerei und Bildhauerkunst* [*Thoughts on the Imitation of Greek Works in Painting and Sculpture*] 241
Witch-doctor 212, 226, 231–233
Women-only day [*Frauentag*] 116
Wunderkammer (cabinet of curiosities) 128, 181–200

Xhosa 212

Zeiller, Gustav 102n12, 109, 118
Zouaves 75
Zulu 209–223, 226, 229–236

www.ingramcontent.com/pod-product-compliance
Lightning Source LLC
Chambersburg PA
CBHW031605210526
45464CB00004B/1435